GENERAL INTERESTS OF HOST STATES IN INTERNATIONAL INVESTMENT LAW

It is a function of sovereign States to take action in order to maintain their financial stability, stimulate economic development or to further their non-economic interests (such as health, the environment and food security). However, such measures can conflict with the rights granted to foreign investors under international treaties. Regulators and policy makers must take States' international commitments towards foreign investors into account when making decisions and when negotiating must also avoid resorting to protectionism in drafting new treaties.

With this tension in mind, this book offers a balanced reappraisal of bilateral treaties and regional agreements on foreign investments. The sensitive issues are examined in the light of the case law of arbitral investment tribunals and other international courts, and the analysis highlights how cross-fertilisation between trade and investment law can assist in resolving conflicts.

GIORGIO SACERDOTI is Professor of International and European Law at Bocconi University, Milan, Italy. He is an internationally recognised expert on both investment and trade law, having been both a member of the WTO Appellate Body and an investment arbitrator at ICSID.

PIA ACCONCI is Professor of European Union Law at the University of Teramo, Italy, where her research focuses on the social responsibility of multinational companies and the relationship between international regulation of trade and investment and non-economic matters such as the protection of public health.

MARA VALENTI is a Lecturer in International Law at the Department of International Studies, University of Milan, Italy, teaching International Organization. Her research focuses on International Investment Law.

ANNA DE LUCA is a Researcher at Bocconi University, Milan, Italy, and a practising lawyer. Her research focuses on International Investment Law and EU Investment Policy.

CAMBRIDGE INTERNATIONAL TRADE AND ECONOMIC LAW

Series Editors

As the processes of regionalisation and globalisation have intensified, there have been accompanying increases in the regulations of international trade and economic law at the levels of international, regional and national laws.

The subject matter of this series is international economic law. Its core is the regulation of international trade, investment and cognate areas such as intellectual property and competition policy. The series publishes books on related regulatory areas, in particular human rights, labour, environment and culture, as well as sustainable development. These areas are vertically linked at the international, regional and national level, and the series extends to the implementation of these rules at these different levels. The series also includes works on governance, dealing with the structure and operation of related international organisations in the field of international economic law, and the way they interact with other subjects of international and national law.

Books in the series

General Interests of Host States in International Investment Law
Edited by Giorgio Sacerdoti, Pia Acconci, Mara Valenti and Anna De Luca

The Law of Development Cooperation: A Comparative Analysis of the World Bank, the EU and Germany
Philipp Dann

WTO Disciplines on Subsidies and Countervailing Measures: Balancing Policy Space and Legal Constraints
Dominic Coppens

Domestic Judicial Review of Trade Remedies: Experiences of the Most Active WTO Members
Müslüm Yilmaz

International Organizations in WTO Dispute Settlement: How Much Institutional Sensitivity?
Marina Foltea

Public Services and International Trade Liberalization: Human Rights and Gender Implications
Barnali Choudhury

The Law and Politics of WTO Waivers: Stability and Flexibility in Public International Law
Isabel Feichtner

African Regional Trade Agreements as Legal Regimes
James Thuo Gathii

Processes and Production Methods (PPMs) in WTO Law: Interfacing Trade and Social Goals
Christiane R. Conrad

Non-Discrimination in International Trade in Services: 'Likeness' in WTO/GATS
Nicolas Diebold

The Law, Economics and Politics of Retaliation in WTO Dispute Settlement
Edited by Chad P. Bown and Joost Pauwelyn

The Multilaterization of International Investment Law
Stephan W. Schill

Trade Policy Flexibility and Enforcement in the WTO: A Law and Economics Analysis
Simon A.B. Schropp

GENERAL INTERESTS OF HOST STATES IN INTERNATIONAL INVESTMENT LAW

Edited by

GIORGIO SACERDOTI

with

PIA ACCONCI

MARA VALENTI

ANNA DE LUCA

CAMBRIDGE
UNIVERSITY PRESS

CAMBRIDGE
UNIVERSITY PRESS

University Printing House, Cambridge CB2 8BS, United Kingdom

Cambridge University Press is part of the University of Cambridge.

It furthers the University's mission by disseminating knowledge in the pursuit of education, learning and research at the highest international levels of excellence.

www.cambridge.org
Information on this title: www.cambridge.org/9781107050235

First published 2014

A catalogue record for this publication is available from the British Library

Library of Congress Cataloguing in Publication data
General interests of host states in international investment law / edited by Giorgio Sacerdoti with Pia Acconci, Mara Valenti, Anna De Luca.
p. cm. – (Cambridge international trade and economic law ; 13)
Includes bibliographical references and index.
ISBN 978-1-107-05023-5 (hardback)
1. Investments, Foreign (International law) 2. Investments, Foreign–Law and legislation. 3. Arbitration and award, International. I. Sacerdoti, Giorgio, editor of compilation author.
K3830.G46 2014
346′.092–dc23
2013044150

ISBN 978-1-107-05023-5 Hardback

CONTENTS

CONTRIBUTORS

PIA ACCONCI **(Co-editor)** is a professor of International Investment Law and European Union Law at the University of Teramo, Italy. She holds a PhD in International Economic Law from the University of Bergamo. She was awarded the special prize 'eccellenza nella ricerca' ('Excellency in Research') at Bocconi University, Milan in 2002. She was a member of the ILA Committee on the Law of Foreign Investment from 2004 to 2008. She has been a member of the editing staff of the *Italian Yearbook of International Law* since 2005. She has authored many works, in particular two books: *Il collegamento tra Stato e società in materia di investimenti stranieri* (*The Link between State and Company in the Field of Foreign Investments*, CEDAM, 2002) and *Tutela della salute e diritto internazionale* (*Health Protection and International Law*, CEDAM, 2011). Her writings mainly concern international investment law, corporate social responsibility in international law and European Union law, human rights protection and health issues in international law.

MICHELE BARBIERI is currently with an international financial and tax consultancy in Luxembourg. He holds a PhD from Bocconi University, Milan, where he was a research assistant in International and EU Law. Previously he was a visiting lecturer in International Investment Law at the Belarus State Economic University, where he contributed to the reform of the investment code of Belarus.

ARNO DAL RI JUNIOR is a professor of International Law at Universidade Federal de Santa Catarina, Brazil. He earned a PhD in International Law and Economics from Bocconi University, Milan, and a Master's degree in European Union Law and Policies from the University of Padova, Italy.

PAULO POTIARA DE ALCÂNTARA VELOSO teaches International Law at Faculdade de Ciências Sociais de Florianópolis (CESUSC), Brazil. He is a PhD candidate at Universidade Federal de Santa Catarina, Brazil, and a researcher with the Research Groups in International Law *Ius Gentium* and in History of Law *Ius Commune* (UFSC/CNPq).

ANNA DE LUCA (**Co-editor**) is a research fellow at Bocconi University in Milan and holds a PhD from the State University of Milan. She specialises in international investment law and arbitration, and EU investment policy. She is a member of the editorial committee of the *Rivista dell'Arbitrato* and a practising lawyer in the field of investment arbitration as a member of the Milan Bar. Besides several articles in international yearbooks and Italian law reviews, she authored in 2013 *La competenza dell'Unione europea sugli investiment esteri* (Giappichelli, Torino).

ANTONIETTA DI BLASE is Professor of International Law at Roma Tre University Law School. Previously Prof. Di Blase taught International Law at the Universities of Bologna, LUISS in Rome and Camerino, where she was also Dean of the Law School. She has published widely in the area of international law and international economic law.

DOMENICO DI PIETRO practises international arbitration both as counsel and as an arbitrator in Rome where he lectures on International Arbitration at Roma Tre University. He was a fellow of the Center for Transnational Litigation and Commercial Law at New York University School of Law. He is qualified to practice in Italy and in England and Wales.

CLAUDIO DORDI, PhD, is Associate Professor of International Law at Bocconi University, Milan. He has worked as a consultant for a number of international organisations (APEC, ASEAN, EU, UNCTAD, UNDP, World Bank). He has taught and researched in a number of American, European and Asian universities and has published in the main international economic law journals. Since 2008 he has also been Technical Assistance Team Leader of the EU Multilateral Trade and Investment project in Vietnam.

MARTINA GUIDI holds a PhD in International and EU Law. She is currently a Research Fellow at LUISS University in Rome. Her writings mainly concern corporate social responsibility, the protection of the environment and of human rights in international and European Union law.

JÜRGEN KURTZ is an associate professor and Director of the International Investment Law Program of the Institute for International Law and the Humanities at the University of Melbourne. He researches and teaches in the various strands of international economic law including WTO and investment law on which he has published in leading international law journals. He teaches annually at the Academy of International Trade and Investment Law in Macau, and at Master programmes at Universidade Catolica in Portugal, at the University of Barcelona and at the Singapore International Arbitration Academy. He was recently appointed F. Braudel Senior Fellow at the European University Institute.

AGOSTINA LATINO is Research Fellow in International Law at the University of Camerino, Italy, and lectures in International Economic Law at Roma Tre University. She holds an LLM and an MBA from LUISS University in Rome and a PhD from the University of Bari, Italy.

PAOLA MARIANI is Associate Professor of International Law and EU Law at Bocconi University, Milan, where she has been in charge of the courses of private international law and EU law since 2001. Mariani's research interests focus on the international fight against corruption, EU external relations, EU private international law and the EU internal market, on which subjects she has published in Italian and European journals.

ELSA MILANESI is a researcher and lecturer in European Law at the University of Milan (Political Sciences). Her publications cover subjects in international law and EU law, the latter mainly focused on the fiscal policy of the European Union.

FEDERICO ORTINO PhD is Reader in International Economic Law at King's College London. He joined King's in 2007. He is a member of the ILA Committee on International Trade Law; founding Committee Member (and now Co-treasurer) of the Society of International Economic Law; consultative member of the Investment Treaty Forum; editorial board member of the *Journal of International Economic Law*, the *Yearbook on International Investment Law and Policy* and the *Journal of International Dispute Settlement*.

ALESSANDRO PERFETTI holds a PhD from the University of Teramo, Italy, where he is a teaching Fellow. He specialised in European Union law and has written in Italian academic journals on anti-dumping, corporate social responsibility, food security, customs cooperation and foreign investment regimes.

EMANUELA PISTOIA is Associate Professor of European Union Law at the University of Teramo, Italy. She holds a PhD in International Organizations. Her research interest in the area of non-economic values in EU economic law covers corporate social responsibility. She has published on environmental performance certification in the EU ('Ecolabel') and on the support to CSR by means of legal instruments in the EU system.

MATILDE RECANATI holds a PhD from Macerata University, Italy, and is currently Research Fellow at Bocconi University in Milan. Her area of expertise is international economic law, specifically in that of international trade and investment on which she has published articles in books and journals both in Italian and non-Italian publications. Before Bocconi she practised with international law firms in Hong Kong and Shanghai.

GIORGIO SACERDOTI **(Editor)** has been Professor of International Law at Bocconi University in Milan since 1986, holding also the Jean Monnet Chair in European Law. He was a member of the WTO Appellate Body from 2001 to 2009 and its chairman in 2006–7. Previously he had been the Vice President of the OECD Working Group on Bribery in International Business Transactions (1995–2001) where he was one of the negotiators of the 1997 OECD Anti-bribery Convention. He is on the ICSID Roster of arbitrators (designated by Italy) where he has chaired various tribunals in high profile cases. An editor of the *Italian Yearbook of International Law*, he has lectured extensively in universities and at conferences around the world including as Senior F. Braudel Fellow at the European University Institute in 2012. He has authored more than 150 works in his fields of interest, combining his international trade and investment law expertise, including the first course on investment law at the Hague Academy in 1994. He is also active in international commercial arbitration as an independent arbitrator and as counsel to *Eversheds Bianchini* in Milan.

HAI YEN TRINH has been a lecturer in International Law at the Diplomatic Academy of Vietnam since 2001. She has also been a visiting lecturer at the Hanoi University of Law and the Hanoi University and Vietnam Academy of Social Sciences. Trinh graduated in International Relations from Vietnam's Institute for International Relations and completed a Master's degree in Law and Diplomacy at the Fletcher School of Law and Diplomacy, Tufts University (USA) and a PhD degree in Law at the National University of Singapore.

MARA VALENTI **(Co-editor)** is a researcher in International Law at the University of Milan focusing on international investment law. She is the author of *Gli standard di trattamento nell'interpretazione dei trattati in materia di investimenti stranieri* (Giappichelli, Torino, 2009). She is a lecturer on the Law of International Organizations at her university and teaches at the PhD in International Law and Economics at Bocconi University, Milan. She holds a PhD in International Law and Economics from Bocconi and a Diplome d'Etudes Supérieures in EU Law from Université Paris 1 – Panthéon Sorbonne.

FRIEDL WEISS is a professor in the Department of European, International and Comparative Law of the University of Vienna. He was formerly a lecturer at LSE, London, and a professor of International (Economic) Law and Organisations at the University of Amsterdam where he was also Director of the Amsterdam Law School. His publications include *EU Recht* (co-authored and co-edited with G. Hafner and A. Kumin; Mainz, 2013); *Free Movement of Persons within the European Community* (with Frank Wooldridge, European Monographs, Kluwer, 2nd edition 2007); *International Law and Sustainable Development: Principles and Practice* (co-edited with Nico Schrijver; Brill, 2004).

EDITORS' PREFACE

This volume brings together sixteen specialists, mostly academics but also practising lawyers in the field of international investment and trade law. The focus of their contribution is primarily the 'protection' of general interest of host States under bilateral investment treaties and other agreements, and on how to reconcile this concern with the traditional primary focus of those treaties, namely the protection of foreign investors.

The issue of safeguarding the policy space of host States when they adopt general regulations and measures in the pursuit of public interest which are liable to prejudice and discriminate against foreign investors has come to the forefront with the recent economic and financial crises. Prudential and other urgent measures for the preservation of financial stability and the viability of the banking system have been accused of having discriminated against foreign business entities and investors. Already before the crisis, the challenge of general measures by aggrieved investors in high profile arbitral litigations, resulting in huge amounts being awarded to claimants at the cost of host States' budgets, has raised the issue of the proper limits of the protection afforded by Bilateral Investment Treaties (BITs) against general measures and regulation that may qualify as indirect expropriation. This would extend treaty coverage well beyond the traditional core protection against arbitrary, discriminatory and confiscatory measures.

As a result, the very legitimacy of BITs and of the direct arbitral dispute settlement process they establish has been questioned. A few countries are opting out from the system or at least signalling their rejection of direct investor–State arbitration. This would mean re-politicising investment disputes and discriminating against investors from weaker countries unable to obtain effective diplomatic protection from their home States. The process of negotiating new treaties goes on, however, to the point of involving the two largest world economies, the United States and China. The trend includes major regional trade agreements comprising investment chapters, on the model of NAFTA, being negotiated in the

Transatlantic and Transpacific arenas as well as in the Far East. In all of these negotiating fora, new clauses are being devised, with a view to shielding host States from potentially abusive claims by investors against bona fide non-discriminatory general regulation in the public interest. This evolution puts pressure on arbitral case law and should encourage both treaty negotiators and arbitrators to look at WTO law and its jurisprudence for a model of a multilateral, more balanced and legitimate system.

Finally, given the active role of the European Parliament in shaping the investment policy of the European Union, the EU may well become not just a new actor but a new type of actor in the evolution of investment law and policies. Current negotiations of investment chapters in free trade agreements and economic partnership agreements between the EU and major trade partners can contribute to the emergence of a new pattern in international investment law that is more deferent to the general interests of host States.

This collection of chapters investigates systematically these current pressing issues from a variety of points of views. Most of them stem from a collective research on the evolution of international investment law, financed by the Italian Ministry of Education and University (PRIN project 2008–12, Grant No. 602366). The European dimension has been added, with chapters by authors from various other countries, thanks to the participation of Bocconi University through its International Law and Economics programme of the PhD school in the Marie Curie 'DISSETTLE' (economic dispute settlement) doctoral and post-doctoral programme, financed by the European Commission (Grant No. 264633). This project links the Geneva Graduate Institute, Université Libre of Brussels and the Universities of St Gallen, Warsaw and Bocconi, focusing on both the legal and economic dimensions of investment, trade and competition international dispute settlement. The Editors thank Dr Geraldo Vidigal and Dr Emily Lydgate, the DISSETTLE researchers at Bocconi University, for their valuable assistance with the final revision of the volume.

PART I

General interests of host States in the application of investment treaties

1

The application of BITs in time of economic crisis: limits to their coverage, necessity and the relevance of WTO law

GIORGIO SACERDOTI

1. Introduction

The limits to the coverage of investment protection provisions in Bilateral Investment Treaties (BITs) and more generally in International Investment Agreements (IIAs) have attracted increasing attention recently.[1] There are various reasons for this development.

First of all, the increase in the number of BITs in place and their growing invocation by aggrieved foreign investors in direct arbitration against host States has shifted the focus from the content of individual provisions to a reflection on their scope in general. Secondly, economic crises have led to renewed intervention by States in the economy, at times affecting negatively foreign investors in particular. The question of whether or in what respect the granting to foreign investors through BITs of fair and nondiscriminatory treatment and specific commitments may limit the discretion of governments in adopting needed anticrisis measures, which may entail differential treatment of creditors and limitations to previous benefits, has naturally surfaced. Although the measures adopted by many economies to face the financial crisis that exploded in 2008 have not given origin to major disputes yet, the issue is not merely academic or relevant only for the drafting of new treaties.[2]

1 For simplicity we will refer here to BITs (Bilateral Investment Treaties) to refer also generally to investment chapters of broader agreements (such as the investment chapters of the NAFTA and KORUS) and to the four investment agreements signed by ASEAN countries between themselves, with Australia and New Zealand, with Korea and with China in 2009, often referred to as International Investment Agreements (IIAs).

2 See: Bjorklund (2009); Van Aaken and Kurtz (2009, 2010); Kurtz (2010). As to the relevance of international monetary and financial rules for the interpretation and application of BITs, such as found in the IMF, the GATS and its Annex on Financial Services, and the OECD Liberalization Codes, see Sacerdoti (2013).

The debate has started with the investment disputes generated by the economic crisis of Argentina in 2001 related to the measures taken during the crisis and in its aftermath. The de-dollarization of that economy, the restructuring of public debt and the freezing of public tariffs have been challenged by a number of foreign investors as being in breach of relevant BITs entered into by Argentina in the previous decade. In these cases Argentina has invoked the crisis as the basis for its defense that the relevant BIT's provisions were inapplicable, or that their application should take into account the situation of crisis. Ensuing awards and annulment decisions of some of them at the International Centre for Settlement of Investment Disputes (ICSID) have given divergent answers, showing different approaches and interpretations of similar or identical texts by different arbitral tribunals and *ad hoc* committees.[3] Notwithstanding a certain trend to coherence in some respects, conclusions reached remain apart on several issues.

Similar cases concerning other countries could occur in the future when governments feel compelled to give precedence to coping with pressing needs of economic stability at the price of sacrificing foreign investors' rights and expectations, even if backed by treaty assurances.[4] From a different point of view, it is important for (prospective) investors to understand how much protection is granted by these treaties in cases of crisis and how good fair treatment and protection from expropriation clauses are in order to cover them from encroachment by host States in these situations. The issue is whether the guaranteed treatment and rights may be invoked irrespective of any unexpected economic evolution, even if resulting in a situation of dire crisis and emergency, or whether in such a situation host States' actions may be admitted as a legitimate, possibly necessary, exercise of State regulatory powers of the economy in the pursuit of paramount noneconomic objectives.[5]

3 For a critical view of these divergences see Crivellaro (2011).

4 There have been indications in the press of the introduction of investment cases against Greece and Cyprus under the BITs of those countries challenging measures taken in the recent crises; see "Crisis in Cyprus. Will bank depositors find shelter under BITs?" 2013 *Global Arbitration Review*, 8(3), 7.

5 More generally, even the constitutional commitments to spending discipline under the 2012 "Fiscal Compact" (Treaty on Stability, Coordination and Governance), between twenty-five members of the European Union allow relaxing the agreed discipline in "exceptional circumstances." Art. 3(3)(b) defines them as "an unusual event outside the control of the Contracting Party, which has a major impact on the financial position of the general government or to a period of severe economic downturn." The implementing Italian constitutional provision allows accordingly derogations in case of "exceptional events, among which [are] serious economic recession, financial crises, major natural disasters."

These crucial issues concerning on the one hand the value of the BIT for investors, and on the other the hurdles that these treaties may impose to governments struggling to cope with a crisis, have been raised first jurisprudentially on a case-by-case basis, with hardly any support from precedents and literature.[6]

In view of the existing stock of BITs in force, it is unlikely that the issue will be resolved promptly through replacement or amendment, that is, updating of existing BITs. It will thus be for adjudicators in case of disputes concerning specific or general regulatory measures taken by host States to give a case-by-case answer by interpreting existing provisions, mostly not focused on the issue of their application in time of economic crisis.

Our analysis will proceed reviewing in turn:

- the type of measures to which States may resort and have resorted, as well as BITs, protection standards that may be affected thereby (Section 2);
- the relevant BITs, provisions as to their coverage, including specific exceptions (such as the "non-precluded measures" provision in Art. XI of the US–Argentina BIT) that may limit their application in time of economic crises (Sections 3 and 4);
- the relevance of the defense of necessity, especially as applied in the Argentinean cases (Section 5);
- the reference to WTO law for interpretative purposes in order to balance investors' expectations and the protection of general interest of host States (Section 6).

2. Measures taken in respect of economic and financial crises affecting foreign investors' rights and BITs' protection

There is not a single definition of "economic crisis."[7] Economic, financial and banking crises are different phenomena but may be closely related, one prompting the other. In the context of the present chapter it is the

6 Only three international decisions, rather far dating, are known to have addressed such issues, *Ottoman Public Debt Arbitration* (1925) 1 UNRIAA 529; *Serbian Loans* (1929) PCIJ Ser. A No. 20 and *Brazilian Loans* (1929) PCIJ Ser. A No. 21. For a critical view of their use by the ILC in drafting the provision on necessity (Art. 25) of the ILC Draft Articles on State Responsibility see Sloane (2012) 106 AJIL 447. For an historical overview, see Sacerdoti (1972), 132 ff.

7 For a review see IMF (2008), "World Economic Outlook. Financial Crises: Causes and Indications," 74 ff.

"extraordinary" measures taken by governments in those situations, to prevent or cope with a crisis, that interest the most.

Past crises, including situations of severe balance of payment problems, offer a broad picture of measures that may affect treaty rights of foreign investors. The recent financial crisis offers further examples. Measures involved may be of the following type:

- limitations of current payments;
- limitations of capital transfers;
- rescue/reorganization of (only) selected national financial institutions ("too big to fail");
- sovereign default and debt restructuring;
- currency redenomination;
- prudential measures for the stability of the financial sector and/or specific intermediaries.[8]

Such measures might breach the fair and equitable treatment standard, requiring a tribunal to evaluate whether normative or regulatory changes, or rather their impact on the investor, were fair or not.[9] These measures may entail also violation of nondiscrimination (national treatment) obligations, as has been hinted in respect of US and EU measures in support of domestic financial institutions in crisis.[10] In more radical instances restrictive measures may amount to indirect expropriation through regulation ("regulatory taking").[11] The distinction between breach of the fair

8 Adoption of such measures implies normally using the flexibilities allowed by international monetary and financial regulation (EU, GATS, IMF, OECD), following the procedure prescribed and obtaining the support of the competent institutions; see Sacerdoti (2013). Prudential measures are those taken "with respect to financial services, including measures for the protection of investors, depositors, policy holders or persons to whom a fiduciary duty is owed by a financial institution or enterprise, or to ensure the integrity and stability of the financial system." See OECD, Negotiating Group on the Multilateral Agreement on Investment (MAI), "The Treatment of Prudential Measures in the MAI," DAFFE/MAI/EG5(96)1, October 7, 1996, available at: www.oecd.org/daf/mai/pdf/eg5/eg5a961e.pdf. See generally Viterbo (2012).

9 Several ICSID tribunals have taken this approach. See in this respect *Generation Ukraine* v. *Ukraine*, ICSID No. ARB/00/9, Award, September 16, 2003, 20.37; *MTD Equity SDN and MTD Chile S.A.* v. *Republic of Chile*, ICSID No. ARB/01/7, Award, May 25, 2004, 178; *Parkerings-Compagniet* v. *Lithuania*, ICSID No. ARB/05/8, Award, September 11, 2007, 308; *Paushok* v. *Mongolia*, UNCITRAL Award, April 28, 2011, 305.

10 See communication from the EU Commission on the application, from January 1, 2012, of State aid rules to support measures in favor of banks in the context of the financial crisis, OJ 2011/C 356/02.

11 In *Saluka Investments B.V.* v. *Czech Republic*, UNCITRAL Award on Jurisdiction, March 17, 2006, 465–467, the legitimacy of a measure addressed to the support of a domestic

and equitable treatment standard (FET) and indirect expropriation is typically based on the level of incidence on the right to property.[12]

On the other hand these measures may be legitimate regulatory action, not entailing any breach of a BIT, also in the light of the specific language of certain instruments. Thus the European Convention of Human Rights (ECHR/CEDU) excludes from the protection against expropriation non-discriminatory regulatory action adopted in the general interest.[13] In the same vein, the US 2004 BIT Model provides that nondiscriminatory regulatory actions to protect legitimate public welfare objectives (health, safety, environment) do not constitute indirect expropriation "except in rare circumstances."[14] Finally these measures may be carved out from the coverage of a treaty by an "essential interests" clause, as will be examined hereunder.

Measures affecting foreign investments protected under a BIT or an IIA taken in time of an economic crisis raise the question of the relevance of the object and purpose of BITs for the interpretation and hence the application of such treaties in emergency situations.

financial institutions to the detriment of other foreign similar entities was found in breach of FET.

12 Investment case law is rather consistent in this respect. See as to Argentina's measures taken during the 2001 crisis: *LG&E* v. *Argentina*, ICSID Case No. ARB/02/1, Decision on Liability, October 3, 2006, 191, where it is stated that "[i]nterference with the investment's ability to carry on its business is not satisfied where the investment continues to operate, even if profits are diminished. The impact must be substantial in order that compensation may be claimed for the expropriation"; *BG Group Plc* v. *Argentina*, UNCITRAL, Award, December 24, 2007, 258–266; *Enron* v. *Argentina*, ICSID Case No. ARB/01/3, Award, May 22, 2007, 245. See also *Tecmed* v. *Mexico*, ICSID Case No. ARB (AF)/00/2, Award, May 29, 2003, 115; *CME Czech Republic B.V.* v. *Czech Republic*, UNCITRAL, Partial Award, September 13, 2001, 604; *Goetz and others* v. *Burundi*, ICSID Case No. ARB/95/3, Award, February 10, 1999. Beyond ICSID see *Starrett Housing Corp.* v. *Iran*, Award, August 14, 1987, 4 Iran–US CTR 122, 154–157; *Tippets, Abbett, McCarthy, Stratton* v. *TAMS-AFFA Consulting Engineers of Iran*, Award, June 29, 1984, 6 Iran–US CTR 219, 255. For doctrinal views see Leben (2006), 173; Dolzer and Schreuer (2008), 96–101.

13 See Protocol to the Convention for the Protection of Human Rights and Fundamental Freedoms, as amended by Protocol No. 11, Paris 20 March 1952, Art. 1: "The preceding provisions shall not, however, in any way impair the right of a State to enforce such laws as it deems necessary to control the use of property in accordance with the general interest or to secure the payment of taxes or other contributions or penalties."

14 *2004 US Model BIT, Annex B*, available at: www.state.gov/documents/organization/117601.pdf. See also Canada, *Foreign Investment Promotion and Protection Agreement Model*, 2003, available at: italaw.com/documents/Canadian2004-FIPA-model-en.pdf.

The basic question is whether, in the absence of a specific clause, the relevant standards – fair and equitable treatment, nondiscrimination and the prohibition of indirect expropriation – may, or should be applied differently in respect of measures taken to avert or cope with an economic crisis.[15] The issue is how to balance the purpose of protecting covered investment by ensuring stability and predictability of the investment regime of the contracting States with other noneconomic values and concerns of host States, especially when they face major crises.[16]

As stated recently by an investment tribunal, it is obvious that the stability established by a BIT cannot be total "especially when extraordinary circumstances appear."[17] Case law shows that the issue is far from settled. In the absence of specific exceptions for measures taken in case of crisis in the relevant BIT, various arbitral tribunals have expressed different views, notably as to whether and how Argentina's 2001 crisis was relevant for evaluating whether certain measures affecting foreign protected investors were fair or not.[18]

15 For an application of this approach see *Total* v. *Argentina*, ICSID Case No. ARB 04/0, Decision on Liability, December 27, 2010, 160–165. The arbitrators held there that an investor in utilities in Argentina could not have a "legitimate expectation" that the dollar peg of the tariffs would be maintained also in case of a crisis such as Argentina went through (in absence of explicit promises to that effect). The BIT at issue, between France and Argentina, does not contain a "security exception" or "non-precluded measures" clause.

16 See *Total* v. *Argentina* (fn 15) 115, based on a detailed analysis of the preamble of the France–Argentina BIT:

> signatories of such treaties do not thereby relinquish their regulatory powers nor limit their responsibility to amend their legislation in order to adapt it to change and the emerging needs and requests of their people in the normal exercise of their prerogatives and duties. Such limitations upon a government should not lightly be read into a treaty which does not spell them out clearly nor should they be presumed.

For a different view see *Occidental Exploration and Production Company* v. *The Republic of Ecuador*, LCIA Case No. UN 3467, Final Award, July 1, 2004, which relies explicitly on the language of the preamble of the US–Ecuador BIT in order to hold that "the stability of the legal and business framework is thus an essential element of fair and equitable treatment."

17 *El Paso Energy International Company* v. *Argentina*, ICSID Case No. ARB/03/15, Award, October 31, 2011, 614–615 (with reference to the preamble of the US–Argentina BIT).

18 In *British Gas (BG) Group* v. *Argentina* (fn 12), issued under the UK–Argentina BIT (which does not contain an essential security exception), the Tribunal took a strict view of the legal principles applicable to the matter. On the other hand the *Total* Tribunal (fn 15) under the France–Argentina BIT (not containing such a provision either) took a more flexible position as recalled at fn 15. The *BG* Award found that pesification (dedollarization) of tariffs established in dollars was a breach of the fair and equitable treatment, while the *Total* Decision held the contrary. For an "intermediate" position

Two different approaches have been proposed in respect of the application of BITs in case of economic and financial crisis.[19] According to the first approach, the protection afforded by BITs should be upheld when it is most needed, that is when a government might incline to have foreign investors paying the highest price in case of crisis disregarding previous commitments. According to the other view, a government's discretionary policy space should be safeguarded precisely when the general interest is most endangered.

3. Limitations to the coverage of BITs relevant to their application in case of crisis

We come now to limitations to the application of BITs stemming from general or specific limits to their coverage spelled out in their text, which may affect their coverage *ratione* (a) *personae*, (b) *temporis*, (c) *materiae*, (d) *loci*.

In case of dispute, the limits of coverage are in principle relevant as a jurisdictional limit since a tribunal has no competence to entertain a dispute if the matter submitted to it is outside the boundaries of the subject matter that contracting States have regulated in the treaty. Viewed differently, the claimant would lack the substantive right it invokes because the treaty does not attribute such rights to investors of either party.[20]

There is an abundant case law on those limits being raised in investment disputes, leading to decisions upholding or declining jurisdiction as the case may be. Relevant boundaries are not always clear: in several well-known cases there have been split decisions by the tribunals on the matter, leading to forceful dissents.[21] Such jurisdictional issues concern,

see *National Grid* v. *Argentina*, UNCITRAL Award, November 3, 2008, also an award under the UK–Argentina BIT.

19 See Burke-White and von Staden (2007).

20 Rule 41 of the ICSID Arbitration Rules defines an objection to jurisdiction as one "that the dispute is not within the jurisdiction of the Centre or, for other reasons, is not within the competence of the Tribunal" as a Preliminary Objection to be raised "as early as possible" in the proceedings.

21 See *Tokios Tokeles* v. *Ukraine*, ICSID Case No. ARB/02/18, Decision on Jurisdiction, April 29, 2004, in which jurisdiction was upheld notwithstanding the fact that the Lithuania-based claimant company was owned by Ukrainian nationals, against the dissent of the president of the Tribunal, Professor Prosper Weil, who resigned thereafter; *Abaclat and Others* v. *Argentina*, ICSID Case No. ARB/07/5, Decision on Jurisdiction and Admissibility, August 4, 2011, in which jurisdiction was upheld against the dissent of arbitrator Professor Georges Abi-Saab, who also resigned thereafter.

as to (a), whether the claimant is a national of the other party to the BIT.[22] As to the temporal issue (b), an issue which has been raised more than once is whether the investment was made or the alleged breach occurred before or after the entry into force of the treaty when the relevant BIT contains a temporal limit in that respect.[23] As to subject matter jurisdiction (c): the issue is whether the dispute concerns the subject matter to which the treaty applies, such as an "Economic Activity in the Energy Sector" under the Energy Charter Treaty.[24] A similar issue is whether the dispute pertains to a subject matter which is explicitly excluded, such as sometimes taxation[25] or gambling.[26] Finally, the territorial requirement (d) is relevant as to whether the investment was made "in the territory" of the host State, as defined in the BIT.[27]

Some limitations are specifically relevant in respect of measures that may be enacted in time of crisis, even if such limitations may not have been intended to protect signatories from obligations limiting their discretion to take measures in such a situation. This is the case of provisions that exclude from coverage the financial sector or financial assets, such as treasury bills or bonds issued by public entities. Some BITs exclude explicitly sovereign debt from the treaty's coverage.[28] NAFTA in contrast

22 See *Soufraki* v. *UAE*, ICSID Case No. ARB/02/7, Award, July 7, 2004, under the BIT between Italy and the UAE, where the Tribunal found it lacked jurisdiction because the claimant had lost his Italian nationality before the alleged breach had occurred.

23 See *Jan de Nul* v. *Arab Republic of Egypt*, ICSID Case No. ARB/04/13, Decision on Jurisdiction, June 16, 2006. Another issue of temporal application of a BIT may concern the date when the dispute arose when the treaty does not cover those that arose before its entry into force, see *Lucchetti* v. *Peru*, ICSID Case No. ARB/03/4, Award, February 5, 2005.

24 Energy Charter Treaty, Art. 1 (Definitions) (6).

25 In *El Paso* v. *Argentina* (fn 17) 291, the Tribunal took note that as to tax matters Art. XII(2) of the US–Argentina BIT excludes, except in special and limited cases (such as indirect expropriation which was not found *in casu*), any review of possible violation of the fair and equitable treatment, while Art. XII(1) "creates only a best-effort obligation."

26 See for instance the exclusion of gambling from the scope of the US–Republic of Korea Free Trade Agreement, Letter from Hyun Chong Kim to Susan Schwab, June 30, 2007, available at: www.ustr.gov/sites/default/files/uploads/agreements/fta/korus/asset_upload_file993_12732.pdf

27 See *Abaclat and Others* v. *Argentina* (fn 21) 379–380, holding that the investment in bonds issued by Argentina abroad complied with the territorial coverage of the BIT between Italy and Argentina as "investments made in the territory of the Contracting Parties" because of the contribution made to Argentina's economy. For a critical view see De Luca (2012). For the general proposition that restructuring of foreign public debt should not be covered by BITs and their arbitration clauses, but rather left to the traditional methods used in case of States' default, see Waibel (2007).

28 Canada–Colombia FTA (2008), Art. 838, fn 11; Australia–Chile FTA (2008), Art. 10(1)(j)(iii); Azerbaijan–Croatia BIT (2007). See generally UNCTAD, "Sovereign Debt

excludes debt securities of State enterprises but is silent about government bonds. Such limits to the coverage of a BIT or an IIA exclude from the protection of the treaty in case of crisis investors who have suffered losses from measures (for instance debt restructuring) that, in the abstract, might be in violation of a treaty-standard, as expropriation without the prescribed compensation, or as unfair or discriminatory treatment.

4. Exceptions applicable in cases of economic crisis: "non-precluded measures" under the "essential security" clause of US BITs and the defense of necessity

BITs may contain general limits or specific clauses that may restrict their application in case of a crisis. This is the case of the clause of the various subsequent US Models of BITs, allowing the adoption at certain conditions of "non-precluded measures" in cases of emergencies. Such a text is also found in Art. XI of the BIT between the USA and Argentina of 1991 and has been invoked by Argentina in the disputes initiated by US investors who had suffered losses in the Argentinean financial crisis of 2001. An abundant though contradictory case law is thus available.[29]

Based on a clause of the US Model BIT, which in its substance dates back to the first such model and is present also in the more recent models of 2004 and of 2012,[30] Art. XI stipulates "This Treaty shall not preclude the application by either Party of measures necessary for the maintenance of public order ... or the protection of its own essential security interests." Since the exclusion of nonprecluded measures in the text of Art. XI rests on the measure at issue being "necessary," a key point in the case law has been whether Art. XI set forth a specification of the customary defense of necessity precluding wrongfulness, or whether it is a "self-standing" provision.

Restructuring and International Investment Agreements," IIA Issues Note No. 2 (UNCTAD 2011), 4.

29 This should not be surprising since arbitral investment tribunals have no obligation to follow precedents (not even as between ICSID tribunals), notwithstanding the desirability of consistent interpretation, especially by Annulment Committees under Art. 52 ICSID Convention *inter se*. See generally Sacerdoti (2011).

30 The "Essential Security" clause in the 2004 US Model BIT (Art. 18), unchanged in the 2012 Model, expressly states that the clause is "self-judging" ("Nothing in this treaty shall be construed ... (2) to preclude a Party from applying measures that it considers necessary ..."), while such a mention is not found in US BITs dated before 1992. All ICSID arbitral tribunals which have dealt with the issue have concluded that Art. XI is not self-judging. The 2012 Model BIT is available at: www.state.gov/e/eb/ifd/bit/index.htm.

In accordance with the first viewpoint a party's conduct can be excused under Art. XI only if it meets all the requirements of Art. 25 of the ILC Draft Articles on State Responsibility dealing with Necessity. Under the second viewpoint, Art. XI would operate instead as an exception to the application of the relevant primary treaty obligation, such as that of providing fair and equitable treatment to US investors by Argentina under the BIT.[31]

The official commentary by the International Law Commission (ILC) makes it quite clear that recourse to this defense is subject to a number of strict conditions. Most relevant as to acts taken in respect of an economic crisis is the requirement that the act be the "only way" for the State to safeguard an essential interest "against a grave and imminent peril." Moreover necessity cannot be invoked when "the State has contributed to the situation of necessity." Finally Art. 27(b) leaves open the "question of compensation for any material loss caused by the act in question."

In view of those requirements there are various hurdles, the first being that the act be "the only way" available to the State. This is an almost impossible requirement to meet: usually authorities have the option, at least on paper, to choose between adopting different economic measures. The evaluation of which one is required or may be more effective, can rarely make unanimity *ex ante*. Similarly, in hindsight there is rarely agreement on whether the solution enacted was the most appropriate and on which other might have been more effective. Economists tend to suggest different economic recipes in order to get a country out of a crisis, entailing a different burden-sharing among different groups of the population and of economic actors, the choice ultimately being dependent on political feasibility and expediency.[32] The second requirement, that the measures enacted be directed "against a grave and imminent peril" in order not to entail international responsibility, appears to be impractical in respect of economic crises. Since they develop progressively, this requirement may encourage inaction: under a strict reading, a State should let the situation

31 The issue has been framed in this way, the only one correct, by the Ad Hoc Committee which reviewed critically (but did not annul) the *CMS* v. *Argentina* Award. See *CMS* v. *Argentina*, ICSID Case No. ARB/01/18, Decision of the Annulment Committee, September 25, 2007.

32 This resulted clearly in respect of the crisis of Argentina in 2001 both as to the *ex ante* different suggestions made to its authorities by the IMF compared to other qualified observers, and *ex post*. See respectively Blustein (2006), and IMF Independent Evaluation Office (2004), 'The IMF and Argentina 1991–2001.

become desperate, up to the ultimate peril, in order to be able to enact remedial measures contrary to previous international commitments without incurring responsibility!

Case law shows that the most difficult test to pass for a State invoking necessity in respect of an economic crisis is the further condition that "the State has not contributed to the situation of necessity." Causation in economic matters does not lend itself however to a strict deterministic evaluation, otherwise than in exact sciences.[33] Some contribution, normally a noninsignificant one, by the country concerned will almost always be found, except in the most extreme instances, amounting to *force majeure* or due to the unlawful use of force against such State.[34] A review of cases shows moreover that arbitral tribunals are at pains to make economic evaluation of this kind, notwithstanding the use of (mostly party-appointed) economic experts, whose contribution the jurists sitting on the bench are most of the time badly equipped to evaluate critically.[35]

33 See the statement in the *Continental Casualty Co.* v. *Argentina* Award, ICSID Case No. ARB/03/9 Award, September 5, 2008, note 356, quoted with approval in the *El Paso* Award (fn 17) 665, that "in economic matters, the analysis of causation … does not lend itself to the same scientific analysis as in the domain of the so-called exact sciences and of natural phenomenon." The ability of an *ad hoc* investment tribunal to adjudicate such complex economic-social issues is problematic. Moreover tribunals are constrained by the quality of the evidence supplied by the parties, whereas judging such questions of public policy ought not depend on the persuasiveness of the parties satisfying their burden of proof in a given litigation.

34 For a cautious description of the various causes that have been at the origin of Argentina's crisis see IMF Independent Evaluation Office (fn 32), 8, 14, relied upon by the *Continental* Award (fn 33), note 356.

35 As highlighted hereafter, in cases brought against Argentina by US investors (*Enron* v. *Argentina*, ICSID Case No. ARB/01/3, Decision on Jurisdiction, August 2, 2004; *Sempra* v. *Argentina*, ICSID ARB/02/16, Award, September 28, 2007; *CMS* v. *Argentina*, ICSID Case No. ARB/01/8, Award, May 12, 2005), ICSID awards have denied on various grounds the applicability of the customary defense of necessity, holding its requirements applicable also to Art. XI of the US–Argentina BIT. The *National Grid* (fn 18) and *BG* (fn 12) Awards (UNCITRAL awards applying the UK–Argentina BIT) have also denied the customary defense. As to the other awards under the US–Argentina BIT, the *LG&E* Award (fn 12) has recognized necessity for a limited period of time. The *Continental* Award (fn 33) has upheld this defense under the Art. XI of the US–Argentina BIT. *El Paso* (fn 17) has considered the defense of necessity unavailable because of the contribution of Argentina. It must be noted that *Enron* and *Sempra* have been annulled because of methodological flaws in their analysis on necessity. The reasoning of the *CMS* Tribunal was heavily criticized by the Ad Hoc Committee which refrained however from annulment. The *BG* Award has been annulled on appeal in the US (DC Cir. January 17, 2012), because the arbitral tribunal was found to have improperly assumed jurisdiction in disregard of the domestic recourse exhaustion clause of the UK–Argentina BIT. The US Supreme Court however granted *certiorari* in Spring 2013.

5. The Argentinean disputes case law

The difficulties highlighted above emerge clearly from the different answers given to the applicability of Art. XI of the US–Argentina BIT and as to its relation with customary defense of necessity by different tribunals.

(a) Initial case law: Art. XI as a specification of necessity under customary law

Looking at these decisions chronologically, the *CMS* v. *Argentina* Award has reasoned that the BIT

> is clearly designed to protect investments at a time of economic difficulties or other circumstances leading to the adoption of adverse measures by the Government. The question is however how grave these economic difficulties might be. A severe crisis cannot necessarily be equated with a situation of total collapse. And in the absence of such profoundly serious conditions it is plainly clear that the treaty will prevail over any plea of necessity.[36]

Emergency and necessity might acquire a different meaning according to the Tribunal only if the economic difficulties "invite catastrophic conditions in terms of disruption and disintegration of society, or are likely to lead to a total breakdown of the economy."

The *CMS* Tribunal also held that the measures adopted by Argentina were not "the only way" for Argentina to safeguard its interest and that the further requisite that the State had not contributed to the situation of necessity was not met. The treatment of necessity in the *CMS* Award was severely criticized by the Annulment Committee before which Argentina had challenged it. In the Committee's view the Tribunal had wrongfully applied Art. XI, considering it an instance of the customary defense of necessity, but had not failed to apply it all together, which would have warranted the annulment of the award under Art. 52(1)(b) of the ICSID Convention.[37]

The approach taken by the *CMS* Tribunal as to the scope of Art. XI was followed by the Tribunals which decided the *Enron* v. *Argentina* and the

36 *CMS* v. *Argentina* (fn 35) 315.

37 *CMS* v. *Argentina* (fn 31) 135, Annulment. The Committee noted, at 123, that Argentina itself had not clearly distinguished in its pleadings between Art. XI and the customary defense, and their respective requirements.

Sempra v. *Argentina* disputes. Both Awards considered that Art. XI had to be interpreted in accordance with the requirements of the defense of necessity under customary international law. Both came to the conclusion that in any case Argentina could not invoke necessity in respect to the crisis and the measures it had taken in that context, since it had contributed to the crisis. Moreover the *Enron* Decision considered that Argentina's crisis was not grave enough to trigger Art. XI. According to the *Sempra* Tribunal, instead, the economic crisis was potentially sufficiently grave to fall within the scope of Art. XI,[38] but Argentina could have resorted to different measures to cope with the crisis.[39]

Both Awards have been annulled, differently from the outcome of the *CMS* annulment proceedings, but on different grounds. The *Sempra* Annulment Committee found that the Tribunal had not just wrongly applied Art. XI, but had failed to apply it all together, when it had equated its applicability with the defense of necessity under customary law.[40] The *Enron* Committee found instead that the Tribunal had not ascertained properly (because of its exclusive reliance on an economic expert rather than on the basis of legal criteria) that the Emergency Law in "pesifying" (de-dollarizing) Argentina's economy was "the only mean to safeguard an essential interest against a grave and imminent peril" as required by Art. 25(1)(a) of the ILC Articles.[41]

(b) Subsequent case law: Art. XI as a carve-out from the BIT's coverage

Two subsequent decisions involving the evaluation of Argentina's crisis in the light of Art. XI and the defense of necessity recognized in part the legitimacy of Argentina's actions following different approaches.

38 *Sempra* (fn 35) 374.

39 *Sempra* (fn 35) 388; *Enron* v. *Argentina* (fn 12). The *Sempra* Award at 378 considered Art. XI to be "lex specialis" in respect of the customary exception. This is in our view a dubious methodological approach once Art. XI and the customary defense are correctly considered operating at different levels, the first as an exception to a substantive treaty obligation, and the other as a defense from wrongfulness. The *Sempra* Tribunal concluded that since "the Treaty itself did not deal with the legal element necessary for a legitimate invocation of the state of necessity … the rule governing such questions will thus be found under customary law." See also *Enron* (fn 12) 333.

40 *Sempra* v. *Argentina*, ICSID Case No. ARB/02/16, Decision by the Annulment Committee, June 27, 2010.

41 *Enron* v. *Argentina*, ICSID Case No. ARB/01/3, Decision by the Annulment Committee, July 30, 2010, 353.

The *LG&E* Tribunal shared the view that the requirements of necessity under Art. 25 of the ILC Articles (noncontribution, "only way") informed the text of necessity under Art. XI of the BIT, but came to opposite conclusions from those reached in *CMS* and *Enron*.[42]

The *LG&E* Tribunal found that Argentina's "essential security interests" were indeed threatened by the crisis, to the point of a risk of total collapse of the government and the State. It considered further that there was "no serious evidence in the record that Argentina contributed to the crisis resulting in the state of necessity." As to the requirement that the measures adopted by Argentina should be "the only means available" to address the crisis, the Tribunal again diverged from the *CMS* and *Enron* Awards which had found that there were other policy alternatives. The arbitrators in *LG&E* held the view that "there may have been a number of ways to draft the economic recovery plan, but still accepted the Argentine response plan as being the only means available."

The *Continental* Tribunal followed in part the approach of the *LG&E* Tribunal but went on making different findings and reaching different conclusions.[43] First of all, the *Continental* Tribunal accepted the view that a serious economic crisis may qualify as affecting the "essential security interest" of a treaty party under Art. XI, even if its first obvious meaning, which the US most likely considered in drafting this model clause, relates to international and military security.[44] The *Continental* Tribunal stressed the conceptual differences between the scope of Art. XI and the defense of necessity under customary international law, in line with the approach of the *CMS* Annulment Committee. Art. XI represents a carve-out rendering the BITs, its protections and remedies inapplicable if that article's conditions are met. The defense under Art. 25 of the ILC text excludes instead wrongfulness when a breach of the substantive obligations at issue has been found.[45]

The *Continental* Tribunal was further of the view that the strict requirements of necessity, as an exceptional defense to avoid responsibility in case of breach of an international obligation, were inapposite to Art. XI. Its language, context and origin, stemming from the US Friendship

42 *LG&E* v. *Argentina* (fn 12) 260 ff.

43 *Continental* v. *Argentina* (fn 33) 160–168. The challenges against this Award by both claimant and Argentina have been rejected by the Annulment Committee Decision of September 16, 2011. The author of this chapter was chairman of the *Continental* and *Total* Tribunals.

44 *Continental* Award (fn 33) 151.

45 *Ibid.*, 162–168.

Commerce and Navigation treaties of the first part of the twentieth century, whose text had also inspired Art. XX of GATT, suggested rather to refer to the standard of interpretation followed in the WTO case law. The Tribunal noted that the WTO case law has extensively dealt with the concept and requirements of necessity in the context of national economic measures derogating to the obligations contained in GATT. The Tribunal therefore considered it appropriate to look at the GATT/WTO jurisprudence, rather than to refer to the requirement of necessity under customary international law.[46]

(c) Interpretation and evaluation of necessity in Art. XI: the reference to GATT

The Tribunal recalled that WTO case law interprets this concept in Art. XX GATT in the sense that a "necessary" measure is, in the continuum, located significantly closer to the pole of "indispensable" than to the opposite pole of simply "making a contribution." In any case the reach of the word "necessary" is not limited to that which is "indispensable" or "of absolute necessity" or "inevitable."[47]

The Tribunal followed the approach of the WTO Appellate Body that

> The necessity of a measure should be determined through "a process of weighing and balancing of factors" which usually includes the assessment of the following three factors: the relative importance of interests or values furthered by the challenged measures, the contribution of the measure to the realization of the ends pursued by it and the restrictive impact of the measure on international commerce.[48]

The Tribunal noted that according to that jurisprudence a measure is not necessary if another treaty-consistent, or less inconsistent, alternative measure, which the member State concerned could reasonably be expected to employ is available. This excludes any measure which is merely theoretical in nature, for instance, where the responding State is not capable of taking it, or where the measure imposes an undue burden on that State, such as prohibitive costs or substantial technical difficulties.[49]

46 *Ibid.*, 192.

47 *Ibid.*, 193 with reference to WTO, Appellate Body Report, *Korea–Beef*, WT/DS/AB/R, June 7, 2001, 161.

48 *Continental* Award (fn 33) 194, quoting the above paragraph of *Korea–Beef*.

49 WTO, Appellate Body Report, *US–Gambling*, 308, referring to Art. XIV GATS, which corresponds to Art. XX GATT.

Those standards are clearly different and more flexible than those to be used in order to ascertain whether the challenged measure was the only one available in the context of necessity as a defense under customary law. On this basis the Tribunal concluded that the crisis met the requirement of Art. XI and that the measures challenged by the claimant were necessary to cope with it.[50] The Tribunal looked also to the issue of whether Argentina had reasonably available alternatives, less in conflict or more compliant with its international obligations, "while providing an equivalent contribution to the achievement of the objective pursued,"[51] to the measures challenged by Continental as inconsistent with the BIT. The Tribunal concluded that the alternatives referred to by the claimant to de-dollarization and the connected temporary transfer restrictions adopted by Argentina were not viable or would not have shielded the investor's assets from the loss it complained of.[52] This reliance on WTO legal concepts has originated a lively legal debate which we address hereunder in Section 6.[53]

(d) Latest developments: back to the customary concept of necessity or resort to general principles?

One of the most recent decisions in the stream of awards concerning Argentina's crisis of 2001, *El Paso* v. *Argentina* in 2011, has taken a view which coincides neither with the earlier cases, which had applied to Art. XI the standards required for necessity as a customary defense against wrongfulness, nor with the decisions of Ad Hoc Committees and of the *LG&E* and *Continental* Tribunals. The *El Paso* Tribunal considered Art. XI "lex specialis" in respect of the defense of necessity under customary law and therefore applied to it the same criteria required for the customary defense.[54] It considered further that reference to the principles reflected in Art. 25 of the ILC Draft was appropriate for "filling *lacunae*" and interpreted Art. XI in the light of the general principles listed in Art. 38(1)(c) of the ICJ Statute relying on Art. 31.3(c) of the Vienna Convention on the Law of Treaties (VCLT).[55]

50 *Continental* Award (fn 33) 197.

51 See WTO, Appellate Body, *Brazil–Tyres*, WT/DS332/AB/R, December 17, 2007, 156.

52 *Continental* Award (fn 33) 223–234.

53 For a criticism of the *Continental* Tribunal approach see especially Alvarez and Brink (2010).

54 *El Paso* Award (fn 17) 616.

55 *Ibid.*, 621–624. The Tribunal considered the UNIDROIT Principles on International Commercial Contracts as evidence of the general character of the principle of non-

The *El Paso* Tribunal stated at paragraph 624 that

> (i) there is a rule of general international law which provides that necessity may not be invoked as a ground for precluding wrongfulness if the State concerned has significantly contributed to creating that necessity; (ii) there also seems to be a general principle of law recognized by civilized nations that necessity cannot be recognized if a Party to a contract has contributed to it. This means that the rule or principle in question may be used, under Article 31(3) of the Vienna Convention, to ascertain the meaning of Article XI of the Argentina–US BIT.

The Tribunal held moreover that Argentina had contributed to the state of necessity, and concluded that it could therefore not avail itself of the defense.[56] The rigorous approach of the *El Paso* Tribunal to the issue of noncontribution makes the availability of the defense of necessity in economic crisis problematic.[57]

In light of the above review of the case law we may conclude that the issue of the protection available to investors under BITs in respect of measures taken by the host State in time of crisis remains open. The answer depends heavily on the features and causes of the crises and the content and impact of the measures. Legally, the strict requirements of necessity as a customary principle, as well as the lack of clarity in texts such as Art. XI of the US–Argentina BIT, resulting in contradictory interpretations, show that this defense is difficult to invoke except in the most exceptional and desperate circumstances. States should therefore consider introducing in BITs appropriate flexibilities and exemptions, such as an Art. XX GATT type clause, if they view themselves as exposed to the relevant risks.

6. The issue of reliance on WTO law

Reference to established WTO concepts concerning exceptions and necessity can represent a useful yardstick to reach balanced solutions. There are a number of valid reasons to refer to WTO law for interpreting concepts found in investment law instruments, when appropriate. Our view is fur-

contribution beyond the ILC codification. The ICSID Tribunal in *Impregilo* v. *Argentina* ICSID Case ARB/07/17, Award, June 26, 2011, 353–359, also held that Argentina had contributed to the crisis through its previous economic and fiscal policies.

56 *El Paso* Award (fn 31) 656 (arbitrator B. Stern dissenting).

57 Arbitrator Stern advocated instead in her dissent reliance on the GATT criteria adopted by the *Continental* Tribunal.

ther that this reference is preferable for structural reasons to reliance on general administrative law principles.

(a) *The different setting of the WTO is not a bar against relying on trade law in investment disputes*

Some authors have considered the reference to WTO law to interpret investment treaties inappropriate in respect of the concept of necessity because of textual differences between Art. XX GATT and Art. XI of the US–Argentina BIT, and because of the different contexts. As to the first criticism, one can point out that once Art. XI is considered a carve-out and not an instance of nonwrongfulness under customary law, defining "necessity" in the light of the most similar provision, namely the one found in a trade instrument sharing the same origin such as the GATT, seems quite justified. Interpretation of the term "necessity," when used as a self-standing concept in treaties dealing with economic matters to refer to an exception in favor of a contracting State against the performance of its obligations towards foreign investors is more appropriately linked to the GATT than to other settings, including that of State responsibility. An objection against using the concept of necessity as developed under Art. XX GATT is based on the fact that BITs lack the antidiscrimination, anti-circumvention prescriptions of the "chapeau" of Art. XX.[58] However, the constant case law of the Appellate Body has been in the direction of separating the analysis of necessity under any of the exceptions listed in Art. XX from the subsequent analysis of whether the domestic measure defended as necessary has been applied in breach of those requirements. Thus also under the GATT ascertaining whether a measure is "necessary to" the legitimate objective pursued is to be analyzed independently from further requirements. Moreover BITs contain a similar requirement that the treatment of protected investors be nondiscriminatory.[59]

More generally the WTO Agreements contain a number of legal-economic concepts which are used also in investment agreements as to the

58 "Subject to the requirement that such measures are not applied in a manner which would constitute a means of arbitrary or unjustifiable discrimination between countries where the same conditions prevail, or a disguised restriction on international trade, nothing in this Agreement shall be construed to prevent the adoption or enforcement by any contracting party of measures."

59 See WTO, Appellate Body, *US–Shrimp*, WT/258/AB/R, October 12, 1998, 115 ff. For a similar rebuttal of the arguments of Alvarez and Brink (2010), see Kurtz (in press), Ch. 5; Mitchell and Henkels (2013)

pursuit of the same objectives, such as nondiscrimination in respect to like products and services.[60] A paramount argument in our view is based on legitimacy: the WTO offers a multilateral setting of comprehensive interconnected agreements and its dispute settlement system represents a multilateral, inter-State (and hence naturally balanced) permanent judicial mechanism (in substance), contrary to the bilateral contest of BITs and their *ad hoc* tribunals. The latter may be thus well advised in appropriate cases to look to the consistent and authoritative jurisprudence of the Appellate Body under the WTO, for interpretative guidance, so as to promote consistency also in investment case law.[61] Since BITs, parties are almost all also members of the WTO and parties to its Agreements, Art. 31(3)(c) of the VCLT, directing an interpreter to take into account also other international rules in force between the parties when interpreting a treaty, is the appropriate basis of such systemic interpretation in context.

(b) The limits of relying on comparative public law principles as an alternative

Some authors have suggested an alternative way to enhance the legitimacy of investment tribunal decisions and their recognition of host States' legitimate concerns[62]: recourse to domestic public law principles, in a comparative dimension, as the proper tool to interpret and apply investment law. Both substantive and procedural arguments have been put forth. As to substance, proponents submit that the relevant standards to ascertain the legality of host States' actions challenged by foreign investors as being in breach of BITs standards can only be found in the generally recognized domestic law principles which govern administrative action. Both from the subjective point of view (the basis for "legitimate expectations" of investors) and from an objective perspective, comparative public law affords the correct standard, balancing the protection of foreign investors with nondiscriminatory application of measures taken to implement governments' obligations towards the public.

From a procedural point of view, it is submitted that investment tribunals perform a function which is akin to judicial review of administrative

60 See Di Mascio and Pauwelyn (2008). The correctness of the reference by arbitral tribunals to WTO law has fueled a lively debate: see Howse and Chalamish (2009), 1087 and Kurtz (2009), 749.

61 See Sacerdoti (2006).

62 See Schill (2010) and the authors contributing to that volume.

decisions in domestic (administrative) law. They should accordingly apply similar standards, including recognizing a margin of discretion to public authorities in evaluating public interest and recourse to proportionality, rather than follow an international commercial arbitration approach, based on strict enforcement of contractual obligations.[63]

The first argument has several merits in relation with specific concepts and standards found in BITs and IIAs in general, for instance as to the requirement of fair and equitable treatment of investors and what constitutes indirect expropriation through regulatory conduct. The parameter of administrative action in democratic and well-governed States may be usually the appropriate yardstick for evaluating the correctness of the conduct of public authorities and the limits of "legitimate expectation" of businessmen interacting with them. This involves assessing proportionality between the objective pursued in the general interest and the burden imposed on specific private parties directly affected as an element of fairness. This does not amount, however, to sharing the view that administrative and public law concepts may replace those of public international law when rights and duties of States, freely negotiated and accepted, are at issue (including those agreed for the benefit of their investors). In international law reference to "general principles" recognized by civilized nations as to the carrying out of administrative action may be the tool to bring public law concepts into international legal relations.[64]

It is, however, as to procedure where those positions are least convincing. International courts, investment tribunals, WTO panels and the Appellate Body have to resolve disputes between parties situated on the same footing, applying international norms agreed by States that reflect their sovereign equality as a fundament of the international community. The unequal position of litigants in domestic disputes when a private party challenges an act or regulation issued in the general interest cannot be transferred as such to the international arena. The principles of administrative discretion, margin of appreciation, deference which are followed

63 See Stone Sweet and Mathews (2008); Kingsbury and Schill (2010).

64 Thus in *Total* (fn 15) in order to ascertain the import of an investor "legitimate expectations" as part of the fair and equitable treatment, the Tribunal considered two elements. First it examined comparatively domestic law in the area, looking at general principles in accordance with Art. 38(1)(c) of the ICJ Statute, reviewing common law and civil law jurisdictions as well as the case law of the ECJ and ECHR. Secondly, as to public international law, it considered the principle of estoppel and the ILC "Guiding Principles applicable to unilateral declarations of States capable of creating legal obligations" (ILC Report A/61/10.2006), *Total* Decision (fn 15), 126–134.

domestically (as well as by the ECJ and the ECHR in such disputes) can have only a limited application in international litigation. This is because the task of adjudicators here is not to "accommodate" individual rights with public action pursuing public interest, protecting the former from any abusive encroachment while being mindful of the responsibility of public authorities. International courts and arbitral tribunals must adjudicate impartially the respective rights and duties of the litigants based on international norms. Similarly, the WTO importing States, whose measures are those normally challenged, do not enjoy a preferential position, absent the recognition in the relevant WTO Agreement of regulatory discretion restricting the standard of review of their actions in disputes.[65] This typical international setting is an objective constraint to the tendency by scholars of domestic public law to devise a global administrative law whose actors would be principally internationally regulatory organizations, though usually lacking the typical regulatory powers of domestic agencies.

Reference to WTO provisions, concepts and jurisprudence thus remains an appropriate tool to approach interpretation of investment law instruments, taking of course into account any difference in the texts, in the light of the object and purpose of the relevant provisions and agreements.

References

Alvarez, J. and Brink, T. 2010. "Revisiting the Necessity Defence: Continental Casualty v Argentina." *Yearbook on International Investment Law and Policy 2010–2011*: 319.

Bjorklund, A. 2009. "Economic Security Defences in International Investment Law." *Yearbook on International Investment Law and Policy 2008–2009*: 479.

Blustein, P. 2006. *And the Money Kept Rolling In (and Out): Wall Street, the IMF, and the Bankrupting of Argentina*. New York: PublicAffairs.

Burke-White, W. and von Staden, A. 2007. "Investment Protection in Extraordinary Times: The Interpretation and Application of Non-Precluded Measures Provisions in Bilateral Investment Treaties." *Virginia J. International L.* 48: 307.

Crivellaro, A. 2011. "Annulment of ICSID Awards: Back to the 'First Generation'?" *Liber Amicorum Serge Lazareff*, Paris: Pédone, 145.

65 See Art. 2.1 of the SPS Agreement allowing all WTO members to freely set their appropriate level of sanitary protection; Art. 17(6)(b) of the Anti-dumping Agreement as to the level of discretion that Panels must allow to national authorities.

De Luca, A. 2012. "Collective Actions in ICSID Arbitration: The Argentine Bonds Case." *IYIL* 21: 211.

Di Mascio, N. and Pauwelyn, J. 2008. "Non-discrimination in Trade and Investment Treaties: Worlds Apart or Two Sides of the Same Coin?" *AJIL* 102: 48.

Dolzer, R. and Schreuer, C. 2008. *Principles of International Investment Law.* Oxford University Press.

Howse, R. and Chalamish, E. 2009. "The Use and Abuse of WTO Law in Investor-State Arbitration: A Reply to Jürgen Kurtz." *EJIL* 20: 1087–1094.

Kingsbury, B. and Schill, S. 2010. "Public Law Concepts to Balance Investors' Rights with States Regulatory Actions in the Public Interest – the Concept of Proportionality," Schill, S. (ed.), *International Investment Law and Comparative Public Law.* Oxford University Press: 75.

Kurtz, J. 2009. "The Use and Abuse of WTO Law in Investor-State Arbitration: Competition and its Discontents." *EJIL* 20: 749–771.

2009. "Adjudging the Exceptional at International Investment Law: Security, Public Order and Financial Crisis." *ICLQ* 59: 325.

in press. *The World Trade Organization and International Investment Law: Converging Systems.*

Leben, C. 2006. "La liberté normative de l'État et la question de l'expropriation indirecte," Leben, C. (ed.), *Le contentieux arbitral transnational relatif à l'investissement.* Limal: Anthemis.

Mitchell, A. and Henkels, C. 2013. "Variation on a Theme: Comparing the Concept of 'Necessity' in International Investment Law and WTO Law." *Chicago J. International L.* 14: 287.

Sacerdoti, G. 1972. *I contratti tra Stati e stranieri nel diritto internazionale.* Milano: Giuffré.

2006. "The Dispute Settlement System of the WTO in Action," Sacerdoti, G., Yanovich, A. and Bohane, J. (eds.), *The WTO at Ten, The Contribution of the Dispute Settlement System.* Cambridge University Press: 35.

2011. "Precedent in the Settlement of International Economic Disputes: The WTO and the Investment Arbitration Models," Rovine, A. (ed.), *Contemporary Issues in International Arbitration and Mediation: The Fordham Papers 2010.* Leiden: M. Nijhoff.

2013. "BIT Protections and Economic Crises: Limits to Their Coverage, the Impact of Multilateral Financial Regulation and the Defence of Necessity." *ICSID Review* 28: 351.

Schill, S. (ed.) 2010. Introduction, *International Investment Law and Comparative Public Law.* Oxford University Press.

Sloane, R. 2012. "On the Use and Abuse of Necessity in the Law of State Responsibility." *AJIL* 106: 447.

Stone Sweet, A. and Mathews, J. 2008. "Proportionality Balancing and Global Constitutionalism." *Columbia J. Transnational L.* 47: 73.

Van Aaken, A. and Kurtz, J. 2009. "Prudence or Discrimination? Emergency Measures, the Global Financial Crisis and International Economic Law." *JIEL* 12: 859.

2010. "Emergency Measures and International Investment Law. How Far Can States Go?" *Yearbook on International Investment Law and Policy 2009–2010*: 505.

Viterbo, A. 2012. *International Economic Law and Monetary Measures. Limits to States' Sovereignty and Dispute Settlement*. Cheltenham: Elgar.

Waibel, M. 2007. "Opening Pandora's Box: Sovereign Bonds in International Arbitration." *AJIL* 101: 711.

2

The protection of general interests of host States in the application of the fair and equitable treatment standard

MARA VALENTI

1. Introduction

The fair and equitable treatment (FET) standard, provided for by most investment treaties, has been a sort of 'sleeping beauty' for many years;[1] quite recently 'kissed awake', it has nowadays become a leading character within the context of foreign investor–State arbitration. Although it has been inserted in bilateral investment treaties (BITs) since the beginning, the FET standard seems to have been discovered only recently by investors complaining about an alleged violation of the applicable treaty by the host contracting State. The reason for this interest in the standard may paradoxically coincide with the reason why it has been so neglected in the past, that is, its inherent ambiguity. Being inherently vague and ambiguous, it seems that initially foreign investors neglected it as a basis for their claims. The more claimants became confident with arbitral proceedings to settle their disputes with the host country, the more they showed an attitude to explore all the opportunities granted by the applicable treaty, clauses providing for FET included.

A 'debate' about the scope of the standard has therefore evolved at different levels: arbitral tribunals applying the standard in their decisions gave rise to a (not always consistent) case-law; scholars supporting or criticizing such decisions advanced their own understanding; and States took position on the issue in their negotiating practice. Such a process has had the effect of contributing to the progressive definition of the standard.

One must acknowledge that a lot has already been said on the subject. However, it seems appropriate at this stage of evolution to assess the question against the background of the new trends in the international

1 For this terminology, see Schreuer (2005b).

investment law as a whole, although the standard may still be open to developments. This study will assess the content that has been given to the FET standard with the aim of pointing out the suitability of the standard to enhance the protection of the general interests of host States.

2. The origins of the clause

One of the first examples in treaty practice of the FET standard is to be found in the Havana Charter. Drafted in 1948 in order to establish an International Trade Organization (ITO), it never entered into force because the very countries which supported it most, eventually did not ratify it. Although the ITO mainly dealt with trade exchanges among member countries, it would have been competent also on issues such as labour rights or investments. According to Art. 11(2), the Organization could make recommendations to promote 'bilateral or multilateral agreements on measures designed: … (i) to assure *just and equitable* treatment for the enterprise, skills, capital, arts and technology brought from one Member country to another'. As it has been acknowledged by the doctrine, such a provision provides for 'even less than a *pactum de contrahendo*'.[2]

A clause providing for FET was contained in the Economic Agreement of Bogotá, adopted by the Conference of the American States in 1948, and which never entered into force. According to Art. 22, 'Foreign capital shall receive equitable treatment. The States therefore agree not to take unjustified, unreasonable or discriminatory measures that would impair the legally acquired rights or interests of nationals of other countries in the enterprises, capital, skills, arts or technology they have supplied.' Capital-importing countries, especially Latin American ones, were likely to perceive the Agreement as being too foreign investor-oriented, and that must have deterred them from ratifying it.[3]

Fair and equitable, or just 'equitable', treatment, was almost invariably provided for in Friendship, Commerce and Navigation Treaties (FCN Treaties) concluded by the US after 1948. Such treaties concerned not only issues of trade and navigation, but also the protection of natural and legal persons having the nationality of one contracting State in the territory of the other contracting State. The standard of treatment at issue was to be accorded by the host contracting State to foreign people, their properties and other interests in its territory.

2 Vasciannie (1999), 108. 3 *Ibid.*

A FET clause has been subsequently enshrined in some draft Conventions dealing with the protection of foreign investments, such as the so-called Abs-Shawcross Convention on Investments Abroad (1959)[4] and the OECD Convention on the Protection of Foreign Property (1967).[5] Although such conventions never entered into force, they exerted an important influence on the subsequent practice of BITs. In fact, the standard has been inserted in most BITs concluded since the 1960s.[6] Its recurrence makes the standard a distinctive feature of BITs, thus showing that the inclusion of such a standard is considered coessential with the purpose of BITs.

The Convention establishing the Multilateral Investment Guarantee Agency (MIGA), whose purpose is to facilitate the flow of foreign investment to developing countries in order to strengthen economic development,[7] mentions 'the availability of *fair and equitable* treatment and legal protection for the investment' among the conditions that the Agency will ascertain in order to decide whether or not to guarantee an investment.[8] While the other conditions required concern the characteristics the foreign investment must have in order to be issued a MIGA guarantee, the above-mentioned provision refers to the 'investment conditions in the host country'. This means that the legal regime existing in the country in which the guaranteed investment will take place is also relevant in the MIGA's decision. The reference to FET in an instrument like the MIGA Convention points out that in order to strengthen the economic development of the host country not only does the soundness of the foreign investment matter, but also does the fairness of the legal system of the host country itself.

4 Reproduced in *Journal of Public Law*, 1960, 116–18.

5 Reproduced in 7 *ILM* (1968), 118–43.

6 BITs that do not contain a FET clause are a minority; see Yannaca-Small (2005), 78, who mentions some Asian countries' BITs (such as those of Pakistan, Saudi Arabia and Singapore).

7 See Preamble of the Convention Establishing the MIGA, reproduced in 6 *ILM* (1985), 1607.

8 According to Art.12(d) of the MIGA Convention, the conditions to be complied with by the foreign investor in order to obtain a guarantee by the MIGA are the following:

> (i) the economic soundness of the investment and its contribution to the development of the host country; (ii) compliance of the investment with the host country's laws and regulations; (iii) consistency of the investment with the declared development objectives and priorities of the host country; and *(iv) the investment conditions in the host country, including the availability of fair and equitable treatment and legal protection for the investment* [italics added].

3. The interplay with the international minimum standard

The issue of the relationship between the FET standard and the minimum standard of treatment of aliens and their property has long been debated and has drawn the attention of those – arbitrators, scholars and State negotiators – who had to handle the FET standard, somehow shifting the attention from the analysis of the standard in itself, as a free-standing obligation.

Such an interest for the relationship between the two standards stemmed from the wording of some international investment agreements (IIAs) providing for the two standards in the same clause, most of the time connecting one to the other. The issue has been addressed mainly within the framework of the North America Free Trade Agreement (NAFTA) in relation to Art. 1105,[9] which is entitled 'Minimum Standard of Treatment' and which requires the host contracting State to 'accord to investments of investors of another Party treatment in accordance with international law, including fair and equitable treatment and full protection and security'.

Looking back at the origins of both principles, however, one can realize that the FET standard and the international minimum standard are distinct and autonomous.

Unlike the FET, the international minimum standard did not originate as a treaty clause: its existence as a customary rule has long been debated between two different groups of States. Industrialized countries basically advanced the standard against the national treatment advocated by developing countries as the standard of treatment to be accorded to aliens and their goods according to international law. The principle appears thus as a 'standard of competency',[10] which serves to determine the threshold treatment to be accorded to a foreigner when the one granted by the domestic legislation of the host country falls below a given level.[11]

The new standard, however, did not win the support of developing countries, since it was perceived as an unjustified interference in their sovereign right to regulate all economic activities on their territory. Developing countries stated their opposition to the international minimum standard. To that purpose, they managed to make the General Assembly of the UN adopt the Charter of Economic Rights and Duties of States.[12]

9 Such jurisprudence has been extensively studied and commented upon; see *i.a.* Laird (2003), 185–214.

10 Falsafi (2007), 335. 11 Roth (1949), 83.

12 A/RES/3281(XXIX), *UN General Assembly Charter of Economic Rights and Duties of States*, 12 December 1974, in *ILM* 1975, 251–61; see, in particular, Art. 2(2)(a) and (b).

The positions taken within the UN by developing countries, however, have been compromised in the context of bilateral relationships, where their bargaining power was weaker than as a whole. Although most BITs do not contain a provision requiring the host contracting State to treat the foreign investor 'in accordance with international law', the very fact that developing countries concluded such treaties testifies their willingness to regulate the activities carried on by foreigners on their territories in compliance with international undertakings.

As we have already noted, a FET clause is, on the contrary, regularly inserted into BITs. According to some authors, States considered the FET standard as equivalent to the minimum standard of treatment of aliens. In other words, they are supposed to insert a FET clause into their BITs having in mind the minimum standard. This would be supported by some statements made by negotiators or governmental legal advisors, such as those quoted by J. C.Thomas.[13] The same conclusion could be drawn by considering that the FET standard was almost invariably provided for in BIT clauses together with full protection and security, a well-established principle of customary international law.

According to another view, however, a literal interpretation of the FET clause itself would lead to a different conclusion. Whenever the clause providing for the FET does not contain any reference to international law nor does it mention full protection and security, it could be inferred that, in the mind of such treaties' drafters, the FET was considered as a free-standing obligation.[14]

The variety of different formulations of the treaty clause providing for FET militates against attempts at generalization.[15] In some cases, the provision commits to both the FET and the treatment required by international law, without any textual connection between the two.[16]

13 Thomas (2002), 54.

14 This opinion has been firstly asserted by Mann (1981), 244. Dolzer and Stevens (1995) at 60 submit 'that the fact that parties to BITs have considered it necessary to stipulate this standard as an express obligation rather than relied on a reference to international law and thereby invoked a relatively vague concept such as the minimum standard, is probably evidence of a self-contained standard'. Schreuer (2005a) at 360 maintains:

> As a matter of textual interpretation, it is inherently implausible that a treaty would use an expression such as 'fair and equitable treatment' to denote a well-known concept such as the 'minimum standard of treatment in customary international law'. If the parties to a treaty want to refer to customary international law, it must be presumed that they will refer to it as such rather than using a different expression.

15 For a useful overview, see UNCTAD (2004).

16 Art. 10 of the ECT, e.g., requires the contracting Parties: 'to accord at all times to Investments of Investors of other Contracting Parties fair and equitable treatment.

In other cases, the clause providing for FET requires that it be granted 'in accordance with (the principles of) international law'.[17]

In NAFTA, the link between the two standards is strengthened by considering the FET standard as subsumed under the other one. As we have seen, Art. 1105 requires to accord 'treatment in accordance with international law, including fair and equitable treatment and full protection and security'.[18] In the 2004 version of the US Model BIT, the relevant provision – now entitled 'Minimum standard of treatment' – is worded in the same manner as NAFTA's Art. 1105, but it specifies that the treatment granted is to be 'in accordance with *customary* international law'.[19]

One must take into account, moreover, that there are IIAs which provide only for FET without any reference whatsoever to international law.

The practice of States in the drafting of their investment treaties, just briefly outlined, reveals that different opinions exist with respect to the relationship between the FET and the international standard of treatment. Given such lack of uniformity, we are inclined to consider the FET as a free-standing obligation with respect to the international minimum standard. The scope of the former, then, essentially depends on the

... In no case shall such Investments be accorded treatment less favourable than that required by international law, including treaty obligations.'

17 See, e.g., Art. 3 of the BIT between Argentina and France (1991) which reads as follows: 'Each contracting Party shall undertake to accord in its territory and maritime zone just and equitable treatment, in accordance with the principles of international law, to the investments of investors of the other Party.'

18 On 31 July 2001, NAFTA member States, gathered within the Free Trade Commission, adopted the 'Notes of Interpretation of certain Chapter 11 Provisions'. As far as Art. 1105(1) is concerned, they asserted that it

> prescribes the customary international law minimum standard of treatment of aliens as the minimum standard of treatment to be afforded to investments of investors of another Party. 2. The concepts of 'fair and equitable treatment' and 'full protection and security' do not require treatment in addition to or beyond that which is required by the customary international law minimum standard of treatment of aliens. 3. A determination that there has been a breach of another provision of the NAFTA, or of a separate international agreement, does not establish that there has been a breach of Article 1105(1).

19 (Italics added.) Such a solution reveals the concern of States like the US about a far-reaching application of the FET standard. The reference to customary international law is useful to put the standard back to the higher parameters of the minimum standard of treatment. The US stance is a telling argument in favour of the self-standing nature of the FET standard. The specification added by the new Model BIT would not be necessary if the two principles were already one and the same. On the 2004 US Model BIT, see *i.a.*, Juillard (2004), 669–82; Kantor (2004), 383–96. On 20 April 2012 a new version of the US Model BIT was released. The provision on the minimum standard of treatment, however, has remained unchanged.

wording of the treaty clause providing for it and is thus a matter of treaty interpretation. Obviously, when the two standards are linked together within the same treaty provision, problems of construction may arise. However, this one is also a matter of treaty interpretation.[20]

Such an opinion, however, is not shared by all scholars, nor by arbitral tribunals dealing with the issue. In particular, foreign investors as claimants, on the one hand, and host States as respondents, on the other hand, have advanced different and opposing views on the issue: the former contend that the two standards are different and therefore that the FET is an autonomous principle, which is to be given its 'plain meaning'; the latter, on the contrary, tend to maintain that the two standards coincide, thus aiming at lowering the scope of the FET standard to the level of treatment required by customary international law.[21]

Whether or not the FET standard has attained, or is about to attain, customary nature is a completely different matter. In this regard, one must acknowledge that its insertion into BITs is a widespread practice of States. However, it is not easily proven that such a practice is backed by a sense of legal obligation (*opinio juris*), which must also be found before concluding by stating the customary status of the rule. Given the uncertainty surrounding the subjective element of custom with reference to the FET, we do not believe that it has already attained the customary status.[22] In our opinion, however, the evolution that the standard has undergone, especially the progressive definition of its content by the arbitral practice and scholarly conceptualization, reveals that it would be ready to take this qualitative step.

20 Schreuer (2005a), 364:

> Overall, the better view would seem to be that in the absence of a clear indication to the contrary, the fair and equitable treatment standard contained in BITs is an autonomous concept. Depending on the specific wording of a particular treaty, this concept may well overlap with or even be identical to the minimum standard required by international law. The meaning of a clause providing for fair and equitable treatment will ultimately depend on its specific wording.

21 Vasciannie (1999) at 103–5 well illustrates the shortcomings of both approaches. Kläger (2010) at 438 *et seq.* reveals that: 'Recent arbitral jurisprudence has attempted to overcome the gap between these two approaches by applying a juristic artifice.' The author acknowledges that the new line of jurisprudence 'has certainly cleared the path for the next developmental phase of fair and equitable treatment, which is the shaping of the norm's content through an increased number of arbitral awards, while at least implicitly recognizing fair and equitable treatment as a norm with a self-contained existence'.

22 *Contra* Tudor (2008), 80–5.

4. The appropriate methodology to construe the FET standard

Once it has been established that the FET is a genuine treaty obligation and is not subsumed under international law, the starting point for its construction consists in interpreting the clauses providing for FET in accordance with the general rule on treaty interpretation, codified in Art. 31 of the Vienna Convention on the Law of Treaties (VCLT).[23] Such clauses simply state that foreign investors are to be granted a fair and equitable treatment by the host contracting State. Usually, no other specification is found.

As we shall see in detail below, a literal interpretation outlines the very nature of the standard, revealing its suitability to pursue the ultimate aim of the investment treaty, namely affording protection to foreign investors, thereby promoting the investment inflows hopefully beneficial to the host country. Interpreting a FET clause according to the general rule on treaty interpretation, however, will not lead to a satisfactory result since it cannot define its exact content. At the most, the general framework of the standard will be outlined. To fill with content such a framework, further steps should be taken.

The appropriate methodology to deal with the standard consists then in distinguishing different fact-specific situations to which it applies and in identifying the ensuing obligations. Such a content-giving operation, which is typical with respect to the general principles of law, is usually carried out through judicial assessment, but it may also be conducted by means of theoretical thinking. As we will try to show hereafter, arbitral tribunals applying FET clauses in specific disputes have progressively clarified the constitutive elements of the standard. Such elements can be viewed as more specific obligations in which the principle is deemed to materialize depending on the circumstances of the case. Stability, consistency, predictability and transparency of the host country's legal framework; protection of the investor's legitimate expectations; procedural fairness and due process are the obligations that have been mostly considered to be inherent to FET.

23 Art. 31 VCLT provides as follows: 'A treaty shall be interpreted in good faith in accordance with the ordinary meaning to be given to the terms of the treaty in their context and in the light of its object and purpose.'

4.1 *The textual interpretation of the clause in light of its purpose: the balancing nature of the standard*

Thus, defining 'fair and equitable treatment' is not an easy task. An arbitral tribunal has deemed the expression to mean: 'just, even-handed, unbiased, legitimate'.[24]

Literally speaking, the host State's conduct towards the foreign investor can be considered fair and equitable when it is not merely lawful, but also reasonable given the circumstances of the case. First of all, the law-conforming requirement of the standard requires that the foreign investor be treated in accordance with the law, that is to say not arbitrarily. At the same time, however, equitable considerations must be included in the assessment of the compliance of the host State's conduct with the standard and may serve as a corrective element to the law-conforming requirement.

The most convincing textual interpretation of 'fair and equitable treatment' has been given, in our opinion, by Carreau and Juillard:

> après que l'on aura constaté qu'étymologiquement, le traitement juste n'est autre que celui qui est conforme au droit, et que le traitement équitable n'est autre que celui qui est conforme à l'équité, on n'aura guère progressé. Il semble bien, d'une part, que par *traitement juste*, on puisse entendre deux choses: le traitement assuré à l'investissement international ne saurait violer le traitement que lui accorde le droit national; le traitement accordé à l'investissement par le droit national ne saurait violer le traitement qu'exigent l'ensemble des sources combinées du droit international. En bref, il y aurait traitement juste lorsque le droit interne tiendrait ce qu'il a promis, et, lorsqu'en tenant ce qu'il a promis, le droit interne satisferait les exigences du droit international. Il semble bien, d'autre part, que par *traitement équitable* on puisse entendre que la règle de traitement ménage leur part légitime aux intérêts des parties en cause dans une opération d'investissement international. Le traitement équitable serait donc celui qui assurerait un équilibre satisfaisant entre les intérêts de l'investisseur, d'un premier côté, de l'État de nationalité de cet investisseur, d'un deuxième côté, et de l'État de territorialité de l'investissement, d'un troisième côté, puisque tous les trois sont parties prenantes à l'opération d'investissement. À l'intérieur de ce principe correctif du droit interne qu'est le standard international du traitement juste

24 *MTD Equity SDN and MTD Chile S.A.* v. *Republic of Chile*, ICSID Case No. ARB/01/7, Award, 25 May 2004, 113. To adopt such an interpretation the tribunal looked it up in the *Concise Oxford Dictionary*.

> et équitable, l'exigence de la conformité au droit se trouverait donc, elle-même, corrigée par l'exigence de la conformité à l'équité.[25]

Such an interpretation immediately points to the balancing nature of the standard itself. If 'fair' means in accordance with the law, and 'equitable' means to be able to take into account the different interests involved in an investment operation, then the standard basically serves the purpose of assessing whether the host State's conduct towards the foreign investor is *not only* lawful *but also* adequate to the circumstances. Those circumstances may concern either the specific situation existing in the host State or the behaviour of the foreign investor itself and may mitigate a strict assessment of the law-conforming requirement of the standard, thus functioning as a corrective to that requirement.

In this respect, the clause perfectly fits the purpose of any investment treaty which has a twofold nature: to grant a certain protection to foreign investors by the host contracting State, thereby promoting investments from abroad that hopefully will bring some economic benefit to the host contracting State. The clause appears thus well suited to achieve that goal by balancing the inherently conflicting interests involved in a transnational investment operation. As we will see hereunder, the way in which the standard has been applied in arbitral practice has confirmed the balancing attitude revealed by the textual interpretation.

4.2 The construction of the standard on a case-by-case basis: the role of arbitral jurisprudence and scholarly literature

The textual interpretation of the clause in light of its purpose, however, does not lead to a satisfactory result, since it does not define the normative content of the standard. What obligations does it entail for a host State? When exactly is the host State's conduct towards the foreign investor to be considered unfair and inequitable? An abstract interpretation of the clause does not tell it to us. This is the reason why one must consider the question from a practical point of view and identify the fact-specific situations in respect of which the fair and equitable treatment standard is relevant and determinative. The need to assess the alleged violation of the standard on a case-by-case basis has been stressed early by the

25 Carreau and Juillard (2007), 463 *et seq*. Such a definition dates back to the first edition of the textbook, that is, years before a case-law was developed in this respect. It already contains the basic features that subsequently arbitral tribunals applying the clause to the dispute at hand have developed.

doctrine.[26] The development of a 'first generation of judicial decisions'[27] on the topic and the scholarly literature published in recent years were an enormous help in accomplishing the task.

Thanks to arbitral tribunals applying a FET clause to the dispute at hand, the so-called 'constitutive elements' of the FET standard have emerged. Such elements are more specific obligations in which the principle concretizes depending on the circumstances of the case.

Arbitral tribunals have not always spelled out the grounds for resorting to such elements. This lack of theoretical justification has already been criticized by the doctrine.[28] However, some efforts have been made in that regard. Schill argues that the constitutive elements are principles existing in domestic legal systems 'as an embodiment of the rule of law'.[29] Wälde refers to 'objective rules and principles reflecting, in an authoritative and universal or at least widespread way, the contemporary attitude of modern national and international economic law'.[30]

In fact, principles like the stability of the legal framework, the protection of legitimate expectations and due process of law can be inferred from any legal system based on the rule of law, that is, one in which the regulatory power is never exercised arbitrarily. In our opinion, they can be considered as principles '*recognized by civilized nations*' within the meaning of Art. 38 of the ICJ Statute. When interpreting a FET clause, therefore, resorting to them can be justified by making reference to Art. 31(3)(c) VCLT.[31]

Although the arbitral practice developed so far may not be completely satisfactory from a theoretical point of view, since it does not clarify the reasons on the grounds of which the decisions are taken, it has played a fundamental role in shaping the content of the standard. As has been pointed out in the doctrine, 'reliance on previous jurisprudence will serve

26 Sacerdoti (1997), 341.

27 Dolzer (2005), 88. See also Schreuer (2005b), who acknowledged that arbitral practice 'is still at an early stage of development'.

28 Kläger (2011), 112. 29 Schill (2006), 10.

30 See Wälde, *Separate Opinion* in *International Thunderbird Gaming Corporation* v. *The United Mexican States*, UNCITRAL, Award, 26 January 2006, 30.

31 Also Kläger (2011), at 110 *et seq.* stresses the importance of the recourse to Art. 31(3)(c) VCLT and of an 'integrative construction of fair and equitable treatment'. According to the author, 'other international law norms' are useful for 'deliver[ing] arguments for particular construction of fair and equitable treatment'. He further assumes that 'all principles of fair and equitable treatment have a footing in the sources of international law', thus allowing the FET standard to act as a *gateway* to other international law systems. The A., however, seems to follow the same line of reasoning used by Wälde, considering that the constitutive principles 'have an existence at a more abstract level', Kläger (2011), 278.

as a useful guide for those authorities which give content to the clause'.[32] This is not to say that arbitral decisions serve as precedents. This means that the construction of the standard made by previous tribunals substantially contributes to better defining its scope. It is indeed the non-existence of the theory of precedent in international law that calls for an evaluation of the jurisprudence.[33]

Another question is whether a comprehensive definition of the standard is possible or even desirable. There are two different positions on the issue.

On the one hand, it has been asserted that

> the legal discussion on fair and equitable treatment seems to focus on the simplification of fair and equitable treatment, in order to split this bulky provision into an easily manageable set of factors, rules and precedents. At the end of such a process of lowering complexity, one might expect a fully differentiated set of criteria, indicating in any possible case whether or not there has been an infringement of fair and equitable treatment.

However, the opinion goes on to state, 'a complete specification of fair and equitable treatment appears not to be feasible solely by means of case law'. Hence 'a comprehensive doctrinal concept needs to go beyond a mere analysis of case law and be capable of indicating, ... [in new fact situations], what justificatory arguments are admissible'.[34]

A prominent scholar, on the other hand, suggests that 'an attempt to reach a general definition may not be the best way to give meaning to this [fair and equitable] term'.[35] Qualifying the FET as a 'broad legal concept',

32 Dolzer (2005), 88. See also Carreau and Juillard (2007), 478; Schreuer (2005a), 357. In the same vein, the arbitral tribunal in *Saluka Investment BV* v. *Czech Republic*, UNCITRAL, Partial Award, 17 March 2006, 284:

> The standards formulated in Article 3 of the Treaty, vague as they may be, are *susceptible of specification through judicial practice* and do in fact have sufficient legal content to allow the case to be decided on the basis of law. Over the last few years, a number of awards have dealt with such standards yielding a fair amount of practice that sheds light on their legal meaning (italics added).

33 The FET standard otherwise risks to be considered as 'a catch-all provision'; see Dolzer (2005), 88. The role of scholarly systematization is pointed out also by the arbitral tribunal in the *Saluka* case (see fn 32), which in a footnote adds to the passage just quoted that 'Guidance may also be derived by comprehensive surveys that have recently taken stock of States' treaty practice, arbitral jurisprudence, relevant literature and documents prepared by international organisations.'

34 Kläger (2011), 119–22.

35 Schreuer (2005b). In 2005, the author acknowledged that the concept was 'still in its infancy' and that future developments of the practice would have made 'further categories' to emerge.

the author considers the identification of 'typical fact situations' to which the principle applies as 'a more promising method' to deal with in order to give it a content. 'An examination of these more concrete applications permits an analysis of the concept of fair and equitable treatment in the light of typical fact situations. This analysis leads to more concrete principles that are *covered by* the fair and equitable treatment standard.'[36]

Whether or not one believes that a general definition should finally be given, the way in order to be able to handle the concept is represented by an assessment of the different elements being part of the FET standard.[37]

5. The 'constitutive elements' of the standard

Before entering into the details of the 'constitutive elements' of the standard applied so far in arbitral practice, it seems useful to recall the definition of FET firstly enunciated by the *Tecmed* tribunal.

> The Arbitral Tribunal considers that this provision of the Agreement, in light of the good faith principle established by international law, requires the Contracting Parties to provide to international investments treatment that does not affect the basic expectations that were taken into account by the foreign investor to make the investment. The foreign investor expects the host State to act in a consistent manner, free from ambiguity and totally transparently in its relations with the foreign investor, so that it may know beforehand any and all rules and regulations that will govern its investments, as well as the goals of the relevant policies and administrative practices or directives, to be able to plan its investment and comply with such regulations. ... The foreign investor also expects the host State to act consistently, i.e. without arbitrarily revoking any preexisting decisions or permits issued by the State that were relied upon by the investor to assume its commitments as well as to plan and launch its commercial and business activities. The investor also expects the State to use the legal instruments that govern the actions of the investor or the investment in conformity with the function usually assigned to such instruments, and not to deprive the investor of its investment without the required compensation.[38]

36 Schreuer (2005a), 373 (italics added); Dolzer and Schreuer (2008), 133.

37 This conclusion could in substance be shared, in our opinion, also by authors like Kläger (2011), who at 116, talking about 'Topoi *in arbitral jurisprudence*', refers to the elements of the FET standard and admits their role in 'filling the concept of this norm with a sense of content'.

38 *Tecnicas Medioambientales Tecmed S.A.* v. *The United Mexican States*, ICSID Case No. ARB(AF)/00/2, Award, 29 May 2003, 154.

Although it has been criticized as excessively pro-investor,[39] such a definition already contained all the elements that are now considered firmly rooted in the standard. Subsequent tribunals have recalled such elements making reference to the 'different components' that the standard 'comprises',[40] to the 'concrete principles' that the standard 'encompasses'[41] or to the 'different factors ... forming part of the FET standard'.[42]

As it will be shown below, the more the jurisprudence evolved, the more the different elements have been considered interconnected with each other in the tribunals' assessment of the host State's conduct for the purposes of the standard. Although the close interdependence characterizing the elements militates against attempts at classification, we will address each element or group of elements separately.

5.1 *The stability, consistency, predictability and transparency of the regulatory framework*

The stability of the legal and business regime in force in the host country has been considered as 'an essential element' of the standard.[43] In fact, the elements of stability, coherence and predictability can be considered together as part of a single concept. Moreover, as we shall see, they are to be appreciated in light of other elements, such as the protection of the legitimate expectations of the foreign investor and transparency.[44]

A distinction has been made by the doctrine between the different aspects of stability 'on which the investor is entitled to rely' for the purposes of the FET standard. Firstly, the stability resulting from the

39 See Roberts (2010), 223 and references quoted at fn 213.

40 *Biwater Gauff (Tanzania) Ltd.* v. *United Republic of Tanzania*, ICSID Case No. ARB/05/22, Award, 24 July 2008, 602.

41 *Rumeli Telekom A.S. and Telsim Mobil Telekomikasyon Hizmetleri A.S.* v. *Republic of Kazakhstan*, ICSID Case No. ARB/05/16, Award, 29 July 2008, 609.

42 *Bayindir Insaat Turizm Ticaret Ve Sanayi A.Ş.* v. *Islamic Republic of Pakistan*, ICSID Case No. ARB/03/29, Award, 27 August 2009, 178.

43 *Occidental Exploration and Production Company* v. *Ecuador*, London Court of International Arbitration, Award, 1 July 2004, 183. *CMS Gas Transmission Company* v. *The Argentine Republic*, ICSID Case No. ARB/01/8, Award, 12 May 2005, 274.

44 Dolzer and Schreuer (2008) at 133 *et seq.* deal with *transparency* and the *protection of the investor's legitimate expectations* under the same heading of *stability*, acknowledging that they 'are closely related' and 'by now firmly rooted in arbitral practice'. Newcombe and Paradell (2009) at 287 stress that 'the element of *stability* and *predictability* have arisen in contexts where there was reliance on *specific representations or undertakings* and the investors in question had acquired investments with those *legitimate expectations*' (italics added).

applicable rules of the domestic legal system, including the international undertakings of the host State ('legislation and treaties'); secondly, the confidence specifically given through public authorities' assurances ('executive assurances') or, thirdly, by a contractual undertaking.[45]

The first cases in which the elements of consistency and transparency of the legal framework have been resorted to by arbitral tribunals fit more in the second category of stability mentioned above. The violation of such a principle was mainly due to the lack of coherence in the public officials' conduct towards the investor. In other words, it was not the legal regime as such which fell short of that requirement, but the manner in which the rules were implemented in the case at issue that frustrated the legitimate expectations of the investor/claimant.

The first case ever was *Metalclad* v. *Mexico*.[46] The tribunal basically decided that the respondent State did not treat Metalclad fairly and justly because of the inconsistent decisions taken at the federal and local levels. Interestingly, the tribunal also seemed to take into consideration the behaviour of the foreign investor with respect to the planning and the management of its investment. In fact, Metalclad began building the landfill station because of the assurances received by the federal officials; Metalclad went on building its site acting in a transparent manner and making the public authorities aware of the work progress. The tribunal then acknowledged that, given such a sound conduct, 'Metalclad was entitled to rely on the representations of federal officials'.[47]

The tribunal in the *Metalclad* case followed an approach that other tribunals will follow thoroughly: the assessment of the host country's conduct according to the FET standard must take into account also the behaviour of the foreign investor within that country. As we shall see, the evaluation of the foreign investor's behaviour serves the purpose of giving the proper weight to equitable considerations in the assessment of the alleged violation of the standard.

The subsequent case in which the FET standard was invoked was *Tecmed*.[48]

Here again, when assessing the alleged violation of the standard by the host country, the tribunal took into account also the manner in which the

45 Dolzer and Schreuer (2008), 134; Kläger (2011), 169–86.

46 *Metalclad Corporation* v. *The United Mexican States*, ICSID Case No. ARB(AF)/97/1, Award, 30 August 2000.

47 *Metalclad* (fn 46), at 89 the tribunal added that 'Metalclad was merely acting prudently'.

48 See *supra* fn 38.

foreign investor behaved. The tribunal pointed out that the complained decision not to extend the operating licence was taken 'regardless of the company in charge of the operation and regardless of whether or not it was being properly operated'.[49] The tribunal seemed to state that, in some circumstances, the way in which the foreign investor manages its investment could play a role in the assessment of the compliance of the host country's conduct with the FET standard, eventually excluding or limiting its responsibility. Such an application appears to be perfectly in line with the theoretical construction of the standard as a principle apt to balance the conflicting interests involved in an investment operation.

The role played by the foreign investor's behaviour in the assessment of the alleged violation of the FET standard was further pointed out in the *MTD* case.[50] The tribunal found that the respondent State violated the standard because of the incoherent conduct of the Chilean officials, in particular through the approval of the investment project which was contrary to the urban policy.[51]

The tribunal, however, also inquired into the investor's behaviour to ascertain whether it sought 'adequate professional advice' in order to put in place wise business decisions.[52] According to the tribunal, MTD showed a 'lack of diligence' in that respect, since it took some risks 'irrespective of Chile's action'.[53] As a consequence, the tribunal considered that 'the Claimants should bear part of the damages suffered'.[54]

5.1.1 Stability in the host State's legislation

In some cases, the claimants complained that the changes brought to the legislation in force when their investment was made either rendered the investment profitless or had the effect of preventing its continuation. The tribunals hearing such cases progressively shaped the notion of stability of the host country legal system, on which the foreign investor is entitled to rely for the purposes of the FET standard.

The conflict of interests under consideration here is between the investors' quest for stability and the host country's sovereign power to legislate. The investors need stability in order to plan their business at best. The host State needs flexibility in policy-making in order to meet its societal demands and, in case, to adapt to changing circumstances. The FET

49 *Tecmed* (fn 38) 164 *in fine*. 50 See *supra* fn 24.
51 *MTD* (fn 24) 164 *et seq*. 52 *MTD* (fn 24) 164.
53 *MTD* (fn 24) 168–78, 242. 54 *MTD* (fn 24) 243.

standard is well suited to meet both concerns. The point is where to strike the balance.

The answer lies in the 'specific commitment' requirement, according to which the foreign investor, in order to be entitled to legitimately expect regulatory stability in the host country, must have received some assurance to that end by the host country itself. Assurances of that kind may be given by contract or through specific representations by the competent authorities. A reversal of those assurances can entail a breach of the standard. In other words, the compliance with the standard cannot go so far as to entail an obligation for the host country to 'freeze' its foreign investor-friendly legal regime. Only when the host country undertakes some commitment to that end, may the foreign investor legitimately expect regulatory stability. Specific commitment and legitimate expectation appear thus closely interconnected for the purposes of the FET standard.

In the *Parkerings* v. *Lithuania* case,[55] the tribunal stated that:

> The expectation is legitimate if the investor received an explicit promise or guaranty from the host State, or if implicitly, the host State made assurances or representations that the investor took into account in making the investment. Finally, in the situation where the host State made no assurance or representation, the circumstances surrounding the conclusion of the agreement are decisive to determine if the expectation of the investor was legitimate.[56]

Then, the tribunal recalled the 'State's undeniable right and privilege to exercise its sovereign legislative power'. It went on by stating:

> A State has the right to enact, modify or cancel a law at its own discretion. Save for the existence of an agreement, in the form of a *stabilisation* clause or otherwise, there is nothing objectionable about the amendment brought to the regulatory framework existing at the time an investor made its investment. As a matter of fact, any businessman or investor knows that laws will evolve over time. What is prohibited however is for a State to act unfairly, unreasonably or inequitably in the exercise of its legislative power.[57]

The tribunal concluded its construction of the standard in light of the principle of the protection of the legitimate expectations giving due weight to the investor's own conduct:

55 *Parkerings-Compagniet AS* v. *Republic of Lithuania*, ICSID Case No. ARB/05/8, Award, 11 September 2007.

56 *Parkerings* (fn 55) 331.

57 *Parkerings* (fn 55) 332 (italics not added).

> In principle, an investor has a right to a certain stability and predictability of the legal environment of the investment. The investor will have a right of protection of its legitimate expectations *provided it exercised due diligence* and that its legitimate expectations were reasonable in light of the circumstances. Consequently, an investor must anticipate that the circumstances could change, and thus structure its investment in order to adapt it to the potential changes of legal environment.[58]

Turning to the concrete application of the FET standard to the dispute at hand, the tribunal found that, although the regulatory changes impaired the claimant's business, the host State's conduct did not amount to a violation of the standard.[59] To come to such a conclusion, the tribunal considered, firstly, that the public authorities did not give any explicit assurance to the foreign investor that the legal regime would remain unchanged;[60] secondly, that the claimant was aware of investing in 'a country in transition'[61] and finally that it 'took the *business risk*' associated with its investment.[62]

In the *AES* case,[63] the alleged violation of the FET standard provided for by Art. 10 of the ECT was due to the reintroduction in Hungary of administrative pricing through the amendment of the Electricity Act of 2001. According to the claimants, such a measure undermined the stability of the legal framework 'upon which [they] had legitimately relied'[64] when deciding to make their investment. The tribunal's enquiry focused on 'whether: (a) there were government representations and assurances made or given to Claimants at that time, and upon which they relied, of the sort alleged; and (b) Hungary acted in a manner contrary to such representations and assurances'.[65] Since it found that 'Hungary made no representations/gave no assurances of a nature that go at the heart of Claimants' complaint',[66] the tribunal concluded that they could not expect 'that a regime of administrative pricing would not be reintroduced'.[67]

On the stability of the legal and business framework, the tribunal held that: 'A legal framework is by definition subject to change as it adapts to new circumstances day by day and a state has the sovereign right to exercise its powers which include legislative acts.'[68] When no specific

58 *Parkerings* (fn 55) 333 (italics added). 59 *Parkerings* (fn 55) 338.

60 *Parkerings* (fn 55) 334. 61 *Parkerings* (fn 55) 335.

62 *Parkerings* (fn 55) 336 (italics not added).

63 *AES Summit Generation Ltd AES-Tisza Eromu Kft* v. *Hungary*, ICSID Case No. ARB/07/22, Award, 23 September 2010.

64 *AES* (fn 63) 9.1.5. 65 *AES* (fn 63) 9.3.17. 66 *AES* (fn 63) 9.3.18.

67 *AES* (fn 63) 9.3.26. 68 *AES* (fn 63) 9.3.29.

commitment is taken, like in the case at stake, such sovereign right can hardly be limited. The tribunal added that '[T]his is because any reasonable informed business person or investor knows that laws can evolve in accordance with the perceived political or policy dictates of the times.'[69]

The disputes that originated from the economic and financial crisis which hit Argentina in 2001–2 can also be considered under this application of the FET standard. In those cases, it was the repeal of the rules that had been specifically enacted in order to attract foreign investors that entailed a violation of the FET clause of the relevant BIT. In fact, such rules, for the manner in which they had been designed, were to be assumed to contain *per se* a promise to stability. In other circumstances, according to the standard, when the regulatory framework is perceived by foreign investors simply as favourable, the discretion of the host State to later modify it would be broader.

The tribunals established to hear such disputes had to assess the legitimacy under the applicable BIT of some measures taken in order to face the severe situation, such as the freezing of tariff adjustments provided for by agreements in the public services sector, the devaluation of the Argentine peso and the elimination of exchange parity with the US dollar, the currency in which the above-mentioned agreements were denominated. The regulatory framework under which the investments in public services were made had been specifically tailored in the 1990s in order to attract foreign investments. The emergency situation, which Argentina underwent ten years later, radically changed the business environment. According to the respondent State, the measures adopted should have been considered reasonable in the circumstances and would not have entailed its responsibility under the applicable BIT.

The first case of the series to be settled was *CMS*.[70] The tribunal found that the complained measures completely 'altered the legal and business

69 *AES* (fn 63) 9.3.34. To complete the assessment of the claimants' complaint about the alleged violation of the FET standard, the tribunal had to look into the manner in which the legislative changes had been brought. In fact, although the State is entitled to change its legislation at will, provided that it has not undertaken commitments to the contrary, the way in which it exercises such power matters. The reasonableness of the measures taken and the transparency of the implementing process are all factors according to which the legitimacy of the State's conduct will be assessed for the purposes of the standard. In the case at issue, the tribunal did not find that 'the process of implementing the Price Decrees was so flawed as to amount to a breach of the fair and equitable standard of the ECT'; *AES* (fn 63), 9.3.41. For a discussion of the procedural fairness element of the FET standard, see *infra* 5.3.

70 See *supra* fn 43.

environment under which the investment was decided and made'.[71] It underlined that the guarantees given under that legal framework 'were crucial for the investment decision'.[72] Then, the tribunal pointed out that the stability of the legal framework required by the standard did not mean that it had 'to be frozen, as it can [could] always evolve and be adapted to changing circumstances'.[73] However, if the State undertook 'specific commitments to the contrary', it could not completely disregard that framework.[74] This is what Argentina did in the case at issue, according to the tribunal.

Other tribunals established to hear similar disputes originated from the Argentina crisis followed the same approach and came to the same conclusion:[75] the respondent State violated the FET clause of the applicable BIT, since it radically changed the regulatory framework that had been specifically enacted in order to attract foreign investors.

It is interesting to note that the emergency situation that the respondent State underwent did not play a major role in the tribunal's assessment of the alleged violation of the FET standard, thus giving rise to a typically investor-oriented construction of the standard. The issue instead was dealt with when assessing the state of necessity defence advanced by Argentina to justify the measures taken to face the crisis.[76]

The construction of the standard made in the above-mentioned decisions reflects the deep consonance between the standard and the ultimate aim of international investment law as a whole,[77] at least as it has been traditionally conceived. Although the FET standard will 'not be understood to amount to a stabilization clause',[78] the regulatory discretion of the host State will be limited by compliance with the standard. Such a limitation is the price to pay to attract foreign investments in the country.

71 *CMS* (fn 43) 275. 72 *Ibid.* 73 *CMS* (fn 43) 277. 74 *Ibid.*

75 See e.g. *LG&E* v. *Argentine Republic*, ICSID Case No. ARB/02/1, Decision on Liability, 3 October 2006, 132–9; *Enron Corporation and Ponderosa Assets L.P.* v. *Argentine Republic*, ICSID Case No. ARB/01/3, Award, 22 May 2007, 264–8.

76 The tribunals, however, reached different conclusions on the point. For a discussion, see, *i.a.*, Schill (2007), 265–86; Valenti (2008), 114–35; Binder *et al.* (2009), 608–30; Kurtz (2010a), 200–17, Kurtz (2010b), 325–71.

77 The *CMS* tribunal, at 277 *in fine*, acknowledged that: 'The law of foreign investment and its protection has been developed with the specific objective of avoiding such adverse legal effects.'

78 Dolzer (2005), 105. See, also, *Impregilo S.p.A.* v. *Argentine Republic*, ICSID Case No. ARB/07/17, Award, 21 June 2011, at 291: 'The legitimate expectations of foreign investors cannot be that the State will never modify the legal framework, especially in times of crisis, but certainly investors must be protected from unreasonable modifications of that legal framework.'

The arbitral tribunal established to hear the *Total* case,[79] however, came to a quite different conclusion. It distinguished between two sets of measures that negatively affected the claimant. On the one hand, the tribunal assessed the compliance with the FET standard of the pesification of the economy, the de-dollarization of the tariffs and the abolishment of the tariff adjustment mechanism. On the other hand, the tribunal considered the freezing of the tariffs since 2002. So far as the first set of measures was concerned, the tribunal found that they could not 'be considered unfair in the circumstances',[80] thus showing to take into account the economic situation of the host State in the assessment of its abidance by the standard. So far as the second measure was concerned, on the contrary, the tribunal found a violation of the FET clause.[81]

The *Total* tribunal had previously pointed out that the foreign investor can legitimately expect that no change would be introduced to the rules in force at the time of investing 'if the host State has explicitly assumed a specific legal obligation for the future such as by contracts, concessions or stabilisation clauses on which the investor is therefore entitled to rely as a matter of law'.[82] The tribunal added that legitimate expectations of the investors may also be created by public authorities announcing 'officially their intent to pursue a certain conduct in the future'.[83] Recalling previous arbitral decisions and scholarly literature, the *Total* tribunal, then, defined the role played by the specific commitments requirement in the assessment of the stability element included in the FET standard. This role consists in limiting the sovereign power of States 'to adapt the legal framework to changing circumstances'.[84]

5.1.2 Stability as a result of contractual undertakings

Compliance with contractual undertakings is expected in any legal system that generally abides by the *pacta sunt servanda* rule.[85] Considering the compliance with contractual undertakings as part of the stability element of the FET standard, however, is quite a delicate operation. The issue concerns more specifically the respect for contracts according to

79 *Total S.A. v. Argentine Republic*, ICSID Case No. ARB/04/1, Decision on Liability, 27 December 2010.

80 *Total* (fn 79) 164. The Tribunal further held that there had been no 'specific promise' to Total, which moreover bought the affected investment from other foreign investors shortly before the crisis.

81 *Total* (fn 79) 175.

82 *Total* (fn 79) 117.

83 *Total* (fn 79) 118.

84 *Total* (fn 79) 119.

85 Dolzer and Schreuer (2008), 140.

domestic law and is eventually dealt with by an umbrella clause inserted in the relevant BIT. The question here is whether, in the absence of an umbrella clause, a breach of its contractual undertakings by the host contracting State may entail a violation of the FET clause.

As acknowledged by the doctrine, the arbitral tribunals that had to pronounce on the matter have not yet outlined a consistent approach.[86]

The contractual stability that would come within the scope of the FET standard covers not only State contracts but also contracts between the foreign investors and other partners.[87] So far as the former are concerned, some tribunals have advanced the argument that the infringement of the contractual relationship must be done in the exercise of the host State's sovereignty. In other words, the complained conduct must be qualified as an act *iure imperii*.[88] So far as the latter are concerned, it is not entirely clear to what extent the State's conduct in this last regard can be challenged as a breach of FET.

86 Dolzer and Schreuer (2008), 140 *et seq.*:

> The authority offered by judicial practice on this point is not entirely uniform. Tribunals seem to be agreed that a failure to perform a contract may amount to a violation of the FET standard. ... But the existing case law leaves open the question whether any violation of a contractual obligation by the host state or one of its entities automatically amount to a violation of the FET standard.

See also Kläger (2011), 185: 'the presented cases suggest that fair and equitable treatment generally protects contractual stability. ... However, the degree to which the principle of contractual stability is protected under fair and equitable treatment has not yet become very clear.'

87 See e.g. *CME Czech Republic B.V.* v. *Czech Republic*, UNCITRAL, Partial Ward, 13 September 2001, 611; *Alpha Projektholding GmbH* v. *Ukraine*, ICSID Case No. ARB/07/16, Award, 8 November 2010, 422. In the well-known *CME* case, the tribunal found that the actions and inactions taken by the Media Council – the competent authority in the broadcasting sector – constituted interferences in the contractual relationship of the foreign investor with the local partners which substantially deprived the claimant's investment of any value. This mainly amounted to an indirect expropriation in violation of the applicable BIT (The Netherlands–Czech Republic BIT); at 607 and 609. The same facts, according to the tribunal, constituted also a violation of the FET clause of the BIT. However, another tribunal, established at the request of the US owner of the Dutch company complaining about the same facts, reached a different conclusion. It held that the Respondent did not violate the almost similar provisions of the applicable BIT (US–Czech Republic BIT); *Ronald S. Lauder* v. *The Czech Republic*, UNCITRAL, Final Award, 3 September 2001, 300–4.

88 *Consortium RFCC* v. *Kingdom of Morocco*, ICSID Case No. ARB/00/6, Award, 22 December 2003, 51. *Impregilo S.p.A.* v. *Islamic Republic of Pakistan*, ICSID Case No. ARB/03/3, Decision on Jurisdiction, 22 April 2005, 260. *Duke Energy Electroquil Partners and Electroquil S.A.* v. *Republic of Ecuador*, ICSID Case No. ARB/04/19, Award, 19 August 2008, 345. *Bayindir* (fn 42) 180.

5.2 *The protection of the foreign investor's legitimate expectations*

As we have seen from the examples quoted above, the elements of the stability of the legal framework and of the protection of the legitimate expectations of the foreign investors are closely interconnected. In particular, the latter serves the purpose of establishing the extent of the required stability for the purposes of the standard. In other words, the existence of expectations on the part of the foreign investor, which can be considered legitimate if created by specific commitments taken by the host country, is the yardstick by which the stability of the host country's legal system is to be assessed.

The protection of the foreign investor's legitimate expectations has been considered as one of the constitutive elements of the FET standard since the beginning.[89] However, it has been progressively given a more relevant role in arbitral jurisprudence. It has even been defined as 'the dominant element of that standard'.[90] Professor Wälde acknowledged such an evolution in his Separate Opinion in the *Thunderbird* case:[91] 'One can observe over the last years a significant growth in the role and scope of the legitimate expectation principle, from an earlier function as a subsidiary interpretative principle to reinforce a particular interpretative approach chosen, to its current role as a self-standing subcategory and independent basis for a claim under the "fair and equitable standard" as under Art. 1105 of the NAFTA.'[92]

In the *Thunderbird* case the claimant, a Canadian corporation with its seat in California, was engaged in the business of operating gaming facilities. Wishing to enter the Mexican market, Thunderbird requested an official opinion to the competent authorities. In such a request (*Solicitud*, 3 August 2000), it described its game machines as

> devices for recreation which have been designed for the enjoyment and entertainment of its users. In these games, *chance and wagering or betting is not involved*, but the skills and abilities of the user who has to align different symbols on the machine screen by touching the screen or pushing buttons in order to stop the wanted symbol from several other symbols which spin in a sequential manner in each of the lanes or squares of each video game.[93]

89 See the definition firstly enunciated by the *Tecmed* tribunal (fn 38).
90 *Saluka* (fn 32) 302.
91 *International Thunderbird Gaming Corporation* v. *the United Mexican States*, UNCITRAL, Award, 26 January 2006.
92 Wälde, *Thunderbird*, Separate Opinion (fn 30) 37.
93 *Thunderbird* (fn 91) 50 (italics added).

In its formal response to Thunderbird (*Oficio*, 15 August 2000), the authority, first of all, recalled that legislation in force 'prohibit[ed] gambling and luck related games within the Mexican territory'.[94] It, then, simply stated that if the gaming machines that Thunderbird intended to install had the characteristics it mentioned in its *Solicitud*, and were based on the user's ability or skilfulness and not on luck or gambling, they could not be prohibited.[95] Interpreting the answer received in its favour, Thunderbird opened some facilities in Mexico. Not long thereafter, however, the competent authority ordered their closure with the reason that the gaming machines installed were 'prohibited gambling equipment'.

What is interesting in the tribunal's reasoning is that it autonomously dealt with the issue of legitimate expectations, that is, before assessing the compliance of the respondent State's conduct with the obligations which were allegedly violated. The tribunal wondered whether the *Oficio* could have reasonably created some expectations on the part of Thunderbird that in turn influenced its decision to invest in Mexico.[96]

To come to the conclusion that the *Oficio* had not generated any legitimate expectation upon which the investor could reasonably rely, the tribunal scrutinized the *Solicitud* itself, thus showing that the investor's behaviour matters when dealing with the issue. The tribunal found that the information contained in the *Solicitud* was 'incomplete and … inaccurate' since it denied that the machines involved luck and betting or any agreement to handle an amount of money. In fact, the representations made by the claimant did not disclose the real nature of the games.[97] As a consequence, the answer given by the authorities on that erroneous basis could not create any legitimate expectation.

The *Thunderbird* tribunal defined legitimate expectations as a concept which relates 'to a situation where a Contracting Party's conduct creates reasonable and justifiable expectations on the part of an investor (or investment) to act in reliance on said conduct such that a failure by the NAFTA Party to honour those expectations could cause the investor (or investment) to suffer damages'.[98]

Given the false representation of reality given by Thunderbird, the public authorities' decision to prevent its facilities from working could not be considered as a reversal of previous assurances. The complained measure, on the contrary, appeared perfectly in line with the policy choices of the respondent State, whose legislation unequivocally prohibited

94 *Thunderbird* (fn 91) 55. 95 *Ibid.* 96 *Thunderbird* (fn 91) 137–67.
97 *Thunderbird* (fn 91) 151–3. 98 *Thunderbird* (fn 91) 147.

game activities based on luck and gambling. The tribunal did not pronounce about the appropriateness of such a regulation; it limited itself to assess whether it had been implemented consistently towards the foreign investor. Concluding that the State accorded to the investor the treatment it deserved under the circumstances, the tribunal showed to pay particular attention to the way in which Thunderbird behaved in its relationship with the public authority.

The subsequent *Saluka* case[99] well illustrates the need to take into consideration the pursuance of public interests by the host country in the assessment of the alleged violation of the FET standard. The dispute between the Dutch subsidiary of the Japanese corporate group Nomura and the Czech Republic concerned the banking sector, and in particular its process of privatization. Nomura's participation in IPB, one of the most important Czech banks, dates back to 1998. The shares acquired had later been transferred to the Dutch subsidiary Saluka Investments BV, which was the claimant in the case at issue. Since 1998, the banking sector in the Czech Republic has undergone a crisis. Nomura committed to finding solutions to the debt problem. In particular, it proposed Allianz/UniCredito as a strategic partner. Its proposals, however, were rejected by the government which, warned by the governor of the central bank about the seriousness of the IPB situation, decided instead to impose forced administration, coupled with a quick sale to the domestic bank CSOB. Afterwards, moreover, Saluka's right to dispose of its shares in IPB was suspended. Before the UNCITRAL tribunal established upon its request, Saluka complained about several violations of the relevant BIT, including the obligation to accord a FET.

The tribunal's construction of the standard reveals the evolution that it has undergone since the first period of its application. Recalling the customary rules on treaty interpretation 'laid down' in the VCLT, the tribunal firstly made reference to the ordinary meaning and acknowledged that it could not lead to a satisfactory result in view of its application to the case at hand.[100] The tribunal, secondly, took into consideration the context in which the clause was inserted and, in particular, looked into the preamble of the BIT, which, in its opinion, linked the standard with the overall objectives of the treaty.[101] The tribunal, thirdly, considered the object and purpose of the treaty, maintaining that 'the protection of foreign investments is not the sole aim, but rather a necessary element

99 See *supra* fn 32. 100 *Saluka* (fn 32) 297.
101 *Saluka* (fn 32) 298.

alongside the overall aim of encouraging foreign investment and extending and intensifying the parties' mutual economic relations'. This led the tribunal to stress the need for 'a balanced approach to the interpretation of the Treaty's substantive provisions'.[102]

The tribunal warned about the risks entailed by an excessively investor-oriented interpretation of the principle, since it 'would impose upon host States obligations which would be inappropriate and unrealistic'. The expectations that are to be protected according to the principle 'cannot exclusively be determined by foreign investors' subjective motivations and considerations'; they 'must rise to the level of legitimacy and reasonableness *in light of the circumstances*'.[103] In order to determine whether the investor's expectations are justified and reasonable, the tribunal stated that 'the host State's legitimate right subsequently to regulate domestic matters in the public interest must be taken into consideration as well'.[104] More explicitly, the tribunal went on stating that the finding of a breach of the FET standard 'requires a *weighing* of the Claimant's legitimate and reasonable expectations on the one hand and the Respondent's legitimate regulatory interests on the other'.[105]

In our opinion, this is the central point in the construction of the standard: without entering into the policy choices at the basis of domestic legislation, in order to comply with the standard, the rules must be transparent and implemented consistently so that they can be assessed by foreign investors, using the proper diligence. The tribunal in the *Saluka* case seemed to state that it is the way in which the measures are taken and implemented that can be assessed according to the standard, and not the decision to take those measures as such. Such a construction seems to put aside the element of stability, which played an important role in other arbitral decisions. However, the need to assess the disputed measures 'in light of the circumstances of the case at hand' places that element too in the right position. Stability does not mean absolute immutability. Especially when the regulated sector undergoes a critical situation, like in the case under analysis, interested business operators cannot expect the government not to react to face difficulties.

When it turned to the concrete application of the standard, the tribunal had to assess quite a complex factual situation. Different facts came under

102 *Saluka* (fn 32) 300: 'This is a more subtle and balanced statement of the Treaty's aims than is sometimes appreciated.'

103 *Saluka* (fn 32) 304 (italics not added).

104 *Saluka* (fn 32) 305.

105 *Saluka* (fn 32) 306 (italics added).

review for the purposes of the standard.[106] The tribunal found that the respondent State violated the FET standard as far as certain aspects were concerned,[107] but that it did not fail to ensure a consistent legal framework for Saluka's investment. The reason behind such a decision lies in the fact that the measures taken could not be considered unpredictable for a wise business operator.[108]

What emerges from the considered case-law is that the assessment of the legitimate expectations element, which apparently should lead to a more investor-oriented application of the standard, served the purpose of taking into consideration also the interests of the host country. In the assessment of the respondent State's compliance with the standard a significant role has been played by considerations related to the State's legitimate right to regulate the relevant economic sector and to the behaviour taken by the foreign investor itself. Such an approach made it possible to balance the different interests involved into the disputed investment relationship, allowing the standard to express its very nature.

The *Total* tribunal, which, as underlined above, thoroughly analysed the protection of the legitimate expectations, put it clearly that: 'The balance between these competing requirements and hence *the limits of the proper invocation of "legitimate expectations"* in the face of legislative or regulatory changes has been based on a weighing of various elements pointing in opposite directions.'[109]

5.3 Procedural fairness and due process

The elements of procedural fairness and due process are closely interconnected with the element of transparency of the legal system. While transparency concerns the manner in which the rules applicable to the foreign investor are framed and made known to the interested parties, due process has more to do with the way those rules are implemented and respective violations ascertained at the domestic level. Basically, administrative procedures come under scrutiny in that respect.

The cases mentioned above concerning the first applications of the FET standard are good examples of the host country's conduct that may fall

106 The acts of the respondent State whose compliance with the standard was to be assessed are listed at 310 of the *Saluka* Award.

107 *Saluka* (fn 32) 498–9.

108 *Saluka* (fn 32) 500.

109 *Total* (fn 79) 121 (italics added).

short of the due process requirement of the standard.[110] In subsequent cases, while focusing mainly on the stability of domestic legislation, the tribunals also dealt with the implementing procedure.

In the *Lemire* case,[111] the dispute concerned the radio broadcasting sector and the procedures for awarding frequencies in Ukraine. The tribunal reported that Ukraine refuted the charges of violation of the FET clause by maintaining that the 'Claimant did not behave as a diligent businessman'.[112] It is interesting that the tribunal made it plain that: 'Ukraine is an independent and sovereign state ... The Arbitral Tribunal naturally respects the legislative function of the Ukrainian Parliament. It certainly is not the task of this Arbitral Tribunal, constituted under the ICSID Convention, to review or second-guess the rules which the representatives of the Ukrainian people have promulgated.'[113] The tribunal also stressed the State's interest in regulating the media sector by taking into consideration 'a number of legitimate public policy issues'.[114]

When looking into the procedure for the awarding of licences, the tribunal found 'some shortcomings'[115] related to the independence of the members of the adjudicating body, 'the absence of formal valuation of the applications for licences against clearly established criteria', 'the absence of reasoning' for the decisions taken and 'the lack of transparency'.[116] According to the tribunal, such shortcomings in the procedure would 'facilitate arbitrary decision making'.[117] The tribunal finally came to the conclusion that some decisions taken according to this procedure 'did not meet the FET standard provided for in the BIT'.[118]

In the 2004 US Model BIT, due process is dealt with together with the denial of justice. Art. 5, devoted to the 'Minimum Standard of Treatment',

110 See *supra* 5.1. See also *Rumeli* (fn 41) 618, where the elements of transparency and due process are linked in the tribunal's assessment of the alleged violation of the FET clause of the applicable BIT.

111 *Joseph Charles Lemire* v. *Ukraine*, ICSID Case No. ARB/06/18, Decision on Jurisdiction and Liability, 14 January 2010.

112 *Lemire* (fn 111) 228; the tribunal reported two additional grounds advanced by the respondent State: 'Gala Radio did not take advantage of available remedies' and 'Claimant abused its position as a foreign investor'.

113 *Lemire* (fn 111) 240; the tribunal went on saying: 'The powers of this tribunal are much more limited: they only encompass the authority to decide on a case-by-case basis whether Ukraine has violated certain guarantees, offered to American investors under the BIT, and to establish the appropriate remedies.'

114 *Lemire* (fn 111) 241. 115 *Lemire* (fn 111) 315.

116 *Ibid.* 117 *Lemire* (fn 111) 316.

118 *Lemire* (fn 111) 421. On the assessment of the element under consideration, see also the already mentioned *AES* case, *supra* fn 63.

specifies that: '"fair and equitable treatment" includes the obligation not to deny justice in criminal, civil, or administrative adjudicatory proceedings in accordance with the principle of due process embodied in the principal legal systems of the world'.

Even without such a specification, some tribunals have been asked to ascertain whether the measure complained about – be it a long protraction in the adjudicative proceedings[119] or the noncompliance with domestic courts' rulings in favour of the investor[120] – entailed a denial of justice in breach of the FET clause.

Denial of justice is a well-established concept in international law.[121] In particular, with reference to the customary obligation of full protection and security, it is supposed to occur when the domestic remedies have been exhausted in vain by the injured person, thus entailing the international responsibility of the host State.

With reference to the FET standard, however, the scope of the obligation not to deny justice has yet to be defined. Although it has been qualified as a 'vital element' of FET,[122] procedural fairness – denial of justice included – in fact still has a 'relative weight'[123] in the assessment of the compliance with the FET standard of the host State's conduct, in comparison with the other elements. Having to do with the administration of justice, which also concerns in general citizens and domestic investments, it is unlikely for such an element to play a major role in the construction of the standard any time soon.

6. Conclusions

The FET standard appears to have undergone an evolution since its original insertion into BITs. Such an evolution concerns, first of all, the fact that from a 'sleeping beauty' it has become one of the provisions most frequently invoked by foreign investors complaining about an alleged violation of the applicable treaty by the host contracting State. Secondly,

119 See e.g. *Victor Pey Casado and others* v. *Chile*, ICSID Case No. ARB/98/2, Award, 22 April 2008.

120 See e.g. *Waguih Elie George Siag and Clorinda Vecchi* v. *Egypt*, ICSID Case No. ARB/05/15, Award, 1 June 2009.

121 See, *i.a.*, Bronwlie (2003), 506; Paulsson (2005). For an assessment of the issue within the context of international investment law, see Bjorklund (2006), 810–95; Francioni (2009), 729–47.

122 Schreuer (2005a), 381.

123 Kläger (2011), 227.

the standard has been the object of a progressive definition thanks to both arbitral practice and scholarly literature.

The construction of the standard has been the outcome of a process consisting, on the one hand, of the interpretation of the treaty clause providing for it; on the other hand, of a content-giving operation which is typically called for in respect to general principles of law.

A textual interpretation of the clause in light of its purpose reveals the very nature of the standard: a double-facet rule well suited to balance the inherent conflicting interests involved in a transnational investment.

The content-giving operation made through judicial assessment and theoretical thinking has highlighted the so-called constitutive elements of the standard, that is, more specific obligations in which it concretizes, depending on the circumstances of the case at issue.

The application of a FET clause by an arbitral tribunal, however, remains a difficult task. In our opinion, there is an image that well illustrates such an operation: it is like an acrobatic exercise, whose performance depends on various factors. Arbitrators seem like tightrope walkers who have to balance and counter-balance different elements to find their equilibrium.

On the one hand, the foreign investor's entitlement to regulatory stability and to a consistent implementation of the applicable rules depends on its expectations; those expectations in order to be considered legitimate must be based, in turn, on some specific commitment undertaken by the host State. On the other hand, the behaviour of the foreign investor itself also matters in the assessment of the host country's compliance with the standard. A wise businessman knows that the circumstances existing at the time the investment is made may change over time, and he has to anticipate those changes. The FET standard cannot be used as an insurance guarantee against the risks of an unsound business strategy, even though it may bring the host State's conduct into scrutiny. Moreover, on the same side of the scale, one must consider that the power to legislate and to change its legislation in order to adapt to the circumstances remains a fundamental privilege of the State.

In short, a tribunal required to apply the FET standard has to weigh up all the factors involved in light of the circumstances of the case at hand. This is exactly what the scholarly literature has been saying since the 'awakening' of the standard. The case-law rendered so far has disclosed the different factors which make up the standard, filling it with content. The pattern that has emerged is, in my opinion, an adequate tool in the hands of the arbitrator to handle the FET standard. The latter lastly appears as a principle whose application should not always be made to the host State's disadvantage and to the benefit of the foreign investor alone. Contrary to the long-standing investor-oriented approach, the standard thus seems to be in line with – and to contribute to – the recent trend affecting international investment law as a whole.

References

Binder, C., Kriebaum, U., Reinisch, A. and Wittich, S. (eds.) 2009. *International Investment Law for the 21st Century: Essays in Honour of Christoph Schreuer*. Oxford University Press.

Bjorklund, A. K. 2006. 'Reconciling State Sovereignty and Investor Protection in Denial of Justice Claims.' *Virginia Journal of International Law* 47: 810–95.

Bronwlie, I. 2003. *Principles of Public International Law*. Oxford University Press.

Carreau, D. and Juillard, P. 2007. *Droit international économique*. Paris: Dalloz.

Dolzer, R. 2005. 'Fair and Equitable Treatment: A Key Standard in Investment Treaties.' *The International Lawyer* 40: 87–106.

Dolzer, R. and Schreuer, C. 2008. *Principles of International Investment Law*. Oxford University Press.

Dolzer, R. and Stevens, M. 1995. *Bilateral Investment Treaties*. The Hague: Martinus Nijhoff Publishers.

Falsafi, A. 2007. 'The International Minimum Standard of Treatment of Foreign Investors' Property: A Contingent Standard.' *Suffolk Transnational Law Review*: 317–63.

Francioni, F. 2009. 'Access to Justice, Denial of Justice and International Investment Law.' *EJIL* 20: 729–47.

Juillard, P. 2004. 'Le nouveau modèle américain de traité bilatéral sur l'encouragement et la protection réciproques des investissements.' *Annuaire Français de Droit International* 50: 669–82.

Kantor, M. 2004. 'The New Draft Model US BIT: Noteworthy Developments.' *Journal of International Arbitration* 21: 383–96.

Kläger, R. 2010. 'Fair and Equitable Treatment: A Look at the Theoretical Underpinnings of Legitimacy and Fairness.' *JWI&T* 11: 435–55.

2011. *Fair and Equitable Treatment in International Investment Law*. Cambridge University Press.

Kurtz, J. 2010a. 'The Paradoxical Treatment of the ILC Articles on State Responsibility and Investor-State Arbitration.' *ICSID Review* 25: 200–17.

2010b. 'Adjudging the Exceptional at International Investment Law: Security, Public Order, and Financial Crisis.' *ICLQ* 59: 325–71.

Laird, I. A. 2003. 'NAFTA Chapter 11: Betrayal, Shock and Outrage. Recent Developments in NAFTA Article 1105.' *Asper Review of International Business and Trade Law*: 185–214.

Mann, F. A. 1981. 'British Treaties for the Promotion and Protection of Foreign Investments.' *BYIL* 51: 241–50.

Newcombe, A. and Paradell, L. 2009. *Law and Practice of Investment Treaties*. The Netherlands: Kluwer Law International BV.

Paulsson, J. 2005. *Denial of Justice in International Law*. Cambridge University Press.

Roberts, A. 2010. 'Power and Persuasion in Investment Treaty Interpretation: The Dual Role of States.' *AJIL* 104: 179–225.

Roth, A. H. 1949. *The Minimum Standard of International Law Applied to Aliens*. Leiden: A. W. Sijthoff.

Sacerdoti, G. 1997. 'Bilateral Treaties and Multilateral Instruments on Investment Protection.' *RCADI* 269: 255–460.

Schill, S. W. 2006. 'Fair and Equitable Treatment under Investment Treaties as an Embodiment of the Rule of Law.' *IILJ Working Paper*.

2007. 'International Investment Law and the Host State's Power to Handle Economic Crises.' *JIA* 24: 265–86.

Schreuer, C. 2005a. 'Fair and Equitable Treatment in Arbitral Practice.' *JWI&T* 6: 357–86.

2005b. 'Fair and Equitable Treatment.' *BIICL*, Investment Treaty Forum.

Thomas, J. C. 2002. 'Reflections on Article 1105 of NAFTA: History, State Practice and the Influence of Commentators.' *ICSID Review* 17: 21–101.

Tudor, I. 2008. *The* Fair and Equitable Treatment Standard *in the International Law of Foreign Investment*. Oxford University Press.

UNCTAD, 2004. *International Investment Agreements: Key Issues, Volume I*, New York and Geneva: UNCTAD, 209–33.

Valenti, M. 2008. 'Lo stato di necessità nei procedimenti arbitrali ICSID contro l'Argentina: due soluzioni contrapposte.' *Rivista di Diritto Internazionale*. 114–35.

Vasciannie, S. 1999. 'The Fair and Equitable Treatment Standard in International Investment Law and Practice.' *BYIL* 69: 99–164.

Yannaca-Small, C. 2005. 'Fair and Equitable Treatment Standard in International Investment Law', in OECD, *International Investment Law. A Changing Landscape*. Paris: OECD, 73–125.

3

Indirect expropriations and regulatory takings: what role for the "legitimate expectations" of foreign investors?

ANNA DE LUCA

1. Introduction

The aim of this chapter is to analyze the role of "legitimate expectations" of foreign investors in international investment rules governing indirect expropriations (or creeping expropriations or regulatory expropriations). The issue is not just a theoretical one. To the contrary, what role foreign investors' expectations should play (if any) vis-à-vis indirect expropriations is a practical issue if one looks not only at the investment case-law but also at the most recent State practice on international protection of investments. A definition of indirect expropriation is provided in Section 2. A brief overview of the role of legitimate expectations of foreign investors in investment case-law and State practice is provided in Section 3. In this respect, the concept of legitimate expectations will be discussed in connection with the *Tecmed* case and the US practice, annexing interpretative notes on indirect expropriation to its BIT provisions on expropriation. In Section 4 some key features of the case-law of the Court of Justice of the European Union (CJEU) and the US Supreme Court in respect of the protection of individuals' economic expectations vis-à-vis regulatory actions are outlined. In Section 5 the conclusion is drawn that the reference to investors' legitimate and reasonable expectations in the context of regulatory expropriation claims can pave the way to the use of the doctrine to restrict the scope of the international protection of foreign investors, as opposed to the asserted too far-reaching protection of foreign investments granted by the doctrine of legitimate expectations in the context of denial of fair and equitable treatment claims.

2. Definition of indirect expropriation

It is well established under customary international law (as well as treaty law) that the protection of foreign investors from expropriation encompasses not only formal and direct takings but also indirect takings.[1] A direct expropriation occurs through an official act, which takes or transfers the title of property of the foreign investor concerned. Under customary international law even a measure, which does not have all the features of a formal expropriation, could be considered as equivalent to an expropriation if an effective deprivation of the investment is thereby caused. For a tribunal to find an effective deprivation, even if formal title continues to be held, an almost complete loss of value of the property (such as when the property affected is rendered worthless by the measure, as in the case of direct expropriation) is required.[2] Hence under classic international law, an expropriation "includes every measure which consists of or directly or indirectly results in the total or partial deprivation of private patrimonial rights, either temporarily or permanently."[3] This is supported by the general direction of the

1 As outlined by Garcia-Amador, ILC Special Rapporteur, in its Fourth Report on State Responsibility (1959), UN Doc A/CN.4/119, at 39, "The patrimonial rights of private individuals may be 'affected' by the State not only through acts of expropriation strictu sensu, but also in other ways and for different reasons and purposes."

2 *Ibid.*, at 40.

3 See also the definition of taking of property and use thereof under Art. 10.3(a) and (b) of the Harvard Draft Convention on International Responsibility of States for Injuries to Aliens of 1961 (Sohn and Baxter (1961), 553). According to Art. 10.3(a) of the Harvard Draft Convention on International Responsibility of States for Injuries to Aliens of 1961 "a taking of property includes not only an outright taking but also any such unreasonable interference with the use, enjoy, or dispose of the property as to justify an inference that the owner thereof will not be able to use, enjoy, or dispose of the property within a reasonable period of time after the inception of the interference." According to Art. 10.3(b) of the Harvard Draft Convention on International Responsibility of States for Injuries to Aliens of 1961 a taking of the use of property "includes not only an outright taking of use but also any unreasonable interference with the use or enjoyment of property for a limited period of time" Reinish (2008).

case-law under BITs,[4] other international jurisprudence[5] and scholarly legal opinions.[6]

An indirect expropriation substantially deprives the investor of the economical use and enjoyment of its property rights.[7] Measures having that effect are indirect expropriations, also when adopted in the form of a legislative enactment and aimed at pursuing legitimate general interests. In the Commentary to Art. 3 of OECD Draft Convention on the Protection of Foreign Property, such measures otherwise legitimate but for their substantially destructive effects on economic profitability of foreign investments are identified as "creeping nationalizations"[8] and entail States'

4 See, *inter alia*, *Sempra Energy International* v. *The Argentine Republic*, ICSID Case No. ARB/02/16, Award, September 28, 2007, at 285 where the Tribunal stated that "a finding of indirect expropriation would require more than adverse effect. It would require that the investor no longer be in control of its business operation, or that the value of the business have been virtually annihilated." See also *LG&E* v. *Argentina*, ICSID Case No. ARB/02/1, Decision on Liability, October 3, 2006, at 191 where it is stated that "[i]nterference with the investment's ability to carry on its business is not satisfied where the investment continues to operate, even if profits are diminished. The impact must be substantial in order that compensation may be claimed for the expropriation"; *BG Group Plc* v. *Argentina*, UNCITRAL, Award, December 24, 2007, at 258–266 and *Enron Corporation and Ponderosa Assets, L.P.* v. *Argentine Republic*, ICSID Case No. ARB/01/3, Award, May 22, 2007, at 245. *Técnicas Medioambientales Tecmed, S.A.* v. *The United Mexican States*, ICSID Case No. ARB (AF)/00/2, Award, May 29, 2003, at 115; *CME Czech Republic B.V.* v. *Czech Republic*, UNCITRAL, Partial Award, September 13, 2001, at 604; *Goetz and others* v. *Burundi*, ICSID Case No. ARB/95/3, Award (Embodying the Parties' Settlement Agreement), February 10, 1999, at 124.

5 See *Starrett Housing Corp.* v. *Iran*, Award, August 14, 1987, 4 Iran–US C.T.R. 122, 154–157; *Tippets, Abbett, McCarthy, Stratton* v. *TAMS-AFFA Consulting Engineers of Iran*, Award, June 29, 1984, 6 Iran–US CTR 219, 225–226. See also *German Interests in Polish Upper Silesia* (Ger. v. Pol.), 1926 PCIJ ser A, No. 7, Judgment, May 25, 1926, at 14–45; and *Norwegian Shipowners' Claims* (Nor. v. US), Award, October 13, 1922, 1 RIAA 307. Christie (1962), 311, observing with reference to the Norwegian Claims and the German Interests in Polish Upper Silesia cases, that "the two cases taken together illustrate that even though a State may not purport to interfere with rights to property, it may, by its actions, render those rights so useless that it will be deemed to have expropriated them."

6 See Leben (2006), 173–175; Dolzer and Schreuer (2008), 96–104.

7 Art. 3 OECD Draft Convention on the Protection of Foreign Property of 1967 states that:

> No party shall take any measures depriving, directly or indirectly, of his property a national of another Party unless the following conditions are complied with: (i) The measures are taken in the public interest and under due process of law; (ii) The measures are not discriminatory or contrary to any undertaking which the former may have given, and (iii) The measures are accompanied by provision for the payment of just compensation …

8 Notes and Comments to Article 3 OECD Draft Convention on the Protection of Foreign Property, at 3(b), available at www.oecd.org/investment/internationalinvestmentagreements/39286571.pdf

obligation to pay compensation. In the wording of the Commentary, they are measures otherwise legitimate, which are

> applied in such a way as to deprive ultimately the alien of the enjoyment or value of his property, without any specific act being identifiable as outright deprivation. As instances may be quoted excessive or arbitrary taxation; prohibition of dividend distribution coupled with compulsory loans; imposition of administrators; prohibition of dismissal of staff; refusal of access to raw materials or of essential export or import licenses ...[9]

It is widely held that, as a rule, State regulatory actions aimed at the protection of non-trade values (public health, morality, environment) might justify "even severe, although by no means complete, restrictions on the use of property."[10]

2.1 *BIT provisions on expropriation*

Standard provisions on expropriation of BITs (at least the ones of the European Models of BITs) endorse the same approach and cover every measure, which consists of, or directly or indirectly results in, the total or partial permanent deprivation of private patrimonial rights.[11] An

9 *Ibid.* See also American Law Institute (ed.), Restatement (Third) of the Foreign Relations Law of the United States § 712 comment g.

10 In this respect, Christie (1962), 331 and footnote 5 where the prominent scholar emphasizes that "the mere fact that an alien still has a 'record' title will not avoid a conclusion of expropriation where the restrictions on use are complete or almost complete."

11 Article 5(2) Argentina–France BIT states that: "The Contracting Parties shall not take, directly or indirectly, any expropriation or nationalization measures or any other equivalent measures having a similar effect of dispossession, expect for reasons of public necessity and on condition that the measures are not discriminatory or contrary to a specific undertaking." Art. 4(2) German Model BIT of 2008 provides that:

> Investments by investors of either Contracting State may not directly or indirectly be expropriated, nationalized or subjected to any other measure the effects of which would be tantamount to expropriation or nationalization in the territory of the other Contracting State except for the public benefit and against compensation. Such compensation must be equivalent to the value of the expropriated investment immediately before the date on which the actual or threatened expropriation, nationalization or other measure became publicly known. ... The legality of any such expropriation, nationalization or other measure and the amount of compensation must be subject to review by due process of law.

On partial expropriation, namely the expropriation of just some fundamental economic rights, protected under the BIT, over the overall bundle of economic rights constituting the investment see *Middle East Cement Shipping and Handling Co. S.A. v. Arab Republic*

expropriation could be found even where control over the investment remains in the hands of the foreign investor provided that the value or the economic profitability of the investment has been substantially destroyed or neutralized in some other way.[12] Therefore BIT provisions on expropriations also cover in the abstract the so-called regulatory takings, namely State regulations aimed at protecting public welfare objectives, when they indirectly have an equivalent effect to expropriations, and result in an effective and substantial deprivation of the investment of the foreign investor claiming under the BIT.[13] These measures of general application, that States generally claim to be noncompensable, should, however, be considered as unlawful under BITs, unless they are taken in the public interest and under due process of law, they are not discriminatory (or not contrary to a specific undertaking) and, above all, they provide the affected investor with just compensation, in line with customary international law.[14]

3. The role of legitimate expectations in international investment law vis-à-vis indirect expropriations

3.1 *The investment case-law: The* Tecmed *case as an illustrative example*

It is well-known that the concept of legitimate expectations of investors have played a significant role in guiding arbitral tribunals in interpreting and applying the absolute BIT standards of protection. This

of Egypt, Award, April 12, 2002, at 101, 105, 107, 127; *Eureko B.V.* v. *Poland*, Partial Award, August 19, 2005, at 239–241.

12 *Consortium RFCC* v. *Kingdom of Morocco*, ICSID No. ARB/00/6, Award, December 22, 2003, at 69.

13 Clause 4 of the Protocol to the 1994 Italy–Peru BIT ["Sarà considerata nazionalizzazione o esproprio di un investitore di una delle Parti Contraenti ogni misura di nazionalizzazione e esproprio di merci o diritti appartenenti ad un'impresa controllata dall'investitore, come pure la sottrazione di risorse finanziarie o di altri beni all'impresa o, viceversa, ogni misura che riduca sostanzialmente il valore della stessa"]. With similar wording also Italy–Kazakhstan BIT 1994, Clause 4 of the Protocol; Italy–Saudi Arabia BIT 1996, Clause 4 of the Protocol; Italy–Georgia BIT 1997, Clause 4 of the Protocol.

14 Manciaux (2004), 457, observing that the form, taken by expropriatory measures under domestic legal systems (legislative acts or administrative acts), has little practical significance from the standpoint of international law; Newcombe and Paradell (2009), 327 observing that "the focus of the expropriation analysis is on the extent of the deprivation that the investor suffers and, to a far lesser degree, on the form or content of the state measure or the intent of the state" Reinisch (2012), 279–285.

notwithstanding, the contours of the doctrine of protecting "legitimate expectations," developed and accepted by many (but not all) legal systems as a public or administrative law device protecting individuals from the withdrawal of administrative measures conferring upon them "vested rights"[15] (rather than from State measures of general application),[16] still appears to be quite blurry when applied in the context of foreign investment protection. This is especially the case when treaty-based tribunals have to evaluate changes effected by host States in the general legal framework through legislative measures or unilateral regulations of a normative or administrative nature. Furthermore, in the context of denial of fair and equitable treatment claims, some arbitral tribunals questioned the relevance of the doctrine of legitimate expectations vis-à-vis legislative measures or unilateral regulation of a normative or administrative nature, in the absence of specific stabilization "promises" or guarantees of stability worded in clear and not ambiguous terms and specifically addressed to the foreign investor concerned.[17] The role of legitimate expectations of foreign investors in the context of the fair and equitable treatment standard will not be discussed here.[18] In this

15 As stated by the ECJ in some joined cases of the 1950s, related to administrative acts appointing Community officials, after a comparative review of the law of the (at that time) six Member States governing the revocability of administrative measures giving rise to individual rights, "an administrative measure conferring individual rights on the person concerned cannot in principle be withdrawn, if it is a lawful measure; in that case, since the individual right is vested, the need to safeguard confidence in the stability of the situation thus created prevails over the interests of an administration desirous of reversing its decision." (Joined cases 7/56 and 3-7/57, *Algera and others* v. *Common Assembly of the European Coal and Steel Community*, 1957 *ECR* 56, 56.)

16 *Total S.A.* v. *Argentina*, ICSID Case No. ARB/04/1, Decision on Liability, December 27, 2010, at 128–130. In legal literature Snodgrass (2006), 36–39.

17 See *Total S.A.* v. *Argentina*, ICSID Case No. ARB/04/1, Decision on Liability, December 27, 2010, at 113–123 and at 319–331. The Tribunal observes at 117 that

> In the absence of some "promise" by the host State or a specific provision in the bilateral investment treaty itself, the legal regime in force in the host country at the time of making the investment is not automatically subject to a "guarantee" of stability merely because the host country entered into a bilateral investment treaty with the country of the foreign investor.

See also, *inter alia*, *Toto Costruzioni Generali S.p.A.* v. *The Republic of Lebanon*, ICSID Case No. ARB/07/12, Award, June 7, 2012, at 150–166 and at 242–246; *El Paso Energy International Company* v. *The Argentine Republic*, ICSID Case No. ARB/03/15, Award, October 31, 2011, at 233–243 (with regard to the interpretation of BIT provision protecting foreign investors from indirect expropriation), and at 350–358 and 364–374 (with regard to the interpretation of the FET standard); *Impregilo S.p.A.* v. *The Argentine Republic*, ICSID Case No. ARB/07/17, Award, June 21, 2011, at 290–291.

18 On the topic see Potestà (2013).

respect, it is sufficient to say that the concept has been the object of growing criticisms for its pro-investment bias[19] as well as for methodological reasons.[20] Furthermore, as observed by Dolzer and Schreuer, "it is arguable whether the concept of legitimate expectations is part of the general principles of law."[21]

Irrespective of the role of the concept of legitimate expectations in the context of fair and equitable treatment, some tribunals in the context of regulatory expropriation claims have also referred to the concept. The *Tecmed* v. *Mexico* case illustrates the role of investors' expectations vis-à-vis indirect expropriation. To more precise, the case illustrates the role that the concept might play in prospect in the context of BIT provisions protecting investors from indirect expropriation, as outlined below.[22]

After having already found that the denial by host State authorities to renew the permit to operate the landfill has caused the substantial and permanent deprivation of the value of the foreign investor's investment, the *Tecmed* Tribunal also considers as necessary under its analysis of the regulatory expropriation claim to "determine whether such measures are reasonable with respect to their goals, the deprivation of economic rights and the legitimate expectations of who suffered such deprivation."[23] According

19 Just to mention some of these criticisms see in investment case-law, *MTD Equity Sdn. Bhd. and MTD Chile S.A.* v. *Republic of Chile*, ICSID Case No. ARB/01/7, Decision on Annulment, March 21, 2007, at 67 where the ad hoc Committee, addressing the criticisms from the Respondent's legal experts to the *Tecmed* standard, states that

> the TECMED Tribunal's apparent reliance on the foreign investor's expectations as the source of the host State's obligations (such as the obligation to compensate for expropriation) is questionable. The obligations of the host State towards foreign investors derive from the terms of the applicable investment treaty and not from any set of expectations investors may have or claim to have. A tribunal which sought to generate from such expectations a set of rights different from those contained in or enforceable under the BIT might well exceed its powers, and if the difference were material might do so manifestly.

20 See the Separate Opinion of Arbitrator Pedro Nikken in the case *Suez, Sociedad General de Aguas de Barcelona, S.A. and Vivendi Universal, S.A.* v. *Argentine Republic*, ICSID Case No. ARB/03/19, Decision on Liability, July 30, 2010.

21 Dolzer and Schreuer (2012), 115. But see also Snodgrass (2006), 56 concluding for the recognition of a general principle of law that legitimate expectations of investors should be protected.

22 *Técnicas Medioambientales Tecmed, S.A.* v. *The United Mexican States*, ICSID Case No. ARB (AF)/00/2, Award, May 29, 2003. See also *Metalclad Corporation* v. *The United Mexican States*, ICSID Case No. ARB(AF)/97/1, Award, August 30, 2000, at 103.

23 *Técnicas Medioambientales Tecmed, S.A.* v. *The United Mexican States*, fn 8, at 122. In this respect, the *Tecmed* Tribunal heavily relies, on the one hand, upon an inapposite ECHR case-law and, on the other, upon a too subjective concept of investors' expectations as an object of international protection (at 41, 88, 89, 90, 149).

to the *Tecmed* Tribunal, "[T]here must be a reasonable relationship of proportionality between the charge or weight imposed to the foreign investor and the aim sought to be realized by any expropriatory measure."[24]

In this respect, it can be questioned whether a proportionality test, such as the one above, should find any place in the examination of indirect expropriation claims, in the case that a substantial deprivation of the value of the investment is found.[25]

The reference to the concept of legitimate expectations and proportionality test does not lead the *Tecmed* Tribunal to rule in favor of the host State. Nevertheless, the application of the proportionality test can possibly free the host State from its obligation to provide the investor with compensation, even in the event that a substantial or complete deprivation of the value of the investment has occurred.

3.2 State practice

A particularly qualified concept of investors' "expectations" is explicitly mentioned in the US Model BIT of 2012 (as well as in the US Model BIT of 2004) among the factors investment tribunals have to consider in order to determine whether an action (or a series of actions) by a State constitutes an indirect expropriation. In the US Model BIT of 2012 "the extent to which the government action interferes with distinct, reasonable investment-backed expectations" is listed together with "the economic impact of the government action" and "the character of the government action" as a yardstick for a tribunal to determine whether an indirect expropriation has occurred.[26] The US practice, annexing the above interpretative

24 *Ibid.*

25 In this respect, see also Mairal (2010), 446.

26 US Model BIT of 2012, Annex B.4 clarifies that

> The second situation addressed by Article 6 [Expropriation and Compensation] is indirect expropriation, where an action or series of actions by a Party has an effect equivalent to direct expropriation without formal transfer of title or outright seizure.
>
> (a) The determination of whether an action or series of actions by a Party, in a specific fact situation, constitutes an indirect expropriation, requires a case-by-case, fact-based inquiry that considers, among other factors:
>
> (i) the economic impact of the government action, although the fact that an action or series of actions by a Party has an adverse effect on the economic value of an investment, standing alone, does not establish that an indirect expropriation has occurred;
>
> (ii) the extent to which the government action interferes with distinct, reasonable investment-backed expectations; and
>
> (iii) the character of the government action.

note to treaty clauses on indirect expropriation, reproduces *verbatim* the principles developed by the US Supreme Court in the context of regulatory taking claims under the Due Process and Taking Clauses (as outlined in Section 4).

The US practice on the point elucidates the US position that the protection of foreign investors' economic interests under the law governing indirect expropriation should not be above the protection granted by the US Supreme Court to individuals' economic interests and rights at the domestic level. The interpretative note (rather than reflecting the level of protection of aliens from indirect expropriations under customary international law or provisions on expropriation of other BITs) seems to be a contemporary proposal of the Calvo doctrine in an American fashion.

An additional element should be mentioned. The above position that investors' reasonable expectations can be relevant to a claim of regulatory expropriation – but are not legally relevant to claims of denial of fair and equitable treatment under the customary law minimum standard of treatment) – is coherently put forward by the US also in the NAFTA context.[27]

(b) Except in rare circumstances, non-discriminatory regulatory actions by a Party that are designed and applied to protect legitimate public welfare objectives, such as public health, safety, and the environment, do not constitute indirect expropriations.

With almost identical wording see Canada Model BIT of 2004, Annex B.13(1) clarifying that:

a) Indirect expropriation results from a measure or series of measures of a Party that have an effect equivalent to direct expropriation without formal transfer of title or outright seizure;
b) The determination of whether a measure or series of measures of a Party constitute an indirect expropriation requires a case-by-case, fact-based inquiry that considers, among other factors:
    i) the economic impact of the measure or series of measures, although the sole fact that a measure or series of measures of a Party has an adverse effect on the economic value of an investment does not establish that an indirect expropriation has occurred;
    ii) the extent to which the measure or series of measures interfere with distinct, reasonable investment-backed expectations; and
    iii) the character of the measure or series of measures;
c) Except in rare circumstances, such as when a measure or series of measures are so severe in the light of their purpose that they cannot be reasonably viewed as having been adopted and applied in good faith, non-discriminatory measures of a Party that are designed and applied to protect legitimate public welfare objectives, such as health, safety and the environment, do not constitute indirect expropriation.

27 In this respect, *inter alia*, see *Grand River Enterprises Six Nations, Ltd., et al.* v. *United States of America*, UNCITRAL case (NAFTA), Award, January 12, 2011, at 127.

4. The role of legitimate expectations vis-à-vis indirect expropriations in the US and EU legal systems

In the US and EU legal systems the role for "legitimate expectations" of individuals and their protection vis-à-vis indirect expropriations is very limited. More specifically, the concept of legitimate expectations plays a limited role in protecting individuals when legislative acts involving choices of economic policy impair their economic interests and rights. The doctrine has been considered as a basis for a successful annulment action and, even more rarely, for compensation or indemnification of individuals when legislative actions by a State were at stake.

This is the case with the EU legal system if one looks at the case-law of the Court of Justice of the EU under the European Union's noncontractual liability regime (Article 340(2) TFEU).[28] The Court has granted a limited protection under Article 340(2) TFEU to individuals (whatever expectations they might have), when EU legislative acts impair their economic interests and rights.[29] In the Court's wording in the joint cases *FIAMM* and *Fedon*, "[A]s regards, more specifically, liability for legislative activity, ... the public authorities can only exceptionally and in special circumstances incur liability for legislative measures which are the result of choices of economic policy."[30] As a result, notwithstanding that the

28 Art. 340(2) TFEU (ex Art. 288(2) TEC) provides as follows: "In the case of non-contractual liability, the Union shall, in accordance with the general principles common to the laws of the Member States, make good any damage caused by its institutions or by its servants in the performance of their duties."

29 See 5/171, *Aktien-Zuckerfabrik Schöppenstedt* v. *Council of the European Communities*, 1971 *ECR* 975, at 11 where the ECJ states that:

> the non-contractual liability of the community presupposes at the very least the unlawful nature of the act alleged to be the cause of the damage. Where legislative action involving measures of economic policy is concerned, the community does not incur non-contractual liability for damage suffered by individuals as a consequence of that action, by virtue of the provisions contained in Art. 215, second paragraph, of the treaty, [now Art. 340(2) TFEU] unless a sufficiently flagrant violation of a superior rule of law for the protection of the individual has occurred. For that reason the court, in the present case, must first consider whether such a violation has occurred.

See, *inter alia*, T-184/95, *Dorsch Consult* v. *Council*, 1998 *ECR* II-667, at 76–77; Joined Cases C- 120/06 P and C-121/06 P, *Fabbrica italiana accumulatori motocarri Montecchio SpA (FIAMM) and Others* v. *Council of the European Union and Commission of the European Communities*, and *Giorgio Fedon & Figli SpA, Fedon America, Inc.* v. *Council of the European Union and Commission of the European Communities*, 2008 *ECR* I-6513, at 171–175 and at 181–183.

30 C-120/06 P and C-121/06 P *FIAMM* v. *Council and Commission* and *Fedon* v. *Council and Commission*, fn 29, at 171 with reference to Joined Cases C-83/76, 94/76, 4/77, 15/77

principle of protection of legitimate expectations is considered as a well-established fundamental principle of the EU, according to the Court,

> traders are not justified in having a legitimate expectation that an existing situation which is capable of being altered by the Community institutions in the exercise of their discretionary power will be maintained, particularly in an area such as that of the common organization of the markets, the objective of which involves constant adjustment to reflect changes in economic circumstances.[31]

More specifically, the EU could be held liable under Article 340 TFEU for the adoption of a legislative measure only when "a sufficiently serious breach of a superior rule of law for the protection of the individual has occurred."[32]

and 40/77 *Bayerische HNL Vermehrungsbetriebe and Others* v. *Council and Commission*, 1978 *ECR* 1209, at 5.

31 C-104/97 P *Atlanta AG and Others* v. *EC*, 1999 *ECR* I-6983, at 52. As observed in legal literature in respect of the EU's noncontractual liability for its legislative acts and the contents and import of the principle of individuals' legitimate expectations, "per mitigare le conseguenze di questa impostazione, peraltro, la Corte ha interpretato estensivamente i poteri discrezionali delle istituzioni comunitarie nelle scelte di politica economica e monetaria, richiamandosi ai principi generali comuni degli Stati membri, ove essa ha rilevato una concezione della responsabilità dei pubblici poteri per gli atti normativi di politica economica" (see Venturini, G. 2001. "Art. 288," Pocar, F. [ed.], *Commentario breve ai Trattati della Comunità e dell'Unione Europea*, Cedam: 973 ff., 974–976 in general and 975, where the above quotation is to be found). In this respect, see also Hartley (2007), 447. For an overview of the EU's noncontractual liability regime for its normative acts on the basis of the general principles common to the laws of the Member States see Grossrieder Tissot (2001).

32 See C-120/06 P and C-121/06 P *FIAMM* v. *Council and Commission* and *Fedon* v. *Council and Commission*, fn 29, at 172. The Court explains its restrictive approach on the EU's liability for legislative measures seriously affecting individuals' economic interests and rights on the basis of two considerations. It is worth reporting *in extenso* the considerations made by the Court:

> First, even where the legality of measures is subject to judicial review, exercise of the legislative function must not be hindered by the prospect of actions for damages whenever the general interest of the Community requires legislative measures to be adopted which may adversely affect individual interests. Second, in a legislative context characterized by the exercise of a wide discretion, which is essential for implementing a Community policy, the Community cannot incur liability unless the institution concerned has manifestly and gravely disregarded the limits on the exercise of its powers (see, in particular, Brasserie du pêcheur and Factortame, paragraph 45).

See also Case T-135/01 *Fedon & Figli and Others* v. *Council and Commission*, 2005 *ECR* II-29, at 78–82.

In this respect, it is worthy of note that the CJEU has not denied in the abstract that an EU legislative measure seriously affecting the very substance of property rights and individuals' freedom to pursue economic activities could give rise to the EU's noncontractual liability.[33] This notwithstanding, by adopting a restrictive concept of property rights and economic interests deserving legal protection from the European Union's regulatory measures the Court has never substantively found the EU's noncontractual liability. In the Court's view, "an economic operator cannot claim a right to property in a market share which he held at a given time, since such a market share constitutes only a momentary economic position, exposed to the risks of changing circumstances."[34] The Court goes on to state that "the guarantees accorded by the right to property or by the general principle safeguarding the freedom to pursue a trade or profession cannot be extended to protect mere commercial interests or opportunities, the uncertainties of which are part of the very essence of economic activity."[35]

The US Supreme Court appears to follow a similar approach in its case-law under the Takings and Due Process Clauses. The case *Concrete Pipe & Products of California* v. *Construction Laborers Pension Trust for Southern California*[36] illustrates the point. Concrete Pipe argued that a legislative act of 1980, amending the previous law of 1974 on multiemployer pension schemes imposing new financial burdens on employers who decided to withdraw from the schemes, violates substantive due process and takes Concrete Pipe's property without compensation.

33 See C-120/06 P and C-121/06 P *FIAMM* v. *Council and Commission* and *Fedon* v. *Council and Commission*, fn 29, at 184 where the Court states that

> a Community legislative measure whose application leads to restrictions of the right to property and the freedom to pursue a trade or profession that impair the very substance of those rights in a disproportionate and intolerable manner, perhaps precisely because no provision has been made for compensation calculated to avoid or remedy that impairment, could give rise to non-contractual liability on the part of the Community.

34 C-120/06 P and C-121/06 P *FIAMM* v. *Council and Commission* and *Fedon* v. *Council and Commission*, *supra* note 150, at 185 with references to Case C-280/93 *Federal Republic of Germany* v. *Council of the European Union*, 1994 *ECR* I-4973, at 79 and Case C-295/03 P *Alessandrini Srl and Others* v. *Commission of the European Communities*, 2005 *ECR* I-5673, at 88.

35 C-120/06 P and C-121/06 P *FIAMM* v. *Council and Commission* and *Fedon* v. *Council and Commission*, fn 150, at 185 with references to Case 4/73, *J. Nold, Kohlen- und Baustoffgroßhandlung* v. *Commission of the European Communities*, 1974 *ECR* 491, at 14.

36 *Concrete Pipe & Products of California* v. *Construction Laborers Pension Trust for Southern California*, US 602 (1993).

With regard to due process, under the case-law of the Court: 'It is by now well established that legislative Acts adjusting the burdens and benefits of economic life come to the Court with a presumption of constitutionality, and that the burden is on one complaining of a due process violation to establish that the legislature has acted in an arbitrary and irrational way."[37] Moreover, the Court goes on to state: "[I]t may be that the liability imposed by the Act ... was not anticipated at the time of actual employment. But our cases are clear that legislation readjusting rights and burdens is not unlawful solely because it upsets otherwise settled expectations."[38] In this respect, the Court makes clear that this is true even if the legislation at stake has retroactive effects.[39]

According to the Court, the detrimental retroactive effects of a legislation are not sufficient for an appellant to succeed in taking and due process claims. In fact, the matter before the Court is (rather than one of retroactivity) one of rationality and proportionality. In respect of the test to be applied in order to balance means and ends, the Court calls for the applicability to economic legislations of a so high deferential standard of review as to constitute a practically impossible threshold to meet.[40] After having rejected the violation of due process claim of the appellant and asserted that "'it would be surprising to discover' the challenged statute nonetheless violating the Taking Clause,"[41] the Court identifies the relevant factors of the fact-based inquiry necessary to determine a regulatory taking claim under the Takings Clause. Besides the nature of the governmental action and the severity of its economic impact[42] is the degree of interference with individuals' "reasonable investment-backed expectations."

37 *Ibid.*, at 637 with reference to the previous cases *Ferguson* v. *Skrupa*, 372 US 726 (1963) and *Williamson* v. *Lee Optical Co.*, 348 US 483, 487–488 (1955).

38 *Ibid.*, at 637–638 with reference to *Fleming* v. *Rhodes*, 331 US 100 (1947), *Carpenter* v. *Wabash R. Co.*, 309 US 23 (1940); *Norman* v. *Baltimore & Ohio R. Co.*, 294 US 240 (1935); *Home Bldg. & Loan Assn.* v. *Blaisdell*, 290 US 398 (1934); *Louisville & Nashville R. Co.* v. *Mottley*, 219 US 467 (1911).

39 *Ibid.*, at 637–638 with reference to *Lichter* v. *United States*, 334 US 742 (1948); *Welch* v. *Henry*, 305 US 134 (1938); *Funkhouser* v. *Preston Co.*, 290 US 163 (1933).

40 *Ibid.*, at 639 where the Court states that "In any event, under the deferential standard of review applied in substantive due process challenges to economic legislation there is no need for mathematical precision in the fit between justification and means. See Turner Elkhorn, 428 US, at 19." In respect of the standard of review in Takings Clause cases the Court refers to a quite similar balancing test entailing just "rough proportionality" between ends and means. See *Dolan* v. *City of Tigard*, 512 US 374, 391 (1994). In legal literature, Snodgrass (2006), 46 observes that both tests are not "particularly searching review."

41 *Ibid.*, at 641. 42 *Ibid.*, at 643–644 and 645, respectively.

With regard to the degree of interference with Concrete Pipes' "reasonable investment-backed expectations" and the definition thereof, the Court clarifies that "'[t]hose who do business in the regulated field cannot object if the legislative scheme is buttressed by subsequent amendments to achieve the legislative end.'"[43] Given that legislations readjusting rights and burdens are not unlawful solely because they upset otherwise settled expectations, even in the case that they have detrimental retroactive effects, it is the position of the Court that individuals' reliance on normative provisions of a general application is misplaced because there can be no reasonable basis to expect that legislation would never be changed by subsequent laws.[44]

5. Conclusion

Given that the protection of legitimate expectations is very limited vis-à-vis regulatory takings under the domestic systems above reviewed, it is questionable whether the doctrine of legitimate expectations (and the proportionality analysis it entails) should play any role in the law governing indirect expropriations.

First of all, the balancing between the protection of individuals' economic rights and interests and the right of States to regulate in the public interest as well as the deferential standard of review applied by national courts to State regulatory actions do not seem to reflect the level of protection of foreigners vis-à-vis indirect expropriation under customary international law. In fact, when State regulatory measures impair the very substance of economic rights of aliens, compensation is due. This is true even admitting that the concept has become one of the general principles of law mentioned in Article 38(1)(c) of the Statute of the International Court of Justice as a source of international law. In investment case-law the concept has been mainly linked to the fair and equitable treatment standard. In this regard, the application of the doctrine of legitimate expectations might be reasonable and appropriate since investment tribunals judge less

43 *Ibid.*, at 645 quoting *FHA* v. *The Darlington, Inc.*, 358 US 84, 91 (1958).

44 *Ibid.*, at 646 where the Court stats that

> Because "legislation readjusting rights and burdens is not unlawful solely because it upsets otherwise settled expectations ... even though the effect of the legislation is to impose a new duty or liability based on past acts," Turner Elkhorn, 428 US, at 16, Concrete Pipe's reliance on ERISA's original limitation of contingent liability to 30% of net worth is misplaced, there being no reasonable basis to expect that the legislative ceiling would never be lifted.

impairing measures than the ones that could amount to a breach of a BIT provision on indirect expropriation.

Secondly, it is true that it is widely held that mere commercial interests or opportunities do not generally deserve international protection and no protection should be granted to economic operators against ordinary business risks, such as those of changes in the market conditions.[45] Furthermore, it might be also the case that domestic legal systems (and more specifically Member States' legal systems and the US legal system) do not generally grant economic operators any protection from legislative measures by adopting a restrictive concept of property rights and economic interests deserving legal protection.

Nevertheless, it is still remains the case that under both BITs and general international law on protection of foreigners' property rights, as interpreted and applied by the ECHR,[46] international protection is granted to foreign economic operators from regulatory changes even when they are introduced by legislative measures in certain instances. As Judge Higgins observed in respect of the usefulness of a distinction between noncompensable bona fide regulation and taking for a public purpose:

> Is this distinction intellectually viable? Is not the State in both cases (that is, either by a taking for a public purpose, or by regulating) purporting to act in the common good? Under international law standards, a regulation that amounted (by virtue of its scope and effect) to a taking, would need to be "for a public purpose" (in the sense of a general, rather than for a private interest). And just compensation would be due.[47]

45 In this respect, see in investment arbitration case-law *Maffezini* v. *Spain*, ICSID Case No. ARB/97/7, Award on the Merits, November 13, 2000, at 64 where the Tribunal emphasizes that:

> Bilateral Investment Treaties are not insurance policies against bad business judgments. While it is probably true that there were shortcomings in the policies and practices that SODIGA and its sister entities pursued in the here relevant period in Spain, they cannot be deemed to relieve investors of the business risks inherent in any investment. To that extent, it is clear that Spain cannot be held responsible for the losses Mr. Maffezini may have sustained any more than would any private entity under similar circumstances

and *MTD Equity Sdn. Bhd. & MTD Chile S.A.* v. *Chile*, ICSID Case No. ARB/01/7, *award* (May 25, 2004) at 178 where the Tribunal states that: "The BITs are not an insurance against business risk and the Tribunal considers that the Claimants should bear the consequences of their own actions as experienced businessmen."

46 In this respect, see the leading case *James and Others* v. *United Kingdom*, Judgment, February 21, 1986, 1986 ECHR 2 Series A no. 98, at 63. See also *Lithgow* v. *United Kingdom*, Judgment, July 8, 1986, available at: http://cmiskp.echr.coe.int/tkp197/search.asp, at 116.

47 Higgins (1982), 331.

Finally, an additional point should be made. The scope of the legal protection granted to investors is strictly dependent on what is deemed to deserve legal protection under any given legal system. The domestic systems reviewed above adopt a restrictive concept of property rights and economic interests deserving legal protection, which excludes goodwill. In respect of customary international law, "[W]hether property rights in the nature of good-will … can be subject of a taking for which a compensation must be paid is a question which has plagued the writers."[48] The issue of whether under general international law goodwill could be indirectly expropriated had been considered as an open question in the 1960s.[49]

With respect of treaty law, a distinction between US BITs and EU Member States' BITs must be made. Contrary to the US Model BIT of 2012,[50] BITs of Member States still list a wide range of tangible and intangible assets, economic rights and interests as protected investments. Among covered investments are not only movable property and immovable property (any ownership right therein included), shares, intellectual and industrial property rights, and any economic rights conferred by contract, but also any economic rights conferred by law and goodwill.[51]

The reference to "distinct, reasonable investment-backed expectations" of investors in the US practice seems to be intentional and coherent with the exclusion of goodwill and licenses, authorizations, permits, and similar rights, conferred pursuant to domestic law, which "do not create

48 Christie (1962), 319 reviewing the different positions taken by international law scholars at that time.

49 *Ibid.*, 319–322, where the author discusses the international case-law (the Oscar Chinn case included), concluding that the question must be considered still open, and 335 where the author concludes in favor of States' obligation to pay compensation in cases of indirect expropriation of goodwill. See also The Oscar Chinn case, PCIJ, 1934, Series A/B, No. 63, at 88 where with reference to a claim of the UK of breach by Belgium of the general principles of international and in particular of respect for vested rights in respect of Mr. Chinn because of the introduction of a de facto monopoly of the fluvial water transportation service the Court states that it

> is unable to see in his original position – which was characterized by the possession of customers and the possibility of making a profit – anything in the nature of a genuine vested right. Favourable business conditions and good-will are transient circumstances, subject to inevitable changes; the interests of transport undertakings may well have suffered as a result of the general trade depression and the measures taken to combat it.

50 US Model BIT of 2012, Art. 1. The same definition was contained in the US Model BIT of 2004.

51 See, for example, Italian Model BIT of 2003, Art. 1(1); German Model BIT of 2008, Art. 1(1); France Model BIT of 2006, Art. 1(1); and UK Model BIT of 2005, Art. 1(1).

any rights protected under domestic law" from the investments protected under BITs.[52] The reference has the purpose of equating the international protection of investors vis-à-vis indirect expropriation to the domestic protection pursuant to US case-law. As far as concerns the provisions on expropriation of Member States' BITs (at least as worded at the moment), the concept of legitimate expectations of foreign investors vis-à-vis regulatory expropriation claims, entailing the application of a proportionality test, might narrow the international protection of foreign investors from indirect expropriation, in contrast with an interpretation in accordance with Art. 31 of the Vienna Convention on the Law of Treaties of 1969.

References

Christie, G.C. 1962. "What Constitutes a Taking of Property under International Law." *British Yearbook of International Law* 38: 307–338.

Dolzer, R. and Schreuer, C. 2008. *Principles of International Investment Law.* Oxford University Press.

2012. *Principles of International Investment Law.* Oxford University Press.

Grossrieder Tissot, S. 2001. "'La responsabilité de la Communauté européenne du fait de l'activité normative de la Commission." *Revue trimestrielle de droit européen* 37: 91–122.

Hartley, T.C. 2007. *The Foundations of European Community Law: An Introduction to the Constitutional and Administrative Law of the European Community.* Oxford University Press.

Higgins, R. 1982. "The Taking of Property by the State: Recent Developments in International Law." *RCADI* 176: 259–392.

Leben, C. 2006. "La liberté normative de l'État et la question de l'expropriation indirecte," Leben, C. (ed.), *Le contentieux arbitral transnational relative à l'investissement.* Paris; Brussels: Anthemis: 163–183.

Mairal, H.A. 2010. "Legitimate Expectations and Informal Administrative Representations," Schill, S.W. (ed.) *International Investment Law and Comparative Public Law.* Oxford University Press: 413–415.

Manciaux, S. 2004. *Investissements étrangers et arbitrage entre États et ressortissants d'autres États.* Paris: Lexis Nexis.

Newcombe, A. and Paradell, L. 2009. *Law and Practice of Investment Treaties: Standards of Treatment.* Austin, TX: Kluwer Law International BV.

Potestà, M. 2013. "Legitimate Expectations in Investment Treaty Law: Understanding the Roots and the Limits of a Controversial Concept." *ICSID Review* 21: 1–35.

52 US Model BIT of 2012, fn 2.

Reinisch, A. 2008. 'Expropriation', Muchlinski, P., Ortion, F. Schreur, C., *The Oxford Handbook of International Investment Law*, Oxford University Press: 407–458.

Reinisch, A. 2012. 'Is expropriation ripe for codification? The example of the non-discrimination requirement for lawful expropriations', Reinisch, A., Bjorkland, A. K., *International Investment Law and Soft Law*, Edward Elgar: 271–304.

Snodgrass, E. 2006. "Protecting Investors' Legitimate Expectations: Recognizing and Delimiting a General Principle." *ICSID Review*: 1–58.

Sohn, L.B. and Baxter, R.R. 1961. "Responsibility of States for Injuries to the Economic Interests of Aliens: II. Draft Convention on the International Responsibility of States for Injuries to Aliens." *American Journal of International Law* 55: 548–584.

4

Trade and investment law: what relations?*

FRIEDL WEISS

1. Preliminary remarks

Due to the skeptical tongue-in-cheek title "what relations?," expectations of any kind of relations between the regulatory systems of trade and investment will probably be low. Yet as they are, like European Union law,[1] necessarily embedded in public international law, interlinkages, even interactions between them exist of course, scattered and inchoate in the treaty-making and adjudicative practice of a globalized economy,[2] and the object of lively, occasionally zealously reformist academic debate of methods for reconciling differences between them. This chapter will not seek to revisit let alone rehearse the academic or intergovernmental debates[3] on whether or not this particular manifestation of evolutionary fragmentation has in practice become so intolerably troublesome that it needs "fixing." Instead, after some introductory contextual matters it will, inevitably in broad terms, consider the only two possible but not mutually exclusive ways through which such reconciliation of incompatibilities could conceivably be achieved: treaty-making and adjudication.

* Parts of this chapter have previously appeared in Muchlinski et al. (2008), "Trade and Investment," 182–223. I would like to thank Ioanna Gouvala for her valuable assistance in finalizing the manuscript for this chapter.

1 Case C-112/00, *Schmidberger* [2003] ECR I-5650; C-60/00, *Carpenter* [2002] ECR I-6279.

2 See WTO, Doha Ministerial Declaration of November 14, 2001, WT/MIN(01)/DEC/1, 41 ILM746 (2002), 20–22. See also the Ministerial Declaration of December 15, 1993 on the Contribution of the WTO to Achieving Greater Coherence in Global Economic Policymaking referring, *inter alia*, to "a need for an adequate and timely flow of ... real investment resources to developing countries," at 2.

3 See, for example, the EU's active participation in work on international investment issues conducted in such fora as the OECD, UNCTAD, WTO, G8, IMF; UNCTAD's most recent Issue Note No. 3/June 2013 on "Reform of Investor Dispute Settlement: In Search of a Roadmap."

2. Introduction

2.1 A historical sketch

Once freed from the shackles of mercantilist doctrine, trade agreements based on David Ricardo's as yet in principle un-falsified paradigm of comparative advantage became the first vehicle of choice for mutual gain of economic welfare.

The Industrial Revolution transformed the economies first of Britain and later of Western Europe into mass producers of inexpensive manufactures. By the second quarter of the nineteenth century, the leading European countries were trying to establish markets for their manufactures on the one hand, and to secure cheap and abundant sources of foodstuffs and raw materials on the other. This involved an unprecedented expansion of trade, a trend which was further accelerated by technological revolution in overseas transportation. Export of capital from the industrialized European countries followed, both in form of loans to governments in Latin America, Asia and Africa, and through direct investment in infrastructure such as railroads aimed at expanding trade.[4] Investment then was supportive of trade.

After World War II States pursued the paramount objective of making law, never war again. Above all, international society needed order and socio-economic reconstruction through better rules. Thus, institutions for multilateral rule-based cooperation emerged, as did common rules of conduct for peaceful co-existence (UN), monetary, financial and development matters (IMF, IBRD) and for trade relations (ITO). Investment, though adumbrated in the abortive ITO's comprehensive socio-economic Havana Charter,[5] was not at first a priority for rule – indeed policy making. It was only in the process of de-colonization, and after progress in trade liberalization was made, that the potential of investment as an instrument of economic and technological development was officially recognized.

Today, however, "it seems that international law develops more rapidly than international society does."[6] Consequently, we witness much

4 Pamuk (1987), 2–3.

5 Arts. 11(2)(a)(ii) and 12. Prior to the Havana Charter, bilateral "Treaties on Friendship, Commerce and Navigation" already covered both trade and investment liberalization; see Coyle (2013), 302 ff.

6 Crawford (2011) 224; Simma and Paulus (1998), 266.

doom-mongering talk and diagnostics of crises[7] or collapse of this or that legal system or socio-economic construct, including most recently the much debated fragmentation of international law and of its sub-systems. In response, many assert or propose greater normative unity in international law. Some, as happened previously from time to time,[8] strive for a still largely elusive "International Community" based on a community of interests in international society,[9] generally postulating either the harmonization of international law,[10] or the strengthening of a common quest for unity of law.[11] Yet others argue in favor of the recognition of inter-regime conflict as essentially political conflict between incommensurable systems for prioritizing global values,[12] while some joined debates on "constitutionalism," on certain fundamental values,[13] matters of common concern,[14] mechanisms of solidarity and on various aspects of public goods.[15]

While the Doha Round of multilateral trade negotiations, now in its twelfth year, has been all but formally written off as a failure, a similar perception of an international investment regime in crisis has also triggered a flurry of academic debates. Many commentators concur that certain aspects of investment law need "fixing." Some consider the investment regime and investor–State dispute settlement seriously flawed by its pro-investor bias and "privatized" method of dispute settlement, compared to commercial arbitration. Others, therefore, see it even as the enemy of the State as repository of the public interest, especially in situations of emergency or crisis.[16] Of course, the investment regime also has its defenders, concerned more with its repair than abolition. One of them, an eminent investment law scholar who attributes the perceived lack of systemic harmony to differences in treaties applicable to relationships between host States and investors of different nationalities, recommends various types

7 See, e.g., Domingo (2009), 1543 ff. 8 See, e.g., Verdross and Simma (1983).

9 Weiss (2011), 406–408; see also Rao (2011), 326–338.

10 Diller and Levy (1997), 663–696.

11 Bronckers (2007), 51–74; Cottier (2007), 99–122; Lavranos and Vielliard (2008), 205–234.

12 Khrebutkova (2008), 51 ff. 13 Simma (1994), 233.

14 See also the Declaration of Judge Simma on the Advisory Opinion: *Accordance with International Law of The Unilateral Declaration of Independence in Respect of Kosovo*, 1–3.

15 See, e.g., Maskus and Reichman (2005), 4 ff.

16 See the so-called Osgoode Hall Statement on the International Investment Regime of August 31, 2010, available at http://papers.ssrn.com/sol3/papers.cfm?abstract_id=1466980.

of action to foster harmony derived from interpretation including the introduction of a novel preliminary reference procedure.[17]

Some, including this author, examined key features of the disparate epistemic systems of trade and investment law and surveyed some such attempts as have hitherto been made to build bridges between them.[18]

As a follow-up, this chapter seeks to highlight instances of case practice of investment arbitration and trade dispute settlement, perhaps including interpretative pontoons on either or one or the other side or, perhaps, just on no man's land.

2.2 *Fragmentation*

The much lamented phenomenon of the fragmentation[19] of international law, or even of its very "fragments" such as investment law itself, its lack of coherence, consistency and predictability and hence legitimacy, has prompted intergovernmental scrutiny and concern.[20] It has also attracted an abundance of scholarly analysis and comment, theoretical and practical, and numerous suggestions for remedial action toward "de-fragmentation," whether generally for regime interaction,[21] coordination of international treaties,[22] judicial integration for the stability and reliability of the international legal system,[23] or more particularly for greater coherence in investment law,[24] or more structured regime interaction between trade and investment regulation.[25]

Yet the metaphor of "fragmentation" is of course itself flawed, as it conjures up an imagined erstwhile harmoniously coherent system of international law, some paradise lost through fragmentation. In reality though such a paradise never existed and will remain elusive, with every concluded treaty exacerbating its very "fragmented" complexity. The traditional and simplistic image of the international community consisting of sovereign and equal States governed by rules coordinating their conduct was always inaccurate, conceptually and practically. Not only was equality amongst States of different endowment with material wealth and

17 Schreuer (2013), 402. 18 Weiss (2008a), 184.

19 One commentator at a recent academic conference described "fragmentation" and "constitutionalization" as "hypochondria," and "faith healing" respectively.

20 E.g., cross references in some constitutive treaties to others (Art. XII GATT); IOs' decisions on cooperation (WTO–ILO on labor standards); Uruguay Round Ministerial Declaration on Coherence in IEL.

21 Young (2012), 85 ff. 22 See, generally, Matz (2005), 233 ff.

23 Webb (2013). 24 Schreuer (2013), 391–402.

25 Footer (2013), 116 ff.

power notoriously fictitious,[26] but even the apparent exclusivity of sovereign States as actors under international law was never complete as other, lesser actors too were admitted or tolerated to some extent (international organizations, corporations, individuals, Holy See),[27] not to mention the multitude of non-State actors and their potential contribution to "State practice."[28] According to the ILC's much debated Report on the subject of the fragmentation of international law, it is but the result of normative differentiation in specialized areas of international law having attained legal significance, especially when accompanied by the emergence of specialized and (relatively) autonomous rules or rule-complexes, legal institutions and spheres of legal practice. Thus, "general international law" has become interspersed with such notoriously specialist systems as "trade law," "human rights law," "environmental law," "law of the sea," "European law" and even such exotic and highly specialized knowledge as "investment law" or "international refugee law," etc. – each possessing its own principles and institutions.[29]

2.3 *Economic perspective*

Economists consider international trade and investment to be complements, even twins,[30] not substitutes. They have worked out that, at the level of the firm, the invest or export decision will have a pro-export bias when the targeted market is in a high-cost country, and a pro-investment bias when it is in a low-cost country, a conclusion apparently consistent with the high ratio of US subsidiary sales to exports and with the low ratio of foreign investments in the US in relation to imports.[31] Over the past decades, national policies toward foreign direct investment (FDI) have been liberalized worldwide, reflecting a more positive perception of the role of FDI in host countries' development.[32] Started by the 1959 private

26 Weiss (2008b), 272 ff.

27 See the seminal Article by Schreuer (1993), 449.

28 In *Japan – Measures Affecting Consumer Photographic Film and Paper* a GATT Panel expressed the view that "the fact that an action is taken by private parties does not rule out the possibility that it may be deemed governmental if there is sufficient governmental involvement with it," BISD 35S/116; for other possible instances of State practice through civil society, see Weiss (2012), 346.

29 International Law Commission (ILC), Report of the Study Group of the ILC: "Fragmentation of International Law: Difficulties Arising from the Diversification and Expansion of International Law," finalized by Martti Koskenniemi, A/CN.4/L.682, April 13, 2006; 61 UN GAOR Supp. No. 10, 400, UN Doc. A/61/10 (2006).

30 DeAnne (1991). 31 Hirsch (1976), 267. 32 De Sterlin (2005), 437–483.

initiative of the Abs/Shawcross group and taken up by the OECD in 1967, treaties for the promotion and protection of investments – all very similar in nature, content, structure, even wording – proliferated.[33] Clearly, as is widely recognized, foreign investors are often also traders, approximately one third of global trade flows being intra-firm flows, between subsidiaries or affiliates of a corporation located in different countries.[34] Governmental measures may affect trade between them, but at the same time also an "investment" of a foreign investor.[35] Yet trade and investment have for a considerable time co-existed side by side, as separate concerns. At different times, either of them functioned as the principal vehicle for global economic integration.[36] Evidently, liberated and regulated international trade and liberated and protected investment have evolved to become the twin pillars of the modern international commercial system. This economic welfare function was clearly recognized in a recent joint WTO–UNCTAD–OECD Report which implores G-20 members to strengthen the global trading and investment system as an insurance policy against protectionism.[37] Unsurprisingly, therefore, in the more recent treaty practice of Preferential Trade and Investment Agreements (PTIAs), both sets of rules feature in the same instrument, seen by some as a possible way forward.[38]

2.4 *Co-existence of separate rules*

Thus, trade and investment co-existed based on separate not integrated rules, though sometimes in the same international agreement.[39] Standard setting approaches for both trade and investment constituted retrospective attempts to discipline governments in the exercise of their near unfettered sovereign regulatory powers. The first, the GATT, was designed to stem self-destructive governmental trade protectionism of the kind that had triggered the worldwide depression, political radicalization and ultimately World War II.

The second, investment protection, sought to liberate individual investors from the vagaries of diplomatic protection in disputes with host States concerning their investment.

33 Mann (1981), 541 ff. 34 See, e.g., WTO (1996).
35 Verhoosel (2003), 494. 36 Shenkin (1994), 544.
37 Reports on G-20 Trade and Investment Measures, May 31, 2012.
38 Hofmann et al. (2013)
39 For further details of historical antecedents see Weiss (2008a), 184.

Pursuant to the ultimately abortive Havana Charter for an International Trade Organization (ITO), both were at first destined to develop alongside one another within the same multilateral institutional and procedural framework.[40] In 1997 the attempt by OECD countries to eliminate the patchwork of the then more than 1300 bilateral investment treaties through a multilateral instrument, the Multilateral Agreement on Investment (MAI), likewise failed.

However, the contracting parties of the residual GATT subsequently focused primarily on removing protectionist barriers to trade in goods while investment activities emerged only a few decades later as a vehicle for economic development based on a growing number of bilateral investment treaties (BITs).[41]

It was only by the early 1980s, after investment activities had emerged as a vehicle for economic development that the United States and other capital-exporting countries proposed to subject investments to the disciplines of the GATT so as to remove what they considered the trade-restricting and distorting effects of performance requirements. DCs were opposed to the initiative, pointing to the lack of jurisdiction for investment policy. However, in a dispute in which the US challenged the GATT legality of the Canadian Foreign Investment Review Act ("FIRA"), the GATT Panel held that GATT rules, in particular the national treatment obligation in Art. III GATT, were applicable to certain trade-related investment measures to the extent that they affected trade. Despite the polarization of positions of developed and developing countries, an agreement on trade-related investment measures ("TRIMs") emerged from the Uruguay Round trade negotiations.[42]

As a result, both trade and investment rules evolved somewhat "autistically," unsynchronized, haphazardly, in leaps and bounds and relative isolation from one another, reflecting both needs of States and shifts in State interests and economic development policy preferences. But while the interpretation and application of trade law of the covered agreements through GATT and WTO panels and especially the permanent WTO Appellate Body (AB) exhibits a certain degree of continuity, consistency

40 Dattu (2000), 275–316.

41 See the Press Release No. 12/391 of October 13, 2012, of the IMF: "We reaffirm our commitment to avoid any form of trade and investment protectionism," 26th Meeting of the International Monetary and Financial Committee Chaired by Mr. Tharman Shanmugaratnam, Deputy Prime Minister of Singapore and Minister for Finance.

42 De Sterlin (2005), 439.

and hence predictability, investment law as determined by *ad hoc* arbitral tribunals struggles to evolve a coherent set of principles and rules for reliable guidance of the investment community, investors, host and home States. However, occasional attempts have been made to overcome the deficit of coherence as well as the "conceptual apartheid" separating the trade and investment treaty systems. This occurred directly in some instances of treaty-making and indirectly by some recent investor–State arbitration panels, particularly by those which invoked interpretations of the most favored nation and national treatment clauses established by WTO panels and the WTO, to interpret relevant investment treaty provisions in issue.

And why, indeed, should the interpretation of comparable legal concepts featuring both in trade and investment treaties not benefit from an application of settled practice first developed in trade disputes? As was observed in *Continental Casualty Company* v. *The Argentine Republic* with regard to Art. XI of the US–Argentina BIT:

> Since the text of Art. XI derives from the parallel model clause of the US FCN treaties and these treaties in turn reflect the formulation of Art. XX(g) GATT 1947, the Tribunal finds it more appropriate to refer to GATT and WTO case law which has extensively dealt with the concept and requirements of necessity in the context of economic measures derogating to the obligations in GATT, rather than to refer to the requirement of necessity under customary international law.[43]

Before considering some examples of these instances, it is appropriate to highlight the marginal status of investment amongst provisions of WTO trade agreements.

3. Investment amongst trade rules

Although, as mentioned above, rules on trade and on FDI share the common objective of "liberalization" from governmental restrictions, they nonetheless developed separately, in response to predominant needs, historically and economically. Yet their complementarity has never been lost sight of: neither regime could conceivably be considered "self-contained" vis-à-vis the other.[44]

43 *Continental Casualty* v. *The Argentine Republic*, ICSID No. ARB/03/9, Award September 5, 2008, 192; see also Coyle (2013), 302.

44 For critical view of this and other terminology drawn from international relations theory, see Weiss (2007), 51–71.

Indeed awareness of linkages between trade and investment is evident from a number of references to investment contained in several WTO Agreements, directly or indirectly. Governmental trade measures which affect intra-firm trade, i.e., trade between subsidiaries of a corporate entity, may also impact on the "investment" of a foreign investor. Such trade measures may constitute breaches of a number of WTO Agreements. Despite opposition, from DCs, the Uruguay Round introduced an "investment" dimension in multilateral trade rules, obligations imposed on governments of WTO Members with respect to the treatment of foreign nationals or companies in their jurisdiction. These are, most importantly, the GATS and the TRIPS but also the Agreement on Government Procurement (AGP), all of which impose obligations on WTO Members with respect to the entry and treatment of foreign persons and enterprises or to the protection of their property rights. Other WTO Agreements, the TRIMS and the Agreement on Subsidies and Countervailing Measures (SCM), operate indirectly by merely restricting the ability of WTO Members to apply investment incentives or to influence the operations of foreign investors. Suffice it to briefly survey the main multilateral agreements amongst them, the TRIMS, the GATS and the TRIPS agreements.

3.1 The TRIMS Agreement

The TRIMS Agreement, essentially a codification of GATT Panel case-law under GATT Arts. III and XI ("FIRA"), seeks to regulate government-imposed investment restrictions,[45] especially potentially trade-restricting and distorting performance requirements imposed by host countries. Other instruments too may directly affect the volume or even the composition of trade, for example export subsidies, import entitlements, local content rules and manufacturing requirements (which require that certain components be domestically manufactured). Likewise, trade-balancing requirements which restrict the quantity of imported goods that can be used if an MNC does not meet its export target violate the national treatment obligation. Tax incentives too may be used to attract FDI, so as to persuade firms to favor FDI rather than exports as a method of foreign market penetration.

45 Curtiss (2003), 233–255.

However, the TRIMS Agreement is narrow in scope. It applies only to trade in goods, doesn't provide any new rules prohibiting all of these TRIMS, but merely prohibits TRIMS deemed inconsistent with GATT Arts. III and XI.

3.2 *The GATS*

The GATS contains no general rules on investment. In fact investment as such is only mentioned in two of its provisions.[46] Investment through FDI is only covered by "commercial presence," the third of the four modes of supply of a service through which the GATS concept of trade in services is defined depending on the origin of the service supplier and consumer and on the degree and type of their territorial presence when the service is delivered.[47] Commercial presence, the GATS investment provision, though akin to FDI, is narrower than the asset-based approach. Although the core GATS principles – the general obligation to accord MFN treatment[48] and the negotiated specific commitments regarding market access (Art. XVI) and national treatment (Art. XVII) – do not directly relate to FDI, they provide, nonetheless, standards for the regulatory treatment of foreign service suppliers (Art. VI) and thus protection against these types of prohibited discrimination. But the GATS provisions on investment, essentially those on "commercial presence," are subsidiary to its liberalization provisions, and serve to avert hidden protectionism and to protect investments which are an integral part of services such as banking. Thus, barriers to FDI in services are for the first time covered by a binding multilateral agreement, albeit subject to restrictions on balance of payments (Art. XII) and to general exceptions (Art. XIV). Furthermore, the GATS commitments only apply to the extent to which Members have expressly agreed, through their negotiated GATS commitments, to open their markets in respect of particular service industries. Many have chosen not to

46 "Aggregate foreign investment": Art. XVI(2)(f) on Market Access; "collective investment management," "investment and portfolio research and advice," Art. 5(a)(xiii) and (xvi) on Definitions, Annex on Financial Services.

47 "Commercial presence" means any type of business or professional establishment, including through: (i) the constitution, acquisition or maintenance of a juridical person, or (ii) the creation or maintenance of a branch or a representative office, within the territory of a Member for the purpose of supplying a service, Art XXVIII(d).

48 Art. II GATS on MFN treatment has been interpreted by the WTO Appellate Body as including de facto as well as de jure discrimination: *EC Bananas III*, WT/DS27/ABR, 233–234.

include many service sectors. Therefore, the practical impact of the GATS on FDI is limited. It is also noteworthy that the GATS does not provide protection against nationalization, nor standards for compensation.

3.3 The TRIPS Agreement

The TRIPS Agreement stipulates that Members "shall not be obliged to implement in their domestic law more extensive protection than is required by this Agreement . . .," a provision on uniform minimum standards for the protection of intellectual property rights (IPRs) of nationals of other Members.[49] Obviously, an increasingly important share of the assets of multinational enterprises consists of intangible assets and virtually all modern investment agreements containing standards for the promotion and protection of foreign investment include IPRs within the definition of investment.[50] Clearly the TRIPS Agreement requires certain guarantees of judicial protection and domestic remedies for foreign intellectual property right holders.[51] It therefore has a bearing on FDI considering that the definition of IPRs and compliance with international standards and procedures constitute part of the framework within which foreign investment takes place. Less certain, however, is the impact of the Agreement on the flow of foreign investment. While a stable and reliable legal environment and better investment climate may generally attract increased flows of FDI, lack of or inadequately enforced IPRs may also encourage FDI.

This brief summary survey of pertinent WTO Agreements evidently confirms the near total absence of provisions on investment and hence the absence of relations within the system of rules governing multilateral trade. Time and again after failed attempts to conclude multilateral trade or investment agreements,[52] bilateralism and various forms of regionalism have sprouted, by default as it were. As for trade, this trend is likely to continue, possibly accelerated after the scanty deal of the Doha Round.

49 Art. 1(1) TRIPS.

50 See, e.g., Art. 1(e)(iv) Hong Kong–Australia BIT 1993; Gestrin and Rugman (2005), 315.

51 Arts. 3, 42–49 TRIPS.

52 Decision by the General Council of the WTO of August 1, 2004, at Cancun that "relationship between Trade and Investment, Interaction between Trade and Competition Policy and Transparency in Government Procurement ... mentioned in the Doha Ministerial Declaration ... will not form part of the Work Program ... and no work towards negotiations on any of these issues will take place ... during the Doha Round."

Similarly, States are increasingly shifting towards framing investment rules within regional framework arrangements.[53]

Regional integration efforts and arrangements have likewise proved effective in attracting FDI. They offer a larger potential market to investors, contribute to macroeconomic and political stability, often involve regulatory reforms favorable to foreign investors, and facilitate harmonization and enforcement of standards and regulations.[54] For instance, using its exclusive competence under Art. 207 TFEU,[55] the EU is currently negotiating on investment, including investment protection, as part of Preferential Trade and Investment Agreements with Canada, India, Singapore, Japan, and soon likely toward a controversial "Transatlantic Trade and Investment Partnership" (TTIP) with the US. Similarly, negotiations toward a Transpacific Partnership Agreement (TPPA) will include provisions on investment and investor-State arbitration.[56] While both efforts may well formally restrict the modest gains of the Doha Round, it is nonetheless recognized, though by no means universally, that in the long run, a multilateral framework of rules can further contribute to improvements in the investment climate.

4. Bridging the trade–investment divide: instances of investor–State arbitration practice

International law does not preclude foreign investors from initiating both arbitration proceedings against a host State under an applicable BIT as well as "diplomatic protection" through WTO dispute settlement proceedings launched by their own State. This could occur when WTO law is "applicable" to the investment dispute, such as when a BIT regulatory standard is defined by reference to international law applicable between the parties including provisions of WTO Agreements which an arbitral tribunal is required to apply. An investor may then be able to invoke the inconsistency of a regulatory measure with provisions of WTO Agreements. For instance, Philip Morris Asia Limited recently claimed that the Australian Tobacco Plain Packaging Bill 2011 will not be fair and

53 See e.g. China–Japan–Korea Trilateral Investment Treaty 2012.

54 Weiss (2008a), 206.

55 Weiss and Steiner (2013), 359 ff.; De Luca (2010–2011), 165–215.

56 Art. 12 TPPA; negotiating parties are New Zealand, Singapore, Chile, Brunei, the US, Australia, Peru, Vietnam and Malaysia. Japan, Canada, Mexico and others have shown interest. TPPA is designed to be much more than a trade agreement; trade in fact is only a small part of it.

equitable, contrary to the Hong Kong–Australia BIT of 2011[57] as it will, *inter alia*, contravene Australia's obligations under the TRIPS and TBT Agreements.[58] Alternatively, where WTO law cannot be said to be applicable to the investment dispute, it may still indirectly constitute the context for the interpretation of the BIT regulatory obligation.[59]

Such a double strategy has never, however, been pursued in practice due to apprehension that WTO proceedings could more swiftly be completed and through DSB findings and recommendations materially preempt subsequent investor–State arbitral proceedings.

Instead, for a period of time it seemed that some investor–State arbitration panels sought to use interpretations of most favored nation and national treatment clauses established by WTO panels and the WTO Appellate Body (AB), to interpret relevant investment treaty provisions before them.

However, this laudable and initially apparently welcome, if somewhat contextually naive opening towards cross-fertilizing "borrowing" from WTO dispute settlement practice, has been haphazard, inchoate, altogether problematic, and probably abandoned again in investor–State arbitration, at least for the time being.

Nonetheless, in the absence of customary law content of either the MFN and/or national treatment clauses, such interpretative outreach, so to speak, remains a potentially useful indirect approach to the integration of these like concepts in the disparate trade and investment treaty regimes. Generally speaking, legal transplants have frequently been advocated, sponsored and used to improve the quality of legal systems.

Legal systems are considered public goods and, in addition to justice and fairness, are commonly valued for the characteristics of continuity, certainty, consistency, stability and predictability. Since Hersch Lauterpacht's seminal writing in the 1930s, we know that judicial and arbitral bodies contribute to the international rule of law by consistent decision-making thereby rendering international law functionally complete.[60] Adjudicative bodies themselves are, of course, aware of their role in maintaining these values and consider instances of inconsistency

57 Art. 2(2), "umbrella" clause.

58 See Written Notice of Arbitration by Philip Morris Asia Ltd., November 21, 2011, 6–7, and Australia's Response of December 21, 2011, 33 and 57–58, cited from www.italaw.com/cases/851.

59 Art. 31(3)(c) VCLT: "any relevant rules of international law applicable in the relations between the parties."

60 See, generally, Lauterpacht (1933).

problematic. Thus, the AB cited from an ICSID arbitral tribunal recognizing that "consistency of jurisprudence is valued also in dispute settlement in other fora."[61]

Obviously, State practice upon which international law mainly rests[62] develops in many different municipal legal settings, reflecting different societal values at different levels of development. Legal transplants, involving entire codes or at least principles, rules and techniques imported from other countries, sometimes help to bridge developmental gaps.[63] For a variety of reasons including commercial self-interest, governmental agencies support legal reform in other countries, as do certain international organizations as a condition for their (financial) assistance with the implementation of development projects of DCs. Alternatively, adjudicative instances take inspiration from the work and approaches developed by others, or from other legal regimes. For instance, in The *Wimbledon* case, it might be recalled, a majority of the PCIJ interpreted provisions of the Treaty of Versailles relating to the Kiel Canal by comparison with the regimes determining the legal status of the Suez and Panama canals.[64] Notoriously, the WTO's AB has not been shy to cite decisions of other international tribunals, including those of the European Court of Justice and of the European Court of Human Rights, at least as some kind of *obiter dicta*.[65] Some might even remember the United Kingdom's Court of Appeal Case of *Trendtex* in which the legendary Lord Denning, Master of the Rolls, extensively analyzed and relied on judicial and treaty practice of other States on restrictive sovereign immunity.[66] So why should the device of borrowing or transplanting legal analysis and reasoning not also be deemed potentially useful in and by other adjudicative fora, including investor–State arbitration? After all, international law knows

61 AB Report in *US–Final Anti-Dumping Measures on Stainless Steel*, WTO Doc. WT/DS344/AB/R(2008), 160, fn 313, citing from *Saipem* v. *Bangladesh*, ICSID Case No. ARB/05/70, at 67.

62 Holland (1898), 152: "The Law of Nations is but private law 'writ large'"; see, generally, Lauterpacht (1927).

63 Watson (1993), 95.

64 See Case *S.S. Wimbledon* (*UK* v. *Japan*), 1923 P.C.I.J. (ser. A) No. 1 (Aug. 17), at 37, or for the respective treaties see the Convention of Constantinople of October 29, 1888 (Suez Maritime Canal) and the Treaty between Great Britain and the United States of November 18, 1901, the Hay-Pauncefote Treaty and the Treaty between the United States and the Republic of Panama of November 18, 1903.

65 Weiss (2009) 185–99.

66 *Trendtex Corporation* v. *Central Bank of Nigeria*, [1977] 2 W.L.R.

no *stare decisis* of any kind. Suffice it to examine critically some of these instances of investor–State arbitration.

There are several reasons justifying a brief summary analysis of Chapter 11 of NAFTA.[67] First, NAFTA Chapter 11 clearly contains by far the most comprehensive and detailed rules on FDI of all treaties to date, though it does not go as far as the Treaty on the Functioning of the EU (TFEU) with respect to the right of establishment and the free movement of capital. Secondly, since drafters of the MAI significantly have drawn inspiration from its provisions, it is likely that negotiators of any future WTO Agreement are bound to appraise its impact carefully and critically, even though it was clear in WTO discussions on investment that any WTO Agreement on investment would not be based on the NAFTA model but rather on that of the GATS; that it would not have dealt with investment protection; and that it would have provided for a positive list approach to market access commitments. Thirdly, the many recent investor arbitral challenges – mostly based on ICSID's additional facility rules – brought under Chapter 11 against regulatory measures adopted by NAFTA States may provide useful material and insights for re-framing the delicate relationship between a prospective WTO investment agreement and regulatory autonomy. More generally, an analysis of even a small sample of such arbitral case-law will permit an empirically more objective assessment of the potential advantages or otherwise of following the Chapter 11 approach as a model for a WTO investment agreement. Of all possible host State discriminatory regulatory measures, Chapter 11 aims particularly at subjecting to its disciplines pre- and post-admission restrictions. Far fewer of its provisions seek to limit the use of investment incentives.

The scope of application of Chapter 11, one of NAFTA's central components, is set out in Art. 1101. It provides that all Chapter 11 disciplines apply to measures of NAFTA States relating to both "investors" and "investments." Furthermore, disciplines regarding performance requirements (Art. 1106) and environmental measures (Art. 1114) are applicable to all investments, including domestic and investments from non-NAFTA countries. Article 1139 NAFTA, as was mentioned above, contains a very broad, asset-based definition of "investment" that goes beyond FDI and which has been stretched further by certain arbitral awards. Thus, unlike the GATS, it includes portfolio investment – equity security – without any percentage limitation on ownership, and also includes beneficial

67 See, generally, Staff and Lewis (2003), 301 ff.

ownership of the underlying interest.[68] However, there are also limiting factors. One stems from the definition of investment by reference to an exhaustive list of interests that would qualify as "investment." Others operate as limiting factors within the definition of certain listed interests.[69] By contrast, the MAI definition of investment was based on a non-exhaustive list of interests.

Liberalization from national investment restrictions is mainly pursued through the application of non-discriminatory standards of treatment.[70] Following US BIT practice, investors enjoy the better of national and MFN treatment. Uniquely relevant NAFTA disciplines also cover the pre-admission phase as well as the post-admission situation of established investments in a NAFTA State. In accordance with NAFTA's top-down approach, the liberalization commitments cover all economic sectors and national laws of NAFTA States, unless these are specifically exempted through negative lists of nonconforming measures.[71] This strict approach differs from the somewhat hybrid approach open to WTO Members which can make either horizontal, all-encompassing commitments to the national treatment obligation in Art. XVII GATS (as well as to market access), covering all sectors, or commitments in only particular sectors. Owing to this measure of discretion allowed WTO Members, scheduled liberalization commitments under the GATS have hitherto been rather modest. In addition to imposing non-discriminatory standards of treatment, NAFTA liberalization commitments also encompass the prohibition on the use of certain performance requirements by NAFTA States. These include, for example, technology transfer requirements which, by contrast, are not expressly covered by the TRIMS Agreement (Art. 1106(f)).

Although provisions for investment protection have featured for a long time in BITs of developing host States, their incorporation in multilateral

68 Lit (e) of the definition of investment includes "an interest in an enterprise that entitles the owner to share in income or profits of the enterprise."

69 Lit (d) only covers intra-firm debt flows of a relatively long-term duration or intra-enterprise loans of at least three years' maturity, thereby excluding short-term debt; see also limitations in lits (h), (i), and (j) of Art. 1139.

70 Arts. 1102–1104, 1106 NAFTA.

71 A "top-down" or negative list approach requires countries to negotiate a reservation for a particular investment or measure. The requirement to negotiate as opposed to just listing its exceptions places potentially considerable pressure on countries; NAFTA follows the top-down negative list approach but does not require the negotiation of such listing, of Art. 1108 NAFTA on reservations and exemptions, Annexes I–IV; for a description of the bottom-up or positive list approach, see also fn 34 *supra*.

instruments is still resisted by them.[72] However, despite a dramatic decline of instances of direct FDI expropriation in DCs, the NAFTA Agreement includes very strong guarantees of investment protection, including an obligation to pay compensation.[73] Short of outright direct expropriation, other regulatory measures "tantamount to nationalization or expropriation" may have an incremental impact on an investor comparable to direct expropriation, amounting to "indirect expropriation." Indeed, a number of investors have challenged seemingly normal regulatory measures in Chapter 11 arbitration proceedings as being "tantamount to nationalization."[74] Additional protection is available under Art. 1105 which provides investors with a minimum standard of treatment "in accordance with international law, including fair and equitable treatment and full protection and security." That is to say that even if a NAFTA State treats foreign and domestic investors equally, an arbitral tribunal may find that the actual treatment violates the international law standard. Consensus is, however, lacking on the exact standard required. Consequently, and in the absence of NAFTA textual guidance on the interpretation of the ambivalent terms used in Art. 1105, investors have resorted to arbitral challenges of regulatory measures under this provision as an alternative to a challenge based on Art. 1110.

Although the NAFTA Agreement does not directly restrict the use of investment incentives despite their discriminatory aims and distorting effects, Art. 1114 NAFTA nonetheless seeks to limit the ability of NAFTA States to engage in a proverbial regulatory "race to the bottom" by lowering their health, safety and environmental standards as an investment inducement. This provision though is a far cry from the much broader general exception of Art. XX GATT and the abundant WTO Panel and Appellate Body case-law struggling to interpret it consistently.[75]

Apart from this, NAFTA arbitral case law has considered directly the meaning of the main standards of treatment: national, MFN, fair and equitable treatment.[76] This has given rise to certain links and analogies with WTO arbitral decisions. National treatment seeks to ensure equality of competitive opportunities for both national and international

72 Guzman (1998), 639 ff. 73 Art. 1110(1) NAFTA.

74 Reinisch (2008), 407 ff; Wälde and Kolo (2001), 819 ff; Muchlinski (2008), 31 ff.

75 See WTO Appellate Body (2005), 163–176.

76 HA standards regularly at issue also include: scope of coverage, definitions of investors and investments, admission and establishment commitments, host country operational measures, transfer of funds and the taking of property.

investors, the so-called "level playing field." While the national treatment standard has primarily originated in trade treaties, it has become one of the main general standards used to secure a certain level of treatment for FDI in host countries. As a relative standard, contingent upon the treatment given to other investors and their investments, in most BITs it typically applied to investors only after they had entered a host country, that is, only to the post-establishment phase of an investment. However, more recent IIAs have extended it to the pre-establishment phase of an investment, which goes beyond its use in Art. III GATT. Direct investor–State dispute resolution procedures offer investors a convenient process through which to enforce commitments made by State signatories of investment agreements. By contrast, individual traders benefit only indirectly from the removal of trade barriers when WTO Members comply with their obligations under covered agreements in compliance with rulings of the intergovernmental WTO system of dispute settlement.

It has taken the GATT/WTO system of multilateral rules and adjudication some time to shed the preposterous tag once artificially affixed to them by certain academic writers of being a "self-contained regime" isolated, if not shielded, from international law.[77] However, in more recent WTO dispute settlement practice, the wider international law context is increasingly recognized, if not yet openly embraced, though the notion of a "self-contained regime" lingers with respect to investment treaty arbitration, possibly due to the unresolved tension regarding the role of the investment treaty arbitrator vis-à-vis the regulatory sovereignty of States.[78] Thus, as is common practice worldwide, panels and the Appellate Body have, at least for the purpose of interpretation of WTO covered agreements, referred to international law sources extrinsic to the WTO, including decisions of other international courts and tribunals. Customary international law, as has been highlighted on several occasions, provides the normative background to the operation of a special

77 In a seminal article which triggered a controversial debate over the last decade, Pieter-Jan Kuyper expressed the view that the WTO "has moved decisively in the direction of … a self-contained regime": see Kuyper (1994), 252; for an important attempt at a refutation of this position see Pauwelyn (2003), 316 and *passim.*; most recently, Bruno Simma and Dirk Pulkowski appear to have ended the debate for the time being, concluding a brief analysis of the WTO dispute settlement system with the view that "arguably, not even the WTO is completely decoupled from the secondary rules governing the consequences of breaches under general international law" (2006), 523.

78 Foster (2012), 1–34.

regime,[79] as is also confirmed in WTO case law.[80] As one WTO dispute settlement panel pointed out:

> customary international law applies generally to the economic relations between WTO Members. Such international law applies to the extent that the WTO treaty agreements do not "contract out" from it. To put it another way, to the extent that there is no conflict or inconsistency, or an expression in a covered WTO agreement that implies differently, we are of the view that the customary rules of international law apply to the WTO treaties and to the process of treaty formation under the WTO.[81]

Admittedly, such references have been relatively sparse and cautious and apparently have not so far included the examination of overlapping treaty issues[82] or references to the case-law of investment arbitration tribunals.

Conversely, investors and NAFTA Parties have argued over the scope and meaning of the "treatment in accordance with international law" standard of Art. 1105 NAFTA, the former pointing to Art. 38 of the Statute of the ICJ,[83] the latter referring to the more restrictive standard defined by customary law as laid down in the 1926 *Neer* Award.[84] It was in *S.D. Myers* that the possibility of incorporating obligations under the WTO Agreement by reference to Art. 1105 was first discussed. In some *dicta* the Tribunal held that while a breach of a rule of international law may not be decisive to determine that a foreign investor has been denied "fair and equitable treatment," "the fact that a host Party has breached a rule of international law that is specifically designed to protect investors will tend to weigh heavily in favour of finding a breach of Art. 1005."[85] In

79 Case concerning the Right of Passage over Indian Territory (Prel. Objections), *Portugal* v. *India*, 1957, ICJ Reports 125; Case concerning the Gabcikovo-Nagmymaros Project, *Hungary* v. *Slovakia*, 1997, ICJ Report 7.

80 AB Report, *United States – Import Prohibition of Certain Shrimp and Shrimp Products*, WT/ DS58/AB/R, November 6, 1998; AB Report, *EG – Measures Concerning Meat and Meat Products (Hormones)*, WTiDS26/AB/R, WT/DS48/AB/R, February 13, 1998.

81 Panel Report, *Korea – Measures Affecting Government Procurement*, WT/DSI63/R, 183, 7.96.

82 In the case of *Mexico – Tax Measures on Soft Drinks and Other Beverages*, the AB declined to examine NAFTA provisions as well as PCIT case-law; AB Report WT/DS308/AB/R, March 6, 2006.

83 *Pope & Talbot Inc.* v. *The Government of Canada*, April 10, 2001, 107; ADF United States, June 27, 2002, 213.

84 "... the treatment of an alien, in order to constitute an international delinquency, should amount to an outrage, to bad faith, to willful neglect of duty, or to an insufficiency of governmental action so far short of international standards that every reasonable and impartial man would readily recognize its insufficiency," October 15, 1926, RIAA, vol. IV, 60–66.

85 *S.D. Myers* v. *Canada*, Partial Award, November 13, 2000, 264.

a concurring separate opinion one of the arbitrators went further, taking the view that the interpretation and application of Art. 1105 must also take into account the "letter or spirit of widely, though not universally, accepted international agreements like those in the WTO system and those typical of BITs," and that regional agreements such as the GATT – as pointed out in the *Shrimp/Turtle* Case – and NAFTA "recognize a broader principle of transparency and regulatory fairness in the making of regulation" that "should be considered part of 'international law' referred to in Art. 1105," inviting "interpreters of Article 1105 to look to the 'state of the art' in international trade agreements to determine the content of the minimum international standard, rather than relying on personal subjective notions of what is 'fair,' 'equitable' or 'full protection and security'."[86] The NAFTA Free Trade Commission subsequently issued "Notes of Interpretation of Certain Chapter 11 Provisions," stating, *inter alia*, that "a determination that there has been a breach of ... a separate international agreement, does not establish that there has been a breach of Art. 1105(1)."[87] Undeterred, several investors invoked Art. 1105 NAFTA as a vehicle for the incorporation of WTO obligations into that provision, arguing that regulatory measures in breach of WTO obligations – SPS Agreement,[88] Anti-Dumping and SCM Agreements[89] – amount to treatment not "in accordance with international law."

In any event, in interpreting Art. 1102 NAFTA on national treatment the Tribunal in *S.D. Myers, Inc.* v. *Government of Canada*,[90] deemed it instructive to follow the reasoning employed in the well-settled case-law of WTO dispute settlement bodies. Art. 1102 NAFTA bars discrimination by a State or province, against foreign investors and their investments with respect to the establishment, acquisition, expansion, management, conduct, operation, and sale or other disposition of investments. Each party is required to accord investors and investments of another party "treatment no less favourable than it accords, in like circumstances to its own investors" or their investments. In its Art. 102(2) NAFTA provides internal guidance for its interpretation by obliging the parties to "interpret and apply the provisions of the Agreement in the light of its objectives set out

86 Bryan Schwartz Concurring Opinion, November 12, 2000, 256–258.
87 NAFTA FTC, July 31, 2001.
88 Notice of Arbitration, *Kenex Ltd.* v. *United States*, January 14, 2002, 23(d).
89 Notice of Arbitration and Statement of Claim, *Canfour* v.*United States*, July 9, 2002, 62 and 122(4).
90 40 ILM (2001) 1408. See also discussion in Kurtz (2002), 745–749.

in paragraph 1 and in accordance with applicable rules of international law," that is, the Vienna Convention on the Law of Treaties.[91]

In interpreting the phrase "like circumstances," the Tribunal followed long-established GATT/WTO case-law in finding that national treatment in the investment area encompasses both *de jure* and *de facto* discrimination, that is, a measure which is on its face discriminatory, as well as in its practical effect. The tribunal found that an evidently non-discriminatory ban on all exports of certain hazardous waste from Canada, that is, whether by domestic or foreign investors, was nonetheless de facto discriminatory and thus in breach of the national treatment obligation, as it "created a disproportionate benefit for nationals over non-nationals."[92]

Yet, somewhat inconsistently, the Tribunal failed to apply its own test to the facts. Instead it conjured up another test, protectionist intent on the part of the Canadian government, to establish a breach of Art. 1102; rather than environmental grounds. This approach is questionable, particularly in light of the evolution of relevant GATT/ WTO case-law grappling with "intent" to ascertain national treatment. Initially, an un-adopted GATT Panel Report[93] introduced the so-called "aims and effects" test for determining "likeness" of products under GATT Art. III.[94] Subsequently, however, a WTO panel firmly rejected the "aims and effects" theory as irrelevant, with respect to both the national treatment standards on internal taxation of Art. III: 2 of the GATT 1994[95] and the "treatment no less favorable" standard in Art. XVII GATS.[96]

Although the Tribunal in *S.D. Myers* recognized that, while important, protectionist intent is not necessarily decisive on its own for a breach of Art. 1102 NAFTA, it failed to consider, let alone follow, the long-standing GATT/WTO rejection of "intent" inherent in the discarded "aims and effects" approach. It is noteworthy, however, that it was perhaps because the "disproportionate benefit" test has no corresponding equivalent in GATT/WTO case-law on GATT Art. III on national treatment that it

91 *Pope & Talbot*, Interim Award on the Merits Phase 1, June 26, 2000, 65.

92 *S.D. Myers Inc* v. *Government of Canada*, Partial Award, 252, November 13, 2000.

93 GATT Panel Report, *US – Taxes on Automobiles*, October 11, 1994, DS3l/R, 5.8 ff.

94 This test originated in the text of Art. III: 1 GATT according to which internal taxes or charges or other regulations should not be applied to imported or domestic products so as to afford protection to domestic production.

95 WTO Panel Report, *Japan – Alcoholic Beverages 11*, WT/DS58/R, WT/DSI0/R, WT/DS11/R, November 1, 1996, 6.16.

96 WTO Appellate Body Report, *EC – Bananas III (Ecuador)*, WT/DS27/AB/R, 241.

was promptly rejected in the later case of *Pope and Talbot* brought against Canada.[97]

A different approach to the determination of a possible breach of Art. 1102 on national treatment was taken in a separate opinion by one of the arbitrators. In order to establish a proper balance between regulatory autonomy and the liberalization and protection provisions of NAFTA, the arbitrator sought to interpret the phrase "in like circumstances" in Art. 1102 NAFTA in light of GATT/WTO case-law on GATT Art. XX containing GATT's general "public value" exceptions. However, the use of the phrase "in like circumstances" as a basis for a respondent government's justification of legitimate regulatory measures with limited effects on free trade and investment goals, though perhaps imaginative, appears somewhat contrived insofar as it transplants GATT's model of a general exception trumping all other GATT provisions to Art. 1102 NAFTA. It is also problematic since GATT/WTO case-law is both abundant and far from "settled." Several interpretative issues arising from GATT/WTO case-law should in fact be mentioned in this context. Generally, in the case *US–Gasoline,* the AB established that Art. XX GATT is subject to a two-tiered analysis which involves "first, provisional justification by reason of characterization of the measure under Art. XX(g);[98] second, further appraisal of the same measure under the introductory clauses of Art. XX."[99] In *EC–Asbestos,* the AB emphasized that "Article XX(b)[100] allows a Member to 'adopt and enforce' a measure, *inter alia,* necessary to protect human life or health, even though that measure is inconsistent with another provision of the GATT 1994." It also held that GATT Arts. III: 4 and XX(b) are distinct and independent provisions, each to be interpreted on its own. Under Art. III: 4, consequently, evidence relating to health risks may be relevant in assessing the competitive relationship in the market-place between allegedly "like" products. On the other hand, the same or similar evidence serves a different purpose under Art. XX(b), namely that of assessing whether a member has a sufficient basis for adopting or enforcing a WTO-inconsistent measure on the grounds

97 In the Matter of an Arbitration under Chapter 11 of the NAFTA between *Pope and Talbot*, Award on the Merits of Phase 2, April 10, 2001, 43–72.

98 Art. XX(g) GATT deals with the general exception of measures "relating to the conservation of exhaustible natural resources."

99 *United States – Standards for Reformulated and Conventional Gasoline*, AB Report WT/DS2/AB/R, 22.

100 Art. XX(b) GATT provides a general exception for measures "necessary to protect human, animal or plant life or health."

of human health.[101] In any case, a measure in question would only be justified if there is "no alternative measure that would achieve the same end and that is less restrictive of trade than a prohibition."[102]

In *Methanex,* another case involving a key ruling on national treatment, a Canadian company challenged Californian regulations on gasoline additives and, as in *S.D. Myers,* sought to base its case for breach of the national treatment obligation of Art. 1102 on an alleged protectionist intent or purpose pursued by the Californian measures. By further claiming that a breach of Art. 1102 would of itself ground a breach of Article 1005 NAFTA, which defines the minimum standard of treatment by reference to both customary and treaty-based international law, *Methanex* also suggested that the "like product" analysis and the specific exceptions to free trade disciplines thereto available in the GATT/WTO framework of trade law should also be applied to the Chapter 11 analysis. This view was expressly rejected by the Tribunal. It declined to be bound by the trade law analysis, based on different language in trade and investment provisions in NAFTA and in trade law and investment law more generally.[103] The Tribunal also stated that the like circumstances test necessitated a comparison of the foreign investor to those most closely comparable domestically, which meant comparing *Methanex*, as a manufacturer of methanol, to other US-based manufacturers of methanol and not, as *Methanex* suggested, to manufacturers of all or any other gasoline additives. By thus interpreting the notion of "in like circumstances" more narrowly, the Tribunal avoided some of the confusion still implicit in the "accordion-like"[104] approach to the like products test in trade law. *Methanex* thus narrowed the scope for possible challenges of WTO-inconsistent regulatory measures under Chapter 11. By referring to the FTC statement on the interpretation of Art. 1105, the Tribunal in the subsequent case of *Mondev Ltd.* excluded that possibility expressly,[105] while recognizing the evolutionary potential of Art. 1105(1) and that the content of current international law is "shaped by the conclusion of more than two thousand bilateral investment treaties and many treaties of friendship and commerce."[106] Yet even if by applying the WTO Agreement, its

101 *EC – Measures Affecting Asbestos and Asbestos-Containing Products,* AB Report WT/DS135/AB/R, 115.

102 *Ibid.*, 172.

103 See comment by Mann (2005), 4–5.

104 See *supra* fn 98, 8.5–6.

105 *Mondev* v. *United States,* ICSID Case No. ARB (AF)/99/2, Final Award, October 11, 2002, 121.

106 *Ibid.*, 125.

breach may not be sufficient to establish a breach of Art. 1005(1) NAFTA, it undeniably belongs to the category of "relevant rules" to be taken into account together with the context in the sense of Art.31(3)(c) VCLT.[107]

5. Concluding remarks

The issue of consistency, broadly, concerns the question of whether adjudicatory bodies are tackling or resolving the same or similar issues in the same way in successive cases. Traders and investors alike crave security and predictability. Consistent interpretations help meet this demand while enhancing systemic legitimacy and a perception of fairness of the dispute settlement system and its greater cost-effectiveness.

Lack of consistency in awards of institutionally unstructured and *ad hoc* panels of different arbitrators has seriously troubled the investment law community. Indeed this is a serious concern as much of the subject of investor–State arbitration touches upon important public interest issues. For the time being, prospects of an AB-type review of investor–State arbitration awards on issues of "law and legal interpretation" remain dim at best. To some, arbitration panels reaching out for the interpretative fruits of the AB and WTO dispute settlement panels must have appeared a worthwhile, though "second best" effort towards securing consistency of interpretations in investment law.

References

Bronckers, B. 2007. "The Relationship of the EC Courts with other International Tribunals. Non-Committal, Respectful or Submissive?" Monti, M. et al., *Economic Law and Justice in Times of Globalisation/Wirtschaftsrecht und Justiz in Zeiten der Globalisierung: Festschrift for Carl Baudenbacher*. Baden-Baden: Nomos: 51–74.

Cottier, E.G.T. 2007. "The Judge in International Economic Relations," Monti, M. et al., *Economic Law and Justice in Times of Globalisation/Wirtschaftsrecht und Justiz in Zeiten der Globalisierung: Festschrift for Carl Baudenbacher*. Baden-Baden: Nomos: 99–122.

Coyle, J.F. 2013. "The Treaty of Friendship, Commerce and Navigation in the Modern Era." *Columbia Journal of Transnational Law* 51: 302–359.

Crawford, J. 2011. "Responsibility for Breaches of Communitarian Norms: An Appraisal of Article 48 of the ILC Articles on Responsibility of States for

107 Sinclair (1984), 139; cited by Verhoosel (2003), 506.

Internationally Wrongful Acts," Fastenrath, Geiger, Khan, Paulus, von Schorlemer and Vedder (eds.): 224–240.

Curtiss, R. 2003. "Agreement on Trade-Related Investment Measures: A Five-Year Review," Campbell, D. and Woodley, S. (eds.), *The Comparative Law Yearbook of International Business*. The Netherlands: Kluwer Law International: 233–255.

Dattu, R. 2000. "A Journey from Havana to Paris: The Fifty-Year Quest for the Elusive Multilateral Agreement on Investment." *Fordham International Law Journal* 24: 275–316.

DeAnne, J. 1991. "Foreign Direct Investment: The Neglected Twin of Trade." *Occasional Paper No.33*. Washington, D.C.: Group of Thirty.

De Luca, A. 2010–2011. "New Developments on the Scope of the EU Common Commercial Policy Under the Lisbon Treaty," Sauvant K.P. (ed.), *Yearbook on International Investment Law & Policy*. Oxford University Press: 165–215.

De Sterlin, M.L. 2005. "The Agreement on Trade-Related Investment Measures," Macrory, P.F.J., Appleton, A.E. and Plummer, M.G. (eds.), *The World Trade Organization: Legal, Economic And Political Analysis. Volume I*. New York: Springer: 437–484.

Diller, J. and Levy, D.A. 1997. "Child Labour, Trade and Investment: Toward the Harmonization of International Law." *AJIL* 91: 663–696.

Domingo, R. 2009. "The Crisis of International Law." *Vand. J. Transnat'l L.* 42: 1543–1593.

Fastenrath, U., Geiger, R., Khan, D.-E., Paulus, A., von Schorlemer, S. and Vedder, C. (eds.) 2011. *From Bilateralism to Community Interest: Essays in Honour of Judge Bruno Simma*. Oxford University Press.

Footer, M. 2013. "On the Laws of Attraction: Examining the Relationship between Foreign Investment and International Trade," Echandi, R. and Sauvé, S. (eds.), *Prospects in International Investment Law and Policy (World Trade Forum)*. Cambridge University Press, 105–138.

Foster, C.E. 2012. "Adjudication, Arbitration and the Turn to Public Law 'Standards of Review': Putting the Precautionary Principle in the Crucible." *Journal of International Dispute Settlement*: 1–34.

Gestrin, M. and Rugman, A. 2005. "Rules for Foreign Direct Investment at the WTO: Building on Regional Trade Agreements," Macrory, P.F.J., Appleton, A.E. and Plumeer, M.G. (eds.), *The World Trade Organization: Legal, Economic and Political Analysis. Volume II*. New York: Springer: 313–324.

Guzman, T. 1998. "Why LDCs Sign Treaties that Hurt Them: Explaining the Popularity of Bilateral Investment Treaties." *Virginia J. of International L.* 38: 639–688.

Hirsch, S. 1976. "An International Trade and Investment Theory of the Firm." *Oxford Economic Papers* 28(2): 258–270.

Hofmann, H., Tams, T. and Schill, S. (eds.) 2013. *Preferential Trade and Investment Agreements: A New Ordering Paradigm for International Investment Relations?* Frankfurt University Press.

Holland, T.E. 1898. *Studies in International Law and Diplomacy.* Oxford: Clarendon Press.

Khrebutkova, A. 2008. "A Call to Freedom: Toward a Philosophy of International Law in an Era of Fragmentation." *JILIR* 4: 51–104.

Kurtz, J. 2002. "A General Investment Agreement in the WTO? Lessons from Chapter 11 NAFTA and the OECD Multilateral Agreement on Investment." The University of Melbourne, Faculty of Law and Legal Theory, Research Paper No. 42. *University of Pennsylvania Journal of International Economic Law* 23: 713–789.

Kuyper, P.J. 1994. "The Law of GATT as a Special Field of International Law: Ignorance, Further Refinement or Self-Contained Regime of International Law?" *Netherlands Yearbook of International Law* 25: 227–257.

Lauterpacht, H. 1927. *Private Law Sources and Analogies of International Law: With Special Reference to International Arbitration.* London: Longmans, Green and Co. Ltd.

1933. *The Function of Law in the International Community.* Oxford: Clarendon Press.

Lavranos, N. and Vielliard, N. 2008. "Competing Jurisdictions between MERCOSUR and WTO." *The Law and Practice of International Courts and Tribunals* 7: 205–234.

Mann, F.A. 1981. "British Treaties for the Promotion and Protection of Investments." *BYIL* 52: 541.

Mann, H. 2005. "The Final Decision in *Methanex* v. *United States*: Some New Wine in Some New Bottles." *IISD*: 1–15, available at: www.iisd.org.

Maskus, K. and Reichman, J.H. 2005. *International Public Goods and Transfer of Technology Under a Globalized Intellectual Property Regime.* Cambridge University Press.

Matz, N. 2005. *Wege zur Koordinierung völkerrechtlicher Verträge: Völkervertragsrechtliche und institutionelle Ansätze.* Berlin-Heidelberg: Springer.

Muchlinski, P. 2008. "Policy Issues," Muchlinski, Ortino and Schreuer (eds.): 3–48.

Muchlinski, P., Ortino, F. and Schreuer, C. (eds.). 2008. *The Oxford Handbook of International Investment Law.* Oxford University Press.

Pamuk, S. 1987. *Ottoman Empire and European Capitalism, 1820–1913.* Cambridge University Press.

Pauwelyn, J. 2003. *Conflict of Norms in Public International Law: How WTO Law Relates to Other Rules of International Law.* Cambridge University Press.

Rao, P.S. 2011. "The Concept of 'International Community' in International Law and the Developing Countries," Fastenrath, Geiger, Khan, Paulus, von Schorlemer and Vedder (eds.): 326–338.

Reinisch, A. 2008. "Expropriation," Muchlinski, Ortino and Schreuer (eds.): 407–458.

Schreuer, C. 1993. "The Waning of the Sovereign State: Towards a New Paradigm for International Law?" *EJIL* 4: 447–471.

2013. "Coherence and Consistency in International Investment Law," Echandi, R. and Sauvé, S. (eds.), *Prospects in International Investment Law and Policy, World Trade Forum*. Cambridge University Press: 391–402.

Shenkin, T.S. 1994. "Trade-Related Investment Measures in Bilateral Investment Treaties and the GATT: Moving Toward a Multilateral Investment Treaty." *University of Pittsburgh Law Review* 55: 541–606.

Simma, B. 1994. "From Bilateralism to Community Interest in International Law." *RCADI* 250: 217–384.

Simma B. and Paulus, A. 1998. "The 'International Community': Facing the Challenge of Globalization. General Conclusions." *EJIL* 9: 266–277.

Simma, B. and Pulkowski, D. 2006. "Of Planets and the Universe: Self-Contained Regimes in International Law." *EJIL* 17: 483–529.

Sinclair, I. 1984. *The Vienna Convention on the Law of Treaties*. Manchester University Press.

Staff, M.J. and Lewis, C.W. 2003. "Arbitration under NAFTA Chapter 11: Past, Present, and Future." *Houston J. of International L.* 25: 301.

Verdross, A. and Simma, B. 1983. *Universelles völkerrecht. theorie und praxis*, 3rd edition. Berlin: Duncker & Humblot.

Verhoosel, G. 2003. "The Use of Investor-State Arbitration under Bilateral Investment Treaties to Seek Relief for Breaches of WTO Law." *JIEL* 6: 493–506.

Wälde, T. and Kolo, A. 2001. "Environmental Regulation, Investment Protection and 'Regulatory Taking' in International Law." *ICLQ* 50: 811–848.

Watson, A. 1993. *Legal Transplants. An Approach to Comparative Law*. 2nd edition Athens, GA: University of Georgia Press.

Webb, P. 2013. *International Judicial Integration and Fragmentation*. Oxford University Press.

Weiss, F. 2007. "Coalitions of the Willing: The Case for Multi-Lateralism vs Regional and Bilateral Arrangements in World Trade," Calliess, C., Nolte, G. and Stoll, P.-T. (eds.), *Coalitions of the Willing: Avantgarde or Threat?* Cologne: Carl Heymanns Verlag: 51–71.

2008a. "Trade and Investment," Muchlinski, Ortino and Schreuer (eds.): 182–223.

2008b. "The Principle of Non-Discrimination in International Economic Law: A Conceptual and Historical Sketch," Buffard, I., Crawford, J.,

Pellet, A. and Wittich, S. (eds.), *International Law between Universalism and Fragmentation. Festschrift in Honour of Gerhard Hafner.* The Hague: Martinus Nijhoff: 269–286.

2009. "Inherent Powers of National and International Courts: The Practice of the Iran-US Claims Tribunal," Binder, C., Kriebaum, U., Reinisch, A. and Wittich, S. (eds.), *International Investment Law for the 21st Century. Essays in Honour of Christoph Schreuer.* Oxford University Press: 185–199.

2011. "Sketching 'Community Interest' in EU Law, an Essay in Honour of Judge Bruno Simma," Fastenrath, Geiger, Khan, Paulus, von Schorlemer and Vedder (eds.): 406–416.

2012. "Finanzkrise und internationales öffentliches Recht," *Paradigmen im internationalen recht. Implikationen der weltfinanzkrise für das international recht. Berichte der deutschen gesellschaft für völkerrecht.* Heidelberg: C.F. Müller: 335–367.

Weiss, F. and Steiner, S. 2013. "The Investment Regime under Article 207 TFEU: A Legal Conundrum. The Scope of 'Foreign Direct Investment' and the Future of Intra-EU BITs," Baetens, F. (ed.), *Investment Law within International Law.* Cambridge University Press: 754–791.

WTO. 1996. Report on "Trade and Foreign Direct Investment," available at www.wto.org/english/news_e/pres96_e/pr057_e.htm.

WTO Appellate Body. 2005. *Repertory of Reports and Awards, 1995–2004.* Cambridge University Press: 163–176.

Young, M.A. 2012. "Regime Interaction in Creating, Implementing and Enforcing International Law," Young, M.A. (ed.), *Regime Interaction in International Law: Facing Fragmentation.* Cambridge University Press: 85–110.

5

On the evolution and slow convergence of international trade and investment law

JÜRGEN KURTZ

1. Introduction

Modern international law protections for foreign trade and investment were born roughly of the same period. In the immediate decades following the Second World War, States parties agreed to a multilateral compact to liberalise barriers to foreign trade (in the General Agreement on Tariffs and Trade 1947) and also entered into treaty protections for foreign investment (beginning with the 1959 West Germany–Pakistan Bilateral Investment Treaty). Yet the inception of these sub-disciplines of international economic law was always grounded in highly distinct strategic imperatives. Their evolution too has been marked by institutional divergence and often, at least among a certain group of actors that inhabit the separate fields and even within separate government departments, a perception of the other as irrelevant (at best) or deep distrust (at worst).

Of course, these systems share a fundamental commonality compared to the majority of the remainder of public international law. The jewel in both crowns is a dispute settlement system that actually 'works' measured at the very least by the superficial proxies of activation, jurisdiction and compliance.[1] Yet behind that common façade, the differences are classically thought to outweigh similarities. Distinct historical pathways have firstly led to significant variances in treaty form, institutional culture and centralisation. Up until the mid- to late 1990s, international trade law had

1 On deeper analysis though, compliance across both systems continues to be contested. In the WTO, we have the spectacle of States delaying the requirement to bring measures in conformity with their WTO obligations, at least within those cases triggering delicate socio-cultural choices (such as import of hormone-treated beef). That in turn has given rise to the question of whether the WTO remedy structure should be amended to allow for more flexible structures such as efficient breach. See Schwartz and Sykes (2002). In investment law, the classic assumption of hard enforcement via the ICSID Convention has also been weakened in recent years through Argentina's insistence that ICSID awards be proved through the Argentine judicial process. On this, see *The Economist* (2012).

been largely constituted on a centralised multilateral basis with Geneva as an institutional nucleus, especially since the formation of the World Trade Organization in 1994. The bilateral network of investment treaties, on the other hand, is highly diffuse with no real common institutional core although counter-balanced with a natural gravitational pull towards established and emerging arbitration centres such as London, Paris, Washington, Hong Kong and Singapore. Secondly and relatedly, there has always been a degree of sociological separation within the communities that inhabit the two fields. In many States, different government departments have had exclusive carriage for trade versus investment matters. Coupled with the usual tendency of many civil servants to jealously defend allocated governmental authority, the upshot is often a regrettable although predictable failure to communicate across the disciplinary divide. Private practitioners too have had a much stronger role in investment than trade law, largely because of a fundamental difference across dispute settlement structures. The WTO follows the usual public international law default of State-to-State dispute settlement, which has tended to constrain (in fact but not in law)[2] the opportunities for private legal counsel to appear in WTO dispute settlement. While State-to-State dispute settlement is present in most modern investment treaties, those treaties also offer a powerful augmentation. Foreign investors (from a signatory home State) are also afforded standing to claim breach of the underlying treaty bargain by the signatory host State. In many countries, especially across North America, enterprising private practitioners quickly identified the new and powerful legal opportunities embodied in the investment treaty network that could be offered and marketed to their clients. Needless to say, they occupy a very different world and incentive matrix than their (mainly government) counterparts engaged in the negotiation and resolution of trade issues and disputes.

Of course, the mere fact that foreign investors are parties to investor–State dispute settlement does not in any way lessen the status of international investment law as an integral part of the public international law universe. Various international regimes similarly accommodate non-State actors as either complainants or respondents in dispute settlement, including both human rights protections and international criminal law.

2 It is important here to note that the Appellate Body has ruled that private legal counsel can attend and plead in WTO proceedings at the appellate level. See WTO Appellate Body, *European Communities – Regime for the Importation, Sale and Distribution of Bananas*, WT/DS27/AB/R, 9 September 1997, AB-1997–3.

It would be implausible to characterise these regimes as carve-outs to public international law, and the investment treaty network is no different. What is more important, but less analysed, are the implications of States parties choosing arbitration as the adjudicatory model to frame investor–State dispute settlement. That fundamental choice has positioned the system, at least from the perspective of some, closer to the private rather than public law end of a spectrum.[3] This view has been strongest among the legal constituency (other than the negotiators) naturally attracted to this field being those legal practitioners who have worked in commercial arbitration in the past. They then come to this new construct with an existing set of habits and practices, without always considering whether those methods are appropriate for resolving a dispute under a broadly worded treaty compared to an individually negotiated contract. Yet that assumption is a superficial one that relies mainly on the title and thus characterisation of the treaty dispute settlement system simply as falling within the genus of 'arbitration'. The conflation with private law constructs is especially misleading when one considers the long history of the emergence of investment treaty protections whereby a range of States parties (as capital exporters) strategically constructed the new treaty device to counter downward shifts in customary international law protections for foreign property. This is a system, very simply and fundamentally, with deep and complex roots in the various sources of public international law. Consider in this respect a fundamental and telling difference in the pedagogy of international trade versus investment law. A teacher can quite respectably and accurately begin any course on trade law with its emergence as a modern set of treaty protections in 1947 without any real attention to customary law (outside of the usual framework mechanisms such as the rules on treaty interpretation). Such an approach would be impossible in

3 Consider this telling statement from the *Romak* v. *Republic of Uzbekistan* Tribunal claiming that, just as with commercial arbitration, the reasoning employed in investor–State arbitration is of no value at all for other stakeholders (than the disputing parties) and future claims:

> Ultimately, the Arbitral Tribunal has not been entrusted, by the Parties or otherwise, with a mission to ensure the coherence or development of 'arbitral jurisprudence'. The Arbitral Tribunal's mission is more mundane, but no less important: to resolve the present dispute between the Parties in a reasoned and persuasive manner, irrespective of the unintended consequences that this Arbitral Tribunal's analysis might have on future disputes in general.

Romak S.A. v. *Republic of Uzbekistan*, PCA Case No. AA280, Award, 26 November 2009, 171. For a similar view, see *AES Corporation* v. *Argentine Republic*, ICSID Case No, ARB/02/17, Decision on Jurisdiction, 26 April 2005, 30–1.

investment law where some of the modern treaty formulae clearly modify existing customary rules (such as diplomatic protection) while also transplanting substantive standards from contested debates on customary international law that revert back to the late nineteenth and early twentieth centuries.[4]

By comparison with the (mistaken) views of select actors in investment law and arguably paradoxically, there is a tendency to view the WTO as reflective of a much deeper public law vision. That view is formally grounded in the fact that standing in WTO dispute settlement is largely confined to States – whether as complainants, respondents or third parties – which have inherent incentives to maintain a certain set of regulatory freedoms. But it is more fundamentally reflective of the sophisticated balance struck right at the outset of the formation of the GATT in 1947 between obligations (constraining State conduct) and flexibilities (permitting intervention where necessary for public values and short-term political imperatives). John Ruggie has memorably described the GATT negotiations as reflecting a bargain of 'embedded liberalism' with the extensive flexibilities comprising a sub-set of shared social purposes among GATT members that has contributed significantly to the resilience of State commitment to the trade law regime.[5] These flexibilities include, for instance, the right of GATT members to take short-term emergency action departing from their GATT commitments where unforeseen developments coupled with the effect of their GATT commitments cause or threaten serious injury to domestic producers.[6] Safeguard measures of this sort are an inherent recognition of the enormous political challenges faced by States when liberalising trade barriers, which may require short-term breathing space (as a matter of shoring up political support for liberalisation) and/or the ability to implement mechanisms to enable

4 On the latter, consider the famous insistence of US Secretary of State Cordell Hull in 1938 that Mexico's expropriation of American oil interests required as a matter of customary international law, 'adequate, effective and prompt payment for the properties seized': see 'Mexico–United States: Expropriation by Mexico of Agrarian Properties Owned by American Citizens', *American Journal of International Law Supplement* 33: 191–201. Compare this customary claim with the later treaty obligation in Art. III(1) of the 1994 US Model BIT that expropriation of foreign investment be subject to a number of conditions including 'prompt, adequate and effective compensation': 1994 US Model BIT, extracted in McLachlan, Shore and Weiniger, *International Investment Arbitration*, 388 ('1994 US Model BIT').

5 Ruggie (1998).

6 General Agreement on Tariffs and Trade, 30 October 1947, 55 UNTS 194, Art. XIX ('GATT').

transition of affected industry and workers to more competitive sectors of the domestic economy. Perhaps most famously of all, the GATT elevated certain core public values over and above the immediate project of trade liberalisation in clear contrast to the dominant focus on investment protection classically found in most early BITs concluded in the 1960s to late 1980s. Member States have the explicit right under GATT Art. XX to depart from their treaty commitments where, for instance, it is 'necessary to protect human, animal, plant life or health'.[7]

Yet despite the nuanced treaty bargain struck in the early years of the international trading system, its judicial arm has not always faithfully endorsed that vision. Michael Trebilcock, Robert Howse and Antonia Eliason have insightfully analysed and compared the dramatically different interpretative practices of early GATT panels with the later WTO Appellate Body when ruling on key parts of GATT Art. XX.[8] For Howse in particular:

> The tendency of panels to assume they understood the general purpose of a provision, and to give sense to it in light of that purpose, without regard to individual words and phrases, almost always resulted in rulings tilted towards one particular value among the competing values at stake, namely that of liberal trade – since the purpose invariably understood by the panel was the greatest possible discipline on barriers to trade.[9]

Indeed, it is only *after* the formation of the WTO Appellate Body that one can discern a clear break from the questionable hermeneutic practices of the GATT era. The Appellate Body has consistently endorsed the customary taxonomy of interpretative practices codified by Arts. 31–2 of the Vienna Convention on the Law of Treaties ('VCLT').[10] Although there are certain downside effects of the 'juridification' of trade law,[11] the Appellate Body's principled insistence on examining the objective bargain struck between WTO members as presented by the treaty text, in light of key contextual indicators (including the architecture of the treaty under review) and against teleological expressions (set out in preambular references) have greatly contributed to the integrity of trade law jurisprudence.

There is, of course, no equivalent of the WTO Appellate Body to insist on principled hermeneutics when it comes to investor–State arbitration. Not surprisingly then, some of the arbitral practices at play echo the crude

7 *Ibid.*, Art. XX(b). 8 Trebilcock, Howse and Eliason (2012), 664–98.
9 Howse (2001), 52–3.
10 Vienna Convention on the Law of Treaties, 23 May 1969, 1155 UNTS 331 ('VCLT').
11 See especially Weiler (2008), 191–207.

adjudicatory habits employed by GATT panels prior to the emergence of the WTO. A stubborn tendency to preference outcome over process characterises investor–State arbitral reasoning as is often naturally and justifiably the case in commercial arbitration. In the latter, the goal is often to craft an efficient end outcome acceptable to both parties where the reasoning to justify that output is of little interest to the disputants and, unless the contract at issue engages key public services, of little resonance to stakeholders other than the disputants. But far more problematically when it comes to investment treaty interpretation, a certain group of arbitrators will typically defend their aggressive and expansive readings in light of *their* personal view of the role of investment treaties rather than – as required by the VCLT – grounding an approach in light of the objectives explicitly articulated by the States parties. Consider this telling statement of the *Enron* v. *Argentina* Tribunal assessing when and how a dedicated exception in the 1991 US–Argentina BIT should apply:

> [T]he object and purpose of the Treaty is, as a general proposition, to apply in situations of economic difficulty and hardship that require the protection of the internationally guaranteed rights of its beneficiaries. To this extent, any interpretation, resulting in an escape route from the obligations defined cannot be easily reconciled with that object and purpose. Accordingly, *a restrictive interpretation of any such alternative is mandatory.*[12]

The order of this reasoning reveals a fundamental flaw that evokes the problematic interpretative practices of the GATT era described by Howse. The *Enron* Tribunal begins by asserting its own claim as to the dominant purpose of the treaty, being one of protection of the rights of investors. This is by no means an outlier award: similar untested assumptions are at play throughout the jurisprudence of investor–State arbitral tribunals.[13] The tribunal then fashions a default, highly restrictive interpretative preference to comply with that claimed dominant purpose that eviscerates much of the flexibility inherent in the exception's role as part of the treaty bargain struck between the States parties.

This type of methodology simply ignores the rules and sequencing of steps on treaty interpretation at international law. Under Art. 31(1) of the VCLT, an adjudicator must begin with the text of the treaty provision in

12 *Enron Corporation Ponderosa Assets LP* v. *Argentine Republic*, ICSID Case No. ARB/01/3, Award, 22 May 2007, 331 (emphasis added).

13 See, e.g., *Azurix Corp* v. *Argentine Republic*, ICSID Case No. ARB/01/12, Award, 14 July 2006, 372; *SGS Societe de Surveillance* v. *Republic of the Philippines*, ICSID Case No. ARB/02/6, Decision on Jurisdiction, 29 January 2004, 116.

question. A given textual reading should then be considered in light of context and the object and purpose of the treaty under review. The initial role of the treaty text in this interpretative setting is not one that condemns an interpreter to simple and arid textualism. But it does have an important disciplinary function as it prevents the adjudicator from preferencing their own intuitive sense of how the system should work over objective expressions of party intent in the treaty text, a critical feature that has been fundamentally recognised by the WTO Appellate Body.[14] By contrast, the *Enron* Tribunal subverts this order of interpretation, bypassing the text entirely as the start-point in the interpretative process. In any event, the stubborn claim in the jurisprudence to a dominant purpose of investment protection is itself open to legitimate contestation. On close examination, the objective expressions of purpose in the preambular recitals of typical investment treaties reveal a concern for the interests of multiple stakeholders and values beyond an exclusive focus on the protection of foreign investors. Indeed tellingly, other cases within the system have belatedly begun to adopt more rigorous approaches to treaty interpretation akin to that employed by the WTO Appellate Body and have actively identified and grappled with the multiple values referenced in the preambular recitals of investment treaties.[15]

2. Pathologies

These many variances have produced a range of troubling pathologies to date. When it comes to investment arbitration, poor interpretative methods (strikingly at odds with that of the WTO Appellate Body) have led to widely inconsistent and unpredictable outcomes. The reflexive objection that investment arbitration falls within a genus that is appropriately limited to particularistic and retrospective resolution of disputes is weakened under close observation. States can be, and often are, repeat players in the

14 WTO Appellate Body, *United States – Import Prohibition of Certain Shrimp and Shrimp Products*, WT/DS58/AB/R, 12 October 1998, AB-1998–4, 121–2 (where the Appellate Body criticises the Panel for 'constructing an *a priori* test' that has no basis in the text of the treaty clause at issue).

15 See, e.g., *Saluka Investments BV* v. *Czech Republic*, UNCITRAL Arbitration, Partial Award, 17 March 2006, 296–308 (in its review of the preambular recitals of the subject investment treaty, the Arbitral Tribunal ruled: 'This is a more subtle and balanced statement of the Treaty's aims than is sometimes appreciated. The protection of foreign investment is not the sole aim of the Treaty, but rather a necessary element alongside the overall aim of encouraging foreign investment and extending and intensifying the parties' economic relations').

investment system and as such, they have inherently legitimate reasons to understand their prospective risk profile when regulating as a matter of potential investment treaty breach. There is, in short, a fundamental conceptual difference between commercial arbitration (based on a specifically negotiated contract between key parties) and investment arbitration (where the potentially broad subject-matter of the dispute can encompass general legal regulation passed at some later stage after the entry into the BIT). While these may indeed fall within the same genus, they are necessarily distinct species. Inconsistency (both in method and outcome) however should be distinguished from incoherence. As touched upon earlier, a certain set of arbitral awards have simply ignored the parameters of the treaty bargain and instead created strained and largely implausible legal constructions.[16] The tolerance of States parties when it comes to incoherence is rapidly eroding. While some may be content to limit their reaction to intervention (via contemporaneous or prospective treaty change),[17] others are simply exiting the network (in whole or in part) altogether.[18] Against a matrix of the resilience of State commitment with the workings of third party adjudication, investment treaty arbitration compares decidedly poorly with WTO dispute settlement.

Yet the WTO too is faced with a set of enormous systemic challenges. The year 2001 witnessed the launch of the Doha Development Round of WTO negotiations and there is little reason to expect conclusion of those long-running negotiations any time soon. States parties are instead bifurcating their treaty commitments on international trade by supplementing their multilateral WTO obligations with bilateral and regional free trade

16 Compare *Pope & Talbot Inc.* v. *Canada*, UNCITRAL Arbitration, Award on the Merits of Phase 2, 10 April 2001, 110–11; *S.D. Myers, Inc.* v. *Canada*, UNCITRAL Arbitration, Partial Award, 13 November 2000, 259–69 (both ruling that NAFTA Art. 1105 adopts an additive component that extends beyond the scope of protection at customary international law) with *United Mexican States* v. *Metalclad Corp.* [2001] BCSC 664, 64–6 (criticising the *Pope & Talbot* and *Myers* Awards on the interpretation of NAFTA Art. 1105 as ignoring the plain text of that treaty provision).

17 NAFTA Free Trade Commission, 'Notes of Interpretation of Certain Chapter 11 Provisions', 31 July 2001, B(1)-(2) (confirming that NAFTA Art. 1105(1) 'prescribes the customary international law minimum standard of treatment' and that 'the concepts of "fair and equitable treatment" and "full protection and security" do not require treatment in addition to or beyond that which is required by the customary international law minimum standard of treatment of aliens').

18 Until recently, this strategy has been confined to a handful of Latin American States such as Bolivia, Ecuador and recently Venezuela. But in 2011, the Australian government announced that it would no longer include investor–State arbitration provisions in future bilateral and regional trade agreements. For an analysis of the Australian policy shift, see Kurtz (2012).

agreements (FTAs). Critically, the latter often combine investment and 'WTO-plus' trade commitments under a common umbrella evidencing a particularly tangible connection between the two fields. There are complex questions as to the institutional and substantive role of WTO law and dispute settlement across the growing universe of these FTAs. These include not only the contested issue of whether WTO dispute settlement organs may appropriately consider other trade commitments of WTO members during adjudication,[19] but also the degree of influence of WTO jurisprudence in FTA adjudication including during investor–State arbitration (within a given investment chapter in that FTA).[20]

Despite these growing connections, there is a troubling ignorance of the WTO in texts devoted to investment law, and vice versa. In the most insightful books dealing with the WTO, investment issues (other than those directly implicated by the WTO treaties) are covered summarily within a few pages usually characterised as part of a future reform agenda for WTO coverage.[21] When it comes to investment texts, any discussion of WTO law is normally a truncated suffix to national treatment analysis.[22] As a related point, one can identify fundamentally different methodologies among various authors in how they approach the two systems. The exponential growth of arbitral case law has fuelled an understandable desire among the practising community in commercial arbitration to be the first to enter and establish authority often as a way of building market in this new and lucrative field. This desire often cashes out as an uncritical acceptance of the merits of individual treaty norms across much of the burgeoning literature. Many of these new investment law authors engage the case law technically and doctrinally in order to synthesise and thereby minimise areas of conflict. That avenue is effectively foreclosed in the case of the WTO given the important systemic role of the Appellate Body in offering a rigorous proxy for qualitative assessment of jurisprudential

19 To date, the Appellate Body has resisted this at least in part of its jurisprudence. See WTO Appellate Body, *Mexico – Tax Measures on Soft Drinks and Other Beverages*, WT/DS308/AB/R, 6 March 2006, AB-2006-10, 75 (ruling that '"laws or regulations" within the meaning of Article XX(d) refer to the rules that form part of the domestic legal order of the WTO Member invoking the provision and do not include the international obligations of *another* WTO Member').

20 For thoughtful criticism of the use of WTO law on exceptions in investor–State arbitration (but in relation to one particular exception category in a BIT rather than an investment chapter in an FTA), see Alvarez and Brink (2011).

21 See, e.g., Van den Bossche (2008). 702–6. But for a notable exception to this trend, see Trebilcock, Howse and Eliason (2012). 566–604.

22 See, e.g., Dolzer and Schreuer (2008). 184–6.

evolution. But it then raises precisely the question of what factors should be taken into account when sorting and reviewing the rapidly growing mass of arbitral cases. There is also typically little consideration in many investment treaty manuscripts of disciplines other than law in attempting to probe and test the contemporary justifications for particular investment protections. This offers an especially stark contrast with the WTO, where inter-disciplinary insights (especially from economics) fuel powerful and compelling critiques of legal mechanisms including the right of WTO members to impose anti-dumping and countervailing duties.[23] International investment law is instead a field populated almost exclusively by lawyers, which has resulted in a highly distinct and troubling thinness to the analysis of legal protections aimed fundamentally at economic and political issues.

3. Five convergence factors

This divergence between the two systems, embedded both in variances in treaty text, jurisprudence and across stakeholder perceptions and methodologies, is increasingly neither desirable nor feasible. Five critical factors are pushing them together with, as yet, uncertain trajectories and end-points.

Firstly, both systems share significant common legal terrain. Indeed, the usual assumption (at least among investment lawyers) of hermetic separation breaks down under close and careful observation. Consider, for example, the manner in which foreign investment in the services sector is regulated extensively within the WTO. There are four distinct modes of service supply defined in the WTO General Agreement on Trade in Services (GATS), which notably include the provision of services through commercial presence – comprising direct investment – by a foreign supplier.[24] Indeed, the coverage of foreign investment issues (as usually defined in a classic BIT) in the WTO extends far beyond the GATS. The WTO Agreement on Trade-Related Investment Measures (TRIMs) disciplines the use of particular performance requirements imposed by States on foreign investors that distort trade, including the obligation to source goods from local suppliers.[25] Many BITs also explicitly include intellectual property within the scope of assets protected by the

23 See, e.g., Sykes (2007).

24 Marrakesh Agreement Establishing the World Trade Organization, 15 April 1994, 1867 UNTS 154, Annex 1B, Art. I(2)(c) ('WTO Agreements').

25 WTO Agreements, Annex 1A.

substantive treaty provisions.[26] In a similar vein, the WTO Agreement on Trade-Related Intellectual Property Rights (TRIPS) requires WTO members to protect various forms of intellectual property as a form of investment in their domestic jurisdictions (although these obligations are balanced against key flexibilities for State conduct).[27]

Across this common legal terrain, both systems have *always* shared a respectable number of dedicated core protections. This includes, most notably, restrictions against State discrimination in the form of both national and most-favoured-nation treatment (for foreign goods and investors). Indeed, some of the earliest cases in the GATT illustrate the manner in which trade law prohibitions on discrimination against foreign goods can be employed to protect foreign investment. In *Canada – Administration of the Foreign Investment Review Act* (*FIRA*), a GATT Panel ruled that the Canadian practice of enforcing certain undertakings given by foreign investors in order to gain regulatory approval to invest in Canada breached the obligation of national treatment in GATT Art. III(4).[28] In particular, the GATT Panel found that undertakings by foreign investors to purchase goods of Canadian origin without any qualification excluded the possibility for those investors to purchase available imported products so that the latter were clearly treated less favourably than domestic products in contravention of Art. III(4).[29] The GATT Panel Report in *FIRA* is an early portent of the protection afforded by international trade law to foreign investors. The TRIMS Agreement in the WTO now explicitly disciplines a range of performance requirements (including the local content conditions at play in *FIRA*) and those dedicated protections were successfully invoked in later WTO proceedings against Indonesia.[30] States parties have also turned their mind to managing potential conflicts between investment treaty norms and WTO law. For instance, the grant of compulsory licence of intellectual property rights is a crucial flexibility under the TRIPS Agreement[31] but could also be interpreted as an expropriation of those rights where the relevant WTO Member State is also a party to a BIT. Newer bilateral trade and investment treaties now specifically

26 1994 US Model BIT, Art. 1 (definition of 'investment' setting out an illustrative list of forms including '(f) intellectual property rights').

27 WTO Agreements, Annex 1C ('TRIPS').

28 GATT Panel Report, *Canada – Administration of the Foreign Investment Review Act*, 7 February 1984, GATT BISD 30S/140.

29 *Ibid.*, 5.8–9.

30 WTO Panel Report, *Indonesia – Certain Measures Affecting the Automobile Industry*, WT/DS54/R, 2 July 1998.

31 TRIPS, Art. 31.

exclude the issue of a compulsory license from guarantees of compensation in the event of expropriation, thereby minimising the possibility of friction between the two legal systems.[32]

Relatedly, States parties have begun to shape their investment treaty commitments to shift away from simply *constraining* State action (through obligations) to also inserting *flexibilities* (via exceptions) for legitimate State regulation, vis-à-vis foreign investors and their investments. In this strategic goal, the negotiators are often employing key flexibilities within the WTO as a model to guide their reform efforts. Thus, many modern investment treaties include generalised exception provisions whose language is strictly or loosely based on the carve-outs for, *inter alia*, environmental and health regulation in GATT Art. XX and GATS Art. XIV. Canada, for instance, has included such a WTO-type exception in every investment treaty it has signed since the adoption of the NAFTA.[33] There are similar exceptions in the investment chapters of FTAs negotiated by Japan, Australia and the ASEAN States.[34] On occasion, States have even moved beyond simply borrowing the architecture of the WTO exceptions as a guide to structure a similar set of carve-outs in the investment treaty. In a range of FTAs, the WTO exceptions are directly incorporated into investment chapters by reference.[35] This raises a highly sensitive question of whether Member States are only channelling the text of WTO exceptions or also seeking to import the complex suite of jurisprudence of the WTO panels and Appellate Body that have interpreted those exceptions.

Indeed, FTAs are proving to be a laboratory for a range of creative, albeit uncertain, experimentations. In the Thailand–Australia FTA, the Member States have elected to use a conservative GATS positive-list structure for scheduling pre-establishment commitments on foreign investment while retaining the traditional negative-list approach for post-establishment commitments.[36] And when we move to the ASEAN treaties, there is explicit articulation of the GATT-based concept of special and

32 See, e.g., United States–Singapore Free Trade Agreement, 6 May 2003, USTIF: www.state.gov/documents/organization/202293.pdf, Art. 15.6(5) (Investment).

33 Levesque (2006), 271.

34 Agreement Between Japan and Republic of the Philippines for an Economic Partnership, signed 9 September 2006, Art. 99; Singapore–Australia Free Trade Agreement, 17 February 2003, [2003] ATS 16, Art. 19; ASEAN Comprehensive Investment Agreement, signed 26 February 2009, Art. 17 ('ACIA').

35 See, e.g., Agreement Establishing the ASEAN–Australia–New Zealand Free Trade Area, signed 27 February 2009, [2010] ATS 1, Ch. 15, Art. 1(2).

36 Australia–Thailand Free Trade Agreement, 7 May 2004, [2005] ATS 2, Art. 904 (pre-establishment national treatment); 907 (post-establishment national treatment).

differential treatment to differentiate the investment treaty obligations of the newer (less developed) and older (more developed) ASEAN members.[37] Within investment law, the traditional assumption is that developing States should be fully responsible for weaknesses in governance structures where these constitute wrongful harm to a foreign investor, rather than the WTO-based idea that development status might variegate the depth of a given international law commitment. Equally strikingly, the ASEAN States created a broad emergency safeguard measure modelled on GATT Art. XIX to deal with the disruptive societal effects of sudden capital withdrawal[38] whose origins can be traced to the particular experience of many of those States in responding to the 1998 Asian financial crisis.[39] Taken together, these features may well evidence the positive use of FTAs as laboratories for experimentation especially for States with a thickly shared set of cultural traditions, customs and ideologies.[40]

As a second convergence factor, the exact same measure can fall within the jurisdictional reach of both systems, invoke a common legal norm and may even be adjudicated in parallel or concurrently. For instance, a Mexican tax on high-fructose corn syrup as a soft drinks sweetener triggered national treatment claims both by the US as a State party in the WTO[41] and by a range of American investors under the investment chapter of NAFTA.[42] Parallel proceedings across both systems will often engage the most sensitive forms of State regulation. Consider in this respect the 2011 Australian law imposing plain packaging on tobacco products. That measure swiftly triggered a claim for breach by Philip Morris of Australia's obligation under the Hong Kong–Australia BIT[43] with the Dominican Republic commencing formal dispute settlement proceedings against

37 ACIA, Art. 23 (Special and Differential Treatment for the Newer ASEAN Member States).

38 *Ibid.*, Art. 4(c) and (d).

39 Indeed, some of those ASEAN States were subject to investment treaty challenge based on their particular responses to the crisis. For such a treaty challenge whose genesis lies in the Malaysia restriction of capital outflows in the aftermath of the crisis; see *Philippe Gruslin* v. *Malaysia*, ICSID Case No. ARB/99/3, Award, 27 November 2000.

40 Cho (2001). 432–4; Hirsch (2008).

41 WTO Panel Report, *Mexico – Tax Measures on Soft Drinks and Other Beverages*, WT/DS308/R, 7 October 2005; WTO Appellate Body, *Mexico – Tax Measures on Soft Drinks and Other Beverages*, WT/DS308/AB/R, 6 March 2006, AB-2006–10.

42 *Archer Daniels Midland Co. and Tate & Lyle Ingredients Americas, Inc.* v. *Mexico*, ICSID Case No. ARB (AF)/04/5, Award, 21 November 2007; *Corn Products International, Inc.* v. *Mexico*, ICSID Case No. ARB (AF)/04/1, Decision on Responsibility, 15 January 2008.

43 *Philip Morris Asia Ltd* v. *Australia*, Notice of Arbitration under the Arbitration Rules of the United Nations Commission on International Trade Law, 21 November 2011.

Australia in the WTO for breach of the GATT, TRIPS and the Agreement on Technical Barriers to Trade. These two legal avenues are deeply related in this factual matrix especially given Philip Morris' novel claim that breach of Australia's obligations under the TRIPS (as well as other WTO norms) is an independent cause of infringement of the BIT.[44] It is thus practically impossible to simply ignore the factual and legal issues, arguments and rulings that occur across both systems.

Indeed, this pressing imperative has already been on display in a set of proceedings brought in the WTO and under investment treaties. In *Canfor Corporation and Terminal Forest Products Ltd.* v. *United States of America* for instance, Canadian producers of softwood lumber claimed that various aspects of countervailing duties and anti-dumping measures adopted by the US relating to softwood lumber products breached the provisions of the investment Chapter 11 of the NAFTA.[45] The *Canfor* Tribunal was faced first with a difficult jurisdictional question of the relationship between the rights conferred on foreign investors to bring arbitration claims under NAFTA Chapter 11 and the dedicated provisions regulating dispute settlement on anti-dumping and countervailing duties in NAFTA Chapter 19. After exhaustive and painstaking analysis, the Tribunal ruled that 'Chapter 11 does not apply with respect to the antidumping and countervailing duty law of a State Party to the NAFTA'.[46] This part of the ruling would thus seem to signal the death-knell of the claims made by the Canadian companies against the US given that those claims seemed to relate entirely to those US trade remedies. But the Tribunal was prepared to accept jurisdiction over one key component of the US scheme in question – the Byrd Amendment – partly because of the US's *own* legal characterisation of that scheme in defending a claim brought against it in the WTO. Among other things, the Byrd Amendment distributed duties assessed under anti-dumping or countervailing orders imposed by the US to affected domestic producers.[47] For the *Canfor* Tribunal, the US's failure to comply with the notification conditions in NAFTA Art. 1902(2) was taken as a strong indication that the Byrd Amendment did not comprise an anti-dumping and countervailing duty law for the purpose of NAFTA Chapter 19.[48] But the Tribunal also went on to note that 'the

44 *Ibid.*, 7.17 (claiming that the umbrella clause in Art. 2(2) of the Hong Kong–Australia BIT encompasses Australia's obligations 'enshrined in TRIPS, the Paris Convention and TBT').

45 *Canfor Corporation and Terminal Forest Products Ltd.* v. *United States of America*, UNCITRAL, Decision on Preliminary Question, 6 June 2006.

46 *Ibid.*, 273. 47 *Ibid.*, 276. 48 *Ibid.*, 297–323.

conduct of the United States that was contemporaneous with, or proximate to, enactment of the Byrd Amendment is supportive of this conclusion, because it leads to the presumption that apparently the United States did not itself consider the Byrd Amendment to constitute a part of its antidumping law'.[49] The Tribunal noted[50] that in WTO proceedings the US had explicitly asserted that '[t]he CDSOA [Byrd Amendment] is a government payment programme', and '[t]he CDSOA has nothing to do with the administration of the antidumping and countervailing duty laws'.[51] The *Canfor* Tribunal in turn ruled:

> While the conduct of the United States before the WTO and the findings of WTO Panels and its Appellate Body have no binding effect upon this Tribunal they constitute relevant factual evidence which the Tribunal can and should appropriately take into account, especially in the case of positions advocated by the United States before the WTO that amount to admissions against interest for purposes of this NAFTA case.
>
> The United States' conduct at the time of enactment and before the WTO, therefore, leads the Tribunal to conclude that the Byrd Amendment does not come within the purview of the words 'with respect to a Party's antidumping law or countervailing duty law' under Article 1901(3). The presumption of good faith under international law as far as compliance with treaty obligations is concerned is supportive of this conclusion.[52]

Thirdly, the very prospect of parallel or related proceedings is driven by the fundamental economic fact that trade and foreign investment is increasingly inter-dependent. Of course, they can – as is often classically assumed – be strict substitutes. In particular, FDI is a substitute where the motivation to commence local production in a host State is to 'jump' (bypass) a high tariff wall or other trade barrier that renders exports unprofitable or impossible.[53] To be sure, tariffs are increasingly less relevant as the underlying motivation for this form of FDI, given the significant reduction in tariff protection especially for industrial products in developed countries. But it is important to bear in mind that non-tariff barriers such as anti-dumping duties constitute equally significant obstacles to export and thereby naturally favour FDI. The empirical evidence has shown, for instance, that anti-dumping duties and safeguard actions

49 *Ibid.*, 324. 50 *Ibid.*, 325.

51 WTO Panel Report, *United States – Continued Dumping and Subsidy Offset Act of 2000*, WT/DS217/R, 16 September 2002, 4.501–2.

52 *Canfor Corporation and Terminal Forest Products Ltd* v. *United States of America*, UNCITRAL, Decision on Preliminary Question, 6 June 2006, 327–8.

53 WTO Working Group on the Relationship Between Trade and Investment, *The Relationship Between Trade and Foreign Direct Investment*, 8.

have strongly influenced Japanese FDI into the US.[54] FDI can thus still be undertaken by an economic actor as a means of rationally reducing the sizeable risk of contingent trade protection which by its very nature is inherently protectionist.[55] There are clear examples of this type of FDI across the arbitral case law. In *Archer Daniels Midland Co. and Tate & Lyle Ingredients Americas, Inc.* v. *Mexico* for instance, the American company concerned *both* exported high-fructose corn syrup (HFCS) from its operations in the US (from 1994) *and* established a plant in Mexico to produce HFCS for sale in the Mexican market (from 1995).[56] The latter form of production was in turn immune from the anti-dumping duties and import restrictions imposed by Mexico on HFCS over the course of 1998 to 2002.[57] The presence of contingent trade protection of this sort can play an important role in understanding the purpose of a host State in promulgating later measures that target foreign investors but have the same overall purpose of insulating domestic production from foreign competition.

More recently, FDI is a complement rather than substitute to cross-border trade in goods and services. In particular, FDI that is efficiency-seeking will locate different stages of a production process so as to minimise overall production cost. For example, energy-intensive processing is located wherever energy costs are low; labour-intensive stages in countries with low labour costs; human capital stages in countries with an abundance of skilled labour and so on.[58] This type of FDI 'is by its very nature trade-creating' because '[b]y subdividing the production process in vertical stages between countries, trade is obviously created (compared to the situation where all stages are undertaken in one country)'.[59] This is no minor or tangential economic fact. Approximately half of the world's trade today takes place between affiliates of multinational enterprises trading intermediate goods and services.[60] Indeed, the economic reality of globalisation of production and distribution is embedded in the very text of the WTO. The

54 Azrak and Wynne (1995). 55 Bhagwati, Dinopoulos and Wong (1992).

56 *Archer Daniels Midland Co. and Tate & Lyle Ingredients Americas, Inc.* v. *Mexico*, ICSID Case No. ARB (AF)/04/5, Award, 21 November 2007, 53.

57 *Ibid.*, 72–6.

58 WTO Working Group on the Relationship Between Trade and Investment, *The Relationship Between Trade and Investment*, 4.

59 *Ibid.*, 7.

60 European Commission, *Communication from the Commission to the Council, the European Parliament, the European Economic and Social Committee and the Committee of Regions: Towards a Comprehensive European International Investment Policy* COM(2010)343, 7 July 2010, 3.

constraints on performance requirements (that States often seek to impose on foreign investors) in the TRIMS Agreement are premised on the fundamental notion that such investment measures (like the obligation to source domestic content struck down in *FIRA* and *Indonesia – Certain Measures Affecting the Automobile Industry*) can significantly impact on market access for foreign goods.[61] At the other end of the spectrum, restrictions on the import and export of goods and services can deeply influence the operation and value of foreign investment as revealed in the complicated factual matrix of many of the softwood lumber cases brought before the NAFTA including *Pope & Talbot Inc.* v. *Canada*[62] and *Merrill & Ring Forestry L.P.* v. *Canada*.[63] In *Pope & Talbot Inc.* for instance, the foreign investor's very ability to export softwood lumber from its plantations in Canada was curtailed by the implementation of a quota arrangement pursuant to bilateral agreement between the US and Canada settling an entrenched trade dispute between those countries.[64]

Fourthly, we are now beginning to find cross-fertilisation of jurisprudence. Both systems are structurally marked by the heavy activation of formalised systems of dispute settlement in the late 1990s. Adjudicators are now drawing on jurisprudence from one system when constructing readings on treaty obligations in the other. Indeed, we are *already* witnessing problematic transplant when it comes to the use of WTO law in investment arbitration. Investment treaty adjudicators are drawing extensively on WTO jurisprudence especially when defining readings on national treatment in investment law. Some of the early case law does this sensitively by extensively reviewing the jurisprudence surrounding the national treatment GATT Art. III before crafting individual juridical approaches.[65] But other cases are far less rigorous in their review yet define their entire reading in opposition to misperceptions of the breadth or limitation of national treatment in the law of the WTO.[66] When one

61 WTO Agreements, Annex 1A.

62 *Pope & Talbot Inc.* v. *Canada*, Award on the Merits of Phase 2, UNCITRAL, 10 April 2001.

63 *Merrill & Ring Forestry L.P.* v. *Canada*, UNCITRAL Arbitration, Award, 31 March 2010.

64 *Pope & Talbot Inc.* v. *Canada*, UNCITRAL Arbitration, Award on the Merits of Phase 2, 10 April 2001, 18–29.

65 See, e.g., *S.D. Myers Inc.* v. *Canada*, UNCITRAL Arbitration, Partial Award, 13 November 2000, 244–50; *Pope & Talbot Inc.* v. *Canada*, UNCITRAL Arbitration, Award on the Merits of Phase 2, 10 April 2001, 45–79.

66 *Occidental Exploration and Production Co.* v. *Ecuador*, UNCITRAL Arbitration, Final Award, 1 July 2004, 174–6; *Methanex Corp.* v. *United States of America*, UNCITRAL Arbitration, Final Award, 3 August 2005, pt IV, ch. B, 28–30.

unpacks the complicated arbitral jurisprudence on national treatment, misuse of WTO law is *the* controlling factor for critical inconsistency in the legal tests applied to that norm.[67]

The national treatment case law is by no means an isolated incidence of cross-fertilisation. For example, the *Continental Casualty Co.* arbitral Award is characterised by careful and sophisticated use of WTO exceptions jurisprudence to guide adjudication of a somewhat similar (but not identical) investment treaty exception.[68] By contrast, earlier cases simply conflate the treaty exception with the customary plea of necessity, an approach that has been criticised by an ICSID Annulment Committee as constituting 'manifest error of law'.[69] Indeed, this part of the emerging arbitral case law reveals a hidden and fascinating parallel between the two systems. Positively, there is no mechanism to correct for legal error in investment arbitration, while legal review of this sort is precisely the mandate of the WTO Appellate Body.[70] The annulment process for arbitration conducted under the auspices of ICSID only allows awards to be annulled based on critical and serious due process flaws.[71] Yet despite this significant variation in institutional mandate, a number of ICSID Annulment Committees (constituted in the cases brought against Argentina) have interpreted their powers creatively (or for those opposed, aggressively) to overturn awards where legal error has poisoned an analytical sequence.[72] In an even further parallel, other annulment committees have isolated – as has classically the WTO Appellate Body – flaws in the application by

67 For an exploration of this argument with a specific focus on the use of WTO law by investor–State arbitral tribunals when ruling on whether competition is a necessary condition of likeness under the obligation of national treatment see Kurtz (2009).

68 For an account supporting the *Continental* Tribunal's interpretative method as well as its substantive rulings, see Kurtz (2010). But for an opposing account that is deeply critical of the *Continental* Award, see Alvarez and Brinks (2011).

69 *CMS Gas Transmission Co.* v. *Argentine Republic*, ICSID Case No. ARB/01/8, Decision of the Ad Hoc Committee on the Application for Annulment, 25 September 2007, 130.

70 WTO Agreements, Annex 2, Art. 17(6) ('An appeal shall be limited to issues of law covered in the panel report and legal interpretations developed by the panel').

71 Convention on the Settlement of Investment Disputes Between States and Nationals of Other States, 18 March 1965, 575 UNTS 159, Art. 52(1) (setting out five grounds for annulment as: (a) tribunal was not properly constituted; (b) manifest excess of powers; (c) corruption; (d) serious departure from a fundamental rule of procedure; (e) failure to state reasons).

72 *Sempra Energy International* v. *Argentine Republic*, ICSID Case No. ARB/02/16, Decision on the Argentine Republic's Application for Annulment of the Award, 29 June 2010, 205 (concluding that there was 'error in law'); 206–10 (finding that such amounted to a failure to apply the applicable law thereby annulling the underlying award).

arbitral tribunals of the hermeneutic techniques mandated by the VCLT.[73] This growing phenomenon of cross-fertilisation of method and substance is commonly assumed to flow largely from the established law of the WTO to that of investor–State arbitration. While this is indeed the dominant direction, the WTO Appellate Body has recently cited an investor–State arbitral award on the systemic issue of the precedential value of past Appellate Body reports.[74]

Cross-fertilisation, in turn, is causative (at least in part) of a fifth and sociological dimension being the movement of actors across the two fields. The *Continental* Award with its heavy use of WTO law is visible proof of this phenomenon, given the presidency of that Tribunal by a former WTO Appellate Body member.[75] Nor is *Continental* an outlier. In *Abalclat,* another former WTO Appellate Body member issued a stinging dissent of 'this excessively long award, its style of turning around the main issues and drowning them into an ocean of minutia and elaborated details, rather than confronting them formally and treating them thoroughly'.[76] Adjudicators are not the only group that have begun to migrate between the two systems. The shift to cover both trade and foreign investment issues in modern free trade agreements is a particularly important development measured by the use of WTO-based ideas to guide reform of investment commitments. The fertilisation of those ideas is not surprising in the FTA context when one considers the intermingling of different government actors and departments under a common negotiating umbrella. Scholars too have begun to navigate and shape disciplinary boundaries including when acting as expert witnesses on WTO law before investor–State arbitral tribunals.[77]

73 *Fraport AG Frankfurt Airport Services Worldwide* v. *Republic of the Philippines,* ICSID Case No. ARB/03/25, Decision on the Application for Annulment of Fraport AG Frankfurt Airport Services Worldwide, 23 December 2010, 73–118 (carefully reviewing the hermeneutic flaws by the *Fraport* Tribunal against the customary rules on treaty interpretation codified in the VCLT).

74 WTO Appellate Body, *United States – Final Anti-Dumping Measures on Stainless Steel from Mexico,* WT/DS344/AB/R, 30 April 2008, AB-2008–1, 160, fn 313.

75 *Continental Casualty Co.* v. *Argentine Republic,* ICSID Case No. ARB/03/9, Award, 5 September 2008.

76 *Abalclat and Others* v. *Argentine Republic,* ICSID Case No. ARB/07/5, Decision on Jurisdiction and Admissibility, 28 October 2011, Dissenting Opinion, Professor Georges Abi-Saab, 3.

77 See, e.g., *Methanex Corp.* v. *United States of America,* UNCITRAL Arbitration, Final Award, 3 August 2005, pt IV, ch. B, 5 (regarding the expert opinion on WTO law by Dr Claus-Dieter Ehlermann, a former member of the WTO Appellate Body).

4. Future evolution

In thinking of the future engagement between the two fields, there are at least three possible outcomes that might flow from the convergence factors surveyed above.

A first, albeit unlikely, prediction would begin from a strongly pluralist premise. It would emphasise the political factors that led to the existence of distinct and diverse normative systems for trade and investment at international law. Based on those factors, a strong pluralist approach could deny the possibility of a shared, universally orientated system of values uniting the two fields. This is de facto a defence of the state of play during the late 1980s to mid-1990s, which predates most of the five convergence factors surveyed above and thus marked the high point of separation of both systems. That period also marks the strongest iteration of the BIT model before the recalibration (mainly by developed States) to pare back those extensive protections (through the late 1990s onwards). It is difficult to escape the impression that some of the practitioners in the investment law field are understandably (if not justifiably) attracted to this research model, precisely because the recalibration of investment treaties (including via the use of WTO-based flexibilities) limits the market opportunities offered to them by the older and stronger BIT model.

It is tempting to dismiss the pluralist account as implausible, especially given the manner in which States parties are using WTO-based ideas to frame newer investment commitments. To put it crudely, States parties have cast their votes and it is in a very different direction to those who would like to see the clock turned back. Nonetheless, there may well be some value in the meta directions of this research model in testing the rationality of some of the WTO-inspired reform of investment treaty commitments, especially for both suitability and redundancy.[78] Yet those attracted to this pluralist account must still in some ways respond directly to fundamental changes in State practice. Even with the occasional flaw, the recalibration strategy shows that States are questioning the contemporary justification for select investment treaty disciplines. This, of course, raises the very issue of what justifications can be found in disciplines other than law for constraints on host State action vis-à-vis foreign investment. Yet the willingness of authors to address that obvious need would seem to be influenced by which side of a sociological divide they sit on within the investment commitment. One thing is however certain; it

78 For an approach along these lines, see Newcombe (2011).

will no longer suffice to simply point to the historical antecedents (which were themselves deeply contingent) of strong investment treaty protections as a sufficient justification for their continued operation.

An alternative prediction – that would sit naturally at the opposite end of a spectrum – would be one of full convergence between the two fields. Those attracted to this possibility would advocate for some form of systemic unity, with an agreed set of basic rules and principles to govern the shared realm. Proponents would point to the obvious path dependence that has separated the twins of international economic law and position the research question as 'not to merely contemplate how to somehow reconcile the procedural and substantive technicalities of international trade and investment law, a formidable challenge in itself, but rather to more ambitiously reconceive (for lack of a better word) the two fields as one'.[79]

There is of course an immediate challenge facing those attracted to this normative trajectory: There is little political appetite among States parties for this type of aggressive treaty reform. For instance, a significant portion of the WTO membership (especially developing States) have explicitly opposed the inclusion of investment as a full negotiating item at both the Singapore (1996) and Cancun (2003) Ministerial meetings.[80] Even within the smaller cohesive grouping of the OECD, its Member States were unable to complete negotiations towards a Multilateral Agreement on Investment in the mid- to late 1990s. Moreover, those attracted to this hypothesis would need to concede that some level of differentiation would continue to be required. A first, albeit obvious, limit is at the level of the norm itself. Certain treaty provisions (in both systems) are highly specific to a given form of economic exchange. A protection against expropriation, for instance, is only relevant where the mode of production is located within the State that seeks to expropriate the economic value of those assets. There is then little value in engaging in comparison with the parts of the WTO that are premised entirely on cross-border exchange of assets. A more appropriate comparator would be the way in which domestic constitutional protections guarantee compensation in the event of takings or acquisition of private property. This constraint is not entirely an absolute given that there is an important role in minimising system friction between international trade and investment law such as in the recognition by States parties in their newer investment treaties that issuance of a compulsory licence (permitted under WTO law) should not trigger a claim of expropriation of the protected patent (under investment law). The

79 Broude (2013). 80 On the latter, see Kurtz (2004).

same qualification holds true for anti-dumping duties. These are expressly limited to cross-border exchange of goods and, superficially at least, there is little benefit in engaging in comparative analysis. Nonetheless, as flagged earlier, the imposition of anti-dumping duties can be a critical (even causative, if overturned by a WTO panel) part of the story of later investment-restrictive measures. Where that is the case, an adjudicator who is schooled in the nuances of both systems can and should recognise that the substitute measure may well be presumptively protectionist.

Yet perhaps more fundamentally, those attracted to the convergence hypothesis should guard themselves against the tempting and intuitive idea that the WTO model frames any unification of the two fields. The Uruguay Round of negotiations from 1986 to 1994 that led to the formation of the WTO were themselves influenced by a particularly aggressive vision of the role of the market vis-à-vis the State. One can detect a distinct chastening of the views of natural defenders of a strong market model in light of the 2008 global financial crisis, not least the US and now particular Member States of the European Union. Care then should be taken when reconceiving the two fields by being mindful of deep contestation within WTO law on select issues. In particular, the mere omission of a discipline in one system and its presence in another may not necessarily suggest it has a logical place in the former. A good, possibly even representative, example here is subsidies that are lightly regulated (if at all) in investment law while subject to deep limitations as a matter of WTO law. For Broude, 'the treatment of subsidies in investment law is inconsistent and underdeveloped' and '[t]his pales in comparison to the [WTO Agreement on Subsidies and Countervailing Measures] sophisticated mechanisms with respect to subsidies'.[81] Yet some commentators have cast doubt, from an economic perspective, on the very ability of a range of legal systems (including but not limited to the WTO) to distinguish socially constructive subsidies from those that are protectionist or otherwise economically objectionable.[82] There are then significant implications implicit in the transport of an overly restrictive (from an economic view) disciplinary model on subsidies from WTO to investment law, especially given that a sizeable number of developing States view subsidisation as an integral part of any developmental strategy.

A third possibility might chart a more modest direction between these starkly opposing poles. It would begin by positing the need for a common body of legal norms in light of a shared set of values, and would position

81 Broude (2013). 82 Sykes (2007).

the judicial actors of both systems as having a significant role in mediating the relationship between the two orders. The common purpose that unites both systems is the fundamental promise to extend and safeguard competitive opportunities to foreign traders and investors. It is not the only goal achieved by each regime but it is arguably the most significant and important from an economic perspective. That instrumental justification for liberal rules on international trade in goods has always been understood. More recently, some economists have argued that it should also act as a benchmark when assessing the contemporary justification of select investment disciplines.[83] Economic analysis only takes us so far, however. There is the still the complex challenge of structuring a legal mechanism that accurately determines the appropriate limits on economically insensible State intervention against the various and myriad ways in which States regulate for legitimate public purposes.

As to the latter, the legal techniques long used in international trade law to guarantee regulatory pluralism between member States have begun to migrate into investment treaties. Indeed, after a long period of stagnation (in investment law at least), States parties are now engaged in a remarkable degree of experimentation with commitments across bilateral and regional investment, trade and economic treaties. The growing heterogeneity of international economic law (across bilateral and regional instruments) reveals a much more sensitive and nuanced tailoring of treaty commitments to underlying State preferences. This, of course, is the opposite side of the coin to the often overblown concerns about fragmentation in the international legal order. It is also worth pointing out that the field of international investment law has always been heterogeneous, at least insofar as there were subtle variances between the 'model BITs' of traditional capital exporters such as the US, the UK, France, Germany and others. But the more recent and deeper heterogeneity – especially across bilateral instruments that combine trade and investment commitments – is causative of growing politicisation as various actors have begun to appreciate the deep public interests implicated by such disciplines. It is often the very nexus between WTO and investment disciplines that sits at the critical juncture of that deep level of politicisation as States parties either transplant legal devices in response (such as WTO-based flexibilities) or the inherent features of a particular system are offered as mechanisms of developing greater legitimacy in the other (such as the value of

83 Stiglitz (2007–8).

centralised appellate review in the WTO, and its strong commitment to principled hermeneutics and de facto *stare decisis*).

The common *telos* and legal terrain uniting the two systems are but one part of their future connection. The shape and degree of their integration will also depend fundamentally on cross-judging and interpretation.[84] International courts and tribunals are capable of talking with each other and this is especially important in the common terrain of international trade and investment law. As we have already seen, there is strong evidence of citation of WTO law in investor–State arbitration with limited practice in the reverse direction. That might lead some to begin from the loose premise that the (usually) older WTO jurisprudence on common norms is necessarily superior select approaches on investment arbitration. Yet any such claim would need to be tested against the full suite of case law in both systems which, given the complexity and enormous growth of such jurisprudence, is no small task. It is however a critical inductive exercise insofar as States parties are unlikely to isolate with precision the sufficient components of breach in their drafting of treaty commitments. The deeply incomplete nature of trade and investment treaties inevitably requires adjudicators to supply those components. And in fact, at least when it comes to a critical common norm of national treatment, it is possible to argue that parts of investment arbitration jurisprudence are superior to their WTO counterparts and may offer a useful guide to the evolution of the latter. This is especially the case on whether and how to construct a test for identification of State purpose as a condition of breach of that legal obligation. This is not to say that the entirety of the national treatment arbitral case law is superior to its WTO counterparts. There are indeed flaws in select arbitral cases on national treatment that, as flagged earlier, have been caused by the mistaken perception of the breadth or narrowness of WTO law on questions such as the role of competition in a national treatment test. Ultimately, however, investigation of those flaws requires qualitative, fine-grained analysis in order to provide scholars, practitioners and adjudicators with a basis for distinguishing between strong and weakly reasoned legal outcomes, a task that is especially important in investment law given the absence of an appellate organ.

84 On the normative implications of cross-judging across international law, see Teitel and Howse (2009).

References

Alvarez, J.E. and Brink, T. 2011. 'Revisiting the Necessity Defence: *Continental Casualty* v. *Argentina*', Sauvant, K. (ed.), *Yearbook of International Investment Law and Policy*. Oxford University Press: 319–62.

Azrak, P. and Wynne, K. 1995. 'Protectionism and Japanese Direct Investment in the United States'. *Journal of Policy Modelling* 17: 293–305.

Bhagwati, J.N., Dinopoulos, E. and Wong, K.-Y. 1992. 'Quid Pro Quo Foreign Investment'. *American Economic Review* 82(2): 186–90.

Broude, T. 2013. 'Investment and Trade: The "Lottie and Lisa" of International Economic Law?', Sauve, P. and Echandi, R. (eds.), *Prospects in International Investment Law and Policy*. Cambridge University Press.

Cho, S. 2001. 'Breaking the Barrier between Regionalism and Multilateralism: A New Perspective on Trade Regionalism'. *Harvard International Law Journal* 42: 419–66.

Dolzer, R. and Schreuer, C. 2008. *Principles of International Investment Law*. Oxford University Press.

The Economist. 2012. 'Come and Get Me: Argentina is Putting International Arbitration to the Test' (18 February, London), 35–6.

Hirsch, M. 2008. 'The Sociology of International Economic Law: Sociological Analysis of the Regulation of Regional Agreements in the World Trading System'. *European Journal of International Law* 19: 277–99.

Howse, R. 2001. 'Adjudicative Legitimacy and Treaty Interpretation in International Trade Law: The Early Years of WTO Jurisprudence', Weiler, J.H.H. (ed.), *The EU, the WTO and the NAFTA: Towards a Common Law of International Trade*. Oxford University Press: 35–70.

Kurtz, J. 2004. 'Developing Countries and Their Engagement in the World Trade Organization: An Assessment of the Cancún Ministerial'. *Melbourne Journal of International Law* 5: 280–97.

2009. 'The Use and Abuse of WTO Law in Investor-State Arbitration: Competition and its Discontents'. *European Journal of International Law* 20: 749–71.

2010. 'Adjudging the Exceptional at International Investment Law: Security, Public Order and Financial Crisis'. *International and Comparative Law Quarterly* 59: 325–71.

2012. 'Australia's Rejection of Investor–State Arbitration: Causation, Omission and Implication'. *ICSID Review* 27: 65–86.

Levesque, C. 2006. 'Influences on the Canadian FIPA Model and the US Model BIT: NAFTA Chapter 11 and Beyond'. *Canadian Yearbook of International Law* 44: 249–98.

Newcombe, A. 2011. 'General Exceptions in International Investment Agreements', Cordonier Segger, M.-C., Gehring, M.W. and Newcombe, A. (eds.),

Sustainable Development in World Investment Law. Riverwoods, IL: Kluwer: 355–70.

Ruggie, J. 1998. 'Embedded Liberalism and Postwar Economic Regimes', Ruggie, J. (ed.), *Constructing the World Polity: Essays on International Institutionalization*. London: Routledge: 62–84.

Schwartz, W. and Sykes, A.O. 2002. 'The Economic Structure of Renegotiation and Dispute Resolution in the World Trade Organization'. *Journal of Legal Studies* 31: 179–204.

Stiglitz, J.E. 2007–8. 'Regulating Multinational Corporations: Towards Principles of Cross-Border Legal Frameworks in a Globalized World Balancing Rights with Responsibilities'. *American University International Law Review* 23: 451–558.

Sykes, A.O. 2007. 'International Trade: Trade Remedies'. Guzman, A.T. and Sykes, A.O. (eds.), *Research Handbook in International Economic Law*. Cheltenham: Edward Elgar: 62–112.

2012. 'The Questionable Case for Subsidies Regulation: A Comparative Perspective'. *Journal of Legal Analysis* 2: 473–523.

Teitel, R. and Howse, R. 2009. 'Cross-Judging: Tribunalization in a Fragmented but Interconnected Global Order'. *New York University Journal of International Law and Politics* 41: 959–90.

Trebilcock, M., Howse, R. and Eliason, A. (eds.) 2012. *The Regulation of International Trade*, 4th edn. Hoboken, NJ: Taylor and Francis.

Van den Bossche, P. 2008. *The Law and Policy of the World Trade Organization: Text, Cases and Materials*. Cambridge University Press.

Weiler, J.H.H. 2008. 'The Rule of Lawyers and the Ethos of Diplomats: Reflections on the Internal and External Legitimacy of WTO Dispute Settlement'. *Journal of World Trade* 35: 191–207.

Wong, K.-Y. 1989. 'Optimal Threat of Protection and Quid Pro Quo Foreign Investment'. *Economics & Politics* 1: 277–300.

6

Sovereign wealth funds as protected investors under BITs and the safeguard of the national security of host States

MICHELE BARBIERI

1. Introduction

In the last decade foreign investments made by sovereign wealth funds (SWFs) have increased in an impressive way and this has contributed to raise fears that they may threaten the national security of the host State. The fact that SWFs are State-owned and State-controlled entities may lead one to assume that their investment decisions are politically rather than commercially driven. For these reasons, several States have decided to adopt measures that aim at ensuring a better protection of their national security in the case of inward investments made by foreign SWFs; nevertheless such measures may jeopardize the ability of SWFs to invest overseas.

When adopting the measures at issue, host States do not operate in a legal vacuum, but, on the contrary, they are obliged to respect existing provisions of international law concerning the protection of foreign investments which are mostly contained in bilateral investment treaties (BITs).

The present contribution attempts to study the extent to which BIT provisions allow States to adopt measures that aim at protecting their national security in respect of foreign investments made by SWFs.

The contribution will be organized as follows. In Section 2 it will try to define the notion of national security of a State; it will study how this could be endangered by inward investments made by foreign entities (especially when they are State-owned and State-controlled, as it is in the case of SWFs) and then the measures the host State may adopt to protect its national security. Section 3 will provide some basic information on SWFs. Section 4 will discuss the functions SWFs are expected to perform in the economy of the States that establish them and it will investigate the political dimension of SWFs in relation to these functions. It will also study when the political dimension of SWFs may raise issues of national security for the recipient States. Section 5 will study whether SWFs should be regarded as investors covered under applicable BITs. Sections 6 and 7 will study the extent to which substantive provisions contained in BITs may be interpreted in a manner not to limit the ability of host States to protect their national security whenever it is in fact threatened by inward investments of SWFs. Finally, Section 8 will briefly discuss under which circumstances the national security clause contained in some BITs may be invoked by host States when they adopt measures that hinder or restrict the investments of SWFs.

2. Sovereign investments, threats to national security and possible responses of host States

For a proper understanding of the applicability of BITs to measures host States may adopt to protect their national security vis-à-vis the investments of foreign SWFs, it is necessary to define some key concepts. They are: first, the concept of national security; second, the possible threats to national security that may be posed by foreign investments, especially when they are made by foreign State entities (such as SWFs); third, the measures adopted by host States to protect their national security. To avoid an excessively abstract discussion, a few quick references to the legislation of certain States will be provided in the course of the present discussion.

The notion of national security may be very broad. First of all, it is related to situations of military crisis, armed attacks carried out by other States or other bodies (such as terrorist organizations), as well as riots or civil disturbances. National security may also be endangered by severe economic crisis as has been pointed out in recent awards given in disputes between Argentina and US investors.[1] However, not every economic crisis raises issues of national security, but only those that reach a particular level of gravity so as to endanger the existence and the integrity of the affected State. The main difficulties reside in assessing in practice the degree of

1 *CMS Gas Transmission Company* v. *The Argentine Republic* ICSID Case No. ARB/01/08, Award, 12 May 2005, 359–60; *LG&E Energy Corp./LG&E Capital Corp./LG&E International Inc.* v. *The Argentine Republic* ICSID Case No. ARB/02/1, Award, 3 October 2006, 238; *Sempra Energy International* v. *The Argentine Republic* ICSID Case No. ARB/02/16, Award, 28 September 2007, 374; *Continental Casualty Company* v. *The Argentine Republic* ICSID Case No. ARB/03/9, Award, 5 September 2008, 175. For a more in-depth analysis, see Alvarez and Khamsi (2008–9), 379–478; Bjorklund (2008–9), 479–504; Hsu (2009), 472–5; Muchlinski (2008–9), 54–8.

severity that an economic crisis must attain in order to be regarded as a real and actual threat to national security.[2]

National security may also be threatened if certain strategic assets come under the control of a foreign investor. If the latter is a foreign government-controlled entity, as is the case of SWFs, then the implications for national security may be even more acute. Defining the notion of strategic assets and strategic sectors is therefore necessary to properly understand the concept of national security and for this purpose it may be useful to refer to applicable domestic laws and regulations.

Some States have developed a list that specifies the sectors to be considered as strategic, while others only refer to more or less detailed criteria.

Russia, for instance, has quite a broad list of strategic industries which includes *inter alia*: the defence, aerospace and nuclear sectors, as well as cryptography, telecommunications, broadcasting, newspapers and all activities related to goods and services connected with the exploration and exploitation of natural resources.[3] In Germany the sectors that are considered strategic are: production of weapons of war, production of military equipment or engines of military vehicles and cryptographic systems used for the transmission of governmental information.[4] France has adopted two lists of strategic sectors: one applies to EU investors, the other to investors from third countries. The first list includes: defence, counter-terrorism, research and development of chemical and biological weapons, IT technologies used for private security purposes and gaming. The second list is longer and also includes, together with the items mentioned in the first list, activities related to military secrets, to the production of weapons and explosives and to procurements by the Ministry of Defence.[5]

In Italy the rules concerning the protection of national security in the case of foreign investments have been recently modified and currently

2 The view that the Argentina economic crisis was sufficiently severe to amount to a threat to the national security of the State was supported in: *LG&E* (fn 1), 231–8; *Continental* (fn 1), 180. Nevertheless, other tribunals reached opposite conclusions when assessing the same issue: *CMS* (fn 1), 355; *Sempra* (fn 1), 348. For a more in-depth analysis of this issue, see Hsu (2009), 472–5; Qureshi (2009), 631–5.

3 Federal law No. 57-FZ of 5 May 2008 ('On Procedures for Foreign Investment in Companies of Strategic Importance for National Defense and Security').

4 Foreign Trade and Payments Act of 27 May 2009 and Regulation Implementing the Foreign Trade and Payments Act of 18 December 1986 as amended on 24 April 2009. See: Alvaro and Ciccaglioni (2012), 27–32.

5 Décret n° 2005–1739 of 30 December 2005, Arts. 2 and 3.

the matter is governed by Decree 21 of 15 March 2012.[6] The new Italian provisions also focus on the industries that possess strategic assets and networks. Therefore, together with the defence and military-related industries, also the energy, transportation and communication sectors are regarded as strategic and may be the object of special measures whose aim is to protect the national security of the host State.[7]

Finally, it must be pointed out that, irrespective of the existence of lists of strategic sectors, many States have special legislation for particularly sensitive industries, given the impact they may have on a country's overall economic and social life: this is the case for instance, for the banking and financial sectors.

After having clarified the concept of national security and of strategic sectors, it is possible to move on to an analysis of the threats to national security the investments of SWFs might entail.

First of all, national security of the host State could be endangered if SWFs invest in the defence or in other dual-use-technology sectors in order to have access to military technology and possibly to secret information related to national security. Another threat to national security could occur if SWFs seize control of strategic sectors, becoming capable of influencing the social, economic and political life of recipient States. Likewise, if they massively invest or divest in certain countries, they could destabilize their financial markets and more in general their economies. As has been explained above, an economic or a financial crisis, when it reaches a certain degree of seriousness, might represent a threat to national security. A related risk emerges when SWFs use their foreign investments in order indirectly to influence companies in which they have invested to adopt strategies that benefit the State to which the SWFs belong at the expenses of the host State. For instance, a SWF might agree to invest in a company subject to the condition that the company in question undertakes to transfer certain facilities or activities to the country to which the SWF belongs. This may entail a reduction of GDP and jobs in the recipient country, together with a significant erosion of its tax base.[8]

6 Decreto-legge of 15 March 2012, n. 21 as converted and modified by the law of 11 May 2012, n. 56.

7 Decreto-legge of 15 March 2012, n. 21, Art. 2.1.

8 The literature on the possible threats posed by SWFs (but also of the benefits their capital may bring or have already brought) is very abundant. See, for instance, the following: Ander (2009); Backer (2007–8), 1801–68; Bahgat (2008), 1189–1204; Barbieri (2010), 272–4; Bassan (2010), 165–201; Bertoni (2010), 81–96; Bhagwati (2008), 25–32; Biard (2008), 68; Das (2008), 1–15; Drezner (2010), 97–116; Feng (2009), 490–501; Gomes (2008), 9–18; Hemphill (2009), 551–6; Kern (2007); Kern (2008), 11–17; Kimmit (2008), 123–26; Lyons

Several States have amended their legislation in order to increase their ability to assess, detect and prevent the threats SWFs may pose to their national security. It must be noted that in many cases the screening and controlling mechanisms which are put in place and which apply to SWFs are the same as are applicable to non-sovereign foreign investors. In other cases, laws or administrative practices provide for specific rules when inward investments are made by governmental entities. Moreover, it must be stressed that in some cases such measures only apply to investments entailing the acquisition of a controlling participation (the latter being defined in domestic legislation) and not to portfolio investments (which, as will be discussed in the following section, represent the large majority of the overseas investments of SWFs). In the remaining part of the present section, a few references to the above-mentioned laws and measures will be made, with the limited purpose of providing some examples and, of course, without attempting to provide an exhaustive review of all relevant State measures.[9]

For instance, in the United States the Committee on Foreign Investments in the United States (CFIUS) is entrusted with the task of reviewing the proposed investments that foreign entities must notify. The CFIUS issues a recommendation to the President of the US as to whether the envisaged transaction is liable to endanger national security. The President then decides whether or not to veto the operation. Since 2007, State-backed entities planning to invest in the US have been obliged to notify the CFIUS. In this way, the control of US authorities over the operations of SWFs is made much more accurate and wide-ranging.[10]

In Australia foreign investors notify their investment proposals to the Foreign Investment Review Board (FIRB). This consultative body is responsible for analysing them and submitting them to the Treasury, which ultimately decides whether to admit the proposed transactions. The Australian government has recently issued guidelines specifying how the existing law should be interpreted in the case of investments made by foreign government-owned entities, as well as the factors that need

(2008), 4–62; Mason (2008), 1321–2; Pasca di Magliano (2009), 79–90; Rose (2008–9), 94; Savona and Regola (2009), 1–100; Seznec (2008), 97–110; Siniscalco (2008), 75–86; Truman (2008a); Wong (2009), 1090–8; Wu and Seah (2008), 33–47.

9 For this purpose, I will mainly rely on a research sponsored by CONSOB (the Italian authority for the supervision of the financial and banking sector and of listed companies): Alvaro and Ciccaglioni (2012).

10 Anwar (2010), 419–66; Carroll (2009), 178; Cooke (2009), 728–82; Feng (2009), 501–7; Gutlin (2010), 765–80; Hsu (2009), 451–77 and in particular 455–6; O'Brien (2008), 1242–4; Sud (2006), 1304–31; Wong (2009), 1088–90. The possibility that SWFs may

to be considered in order to ensure an adequate protection of national security.[11]

In France, too, foreign direct investments in strategic sectors need to undergo a screening procedure prior to their admission. Such procedure consists of an application for authorization made by the foreign investor to the Ministry of the Economy.[12]

In Germany the Ministry of the Economy and Technology is empowered to carry out investigations in the case of foreign investments that entail the acquisition of controlling shares of companies in a way that may endanger domestic national security. Such investigation may be undertaken within three months following the conclusion of the agreement for the acquisition of the shareholding in question and must be concluded within the following two months. If the existence of threats to national security is found to exist, the Ministry is empowered to prevent the transaction, although the decision it takes may be challenged before domestic tribunals. However, a foreign investor may seek assurances in advance as

endanger the national security of recipient countries has been discussed also at the OECD. In the OECD Declaration of 5 June 2008 on Sovereign Wealth Funds and recipient countries policies it was acknowledged that "if SWF investments were motivated by political rather than commercial objectives, they could be a source of concern, and that legitimate national security concerns could arise". In this case, restrictions would be acceptable, but only if measures of "general application to both foreign and domestic investors are inadequate to address legitimate national security concerns." They also dealt with the relation between policies governing foreign investments and national security in the Recommendation of the Council on Guidelines for Recipient Country Investment Policies relating to National Security of 25 May 2009.

This document does not focus on SWFs but does not exclude investments carried out by these State-owned vehicles. It recommends that "if governments consider or introduce investment policies (including measures) designed to safeguard national security, they should be guided by the principles of non-discrimination, transparency of policies and predictability of outcomes, proportionality of measures and accountability of implementing authorities."

11 Guidelines for foreign government investment; 2008; available online at: www.treasurer.gov.au/DisplayDocs.aspx?doc=pressreleases/2008/009.htm&pageID=003&min=wms&DocType=0. This document of soft law provides the elements government authorities must consider in order to assess whether an investment made by foreign governmental entities may threaten Australian national security. The focus should be on the degree of independence of the investor's operations from the relevant foreign government, on the compliance of the investor with the law and common standards of business behaviour, on the risks the transaction in question may hinder market competition, on the impact they may have on Australian government revenue or other policies or its ability to protect its strategic and security interests and, finally on the impact they are likely to have on operations and direction of Australian businesses and their contribution to the Australian economy. See also Alvaro and Ciccaglioni (2012), 26.

12 Décret n° 2005–1739 of 30 December 2005, Art. 4.

to whether the Ministry will regard its transaction as capable of threatening the national security.[13]

In Italy, the foreign investor that acquires a holding in a strategic company is required to notify the government within ten days from the conclusion of the transaction. The government, after having assessed the existence of serious threats to national security, may impose particular obligations upon the investor. It may also veto certain decisions adopted by the boards or general meetings of strategic companies and it is finally empowered to prevent their acquisition by foreign investors.[14]

It must be noted that the majority of the measures surveyed so far entail a screening mechanism, which is performed by government authorities *ex ante*, i.e. when the investment by the SWF is still to be admitted (with the partial exception of the Italian and German screening mechanisms).

Nevertheless, the measures a host State may adopt to protect its national security may apply not only in the phase in which it decides whether to admit foreign investments, but also after they have already been admitted. Very broadly speaking, this is the case, for instance, of measures that suspend or limit the voting rights of foreign SWFs in companies after the acquisition of a shareholding has already been made. Other examples may include the withdrawal or the denial of certain authorizations or certificates which are needed to start or to continue certain business activities. All these measures may adversely affect the investments of foreign investors, including foreign SWFs. Therefore, it is important to analyse whether BITs affect the ability of host States to screen, review and restrict the investments of SWFs before their admission and/or their ability to adopt measures that may adversely affect the investments of SWFs once they have already been admitted.

3. Overview of SWFs

For the purposes of a proper understanding of the applicability of BITs to SWFs, and of the way this might affect the ability of host States to protect their national security against possible threats posed by SWFs, it is also necessary to provide some basic information on these State-owned investment vehicles.

13 Alvaro and Ciccaglioni (2012), 31.

14 Decreto-legge of 15 March 2012, n. 21; cit.; Arts. 1 and 2; Alvaro and Ciccaglioni (2012), 34–9.

Developing a definition of SWFs has proved difficult.[15] In fact, SWFs present very different features and, moreover, it is not always easy to distinguish them from other entities such as State-owned enterprises, State-owned pension funds, central banks and other monetary authorities.[16] The definition of SWFs that will be adopted in the present contribution is the one elaborated by the International Working Group on SWFs (IWG) on the occasion of the adoption of the 'Santiago Principles'.[17] It reads as follows: 'SWFs are defined as special purpose investment funds or arrangements, owned by the general government. Created by the general government for macroeconomic purposes, SWFs hold, manage, or administer assets to achieve financial objectives, and employ a set of investment strategies which include investing in foreign financial assets.' The following elements seem therefore to characterize a SWF. First, it is owned and controlled by State authorities, i.e. by the central government, a ministry, the central bank or also sub-national governments (especially in federal States). Second, the investment strategy of a SWF includes investments in foreign financial assets; for this reason, funds which invest only in domestic assets are excluded from the IMF definition of SWFs. Third, a SWF is established in order to pursue macroeconomic functions in the State to which it belongs.

As has been pointed out *inter alia* in the Santiago Principles,[18] the legal framework governing the creation of SWFs can vary greatly. First of all, SWFs may be established as separate legal entities under public law, with

15 Many definitions of SWFs have been developed. They are similar in many aspects, but the fact that there is not a consensus in literature on a definition of SWFs reveals how difficult such a task is. For an attempt at defining SWFs see, for instance: Bassan (2011), 17–35; Chiarlone (2010), 55–80; Jen (2007); Truman (2008a, 2008b). See also the definition provided by the Sovereign Wealth Fund Institute, the main think tank on SWFs at: www.swfinstitute.org/what-is-a-swf/page.

16 On the difference between SWFs and SOEs see Bassan (2011), 21–3. Nevertheless, especially in non-market economies, SWFs and SOEs may be strictly interconnected and they are often part of a coherent economic and industrial policy. On this aspect, see: Backer (2010–11), 129–30. On the relation between central banks and SWFs see, for instance, ECB (2009). The difference between SWFs and (certain) pension funds is studied in: Blundell-Wignall, Hu and Yermo (2008), 1–17 as well as in: Kern (2007), 2.

17 International working group for sovereign wealth funds, 'Generally accepted principles and practices "Santiago Principles"'. The Santiago Principles is one of the most important official documents dealing with the issue of SWFs. The definition it contains may be regarded as the official one. For more information of the Santiago Principles see, for instance: Cooke (2009), 766–70; Gutlin (2010), 745–80; Wong (2009), 1103–9. For a more in-depth discussion of the events that led to the adoption of the GAPP, see Norton (2010), 645–62.

18 International Working Group for Sovereign Wealth Funds (2008a), 11; International Working Group for Sovereign Wealth Funds (2008b).

full legal capacity and governed by specific legislation.[19] Other SWFs take the form of State-owned corporations, created in accordance with the corporate law of the State to which they belong.[20] Finally, SWFs may consist of pools of assets without a separate legal identity, owned and managed directly by the central bank or by the ministry of economic affairs.[21]

SWFs manage assets estimated to be worth more than US$5 trillion.[22] In principle SWFs are able to invest in virtually any kind of assets: equity and debt instruments, units of funds as well as in any other financial asset. SWFs may also invest in non-financial assets, such as real estate. Possible limitations on the eligible asset classes may be imposed by the legal framework governing the operations of the SWF which is laid down in the legislation of the home State.

Although in recent times a few SWFs have purchased relevant stakes in big companies (which aroused particular interest in the media), in actual fact the large majority of SWFs operations overseas still consists of portfolio (also defined as 'financial') investments.[23] Only a small proportion of the value of the assets under the management of SWFs (an estimated $125 billion) is in the form of foreign direct investments (FDIs).[24] The fact that in the last few years there has been a rise of FDI by SWFs, with a particular activism of SWFs from Libya (until 2011) and the United Arab Emirates,[25] is unlikely significantly to change the proportion of direct and portfolio investments.

19 This is the case of the SWFs established, for instance, by Kuwait, Korea, Qatar and United Arab Emirates (Abu Dhabi Investment Authority, ADIA).

20 SWFs belonging to this category are, for instance, Singapore's Temasek Fund, the Government of Singapore Investment Corporation (GIC) and China Investment Corporation (CIC).

21 This occurs, for instance, in Botswana, Canada (Alberta), Chile and Norway.

22 Data provided by the SWF Institute at the webpage: www.swfinstitute.org/fund-rankings.

23 Portfolio investments, as distinct from direct investments, are those that do not entail the acquisition of control of the target company. It is difficult to assess *in abstracto* the percentage of capital of the target companies to be purchased in order to give control of a company. In actual fact, this also depends on the level of concentration of the shareholding: for instance, in the case of companies with very widespread shareholdings, even ownership of only 5 per cent of the capital may be sufficient to entitle the shareholder to appoint a relevant number of members of the board of directors and to provide it with substantial control over the company. The municipal law of recipient states establishes when acquiring a stake in a company amounts to controlling it. According to statistics of many states and international organizations (including the IMF and UNCTAD) owning more than 10 per cent of the equity amounts to control of the company. As a result, a FDI occurs when more than 10 per cent of the capital of a company is acquired.

24 UNCTAD (2012), 13–16.

25 On the ongoing change of investment strategies of SWFs towards a greater involvement in FDIs see Bassan (2010), 166–7.

Looking at SWFs' acquisition of holdings in foreign firms from 1995 to 2007, 37 per cent of the total transaction volume has been related to North American enterprises and 32 per cent to European-based firms.[26] As regard the industries that are the targets of SWFs' investments, the financial and banking sectors are undeniably the main recipients of SWF capital. In the US other sectors are practically neglected, while in Europe investments have been more diversified, involving services, retailing, industry, commodities, energy and also real estate. Investments in the defence sectors, which are likely to raise particular concern, have played an insignificant role.[27]

4. The macroeconomic functions of SWFs and the political dimension of their investments

SWFs are first of all created in order to perform macroeconomic functions in the home State and for its benefit.

For the purposes of this analysis it can be useful to distinguish between commodity funds, financed by the proceeds from the exploitation of domestic (in most cases exhaustible) natural resources, and non-commodity funds. The latter may be divided into 'forex' funds, financed by big trade-balance surpluses, and fiscal funds, fed by surpluses deriving, for instance, from massive privatizations.[28]

Commodity SWFs may serve the purposes of saving funds and/or of stabilization funds. Saving funds are created to ensure intergenerational savings, i.e. to make sure that future generations of one State may enjoy a proper level of wealth even when the natural resources of that State are depleted. Stabilization funds allow States whose economy is highly dependent on the exploitation of natural resources to set aside in a fund a part of the wealth obtained from the sale of such resources in times when commodity prices are high. Conversely, when commodity prices fall, the State will be able to draw money from the fund. In this way the

26 Kern (2008), 7. On the investments of SWFs in western economies see also Cooke (2009), 732–4; Pasca di Magliano (2009), 70–3. However, it should be pointed out that since 2009 many SWFs have increased the share of their investments in Asia and in emerging markets. For an in-depth discussion of this development see: Barbary, Bortolotti, Fotak and Miracky (2010), 12–15.

27 For a description of the investments of SWFs see, for instance: Kern (2008), 9–12; Siniscalco (2008), 75–86; UNCTAD (2008), 23–4.

28 Funds established as a result of privatizations are a minority and they will not be discussed further in the present contribution.

government budget is protected against sudden shocks of international commodity prices.[29]

Another important category of SWFs is constituted by forex SWFs.[30] They are financed by the reserves of foreign currency held by a State (or, *rectius*, by its central bank), which in turn are often the result of large balance-of-trade surpluses not obtained by the sale of commodities. When reserves of foreign currency exceed a certain threshold, it may be convenient for a central bank to transfer part of them to a SWF, which will invest them according to strategies that are usually different from those traditionally pursued by central banks.[31]

The explanation of the rationale underlying the creation of SWFs allows one to understand that SWFs are set up with a view to pursuing macroeconomic goals, i.e. goals related to the proper management of the revenues obtained from the exploitation of domestic natural resources and to the management of foreign exchange reserves. These undeniably represent public functions. Therefore, when it is argued that SWFs are politically driven, this is of course true if it is meant in the sense that the investments of SWFs must be carried out in a way to pursue macroeconomic and public-policy goals in the countries that have created them. Nevertheless, if these are the political goals SWFs may be interested to achieve when investing abroad, there is no evidence that this may *per se* represent a threat to the national security of the host States.

On the other hand, it cannot be forgotten that States, by means of the investments their SWFs make abroad, might try to pursue other political goals that may instead threaten the national security of the host State. As has been described in the previous section, the main potential threats are related to the possibility that SWFs may seize control of domestic strategic firms or that they invest in the defence or in dual-use technology sectors, in order to have access to foreign military technology and perhaps to secret information related to national security.

However, these worries need to be partially reconsidered. Investments in the military sector are always very small and, in any case, the defence

29 On the functions of commodity SWFs and on the rationale underlying their creation see: Barbieri (2009), 22–8; Griffith-Jones and Ocampo (2008), 8–10; Johnson-Calari (2007); 47–70; Santiso (2008), 6; Summers (2007), 15–28; Wälde (2004), 130–50.

30 The term 'forex', which is adopted in the present contribution, is an abbreviation of foreign exchange and is used, for instance, by Goldstein and Subacchi (2008), 56.

31 On the economics of the creation of forex SWFs see: Beck and Fidora (2008); Butt, Shivdasani, Stendevad and Wyman (2008), 73–83; Gomes (2008), 35–54; Hildebrand (2007), 29–45; Kern (2007), 2; Kern and Reisen (2008), 3; Reisen (2008), 26–8; Subacchi (2007); Summers (2007), 15–28.

sector is already well protected from foreign investors, irrespective of whether they are State or non-State actors. With respect to the fears that strategic firms might fall under the control of foreign governments ready to use them to pursue undue political advantages, a preliminary objection can be made: up to now SWFs have made mainly portfolio investments, which implies that they are not interested in acquiring direct control over foreign companies (and especially of those based in developed countries).

In the current economic crisis, States and companies are often looking for capital and SWFs are able to provide it. Also for this reason, the attitude of most States towards SWFs has changed in the last few years and the investments of SWFs are increasingly welcomed. It is broadly held that the most suitable approach is to admit the investments of SWFs and to adopt measures that might ensure that when they pursue political goals (which, as has been seen above, is inevitable, at least if we consider their macroeconomic functions) this does not result in a threat for the host State.[32]

In any case, it is necessary that measures host States adopt to protect their national security are not inconsistent with the principles of international law provisions for the protection of foreign investments.

5. The applicability of BITs to SWFs

Today, the majority of the international rules on the protection of foreign investments are provided for in BITs.[33] For the purpose of studying whether BITs may limit the discretion of host States in adopting measures aimed at protecting their national security from possible threats posed by the operations of foreign SWFs, it is first necessary to discuss whether BITs may apply, in general, to SWFs. In fact, were the BITs simply not applicable to SWFs, these international instruments would not affect the ability of the host States to adopt measures that aim at protecting their national security and that may limit the rights to which foreign SWFs would have been otherwise entitled as covered foreign investors under BITs.[34]

32 See, *supra*, fn 8.

33 Other international instruments contain provisions governing transnational investments. It is the case, for instance, of treaties establishing economic partnerships or areas of economic integration including free trade areas and customs unions. Nevertheless, in the present contribution, the focus will be on BITs only.

34 The issue of the applicability of BITs to SWFs, and in particular of whether SWFs may be regarded as covered investors under BITs has been analysed more in depth in a previous article of mine. See Barbieri (2011), 735–66.

It is clearly impossible in the present contribution to review all the definitions of 'investor' in every existing BIT.[35]

Some BITs explicitly cover investments made by State entities and State funds of the contracting parties and, in some cases, by the contracting States themselves. Under these BITs, SWFs are to be regarded as covered investors irrespective of whether they are established as government agencies, public entities with separate legal personality or State-owned corporations.

The BIT between the United Kingdom and the United Arab Emirates, signed in Dubai on 8 December 1992 and entered into force in 1994, provides a good example of this category of BITs. Art. 1(e) defines as investor 'any national or company of one of the Contracting parties *or the Government of one of the Contracting Parties, or the Government of any of the Emirates of the United Arab Emirates*' (emphasis added). In addition, it specifies at Art. 1(d)(ii) that the word 'companies', in respect of the United Arab Emirates, shall mean: 'any entity established in accordance with and recognised as a juridical person by the law of the State, such as public and private companies, corporations, business associations, authorities, partnerships, foundations, firms, institutions, establishments, agencies, *development funds*' (emphasis added).

Likewise, the BIT between the United Arab Emirates and Italy, signed in 1995, at Art. 1(2) defines investors as 'il governo di una Parte Contraente ovvero qualsiasi persona fisica o giuridica di una Parte Contraente che effettui investimenti nel territorio dell'altra Parte Contraente'. BITs concluded by Saudi Arabia are even more explicit in including SWFs in the concept of covered investor. For instance, the BIT concluded with Switzerland in 2006 provides at Art. 1(3)(a) that, with respect to Saudi Arabia, the term investor shall mean 'toute entité, avec ou sans personnalité juridique, constituée conformément aux lois du Royaume d'Arabie saoudite et ayant son siège social sur le territoire de celui-ci, telles les sociétés de capitaux, les entreprises, les coopératives, les sociétés, les sociétés de personnes, les établissements, les fonds, les organisations, les associations économiques et entités similaires, que leur responsabilité soit limitée ou non' as well as 'le Gouvernement du Royaume d'Arabie saoudite et ses institutions financières, telles que l'Agence monétaire

For a more general introduction on the concept of investor in BITs see: Sacerdoti (1997), 310–15; Schlemmer (2008), 49–88; UNCTAD (2004), 126–31; UNCTAD (2011), 72–98.

35 A broader review of the BITs which includes SWFs in their scope has been carried out by En Low (2012).

saoudienne (Saudi Arabian Monetary Agency), les fonds publics et autres institutions gouvernementales similaires'.

Other BITs may raise more difficulties of interpretation. In fact they do not refer to States and State entities but only to legal entities established in one of the contracting parties in conformity with its law. However, this concept could be construed in a way to include legal entities owned by States but subjected to corporate law, legal entities governed by public law, and, to a certain extent, also funds which have no separate legal personality but which are owned and managed by other State entities (including the government or the central bank) or State instrumentalities.

For instance, Art. 1(1) of the BIT between Russia and Switzerland provides that

> Le terme 'investisseur' désigne, en ce qui concerne chaque Partie Contractante, … (b) les *entités juridiques*, y compris les sociétés, les sociétés enregistrées, les entreprises, les sociétés de personnes *et autres organisations*, qui sont organisées conformément à la législation de cette Partie Contractante et qui ont leur siège, en même temps que des activités économiques réelles, sur le territoire de cette même Partie Contractante [emphasis added].

The broad formulation of the term 'investor', which is far from being limited to companies, should therefore be construed so as to include the two Russian Funds although they cannot be regarded as companies separate from the Ministry of Finance of the Russian Federation.

The BIT between Italy and China of 1985 does not raise particular uncertainties since at Art. 2(3) it defines 'investor' as: 'residente o società di ciascuna delle parti contraenti che effettua investimenti nel territorio dell'altra Parte Contraente' and adds, at par. 5 that: 'Il termine "società" indica ogni persona giuridica costituita nel territorio di ciascuna Parte Contraente in conformità con le sue leggi e regolamenti ed avente la sua sede entro il suo territorio.' Therefore, in such Chinese BITs it seems that any legal entity incorporated in China and having its seat therein must be regarded as a covered investor. In addition, the fact that the CIC, the main Chinese SWF, has been established as a corporation with its own legal personality and mainly governed by company law, ensures that it is a covered investor under the BIT in question.

It may be concluded that, in most cases, SWFs should not be excluded from the notion of covered investors to be found in BITs. This implies that, in principle, the substantive provisions of BITs concerning the treatment of foreign investors shall apply also to SWFs.

However, it must be underlined that most BITs do not provide for an obligation to admit foreign investments, but only to afford them certain standards of treatment and certain forms of protection in the post-entry phase.[36] Therefore, a State that considers that its national security may be impaired by an investment of a SWF may simply refuse to admit it, without this might entail a breach of the applicable BIT.

Only a minority of BITs provide for an obligation upon contracting parties to admit foreign investments,[37] but even in this case the BITs in question allow the host State to refuse certain categories of investments or of investors.[38] As a result, the ability of host States to restrict the investments of SWFs in order to protect their own national security may be limited by BITs only in relation to measures States apply to those investments of foreign SWFs that have already been admitted.

For these reasons, in most cases it is not necessary to assess the consistency with applicable BITs of the screening mechanisms which have been examined *supra* in Section 1. In fact, such screening mechanisms (with the partial exception of the one put in place in Germany) apply before the admission of the foreign investment. BITs will therefore apply mainly to those measures of host States that affect the investments of foreign investors after they have been admitted.

6. MFN and NT clauses as possible limitations to host States' measures to protect national security

After having concluded that SWFs are covered investors under the majority of existing BITs, it is useful to investigate whether the substantive provisions of such international instruments may be interpreted in a way that

36 Gomez Palacio and Muchlinski (2008), 240–2; Sacerdoti (1997), 328.

37 As is the case of several BITs concluded by the US and by Canada. For instance, the BIT between the US and Kazakhstan provides, at Art. 2.1, that 'Each Party shall permit and treat investment, and activities associated therewith, on a basis no less favorable than that accorded in like situations to investment or associated activities of its own nationals or companies, or of nationals or companies of any third country, whichever is the most favourable'. Likewise, the BIT between the US and Azerbaijan provides at Art. 2.1 that:

> With respect to the establishment, acquisition, expansion, management, conduct, operation and sale or other disposition of covered investments, each Party shall accord treatment no less favorable than that it accords, in like situations, to investments in its territory of its own nationals or companies (hereinafter 'national treatment') or to investments in its territory of nationals or companies of a third country (hereinafter 'most favored nation treatment'), whichever is most favorable (hereinafter 'national and most favored nation treatment').

38 For instance, Art. 2.1 of the US–Kazakhstan BIT specifies that the national treatment and the MFN treatment apply to foreign investors in the pre-entry phase but 'subject to the right of each Party to make or maintain exceptions falling within one of the sectors or matters listed in the Annex to this Treaty'. For a more in depth analysis of these issues see: Gomez Palacio and Muchlinski (2008), 242–3; Muchlinski (2008–9), 40.

leaves a certain margin of manoeuvre to host States to adopt measures that aim at safeguarding their national security and may even impair the investments of foreign SWFs after their admission. The BIT clauses which will be taken into consideration in the present contribution are those on the most favoured nation treatment (MFN), on the national treatment (NT) and on the fair and equitable treatment (FET). In this respect the question whether measures taken only against SWFs would be admissible under these provisions will be analysed.

Both the MFN and the NT clauses aim at preventing discriminatory measures adopted by the host States against the investors of the other contracting party. Broadly speaking, under the MFN clause investors from the other contracting party are to be treated at least as favourably as any investor from any third country in like circumstances. Likewise, the NT clause provides that investors from the other contracting party are to be treated at least as favourably as any investor who is a national of the host State in like circumstances.[39]

When assessing the existence of discrimination, it is indispensable to verify whether two investors are in a similar or comparable situation and then whether they are treated differently. Clearly no discrimination exists when different treatments are accorded to investors in different situations.[40]

Therefore, the key issue that allows one to shed more light on the applicability of the NT and the MFN clause to SWFs is whether an investment made by a SWF can, by its nature, be regarded as comparable or similar to an investment made by a domestic or a third-country investor that is not a SWF.

In an attempt to address this issue, two approaches are in principle available. If the focus is on the functions SWFs perform in the countries to which they belong, then it must be argued that their investments overseas cannot be regarded as similar or comparable to those of any other non-sovereign investor. In fact, as has been pointed out in Section 3, SWFs pursue macroeconomic and political goals and this makes them radically different from other investors. In this case the

39 For a more in-depth discussion of the MFN and of the NT clauses in BITs see: DiMascio and Pauwelyn (2008), 48–89; Muchlinski (2007), 621–5; Ortino (2008), 346–8.

40 Acconci (2008), 365; Grierson-Weiler and Laird (2008), 262; UNCTAD (1999), 28; Valenti (2009a), 139–41. This concept is expressed very well in several arbitral awards. See, in particular: *Antoine Goetz and others* v. *Republic of Burundi* ICSID Case No. ARB 95/3, Award, 10 February 1999, 121; *Parkerings-Compagniet AS* v. *Republic of Lithuania* ICSID Case No. ARB/05/8, Award, 11 September 2007, 290; *Saluka Investments BV (The Netherlands)* v. *The Czech Republic*, UNCITRAL, Award, 17 March 2006, 307.

host State would be virtually free to adopt any measure it deems necessary to protect its national security from possible threats posed by foreign SWFs without this amounting to a breach of the MFN and NT clauses.

On the other hand, if the focus is on the kind of operations SWFs undertake overseas, which consist of financial investments whose aim is also the maximization of risk-adjusted returns, then SWFs are comparable to any other institutional investor that mainly makes portfolio investments. In this case the host State, when it adopts measures aiming at protecting its national security from possible threats posed by foreign SWFs, is obliged to abide by the MFN and NT clauses contained in BITs. Only when the host State is able to prove that the financial investments made by the foreign SWFs do not aim at pursuing economic objectives, but aim at allowing the States to which the SWFs belong to exert undue political and strategic influence on the recipient country, then such investments could not be regarded as comparable to those made by other portfolio investors. In this case, and only in this case, measures aiming at protecting the national security of the host State should not amount to a breach of the MFN and NT clause, because these clauses would not be applicable for the reasons stated above.

This second approach seems to be more consistent with the nature and the purpose of the MFN and NT clauses. If States mean always to exclude the investments of SWFs from the application of such clauses, they should express such intention by including a specific exclusion in the wording of BITs. Lacking such an exclusion, and since BITs and their provisions apply to SWFs and their investments, then also the MFN and NT clauses should in principle apply to SWFs. If the host State adopts measures that aim at protecting its national security and entail discrimination against a SWF from the other contracting party, it does not violate the MFN or NT clauses only insofar as it is able to prove that the objective of the investments carried out by that SWF is not the maximization of financial return but the pursuit of undue political influence.[41]

7. The interpretation of the FET clause in a way to ensure the protection of the national security of the host State

Another provision of substantive law which is contained in BITs and which is related to the standards of treatment that the host State is required to

41 For the concept of undue political influence, which may be exercised also by controlling strategic sectors or by becoming able to affect the economic and political decisions of host States see, *supra*, the analysis developed in Section 2.

accord to foreign investors consists in the fair and equitable treatment (FET) clause.

In brief, a breach of the FET may occur when the host State acts vis-à-vis the investor in bad faith or in an unpredictable, inconsistent or non-transparent way, or if it abuses its right to regulate its domestic affairs with the actual objective of impairing the activities of the foreign investor and when this conduct entails a relevant loss for the investor.[42]

In addition, if the host State through its actions induces the investor legitimately to expect it will be accorded a certain treatment and if later such legitimate expectations are frustrated, this provides further evidence of a violation of the FET.[43]

According to recent developments in international arbitration, when assessing the existence of a breach of the FET, it is necessary to consider not only the conduct of the host State, but also that of the investor. For this purpose, the fair and equitable treatment should be interpreted in a way in which 'equity' is conceived as a counterweight to 'fairness', thus allowing one to assess the conduct of the host State not in absolute terms, but also considering whether it could be regarded as a necessary and legitimate response to the conduct of the investor. According to this approach 'fair' means consistent with the domestic law of the host State which in turn must be consistent with BITs and other applicable sources

42 For a more detailed discussion of the content of the fair and equitable treatment clause see for instance: Ben Hamida (2004), 419–42; Ben Hamida (2008), 999–1034; Fietta (2006), 375–400; Francioni (2009), 729–47; Grierson-Weiler and Laird (2008), 272–90; Knoll-Tudor (2009), 310–43; Krommendijk and Morijn (2009), 422–50; Muchlinski (2006), 527–57; Valenti (2004), 973–90; Valenti (2009a), 183–211; Van Harten and Loughlin (2006), 121–50.

Among the arbitral decisions which provide useful elements for the analysis of the content of the fair and equitable treatment clause and supporting the finding of the present section see, for instance: *Técnicas Medioambientales Tecmed, S.A.* v. *United Mexican States* ICSID Case No. ARB(AF)/00/2, Award, 29 May 2003, 152–74; *Metalclad Corporation* v. *The United Mexican State* ICSID Case No. ARB(AF)/97/1, Award, 30 August 2000, 99; *Occidental Exploration and production company* v. *Ecuador* London Court of International Arbitration, Award, 1 July 2004, 183–5.

43 For the notion of legitimate expectations and transparency see: Ben Hamida (2008), 999–1034; Fietta (2006), 375–400; Gotanda (2003), 1348–80, Kotera (2008), 617–36; Mairal (2010), 413–52; Parisi (2005), 383–426; Reinisch (2008), 432–58. Several arbitral decisions discussed the role of legitimate expectations of the investors and/or of transparency in order to assess whether a breach of the fair and equitable treatment clause has occurred. See, for instance, the following cases: *Continental Casualty Company* v. *Argentine Republic* ICSID Case No. ARB/03/9, Award, 5 September 2008, 257–62; *Tecmed*, 122 and 149–74; *Waste Management, Inc.* v. *United Mexican States* ICSID Case No. ARB(AF)/00/3, Award, 30 April 2004, 159; *Azurix Corp.* v. *The Argentine Republic* ICSID Case No. ARB/01/12, Award, 14 July 2006, 316–23.

of international law. 'Equitable' would mean that all the interests at stake, both those of the investors and of the host State, must be adequately taken into consideration, together with all relevant circumstances that are specific to the case at issue.[44] This interpretation of the concept of fair and equitable treatment has two implications.

The first implication is that the concept of legitimate expectations must not be understood as an absolute concept, but rather in relative terms and more precisely in relation to the situation of the host State. If an investor has unrealistic and unreasonable expectations regarding the business environment of the host State or if it unconsciously and unjustifiably expects it will receive certain favourable treatment, then it cannot claim that the host State should have not frustrated its expectations, since such expectations were neither reasonable nor legitimate.[45] In this case the investor would hardly be able to successfully claim that it has not been accorded fair and equitable treatment.

Based on this interpretation, if a SWF decides to invest in a country in which transactions carried out by State-owned entities are traditionally not welcomed and are subject to unfavourable treatment, then, when it is affected by certain measures of the host State measures, it cannot claim that its legitimate expectations have been frustrated, as it should have been aware of the hostility reserved in the recipient State to investments made by SWFs. To give proof of its good faith the foreign SWF should have at least tried to seek some assurances from the relevant authorities of the recipient State, for instance by entering into special kinds of agreements with that State.[46]

The second important implication is that, if the conduct of a State that adversely affects the activity of the investor is a consequence of some previous illegal or harmful conduct on the part of the investor itself, in this

44 Ben Hamida (2008), 999–1034; Carreau and Juillard (2007), 463–6; Muchlinski (2006), 527–57; Valenti (2009a), 185–211; Valenti (2009b), 83–94. Among ICSID arbitral decisions that deal with these issues and that deserve to be quoted we would draw attention to: *Alex Genin and others* v. *Republic of Estonia* ICSID Case No. ARB/99/2, Award, 25 June 2001, 352–63; *International Thunderbird Gaming Corporation* v. *The United Mexican States*, UNCITRAL, Award, 26 January 2006, 148–66; *Saluka* (fn 40), 297–306; *Parkerings* (fn 40), 320–46.

45 Muchlinski (2006), 542–7.

46 In the US, for instance, such a possibility is granted to foreign investors, including SWFs, by means of the conclusion of a 'mitigation agreement'. For more information on these issues see, for instance: Cooke (2009), 729–82; Feng (2009), 501–7; Gutlin (2010),765–80; Hsu (2009), 451–77 and in particular 455–6; Sud (2006), 1304–31; Wong (2009), 1088–90.

case the latter cannot claim that the State measure in question amounts to a violation of the FET clause.[47]

This allows one to consider as compatible with the FET clause any measure adopted by the host State in order to tackle the effects of the conduct of a foreign SWF whenever the latter means to use its investments in order to pursue political objectives in a way detrimental to the interests of the host State. Therefore, in a hypothetical dispute between a foreign SWF and the host State concerning the alleged violation of the FET clause, the host State could claim that the measure it has adopted, although it may damage the foreign SWF, does not represent a breach of the applicable BIT since it constitutes an appropriate response to the conduct of the SWF itself.

On the other hand, if the host State is left free to determine when the conduct of the foreign SWF allows it to adopt restrictive measures which are, however, consistent with the FET clause, then the host State would enjoy an excessive discretion that might well lead to an arbitrary result. This would ultimately result in depriving the fair and equitable clause of its utility. For this reason, it would be desirable to develop mutually agreed and predictable criteria concerning the conduct of SWFs. If a SWF fails to respect such standards, then there would be a presumption that it is behaving in a way that could in turn justify the host State's adopting measures that would have been otherwise inconsistent with the FET clause.

As indicated above, in 2008 an important document, the so-called 'Santiago Principles', has been adopted with regard to the way SWFs should be managed and the way they should carry out their investments overseas. It must be underlined that the Santiago Principles are not legally binding and, although their adoption has been supported by the IMF, they have been drafted and approved by the SWFs themselves or by their home States. The Santiago Principles represent a collection of best practices that the same SWFs have already implemented, or desire to implement, on a voluntary basis. Notwithstanding this caveat, the Santiago Principles could be used as a benchmark against which to assess whether a SWF is acting fairly for the purposes of interpreting and applying the FET clause.

A full discussion of the content of the Santiago Principles would clearly fall outside the scope of the present research. However, it should be stressed that according to the Santiago Principles, the governance

47 On this point see, *inter alia*, Muchlinski (2006), 540–3.

framework, organization and investment strategies of SWFs should be clear and transparent, to the advantage of both the SWFs' home States and the recipient States. The relations between the SWFs and their home governments as well as the degree of independence of the management should be specified. SWFs should disclose their investment strategies, in particular if they use leverage or financial derivatives and in which way they do so. Moreover they should disclose the extent to which their decisions are subject to other than financial or economic considerations. They should refrain from taking advantage of privileged information or the inappropriate influence they might have in relation to their particular status in competing with private firms. From this very brief review of the Santiago Principles, it emerges that they do not lay down detailed rules on the way SWFs should be established and organized, nor do they provide which investment strategies they should pursue. Nevertheless, they emphasize the fact that SWFs should be transparent and that they should not try to exert undue political influence over the States where they invest.[48]

The notion of undue political influence that SWFs should refrain from exerting is not specified in detail in the Santiago Principles. Further elements, which nonetheless are far from exhaustive, could be obtained from a more in-depth analysis of the related commentaries. For instance, when Principle 2 provides that 'the policy purpose of the SWF should be clearly defined and publicly disclosed', the related commentary underlines that 'a clearly defined policy purpose will also ensure that the operational management of the SWF will conduct itself professionally and ensure that the SWF undertakes investments *without any intention or obligation to fulfill, directly or indirectly, any geopolitical agenda of the government*' (emphasis added). Likewise, the commentary to Principle 6, which concerns the governance framework of SWFs, again stresses the importance that investment 'decisions and operations [of SWFs] are based on economic and financial considerations consistent with its investment policy and objectives, in effect free of political influence or interference'. This concept is repeated in the commentary to Principle 16, where it is stressed that SWF investments should be 'based on economic and financial considerations'.

The conduct of a SWF resulting in a failure to respect the Santiago Principles cannot amount to a breach of a legal obligation. However, to

48 IMF (2008); International Working Group for Sovereign Wealth Funds (2008a), 3; Audit (2008); Kern (2008), 18.

the extent the Santiago Principles contain standards whose validity and desirability is supported *in primis* by the SWFs themselves, then the degree of compliance with them may constitute a benchmark against which to assess the conduct of the SWFs.

If the conduct of SWFs is not consistent with the Santiago Principles, this could bring host States reasonably to consider that the SWFs are behaving in a way that may justify the adoption of special measures against possible threats posed by the SWFs themselves. In other words, State measures adopted to offset the possible adverse effects of the investments of foreign SWFs on their national security should not be regarded as unfair even if they adversely affect the SWFs in question and their investments. In conclusion, the failure of SWFs to comply with the standards laid down in the Santiago Principles would give rise to a presumption that measures adopted by the host State as a response to the conduct of SWFs do not constitute a violation of the FET clause.

8. The applicability of the national security clause

A certain number of BITs contain a national security clause, which may allow host States to adopt measures necessary to protect their national security and which, being inconsistent with the other provisions of BITs, would be otherwise prohibited.

Invocation of the national security clause would be particularly appropriate when threats to the national security of the host States do not arise as a result of some specific conduct of the foreign SWF or in relation to the particular nature of these State-owned investment vehicles. In fact, as has been explained in Sections 5 and 6 of the present contribution, when State measures adversely affecting the foreign SWFs are adopted in order legitimately to discriminate between non-sovereign and sovereign investors (because of their non-comparable situation in the case in question), or as a proper response in case of illegal or harmful conduct on the part of SWFs, then these measures would not be regarded as inconsistent with the MFN, NT and FET clauses. Therefore, if no breach of such clauses occurs, no need to invoke the national security clause will rise to justify the conduct of the host State.

On the other hand, the national security clause is more likely to be invoked when circumstances threatening the national security of the host State and which are independent from SWFs require the adoption of domestic measures that adversely affect the foreign SWFs and are inconsistent with the provisions of the applicable BITs. For the purposes of the present discussion, a quick analysis of the main features of the national security clause is necessary.

Some BITs contain clauses providing for the derogation of all[49] or some[50] of their provisions when it proves necessary for the host State in order to protect its national security.

Many BITs fail to clarify what 'national security' means, while more details defining this concept may be found in other international instruments containing also, but not exclusively, provisions governing transnational investments between contracting parties, such as economic integration or economic cooperation agreements.[51] According to the wording of these international instruments, national security exceptions are mainly intended as pertaining to the military and security sphere. The application of these clauses allows one to consider lawful those host-State measures which, although inconsistent with other provisions contained in the international instruments in question, are nonetheless necessary to limit and control trade and investments in the military and in the dual-sector industry, to prevent nuclear proliferation, or which are adopted in case of war or serious internal disturbances involving the host State, or in order to comply with actions undertaken by a competent international organization with a view to maintaining international peace and security (as in the case, for instance, of host-State measures adopted in order to implement sanctions against a State adopted by the UN Security Council).[52]

49 For instance, Art. 2.3 of the BIT between Hungary and the Russian Federation provides that it 'shall not preclude the application of either Contracting Party of measures, necessary for the maintenance of defence, national security and public order, protection of the environment, morality and public health'.

50 Art. 4.4 of the BIT between Kuwait and Lithuania provides that 'measures that have to be taken for reasons of public security and order, public health or morality shall not be deemed "treatment less favourable" within the meaning of this Article'. The peculiarity of such provision is that the national security exception seems to apply not to all the provisions of the BIT, but only in relation to the non-discrimination clauses.

51 UNCTAD (2009), 85.

52 An example of detailed national security clause contained in an IIA is represented by Art. 2102 of the NAFTA, providing that "none of its provisions shall be construed:

> b) to prevent any Party from taking any actions that it considers necessary for the protection of its essential security interests (i) relating to the traffic in arms, ammunition and implements of war and to such traffic and transactions in other goods, materials, services and technology undertaken directly or indirectly for the purpose of supplying a military or other security establishment, (ii) taken in time of war or other emergency in international relations, or (iii) relating to the implementation of national policies or international agreements respecting the non proliferation of nuclear weapons or other nuclear explosive devices; or (c) to prevent any Party from taking action in pursuance of its obligations under the United Nations Charter for the maintenance of international peace and security."

National security exceptions, especially when they are not interpreted in a narrow sense, can provide a powerful tool in the hands of the host State to avoid compliance with the provisions of the BITs. In order to minimize the risk of this kind of abuse, the same text of BITs could contain some additional requirements that the host State must fulfil in order to claim a security-related exception. One requirement is that measures adopted in order to protect national security exceptions must not be arbitrary or constitute an unjustifiable discrimination.[53] The requirement that measures

The Closer Economic Partnership Agreement between New Zealand and Singapore of 2000 provides further insight into the concept of national security and the measures that may be lawfully adopted to protect it. Its Art. 76 in fact provides that:

> "Nothing in this Agreement shall be construed: (a) as preventing either Party from taking any action which it considers necessary for the protection of its essential security interests, including but not limited to action relating to traffic in arms, ammunition and implements of war and to such traffic in other goods and materials as is carried on directly or indirectly for the purpose of supplying a military establishment, and any action taken in time of war or other emergency in domestic or international relations."

According to Art. 193 of the Economic Partnership Agreement between Chile and Japan of 2007, national security implies the adoption of measures

> "(i) relating to the traffic in arms, ammunition and implements of war and to such traffic in other goods and materials, or such supply of services, as is carried on directly or indirectly for the purpose of supplying or provisioning a military establishment; (ii) taken in time of war or other emergency in international relations; or (iii) relating to fissionable and fusionable materials or the materials from which they are derived."

Another IIA provisions which deserves to be quoted is Art. 6.12 of the Economic Cooperation Agreement between India and Singapore of 2005. It reads as follows:

> "Nothing in this Chapter shall be construed:
> (a) to require a Party to furnish any information, the disclosure of which it considers contrary to its essential security interests; or
> (b) to prevent a Party from taking any action which it considers necessary for the protection of its essential security interests
> (i) relating to fissionable and fusionable materials or the materials from which they are derived;
> (ii) in time of war or other emergency in international relations;
> (iii) relating to the production or supply of arms and ammunition; or
> (iv) to protect critical public infrastructures, including communication, power and water infrastructures, from deliberate attempts intended to disable or degrade such infrastructures; or
> (c) to prevent a Party from taking any action in pursuance of its obligations under the United Nations Charter for the maintenance of international peace and security."

For a general discussion on these issues see UNCTAD (2009), 85–9.

53 For an example of IIA providing for such a requirement see, for instance, Art. 99 of the Economic Partnership Agreement between Japan and the Philippines of 2006. It

for the protection of national security be not adopted in an arbitrary way is set out in detail in other BITs, when they clarify that such measures must be adopted in accordance with the domestic laws of the host States.[54] In addition, it could be required that national security exceptions be not used as disguised restrictions on international investments.[55]

National security clauses may be self-judging or not self-judging. In the first case, they would in principle allow the host State to autonomously and at its discretion judge what is necessary for the protection of its national security. Therefore, in principle, the only condition for the invocation of the self-judging national security exception is that the contracting party concerned considers the measure in question 'necessary', thus excluding any kind of review by arbitral tribunals or other dispute settlement bodies on this issue. On the other hand if the clause is not self-judging, the host State cannot decide on its own if the measure adopted is necessary for the protection of its national security. Non-self-judging clauses provide arbitral tribunals, or other organisms in charge of settling investor–State disputes, with a greater power in assessing whether State measures are actually adopted in a view to protecting national security. Non-self-judging clauses clearly provide a higher degree of stability and protection for investors, since they reduce the risk of an abusive application of the national security clause by the host State. On the other hand, they entrust a body such as an arbitral tribunal with the task of deciding what is necessary for the protection of the national security of the host State. This means that a tribunal which in principle is empowered to apply international law and therefore to have primary expertise in this field, is de facto required to undertake an in-depth political, economic and social analysis of the situation of the host State. Arbitrators would be given the definitive power to assess what constitutes 'national security' for the host State, which events or situations might pose a threat to it, and which State measures are appropriate and proportionate to the purpose of protecting

provides that "measures adopted for the protection of national security are lawful: '[s]ubject to the requirement that such measures are not applied in a manner which would constitute a means of arbitrary or unjustifiable discrimination against the other Party, or a disguised restriction on investments of investors of the other Party in the Area of a Party'". For a more general discussion see UNCTAD (2009), 81.

54 For instance, Art. 12 of the BIT of 2003 between Hungary and India provides that 'nothing in this Agreement precludes the host Contracting Party from taking action for the protection of its essential security interests or in circumstances of extreme emergency in accordance with its laws normally and reasonably applied on a non-discriminatory basis'.

55 UNCTAD (2009), 83–4.

national security. From this point of view it is difficult to believe that an arbitral tribunal could be better equipped to understand what the host State needs for its national security than the host State itself. Without going further into a discussion of the pros and cons of self-judging and non-self-judging clauses, which would fall outside the scope of the present analysis, it is necessary to explain how to distinguish between a self-judging and a non-self-judging clause. Only the former is worded so as to make it clear that it will be the host State that will be entitled to decide what it deems necessary.[56]

On the other hand, non-self-judging clauses do not specify who is empowered to decide what is necessary for the protection of national security.[57] In these cases, it will be the arbitral tribunal, in the case of dispute, to interpret and apply the provision and, as a result, to decide if a measure adopted by one of the contracting parties is really necessary in order to protect its national security.

Therefore, when a BIT fails to specify the exact extent of the concept of national security, it will be the task of the arbitral tribunal to do so, especially in the case of non-self-judging clauses.

9. Conclusions

This contribution has pointed out that, since SWFs are created to pursue macroeconomic (i.e. public and governmental) functions in the home States, from this point of view they may be regarded as politically driven. If

56 For instance, Art. 14 of the BIT concluded between the US and Bahrain provides that: 'This treaty shall not preclude a Party from applying measures which it considers necessary for the fulfilment of its obligations with respect to the maintenance or restoration of international peace or security, or the protection of its own essential security interests.' For a comment, see: Bjorklund (2008–9), 498–500; UNCTAD (2009), 49–55. It must be noted that the US model BIT of 2012 adopts a self-judging clause. In fact, it reads as follows:

> Article 18: Essential Security: Nothing in this Treaty shall be construed: 1. to require a Party to furnish or allow access to any information the disclosure of which it determines to be contrary to its essential security interests; or 2. to preclude a Party from applying measures that it considers necessary for the fulfilment of its obligations with respect to the maintenance or restoration of international peace or security, or the protection of its own essential security interests.

57 For instance, Art. 10 of the US–Kazakhstan BIT provides that: 'This Treaty shall not preclude the application by either Party of measures necessary for the maintenance of public order, the fulfilment of its obligations with respect to the maintenance or restoration of international peace or security, or the protection of its own essential security interests.'

the political objectives they pursue are limited to the proper management of their investments in order to maximize the wealth under their control and, in turn, to ensure that the States that create them have sufficient resources to achieve their governmental functions, then SWFs should not represent a threat to the national security of the States where they invest. Such kinds of threats could rise when the investments of SWFs are politically driven in the sense that they aim at exerting undue political influence on the recipient State. Moreover, threats to national security may arise when SWFs carry out investments in sectors the recipient country considers as strategic. In this case, host States may need to adopt restrictive measures, whose consistency with international law, and in particular with applicable BITs, must nonetheless be assessed.

This contribution has explained that, under the majority of BITs, SWFs should be regarded as covered investors both when they are established as State bodies and when they are incorporated as entities with a separate legal personality from the home State (governed either by public or private law). Therefore, States that decide to adopt measures that aim at protecting their national security against possible threats posed by the investments of SWFs, must do so in a manner consistent with the applicable BITs.

It has been argued that if a State considers that investments made in its territory by a SWF threaten its national security, it is often allowed simply to refuse to admit them. In fact, the majority of BITs do not provide for obligations upon the contracting parties to admit foreign investments, but only to accord them certain standards of treatment once they have decided to admit them. In particular, it has been shown that the host State, after having agreed to admit the foreign investor, is required to accord it NT, MFN and FET treatment.

It has been explained that the NT and MFN treatment could be construed in a way to allow the host State to adopt measures that are less favourable to SWFs compared with other domestic or non-domestic investors when these SWFs, instead of carrying out investments according to financial criteria, pursue undue political objectives in the territory of the host State. In fact, when SWFs act in such a way, they are not comparable to other non-sovereign investors, and for this reason a differential (and less favourable) treatment accorded them should not be regarded as being inconsistent with the MFN and NT clauses.

The present contribution has then discussed also whether a proper interpretation of the FET clause allows the host State to adopt those measures necessary to protect its national security against possible threats that arise in relation to specific conduct on the part of foreign SWFs, including investment in strategic sectors, the pursuit of undue political goals, as well as the failure to disclose relevant information and to respect applicable law and regulations. In other words, the FET cannot be construed in a way to entitle foreign investors to prevent host States from adopting measures that constitute an adequate response to inadmissible conduct and activities undertaken by foreigners.

Finally, it has been recalled that host States in some cases may have recourse to a national security clause, which is contained in a limited number of BITs. Such clauses should be particularly relevant when SWFs, like any other investor, are adversely affected by State measures that are independent of the conduct of the investor itself. It has been pointed out that the wording of BITs seldom allows one to understand clearly and in detail the extent of the concept of national security, which, as a result, is often to be determined by those tribunals (in most cases, arbitral tribunals) responsible for settling disputes between the foreign investor and the host country.

References

Acconci, P. 2008. 'Most-Favoured Nation Treatment', Muchlinski, Ortino and Schreuer (eds.): 363–406.

Alvarez, J.E. and Khamsi, K. 2008–9. 'The Argentine Crisis and Foreign Investors: A Glimpse into the Heart of the Investment Regime'. *The Yearbook on International Investment Law & Policy*: 379–478.

Alvaro, S. and Ciccaglioni, P. 2012. 'I fondi sovrani e la regolazione degli investimenti nei settori strategici', *Discussion Paper*. Roma: CONSOB.

Ander, E.C. 2009. *Take the Money and Run: Sovereign Wealth Funds and the Demise of American Prosperity*. Westport, CT: Praeger Security International.

Anwar, S.T. 2010. 'CFIUS, Chinese MNCs' Outward FDI, and Globalization of Business'. *Journal of World Trade*: 419–66.

Audit, M. 2008. 'Is the Erecting of Barriers Against Foreign Sovereign Wealth Funds Compatible with International Investment Law?'. *Society of International Economic Law*; Working Paper No. 29/08.

Backer, L.C. 2007–8. 'The Private Law of Public Law: Public Authorities as Shareholders, Golden Shares, Sovereign Wealth Funds, and the Public Law Element in Private Choice of Law'. *Tulane Law Review*: 1801–68.

2010–11. 'Sovereign Investing in Times of Crisis: Global Regulation of Sovereign Wealth Funds, State Owned Enterprises and the Chinese Experience'. *Transnational Law and Contemporary Problems*: 5–144.

Bahgat, G. 2008. 'Sovereign Wealth Funds: Dangers and Opportunities'. *International Affairs*: 1189–204.

Barbary, V., Bortolotti, B., Fotak, V. and Miracky, W. 2010. 'Sovereign Wealth Fund Investment Behavior; Semi Annual Report; January–June 2010'. *FEEM* and *Monitor Group.*

Barbieri, M. 2009. 'Developing Countries and Their Natural Resources. From the Elaboration of the Principle of Permanent Sovereignty over Natural Resources to the Creation of Sovereign Wealth Funds'. *UNCTAD – Virtual Institute Digital Library.*

2010. 'A New Challenge for the European Union: Regulating the Investments of Sovereign Wealth Funds While Preserving the Competitiveness of the European Market', *The Improvement of the Architecture of the Economic Relations and the Enhancement of Competitiveness of Russia: Materials of the International Conference of Applied Research*, Moscow, 22 April 2009. MGIMO Press (in Russian).

2011. 'The Settlement of Disputes Between Foreign Sovereign Wealth Funds and Host States Through International Investment Arbitration'. *Diritto del Commercio Internazionale* 25: 735–66.

Bassan, F. 2010. 'Host States and Sovereign Wealth Funds, Between National Security and International Law'. *European Business Law Review* 21: 165–201.

2011. *The Law of Sovereign Wealth Funds.* Cheltenham: Edward Elgar Publishing.

Beck, R. and Fidora, M. 2008. 'The Impact of Sovereign Wealth Funds on Global Financial Markets', *Occasional Chapter Series* 91. European Central Bank.

Ben Hamida, W. 2004. 'L'arbitrage état-investisseur étranger: regards sur les traités et projets récents'. *JDI*: 419–42.

2008. 'La prise en compte de l'intérêt général et des impératifs de développement dans le droit des investissements'. *JDI*: 999–1034.

Bertoni, F. 2010. '"Stepping Stones" or "Stumbling Blocks"', Lossani, Bertoni and Chiarlone (eds.): 81–96.

Bhagwati, J. 2008. 'Sovereign Wealth Funds: Implications for Policy', Rietveld, M. (ed.), *New Perspectives in Sovereign Asset Management.* London: Central Banking Publications: 25–32.

Biard, J. 2008. 'Fonds souverains'. *Revue de Droit Bancaire et Financier*: 63.

Bjorklund, A.K. 2008–9. 'Economic Security Defenses in International Investment Law'. *The Yearbook on International Investment Law & Policy*: 479–504.

Blundell-Wignall, A., Hu, Y. and Yermo, J. 2008. 'Sovereign Wealth and Pension Funds Issues'. *Financial Market Trends:* 1–17.

Butt, S., Shivdasani, A., Stendevad, C. and Wyman, A. 2008. 'Sovereign Wealth Funds: A Growing Global Force in Corporate Finance'. *Journal of Applied Corporate Finance*: 73–83.

Carreau, D. and Juillard, P. 2007. *Droit international économique.* Paris: Dalloz.

Carroll, J.F.F. 2009. 'Back to the Future: Redefining the Foreign Investment and National Security Act's Conception of National Security'. *Emory International Law Review:* 167–98.

Chiarlone, S. 2010. 'I fondi Sovrani', Lossani, Bertoni and Chiarlone (eds.): 55–80.

Cooke, J. 2009. 'Finding the Right Balance for Sovereign Wealth Fund Regulation: Open Investment vs. National Security'. *Columbia Business Law Review*: 728–82.

Das, D.K. 2008. 'Sovereign-Wealth Funds: Assuaging the Exaggerated Anguish about the New Global Financial Players'. *Global Economy Journal*: 1–15.

DiMascio, N. and Pauwelyn, J. 2008. 'Nondiscrimination in Trade and Investment Treaties: Worlds Apart or Two Sides of the Same Coin?'. *AJIL*: 48–89.

Drezner, W. 2010. 'Il potere economico nella politica mondiale', Lossani, Bertoni and Chiarlone (eds.): 97–116.

Dupuy, P-M., Francioni, F. and Petersmann, E.U. (eds.) 2009. *Human Rights in International Investment Law and Arbitration*. Oxford University Press.

ECB. 2009. 'Foreign Asset Accumulation by Authorities in Emerging Markets'. *ECB Monthly Bulletin January 2009.*

En Low, J. 2012. 'State-Controlled Entities as "Investors" Under International Investment Agreements'. *Columbia FDI Perspectives* 80.

Feng, Z. 2009. 'How Should Sovereign Wealth Funds Be Regulated?'. *Brook. J. Corp. Fin. & Com*: 483–511.

Fietta, S. 2006. 'Expropriation and the "Fair and Equitable" Standard. The Developing Role of Investors' "Expectations" in International Investment Arbitration'. *Journal of International Arbitration*: 375–400.

Francioni, F. 2009. 'Access to Justice, Denial of Justice and International Investment Law'. *EJIL* 20: 729–47.

Goldstein, A. and Subacchi, P. 2008. 'I fondi sovrani e gli investimenti internazionali – salvatori o sovvertitori?', *L'Italia nell'economia internazionale. Rapporto ICE 2007–2008*. Roma: ICE: 55–67.

Gomes, T. 2008. 'The Impact of Sovereign Wealth Funds on International Financial Stability – Discussion Paper 2008–14'. *Discussion Paper/Document d'analyse*. Bank of Canada.

Gomez Palacio, I. and Muchlinski, P. 2008. 'Admission and Establishment', Muchlinski, Ortino and Schreuer (eds.): 227–58.

Gotanda, J.Y. 2003. 'Renegotiation and Adaptation Clauses in Investment Contract, Revisited'. *Vanderbilt Journal of Transnational Law*: 1348–80.

Grierson-Weiler, T. and Laird, I.A. 2008. 'Standards of Treatments', Muchlinski, Ortino and Schreuer (eds.): 259–304.

Griffith-Jones, S. and Ocampo, J.A. 2008. 'Sovereign Wealth Funds: A Developing Country Perspective'. Columbia University. Available at: policydialogue.org/files/events/Griffith-JonesSovereign_Wealth_Funds.pdf.

Gutlin, A. 2010. 'Regulating Sovereign Wealth Funds in the US: A Primer on SWFs and CFIUS'. *FIU Law Review*: 745–80.

Hemphill, T.A. 2009. 'Sovereign Wealth Funds: National Security Risks in a Global Free Trade Environment'. *Thunderbird International Business Review*: 551–6.

Hildebrand, P.M. 2007. 'Four Tough Questions on Foreign Reserve Management', Johnson-Calari and Rietveld (eds.): 29–45.

Hsu, L. 2009. 'SWFs, Recent US Legislative Changes and Treaty Obligations'. *Journal of World Trade*: 451–77.

IMF. 2008. *Sovereign Wealth Funds – A Work Agenda*. Washington, DC: IMF.

International Working Group for Sovereign Wealth Funds. 2008a. *Generally Accepted Principles and Practices – 'Santiago Principles'*. Available at: www.iwg-swf.org/pubs/eng/santiagoprinciples.pdf.

2008b. *Sovereign Wealth Funds – Current Institutional and Operational Practices*. Washington, DC: IMF.

Jen, S. 2007. 'The Definition of a Sovereign Wealth Fund'. Morgan Stanley. Available at: www.morganstanley.com/views/gef/archive/2007/20071026-Fri.html#anchor17065580-419f-11de-a1b3-c771ef8db296.

Johnson-Calari, J. 2007. 'Managing Commodity Revenues and Windfall Profits: Investment Income Funds', Johnson-Calari and Rietveld (eds.): 47–70.

Johnson-Calari, J. and Rietveld, M. (eds.) 2007. *Sovereign Wealth Management*. London: Central Banking Publications.

Kern, S. 2007. 'Sovereign Wealth Funds; State Investments on the Rise'. Deutsche Bank Research.

2008. 'SWF's and Foreign Investment Policies – An Update'. Deutsche Bank Research.

Kern, S. and Reisen, H. 2008. 'Commodity and Non-Commodity Sovereign Wealth Funds'. Deutsche Bank Research.

Kimmit, R.M. 2008. 'Public Footprints in Private Markets. Sovereign Wealth Funds and the World Economy'. *Foreign Affairs*: 119–30.

Knoll-Tudor, I. 2009. 'The Fair and Equitable Treatment Standard and Human Rights Norms', Dupuy, Francioni and Petersmann (eds.): 310–43.

Kotera, A. 2008. 'Regulatory Transparency', Muchlinski, Ortino and Schreuer (eds.): 617–36.

Krommendijk, J. and Morijn, J. 2009. '"Proportional" by What Measure(s)? Balancing Investor Interests and Human Rights by Way of Applying the Proportionality Principle in Investor State Arbitration', Dupuy, Francioni and Petersmann (eds.): 422–50.

Lossani, M., Bertoni, F. and Chiarlone, S. (eds.) 2010. *Fondi sovrani: economie emergenti e squilibri globali*. Milano: Francesco Brioschi Editore.

Lyons, G. 2008. 'State Capitalism: The Rise of Sovereign Wealth Funds'. *Law and Business Review of the Americas*: 4–62.

Mairal, H.A. 2010. 'Legitimate Expectations and Informal Administrative Representations', Schill, S.W. (ed.), *International Investment Law and Comparative Public Law*. Oxford University Press: 413–52.

Mason, R. 2008. 'Sovereign Wealth Funds and the Efficient Management of the Wealth of Nations'. *Tax Notes*: 1321–2.

Muchlinski, P. 2006. 'Caveat Investor? The Relevance of the Conduct of the Investor under the Fair and Equitable Treatment Standard'. *ICLQ* 55: 527–57.

2007. *Multinational Enterprises and the Law*, Oxford University Press.

2008–9. 'Trends in International Investment Agreements: Balancing Investor Rights and the Right to Regulate'. *The Yearbook on International Investment Law & Policy*: 35–78.

Muchlinski, P., Ortino, F. and Schreuer, C. (eds.) 2008. *The Oxford Handbook of International Investment Law*. Oxford University Press.

Norton, J. 2010. 'The Santiago Principles for Sovereign Wealth Funds: A Case Study on International Financial Standard-Setting Processes'. *Journal of International Economic Law* 13: 645–62.

O'Brien, J. 2008. 'Barriers to Entry: Foreign Direct Investment and the Regulation of Sovereign Wealth Funds'. *The International Lawyer*: 1232–57.

Ortino, F. 2008. 'Non-discriminatory Treatment in Investment Disputes', Muchlinski, Ortino and Schreuer (eds.): 346–8.

Parisi, M.G. 2005. 'Moving Towards Transparency? An Examination of Regulatory Takings in International Law'. *Emory International Law Review*: 383–426.

Pasca di Magliano, R. 2009. *Fondi di ricchezza sovrana*. Milano: LED.

Qureshi, A.H. 2009. 'The Economic Emergency Defence in Bilateral Investment Treaties; a Development Perspective', Binder, C., Kriebaum, U., Reinisch, A. and Wittich S. (eds.), *International Investment Law for the 21st Century: Essays in Honour of Christoph Schreuer*. Oxford University Press: 631–5.

Reinisch, A. 2008. 'Expropriation', Muchlinski, Ortino and Schreuer (eds.): 407–58.

Reisen, H. 2008. 'Fonds souverains et économie du développement'. *La Vie Économique, Revue de Politique Économique*: 26–8.

Rose, P. 2008–9. 'Sovereigns as Shareholders'. *North Carolina Law Review*: 83–150.

Sacerdoti, G. 1997. 'Bilateral Treaties and Multilateral Instruments on Investment Protection'. *RCADI* 269: 255–460.

Santiso, J. 2008. 'Sovereign Development Funds: Key Financial Actors of the Shifting Wealth of Nations'. OECD Emerging Markets Network Working Paper.

Savona, P. and Regola, P. 2009. *Il ritorno dello Stato padrone: i fondi sovrani e il grande negoziato globale*. Milano: Rubbettino Editore.

Schlemmer, E. 2008. 'Investment, Investor, Nationality and Shareholders', Muchlinski, Ortino and Schreuer (eds.): 49–88.

Seznec, J. 2008. 'The Gulf Sovereign Wealth Funds: Myths and Reality'. *Middle East Policy*: 97–110.

Siniscalco, D. 2008. 'Governi alle porte. Crisi del credito e fondi sovrani'. *Mercato, Concorrenza Regole*: 75–86.

Subacchi, P. 2007. 'Capital Flows and Emerging Market Economies: A Larger Playing Field?'. London: Chatham House.

Sud, G. 2006. 'From Fretting Takeovers to Vetting CFIUS: Finding a Balance in US Policy Regarding Foreign Acquisitions of Domestic Assets'. *Vanderbilt Journal of Transnational Law*: 1304–31.

Summers, L.H. 2007. 'Opportunities in an Era of Large and Growing Official Wealth', Johnson-Calari and Rietveld (eds.): 15–28.

Truman, E.M. 2008a. 'Four Myths about Sovereign Wealth Funds'. Peterson Institute for International Economics.

2008b. 'Sovereign Wealth Funds: New Challenges from a Changing Landscape', Testimony before the Subcommittee on Domestic and International Monetary Policy, Trade and Technology, Financial Services Committee. US House of Representatives, 10 September.

UNCTAD. 1999. *National Treatment*. New York and Geneva: UNCTAD.

2004. *International Investment Agreements: Key Issues*. New York and Geneva: UNCTAD.

2008. *World Investment Report 2008 – Transnational Corporations and the Infrastructure Challenge*. New York and Geneva: UNCTAD.

2009. *The Protection of National Security in IIAs*. New York and Geneva: UNCTAD.

2011. *Scope and Definition*. New York and Geneva: UNCTAD.

2012. *World Investment Report 2012*. New York and Geneva: UNCTAD.

Valenti, M. 2004. 'Il trattamento "conforme al diritto internazionale" degli investimenti stranieri nelle convenzioni internazionali'. *Diritto del Commercio Internazionale* 18: 973–90.

2009a. *Gli standard di trattamento nell'interpretazione dei trattati in materia di investimenti stranieri*. Torino: Giappichelli Editore.

2009b. 'Il contributo dei trattati in materia di investimenti stranieri allo sviluppo del paese ospitante', Venturini, G. (ed.), *Le nuove forme di sostegno allo sviluppo nella prospettiva del diritto internazionale*. Torino: Giappichelli Editore: 83–94.

Van Harten, G. and Loughlin, M. 2006. 'Investment Treaty Arbitration as a Species of Global Administrative Law'. *European Journal of International Law* 17: 121–50.

Wälde, T. 2004. 'Natural Resources and Sustainable Development: from "Good Intentions" to "Good Consequences"', Schrijver, N. and Weiss, F. (eds.), *International Law and Sustainable Development – Principles and Practice*. Leiden: Martinus Nijhoff Publishers: 130–50.

Wong, A. 2009. 'Sovereign Wealth Funds and the Problem of Asymmetric Information: the Santiago Principles and International Regulation'. *Brook. J. Int'l L.*: 1081–109.

Wu, F. and Seah, A. 2008. 'Would China's Sovereign Wealth Fund Be a Menace to the USA?'. *China & World Economy*: 33–47.

PART II

The protection of non-investment concerns in international investment law

7

The integration of non-investment concerns as an opportunity for the modernization of international investment law: is a multilateral approach desirable?

PIA ACCONCI

1. Introductory remarks

After decolonization, the legitimacy of international rules for the protection of aliens was debated within the United Nations (UN) due to the conflicts between the group of developing countries and that of the Western industrialized States. Developing countries considered such rules a legal means to protect the hegemonic approach of colonial powers in Africa, Asia and Latin America. As is well-known, as a part of the New International Economic Order which they were promoting, developing countries insisted that foreign investors be treated in conformity with domestic, rather than international, law, with particular regard to the settlement of foreign investor–host State disputes and to the determination of compensation for expropriations and nationalizations.[1]

These are still highly debated subjects, despite the great number of international treaties, particularly bilateral, which have been concluded to promote and protect foreign investments leading to a corpus of international investment law.[2] Today, among the most debated issues which raise the problem of the legitimacy of international investment law, are those of consistency, transparency and openness. Another debated issue is regulatory diversification. States tend to keep the regulation of economic and non-economic matters separate by concluding different treaties.

A further debated issue is the two tier nature – public and private – of international investment law which involves the activity of a multitude of diverse actors, States, international organizations, multinational enterprises and non-governmental organizations (NGOs), all with different

1 See Sen (1988). 2 See Sacerdoti (1997).

interests and expectations.[3] On account of the variety of actors, interests and expectations, the settlement of foreign investor–host State disputes has become in itself a debated issue. Domestic judges would, in principle, have jurisdiction over such disputes, but these settlements are typically referred to arbitral tribunals.[4]

These issues affect international investment law in both its regulatory and judicial dimensions. Because of these issues and others concerning the procedural aspects of investment arbitration, such as evidentiary issues, in the last ten years, the number of the cases has increased and the topic of international investment law has attracted substantial interest. We have seen many books, collected essays, articles, conferences, workshops and statements from different groups of scholars. This has opened up the debate in academic circles. All these contributions from different perspectives – legal, economic and social – are positive because they have revitalized the field. For academics it is an exciting time.

Within the scope of this chapter I cannot do justice to all the issues. I am going to focus on the reasons why multilateral rules would appear to be appropriate in order to make current international investment law less controversial by integrating non-investment concerns into it. Working on the assumption that many of the issues mentioned above are related to the question of how to reconcile private interests, those of the investors, and public concerns which are referred to in this chapter as 'non-investment interests/concerns', I have grouped together the interests, concerns and needs of local populations, NGOs, consumers, stakeholders and public opinion in general under the term 'public'. Before so doing, I would point out that pursuing integration – as one of the key principles of sustainable development – implies something more than referring to non-investment interests or acknowledging their importance in respect of international instruments dealing with investment.

The activities of many international organizations belonging to the UN system that deal with economic cooperation show the importance of integration as a means to achieve a balance between the protection of private and public interests. That is why such organizations tend to influence international relations, by promoting the protection of non-investment interests within their actions for good governance and development. Several UN resolutions, guidelines and programmes promote the integration of non-investment concerns in the economic policies of Member States. Concerns that are mostly taken into consideration are sustainable

3 See Muchlinski (2008). 4 See Schill (2011).

development, the rule of law, the protection of human rights and of the environment, as well as the control of the sale of harmful substances. This trend especially emerges from the activities that aim to foster the achievement of the Millennium Development Goals and from the documents of the several UN Conferences on Sustainable Development.

The UN Development Programme (UNDP), the World Bank and other international organizations have assisted least developed Member States to modify investment projects in order to integrate non-investment concerns. As from the 1990s, the International Finance Corporation (IFC) and the Multilateral Investment Guarantee Agency (MIGA) of the World Bank have promoted social and environmental friendly foreign investments in the southern half of the world. The establishment of the Inspection Panel within the World Bank in 1993 has also been important in promoting foreign investments in line with the needs of local populations of host countries.[5] International assistance has even led to the termination of investments in the fight against climate change. In 2010, Ecuador and the UNDP came to an agreement to stop the exploitation of oil fields in the Yasuni Region in the interests of local indigenous people. This was made possible thanks to special financial funds made available by other States and private banks.[6]

The integration of non-investment concerns into international investment law would contribute to the establishment of a more favourable climate for foreign investments, because it would bring together the various attitudes and interests of the different parties.

The issue of considering public interests related to non investment concerns within the international investment framework is not new, since already in the early 1990s certain multinational enterprises and international organizations began to collaborate for this purpose during the preparation of the UN Conference on Environment and Development held in Rio de Janeiro in 1992. Large multinational enterprises started to refer to non-investment interests in non-binding codes of corporate conduct and/or principles to promote corporate social responsibility in order to meet public opinion's criticism and expectations. In that period, several industrialized States also started to show that the competitiveness of their economies and that of their investors could be enhanced if the quality

5 See the contributions by Latino and Guidi in this book, as to the activity of the Inspection Panel to ensure the protection of certain non-investment concerns within the World Bank.

6 See UNDP (2011), especially 193 ff.

of their products and investments is perceived as being more politically correct.[7] Since the 2002 UN Johannesburg Conference on sustainable development, the contribution of private parties to the promotion of sustainable and human development has also emerged from the recourse to partnerships among different interested parties. The establishment of such partnerships has become extensive in international economic relations in order to provide technical assistance for specific development needs, such as the access to essential drugs and/or the promotion of food safety. Like corporate social responsibility, these partnerships are expressions of the increasing involvement of private parties in international economic relations.[8] When partnerships are used as a vehicle to provide for technical and financial assistance within the programmes and strategies of the International Monetary Fund and the World Bank, private parties that take part in them are able to influence not only the implementation of international policies on economic matters, but also their regulatory dimension. These efforts made by private parties under the auspices of the UN international organizations and agencies have had an impact on the current international climate for foreign investments.

On the other hand, as I will explain below, a few States have moved towards a regulatory approach that integrates non-investment concerns into their bilateral investment treaties by including special provisions that refer to such concerns as exceptions to regulatory diversification.[9] Resort to such kinds of provisions may be considered a regulatory means of integration. This technique has been implemented in the European Union law to a large extent and with less intensity in the most important international trade agreements, such as the General Agreement on Trade and Tariffs (GATT), the General Agreement on Trade in Services (GATS) and the Trade-Related Intellectual Property Rights (TRIPs) Agreement. In these agreements the protection of a number of non-trade interests, such as the environment and health, is considered a legitimate exception to treaty obligations for the promotion of free trade.[10]

7 See Horn (1980); Rubin (1995).

8 See Darrow (2003); World Bank (2004); Acconci (2012), 599–602. See also the Statement 'Welcoming New Partnerships in International Development Co-operation' issued by the OECD Development Assistance Committee on 6 April 2011 (www.oecd.org/dac/47652500.pdf).

9 As to the increasing relevance of exceptions for the protection of the host State's general interests, see El Boudouhi (2005). Important examples are the 2004 Canada Model BIT, the 2004 and 2012 US Model BIT.

10 Art. XX of the GATT, Art. XIV of the GATS and Art. 27 (2) of the TRIPs Agreement are examples of such a technique.

Besides regulatory developments, the choice of the applicable rules for a specific case and of interpretative criteria on the part of arbitrators has become an important instrument for integration at the judicial level. A number of arbitral tribunals have accepted third-party participation on the part of NGOs and/or representatives of local communities and *amici curiae* submissions in order to improve the transparency and openness of current international investment law. This approach represents another means – a procedural one – to combine different concerns and move towards eventual integration.

After reviewing these developments, I will focus on the reasons why a more global approach is called for.

2. Non-investment interests in international investment agreements

Defining public interests at the level of international law is a long-standing problem to which a solution has not yet been found. In international investment law public interest has been considered as one of the typical requirements that a State has to satisfy if it wishes lawfully to expropriate/nationalize a foreign investment. The majority of investment treaties refer to such a requirement without defining it. As a result, paramount concerns, such as the environment and health, are taken into consideration in investment treaties only in vague terms. They are pushed to one side during the negotiations and given a few lines in international investment agreements, usually in the preamble and in the articles providing for exceptions to treatment standards. Treaties are rather focused on defining and protecting relations between a host State and a foreign investor from an economic point of view. Therefore, it is not surprising that investment treaties tend not to refer to concepts such as corporate social responsibility and/or to other instruments that are apt to impact on the approach of companies towards human and social development.[11]

11 The investment chapters of a few trade agreements refer to international standards of corporate social responsibility as something that the Contracting States should promote. Art. 816 of the 2008 Canada–Colombia FTA Agreement reads as follows:

> Each Party should encourage enterprises operating within its territory or subject to its jurisdiction to voluntarily incorporate internationally recognized standards of corporate social responsibility in their internal policies, such as statements of principle that have been endorsed or are supported by the Parties. These principles address issues such as labour, the environment, human rights, community relations and anti-corruption. The Parties remind those enterprises of the importance

Sustainable development is only mentioned in the preamble, as in the 2004 Model BIT of Canada, if at all.

In any case, a number of BITs concluded by the United States in the 1990s recognize in their preambles that 'the development of economic and business ties can promote respect for internationally recognized worker rights' and underline that their economic objectives 'can be achieved without relaxing health, safety and environmental measures of general application'.[12]

The preamble of the 2004 Model BIT of Canada includes the same non-relaxation clause.

The 2012 Model BIT of the United States, like that of 2004, contains a non-relaxation clause which aims to promote much more integration between the economic objectives of an investment treaty and the safeguard of a number of non-investment interests. This clause runs as follows: '[*d*]*esiring* to achieve these objectives in a manner consistent with the protection of health, safety, and the environment, and the promotion of internationally recognized labor rights'. Recent BITs of other States contain similar non-relaxation clauses.[13]

A more significant attempt to integrate non-investment interests into BITs emerges from treaty clauses which specify that: 'Each Contracting Party recognizes that it is inappropriate to encourage investment by investors of another Contracting Party by relaxing its environmental measures. To this effect each Contracting Party should not waive or otherwise derogate from such environmental measures as an encouragement for the establishment, acquisition or expansion of investments in its territory.'[14]

of incorporating such corporate social responsibility standards in their internal policies.

See also the preambles of several FTA Agreements of the EFTA States, like those concluded with Colombia in 2008, with Albania in 2009, with Peru in 2010 and with China in 2011; as well as the 2012 draft investment chapter of the Trans-Pacific Partnership Agreement, Art. 12.15 *bis* (www.tppinfo.org).

12 In particular, see bilateral treaties concluded by the United States in 1995 with Nicaragua; in 1997 with Azerbaijan and Jordan; in 1998 with Bolivia. See also the 1991 United States–Argentina BIT and the 1992 United States–Russia BIT which however refer only to 'the well-being of workers' and to the promotion of 'respect for internationally recognized worker rights'.

13 See, *inter alia*, the 2002 Netherlands–Namibia BIT; the 2002 Korea–Trinidad and Tobago BIT; the 2003 Finland–Kyrgyzistan BIT; and the 2004 Dutch Model BIT.

14 See the 1995 Switzerland–Mexico BIT, Protocol to Art. 3; the 2004 Model BIT of Canada, Art. 11; the 2008 Canada–Colombia FTA Agreement, Art. 815; and the 2012 trilateral investment treaty among Japan, China and South Korea, Art. 23 concerning envir-

In some cases, following Art. XX of GATT, the protection of public interests like the environment and health is considered a general exception to treaty obligations on the treatment of foreign investments in BITs and FTA Agreements.[15]

For example, Art. 33 of the 2012 BIT between Canada and China reads as follows:

> 2. Provided that such measures are not applied in an arbitrary or unjustifiable manner, or do not constitute a disguised restriction on international trade or investment, nothing in this Agreement shall be construed to prevent a Contracting Party from adopting or maintaining measures, including environmental measures:
>
> (a) necessary to ensure compliance with laws and regulations that are not inconsistent with the provisions of this Agreement;
> (b) necessary to protect human, animal or plant life or health; or
> (c) relating to the conservation of living or non-living exhaustible natural resources if such measures are made effective in conjunction with restrictions on domestic production or consumption.[16]

In addition, in a number of investment treaties, the protection of non-investment interests is considered as an exception to treaty obligations on the prohibition of performance requirements.[17]

Besides the reference to a number of non-investment concerns in preambles and the inclusion of non-precluded measures clauses, in the last decade, a few industrialized countries have inserted special provisions in their investment treaties to protect health, the environment and/or worker rights, as a new way of promoting foreign investments. This is the case of the investment treaties concluded by the United States and Canada. The

onmental measures. See also the 2012 draft investment chapter of the Trans-Pacific Partnership Agreement, Art. 12.15 (2).

15 For reference to public health and/or national security as general exceptions, see the 1994 Bolivia–Mexico FTA Agreement, Art. 3–13 (3); the 2003 Australia–Singapore FTA Agreement, Art. 21 which includes a reference to 'the protection of national treasures of artistic, historic or archeological value'. In addition, see the 2007 Model BIT of Colombia, Art. VII as regards the protection of the environment.

16 Other examples are the 1997 Canada–Armenia BIT, Art. XVII; and the 2004 Model BIT of Canada, Art. 10 (1). The 1998 Switzerland–Mauritius BIT, Art. 11 (3); and the 1999 New Zealand–Argentina BIT, Art. 5 (3). Several Indian BITs, such as the 1995 Germany–India BIT (Art. 12), the 1995 Italy–India BIT (Art. 12), the 1996 Czech Republic–India BIT (Art. 12), and the 1999 Australia–India BIT (Art. 15) refer to 'measures necessary ... for the prevention of diseases or pests'.

17 See the 2003 Australia–Singapore FTA Agreement, Art. 5 (3) (c); the 2012 Model BIT of the United States, Art. 8 (3) (c); and the 2012 draft investment chapter of the Trans-Pacific Partnership Agreement, Art. 12 (7) (3) (c).

most recent Model BITs of the United States – those of 2004 and 2012 – incorporate specific provisions related respectively to the relationships between investment and the environment and investment and labour.

The revised text of Art. 12 in the 2012 US Model BIT is longer than the 2004 text and more complex. The 2012 Art. 12 refers to a wide-ranging concept of the environment, as well as measures that may be adopted for its protection. These measures may be directed to preventing and controlling air pollution, the employment of hazardous and toxic substances, the conservation of 'wild flora and fauna' and/or 'specially protected natural areas'.

In addition, the revised text of Art. 12 establishes a clear relationship between the protection of the environment and health, by specifying that '"environmental law" means each Party's statutes or regulations, or provisions thereof, the primary purpose of which is the protection of the environment, or the prevention of a danger to human, animal, or plant life or health'.

The revised text of Art. 12 also accords great discretion to Contracting States for the protection of the environment within the investment context. According to Art. 12 (3), '[t]he Parties recognize that each Party retains the right to exercise discretion with respect to regulatory, compliance, investigatory, and prosecutorial matters, and to make decisions regarding the allocation of resources to enforcement with respect to other environmental matters determined to have higher priorities'.[18]

The importance of the environment within the framework of the revised US Model BIT further emerges from Art. 12 (7), which acknowledges that the relationship between investment and the environment may concern local communities and the public opinion. This paragraph states that '[t]he Parties confirm that each Party may, as appropriate, provide opportunities for public participation regarding any matter arising under this Article'. It is noteworthy that Art. 12 (7) does not mention the 1998 UNECE Aarhus Convention on 'Access to Information, Public Participation in Decision-making and Access to Justice in Environmental Matters', although this provision is clearly inspired by that Convention.[19]

The revised text of Art. 13 of the 2012 US Model BIT on the relationship between investment and labour is based on international standards

18 See also Art. 12 (5).

19 UNECE – the United Nations Commission for Europe – was established by the UN Economic and Social Council in 1947 to promote pan-European economic integration. Today, fifty-six States, including the United States and a number of non-EU Western and Eastern European States, take part in the UNECE.

of protection. This text, as its 2004 version, is in line with the international Conventions concluded under the aegis of the International Labour Organization (ILO) to protect basic labour rights, insofar as this Article mentions the ILO Declaration on Fundamental Principles and Rights at Work and its Follow-Up and refers indirectly to the standards of protection included in those Conventions.[20] Conventions like the Aarhus Convention and the ILO Conventions are not, however, directly named, possibly in order to avoid treaty cross-fertilization through the US revised Model BIT in favour of the protection of non-investment concerns.

One may wonder why States, like Canada and the United States, show a specific interest in safeguarding their power to protect such concerns in their investment treaties. An important reason is that these concerns are considered public-law issues and as such they are invoked both by industrialized and developing countries, in light of the needs of their populations. Nowadays industrialized States may be either home or host State for investors and domestic public opinion has positive expectations concerning the protection of public concerns not only by national investors abroad, but also by foreign investors at home. States like the United States and Canada have had to face arbitral tribunals as respondent States because of a change in their domestic laws which was directed to protecting a public

20 Art. 13 of the 2012 US Model BIT reads as follows:

> 1. The Parties reaffirm their respective obligations as members of the International Labor Organization ('ILO') and their commitments under the *ILO Declaration on Fundamental Principles and Rights at Work and its Follow-Up*. 2. The Parties recognize that it is inappropriate to encourage investment by weakening or reducing the protections afforded in domestic labor laws. Accordingly, each Party shall ensure that it does not waive or otherwise derogate from or offer to waive or otherwise derogate from its labor laws where the waiver or derogation would be inconsistent with the labor rights referred to in subparagraphs (a) through (e) of paragraph 3, or fail to effectively enforce its labor laws through a sustained or recurring course of action or inaction, as an encouragement for the establishment, acquisition, expansion, or retention of an investment in its territory. 3. For purposes of this Article, 'labor laws' means each Party's statutes or regulations, or provisions thereof, that are directly related to the following: (a) freedom of association; (b) the effective recognition of the right to collective bargaining; (c) the elimination of all forms of forced or compulsory labor; (d) the effective abolition of child labor and a prohibition on the worst forms of child labor; (e) the elimination of discrimination in respect of employment and occupation; and (f) acceptable conditions of work with respect to minimum wages, hours of work, and occupational safety and health. ... 5. The Parties confirm that each Party may, as appropriate, provide opportunities for public participation regarding any matter arising under this Article.

non-investment concern that, according to the claimants (the foreign investors), amounted to a breach of their investment treaties.[21]

In light of increased competition in the investment arena, the changes in the 2012 revised Model BIT of the United States providing for more protection of non-investment concerns may improve the US position because of its willingness, on the one hand, to promote and safeguard social issues at an international law level and, on the other, to attract 'socially oriented' foreign investments to its territory. At the same time, those changes would reduce the likelihood of the United States finding itself as a respondent host State in disputes arising from its need to make its domestic law more consistent with international rules on the protection of the environment, of health and of labour.

The objective of avoiding disputes arising from non-discriminatory regulatory actions is evident in Canada's 2004 Model BIT which includes an important provision concerning the requirements of an indirect expropriation. One of its Annexes provides that '[e]xcept in rare circumstances, such as when an action or a series of actions by a Contracting Party is extremely severe or disproportionate in light of its purpose, non-discriminatory regulatory actions adopted by the Contracting Party for the purpose of legitimate public welfare do not constitute indirect expropriation'.[22]

3. Non-investment concerns in international investment arbitration

In light of its 'private' nature, arbitration may not be a satisfactory mechanism when a dispute arises from the host State's intention to protect public-law concerns/interests.[23] This explains why a new wave of criticism has emerged towards arbitration as the most common mechanism to settle host States–foreign investors disputes. Some States, like Australia, have considered to stop including reference to arbitration in their investment treaties. A few, such as Bolivia, Ecuador and Venezuela, have withdrawn

21 See cases at footnotes 36–8.

22 Annex B.13 (1) of the 2004 Model BIT of Canada. See, in particular, the 2012 Canada–China BIT. See also Art. 2 (c) of the Protocol to the 2012 trilateral investment treaty among Japan, China and South Korea and the 2007 Model BIT of Colombia, Art. VI (2) (c); as well as the 2012 draft investment chapter of the Trans-Pacific Partnership Agreement, Annex 12-D (5).

23 As to the importance of considering international investment law, in particular investment arbitration, as part of a public-law framework, see Van Harten (2007), especially 47.

from the ICSID Convention, while others, such as Argentina, have chosen to remain in the ICSID, by adopting proactive judicial strategies – based on various objections raised during arbitral proceedings – that challenge the present system.

In addition, the complexity of cases and the importance of the issues at stake have brought about demands for more transparency and openness, which imply allowing third parties, such as NGOs, to take part in arbitral proceedings as *amici curiae*. A positive trend towards this objective is that some arbitral tribunals have admitted third-party participation and *amici curiae* appearances by NGOs representing the people of the respondent States.[24] The ICSID procedural rules for arbitration proceedings were amended to this end in 2006.[25] Third parties are able to respond positively to the need of developing countries for technical assistance and capacity-building through their participation in arbitral proceedings, as well as highlighting the relevance of non-investment concerns.

Investors and States not involved in investment disputes may also be interested in more transparency and openness in arbitral proceedings. Even if the rule of precedent does not operate in such proceedings, investment arbitral tribunals tend to refer to the awards of other such tribunals.[26] Thus, these awards become relevant as they may give rise to expectations as to the interpretation and application of investment treaties.

One cannot overstate the active role of arbitrators in the last decades in implementing and sometimes clarifying the basic structure of international investment treaties:[27] this point of view finds support by a number of legal writers who believe that arbitrators might contribute to a change in international investment law with a new approach to the applicable rules.

24 See, *inter alia*, *Methanex* v. *The United States*, NAFTA/UNCITRAL Arbitration, Decision on petitions from third parties to intervene as *amici curiae*, 15 January 2001; *UPS* v. *Canada*, NAFTA/UNCITRAL Arbitration, Decision on petitions from third parties to intervene as *amici curiae*, 17 October 2001; *Vivendi* v. *Argentina*, ICSID Case No. ARB/03/19, order in response to a petition for transparency and participation as *amicus curiae*, 19 May 2005. On the contrary, the ICSID Tribunal of *Aguas del Tunari* v. *Bolivia* (letter, 29 January 2003) and that of *von Pezold* v. *Zimbabwe* (ICSID Case No. ARB/10/15) and *Border Timbers* v. *Zimbabwe* (ICSID Case No. ARB/10/25) did not accept non-disputing parties submissions (see Procedural Order No. 2, 26 June 2012, 56–63).

25 See new Arts. 32 and 37 of the ICSID Arbitration Rules. See Blackaby and Richard (2010), 253–74.

26 See Schreuer and Weiniger (2008), 1188–1206; Schill (2009), 321–39; Sacerdoti (2011).

27 See Salacuse (2009–10), especially 577, 588; Montt (2012), especially 125 ff.

Arbitrators might apply international rules concerning human rights, cultural heritage and the environment together with those on investments, when the circumstances of the case make it appropriate. This would be possible since the ICSID Convention and other international investment treaties, like the NAFTA Treaty, the Energy Charter Treaty and many BITs, provide that the law applying to the merits of a dispute includes international law.

However, in the case-law of investment arbitration, the fact that the law applying to the merits of a foreign investor–host State dispute may include international rules on the protection of non-investment interests in itself tends not to be considered relevant, or at least not expressly relevant. Only a few tribunals have referred to non-investment obligations which the host State was required to observe in implementing its investment obligations, thus acknowledging, in an indirect way, the existence of conflicting rules.[28]

A number of arbitral tribunals, like those established to settle the cases against Argentina regarding water concessions, have instead dismissed the claims of the respondent States to integrate international rules for the safeguard of public concerns into the applicable law. These tribunals have either ignored or refused Argentina's claims to apply international rules on the protection of human rights contained in the 1966 UN Covenant on Economic, Social and Cultural Rights or in the Inter-American Convention on Human Rights. In effect, the investment treaties, contracts and other relevant applicable legal sources in those proceedings did

28 In *Saluka* v. *The Czech Republic* the Tribunal referred to international customary law to deny that the host State's regulatory actions amounted to an expropriation (UNCITRAL Arbitration, Partial Award, 17 March 2006, 261). In other cases the tribunals referred to the ECHRs case-law to ascertain whether or not the host State had expropriated the claimant's property (see, in particular, *Mondev* v. *The United States*, ICSID Case No. ARB(AF)/99/2, Award, 11 October 2002, 143–4; *Tecmed* v. *Mexico*, ICSID Case No. ARB(AF)/00/2, Award, 29 May 2003, 122; *Azurix* v. *Argentina*, ICSID Case No. ARB/01/12, Award, 14 July 2006, 311–12; and *Saipem* v. *Bangladesh*, ICSID Case No. ARB/05/07, Decision on jurisdiction and recommendation on provisional measures, 21 March 2007, 130–2). In *SPP* v. *Egypt*, the Tribunal referred to the 1972 UNESCO Convention concerning the 'Protection of the World Cultural and Natural Heritage' (ICSID Case No. AF/84/3, Award on the merits, 20 May 1992, 150–4). In *Myers* the Tribunal took into consideration the 'Basel Convention on the Control of Transboundary Movements of Hazardous Waste and their Disposal' as a relevant reference point (*Myers* v. *Canada*, NAFTA/UNCITRAL Arbitration, Partial Award, 13 November 2000, 209–17). In *Pope & Talbot* v. *Canada* the Tribunal mentioned WTO case-law in relation to the definition of the field of application of the NAFTA trade regulation (UNCITRAL Arbitration, Award on the merits of phase 2, 10 April 2001, 45–82).

not provide for such an integration and the arbitrators limited themselves to the letter of the law.[29]

Other arbitral tribunals have refused to import a State's international obligations from one treaty system to another to the detriment of the foreign investors as claimants.[30] Also the few cases where the treatment of the foreign investors as human beings was at issue did not have a positive outcome.[31]

The public interest in the protection of non-investment concerns has been taken into consideration in three possible ways.

Firstly, the record of international investment arbitration shows that disputes have arisen when host States have taken regulatory action, by changing their domestic legislation against the foreign investor's interests and expectations for reasons of public interest.

29 See Pannatier and Ducrey (2005); Thielbörger (2009); Marrella (2010). See certain cases against Argentina, e.g. *SAUR* v. *Argentina* (ICSID Case No. ARB/04/4, Decision on jurisdiction and liability, 6 June 2012, 328–32) and *EDF* v. *Argentina* where the Tribunal denied that the respondent State's conduct could be justified in accordance with international *jus cogens* norms concerning 'basic human rights such as life, health, personal integrity and education, which were directly threatened by the socio-economic crisis suffered by Argentina' (ICSID Case No. ARB/03/23, Award, 11 June 2012, 909–14).

30 In particular, in *Spyridon Roussalis* v. *Romania* the claimant investor had argued for the application of the respondent host State's international obligations contained in the European Convention on Human Rights concerning property protection. The Tribunal admitted

> the possibility that the international obligations of the Contracting States mentioned at Article 10 of the BIT could include obligations deriving from multilateral instruments to which those states are parties, including, possibly, the European Convention of Human Rights and its Additional Protocol No. 1. But the issue is moot in the present case and does not require decision by the Tribunal, given the higher and more specific level of protection offered by the BIT to the investors compared to the more general protections offered to them by the human rights instruments referred above. Consequently Article 10 of the BIT cannot, in its own terms and in the instant case, serve as a useful instrument for enlarging the protections available to the Claimant from the Romanian State under the BIT.
>
> (ICSID Case No. ARB/06/1, Award, 7 December 2011, 312)

See also *von Pezold* v. *Zimbabwe* and *Border Timbers* v. *Zimbabwe* (fn 24) as to the relevance of the UN Declaration on the Rights of Indigenous Peoples in the arbitral proceedings, especially 58–9.

31 See *Biloune* v. *Ghana Investments Centre* where the Tribunal decided that it 'lack[ed] jurisdiction to address, as an independent cause of action, a claim of violation of human rights' (Award on jurisdiction and liability, 27 October 1989, 95 *International Law Reports* 184, 203) and *Foresti* v. *South Africa* (ICSID No. ARB(AF)/07/1, Award, 4 August 2010).

The attempts of developing countries, which are still the most numerous host States for foreign investments, to protect non-investment concerns for the benefit of their populations emerges from the ICSID and UNCITRAL arbitral case-law concerning access to water as a basic utility,[32] the management of waste-sites,[33] the protection of health[34] and of archeological and religious sites.[35]

Industrialized countries have also become respondents in arbitral proceedings, due to the fact that they had changed their legislation in order to protect health from the sale of harmful substances,[36] to control air pollution[37] or to preserve cultural sites.[38]

A number of arbitral tribunals have decided in favour of the respondent host State on these issues. A change in the host State's domestic legal framework during the post-establishment phase, due to the need to protect non-investment concerns, such as human rights, cultural heritage and/or the environment, has been considered as a legitimate exercise of the host State's police powers, rather than a regulatory taking, even though the change may constitute a breach of the investment treaty on which an arbitral tribunal's jurisdiction is based. In light of this conclusion, host States have not been ordered to pay compensation to the claimant foreign investors.

This trend may be explained as the protection of such specific concerns is more pronounced than in other fields. As a consequence, when these concerns became a bone of contention in the relations between a host State and a foreign investor, a number of arbitrators considered their protection to be a good reason to derogate from the treatment obligations – in favour of the foreign investor – contained in the investment treaty.

32 See, for example, *Aguas del Tunari* v. *Bolivia*, ICSID Case No. ARB/02/3, Decision on respondent's objections to jurisdiction, 21 October 2005; *Biwater* v. *Tanzania*, ICSID Case No. ARB/05/22, Award, 24 July 2008; and some cases against Argentina, like *Azurix* (fn 28); *Aconquija/Vivendi Universal* v. *Argentina*, ICSID Case No. ARB/97/3, Award, 15 August 2007; and *SAUR* (fn 29).

33 See *Santa Elena* v. *Costa Rica*, ICSID Case No. ARB/96/1, Award, 17 February 2000; *Metalclad* v. *Mexico*, ICSID Case No. ARB(AF)/97/1, Award, 25 August 2000; and *Tecmed* (fn 28).

34 See *Philip Morris* v. *Uruguay*, ICSID Case No. ARB/10/7 (ongoing).

35 See *Parkerings* v. *Lithuania*, ICSID Case No. ARB/05/8, Award, 11 September 2007.

36 See *Myers* (fn 28); *Chemtura* v. *Canada*, NAFTA/UNCITRAL Arbitration, Award, 2 August 2010; *Grand River* v. *The United States*, NAFTA/UNCITRAL Arbitration, Award, 12 January 2011; *Philip Morris Asia* v. *Australia*, UNCITRAL Arbitration (ongoing).

37 See *Methanex* v. *The United States*, NAFTA/UNCITRAL Arbitration, Final Award on jurisdiction and merits, 3 August 2005.

38 See *Glamis* v. *The United States*, NAFTA/UNCITRAL Arbitration, Award, 8 June 2009.

However, this has not happened in a systematic way as only a few arbitral tribunals have allowed this kind of derogation. The *Methanex*, *Glamis*, *Chemtura*, *Parkerings* and *Grand River* cases are particularly noteworthy, as they represent the most far-reaching awards which have been issued in this regard.[39] In *Grand River* the conflict involved two different non-investment concerns, namely the safeguard of the 'privileges' of an indigenous people to export the cigarettes it produces to the United States and the protection of public health through the control of tobacco sales. The UNCITRAL Tribunal dismissed the arguments of the claimants because they did 'not have an investment in the United States' and the conduct of the United States had not breached the NAFTA Treaty on which the Tribunal's jurisdiction was based. The Tribunal however expressed sympathy for the indigenous claimants and did not order them to pay the costs of arbitration.[40]

Secondly, the 'Salini test' has been adopted to define foreign investments in a few cases. The contribution of a foreign investment to the host State's development has thus been considered one of the key defining elements.[41]

39 *Methanex* (fn 37); *Glamis* (fn 38); *Chemtura* (fn 36); *Grand River* (fn 36). In *Saluka* the Tribunal refers to the *Methanex* Award to underline that 'the principle that a State does not commit an expropriation and is thus not liable to pay compensation to a dispossessed alien investor when it adopts general regulations that are "commonly accepted as within the police power of States" forms part of customary international law today' (fn 28) 262. See also *Spyridon Roussalis* where the Tribunal decided that, in relation to the host State's regulation for food safety, '[c]laimant's argument that the State authorities' behavior in conducting too many inspections and imposing too severe penalties, namely suspensions or revocations of operating permits, would amount to a failure to protect its legitimate expectations is not justified'. According to the Tribunal, '[s]uch regulations by a state reflect a clear and legitimate public purpose. In the Tribunal's view, Claimant may not have expected that the State would refrain from adopting regulations in the public interest, nor may Claimant have expected that the Romanian authorities would refrain from implementing those regulations' (fn 30) 691.

40 See *Grand River* (fn 36) 246–7.

41 *Salini* v. *Morocco*, ICSID Case No. ARB/00/4, Decision on jurisdiction, 23 July 2001, 52–8. See also, *inter alia*: *Fedax* v. *Venezuela*, ICSID Case No. ARB/96/3, Decision on objections to jurisdiction, 11 July 1997, 43; *Consortium R.F.C.C.* v. *Morocco*, ICSID Case No. ARB/00/6, Decision on jurisdiction, 16 July 2001, 65. The *ad hoc* annulment Committee in *Mitchell* v. *Congo*, for example, stated that:

> The *ad hoc* Committee wishes … to specify that, in its view, the existence of a contribution to the economic development of the host State as an essential – although not sufficient – characteristic or unquestionable criterion of the investment, does not mean that this contribution must always be sizable or successful; and, of course, ICSID tribunals do not have to evaluate the real contribution of the operation in question. It suffices for the operation to contribute in one way or another to the

Thirdly, the relevance of general principles of law, like abuse of rights[42] or good faith[43] or arbitrariness,[44] has been recognized by other investment arbitration tribunals. In a handful of cases, tribunals have referred to the European Court of Human Rights (ECHRs) case-law to show that their decisions on the application of principles like denial of justice[45] and proportionality[46] in favour of the foreign investor were well-founded.

Investment arbitrators, like any other international judge, observe the few fundamental core principles which are the basis of the unity of international law.[47] A number of ICSID *ad hoc* Committees have also taken

> economic development of the host State, and this concept of economic development is, in any event, extremely broad and also variable depending on the case.
>
> (ICSID Case No. ARB/99/7, Decision on the application for the annulment of the award, 1 November 2006, 33)

Other tribunals, however, rejected the relevance of the contribution of the foreign investment to the host State's development as a key defining element (see, *inter alia*: *L.E.S.I.-DIPENTA* v. *Algeria*, ICSID Case No. ARB/03/08, Award, 10 January 2005, (13) (iv); *L.E.S.I. & ASTALDI* v. *Algeria*, ICSID Case No. ARB/05/3, Decision, 12 July 2006, 72 (iv); *Phoenix* v. *The Czech Republic*, ICSID Case No. ARB/06/5, Award, 15 April 2009, 85–6).

42 In *Saipem* v. *Bangladesh* the ICSID Tribunal referred to the 'prohibition of abuse of rights' as an 'internationally accepted principle' (ICSID Case No. ARB/05/07, Award, 30 June 2009, 161).

43 The Tribunal of *Tecmed* refers to the fair and equitable treatment standard as an expression of good faith (fn 28) 153; whereas the Tribunal of *ADF* v. *The United States* considers the contribution of good faith to be less important for this purpose (ICSID Case No. ARB(AF)/00/1, Award, 9 January 2003, 180–4).

44 See *CMS* v. *Argentina* as to the relevance of the fair and equitable treatment standard against arbitrariness and discrimination (ICSID Case No. ARB/01/8, Award, 20 April 2005, 285–92). With regard to the link between arbitrariness and/or discrimination and the lack of good faith, see also *Lauder* v. *The Czech Republic* (UNCITRAL Arbitration, Award, 3 September 2001, 214–21). In the latter case the Tribunal found that the respondent State had taken a 'discriminatory and arbitrary measure' against the claimant (222). See Stone (2012).

45 The Tribunal in *Mondev* refers to ECHRs case-law on denial of justice in favour of the private investor (fn 28) 139–44. In *Iberdrola* v. *Guatemala* the Tribunal denied that a broader concept of denial of justice than that applied in customary international law could be applied because of the treaty fair-and-equitable-treatment clause (ICSID Case No. ARB/09/5, Award, 17 August 2012, especially 427); whereas in *Oostergetel* v. *Slovakia* the Tribunal decided to analyse 'the Claimants' allegations [of denial of justice] from a procedural and a substantive perspective' (UNCITRAL Arbitration, Final Award, 23 April 2012, 275).

46 A few tribunals have referred to the proportionality test applied by the ECHRs in relation to *de facto* expropriations. See *Tecmed* (fn 28) 122; and *Azurix* (fn 28) 311. See Krommendijk and Morijn (2009).

47 See Fry (2007); McLachlan (2008); von Staden (2011); Lattanzi (2012).

into account the right of defence[48] and the equality of the parties[49] in their decisions on annulment. These decisions show that those Committees may go beyond the field of investment law and clarifying decisions on important points of law are made in annulment proceedings.

4. Might arbitrators contribute to a change in international investment law through interpretation?

Trends in investment treaty practice and arbitral case-law, in principle, show acknowledgement rather than integration of non-investment concerns into the international legal framework on investments. This acknowledgement does not seem to be sufficient to make the international legal framework on investments less controversial. This is why several writers have emphasized that arbitrators might follow innovative interpretations of the applicable rules in accordance with international law,[50] since the interpretation of investment treaties is of marked importance for the integration of non-investment concerns into international investment law. Broad interpretations of the applicable rules – both as to the merits and to the arbitration procedure – would be in line with Art. 31 (3) (c) of the Vienna Convention on the Law of Treaties, as certain writers have already pointed out.[51] Others have proposed the application of interpretative criteria and methods that are applied in public law, such as the standard-of-review criterion.[52]

The issue is how to choose the applicable standard in international investment law. Should such a standard be deferential or reasonable and proportionate? An arbitral investment tribunal shows more deference to a host State, as long as it chooses to combine the standard-of-review and the

48 As to the right of defence, see the Annulment Decisions on *Wena Hotels* v. *Egypt* (ICSID Case No. ARB/98/4, Decision, 28 January 2002, 57); *MTD* v. *Chile* (ICSID Case No. ARB/01/7, Decision, 21 March 2007, 49); *CDC* v. *Seychelles* (ICSID Case No. ARB/02/14, Decision, 29 June 2005, 49); *Azurix* v. *Argentina* (ICSID Case No ARB/01/12, Decision, 1 September 2009, 212); and *Enron Ponderosa* v. *Argentina* (ICSID Case No. ARB/01/3, Decision, 30 July 2010, 193, 195 and 197). The Tribunal of *Lauder* referred to 'the right to a court' (fn 44) 200.

49 As to the equality of the parties, see the Annulment Decisions on *MINE* v. *Guinea* (Case ARB/84/4, Decision, 6 January 1988, 5.06); *Azurix* (fn 48) 213 and *Enron Ponderosa* (fn 48) 193, 195 and 197. The Tribunal of *Metalpar* v. *Argentina* has also referred to the equality of the parties (ICSID Case No. ARB/03/5, Award, 6 June 2008, 153–5).

50 See Brower (2008–2009), especially 378; Wouters and Hachez (2009), especially 318 ff.; Henry (2010), especially 1009–11; Vadi (2013), especially 161–88.

51 See Simma and Kill (2008); Prislan (2012), 462–464.

52 See Burke-White and von Staden (2010).

State's margin-of-appreciation criteria. Proportionality tends to become less relevant when the State's margin of appreciation is considered more important, since an inverted relationship exists between proportionality and a State margin of appreciation.

The margin of appreciation of States is commonly applied by international courts dealing with the protection of human rights, such as the ECHRs, in order to recognize the discretion of States in implementing their international obligations.[53] The question is to define how broad such a margin can be and the level of deference to host States, i.e. respondent States, that arbitral investment tribunals could or should show.[54] As non-investment concerns have not been defined and integrated into international investment law and, by its nature, this margin is variable, a case-by-case approach is the only method currently available.

Reasonableness and proportionality may contribute to find a fair balance between different expectations, interests and concerns, particularly between the host State regulating powers and a foreign investor's rights and expectations.[55]

Whichever method arbitrators might choose in order to integrate non-investment concerns into international investment law – reference to international rules other than those on investments and/or new interpretative criteria or methods, which may result in a broader interpretation of the applicable law, taking account of the human rights and environmental

53 See Shany (2006).

54 For reference to the margin-of-appreciation approach, see, in particular, *Continental Casualty* v. *Argentina* (ICSID Case No. ARB/03/9, Award, 5 September 2008, 181, 187). Against the application of 'the same notions of margins of appreciation [in investment treaties] that apply to' human rights conventions, see *Renta 4* v. *Russia* (SCC No. 24/2007, Award, 20 July 2012, 22). In favour of a deferential margin-of-appreciation, see Van Harten (2007), especially 144–5, who believes that domestic institutions have broad discretionary powers as long as 'governmental decisions are not specifically abusive or discriminatory'; Burke-White and von Staden (2010), especially 690, 711–20, who underline that a deferent standard of review within the ICSID framework should be based on the margin-of-appreciation approach, since '[t]he inherent problem with ICSID tribunals engaging primarily in direct balancing at the heart of proportionality analysis is that they are not well positioned or equipped to engage in law-making, to read the context, and to weigh the policy considerations at play in a particular case', whereas '[w]ithin a constitutional framework, proportionality analysis may be an ideal mechanism for judicial balancing' (717). Others point out that in *Pope & Talbot* the UNCITRAL Tribunal adopted a standard-of-review based on the objectives of the NAFTA Treaty. See Newcombe and Paradell (2009), 178; and Weiler (2005).

55 Besides *Tecmed* (fn 28), see *LG&E* v. *Argentina* (ICSID Case No. ARB/02/1, Decision on liability, 3 October 2006, 195). See Newcombe and Paradell (2009), 363 ff.; Kingsbury and Schill (2010); Henckels (2012).

needs of a host State's population – arbitrators, from inside, can identify and foster the changes that are needed for a peaceful and favourable international investment environment.

Arbitration involves a cost both for a community and a company, but it may be necessary when the letter of the law is not adequate in respect of the complexity of the dispute. Should this be the case, not only local communities and public opinion, but also investors would benefit from innovative approaches by arbitrators.[56] In times of economic crisis a corporate investor is very sensitive to any economic decrease, like a drop in market share, and might accept new attitudes towards the applicable rules if such attitudes were to favour the establishment of an environment based on cooperation between local communities, investors and States. A greater integration of non-investment concerns in international investment law through new attitudes by arbitrators might reduce opposition and the relevant cost, such as administrative delay or even the blocking of an investment project.

5. The interplay of different international obligations as a reason for a multilateral investment treaty

At the beginning of my research I had assumed that should I have been able to find any useful examples of the integration of non-investment concerns into international investment law these examples would have been in favour of host States. This is true at the treaty-law level. There are a few States, in particular the United States and Canada, which promote a certain degree of integration for the protection of the few non-investment concerns that such States wish to keep within their police power.

At the judicial level, there is no definitive trend towards the protection of non-investment concerns.

Some arbitral awards show that when a host State satisfies certain requirements – non-discrimination and the pursuit of a public interest which reflects the need to safeguard historical cultural sites or the local population's public health through the control of the sale of harmful substances – a change in its law to the detriment of a foreign investor may not be considered a deprivation equivalent to an expropriation. In other

56 See Liberti (2007) who thinks that arbitrators should deal with the interplay of issues in international obligations by paying due attention to the differences in the nature and the structure of international rules concerning different fields (especially 850–2); Stern (2011), 174–92; Schreuer and Kriebaum (2011), who believe that a more active role by arbitrators in raising community interests might be appropriate (1096).

arbitral decisions, many of the same non-investment concerns have been considered good reasons, depending on the circumstances of the case, to sacrifice the unilateral interests either of the foreign investor or of the host State.[57]

It is however important to point out that international practice does not seem to be inspired by the idea that the non-investment concerns which have often arisen within the international investment legal framework are protected by specific rules because these concerns have a public collective dimension at an international law level. On account of the fact that the applicable law in investment arbitration proceedings tends to include international law, and independently of the specific claims of one of the disputing parties, arbitrators would be entitled to act as guarantors of these collective concerns should the applicable rules provide for *erga omnes* international obligations. Besides, the international rules on the protection of such concerns would prevail over the international rules for the protection of a foreign investor's interests if those concerns were collective concerns protected by international peremptory norms. *Erga omnes* obligations and/or peremptory norms are still difficult to establish today with regard to the non-investment concerns which have often arisen within the international investment legal framework.[58] This may explain the cautious approach of many arbitrators.

The international investment legal framework appears to have been shaken by the attitude of a few investment arbitral tribunals, by public opinion and discontent which tend towards a possible change in favour of more integration of non-investment concerns into international investment law.

Since the approach of arbitral tribunals is most of the time directed to safeguarding the letter of the law on which their jurisdiction is based and/or the host State's police power, States may encourage the achievement of such a result, by changing the applicable law to this end. This would be in line with the views on State 'positive obligations' expressed by the UN Committee on economic, social and cultural rights in its General Comments, particularly in those on the right to health and the right to water.[59]

57 See, in particular, cases at footnotes 39, 44 and 45.

58 As to the structure of international rules concerning the protection of health, see Acconci (2011), especially 10–16.

59 See the 'General Comment No. 14 on the Right to the Highest Attainable Standard of Health' (11 August 2000, UN Doc. E/C.12/2000/4) and the 'General Comment No. 15 on the Right to Water' (20 January 2003, UN Doc. E/C 12/2002/11).

From a general point of view, the international investment legal framework has produced a good record but at this stage it needs to be renegotiated and restructured for the benefit of all parties concerned with the world perspective and the continuous changes brought about by the diffusion of technology. An appropriate start might be the adoption of binding interpretative guidelines for conflicts between international investment law and international rules on the protection of non-investment concerns. It would be even better if a greater number of States were to integrate non-investment concerns into international investment law by drafting 'model clauses' for recurring issues dealt with by arbitrators as to the relevance of international rules on the protection of non-investment concerns within the international investment framework, with the aim of introducing specific provisions and/or standards.

This can be achieved through new negotiations affecting existing BITs and/or new proposals for a multilateral treaty.[60] In the last decade certain BITs have been renegotiated to make them better instruments to mitigate conflicts of interests between Contracting States on new issues, like the determination of the field of application of most-favoured-nation clauses and of compensation in case of indirect expropriation.[61]

The new Model BIT of the United States, like that of Canada, favours textual solutions for the protection of non-investment concerns with a potential collective dimension, like the environment and health. Such a Model BIT may be seen as a new approach to promoting foreign investments in comparison with 'old' investment treaties still in force today.[62] In the latter the fact that non-investment concerns are mentioned in preambles and/or as exceptions seems to be lip-service to public interests without anything substantial being achieved.

The recent materialization of the 'post-Lisbon Treaty' European Union as a new important player in the international investment arena has generated expectations as to the relevance of public-policy objectives and principles within the international legal investment framework, as if a levelling of the existing playing field were near to being achieved.[63] Arts. 21 of the

60 See Caron (2009), especially 523–4; Wouters and Hachez (2009), especially 340, 344; Miles (2010); Toral and Schultz (2010); Wells (2010); Geiger (2011), 153–73; Markert (2011). In favour of bilateralism, rather than multilateralism, cf. Krishan (2011); while see Yackee (2009) for the proposal of a 'minimalist system of international investment law'.

61 See Peinhardt and Allec (2010–11).

62 'Old' refers to the BITs made up to the late 1990s which have been continuously revised without substantial changes.

63 See Reinisch (2008), 205–6; Brown and Alcover Llubià (2010–11), especially 161.

Treaty on the European Union and 205 of the Treaty on the Functioning of the European Union are considered as highly relevant, since they provide for consistency between the EU external action and the principles and values at the basis of the EU integration process. These principles and values include the rule of law, sustainable development, the protection of human rights and of the environment. So far, these expectations have not been realized.[64] Perhaps the reason is that the current financial crisis has led the EU to be inward- rather than outward-looking.

The debate about the design of the EU common policy framework on investments and the legitimacy of international investment law shows that it is time to ask if it is still sufficient to refer to a 'colonial' concept of foreign investor protection, after passing from a colonial period to a global one in international economic relations. Today, the establishment of a favourable climate for foreign investments depends on the expectations not only as to the treatment of investors, but also the social and environmental dimensions of investments.

If the goal is to integrate on the basis of a balance between economic interests and non-investment concerns, new proposals for a multilateral treaty would seem to be called for. Multilateral rules could harmonize relevant non-investment concerns, such as access to basic services, the protection of health and of the environment, as exceptions in case of political, social and economic turmoil.[65] This would allow multilateral rules to settle potential norm conflicts which have arisen in some arbitral proceedings. In addition, multilateral rules could reduce the number of disputes arising from conflicts between diverse interests, which arise from the interpretation and application of different BITs in force connected by treaty provisions referring to the MFN treatment standard.

Since the conclusion of a multilateral investment treaty would contribute to the coordination of international treaty obligations of States, multilateral investment rules could ensure a balanced implementation of stabilization clauses and the fair and equitable treatment standard so as to meet expectations both of foreign investors and the people living in host States,[66] particularly in poor countries, in order to reach a more equitable share of the benefits from foreign investments.

One of the questions to be answered is whether principles already incorporated in a number of international treaties and acts of UN international organizations, like sustainable development and the precautionary

64 See the contribution by Perfetti in this book. 65 See Choudury (2011).

66 See the contributions by Valenti and De Luca in this book.

principle, should be included in specific provisions of a multilateral investment treaty. These principles would widen the margin of appreciation of host States, as well as the discretionary powers of arbitrators.

Assuming the 'importation' of principles and regulatory solutions found in other international legal frameworks to be appropriate in order, through interpretation, to coordinate the interplay of issues arising in international investment law,[67] multilateral rules would facilitate the resort to systemic interpretation of investment treaties in accordance with Art. 31 (3) (c) of the Vienna Convention on the Law of Treaties which provides that '[t]here shall be taken into account, together with the context … any relevant rules of international law applicable in the relations between the parties'.

The universe of Contracting Parties to a multilateral investment treaty and international treaties on the protection of the environment, of historical and cultural sites and/or of human rights would thus become homogenous. Therefore, the treaty rules on the protection of such non-investment concerns might become relevant in the interpretation of investment treaty rules. This would prevent problems like those which arose in the WTO *EC-Biotech Products* case. In that case the WTO panel did not consider the Biodiversity Convention and its Protocol on Biosafety relevant for the systemic interpretation of the WTO treaties in question, in accordance with Art. 31 (3) (c), since the Contracting States of the Convention and Protocol and those of the WTO treaties were not the same.[68]

6. Concluding remarks

Greater integration of non-investment concerns into international investment law, through the conclusion of a multilateral treaty, might mitigate the diversification of international investment law and reduce its inconsistency. Making international investment law less controversial might reduce lengthy arbitrations, whenever non-investment concerns are relevant to settle a case.[69] Uniformity and consistency in the applicable international rules would facilitate arbitrators.

67 In favour of arbitral and judicial importation at an international law level, see French (2006).

68 See WT/DS291/R, WT/DS292/R and WT/DS293/R, Report of the Panel, 29 September 2006, 7.68–75.

69 See Alvarez (2011), especially 456–7.

Although many discussions are taking place, negotiations towards one multilateral investment agreement or a network of regional investment agreements are not on the agenda. This apparent indifference by States may be due to the fact that the renewal of BITs occurs automatically.[70] However, it is time not only for States to concern themselves with legal definitions to answer popular demands and make investment arbitration less controversial, but also for other actors, like NGOs, to assess the weight of non-investment concerns in the international investment framework.[71] At present, the average time for the settlement of investment disputes is too long for all parties, including possible third parties like NGOs.

One proposal to put multilateral negotiations back on the agenda could be for a convergence of the different ongoing researches and studies into a network with the purpose of designing a model framework for future negotiations. A starting point might be the drafting of 'model clauses' and/or 'model interpretative guidelines' for recurring issues dealt with by different arbitral tribunals. This would speed up proceedings and facilitate the establishment of a more favourable climate for international investments which is something needed in times of economic crisis.

Such 'model clauses' and/or 'model guidelines' might clarify the criteria that would, in cases of conflict, facilitate the combination of a foreign investor's interests and a host State's non-investment concerns. Due to the inconsistency of investment treaties and arbitrations, it is difficult to formulate definitive criteria, although legal writers, international organizations and private associations have made proposals in this connection.[72]

70 As this book goes to press, there are unconfirmed reports that Ecuador wishes to withdraw from all its BITs.

71 See Mann (2011), 22–9. A number of studies in international investment law have been carried out within international organizations, such as the United Nations Conference on Trade and Development (UNCTAD), and private transnational associations, like the International Law Association (ILA) and the International Institute for Sustainable Development (IISD), in the last decade. The amassed data from these studies could be used to identify common features which might represent a starting point for future negotiations.

72 In 2013 UNCTAD published a report to promote 'a new generation of investment policies' ('Investment Policy Framework for Sustainable Development', www.unctad.org) and UNCITRAL published new rules for greater transparency in host States–foreign investors disputes (www.uncitral.org). See also the OECD 'Policy Framework for Investment' (www.oecd.org/daf/inv/mne/pfi.htm). Some writers have suggested what new investment treaty clauses might provide and what international organizations might do to protect both foreign investments and human rights. See Weiler (2004); van Aaken (2009); Kammerhofer (2011); Taillant and Bonnitcha (2011); Prislan (2012); Francioni (2012).

Integration is materializing as an appropriate means since it is based on a balance of different interests and concerns. This emerges from the judicial importation into international investment law of principles and interpretative methods, like proportionality and the standard-of-review, from other international, as well as domestic, legal systems. Even if this kind of 'organic' integration has come about,[73] demonstrating that integration is a useful means, it may be preferable to bring all parties concerned together in a specific forum to devise rules and regulations for a 'more standard' form of integration that incorporates a wide range of values and interests from the economic to the environmental to the ethical. This 'standard' integration might facilitate arbitration in the future.

References

Acconci, P. 2011. *Tutela della salute e diritto internazionale*. Padova: CEDAM.

2012. 'La "green economy" e la realizzazione dei diritti dell'uomo alla base dello sviluppo sostenibile'. *Diritti umani e diritto internazionale* 6: 587–607.

Alvarez, J.E. 2011. *The Public International Law Regime Governing International Investment*. Maubeuge: AIL – Pocket.

Alvarez, J.E., Sauvant, K.P., Ahmed, K.G. and Vizcaíno, G.P. (eds.). 2011. *The Evolving International Investment Regime: Expectations, Realities, Options*. Oxford University Press.

Blackaby, N. and Richard, C. 2010. 'Amicus Curiae: A Panacea for Legitimacy in Investment Arbitration?'. Waibel, Kaushal, Chung and Balchin (eds.): 253–368.

Brower, II, C.H. 2008–9. 'Obstacles and Pathways to Consideration of the Public Interest in Investment Treaty Disputes'. *Yearbook on International Investment L & Policy*: 347–78.

Brown, C. and Alcover Llubià, M. 2010–11. 'The External Investment Policy of the European Union in the Light of the Entry into Force of the Treaty of Lisbon'. *Yearbook on International Investment L & Policy*: 145–64.

Burke-White, W. and von Staden, A. 2010. 'The Need for Public Law Standards of Review in Investor-State Arbitrations'. Schill (ed.): 689–720.

Caron, D.D. 2009. 'Investor State Arbitration: Strategic and Tactical Perspectives on Legitimacy'. *Suffolk Transnational L Review* 32: 513–24.

Choudury, B. 2011. 'Exception Provisions as a Gateway to Incorporating Human Rights Issues into International Investment Law'. *Columbia Transnational L* 49: 670–716.

73 By 'organic' I mean that the current integration has not been pre-devised.

Darrow, M. 2003. *Between Light and Shadow. The World Bank, the International Monetary Fund and International Human Rights Law*. Oxford: Hart Publishing.

El Boudouhi, S. 2005. 'L'intérêt général et les règles substantielles de protection des investissements'. *Annuaire français de droit international* 60: 542–63.

Francioni, F. 2012. 'Diritto internazionale degli investimenti e tutela dei diritti umani: convergenza o conflitto?'. Di Stefano, A. and Sapienza, R. (eds.), *La tutela dei diritti umani e il diritto internazionale*. Napoli: Editoriale Scientifica, 417–35.

French, D. 2006. 'Treaty Interpretation and the Incorporation of Extraneous Legal Rules'. *ICLQ* 55: 281–314.

Fry, J.D. 2007. 'International Human Rights Law in Investment Arbitration: Evidence of International Law's Unity'. *Duke J Comparative and International L* 18: 77–149.

Geiger, R. 2011. 'Multilateral Approaches to Investment: The Way Forward'. Alvarez, Sauvant, Ahmed and Vizcaíno (eds.): 153–73.

Henckels, C. 2012. 'Indirect Expropriation and the Right to Regulate: Revisiting Proportionality Analysis and the Standard of Review in Investor-State Arbitration'. *JIEL* 15: 223–55.

Henry, L. 2010. 'Investment Agreement Claims under the 2004 Model US BIT: A Challenge for State Police Powers?'. *University of Pennsylvania J International L* 31: 935–1011.

Horn, N. (ed.) 1980. *Legal Problems of Codes of Conduct for Multinational Enterprises*. Antwerp; Boston; London; Frankfurt: Kluwer.

Kammerhofer, J. 2011. 'The Theory of Norm Conflict Solutions in International Investment Law'. Cordonier Segger, M.-C., Gehring, M.W. and Newcombe, A. (eds.), *Sustainable Development in World Investment Law*. Alphen aan den Rijn: Wolters Kluwer: 83–98.

Kingsbury, B. and Schill, S.W. 2010. 'Public Law Concepts to Balance Investors' Rights with State Regulatory Actions in the Public Interest – The Concept of Proportionality'. Schill (ed.): 75–104.

Krishan, D. 2011. 'Thinking about BITs and BIT Arbitration: The Legitimacy Crisis'. Weiler and Baetens (eds.): 107–50.

Krommendijk, J. and Morijn, J. 2009. '"Proportional" by What Measure(s)? Balancing Investor Interests and Human Rights by Way of Applying the Proportionality Principle in Investor-State Arbitration'. Dupuy, P.-M., Francioni, F., Petersmann, E.-U. (eds.), *Human Rights in International Investment Law and Arbitration*. Oxford University Press: 422–51.

Lattanzi, F. 2012. 'Introduction', van den Herik, L. and Stahn, C. (eds.), *The Diversification and Fragmentation of International Criminal Law*. Leiden, Boston: Martinus Nijhoff Publishers, 1–20.

Liberti, L. 2007. 'Investissements et droits de l'homme'. Kahn, P. and Wälde, T.W. (eds.), *New Aspects of International Investment Law*. Leiden, Boston: Martinus Nijhoff Publishers, 791–852.

Mann, H. 2011. 'Civil Society Perspectives: What Do Key Stakeholders Expect from the International Investment Regime?'. Alvarez, Sauvant, Ahmed and Vizcaíno (eds.): 22–9.

Markert, L. 2011. 'The Crucial Question of Future Investment Treaties: Balancing Investors' Rights and Regulatory Interests of Host States'. Bungenberg, M. *et al.* (eds.), *International Investment Law and EU Law*. Berlin, Heidelberg: Springer-Verlag, 145–71.

Marrella, F. 2010. 'On the Changing Structure of International Investment Law: The Human Right to Water and ICSID Arbitration'. *International Community L Review* 12: 335–59.

McLachlan, C. 2008. 'Investment Treaties and General International Law'. *ICLQ* 57: 361–401.

Miles, K. 2010. 'International Investment Law: Origins, Imperialism and Conceptualizing the Environment'. *Colorado J International Environmental L & Policy* 21: 1–47.

Montt, S. 2012. *State Liability in Investment Treaty Arbitration*. Oxford and Portland: Hart Publishing.

Muchlinski, P. 2008. 'Policy Issues'. Muchlinski, Ortino and Schreuer (eds.): 3–48.

Muchlinski, P., Ortino, F. and Schreuer, C. (eds.). 2008. *The Oxford Handbook of International Investment Law*. Oxford University Press.

Newcombe, A. and Paradell, L. 2009. *Law and Practice of Investment Treaties*. Alphen aan den Rijn: Kluwer Law International.

Pannatier, S. and Ducrey, O. 2005, 'Water Concessions and Protection of Foreign Investments under International Law'. Weiss, B., Boisson de Chazournes, L. and Bernasconi-Osterwalder, N. (eds.), *Fresh Water and International Economic Law*. Oxford University Press: 289–302.

Peinhardt, C. and Allec, T. 2010–11. 'Devil in Details?'. *Yearbook on International Investment L & Policy*: 837–58.

Picone, P. 2011. 'The Distiction between *Jus Cogens* and Obligations *Erga Omnes*'. Cannizzaro, E. (ed.), *The Law of Treaties Beyond the Vienna Convention*. Oxford University Press: 411–24.

Prislan, V. 2012. 'Non-Investment Obligations in Investment Treaty Arbitration – Towards a Greater Role for States?'. Baetens, F. (ed.), *Investment Law Within International Law: An Integrationist Perspective*. Cambridge University Press: 450–481.

Reinisch, A. 2008. '"Investment and ..." – The Broader Picture of Investment Law'. Reinisch, A. and Knahr, C., *International Investment Law in Context*. Utrecht: Eleven International Publishing: 201–7.

Rubin, S.J. 1995. 'Transnational Corporations and International Codes of Conduct: A Study of the Relationship Between International Legal Cooperation and Economic Development'. *American University International L Review* 10: 1275–89.

Sacerdoti, G. 1997. 'Bilateral Treaties and Multilateral Instruments on Investment Protection'. *RCADI* 269: 251–460.

2011. 'Precedent in the Settlement of International Economic Disputes: The WTO and the Investment Arbitration Models'. Rovine, A. (ed.), *Contemporary Issues in International Arbitration and Mediation: The Fordham Papers 2010*. Leiden; Boston: Martinus Nijhoff Publishers, 225–46.

Salacuse, J.W. 2009–10. 'Investment Treaties Through a Different Lens: A New Global Regime?'. *Yearbook on International Investment L & Policy*: 575–94.

Schill, S.W. 2009. *The Multilateralization of International Investment Law*. Cambridge University Press.

(ed.). 2010. *International Investment Law and Comparative Public Law*. Oxford University Press.

2011. 'Public or Private Dispute Settlement? The Culture Clash in Investment Treaty Arbitration and Its Impact on the Role of the Arbitrator'. Weiler and Baetens (eds.): 23–44.

Schreuer, C. and Kriebaum, U. 2011. 'From Individual to Community Interest in International Investment Law'. Fastenrath, U., Geiger, R., Khan, D.-E., Paulus, A., von Schorlemer, S. and C. Vedder (eds.), *From Bilateralism to Community Interest. Essays in Honour of Judge Bruno Simma*. Oxford University Press: 1079–96.

Schreuer, C. and Weiniger, M., 2008. 'A Doctrine of Precedent?'. Muchlinski, Ortino and Schreuer (eds.): 1188–206.

Sen, B. 1988. 'Investment Protection and New World Order'. *Zeitschrift für ausländisches öffentliches Recht und Völkerrecht* 48: 419–46.

Shany, Y. 2006. 'Toward a General Margin of Appreciation Doctrine in International Law?'. *EJIL* 16: 907–40.

Simma, B. and Kill, T. 2008. 'Harmonizing Investment Protection and International Human Rights: First Steps Towards a Methodology'. Binder, C., Kriebaum, U., Reinisch, A. and Wittich, S. (eds.), *International Investment Law for the 21st Century. Essays in Honour of Christoph Schreuer*. Oxford University Press: 678–707.

Stern, B. 2011. 'The Future of International Investment Law: A Balance Between the Protection of Investors and the States' Capacity to Regulate'. Alvarez, Sauvant, Ahmed and Vizcaíno (eds.): 174–92.

Stone, J. 2012. 'Arbitrariness, the Fair and Equitable Treatment Standard, and the International Law of Investment'. *Leiden J International L* 25: 77–107.

Taillant, J.D. and Bonnitcha, J. 2011. 'International Investment Law and Human Rights'. Cordonier Segger, M.-C., Gehring, M.W. and Newcombe, A. (eds.),

Sustainable Development in World Investment Law. Alphen aan den Rijn: Wolters Kluwer, 57–80.

Thielbörger, P. 2009. 'The Human Right to Water Versus Investor Rights: Double-Dilemma or Pseudo-Conflict?'. Dupuy, P.-M., Francioni, F., Petersmann, E.-U. (eds.), *Human Rights in International Investment Law and Arbitration*. Oxford University Press: 487–510.

Toral, M. and Schultz, T. 2010. 'The State, a Perpetual Respondent in Investment Arbitration? Some Unorthodox Considerations'. Waibel, Kaushal, Chung and Balchin (eds.): 577–602.

UNDP, 2011. *Getting It Right: Lessons from the South in Managing Hydrocarbon Economies*. New York: UNDP.

Vadi, V. 2013. *Public Health in International Investment Law and Arbitration*. London and New York: Routledge.

van Aaken, A. 2009. 'International Investment Law Between Commitment and Flexibility: A Contract Theory Analysis'. *JIEL* 12: 507–38.

Van Harten, G. 2007. *Investment Treaty Arbitration and Public Law*. Oxford University Press.

von Staden, A. 2011. 'Towards Greater Doctrinal Clarity in Investor-State Arbitration: The *CMS*, *Enron*, and *Sempra* Annulment Decisions'. *Czech Yearbook of International L* 2: 207–27.

Waibel, M., Kaushal, A., Chung, K.-H.L., and Balchin, C. (eds.). 2010. *The Backlash against Investment Arbitration: Perceptions and Reality*. Alphen aan den Rijn: Wolters Kluwer.

Weiler, T. 2004. 'Balancing Human Rights and Investor Protection: A New Approach for a Different Legal Order'. *Boston College International and Comparative L Review* 27: 429–52.

2005. 'Good Faith and Regulatory Transparency: The Story of *Metalclad* v. *Mexico*'. Weiler, T. (ed.), *International Investment Law and Arbitration: Leading Cases from the ICSID, NAFTA, Bilateral Treaties and Customary International Law*. London: Cameron May, 701–46.

Weiler, T. and Baetens, F. (eds.). 2011. *New Directions in International Economic Law. In Memoriam Thomas Wälde*. Leiden; Boston: Martinus Nijhoff Publishers.

Wells, L.T. 2010. 'Backlash to Investment Arbitration: Three Causes'. Waibel, Kaushal, Chung and Balchin (eds.): 341–52.

World Bank. 2004. *Partnerships in Development*, Washington, DC: World Bank.

Wouters, J. and Hachez, N. 2009. 'When Rules and Values Collide: How Can a Balanced Application of Investor Protection Provisions and Human Rights Be Ensured?'. *Human Rights & International Legal Discourse* 3: 301–44.

Yackee, J.W. 2009. 'Toward a Minimalist System of International Investment Law?'. *Suffolk Transnational L Review* 32: 303–39.

8

Intellectual property protection in investment agreements and public concerns

ANTONIETTA DI BLASE

1. The role of intellectual property within the framework of the protection of investments

Intellectual property rights (IPRs), being a key element in technology-transfer and production, play a primary role in investment.[1] This means that States, to be attractive towards investors, have to adapt their legislation according to an adequate standard of IP protection.[2] Nevertheless, it may be necessary to introduce limits, through compulsory licences or other measures reducing the use or extent of IP titles, in order to address social needs, public emergencies or health and environmental challenges, which can be generally referred to as 'public concerns'. The reach and legitimacy of such restrictions represent a controversial issue in the light of IP international law rules and their interference with the foreign investors' rights, since they have an impact on expected economic rewards.

Under the Agreement on the Trade-Related Aspects of Intellectual Property Rights (TRIPs), adopted within the framework of the World Trade Organization (WTO), some margins of discretion are provided which give Members the right to derogate from a rigid implementation of the Agreement, under given circumstances.[3] The TRIPs Preamble

1 On the debates within the WTO Committee on Trade and Environment on the role of IP in the transfer of environmentally sound technology see Macmillan (2001), 211–15.

2 An open question is that of the level of IP protection beyond which the promotion of investments and the economic development of a State could be affected: see OECD Report (OECD Working Party of the Trade Committee), 'The Impact of Trade-Related Intellectual Property Rights on Trade and Foreign Direct Investment in Developing Countries', 2003, www.oecd.org/dataoecd/59/46/2960051.pdf, 4) and UNCTAD, 'The TRIPS Agreement and Developing Countries' (*UNCTAD-ICTSD Policy Discussion Paper*, 87), Geneva, 1996, 18. Chaudhuri (2005), 128 is sceptical about the existence of a positive causal relationship between IP protection and foreign investment.

3 We do not refer here to issues left outside the scope of TRIPs, as for instance IPRs exhaustion (Art. 6 TRIPs). On the distinction between limits and exceptions, with reference to GATT, see the contribution by Sacerdoti in this book.

preserves the Members' right to pursue 'the objectives of national systems for the protection of intellectual property, including developmental and technological objectives'. As a consequence, Member States can balance IPRs for individuals or juridical persons against the need to improve and secure international technology transfer as an instrument for social and economic welfare (Art. 7 TRIPs). Members may adopt and amend their national law 'to protect public health and nutrition, and to promote the public interest in sectors of vital importance to their socio-economic development', provided such measures are consistent with the TRIPs provisions (Art. 8.1 TRIPs).

Some TRIPs provisions introduce true 'exceptions', under given conditions: this is the case with respect to compulsory licences, the Member State concerned being left the power to determine autonomously what amounts to a 'national emergency' or 'other circumstances of extreme urgency' (Art. 31 TRIPs). An exception is also provided in Art. 27.2 TRIPs, permitting Member States to exclude the patentability of certain inventions in order 'to protect *ordre public* or morality'.[4] Other limited exceptions to IPRs consisting in introducing restrictions to a registered patent or re-directing the way a trademark is used,[5] or other forms of regulatory controls on the utilization and exploitation of IPRs might be introduced by Member States, provided they are reasonable (Arts. 13 and 30 TRIPs, relating to copyright and patents, respectively) and taking into account the legitimate interests of the owner (Arts. 13 and 17, relating to copyright and trademarks) and of third parties (Arts. 17 and 30). Thus margins of freedom are given to Member States to consider social and welfare needs, health or environmental problems, although the latter do not represent the central focus of the TRIPs Agreement and of the WTO system in general. We can say that public concerns belong to the sphere of the 'flexibilities' of the system.[6]

4 See Vadi (2012), 93–130, on the clash between public health and investment law, and options to reconcile the different interests at stake.

5 The Australian Tobacco Plain Packaging Act 2011 has banned colour, shape and retail 'finish' from the packaging of tobacco products, on the basis that it may render the product too attractive in spite of its negative effects on health. A notice of arbitration was sent to the Attorney General for Australia by Phillip Morris on 21 November 2011 on the basis of the Hong Kong/Australia BIT of 1993. For the same facts, Ukraine, the Dominican Republic and Uruguay have requested consultations under the WTO/DSU, for infringements of TRIPs, but also the Technical Barriers to Trade Agreement (TBT) and GATT: for the case started by Ukraine a panel was established in August 2012 (WT/DS434/11, 17 August 2012).

6 The issue of exclusion from patentability, exceptions and limitations in the national laws has been on the World Intellectual Property Organization (WIPO) agenda since 2009:

In addition to public concerns relating to health or the environment, which may be considered as external limits, in order to keep legislation in line with the general aim of pursuing general interests, IPRs must also be balanced against the aim of trade liberalization and competition. The incorporation of intellectual property rights into the fundamental WTO objectives means that competition must be safeguarded against possible abuses of intellectual property rights, as an inherent limit to IPRs protection.[7] Reference may be made to the Preamble, where the risk that IPRs could become barriers to legitimate trade is mentioned, as well as to Art. 8.2 TRIPs, for measures that States should adopt in order 'to prevent the abuse of IPRs by right holders'. Art. 40 is also relevant in this regard.[8]

In the light of the investment treaties, limitations imposed by a State on investors' IPRs are to be balanced against the right of the investor to 'enjoy protection and security' within the territory of the contracting State, IPRs being included among the assets of the investors.[9] This means that measures denying or restricting the use of those rights are to be considered as a kind of expropriation. Such a perspective has not changed, even if some recent bilateral investment treaties (BITs) and other more comprehensive bilateral or regional free trade agreements (FTAs), that also include provisions on IPRs, make reference to grounds that might permit the adoption of restrictive measures by the host State, especially with regard to public health and the environment, under given conditions. In fact, it cannot be excluded that a potential interaction exists between BITs/FTAs-based investment law and multilateral trade-related IP rules, though the latter seem more inclined to take into account the wide-ranging debate arising within the international organizations (IOs) belonging to the United Nations (UN) system. We refer to the contribution of the main IOs to

see Report by the Secretariat to the XIII session of the Standing Committee on the Law of Patents (Doc. WIPO, SCP/13/3, 4 February 2009), and the responses from seventy-two States (Doc. WIPO, SCP/18/INF/2, 2 April 2012).

7 See Heinemann (2006), 241–3.

8 We refer, in the present chapter, to patents and trademarks, since the problem of possible limits for investors' IPRs has emerged in the practice mainly with reference to those rights.

9 IP is mentioned in the Germany–Pakistan Treaty of 25 November 1959 for the promotion and protection of investments, Art. 8.1 (a). Recent investment agreements generally provide for a detailed list of IPRs. See for instance Art. 1.1 (d) of the 2011 Germany–Pakistan Treaty on the Encouragement and Reciprocal Protection of Investments, which replaces the 1959 Treaty.

provide for a global response to climate change,[10] food security[11] and access to medicines.[12] The emerging trend towards empowering host States to impose limits on investors in the field of IP is evident: the 2001 Doha Declaration, aimed at an expeditious solution to the difficulties of WTO Members with insufficient or no manufacturing capacities in the pharmaceutical sector,[13] is a relevant step forward towards a more flexible interpretation of the international rules on IP.[14] This may influence the attitude of the relevant WTO bodies when settling disputes relating to TRIPs compliance. A TRIPs amendment, adopted by a Decision by the General Council of 6 December 2005 and ratified by a large number of Members – though not yet reaching the two-thirds majority required for its entry into force – should make it easier for poorer countries to obtain cheaper generic versions of patented medicines.[15] It also gives support to the idea that common concerns should be shared by all States, and that they justify possible exceptions to conflicting provisions in international agreements.

An in-depth analysis of the applicable BITs/FTAs rules is beyond the limits of the present work. Moreover, a centralized and homogeneous legal system is lacking in the field of investment law. However, from a summary investigation of the models followed in investment treaties, a different approach emerges in comparison with the TRIPs Agreement as to the weight given to public interests: within the multilateral trade system IPRs are strictly linked with the aim of technological development, progress in knowledge and distinctiveness of products, whereas the protection of foreign investors' tangible and intangible assets represents the core issue of any investment agreement. For these reasons, a conflict may

10 See Maskus, Okediji, Reichman and Roffe (2011), 1–8. Within the UN Framework Convention on Climate Change (UNFCCC), the view has been expressed that IP should improve climate, though no agreement exists at the moment on the level of protection and the option of applying the existing TRIPS flexibilities to enhance climate-related technology transfer.

11 IP has been on the FAO agenda since 2002 in connection with genetic resources.

12 Public health has been at the top of the World Health Organization (WHO) agenda since 1996, in response to the HIV/AIDS epidemic. The debate led to the Revised Drug Strategy (RDS) (WHO Res. 54.11, 2001) and the Global Strategy Plan of Action (GSPOA) for Public Health, Innovation and Intellectual Property (2008), supporting the State's right to deal with health emergencies. See, among others, 't Hoen (2009), 1–160.

13 Declaration on the TRIPs Agreement and Public Health, WTO Ministerial Conference, IVth session, Doha (WT/MIN(01)/DEC/2), 14 November 2001, 4.

14 With reference to patents see Acconci (2011a), 803–28.

15 The term for the acceptance of the Protocol has been extended to 31 December 2013 (Doc. IP/C/58, 2 November 2011).

arise whenever the two different sets of rules must be applied in assessing the host State's policy towards foreign investors, leading to conflicting decisions by investment arbitrators and WTO/DSU bodies.

In the final part of the present chapter, reference will be made to possible developments towards reconciling investors rights and non-trade values in the specific field of IP, in order to foster coherence between the bilateral and the multilateral systems.

2. TRIPs-plus clauses in BITs/FTAs

As highlighted above, public concerns are not the foundation of BITs/FTAs, their aim being instead to ensure that investors reap the expected rewards for their activities. This means that if we refer to the general interest to a shared use of resources and to the availability of environmentally sound technologies, it may happen that the obligations undertaken by the host State could be an obstacle to adopting or changing local legislation where it has the effect of limiting investors' protection.

We refer, in particular, to the rights granted by BITs including provisions on IP protection. Some of the measures restricting the investors' IPRs could be legitimate at the multilateral level, on the basis of the TRIPs flexibilities. It could thus be interesting to compare those margins of flexibility with the bilateral investment rules. A higher level of IP protection in comparison with the regime established through the TRIPs Agreement means a TRIPs-plus regime, limiting the power of the host State to address public interest concerns, which may lead to a clash between the bilateral rules and the aims and principles to be followed at the multilateral level.

Interference by the host State in the IPRs of an investor, when it is not permitted by a BIT/FTA, results in an expropriation of the investor's rights. Since the infringement in question does not amount to a formal transfer or seizure of the IPRs – depriving the investor of his ownership of the IPRs – but has the effect of substantially limiting the economic reward, in the form of the value of IPRs and the expected profits, it is referred to as an 'indirect expropriation'. The concept has been adopted in *Metalclad*, to include any measure that leads to depreciation of the value of property or annulment of reasonably expected benefits.[16] The BIT/FTA

16 *Metalclad* v. *Mexico* (Case No. ICSID ARB(AF)/97/1, Award, 25 August 2000). A wide formulation is also present in *Pope and Talbot* v. *Canada* (UNCITRAL Arbitration, Award in respect of damages, 31 May 2002). These disputes relate to NAFTA Art. 1110 prohibiting not only the physical expropriation of private property, but also indirect takings and measures 'tantamount to nationalization and expropriation'. See also *Tecmed*

arbitrators will decide whether an indirect expropriation has taken place on the basis of the general standards of treatment applicable not only with regard to IPRs, but also to other assets: fair and equitable treatment, non-discrimination, reasonableness and transparency. The same approach is followed in a number of FTAs that include specific provisions relating to IP, whose model is often followed in negotiations with other States, on a regional basis. The result is the enlargement of the host State's commitments beyond the TRIPs rules, thus repealing the limits and flexibilities hitherto permitted by TRIPs.

It is not possible to give an exhaustive review of the different BITs/FTAs clauses providing for enhancement of the level of IP protection.[17] The less recent ones, dating back to the 1960s merely include IP in the list of the investor's rights, thus making no distinction between IP and other assets as possible objects of expropriation in terms of the applicable standards of treatment. In other more recent agreements, specific rules relating to patents provide for the so-called data exclusivity period of five years, to be counted from the date when the product was approved, whether or not it was patented.[18] This means extending the time that generic producers have to wait in order to be able to start the production of an identical non-patented drug. A similar impact may result from the rules providing for a patent extension beyond the TRIPs twenty-year term, to compensate for delay in marketing approval.[19] Other provisions relate to patent exhaustion, which is expressly excluded from the scope of TRIPs (Art. 6 TRIPs). These provisions have the effect of extending the patent rights beyond the first sale of the product or of the process, and restrict the ability of Members to resort to parallel importation, which means excluding the possibility that consumers will benefit from the

v. *Mexico* (ICSID Case No. ARB(AF)/00/2, Award, 29 May 2003, 113). Cf. Hoffmann (2008), 151–70 and Sornarajah (2010), 369–73.

17 A detailed description of the TRIPs-plus provisions in BITs and FTAs is given, among others, by Vivas-Eugui (2003), www.quno.org/geneva/pdf/economic/Issues/FTAs-TRIPS-plus-annex-English.pdf, 1–97 and by Drahos (2003), 7.

18 See for instance Art. 15.10 of CAFTA-DR, signed on 5 August 2004, by the US and five Central American Countries (Costa Rica, El Salvador, Guatemala, Honduras, Nicaragua), and the Dominican Republic (www.ustr.gov/trade-agreements/free trade agreements/cafta-dr-dominican-republic-central-america-fta).

19 US–Australia FTA, Art. 17.9 (8); US–Morocco FTA, Art. 15.9 (7); US–Singapore FTA, Art. 16.7 (7) and (8); CAFTA-DR, Art. 15.9 (6). All these agreements will be gradually reproduced in the framework of the Trans-Pacific Partnership Agreement (TPP), signed in 2005 (draft of the chapter relating to intellectual property rights – 20 February 2011 – at keionline.org/sites/default/files/tpp-10feb2011-us-text-ipr-chapter.pdf).

lower prices of generic goods produced abroad.[20] Limits have also been introduced with respect to compulsory licensing,[21] granting a wider margin of patent protection.

Some treaties, such as the 2004 US-Central American FTA (CAFTA-DR), limit the Members' right under Art. 27.3 (b) TRIPs to exclude biological material from patentable subject matter,[22] and put in place additional conditions for the revocation of patents (Arts. 15.9.2 and 15.9.4).[23] Thus FTA parties are not free to rely on TRIPs flexibilities to modify their legislation:[24] reference to TRIPs flexibilities is made 'subject to' TRIPS-plus FTA through 'freeze-clauses' which prevent the contracting States from adapting their own IP system to a changing economic, technological and social context.

20 US–Morocco FTA, Art. 15.9 (4): 'Each Party shall provide that the exclusive right of the patent owner to prevent importation of a patented product, or a product that results from patented process, without the consent of the patent owner shall not be limited by the sale or distribution of that product outside its territory'; in the US–Australia FTA, Art. 17.9 (4) excludes exhaustion whenever the investor has placed restrictions on importation by contract or other means.

21 US–Australia FTA, Art. 17.9 (7):

> [a] Party shall not permit the use of the subject matter of a patent without the authorization of the right holder except in the following circumstances: (a) to remedy a practice determined after judicial or administrative process to be anticompetitive under the Party's laws relating to prevention of anti-competitive practices; or: (b) in cases of public non-commercial use, or of national emergency, or other circumstances of extreme urgency, provided that: (i) the Party shall limit such use to use by the government or third persons authorized by the government; (ii) the Party shall ensure that the patent owner is provided with reasonable compensation for such use; and (iii) the Party may not require the patent owner to provide undisclosed information or technical know-how related to a patented invention that has been authorized for use in accordance with this paragraph.

See also the US–Singapore FTA, Art. 16.7 (6).

22 See Art. 10.7 (5) CAFTA-DR.

23 US–CAFTA DR Art.15.9 (2), identical to Art. 16.9 (2) of the US–Colombia FTA and US–Peru TPA:

> Nothing in this Chapter shall be construed to prevent a Party from excluding inventions from patentability as set out in Arts. 27.2 and 27.3 of the TRIPS Agreement. Notwithstanding the foregoing, any Party that does not provide patent protection for plants by the date of entry into force of this Agreement shall undertake all reasonable efforts to make such patent protection available. Any Party that provides patent protection for plants or animals on or after the date of entry into force of this Agreement shall maintain such protection.

24 See Art. 8 of the TPP draft, limiting the right to exclude plants and animals from patentability, however authorizing a modified handling of the matter by Contracting States.

3. Non-consistency of TRIPs-plus clauses with the WTO/TRIPs regime

Restricting resort to TRIPs flexibilities in a BIT/FTA could be considered an option for a State: the latter may decide to waive its right when signing a treaty, making the choice of not taking measures that would otherwise be consistent with the TRIPs system. From this point of view, treaty clauses excluding those flexibilities, being the expression of the freedom of a State to waive its own rights, may be considered in line with the TRIPs provisions and there should be no limit to their applicability.

At the same time, the discretion allowed by TRIPs in favour of a less rigid application of the provisions relating to IP, in given circumstances and within certain limits, may be considered as the expression of the need to reach a balance between IP protection and progress in the economic, social, cultural and technological development of the country. Such a balance is essential in making the general commitments resulting from multilateral treaties effective, particularly in relation to developmental and environmental goals. The balancing of public concerns with the protection of IP must be accomplished by the State on a case-by-case basis, since it is only possible for WTO bodies to intervene with reference to the standards of non-discrimination, reasonableness and prohibition of disguised restrictions on trade, in terms of TRIPs. For this reason, Arts. 7 and 8 of the TRIPs Agreement have been referred to as 'a useful bridge that connects the TRIPs regime with those other regimes that may be implicated by the protection and enforcement of intellectual property rights … [they are therefore] important for maintaining the balance in not just the TRIPs regime, but also in the global innovation system'.[25]

From this point of view, the enjoyment of such flexibilities cannot be considered as the expression of a free choice for a State hosting foreign investment, nor can it be placed at the same level as the need to reap profits from the investment.[26]

To this extent, flexibilities represent a vital instrument that cannot be disposed of once and for all, since they are essential in order to attain the

25 Yu (2009), 1039.

26 Worth mentioning here is the declaration by the Indian Delegate at the TRIPS Council Meeting on 8–9 June 2010: 'TRIPS-plus measures cannot be justified on the basis of Art 1.1, since the same provision also states that more extensive protection may only be granted – provided that such protection does not contravene the provisions of this Agreement' (Minutes of the Council for TRIPS Meeting, Agenda Item M – *Enforcement Trends*, IP/C/M/63, 265).

aims and purposes of welfare and technological development.[27] Limiting flexibilities may obstruct measures that the host State could undertake in keeping with general public concerns and may raise problems of consistency with general principles established at the level of international law. Explicit support in favour of the States' efforts to grant public access to pharmaceuticals in the case of insufficient or no manufacturing capacity is expressed by the WTO General Council for TRIPs in the Decision of 6 December 2005, already mentioned, enlarging the exception under Art. 31 (f) TRIPs with respect to compulsory licences in order to remove the duty to direct generic production principally to domestic supply. This Decision strongly emphasizes the WTO Members' right 'to use, to the full, the provisions in the TRIPS Agreement, which provide flexibility' for the purpose of public health protection. The consensus expressed in support of the Declaration and the remarkable number of the acceptances reached seem to align the WTO with the practice of the other multilateral organizations in solemnly endorsing the urgent need to face problems connected with health emergencies, which makes it obligatory for Members to use all possible instruments at hand. This should play a decisive role in the interpretation and application of BIT/FTA provisions relating to investments.[28]

Also within the context of action in favour of higher environmental standards, a conflict between the commitments of a host State towards foreign investors and the duty to abide by the targets established at the global level should be faced giving due regard to the duty of the host State to do whatever necessary to comply with its international obligations.

Apart from considerations connected with the binding force of the rules that have been adopted both inside and outside the TRIPs system, one should not underrate the negative effect on other WTO Members resulting from a regime that risks altering the level of competitiveness in the global market, making them less attractive for investments and the transfer of new technologies. IPRs must not become barriers to legitimate trade. BIT/FTA TRIPs-plus provisions not only may impact on the reciprocal rights and duties of the contracting parties, but may also affect third

27 See Grosse Ruse-Kahn (2011), 31.

28 As the International Law Commission Report on 'Fragmentation of International Law: Difficulties Arising from the Diversification and Expansion of International Law' remarks, with regard to the relevance of the international law principles in the settlement of disputes within the WTO, the practice of the Appellate Body in a number of cases has developed in such a way as to take into account other rules of international law accepted by the disputing States (A/CN.4/L.682, 13 April 2006, 223, 443).

States, making them less competitive in the market for investments, and bringing competition to a level that might well be incompatible with a sound regulation of the market.[29] The need to prevent an abuse of IP and consequent restrictions on competition is the object of the Preamble and of some TRIPs provisions (Art. 8.2 and Art. 40), as we have seen before.

From this point of view, TRIPs-plus provisions may be considered as incompatible with the principle of sound competitiveness, since they risk undermining or limiting the ability of the WTO Members, which are not parties to the bilateral agreement, 'to use the policy space provided by TRIPS'.[30] This effect would be further enlarged through the mechanism of the most favoured nation (MFN) rule, which could be invoked to override exceptions to IPRs.[31] In the light of these considerations, the WTO/DSU, if asked for a decision on the consistency of a measure representing an exception to the duty to protect IP, could consider that measure in keeping with the aims and principles of the TRIPs, even if the same measure might entail a negative impact on the investor and give rise to an infringement of a BIT/FTA, and, consequently, to a claim for indirect expropriation against the host State.

4. The relevance of referral to TRIPs in BITs/FTAs

Some clauses in the 2004 bilateral agreements concluded in conformity with the US Model for a Bilateral Investment Treaty (BIT) – updated in April 2012[32] – seem to uphold some TRIPs flexibilities and mitigate some

29 In the practice of WTO a broad interpretation of anti-competitiveness conduct has been followed: see, among others, the WTO Panel Report *Mexico-Telecom* (WT/DS204/R, 2 April 2004, 7.230 ff.).

30 In order to support the case for non-legitimacy of TRIPs-plus clauses, some authors have argued that a bilateral treaty cannot introduce any limits whatsoever towards third States: in support of this thesis, Mitchell and Voon (2009), 596–9, refer to Art. 41 (b) (i) of the 1969 Vienna Convention on the Law of Treaties, providing that a term of a bilateral treaty between two States also parties of a multilateral agreement may not affect the enjoyment by the other parties of their rights under the multilateral treaty.

31 Correa (2004), 12, refers to MFN clauses in bilateral agreements. According to Abbott (2005), 98, higher standards of IP protection through the MFN rule result in a *de facto* discrimination against the States that are not parties to bilateral agreements. Ranjan (2010), 67–78, claims that Bilateral Trade Agreements (BTAs) and BITs may not restrict TRIPs flexibilities through the MFN rule, and suggests that the GATT exception to MFN where BTAs are entered into under the aegis of Art. XXIV extends to the TRIPS Agreement.

32 The changes introduced in the 2012 US Model BIT are aimed at emphasizing the need to respect transparency and the national environmental law (www.citizen.org/documents/2012-model-bit-changes.pdf). The bilateral agreements which are referred

harsh provisions in FTAs.[33] They ensure that investment standards – especially relating to (indirect) expropriation – do not interfere with the exercise of TRIPs flexibilities.[34] Clauses of the same kind are in almost all investment sections of US FTAs:[35] they not only set out technology transfer requirements and standards of treatment, but also specific exceptions and limitations provided they are allowed under TRIPs. Though these clauses aim at ensuring – to the extent possible – consistency between TRIPs and FTA obligations, it seems that they have a minor impact in comparison with the role that such exceptions play under the TRIPs system.[36]

Under a provision of the EC–Cariforum EPA,[37] the Contracting States committed themselves to granting an adequate and effective implementation of international treaties dealing with IP to which they are parties and of the TRIPs Agreement, which of course means the duty to comply and enforce IPRs according to TRIPs. However, the developmental needs of the Cariforum States are emphasized, and the method of balancing rights and obligations between right-holders and users is referred to, together with the aim of protecting public health and nutrition. It is also explicitly excluded that the Cariforum be construed as impairing the capacity of the signatory States to promote access to medicines. It seems, therefore, that some of the most urgent concerns expressed by the Doha Declaration have been, in a sense, 'internalized' in the agreement, making them subject

to in the text have been signed on the basis of the US 2004 Model BIT, no amendments have been introduced as regards the relevant provisions on IP and indirect expropriation.

33 See Sell (2010–11), 449.

34 2004/2012 US Model BIT, Art. 6.4 (5): 'Expropriation and compensation: 1. Neither Party may expropriate or nationalize a covered investment either directly or indirectly through measures equivalent to expropriation or nationalization, except: (a) for a public purpose; (b) in a non-discriminatory manner; (c) on payment of prompt, adequate, and effective compensation; and (d) in accordance with due process of law and Article 5.' Art. 6.5: 'This Article does not apply to the issuance of compulsory licenses granted in relation to intellectual property rights in accordance with the TRIPS Agreement, or to the revocation, limitation, or creation of intellectual property rights, to the extent that such issuance, revocation, limitation, or creation is consistent with the TRIPS Agreement.'

35 US CAFTA-DR, Art. 10.7 (5) and US 2004/2012 Model BIT, Art. 8.3 (b).

36 Art. 10.2 of the Canada–China Agreement for the Promotion and Reciprocal Protection of Investments of 9 September 2012 makes compensation for compulsory licences depend on lack of compliance with the international agreements in force between the contracting parties, thus binding the arbitrator to rely on a TRIPs-based assessment (www.international.gc.ca/trade-agreements-accords-commerciaux/agr-acc/fipa-apie/china-text-chine.aspx?lang=eng&view=d).

37 Art. 139.2 of the 'Economic Partnership Agreement between the Caribbean Group of the African, Caribbean and Pacific States (Cariforum), of the one part, and the EU and its Member States, of the other part', OJ L 289/I/46, 30 October 2008.

to the methods and rules of interpretation that should be followed when assessing the States' conduct with regard to the protection of investors. A similar approach has been followed in the draft EU–Peru–Colombia FTA,[38] signed in June 2012, where the parties are under an explicit duty to conform to the provisions of the TRIPs Agreement and other multilateral agreements relating to IP.[39] According to Art. 13.2 of the draft EU–India FTA:

> The Parties recognise the importance of the Doha Declaration ... In interpreting and implementing the rights and obligations under this Chapter, the Parties shall ensure consistency with this Declaration. The Parties shall contribute to the implementation and respect the Decision of the WTO General Council of 30 August 2003 on Paragraph 6 of the Doha Declaration on the TRIPS Agreement and Public Health, as well as the Protocol amending the TRIPS Agreement, done at Geneva on 6 December 2005. Nothing in this Agreement shall be so construed as to impair the capacity of the Parties to promote access to medicines and protect public health.[40]

It is beyond any doubt that references to the Doha principles have a stronger impact on the interpretation of TRIPs flexibilities than mere reference to TRIPs, in that they suggest that fundamental public needs must be given due weight when balanced against the investor's IPRs. Considering that the Doha Declaration, and the subsequent Decision of the TRIPs Council of 2005 are part of the TRIPs system, a step further is taken towards the recognition of a role for public concerns, in comparison with the BITs concluded in the 1960s: at that time, non-trade-related issues connected with IP were only mentioned. Today, the TRIPs/Doha approach has a more important role to play in respect of those States which have ratified the 2005 Council Decision: with specific reference to

38 'Trade Agreement between the EU and its Member States, of the one part, and Colombia and Peru, of the other part' (trade.ec.europa.eu/doclib/docs/2011/march/tradoc_147704.pdf).

39 Art. 196.2: 'The provisions of this Title shall complement and specify the rights and obligations of the Parties under the TRIPS Agreement and other multilateral agreements related to intellectual property to which the Parties are party, and therefore, no provision of this Title will contradict or be detrimental to the provisions of such multilateral agreements.' Under Art.197.2 'The Parties recognize the importance of the Declaration of the Fourth Doha Ministerial Conference and especially the Doha Declaration on the TRIPS Agreement and Public Health, adopted on 14 November 2001 by the WTO Ministerial Conference and its subsequent developments.' However, Art. 231 extends protection of pharmaceuticals requiring a minimum of five years of exclusivity of test data.

40 See www.bilaterals.org/IMG/pdf/ip_euindia_july2010.pdf. The EU Commission has later confirmed such an interpretation.

the provisions relating to possible exceptions to IPRs protection, TRIPs/Doha can be considered as relevant as a 'subsequent agreement between the parties regarding the interpretation of the treaty or the application of its provisions' in the sense of Art. 31.3 (a) of the Vienna Convention on the Law of Treaties, which, therefore, 'shall be taken into account, together with the context' in the process of interpreting the TRIPs Agreement.[41] This can represent a turning point also in WTO/TRIPs case-law, which is sometimes elusive as regards public concerns.[42]

Apart from rules applicable to the relationships between different treaties, the Doha principles are also relevant from a different point of view: being supported by the large majority of States, as well as referred to in many agreements, they may have a considerable impact on treaty interpretation by national and international arbitrators, and help generate a wide consistent case-law. It is thus possible to regard certain provisions of the 2004/2012 US Model BIT as evidence of a more open approach to internalizing some flexibilities, which may further influence dispute-settlement practice.[43] According to *Annex* B of the same Model BIT (almost identical to *Annex* B of the Canadian Model BIT), indirect expropriation should be assessed case-by-case in the light of 'the economic impact of the government action, the extent to which the government action interferes with distinct, reasonable investment-backed expectations and the character of the government action'. It excludes that 'non-discriminatory regulatory actions by a Party that are designed and applied to protect legitimate public welfare objectives, such as public health, safety, and the environment' can be generally considered as indirect expropriations.[44] Further, in other investment agreements, a more flexible approach in comparison with the old-generation investment agreements results from a general

41 Given the dimensions of the WTO, it is predictable that the Contracting States of a BIT/FTA will be also Members of TRIPs.

42 See Weiss (2006), 181–9, with reference to *US-Gasoline*, *US-Shrimp*, *US-Gambling* and *EC-Hormones*. Only in *EC-Asbestos* did the WTO Appellate Body find the import ban by the European Community justified to protect human life, also because of the overwhelming scientific evidence of the harm arising from asbestos.

43 See the US 2004/2012 Model BIT, *Annex* A, Art. 4: 'The Parties confirm their shared understanding that "customary international law" generally and as specifically referenced in Article 5 [Minimum Standard of Treatment] and *Annex* B [Expropriation] results from a general and consistent practice of States that they follow from a sense of legal obligation.' On the role of customary international law within NAFTA see Ewing-Chow (2007), 569.

44 US 2004/2012 Model BIT, *Annex* B, Art. 4 (b). The Canadian 2004 Model BIT can be read at http://italaw.com/investment-treaties. *Annex* 10 C of the US-CAFTA-DR Agreement has identical wording.

reference to non-commercial values, even if this is not the subject of a specific provision relating to the adoption by the host State of measures limiting the protection of the investors.[45]

In the light of these considerations, resort to flexibilities, of the same kind as those available under the TRIPs Agreement, may be positively evaluated when founded on reasons of public welfare (i.e. in areas such as antitrust, consumer protection, securities, environmental protection, planning and land use), even if they may have a negative impact on the investor: in this case, they will not give rise to a finding of indirect expropriation;[46] consequently, the problem of compensation should be addressed in the same way as in case of a regulatory takeover.[47] These provisions, which embody principles of law emerging from the practice of IOs, are evidence of a trend towards giving weight to public concerns in the settlement of investor–State disputes, which is significant from the point of view of the consistency of the TRIPs approach with that which might be followed within the framework of bilateral agreements. From this point of view, it is possible to consider BITs/FTAs themselves as an instrument for the further consolidation, though in a sporadic and fragmentary way, of a flexible approach when relying on standards broadly accepted to assess a host State's measures which, though interfering with the investors' assets, are needed to deal with public health or environmental emergencies.[48]

5. Litigation against the host State for infringement of intellectual property in BIT/FTA and in WTO/DSU forums

Arbitral disputes under a BIT/FTA for indirect expropriation of an investor's IPRs would seem to be fairly infrequent.[49] One reason might be that

45 See Acconci (2011b), 409–28, on the trend in investment agreements to give relevance to non-commercial values.

46 See Grosse Ruse-Khan (2011), 22.

47 In *Methanex* v. *The United States* the category of regulatory expropriation, which does not give rise to compensation, is formulated as: '[a] non-discriminatory regulation for a public purpose, which is enacted in accordance with due process, and which affects, *inter alios*, a foreign investor or investment, is not deemed expropriatory and compensable, unless specific commitments had been given by the regulating government to refrain from such regulation' (NAFTA/UNCITRAL Arbitration, Final Award on jurisdiction and merits, 3 August 2005, IV, chapter D, 7).

48 Schwebel (2004), 1–4. Reference can be made to the 'scientific consensus' in evaluating the legitimacy of a regulatory measure by the State: Vadi (2013), 153.

49 In *Plain Tobacco Packaging* (fn 5) the host State involved (viz. Australia), being a party to the WHO Framework Convention on Tobacco Control (FCTC) of 27 February 2005

claims commonly originate from measures affecting the tangible assets of the investor. When those measures are undertaken by the host State for reasons connected with the protection of public health or the environment, lack of litigation could also be explained on the basis that the investor may be reluctant to embrace a position that the local government has viewed with disfavour. In these cases, the threat of litigation is an instrument for the foreign company to deter the local government from restricting the protection of IP,[50] considering also that it might be difficult to quantify the amount of the damage resulting from the limitations imposed by the State.

However, the *Plain Tobacco Packaging* case mentioned above, which is still at the initial stage, brings to the foreground the question of the legal basis of a complaint by an investor as regards his IPRs, in circumstances where the investor is entitled to bring a case to a BIT/FTA tribunal.[51] As already mentioned above, in the framework of a BIT/FTA the host State's conduct may be considered by the arbitrators as an indirect expropriation, because it produces an economic loss due to the reduction of the expected reward and value of IPRs.[52] Under the less recent BITs, where no distinction is made between direct and indirect expropriation,[53] the traditional standards of treatment must be tested, consisting of fair and equitable treatment, reasonableness, due process, good faith and legitimate expectations. Under some bilateral agreements, a similar assessment is made, though on the basis of more flexible standards: thus, even non-discriminatory regulatory actions by a host State, motivated by legitimate public welfare objectives, must be balanced against the investor's interests in protecting his intangible assets.[54] A BIT/FTA tribunal will presumably reject the host State's claims when founded on the need to comply

(www.who.int/fctc/signatories parties/en/index.html), is expected to carry out a policy to reduce tobacco consumption. The same is true for Hong Kong/China, also party to the FCTC.

50 See Rutledge (2012), 16.

51 As is well-known, not all BITs or FTAs provide for the duty on the host State to submit to a tribunal in an investor–State dispute: see, for instance, Art. 11.16 of the US–Australia FTA, providing only for investor–State consultations for the settlement of disputes, unless the investor receives the State's permission to submit the claim to arbitration.

52 See fn 16.

53 Art. 6.1 of the Hong Kong–Australia BIT: 'Investors of either Contracting Party shall not be deprived of their investments nor subjected to measures having effect equivalent to such deprivation in the area of the other Contracting Party except under due process of law, for a public purpose related to the internal needs of that Party, on a non-discriminatory basis, and against compensation.'

54 Giardina (2008), 333–9; Reinisch (2008a), 199–204; Vadi (2013), 59–61.

with multilateral international agreements aiming at the improvement of health or environmental standards. It can be expected that the tribunal will prefer to give weight to practices and recommendations based on customary international rules.

For measures limiting the investor's IPRs, a case might also be brought before a WTO/DSU panel for infringement of TRIPs rules on the initiative of another Member State. The assessment by the WTO/DSU bodies of the host State's conduct would take into account the freedom to balance different competing interests within the limits provided by TRIPs: the interest in encouraging investment, which can be considered as inherent in the aim of promoting technological innovation and economic development, should be balanced against other public goals, such as higher standards in employment, health and the environment. Such an approach might lead to the rejection of a claim for infringement of TRIPs, even if, in a case before BITs arbitrators, the same facts could lead to a declaration of non-compliance by the host State with its commitments towards the investor.

Problems relating to a possible overlap of proceedings may be considered not only with regard to investor–State disputes, but also with reference to inter-State disputes relating to the implementation of a bilateral agreement.[55] Many FTAs provide a choice-of-forum provision granting the complaining State the right to sue the other contracting State before arbitrators or before the WTO/DSU, thus making the exclusion of one of the two forums contingent upon the complaining party requiring reference to a panel.[56] Also in this case, the settlement by FTA arbitrators, on the basis of the agreed standards, could lead to a less favourable outcome for the host State than the WTO dispute-settlement mechanism.[57]

6. The significance for the investor of a WTO/DSU decision on the legitimacy of the host State's conduct

It is now worth considering the problem whether, from the point of view of BIT/FTA arbitrators, it would be relevant to acknowledge the consistency

55 For an overview of concurrent regional and international trade law proceedings see McLachlan (2009), 317–26.

56 A choice-of-forum clause is present in almost all FTAs signed by US: see list by Drahos (2006), 8. The same privilege is provided by NAFTA for disputes between Member States connected with trade, with some exceptions (Art. 2005.4).

57 Drahos (2006), 21, suggests that decisions of bilaterally established panels may have a possible feedback on the WTO system, favouring a claim for profits by companies, to the detriment of DCs.

of the host State's conduct with TRIPs. The question has special interest in relation to a decision given by the WTO/DSU on the host State's compliance with TRIPs.

A WTO decision is declaratory in kind, and is aimed at deciding the existence or non-existence of an infringement by the host State: thus it is not focused on the question of the impact on the economic results for the investor and the consequent duty to compensate. A BIT/FTA tribunal is not entitled to make a decision on the application of the TRIPs rules. However, a WTO/DSU decision that the host State's conduct is in line with the TRIPs rules may be relevant in considering whether the standards of good-faith and reasonableness have been met: in this sense, a WTO decision may possess an indirect relevance for the settlement of an investor–State dispute.[58] As a consequence, should the tribunal decide that the host State has infringed its commitments towards the investor, the charge of indirect expropriation might be downgraded to regulatory expropriation, with the result of a possible reduction in compensation.[59]

Of course, if one accepts such a view, every dispute relating to an investor's IPRs could be the subject of concurrent proceedings before BIT/FTA arbitrators and before the WTO/DSU.[60] There is a chance of a WTO panel's decision being in favour of the host State, when the latter is able to give evidence that the measures in question were aimed at pursuing public concerns. Also the rules applicable to the proceedings before the WTO/DSU are more favourable to the host State: under the WTO/DSU, it is for the complaining State to show that the defendant State is responsible for an infringement of the obligations under the TRIPs Agreement, whereas in BIT/FTA arbitral proceedings the host State in answering the investor's claim must prove consistency with BITs/FTAs provisions of the measures adopted.

Given the special features of the two different procedures, the host State might be interested in accelerating the conclusion of the proceedings

58 The same is true when a comparison is made between a WTO/DSU case and a State v. State dispute on a claim for alleged non-compliance by the host State with the contract, on the basis of an 'umbrella clause' in a BIT.

59 Sometimes the dividing line between regulatory taking and violation is not clear. See *Metalclad* (fn 16) and *Methanex* (fn 47). Authors express divergent opinions on compensation in cases of regulatory expropriation: see, among others, Vadi (2013), 50–1, 80–3.

60 *Plain Tobacco Packaging* (fn 5) has brought about concurrent suits involving Australia, one before the Hong Kong–Australia BIT Tribunal, Phillip Morris Asia having sought the appointment of arbitrators, and others before the WTO/DSU, on claims by Ukraine, Honduras, Dominican Republic, Cuba and Indonesia (Doc. WTO/DS 434; 435; 441, 458 and 467 respectively).

at the multilateral level in order to have a chance of a decision on non-infringement, in order to assure the arbitrator of its good faith and compliance with the required standard of treatment towards of the investor. Moreover, a WTO/DSB decision, being the expression of the general approach of Member States as regards the consistency of a State's conduct with the international rules on IP protection, should lead arbitrators to adopt a wider approach in deciding an investor–State dispute, all the more so when the State's conduct is aimed at pursuing effects that are in keeping with general principles adopted at the international level, or even recommended by IOs. It would be not in line with the principle of consistency of treaty obligations, even of a bilateral nature, to ignore such international developments. There are at least a couple of reasons in favour of such a choice: BIT/FTAs are instruments governed by international law, and cannot be fully considered apart from the WTO rules, which represent the bulk of the international economic principles applicable at the global level, in relation to which there is substantial State participation. This is true, even without considering the need for the arbitrators to give weight to the standpoint of the State to which the investor belongs in the international context: it implies that adequate consideration should be given to a WTO decision.

Another argument in favour of the need to consider the decisions of the WTO/DSU as being relevant can be found when the arbitral award is issued on the basis of an agreement outside the ICSID system. In this case, should the WTO/DSU decision be in favour of the host State, this would give the host State a strong basis on which to refuse enforcement of the arbitral award on the grounds that it is limited by public policy-considerations.[61]

Given the relevance, albeit indirect, of the outcome of such a dispute on the assessment by a BIT/FTA tribunal, the lawyers representing the host State could apply for a stay of proceedings, whenever they are able to make a strong case about the need to deal with important public concerns, in order to avoid the risk of a possible conflict between decisions on the same point. Despite substantial grounds that might be invoked to obtain a stay of proceedings, it seems that it is not possible to rely upon reasons of judicial economy or *forum non conveniens*, which have been held to apply exclusively to concurrent proceedings between private parties before

61 The same would not be possible for an ICSID award, since Art. 54 (1) of the 1965 Washington Convention makes it mandatory for Contracting States to enforce such awards as if they were final national judgments.

national courts or arbitrators.[62] Thus, an investment arbitral tribunal is expected to give a decision based on a pragmatic assessment of what seems to be the most reasonable outcome.

7. The need for consistency between the multilateral system and the bilateral investment rules

The extension of the level of IP protection in favour of the investors under BITs/FTAs risks leading to a weakening of the role of the States in encouraging technology transfer and improving social and economic welfare. However, at the same time, TRIPs flexibilities risk impairing investors' expectations and dissuading investment, without providing a direct effective remedy as under the BITs/FTAs. The clashes between the investor-centred approach followed by arbitrators, founded on the standards of treatment provided for in the applicable bilateral agreements, and the different evaluation of host States' measures under the multilateral rules on IP protection lead to a disharmony which should be overcome in order to give IP the role of a true instrument for innovation and social welfare.

The elements of flexibility present in some BITs/FTAs, such as the recent US and Canadian Model BITs, seem to express the consciousness of the industrialized countries and of their companies about the need to give adequate weight to public concerns and to promote a new approach, without which they may risk appearing as negative profit-oriented actors, at the expense of the fundamental needs of the population, especially in developing countries (DCs). There may also be another reason at the bottom of such an approach: given the effects of the MFN rule, granting the same level of protection to any other investors belonging to a WTO Member, the benefits resulting from TRIPs-plus clauses for the companies belonging to a contracting State in respect to competitors from other countries are *de facto* annulled. This means that companies of industrialized countries might be less active in encouraging their national States to include TRIPs-plus clauses in investment agreements with DCs.

It is thus possible to highlight a general trend towards a more sophisticated way of administering investments. Of course, it should be considered that, however advanced and public-good-oriented bilateral

62 In exceptional cases, doctrines such as good faith, estoppel or abuse of process could be applied to curb genuinely abusive consequential procedures. See, among others, Ligustro (2011), 551–74 and Virzo (2011), 660–7.

agreements may be, they cannot constitute, as such, a system of international investment law. Suffice it to make reference to one of the most debated questions, which has not yet found a uniform answer in arbitral case-law: the duty of the host State to compensate the investor, even when evidence is given that restrictive measures are undertaken on a non-discriminatory basis, where it is acting to pursue public interests. To resolve this and other problems, the interpretation of the relevant provisions of the single BIT/FTA plays a decisive role. The result is the difficulty of figuring out a unitary regime relating to indirect expropriations, including the specific topic of the investor's IPRs.[63]

The idea of a comprehensive agreement on foreign investments – IP protection included – which has been the object of extensive debates *inter alia* within the Organisation for Economic Co-operation and Development (OECD) from 1970 to 1998, has faded away because of the difficulty in reconciling different views about the relationship between international trade and investment law, and has not yet officially resumed.[64]

Nor does the Trade Related Investment Measures Agreement (TRIMs), administered by the WTO, provide for a comprehensive response: the existing 'black list' of measures not in line with the WTO commitments focuses on possible inconsistencies with trade liberalization. No reference is made to IP. This means that TRIMs should be integrated, possibly including a sort of 'white list' of the measures relating to IP, which a State may adopt to limit the rights of the investors, to take into account public concerns.[65]

In the specific field of patents, a different, less controversial, though perhaps less far-reaching mechanism, might consist in a refinement of the present system through the establishment of a multilateral process to evaluate the coherence and consistency of the proceedings followed by WTO Members when registering a patent, in order to ensure that the product or the method of production will be assessed according to acceptable standards, not only in keeping with the need to ensure transparency and non-discrimination, but also in conformity with the goals of

63 According to Schill (2009), 65–120, transnational investment law should be understood as a coherent and multilateral subsystem of international law.

64 The draft Multilateral Agreement on Investment (MAI) can be read at www1.oecd.org/daf/mai/pdf/ng/ng987r1e.pdf. See Sacerdoti (1997), 292–7, and Åslund (2013), 1–8, suggesting the establishment of a MAI within the WTO framework.

65 On the points for criticism as regards the suitability of WTO to deal with investments see Weiss (2008), 199–204.

public policy such as sound environmental parameters.[66] The standards thus fixed at the global level would become mandatory for the competent national patent registration authorities. At the same time the international standard should ensure investors consistency in the duties owed to them by the host State. Such a mechanism, which could prevent investor–State disputes over the limits imposed by the host States on the use and profits of IPRs, might represent a sequel to the current debates within the WIPO, up to now mainly focusing on the comparison between the legal procedures and methods followed within the national systems.[67] It should however be coordinated with the WTO/TRIPs system, in order also to prevent the risk of a proliferation of forums available, which could be detrimental to certainty and predictability.

Another reasonable path, less ambitious than the formulation of new multilateral agreements or amending the existing ones, consists in increasing the general support for flexibilities in IP protection. As we saw before, among the general public interests mentioned in some BITs/FTA, those expressed in the Doha Declaration are definitely supported at the level of the international community and those relating to health will probably be included in TRIPs when the amendment decided by the Council in 2005 will obtain the required number of ratifications. Nevertheless, the 'Doha approach' does not exhaust the policy space for measures aimed at ensuring the public good. It would be profitable to export that method into other fields, for instance to promote environmentally friendly innovation. In this field the debate is still open, the adoption of a Doha-type Declaration raising, among others, problems connected with the involvement of a number of international institutions, including the WTO.[68] Of course, this would not meet all of what is needed to reach a coherent and effective international system for the protection of investors' IPRs. Nevertheless, it could be a further step towards building a wider participation in the benefits of technological progress. To this end, the scientific community and lawyers can play a crucial role.

66 See Tran (2010), 349 and fn 26. On the extension of Art. XX GATT flexibilities to the processes of production, as distinct from the product itself, see Giansanti (2008), 100–52.

67 See the debates at the WIPO Special Committee on the law of patents at www.wipo.int/meetings/en/topic.jsp?group_id=61.

68 According to Abbott (2009), 27, for a Declaration on IPRs and climate change, the UN framework, more specially the UNFCCC, or even more broadly the UN General Assembly would be more appropriate than the WTO.

References

Abbott, F.M. 2005. 'Toward a New Era of Objective Assessment in the Field of Trips and Variable Geometry for the Preservation of Multilateralism'. *JIEL* 8: 77–100.

2009. 'Innovation and Technology Transfer to Address Climate Change: Lessons from the Global Debate on Intellectual Property and Public Health', International Centre for Trade and Sustainable Development (ICTSD). *Issue Paper* No. 24, I–IX: 1–40.

Acconci, P. 2011a. 'The Implementation of the Patent Regulation of the TRIPs Agreement and the Protection of Non-Trade Values. Have Continuous Negotiations Become the Mechanism for Balancing Them?'. Ligustro and Sacerdoti (eds.): 803–28.

2011b. *Tutela della salute e diritto internazionale*. Padova: CEDAM.

Åslund, A. 2013. 'The World Needs a Multilateral Investment Agreement'. Peterson Institute for International Economics, *Policy Brief* No. PB 13–01: 1–8 (www.piie.com/publications/pb/pb13-1.pdf).

Chaudhuri, S. 2005. *The WTO and India's Pharmaceuticals Industry*. Oxford University Press.

Correa, C.M. 2004. 'Bilateral Investment Agreements: Agents of New Global Standards for the Protection of Intellectual Property Rights?'. www.grain.org/article/entries/125: 1–31.

Drahos, P. 2003. 'Expanding Intellectual Property's Empire: The Role of FTAs'. www.grain.org/rights_files/drahos-fta-2003-en.pdf: 7.

2006. 'The Bilateral Web of Trade Dispute Settlement' (unpublished manuscript). wage.wisc.edu/uploads/WTO%20Conference/drahos.pdf: 1–26.

Ewing-Chow, M. 2007. 'Thesis, Antithesis and Synthesis: Investor Protection in BITs, WTO and FTAS'. *University of New South Wales LJ* 30: 548–71.

Giansanti, A. 2008. *La tutela degli interessi non economici nel sistema OMC*. Napoli: Editoriale Scientifica.

Giardina, A. 2008. 'L'arbitrato internazionale in materia di investimenti: impetuosi sviluppi e qualche problema'. Boschiero N. and Luzzatto R. (eds.), *I rapporti economici internazionali e l'evoluzione del loro regime giuridico*. Napoli: Editoriale Scientifica, 333–9.

Grosse Ruse-Kahn, H. 2011. 'Protecting Intellectual Property under BITs, FTAs and TRIPs: Conflicting Regimes or Mutual Coherence?. Max Planck Institute for Intellectual Property and Competition Law, *Research Paper* No. 11–02: 1–34.

Heinemann, A. 2006. 'Antitrust Law of Intellectual Property in the TRIPs Agreement of the WTO'. Beier F.-K. and Schricker G. (eds.), *From GATT to TRIPs*. Cambridge University Press: 241–3.

Hoffmann, A.K. 2008. 'Indirect Expropriation'. Reinisch (ed.): 151–70.

Ligustro, A. 2011. 'Conflitti di giurisdizione e "dialogo tra Corti" internazionali nella prospettiva dell'Organizzazione internazionale del commercio'. Ligustro and Sacerdoti (eds.): 551–74.

Ligustro, A. and Sacerdoti, G. (eds.). 2011. *Problemi e tendenze del diritto internazionale dell'economia*. Liber amicorum *Paolo Picone*. Napoli: Editoriale Scientifica.

McLachlan, C. 2009. Lis pendens *in International Litigation*. Leiden/Boston: Martinus Nijhoff.

Macmillan, F. 2001. *WTO and the Environment*. London: Sweet & Maxwell.

Maskus, K., Okediji, R., Reichman, J. and Roffe, P. 2011. 'Overcoming the Impasse on Intellectual Property and Climate Change at the UNFCCC: A Way Forward'. International Centre for Trade and Sustainable Development (ICTSD), *Policy Brief* No. 11, November 2011: 1–8.

Mitchell, A. and Voon, T. 2009. 'Patents and Public Health in the WTO, FTAs and Beyond: Tension and Conflict in International Law'. *J World Trade* 43: 571–601.

Ranjan, P. 2010. 'Bilateralism, MFN and TRIPS: Exploring Possibilities of Alternative Interpretation'. *International Trade L and Regulation* 13: 67–78.

Reinisch, A. (ed.). 2008a. *Standards of Investment Protection*. Oxford University Press.

2008b. 'Legality of Expropriations'. Reinisch (ed.): 171–204.

Rutledge, P.B. 2012. 'TRIPS and BITs: An Essay on Compulsory Licenses, Expropriation, and International Arbitration'. *North Carolina JL & Technology* 13: 149–63.

Sacerdoti, G. 1997. 'Bilateral Treaties and Multilateral Instruments on Investment Protection'. *RCADI* 269: 251–460.

Schill, S.M. 2009. *The Multilateralization of International Investment Law*. Cambridge University Press.

Schwebel, S.M. 2004. 'The Influence of Bilateral Investment Treaties on Customary International Law'. *ASIL Proceedings* 98 (27): 1–4.

Sell, S.K. 2010–11. 'TRIPs Was Never Enough: Vertical Forum Shifting, FTAs, ACTA, and TPP'. *J Intellectual Property L* 18: 447–78.

Sornarajah, M. 2010. *The International Law on Foreign Investment*. Cambridge University Press: 3rd ed.

't Hoen, E.F.M. 2009. *The Global Politics of Pharmaceutical Monopoly Power. Drug Patents, Access, Innovation and the Application of the WTO Doha Declaration on TRIPS and Public Health*. Diemen: AMB Publishers (www.msfaccess.org).

Tran, C. 2010. 'Using GATT, Art. XX to Justify Climate Change Measures in Claims under the WTO Agreements'. *Environmental and Planning LJ* 27: 349.

Vadi, V. 2012. 'Global Health Governance at a Crossroads: Trademark Protection and Tobacco Control in International Investment Law'. *Stanford J International L* 48: 93–130.

2013. *Public Health in International Investment Law and Arbitration*. London; New York: Routledge.

Virzo, R. 2011. 'Stay of International Proceedings on Ground of Connection between Pending Actions'. Panella, L. and Spatafora, E. (a cura di), *Studi in onore di Claudio Zanghì*. Torino: Giappichelli, 660–7.

Vivas-Eugui, D. 2003. 'Regional and Bilateral Agreements and a TRIPs-plus World'. *TRIPs Issues Papers* 1: 1–40 (www.quno.org/geneva/pdf/economic/Issues/FTAs-TRIPS-plus-English.pdf).

Weiss, F. 2006. 'The Limits of the WTO: Facing Non-Trade Issues'. Sacerdoti, G., Yanovich, A. and Bojanes, J. (eds.). *The WTO at Ten*. Cambridge University Press: 155–90.

2008. 'Trade and Investment'. Muchlinski, P., Ortino, F. and Schreuer, C. (eds.), *International Investment Law*. Oxford University Press: 199–204.

Yu, P.K. 2009. 'The Objectives and Principles of the TRIPs Agreement'. *Houston L Review* 46: 979–1046.

9

Up-keeping non-economic values in development assistance: does the World Bank practise what it preaches? Answers from the Inspection Panel

AGOSTINA LATINO

1. Introduction

Twenty years after its establishment, the Inspection Panel of the World Bank represents an interesting area of study, raising relevant questions regarding the matter of the delicate relationship between loans made by the Bank and the protection of non-economic values, such as fundamental human, social and environmental rights.

At the beginning of the 1990s, both internal and external factors to the Organization led the Bank to reconsider the process of granting loans.

The efficacy of the economic assistance provided by the Bank to its members was questionable and the so-called 'Wapenhans Report' outlines the weak points in the lending procedures in three different respects. In the first place, the loan-approval criteria favoured quantity over quality in the project-proposals. In other words, the Bank appeared to be more driven by the pressure to lend than by the desire for successful project-implementation. In the second place, the complexity of the projects led to the failure of approximately one-third of those financed by the Bank. In the third place, the policies and practices of the Bank revealed a discrepancy between banking and local officers.[1]

1 The Report takes its name from that of the senior economist of the World Bank, Willi A. Wapenhans, who supervised its drafting. The official name of the document is 'Effective Implementation: Keys to Development Impact, Report of the Portfolio Management Task Force, Washington, DC, 3 November 1992'. The Report was written upon the request of the president of the World Bank at that time, L.T. Preston. Its intended scope was much wider, in the wake of the Report by the Morse Commission which investigated the 'Sardar Sarovar Water Project' and showed how the hydroelectric project in Narmada (India) would have a much greater environmental impact than what was foreseen because the Bank had not asked for the environmental impact assessment required by its own lending

Regarding the matter of non-economic values, non-governmental organizations (NGOs) made ever-more pressing remonstrations, defining the Bank a 'black box', due to the lack of transparency in the implementation of operations, for which a higher level of co-responsibility was required.[2]

The response to these critical comments was the Bank Directors' Resolution which gave rise to the Inspection Panel.[3] The innovation of this decision was particularly significant because, for the first time, an economic authority was established within an international organization, to which private claimants could appeal. Furthermore, the Resolution enlightened the advanced opinion of civil society.[4]

The institution of the Inspection Panel responded to the need to ensure that the Bank has acted in accordance with its own policies and operational directives.

The development of the World Bank's first operational standards started in the 1970s. As is known, in the original formulation of the Articles of Agreement there was no reference to environmental or social issues.[5] At

procedures and had not taken measures to guarantee the implementation of the loan conditions which required the Indian government to compensate the people involved before they were moved. In essence, the project called for the construction of a system of dams in the Narmada Valley, with the forced transfer of approximately 250,000 people and the expropriation of nearly 289,113 acres of land. See Huyser (2011), 783–7.

2 Shihata (1992).

3 On 22 September 1993, the Executive Directors of the World Bank decided to establish an independent Inspection Panel (The World Bank Inspection Panel, Res. 93–10, International Bank for Reconstruction and Development; Res. 93–6, International Development Association). The Panel's jurisdiction does not extend to the risk-mitigation or private-sector investment arms of the World Bank. The Bank's private-sector investment arm is the International Finance Corporation (IFC); the risk-mitigation department is the Multilateral Investment Guarantee Agency (MIGA). Instead of being subject to the mandate of the Inspection Panel, these institutions are reviewed by the Office of the Compliance Advisor Ombudsman (CAO). The CAO uses mediation and other dispute resolution methods, followed by compliance audits of questioned projects, and ultimately provides advice to the institutions' senior management about the application and effectiveness of the IFC and MIGA's polices. For further information regarding the Inspection Panel see, among others, Shihata (2000); Alfredsson and Ring (2001); Seatzu (2008). For an analysis of the various proposals advanced during the discussion on the institution of a governing body, see Bradlow (1994).

4 McBeth (2010), 222 ff. Some hold, in a critical sense, that the true aim of the Inspection Panel was to provide the Executive Directors with an instrument that would reinforce the responsibility of the Bank towards the Directors themselves: Rigo Sureda (2004), 141.

5 As opposed to the charter of the European Bank for Reconstruction and Development: Agreement establishing the European Bank for Reconstruction and Development, preamble and Art. II.

first, it was presumed that such demands could easily be met when the loans were approved. In fact, the Articles of Agreement expressly state that the World Bank must pay 'due attention' only 'to considerations of economy and efficiency … without regard to political or other non-economic … considerations'.[6] The result was that the promotion of the decolonized countries' development was expressed by the World Bank solely in economic terms, based above all on GNP growth. During the 1970s, development strategies started to rely on growth, taking into account the negative consequences on the environment only so long as their elimination or minimization were not excessively onerous in economic terms. The first operational standards were elaborated within this framework, sporadically and in relation to each financed project. With the rise of international awareness of the need to comply with sustainable development needs, the original standards began to be consolidated into 'Operational Directives' (ODs), with a more systematic aim of social and environmental protection against the increasingly evident negative impacts of projects financed by the World Bank. In essence, the concept of sustainable growth postulates 'the need to reconcile economic development with protection of the environment',[7] and does not allow the development of a country to occur through the financing of projects with detrimental effects for large sectors of the population.[8]

In any case, such ODs, which included the 'National Environmental Actions Plans', 'Projects on International Waterways' and 'Involving Nongovernmental Organizations in Bank-Supported Activities', were documents with heterogeneous content, in which there were procedural elements, policy directives and practical guidelines set for both the Bank's management and the countries applying for a loan.

Starting from the 1990s, the World Bank reformulated these instruments in order to clarify content and their binding effects. Hence, the original ODs gave rise to three distinct instruments: 'Operational Policies' (OPs),[9] 'Bank Procedures' (BPs)[10] and 'Good Practices' (GPs).

6 Articles of Agreement of the International Bank for Reconstruction and Development, Art. III, section 5 (b). In the same sense, compare Articles of Agreement of International Development Agency, Art. V, section 1 (g); Art. V, section 6.

7 To use the words of the International Court of Justice in the case regarding the Gabčikovo-Nagymaros Project (Hungary/Slovakia), 140.

8 Agenda 21 also invites, among other things, Multilateral Development Banks to ensure that financing contributes not only to economic growth but also to social development and to the protection of the environment in beneficiary countries (Agenda 21, chapter 33, 16, a), UN Doc. A/CONF.151/26 (1992).

9 See go.worldbank.org/3GLI3EECP0.

10 See go.worldbank.org/L2LCRJEHW0.

Based on the 'World Bank Operational Manual',[11] the OPs establish the parameters that Bank operations should comply with, in order to meet the established goals and specify essential exceptions. The BPs, on the other hand, provide the Bank staff with the instructions to put into effect the policies established in the OPs, clarify procedures to follow and specify the required documentation. Finally, the GPs contain suggestions and guidelines for the implementation of policies (tied to precedents in the subject-matter and the context of the sector), along with examples taken from practice.[12]

Only OPs and BPs are binding on the Bank, while the 'Good Practices' are mere recommendations.

Currently, the 'Environmental and Social Safeguard Policies Framework' of the World Bank can count on about ten instruments, among which there are three pillar policies, aimed at elaborating plans of action to remove or, at least, to reduce the negative effects of a project intended to be financed.

First of all, the 'Policy on Environmental Assessment' (OP 4.01) must be considered.[13] The aim of this OP is to ensure that financed projects are environmentally sustainable and in compliance with environmental protection. In effect, OP 4.01 is based on the premise that 'the Bank requires environmental assessment (EA) of projects proposed for Bank financing to help ensure that they are environmentally sound and sustainable'.[14] For this purpose, the World Bank requires the applicant country to conduct an environmental assessment, according to one of four categories (A, B, C, D) set by the OP.[15] In general, the 'environmental assessment' should take into consideration the potential risks and foreseeable impact of the proposed project on the environment; and pay attention to the effects on

11 See go.worldbank.org/DZDZ9038D0.

12 The 'Operational Memoranda' (Op Memos) must also be mentioned. They were formulated beginning in 2004 and constitute interim instructions, intended to elaborate on material in OPs/BPs or ODs. Once the instructions in OP Memos are incorporated into revisions of the pertinent OPs/BPs, the OP Memos are retired (go.worldbank.org/9VJ2LVPR60).

13 This Operational Policy statement was updated in February 2011 to clarify the use of framework instruments and to add strategic environmental and social assessment (SESA) to the list of available instruments. It was previously revised in March 2007 to reflect the issuance of OP/BP 8.00, 'Rapid Response to Crises and Emergencies', and in August 2004 to ensure consistency with the requirements of OP/BP 8.60.

14 OP 4.01, 1. Compare Boisson de Chazournes (2000, 2001).

15 The projects are classified by the World Bank following an environmental screening phase based on the type of project, its size, the area involved and the nature and extent of potential impact on the environment.

the soil, water and air, on human health and social aspects of the project, such as relocation of local communities.[16]

Country/National regulation and international commitments on environmental protection must be taken into account. In fact, the World Bank undertakes not to finance projects and activities that could be in contrast with the international obligations of the country set out in the environmental-assessment document.[17] In particular, if the project falls into category A (i.e. a project with an appreciable negative impact on an area wider than the area directly involved in the activities), the OP requires a comparative analysis of the impact on the environment of the project and of alternative projects (including the 'without-project' case/situation), and requires advice to be taken on the measures to be adopted in order to prevent, mitigate or compensate the negative effects of the project. In addition, the policy of the World Bank for category A projects contemplates that the applicant country should refer to the groups affected by the project and the NGOs regarding the environmental aspects, in order to take into account their positions.[18] Finally, once the decision to finance the project has been made, and during its execution, the Borrower is required to draw up a report on the observance of all the measures agreed with the Bank according to the conclusions and results of the EA. The

16 According to the criteria established in the version revised in February 2011, the assessment 'takes into account the natural environment (air, water and land); human health and safety; social aspects (involuntary resettlement, indigenous peoples, and physical cultural resources); and transboundary and global environmental aspects': OP 4.01, 3. Regarding requests to involve the Inspection Panel in projects with presumed, material prejudice in terms of health, please see Acconci (2011), 113 ff (in particular, fn 63).

17 So, the assessment of the Bank should be based on the analysis of the national legislation and policies, on environmental studies conducted at the local and national level and on the 'obligations of the country, pertaining to project activities, under relevant international environmental treaties and agreements' (OP 4.01, 3). This reference to compliance with international law which is binding for the country benefiting from the loan is found in OP. 4.36, which is specifically dedicated to projects that impact forest conservation. The environmental parameters with which the Bank should comply are found in OP 4.04, 'Natural Habitats', which, although making no express reference to international environmental law, recalls several fundamental principles with which the projects financed by the Bank should comply. According to this OP, the projects should be consistent with the principle of environmental conservation, a fundamental condition to ensure sustainable growth over the long term. This is confirmed by the fact that the beneficiary countries are required by the Bank to adopt a precautionary approach in the management of natural resources.

18 In order for consultations with the interested parties to be profitable, the country must make public, in a timely manner, all the material that could be relevant, in a form and language that is understandable and accessible to the groups to be consulted.

report will be the point of reference for the supervision of the project in its environmental aspects.[19]

The second pillar policy of the World Bank regards 'Involuntary Resettlement' (OP 4.12). Often the projects' implementation involves the relocation of human communities that may cause severe economic, social and environmental imbalances that have to be faced and mitigated through specific defensive measures. Therefore, any relocation should be avoided where possible, and the country is required to record a 'Resettlement Plan' that, *inter alia*, not only adequately informs any individual affected of his options and rights regarding the relocation, but also advises as to alternatives to resettlement. Furthermore, the payment of a proper compensation must be guaranteed for the loss of property and the costs of resettlement. The policy establishes that the payment of due compensation must precede the expropriation of lands and goods. In particular, the policy states that monetary compensation must give way to land-based resettlement strategies if the survival and lifestyle of the people involved are closely linked to their land; if this is the case, the resettlement of those groups will be on either public land, or private lands purchased for this purpose.

If the resettlement plan concerns indigenous populations, any possible alternative must have been taken into consideration. Should the resettlement be unavoidable, a strategy must be planned in consultation with the indigenous groups taking into account both the importance of the land for them, and cultural preferences.[20]

On the other hand, indigenous communities are the subject of a specific policy that represents the third pillar of the safeguard policies, OP 4.10 on 'Indigenous Peoples'.[21] The OP clarifies, in particular, that the development process must ensure respect for the dignity, rights and

19 Regarding this phase, compare OP 13.05, 'Project Supervision'.

20 On this topic see the contribution by Guidi in this book.

21 Previously, the protection of indigenous peoples was entrusted to a simple operational directive, OD 4.20, dating back to 1991. The process of converting the directive began in 1998 and led to the formulation of a first draft of an OP in 2001, which was harshly criticized by indigenous movements. The new text, the fruit of observations and recommendations from civil society, was presented in December 2004 and open for public consultation for a period of ninety days prior to examination by the Board of Executive Directors. All the same, the text, which was eventually approved and took effect on 1 July 2005, was not without bitter controversies. It was widely complained that many demands that had emerged during public consultation were left unheard. In any case, it should be underlined that attention to the problem of protecting indigenous peoples gave rise to wide debate within the system of the World Bank, so much so that the adoption of an *ad hoc* instrument became necessary.

culture of indigenous peoples, and must produce economic and social benefits, culturally compatible with their lifestyle. The Bank undertakes to finance exclusively those projects 'where free, prior, and informed consultation results in broad community support for the project by the affected Indigenous Peoples'.[22]

The provisions of these operative policies should guide financing choices both *ex ante* at the time the decision to finance the project is made, and *ex post* because the safeguard conditions are often expressed in contractual clauses that the borrower country must comply with as a condition of the loan. This mechanism allows the Bank to react to a country's breaches through the usual contractual remedies set out in the 'General Conditions Applicable to Loan and Guarantee Agreements'; in particular, the right to draw funds from the account where the loan has been deposited may be suspended.[23]

The monitoring and control by the Bank of the implementation of protection procedures is vested in the Inspection Panel. In effect, the Inspection Panel's purpose is to ensure that the projects already financed by the Bank comply with its policies and procedures.[24] Moreover, it must be pointed out that the Inspection Panel is not a jurisdictional body, hence it cannot state or define the rights and duties of the borrowers or the Bank, nor can it interpret the Articles of Agreement of the Bank and the loan agreements.[25] The legal status of the Inspection Panel might be that of an 'independent forum',[26] through which groups of individuals may demand that the Bank act according to its operational procedures; or it could be that of an 'almost-independent accountability mechanism'.[27]

22 OP 4.10 and 4.12, expressly referring to protecting human rights, contribute 'to the Bank's mission of poverty reduction and sustainable development by ensuring that the development process fully respects the dignity, human rights, economies, and cultures of Indigenous People', Rigo Sureda (2004), 213–14.

23 General Conditions for Loans, 1 July 2005 (as amended through 15 October 2006), Art. VII, section 7.02. Suspension by the Bank (b) (ii) (siteresources.worldbank.org/INTLAWJUSTICE/Resources/IBRD_GC_0705_1006.pdf).

24 The Inspection Panel was created 'for the purpose of providing people directly and adversely affected by a World Bank-financed project with an independent forum through which they can request the World Bank to act in accordance with its own policies and procedures', World Bank (1994), 1.

25 World Bank (2007), 7.

26 It is the Inspection Panel itself that uses this expression: compare World Bank (1994), introduction.

27 This is the definition coined by Wahi: the author specifies that 'quasi-independent accountability mechanism' is intended as those bodies instituted by international organizations for the purpose of evaluating their policies and to ensure compatibility

The aim of this chapter is to investigate whether, having regard to actual practice,[28] the Inspection Panel is or is not an adequate mechanism to guarantee environmental and social values, since human-rights accountability is also taken into consideration by the World Bank.

2. Composition and jurisdiction of the inspection panel: critical insights

As is known, the Inspection Panel is composed of three members, the inspectors. Their names are suggested by the President of the Bank and subjected to the approval of the Executive Board. The term of office for each inspector lasts five years. The inspectors must be impartial and independent, hence they must come from different member countries of the

with their respective mandates. Said mechanisms have both advantages and disadvantages: '[t]he advantages ... are that they provide semi-independent check on the activities of the institution and they hear grievances from external sources. Their disadvantages stem from the fact that they are only semi-independent because they function within the structure of the institution and their powers are strictly limited by terms of their mandate': Wahi (2005–6), 356. Among the first to analytically question the legal status of the Inspection Panel, please see Nathan (1995). The author uses 'quango' as an acronym for 'quasi-autonomous non-governmental association', 'used to mean a body of uncertain parentage and uncertain future' (137). First off, the author underlines that,

> [t]he fact that: i) the Panel is described as an Inspection Panel rather than a Tribunal; ii) the Panel is very much left to itself in the adoption of its own procedures, rules of evidence and standards of proof; iii) the subject matter could involve highly technical issues; and iv) the Panel is required to submit a report rather than an award, would suggest that the Panel is a team of 'inspectors' conducting a plain enquiry which ends in the filling of a technical report and, therefore, is not intended to be a judicial or quasi-judicial body.
>
> (138)

Then the author underlines that

> [h]owever, the fact that: i) in effect, there is a dispute between an affected party and the Bank; ii) Bank management has to respond to charges within a specified period; iii) the Panel conducts the investigations within the Bank as well as in the country in which the project is located, including hearing testimonies from both sides and iv) the findings of the Panel have some binding character, would signify the creation of a new-quasi-judicial organ, albeit an unconventional one, with severe limitations.
>
> (*ibid.*)

The author arrives at the conclusion that 'the Panel is definitely not a quango – an advisory body which is left largely on its own and ultimately forgotten' (148).

28 The cases submitted to the Inspection Panel to date number eighty-two: compare go.worldbank.org/2HG4E0MLV0.

Bank and may not have held official positions during the last two years, nor may they hold such positions for the next two years.[29]

The Panel can receive inspection requests if there is an adverse effect, real or potential, that prejudices the rights or interests of a group of individuals and that is directly referable to actions or omissions by the Bank that are not in accordance with its operational policies and procedures regarding the design, appraisal or implementation of a Bank-financed project.[30]

In order to be accepted, the request for inspection must satisfy two conditions: first, it must regard an issue that has already been submitted to the Bank's management and the management has not been able to show the compliance of the contested operation with the OPs and BPs; second, the alleged violation of internal Bank procedures must be, in the judgement of the Panel, of a serious character.[31]

The parties that are permitted to appeal to the Panel may not be single individuals, but, rather, groups of two or more people residing in the project area (or their representatives).[32]

The inspection procedures, set out in a document drafted by the Panel itself in 1994,[33] provide that upon receipt of a request, the Panel shall, first

29 The members of the Panel shall be selected based on their 'ability to deal thoroughly and fairly with the requests ..., integrity ..., independence from the Bank's Management, ..., exposure to developmental issues and to living conditions in developing countries'. Compare Res. WB Res. 93–10 and IDA Res. IDA 93–6, 4. It should be noted that the members of the Panel are, however, considered in the resolution to be officials of the same organization which they are inspecting, at the expense of their independence and impartiality: compare paragraph 10.

> In the performance of their functions, members of the Panel shall be officials of the Bank enjoying the privileges and immunities accorded to Bank officials, and shall be subject to the requirements of the Bank's Articles of Agreement concerning their exclusive loyalty to the Bank and to the obligations of sub-paragraphs (c) and (d) of paragraph 3.1 and paragraph 3.2 of the Principles of Staff Employment concerning their conduct as officials of the Bank.

30 The Panel can receive 'a claim that an actual or threatened material adverse effect on the affected party's right or interests arises directly out of an action or omission of the Bank to follow its own operational policies and procedures during the design, appraisal and/or implementation of a Bank financed project', Resolution IBRD 93–10 and Resolution IDA 93–6 (fn 3) 12. Washington, DC.

31 Therein, at 13.

32 The fact that the affected party legitimized to appeal to the Panel cannot be a single individual, but must be an organization, an association or other representation of a collectivity is established at 12. Alongside this hypothesis, it should be mentioned that one of the members of the Board of Executive Directors, in special cases, can present a request for inspection, *ibid.*

33 World Bank (1994).

of all, ascertain whether it has authority (based on whether the applicant is entitled to make the request, whether the subject of the request is relevant and whether the request has been submitted after the loan maturity date, or after at least 95 per cent of the loan has been drawn). Subsequently, the Panel informs the management of the Bank of the request. Hence, the management may respond on the questions raised by the applicants. If the request meets all of the required criteria, the Panel will recommend to the Executive Board that an inspection be conducted. If the Executive Board approves the inspection, the Panel can conduct it, generally through visits *in loco* and direct contact with the applicants, and send a report with its conclusions to the Bank's management and to the Executive Directors. The Executive Directors will decide measures to be adopted on the basis of the Panel's conclusions and the management's recommendations.[34]

After having briefly described the terms of office and the Inspection Panel's procedures, it seems opportune to highlight several critical aspects, which may be grouped as *ratione materiae*, *ratione personae* and *ratione temporis*.

As regards the first group, one must take into consideration that the expression 'project' used in the Resolution instituting the Panel can be understood to include the 'non-project loans' (such as structural adjustment programmes), while a request that is not related to a specific operation of the Bank and, therefore, does not concern any of the three phases of the life of the project (design, appraisal and implementation) cannot be accepted by the Panel, even if the Bank has violated its own operating procedures.[35] In order better to clarify the importance of this initial observation, it might be opportune to recall that World Bank loans can be classified into two types of credit instruments, called respectively investment loans and development-policy loans. Investment loans are financed over the long term, last between five to ten years and are planned to cover costs specific to the implementation of projects for the construction of physical and social infrastructures. Investment loans can be used to finance new projects or to renew or reinforce existing infrastructures. The criteria that the financed projects must meet are the following: compliance with the Articles of Agreement, with the OPs/BPs and with the 'Country Assistance Strategy';[36] solid economic justification; capacity to contribute to the reduction of poverty and the sustainable economic growth of

34 *Ibid.*, 30 ff. 35 Shihata (2000), 105 ff.

36 Those are the strategies elaborated by the Bank with which it plans its programmes of assistance: go.worldbank.org/4M75BI76J0.

the country.[37] The second type of loan is part of the system of operations called 'Development Policy Operations' and was introduced in 2004 to replace structural-adjustment loans.[38] They are the result of rethinking economic assistance, motivated by the awareness that the requirement of a rigid package of reforms that are uniform for all countries cannot guarantee efficient results in terms of development.[39] In substance, the 'development-policy Loans', initially designed to support macroeconomic policy reforms and adjustment to economic crises, have evolved into instruments for dealing with complex institutional questions, such as social and health policies or improving the investment attractiveness of a country, rather than managing public spending or the financial accountability of institutions in a country. 'Development-policy loans', as opposed to structural-adjustment loans, are based on a careful analysis of the beneficiary country and the potential social impact that the financed measures could have.

This second category of loans, which represents on average 20–25 per cent of the Bank's operations over the last decade,[40] cannot be the subject of examination by the Inspection Panel.

Again, in terms of *ratione materiae*, it bears highlighting that the mandate of the Inspection Panel is fairly circumscribed. The mandate includes the OPs and the BPs, but excludes other internal directives of the Bank (such as the Guidelines and Best Practices) and, *a fortiori,* does not grant

37 World Bank, Operational Policy 10.00 – Investment Lending, June 1994, 3 (a), (b), (c). Currently, the activities associated with this type of economic assistance are undergoing a reform, started in 2009, with the purpose of creating more flexible instruments for assistance that guarantee more efficient results. The reform is based on five fundamental points, defined as pillars: 1) dedicate greater attention to results and introduce differentiation in the process of loan approval according to the level of associated risk; 2) change 'supervision' into support for the implementation of the project; 3) elaborate a new loan instrument that can tie disbursement of funds more closely to the results achieved; 4) foresee instruments that can create better working conditions for the national teams that deal with implementing the reforms foreseen by the project; 5) create a policy framework that encompasses all of the investment lending instruments. World Bank, Investment Lending Reform: Concept Note, 26 January 2009, 2 ff.

38 The operative document that defines this new type of loan is Operational Policy 8.60, August 2004.

39 In the words of the Bank, the reform of adjustment lending in 2004 'reflected the need for streamlining conditionality and the Bank's acknowledgement that there is not a single blueprint for reform that will work in all countries': compare web.worldbank.org/WBSITE/EXTERNAL/PROJECTS/0,contentMDK:20120732~menuPK:268725~pagePK:41367~piPK:51533~theSitePK:40941,00.html.

40 The data can be consulted on the following site: digitalmedia.worldbank.org/projectsandops/lendingtools.htm.

them the power to ascertain the existence of violations of international law.[41] The implications for non-economic values is that the Inspection Panel does not have many possibilities of initiating an inspection, except when the policies and procedures of the Bank itself – claimed to have been violated – require the Bank's compliance,[42] since the Panel will be bound to reject all cases alleging violations of non-economic values when they cannot be said to arise from some specific internal procedure.[43] This

41 The impossibility of assessing (non-)compliance with international law on the part of the Bank is underlined by the Panel itself, which expressly declared beyond its authority an inspection request regarding presumed violations of the UN resolutions that imposed economic and commercial sanctions on South Africa. Compare World Bank Inspection Panel, report and recommendation on request for inspection on Lesotho Highlands Water Project, 19 July 1999, 7. There are those who hold that the normative system of the Bank is not one of self-restraint with respect to international law, but rather a subset that, as such, must respect the fundamental rules since non-compliance with these general rules could be noticed by the Inspection Panel, that is a violation of these obligations would constitute an offence imputable to the Bank: compare Crippa (2010). On this topic, see also Benvenuti (2004).

42 The position regarding the Executive Directors is reported by the Inspection Panel in the Report of Case 22: 'in other words, according to the Management response, if human rights issues have "significant direct economic effects" on a Bank financed project, they become a matter of concern to the bank. Otherwise they don't. In this case, Management feels that the project "can achieve its development objectives", so human rights issues are of no direct concern', *Chad-Cameroon Petroleum Development and Pipeline Project*, Management of the Petroleum Economy Project, and Petroleum Sector Management Capacity Building Project, 17 September 2002, 12 (web.worldbank.org/WBSITE/EXTERNAL/EXTINSPECTION*PANEL*/0,contentMDK:22515234~pagePK:64129751~piPK:64128378~theSitePK:380794,00.html).

43 Despite this, projects have been cancelled, as, for example, in the case of Nepal: *Arun III Proposed Hydroelectric Project and Restructuring* of IDA Credit, in 1994, which was the first case faced by the Inspection Panel. It was shown that the dam to be built in Arun would have destroyed forests in the Himalayas and threatened the survival of local populations. In place of the dam, numerous villages developed mini hydropower plants managed collectively. Inspection Panel, *Request for Inspection: Panel Report – Nepal Arun III Proposed Hydroelectric Project* (IDA/SecfM94–378), 16 December 1994, Inspection Panel, *Arun III Hydroelectric Project – Management Response to the Inspection Panel's Investigation Report*, 2 August 1995. Sometimes the State, resentful, decided to stop working with the Bank: see case of 'China Western Poverty Reduction Project' (1999)

> China accepts no conditions beyond Management's original recommendations that had been agreed between Management and my authorities. We appreciate Management's efforts ... that only economic considerations be taken into account in Bank decision making ... It is unacceptable ... that other Bank shareholders would insist on imposing additional conditions on Management's recommendations – namely coming back to the Board for approval again for a project that was already approved last year
>
> (Inspection Panel, 'World Bank Press Release on China Western Poverty Reduction Project', press release 2001/004/EAP, 7 July 2000, go.worldbank.org/7K2VNSGJX0)

occurred, for example, in the case of the *Uganda Third Power Project, Fourth Power Project, and Proposed Bujugali Hydropower Project*, regarding a project financed in Uganda to enhance the hydroelectric system in the country,[44] and also in the case of *Transitional Support for Economic Recovery Credit Operation (TSERO) and Emergency Economic and Social Reunification Support Project*, regarding a project financed in the Congo to improve forest management.[45]

As regards *ratione personae* requirement, we have stated that the applicants must be two or more individuals residing in the project area (or their representatives). The notion of 'affected party' was the subject of clarification, since it is understood to mean 'any two or more people with common interests or concerns'.[46] However, the requisite of territoriality, combined or not with the need to demonstrate that the applicants share a common interest to be defended that affects them directly,[47] seriously limits the number of individuals that can legitimately request an inspection by the Panel and, in any case, denies the possibility of an *actio popularis*.[48]

Finally, in terms of *ratione temporis*, the fact that inspections cannot be conducted into projects for which a sum greater than 95 per cent has

44 Case 24, *Uganda Third Power Project, Fourth Power Project, and Proposed Bujugali Hydropower Project*: among the Operational Policies the Panel considered to have been violated was OD 4.15 – (transformed into OP1 in 2004) – on the topic of reducing poverty (recommendation of the Board of Executive Directors, 7 June 2002, published on web.worldbank.org/WBSITE/EXTERNAL/EXTINSPECTION*PANEL*/0,contentMDK:22515085~pagePK:64129751~piPK:64128378~theSitePK:380794,00.html).

45 Case 37, *TSERO and Emergency Economic and Social Reunification Support Project* (web.worldbank.org/WBSITE/EXTERNAL/EXTINSPECTIONPANEL/0,contentMDK:22513352~pagePK:64129751~piPK:64128378~theSitePK:380794,00.html). Please also see Case 40 *West African Gas Pipeline Project* (regarding a project for the construction of a gas pipeline in Nigeria: recommendation of 27 June 2008, web.worldbank.org/WBSITE/EXTERNAL/EXTINSPECTION*PANEL*/0,,contentMDK:22513059~pagePK:64129751~piPK:64128378~theSitePK:380794,00.html).

46 During 1996 the Board of Executive Directors reviewed the Resolution establishing the Inspection Panel and, on 17 October 1996, it issued 'Clarification of Certain Aspects of the Resolution' (Res. 96–204, the Clarification). Following a second review, on 20 April 1999, the Board issued 'Conclusions of the Board's Second Review of the Inspection Panel' (1999 Clarification). On the nature of Clarifications as gentlemen's agreements, void of binding, legal value, see Adjovi (2001).

47 As in Case 74 *South-West Roads: Western Europe-Western China International Transit Corridor* (regarding a project for a highway in Kazakhstan, 2011). The requester was Bauyrzhan Isaliev, a representative of the non-governmental organization 'National Analytical Information Resource' (NAIR), on his own behalf and on behalf of the NAIR and twenty-four project-affected people (web.worldbank.org/WBSITE/EXTERNAL/EXTINSPECTION*ANEL*/0,,contentMDK:22985149~menuPK:64129250~pagePK:64129751~piPK:64128378~theSitePK:380794~isCURL:Y,00.html)

48 Hansungule (2001), 159.

been disbursed does not take into account the fact that it is usually in the conclusive phases of a project, or even after its conclusion, that the damage suffered by the population residing in the area in question could be objectively verified.[49] For example, the inspection request in the case of *Santa Fe Infrastructure Project and Provincial Road Infrastructure* (2011), Argentina, was not accepted. The applicants claimed that the new path of Road 19, at km 44, was dangerously too close to a school, a chapel and a commercial establishment, thus jeopardizing the lives of the students and others. They added that this situation created difficulties of access and parking near these buildings/premises, and, as a consequence, was also a danger to vehicles passing along the road at high speed. The Panel did not accept the request because at the time it was submitted to the Panel, the disbursement of the loan financing the project exceeded 95 per cent.

3. Concluding observations

The difficulties and the limitations mentioned above are exacerbated by an aspect that permeates all of the activity of the Panel: its lack of independence. In effect, from the actual start of the inspection procedure to the final evaluation of the outcome of the inspection and, if called for, the remedies to adopt, the true power of decision is in the hands of the Executive Directors.[50] The Directors have often taken very defensive positions,[51] denying that the OPs have been violated, bringing into discussion

49 Treakle (2003), 267.

50 The existence of multiple resource providing sponsors coupled with high earnings retentions have given Bank managers enormous freedom to operate autonomously of its formal owners: Burnham (1994). Such managerial autonomy has for years rendered its shareholder governments and their taxpayers ignorant of and powerless over how and where their funds have been deployed: Udall (1998).

51 For example, Case 4, *Brazil: Rondônia Natural Resources Management Project* of 1995. The requesters alleged that a project designed to protect the local ecosystem was in fact having the opposite effect, in particular, that the construction of roads was facilitating deforestation and environmental degradation. Management asserted that the alleged harm was not caused by any failure on the part of the Bank but was the fault of the borrower. Although the Panel recommended an investigation, the Board felt that the degree of harm alleged was unclear. The Board directed the Panel instead to conduct a special factual review of the issue. The Panel was asked to assess allegations that the project, designed to benefit local communities and indigenous peoples and the fragile natural environments they depended on for their livelihood, had not been adequately implemented. The Panel's second report confirmed that extensive environmental harm had been caused in the project area and noted that management's failure to properly supervise the project 'had undoubtedly contributed' to the damage (web.worldbank.org/WBSITE/EXTERNAL/EXTINSPECTIONPANEL/0,contentMDK:22515717~pagePK:64129751~piPK:64128378~theSitePK:380794,00.html).

the applicants' right to make the requests and the conclusions of the Panel itself and, in reality, not adopting effective remedies.[52] As regards the latter aspect, another critical point brought to light by the doctrine is the lack of a protection mechanism for the individuals requesting the inspection from possible repressive measures taken by the country concerned.[53] In fact, in a case in which repressive measures were actually found to have occurred and were brought to the attention of the Bank, the latter took steps to prevent the Panel from dealing with the issue in the formulation of its conclusions.[54]

In the cases handled by the Inspection Panel, respect for non-economic values was often sacrificed to the need of the Bank to comply with its Articles of Agreement in its operations and the relative provisions prohibiting political interference.[55] Often, the Bank's management invoked the principle/concept of 'direct economic effects' as the criterion to use in evaluating whether the Bank could consider its own decisions to be

52 Herein, 254. Circi points out the structural weakness represented by the absence of an appraisal phase for the effective actuation of the measures recommended by the Panel: Circi (2006). Similar considerations are made by Sorel (2009).

53 Ghazi (2005), 221.

54 Umaña, Charmain of the Inspection Panel, affirmed that this type of investigation was obstructed by the Executive Board: compare Umaña (2001), 135. In truth, some negative peculiarities of the inspection procedures were recognized by the Bank itself. The former General Counsel Shihata, for example, notes that at the end of the 1990s, the Panel complained that the Bank management was in the habit of making agreements with the beneficiary country concerning the remedies that the Bank should adopt in the case that violations of internal procedures were ascertained, even before the Panel was able to formulate its recommendations. At the same time, there was strong disagreement with the Executive Board regarding the possibility of abolishing the request to the Executive Directors for authorization to proceed from the Panel, at least in a few cases. The member countries, on the other hand, sustained that the inspection procedures were an evaluation of their conduct, as opposed to that of the Bank, and manifested their disapproval of the public nature of the procedures. In other words, the functional evaluation of the parameters that the Bank is called upon to deny or grant loans was considered by some countries to be interference in their internal affairs. Finally, the groups of individuals that turned to the Panel denounced the fact that they were not consulted appropriately during the inspection phase and were not informed of the outcome of the inspection in their own language: Shihata (2000), 2 ff.

55 As is known, section 10 of Art. IV of the Articles of Agreement, entitled 'Political Activity Prohibited', states: 'The Bank and its officers shall not interfere in the political affairs of any member; nor shall they be influenced in their decisions by the political character of the member or members concerned. Only economic considerations shall be relevant to their decisions, and these considerations shall be weighed impartially in order to achieve the purposes stated in Article I.' It is beyond the scope of this chapter to consider the changing and dynamic interpretation of this disposition: the question of political neutrality on the part of the Bank is, in fact, one of the most debated in this context.

non-economic factors: if the project in question was considered capable of reaching its development goals, the alleged violations of non-economic values do not have direct economic effects, since they can legitimately be left out of consideration.[56] In other words, the practice of the Inspection Panel seems to point to a rift between the statements of the Bank[57] (at times supported by positions actually taken)[58] and operative procedures.

In conclusion, despite the fact that its institution represents a positive example for the accountability of international organizations, the Inspection Panel suffers from several limitations and does not represent a wholly suitable mechanism to guarantee the protection of non-economic values within the framework of the operations conducted by the Bank.

These limitations vary in nature. There are at least four principal limitations.

First, the Panel has no authority to make explicit reference to the compatibility of Bank operations with international regulations regarding the protection of non-economic values.

Second, the Panel lacks any true decision-making power within the Bank.

Third, the inspection procedure is more 'administrative' than judicial in nature, since the applicants are without any active, guaranteed role.

Fourth, the Panel has limited expertise in terms of non-economic values.[59]

These limitations might be overcome in the near future. To this end, at least two strategies might be undertaken. One is to reconsider the role played by the Panel: moving from a merely corrective role (as it is currently) to becoming a mechanism for protection. The other would be to revise the OPs in order to guarantee full inclusion of more non-

56 Compare to fn 37.

57 For example, on the occasion of the fiftieth anniversary of the Universal Declaration of Human Rights, the Bank affirmed that creating conditions for the exercise of fundamental rights is one of the central and inalienable objectives of development and recognized that the Bank itself could take further steps to affirm its role in the promotion of basic rights. In general, for an analysis of international obligations sanctioned by the Pact on Economic, Social and Cultural Rights, and of the actions needed to promote and monitor respecting human rights in the practice of the World Bank, see De Sena (2011).

58 For example, the role played by the President of the Bank for the release of Ngarlejy Yorongar: arrested in 1998 for defamatory accusations against the President of Chad, tortured and then released and arrested again in 2001 immediately after the inspection request sent to the Panel (case 22, fn 42), Yorongar was released only following strong pressure on the government of Chad from the international community, and, in particular, by the President of the Bank.

59 Van Genugten (2003).

economic values. In effect, the adoption of internal operative procedures that directly concern/protect non-economic values on the whole (as far as possible) would be desirable, as expressed in the relevant international instruments, or, at least, provision for careful evaluations (*ex ante* and *ex post*) of the negative impact that Bank-financed projects can have on these rights.[60] One OP on non-economic values can proactively contribute to improving the selection, design, sitting and implementation of programmes and projects, if it is initiated early, if it involves the public, if it evaluates development alternatives and if it is supported by effective monitoring and supervision. The use of an OP on non-economic values would move environmental/social, etc. analysis 'upstream' in the planning process so as better to become an integral part of decision-making; ensuring adequate supervision and monitoring of OP-related measures during the implementation of projects ('downstream' operations); and, at the 'midstream', building necessary design and mitigation measures into the project. In other words, this means that the piecemeal plans that currently exist for non-economic values, and particularly the lack of attention to the protection of fundamental human, social and environmental rights in the Bank's plans, have to be changed. What this suggests is that the problems of the developing world, many of which have been redefined by globalization, need to be confronted in terms of their full complexity: it means understanding both the local and global dimensions of these issues. Sadly, it is doubtful that anything close to such a global consciousness and commitment might be called upon in the practice of the World Bank.

References

Acconci, P. 2011. *Tutela della salute e diritto internazionale*. Padova: CEDAM.

Adjovi, R. 2001. 'Le Panel d'Inspection de la Banque Mondiale: développements récents'. *Actualité et droit international*: 2–9.

Alfredsson, G. and Ring, R. 2001. *The Inspection Panel of the World Bank: A Different Complaints Procedure*. Leiden, Boston: Martinus Nijhoff Publishers.

Benvenuti, P. 2004. 'La tutela giuridica delle istanze sociali nel tempo della globalizzazione'. Orrù, R. and Sciannella L.G. (eds.), *Limitazioni di sovranità e processi di democraticizzazione*. Torino: Giappichelli: 227–44.

Boisson de Chazournes, L. 2000. 'Policy Guidance and Compliance: The World Bank Operational Standards'. Shelton D. (ed.), *Commitment and Compliance:*

60 Boisson de Chazournes (2000).

The Role of Non-Binding Norms in the International Legal System. Oxford University Press: 281–303.

2001. 'Compliance with Operational Standards, the Contribution of the World Bank Inspection Panel'. Alfredsson and Ring (eds.): 67–86.

Bradlow, D.D. 1994. 'International Organizations and Private Complaints: The Case of the World Bank'. *Virginia J International L* 34: 553–613.

Burnham, J.B. 1994. 'Understanding the World Bank: A Dispassionate Analysis'. Bandow, D. and Vásquez, I. (eds.), *Perpetuating Poverty: The World Bank, the IMF and the Developing World*. Washington, DC: The Cato Institute, 75–85.

Circi, M. 2006. 'The World Bank Inspection Panel: Is It Really Effective?'. *Global Jurist Advances* 6: 1–25.

Crippa, L.A. 2010. 'Multilateral Development Banks and the Human Rights Responsibility'. *American University International L Review* 25: 531–77.

De Sena, P. 2011. 'Fondo monetario internazionale, Banca mondiale e rispetto dei diritti dell'uomo'. Ligustro, A. and Sacerdoti, G. (eds.), *Problemi e tendenze del diritto internazionale dell'economia*. Liber Amicorum *in onore di Paolo Picone*. Napoli: Editoriale Scientifica: 829–58.

Ghazi, B. 2005. *The IFM, the World Bank and the Question of Human Rights*. Ardsley Park, NY: Transnational Publishers.

Hansungule, M. 2001. 'Access to the Panel – the Notion of Affected Party, Issues of Collective and Material Interest'. Alfredsson and Ring (eds.): 143–66.

Huyser, K. 2011. 'Sustainable Development Rhetoric and Reform at the World Bank'. Anton, D.K. and Shelton, D.L. (eds.), *Environmental Protection and Human Rights*. Cambridge University Press: 783–7.

McBeth, A. 2010. *International Economic Actors and Human Rights*. London; New York: Routledge.

Nathan, K.V.S.K. 1995. 'The World Bank Inspection Panel – Court or Quango?'. *J International Arbitration* 12: 135–48.

Rigo Sureda, A. 2004. 'The Law Applicable to the Activities of International Developments Banks'. *RCADI* 308: 9–251.

Seatzu, F. 2008. *Il panel di ispezione della Banca Mondiale. Contributo allo studio della funzione di controllo nelle banche internazionali di sviluppo*. Torino: Giappichelli.

Shihata, I.F.I. 1992. 'The World Bank and Non-Governmental Organizations'. *Cornell International LJ* 25: 623–41.

2000. *The World Bank Inspection Panel: In Practice*. Oxford University Press: new edn.

Sorel, J.-M. 2009. 'Institutions économiques internationales et droit international des droits de l'homme: un respect cosmétique en effet miroir'. *La soumission des organisations internationales aux normes internationales relatives aux droits de l'homme: journée d'études de Strasbourg*. SFDI, Institut international des droits de l'homme, Paris: Pedone: 35–56.

Treakle, K. 2003. 'Lessons Learned'. Clark, D., Fox, J. and Treakle K. (eds.), *Demanding Accountability: Civil Society Claims and the World Bank Inspection Panel*. Lanham; Boulder; New York; Oxford: Rowman and Littlefield: 247–8.

Udall, L. 1998. 'The World Bank and Public Accountability: Has Anything Changed?'. Fox, J. A. and Brown, L.D. (eds.), *The Struggle for Accountability: The World Bank, NGOs and Grassroots Movements*. Cambridge, MA: MIT Press: 391–436.

Umaña, A. 2001. 'Some Lessons from the Inspection Panel's Experience'. Alfredsson and Ring (eds.): 127–42.

van Genugten, W. 2003. 'Tilburg Guiding Principles on World Bank, IMF and Human Rights'. Van Genugten, W., Hunt, P. and Mathews, S., *World Bank, IMF and Human Rights*. Nijmegen: Wolf Legal Publishers: 247–55.

Wahi, N. 2005–6. 'Human Rights Accountability of the IFM and World Bank: A Critique of Existing Mechanisms of a Theory of Horizontal Accountability'. *University of California Davis J International L and Policy* 12: 331–407.

Wapenhans, W.A. 1992. *Effective Implementation: Keys to Development Impact, Report of the Portfolio Management Task Force*. Washington, DC: World Bank.

World Bank, 19 August 1994. *World Bank Inspection Panel: Operating Procedures*. Washington, DC: World Bank.

2007. *Inspection Panel: A Staff Guide to the World Bank Inspection Panel*. Washington, DC: World Bank.

10

The protection of indigenous peoples' concerns in World Bank-funded projects

MARTINA GUIDI

1. Development projects and indigenous peoples

The UN Special *Rapporteur* on human rights and fundamental freedoms of indigenous peoples has tackled the impact of large-scale development projects[1] on indigenous peoples,[2] since their identity is bound up with traditional livelihoods and ancestral lands[3] and their rights may pose an obstacle to national or foreign investors in projects affecting those lands. Two hundred and fifty (often foreign or multinational) companies have been identified as creating the risk of endangering indigenous rights; 17 per cent of which have a high risk of negative impact on indigenous-rights issues. Very few companies report voluntarily on areas of non-compliance with indigenous-rights issues, whilst most companies provide a response to allegations of breaches of indigenous rights. Nineteen per cent of companies have a corporate-wide indigenous-rights policy; 15 per cent of companies have adopted a policy that supports free,

1 The term 'development project' is used herein as defined by the Special *Rapporteur* on the Situation of Human Rights and Fundamental Freedoms of Indigenous People in the 2003 Report 'Indigenous Issues: Human Rights and Indigenous Issues', UN Doc. E/CN.4/2003/90 (21 January 2003):

> [a] process of investment of public and/or private, national or international capital for the purpose of building or improving the physical infrastructure of a specified region, the transformation over the long run of productive activities involving changes in the use of and property rights to land, the large-scale exploitation of natural resources including subsoil resources, the building of urban centres, manufacturing and/or mining, power, extraction and refining plants, tourist developments, port facilities, military bases and similar undertakings.

2 Anaya (2010).

3 The relationship between indigenous peoples and their land is reflected in their culture, spirituality, history, social organization, food supply, economy and health. Dannenmaier (2008), 53.

prior and informed consultation of indigenous peoples. Just over 6 per cent of companies have a policy covering involuntary resettlement.[4]

Some local issues now reach a global audience thanks to the increasing effectiveness of indigenous peoples' actions in promoting partnership with non-governmental organizations (NGOs).[5] World-wide visibility for indigenous peoples' concerns have negative repercussions for companies that ignore the 'reputational' risks arising when they come into conflict with indigenous peoples.[6] Allegations against companies include failure to inform or consult, negative impact on traditional ways of life, destruction of sacred sites or impact on health through pollution.

In the last few years the banking sector has been exposed to negative publicity for financing environmentally and socially damaging projects.[7] As a consequence, not only activists and scholars but also International Financial Institutions' (IFIs) boards, management and staff now reject the idea that IFIs can or should make decisions solely based on economic factors.[8] The whole economic investment area seems to be inextricably linked to human-rights issues. An expanded approach to human rights at the IFIs holds the promise of improving consistency of policy between the twin goals of development and human rights.[9]

4 In its paper on 'Indigenous Rights: Risks and Opportunities for Investors' EIRIS has analysed the impact and the response of 250 companies operating in sectors (mining, oil and gas, agricultural producers, forestry and paper) and in countries considered high risk for indigenous rights (www.eiris.org).

5 For example, in February 2009, the UK's Co-operative Bank announced it would fund a legal challenge by the Beaver Lake Cree Nation against oil and gas companies on the basis that tar sands extraction in Canada is destroying indigenous peoples' hunting and fishing lands and resources (www.guardian.co.uk, 26 February 2009). This case is the first time a large-scale litigation seeking to curtail industrial activity based on treaty rights the Alberta Court of Queen's Bench has assumed an ongoing supervisory role in order to ensure that the parties involved (local government and indigenous peoples) 'sit down and negotiate the application of the duty to consult', even if the Court considered itself as having no jurisdiction to make a judicial review of the authorizations to the foreign companies (Memorandum of decision at 70, March 2012, www.raventrust.com).

6 In consumer-facing companies poor performance with regard to indigenous peoples may result in a boycott. An example was the 2008 campaign against De Beers' diamonds in connection with allegations of exploration in the Central Kalahari Game Reserve, home of the indigenous San in Botswana.

7 See Castellino (2005), 89; Daes (2005), 75; Gilbert (2007), 583; Bankes (2009–10), 457.

8 Recent developments with respect to IFI policies relating to human rights, including labour rights and the rights of indigenous peoples, suggest that IFIs themselves recognize their own crucial role with regard to international human rights obligations. According to Bradlow and Hunter (2010), 393, this also leads one to hope that IFIs may move more decisively in the future to define their human rights and related responsibilities.

9 McInerney-Lankford (2010). Similar benefits are likely to follow from the European Bank for Reconstruction and Development's clear endorsement of free, prior and informed

Indigenous peoples' rights[10] number among the human-rights issues that States, companies and their investors should take into account and respect in the context of socially responsible projects and investments,[11] if for no other reason then merely for the financial viability of their project.[12]

2. The World Bank policy on indigenous peoples

The policy-making of the World Bank (WB) exemplifies IFIs' environmentally and socially responsible trend.[13] Safeguard policies[14] were designed to prevent and mitigate undue harm to people and their environment in the development process.[15] While the WB has no operational policies on human rights *per se*, the protection of indigenous peoples' concerns is one of the most overlooked. Its policy on indigenous peoples addresses the rights of those peoples, aiming at 'ensuring that the development process fully respects the dignity, human rights, economies, and cultures of Indigenous Peoples'.[16]

The WB projects may have a significant impact on the social and economic welfare of these peoples, who are among the most disadvantaged and marginalized populations in many areas of the world and are

consent for indigenous peoples (see EBRD's Environment and Social Policy, 'PR 7: Indigenous Peoples' (May 2008), 50–7, www.ebrd.com).

10 See Barsh (1994), 72; Wolfrum (1999), 369; Thornberry (2002); Anaya (2004, 2009); Rodríguez-Piñero (2005); Swepston (2005), 53.

11 MacKay (2010) argues that the internal policies of the IFIs should reflect principles of international law protecting the rights and interests of indigenous peoples, including their rights of free, prior and informed consent.

12 Given the level of NGO and media attention to the issue of indigenous peoples' rights and the introduction of laws and regulation in many countries, companies with strong commitments and effective engagement processes will result in being more competitive in an environment where access to land and resources is becoming increasingly restricted.

13 See, in general, Shihata (1988), 39, 47; Bradlow (1996), 47, 63.

14 In 1997, the WB regrouped ten Operational Policies as specific safeguard policies; among these, OP 4.10 on Indigenous Peoples. The policies were designed to help the Bank address environmental and social issues arising primarily from Investment Lending projects that finance goods, works and services in a broad range of sectors, which constituted the WB's main line of business at that time.

15 In the opinion of Sarfaty (2009), 670, such policies may also create a perverse incentive: for instance, staff members may avoid projects that would benefit indigenous peoples – by redesigning projects to be undertaken in areas lacking an indigenous population – so that they would not be required to complete additional time-consuming and costly tasks under the Bank's policy on indigenous peoples.

16 The WB Operational Policy on Indigenous Peoples, July 2005, OP 4.10, 1, www.worldbank.org. This Bank's policy aims at ensuring that adverse impact on indigenous people is avoided, or minimized when avoidance is not feasible.

vulnerable to changes caused by development projects. Given its day-to-day experience in carrying out development projects that directly or indirectly affect indigenous peoples, the Bank has become a critical international player in the implementation of indigenous-rights standards.

The WB was the first international organization and multilateral development bank engaging in or financing major on-the-ground projects to introduce a policy that set standards for these operations as they affect indigenous peoples.[17] The Operational Policy and Bank Procedures (OP/BP 4.10) on indigenous peoples[18] requires that WB-financed projects are designed not only to avoid adverse impact but, equally important, to provide culturally appropriate benefits for indigenous peoples.[19]

Nevertheless, there is a disjuncture between the articulation of the indigenous peoples' policy and its day-to-day application, because of the WB's difficulties in implementing the policy.[20] The best compliance with the operational policy resulted in the inclusion of specific activities for indigenous peoples in the plan of action, screening and free, prior and informed consultation.[21] Moderate compliance score criteria included evidence of broad community support,[22] the inclusion of specific ethnically disaggregated monitoring data and dissemination of information in appropriate language, form and manner. Agreement on benefit-sharing

17 The WB's first policy on indigenous peoples was adopted in 1982 as Operational Manual Statement (OMS 2.34). By 1987, the WB had begun linking its indigenous-peoples and resettlement policies to its new environmental policies. For more detailed information, see Sarfaty (2005), 1791; and Spiliopoulou Akermark (2005), 93.

18 The Operational Policy 4.10 (endorsed by the WB Board of Executive Directors on 10 May 2005 and in effect from July 2005) and the more technical Bank Procedures 4.10 work in tandem with Operational Policy 4.12 on involuntary settlement (revised February 2011), and other policies on matters such as environmental assessment, natural habitats and forests.

19 As to the policy, see MacKay (2002), 527 and (2005), 65.

20 See the Report prepared by the Independent Evaluation Group (IEG) that provides the outcomes of the portfolio review of projects triggering the WB OP on indigenous peoples in the first three years during which the revised policy was in effect. From July 2005 to June 2008, 132 projects triggered OP 4.10, equivalent to about 12 per cent of the total number of projects approved by the WB during the same period. A positive finding is that, during this period, fifteen operations were self-standing indigenous-peoples projects.

21 See further at 5.

22 While in practice many projects apply the concept of 'broad community support', they need to document it to facilitate verification of compliance with the policy requirement.

of indigenous knowledge and cultural resources, the inclusion of a conflict-resolution mechanism and, when applicable, consideration of indigenous peoples' rights to lands and resources are at the lower end of the ranking.[23] In the few cases where resettlement of indigenous peoples was an issue, the relevant projects did not include such resettlement.

The involvement of the WB Inspection Panel (IP)[24] often leads to quite significant changes in projects and substantial benefits for the affected people and the environment. At the project level, positive outcomes regarding indigenous peoples are an increased attention to indigenous peoples' concerns and livelihoods and the strengthening of the rights and protection for indigenous and traditional communities affected by WB projects. In particular, we may recall rights of full participation and representation; respect for the traditional practices and means of representation of these communities; rights to land tenure, including collective title.[25]

According to the Panel, WB policies[26] should require that WB-financed projects respect international agreements addressing human rights and indigenous peoples when the project country is a party. For example, the Panel found a failure when the WB 'did not adequately consider whether the proposed Project plan and its implementation would be consistent with ILO Convention No. 169'.[27]

23 Many projects targeting or impacting on indigenous peoples do not address issues related to land and resource rights, which are important to the well-being of indigenous peoples.

24 The IP is an independent accountability mechanism (IAM), established in September 1993 by the WB Board of Directors, and it provides a forum for people who believe that they may be adversely affected by Bank-financed operations. On its role see Bradlow (1994), 576–79; Shihata (2000): and Latino in this book.

25 See 'Accountability at the World Bank. The Inspection Panel at 15 Years', Washington, 2009.

26 The WB policies and procedures are not limited to the Bank's social and environmental safeguard policies, but include other Operational Policies, Bank Procedures and Operational Directives, as well as other WB procedural documents, among others, those regarding indigenous peoples.

27 See IP, 'Honduras: Land Administration Project- Investigation Report', 254–8 (www.inspectionpanel.org). The request for inspection concerned a small pilot effort to delimit and establish title to the lands of selected Garífuna and Miskito communities. According to the Garífuna people, as this project was undermining their long-standing struggle to assert collective title over lands lived on and traditionally used by them, WB actions that supported it lead to a violation of the government's commitments under ILO Convention No. 169, an international agreement to which Honduras was a party. About this case, see Herz and Perrault (2009).

3. The IFC's Performance Standards on indigenous peoples

The International Finance Corporation (IFC) has adopted a Policy on Environmental and Social Sustainability[28] and also eight Performance Standards concerning its clients. These Standards, introduced in 2006, provide guidance on how to avoid, mitigate and manage environmental and social risks and impact,[29] including stakeholder-engagement and disclosure obligations on the part of the client, as a way of doing sustainable business.

The requirements related to indigenous peoples are described in Performance Standard 7 (PS7). It aims at establishing and maintaining an ongoing relationship based on 'informed consultation and participation' (ICP) with the indigenous peoples affected by a project throughout the latter's life-cycle, and ensuring the 'free, prior, and informed consent' (FPIC) of affected communities of indigenous peoples, as well as respecting and preserving their human rights, dignity, aspirations, culture, natural-resource-based livelihoods, knowledge and practices. The ultimate aim is to prevent and avoid the adverse impact of projects on communities of indigenous peoples, or, when avoidance is not possible, to minimize and/or compensate for such impact.

The requirements of PS7 have incorporated many of the core elements of ILO Convention 169:[30] the meaning of the terms 'indigenous' and 'tribal peoples'; the importance of consultation;[31] the recognition of the customary rights of ownership and possession over lands; and the lack of a veto over projects. Compliance with ILO Convention 169 not only protects indigenous and tribal peoples' rights, it also benefits private companies implementing projects that affect them, and promotes the interests of private business by laying the groundwork for a positive and socially responsible investment environment.

As the IP did not have jurisdiction over IFC projects, the Compliance Advisor/Ombudsman (CAO)[32] was established in 1999. It is an

28 'International Finance Corporation's Policy on Environmental and Social Sustainability', 1 January 2012 (www.ifc.org).

29 The Performance Standards now encompass all vulnerable groups and related social issues, while continuing to give special attention to the complexity of involuntary resettlement, indigenous peoples and cultural heritage.

30 ILO Convention No. 169 Concerning Indigenous and Tribal Peoples in Independent Countries, 27 June 1989 (1650 UNTS 383).

31 Article 6 of the Convention requires governments to consult indigenous and tribal peoples, and PS7 clause 9 also requires 'free, prior and informed consultation'.

32 The CAO reports directly to the President of the WB Group, completely independent from the line management structure of both IFC and MIGA.

accountability mechanism for the private-sector arms of the WB[33] and a means for promoting and ensuring compliance of IFC and MIGA (Multilateral Investment Guarantee Agency) activities with their environmental and social safeguard policies and procedures. It is worth remembering, first, that the IFC policies and standards are followed by private-sector banks that model their voluntary environmental and social policies accordingly;[34] second, that the CAO deals with private-sector projects where the government is no longer a contracting party to the transaction.

CAO serves as an ombudsman who responds to complaints from people affected or likely to be affected by projects; as an auditor who assesses IFC's (and MIGA's) compliance with environmental and social safeguards; and as an advisor, who highlights deficiencies and suggests ways the IFC/MIGA can improve its environmental policies, procedures and outcomes.[35] In each of these processes, the CAO works with the stakeholders and uses its dispute-resolution expertise to try to bring the parties to an agreement and resolve the problems.[36]

As an independent recourse mechanism, CAO's mandate is to assist IFC and MIGA in addressing complaints by people affected by IFC/MIGA projects, or projects in which those organizations play a role. Among the core issues raised in letters of complaint in 2012, indigenous peoples' rights are invoked in 24 per cent of complaints, in comparison to 17 per cent in previous years since 2000.[37]

According to CAO Operational Guidelines,[38] the criteria to be referred to when conducting audits include IFC/MIGA policies, performance standards, guidelines, procedures and requirements whose violation might lead

33 Pressure for greater IFC and MIGA accountability remained even after the IP institution in 1993. The WB Group was spurred to respond to this pressure by the Pangue Ralco Dam Project on the BìoBìo River in Chile, financed by the IFC. Damming the BìoBìo River displaced fifty-three non-indigenous peoples, and had a negative impact on the region's indigenous communities. An NGO laid a complaint with the WB IP alleging non-compliance with IFC policies, but it rejected the complaint on a jurisdictional issue, since it did not cover IFC activities. An independent report commissioned by the WB Group President concluded that in managing that project the IFC had failed to comply with many of its own policies and procedures. See 'Accountability at The World Bank: The Inspection Panel 10 Years On' (2003), www.worldbank.org; Bissell and Nanwani (2009), 9.

34 The IFC Social and Environmental Policies serve as the model for the Equator Principles, a voluntary set of principles that private-sector international finance institutions adopt to guide their project investment in the developing world.

35 For more detailed information about the CAO's three roles, see Saper (2012), 1296.

36 See Neugebauer III (2003), 1227.

37 See Compliance Advisor Ombudsman (CAO) Annual Report 2012, www.cao-ombudsman.org.

38 CAO Operational Guidelines, 3.3.1.

to adverse social or environmental consequences. Audit criteria may have their origin, or arise from, the environmental and social assessments or plans, host-country legal and regulatory requirements (including its international legal obligations), and environmental, social, health or safety provisions of the WB Group. Conspicuously absent from these standards are international treaties and international customary law. Essentially, CAO is only looking at IFC's or MIGA's performance in relation to IFC/MIGA policies and contractual agreements concluded by IFC/MIGA.[39]

However, in its ombudsman role CAO does not strictly limit itself to comparing IFC/MIGA actions with any specific policies, procedures or rules – as it does in its compliance role – even if it does not explicitly refer to general international law, environmental law or human-rights law. Acting as ombudsman, CAO can take into greater consideration human-rights obligations and implement solutions more respectful of human-rights standards, due to emphasis on mediation and a more flexible approach compared with those of the IP.[40] Thus, while not explicitly considering international norms, CAO is likely to strive for outcomes that better respect the dignity and welfare of local communities. Indirectly, then, CAO strives to reach agreements that generally align with human rights.

Moreover, in its advisory role, CAO has broad leeway to consider international norms as models for the IFC/MIGA to emulate, in response to a need for IFC policies that better reflect international norms and standards on human rights and environmental protection. For instance, CAO recommended that IFC/MIGA update its policies and performance-standards in accordance with the policy framework of business-responsibility for human rights, established by John Ruggie, as the UN Secretary – General's Special Representative on Business and Human Rights.

4. Identification of indigenous peoples

Even after the recent revisions of WB policy and IFC Performance Standards, some key issues relating to indigenous peoples still remain controversial, in relation to the relevant international instruments.[41]

39 In the IFC Paper Pulp Mill project in Uruguay, the CAO demonstrated its inability to look beyond IFC/MIGA policies and safeguards. See Lee (2008), 356–7.

40 McBeth (2009), 1151, but according to the author, on the other hand, 'that flexibility also can understate the importance of human rights as entitlements that cannot simply be bartered away'.

41 The ILO Indigenous and Tribal Peoples Convention No. 169 (1989) was the first binding international convention to address the specific rights of indigenous peoples and to

Countries' definitions of who is indigenous, or their lack of recognition of any indigenous peoples within their borders,[42] sometimes contrast with the classifications made by WB staff.[43] The first WB Indigenous Peoples Policy identified a group as indigenous according to the presence in varying degrees of the following characteristics: (a) a close attachment to ancestral territories and to the natural resources in these areas; (b) self-identification and identification by others as members of a distinct cultural group; (c) an indigenous language, often different from the national language; (d) the presence of customary social and political institutions; and (e) primarily subsistence-oriented production.

It is worth noting that even if WB policy gives greater weight to the 'self-identification' criterion, it does not consider it as the principal criterion for determining indigenous status. The two main criteria of identification still remain the indigenous peoples' maintenance of a social and cultural identity different from those of the national societies, and indigenous peoples' close attachment to their ancestral lands.

In IFC PS7, the term 'indigenous peoples' is used in a generic sense to refer to a distinct social and cultural group possessing certain characteristics as communities or groups of indigenous peoples who maintain a collective attachment, i.e. whose identity as a group or community is linked to distinct habitats or ancestral territories and the natural

outline the legal responsibilities of governments to promote and protect their human rights. The relatively low level of ratification (at December 2012 the Convention has been ratified by twenty countries; see www.ilo.org) indicates the difficulties surrounding this issue. The UN Declaration on the Rights of Indigenous Peoples (UN Doc. A/Res/61/295. 13 September 2007) was approved with 143 Member States voting in favour. See Xanthaki (2007); Charters and Stavenhagen (2009). In addition to these two specific instruments, international instruments on general human-rights protection are used to protect indigenous peoples' rights. For example, Art. 27 of the International Covenant on Civil and Political Rights has been used to contest failure to consult and to assert indigenous peoples' land rights. See Scheinin (2005), 3.

42 There is no universally accepted definition of indigenous peoples. They may be referred to in different countries by such terms as 'indigenous ethnic minorities', 'aboriginals', 'hill tribes', 'minority nationalities', 'scheduled tribes', 'first nations' or 'tribal groups'. See Sanders (1999), 4; Kingsbury (2001); Alfredsson (2005), 163; Scheinin (2005), 3.

43 There are some countries, such as Morocco, whose governments do not recognize ethnic minorities within their borders as indigenous or provide only limited rights for these minorities in their legal systems. Approving a loan in these countries becomes more problematic when there are disagreements within the WB about whether these peoples are in fact indigenous and thus require special protection that countries do not want to institute.

resources therein.[44] But indigenous peoples are considered also communities or groups that have lost collective attachment to such habitats or territories in the project area, because of forced severance, conflict, government resettlement programmes, dispossession of their lands, natural disasters or incorporation of such territories into an urban area.

The IFC Standard pays attention to the real condition of indigenous peoples' life, recognizing that they are often among the most marginalized and vulnerable segments of the population, as social groups that are distinct from mainstream groups in national societies.[45] In many cases, their economic, social and legal status limits their capacity to defend their rights to, and interests in, lands and natural and cultural resources, and may restrict their ability to participate in and benefit from development.

In the early stage of the project, it is fundamental to carry out appropriate screening research in order to determine the possible presence of indigenous communities in areas affected by project, and consequently ensure their meaningful consultation and participation, as required by the WB policy and the IFC Standard.[46]

5. Free, prior and informed consultation

World Bank OD 4.20 highlighted the need of 'informed participation' of indigenous peoples in the decision-making of development projects. In particular, in projects where activities are contingent on establishing legally recognized rights to indigenous peoples' lands and territories, the policy required the borrower to set out a plan of action for the recognition of the customary land rights of indigenous peoples, and required the financed projects that affect indigenous peoples to include a special 'Indigenous Peoples Development Plan' (IPDP). Such a 'culturally

44 As a consequence, indigenous peoples may be very vulnerable to the adverse impact associated with projects that affect the territories in which they live, causing loss of identity, culture and natural-resource-based livelihoods, as well as exposure to impoverishment and diseases.

45 Indigenous peoples are particularly vulnerable if their lands and resources are transformed, encroached upon or significantly degraded. Their languages, cultures, religions, spiritual beliefs and institutions may also come under threat.

46 See Reports on the Honduras Land Administration Project and the Democratic Republic of Congo Forest Operations. To its surprise, the Panel documented in the early stage of the DRC forest-related project failure to carry out appropriate screening research to determine possible presence of indigenous Pygmy communities in areas affected by the project, and failure to ensure their full and meaningful participation in key project actions. The Panel found this non-compliance with WB policy posed significant risks for the Pygmy peoples' safeguard.

appropriate' development plan 'based on the informed participation' of the peoples themselves must aim at ensuring that 'the development process fosters full respect for the ... dignity, human rights, and cultural uniqueness'[47] of indigenous peoples.

After the 2005 revision, the WB Indigenous Peoples Policy requires the borrower to seek 'broad community support' through a process of 'free, prior and informed consultation' of indigenous peoples before deciding to develop any project that targets or affects them.[48] The projects affecting or targeting indigenous peoples are increasingly extending the concept of consultation upstream to the project-design phase, thus expanding the earlier concept of 'informed participation' for the purpose of project-implementation. Broad community support tends to ensure that the design of many projects is more likely to benefit from indigenous knowledge, preferences or priorities, which often ensure that projects are socio-culturally compatible and sustainable. Participatory mapping of indigenous peoples' customary natural resources uses is critical, because indigenous peoples must participate in planning to reduce and possibly avoid restricting their access to non-timber resources, such as firewood, bush meat, forest fruit and medical plants.

The policy requires the borrower to conduct free, prior and informed 'consultation'[49] and to seek broad community support in deciding whether to proceed with the project, but does not recognize the 'right of free, prior and informed consent' of indigenous peoples regarding development projects that affect them. It is important to take into account the fundamental distinction between consultation and consent: only free prior informed consent would guarantee the potential right of indigenous peoples to veto companies' projects.[50]

Conversely, the IFC PS7, such as that updated in 2012, includes a requirement for free prior and informed consent (FPIC) from indigenous

47 Operational Manual OD 4.20, 6.

48 In its 2010 Advisory Note ('Review of IFC's Policy and Performance Standards on Social and Environmental Sustainability and Policy on Disclosure of Information', 16 (2010), www.caoombudsman.org), the CAO recommends that the IFC clarify its standard of ensuring 'broad community support' for a project by making reference to the standard of 'free, prior and informed consultation', which reflects ILO Convention 169's provision on 'free and informed consent'. This Convention is directed at governments, so that its relevance to IFC clients is usually indirect.

49 Recently (March 2012) the Alberta Court said pointedly that 'consultation does not mean "listening" and then doing what one pleases'; it must be more than that (fn 5).

50 FPIC is seen by the UN Declaration as an essential step forward for guaranteeing indigenous peoples' well-being (see Art. 10, UN Declaration). In general, see Ward (2011).

peoples in 'certain circumstances'.[51] However, the circumstances provided are tightly restricted, and they do not meet consent requirements under the UN Declaration on the Rights of Indigenous Peoples.[52] The client will obtain the FPIC of affected indigenous communities in three circumstances: (i) if the client proposes to locate a project on, or commercially develop natural resources on, lands traditionally owned by, or under the customary use of, indigenous peoples, to which adverse impact can be expected; (ii) if the relocation of indigenous peoples from communally held lands and natural resources subject to their traditional ownership or customary use is unavoidable; (iii) where a project may significantly impact on critical cultural heritage that is essential to the identity and/or cultural, ceremonial or spiritual aspects of indigenous peoples' lives.

The revised framework also requires additional consultation for projects that have 'potentially significant adverse impacts' on local communities, but it is still unclear when different consultation or consent requirements are triggered or what processes are adequate to fulfil them.

FPIC will be established through negotiation in good faith between the client and the indigenous peoples' communities. The client will undertake an engagement process with the affected communities of indigenous peoples, that includes an analysis and engagement planning, disclosure of relevant information,[53] consultation and participation,[54] in a culturally appropriate manner. Consultations with indigenous peoples must be carried out in a way that is suitable for the rights and needs of those peoples, providing relevant information prior to consultation in a culturally appropriate manner, form and language, when necessary ensuring translation of relevant documents.[55]

51 The positive changes seen on FPIC as regards the IFC Performance-Standards framework for the private sector could be extended to the public-sector arms of the WB Group as part of the ongoing safeguard review.

52 According to this UN Declaration, 'free prior informed consent' is necessary for projects which will heavily disrupt natural landscapes throughout the operating life of such projects. Setting such a framework is of paramount importance as indigenous peoples rarely have the ability in practice to veto development projects that affect them.

53 Disclosure of relevant information and participation of affected communities and persons will continue during the planning, implementation, monitoring and evaluation of compensation payments, livelihood-restoration activities and resettlement to achieve outcomes that are consistent with the objectives of PS5.

54 Private-sector projects can create opportunities for indigenous peoples to participate in and benefit from project-related activities that may help them fulfil their aspiration for economic and social development.

55 The IP found a double failure of compliance with the WB Policy in the case that the project did not include critical means of improving indigenous smallholder-livelihoods,

Such an appropriate approach should also identify how indigenous peoples choose to represent themselves in dealing with outside entities and organizations, improving the level of their direct participation in the Bank's staff meetings with affected communities. In light of the IP findings, the designed and later implemented consultation process should adequately reflect the way in which indigenous peoples represent themselves, as being in compliance with the Bank's policy regarding them.[56] Shortcomings in consultations with the affected populations have often been a significant issue, in particular failure adequately to account for local structures of representation.[57]

In order to improve the proper division of roles between the Bank and the borrower in the consultation processes, several meetings during the planning of the project are recommended to give affected peoples the opportunity to provide comments and express their concerns about the project. It is also necessary to provide sufficient time for indigenous peoples' decision-making processes, even if FPIC does not necessarily require unanimity and it may be achieved even when some individuals or groups within the community explicitly disagree.

The requirement of FPIC applies to project-design, implementation and expected outcomes in the light of their impact on communities of indigenous peoples. Decision-making processes that take into account the views of affected indigenous communities improve project-design and facilitate its operation over time.

6. Indigenous peoples' ancestral lands and resettlement

Due to the importance attached to indigenous peoples' cultural, spiritual and economic relationship to their land, the clear definition and protection of the rights of indigenous peoples to land and natural resources facilitates the planning and implementation of private-sector projects and

and during the consultation process relevant information was not provided in a culturally appropriate manner, form and language to achieve broad community support (see Investigation Report related to the Papua New Guinea Smallholder Agriculture Development Project issued on September 2011).

56 See the IP Report 39933-HN, 12 June 2007 and also the IP Progress Report of 9 March 2009.

57 As regards WB-financed land and forest management projects, the IP has received such complaints by Pygmy people in the Democratic Republic of Congo, Garífuna people in Honduras, Naso and Ngobe-Bugle people in Panama and representatives of indigenous groups from the Preah Vihear, Stung Treng and Oddar Meanchey Provinces in Cambodia.

reduces the risk of conflicts over lands and resources.[58] The IP has often highlighted risks to collective land rights while noting that land and forest management is complex, difficult to implement effectively and often politically controversial.

As the IP investigations confirmed, land and forest management projects, if not appropriately planned, appraised, monitored and supervised, inherently risk having a serious negative impact on the livelihoods and cultures of indigenous peoples.[59] For instance, the cultivation and production of palm oil continues to cause considerable social tensions between private-sector operators and communities, when palm-oil production activities include clearance of land and forests, acquisition of land without due process for indigenous communities, and repressive action.[60] While recognizing that, under the right conditions, certain projects can contribute to positive development, some communities see them as a threat to their livelihood.

As a consequence, the IP has asserted that special attention should be paid to areas of particular cultural and spiritual significance. Nevertheless, WB policy does not prohibit physical relocation of indigenous peoples altogether, but requires the borrower to explore alternative project-designs to avoid it, and when not feasible, to seek the broad support of the affected communities. Relocation may therefore be considered an exceptional measure in extreme and extraordinary cases.

For indigenous peoples, forcible relocation can be disastrous, by severing their various relationships with the ancestral lands.[61] According to relevant international instruments, strict standards of scrutiny are required and indigenous peoples' free, prior and informed consent must

58 For further details see IFC, 'ILO Convention 169 and the Private Sector: Questions and Answers for IFC Clients', March 2007, www.ifc.org.

59 In the Cambodia Forest Project, the Panel found that the project 'did not give adequate attention to the vital interests of local communities and indigenous peoples in forest resources, and to the contested nature of the forest domain', and failed to identify and make plans to protect resin trees that belonged, and were of high economic value, to the forest communities.

60 See the indigenous peoples' complaint alleging that the Wilmar Group's palm-oil production activities in West Kalimantan include clearance of land and forests, acquisition of land without due process, but with repressive actions, among others. See Office of the Compliance Advisor/Ombudsman, 'Audit Report: CAO Audit of IFC's Investments in Wilmar Trading (IFC 20348), Delta-Wilmar CIS (IFC 24644), Wilmar WCap (IFC 25532), Delta-Wilmar CIS Expansion (IFC 26271)', 2.1.4–7, 3.2.1, C-I-R6-Y08-F096 (19 June 2009), www.cao-ombudsman.org.

61 See Udall (1995).

be obtained.[62] In recognition of indigenous peoples' vulnerability to the loss of, alienation from or exploitation of, their land and access to natural and cultural resources, international law treats 'involuntary resettlement' as a serious human-rights concern.[63]

Moreover, the same instruments ask for high-profile attention to the further marginalization of minority indigenous populations resulting from the increased migration that WB financing may cause.[64] Consequently, management across the WB should take better account of the often unanticipated effects on indigenous populations, whether through displacement or loss of representation.

According to the IFC PS7, the client has to ensure indigenous peoples: (i) continued access to natural resources, identifying the equivalent replacement resources, or, as a last option, providing compensation and identifying alternative livelihoods if project development results in the loss of access to, and the loss of, natural resources independently of land-acquisition under the project; (ii) fair and equitable sharing of benefits associated with project where the client intends to utilize natural resources that are central to the identity and livelihood of affected indigenous communities and their usage could thereby exacerbate livelihood risk.

In doing so, the adverse impact on affected communities of indigenous peoples should be avoided where possible. If adverse impact is unavoidable, the client must minimize, restore and/or compensate for such impact in a manner appropriate to its nature and scale and the vulnerability of the affected communities.[65] The client has to offer indigenous peoples compensation and due process in the case of commercial development of their land and natural resources, together with culturally appropriate sustainable development opportunities, including provision of land-based compensation or compensation in kind in lieu of cash compensation where feasible.[66]

62 Article 10 of the above-cited 2007 UN Declaration states that 'Indigenous peoples shall not be forcibly removed from their lands or territories. No relocation shall take place without the free, prior and informed consent of the indigenous peoples concerned and after agreement on just and fair compensation and, where possible, with the option of return.'

63 The UN Declaration is particularly relevant for indigenous peoples' safeguard against investments in their ancestral lands as it underscores that the basic economic right to ancestral homelands and the livelihoods that depend on them are closely linked to indigenous human rights.

64 As, for example, in the China Western Poverty Reduction Project.

65 See Francioni (2008), 33; Lenzerini (2008).

66 Engaged with ancestral land claims of indigenous peoples impacted by mining (the Ambuklao-Binga Hydro Project case in the Philippines, 2012), the intervention of the

As regards compensation, the IP has often found that the WB failed to observe policy-requirements for the supervision of the resettlement programme, and that indigenous peoples displaced would not be adequately compensated. In most cases, in the opinion of the Panel, there is no way of compensating indigenous communities for losses of traditional and healthy life with nutritionally adequate food supply in their ancestral land.[67]

7. Concluding remarks

Many of the existing WB safeguard policies address human-rights-related issues, such as indigenous peoples, but also cultural property, environmental assessment, forests, natural habitats and the safety of dams or involuntary resettlement. Although not couched in the language of rights,[68] these policies acquire a quasi-legal nature to the extent that a breach of them can be claimed by affected communities in proceedings before the IP, potentially leading to remedial measures. The IP's existence contributes to increasing attention to WB policies and procedures. As the IP has highlighted, since human rights are embedded in many of the WB safeguard policies for managing Bank-financed projects, economic issues and human rights have become inextricably linked.

WB operational policies are therefore becoming widely accepted standards[69] among other development banks,[70] as well as institutions engaged

CAO enabled use of the lands to be transferred back to indigenous community management and the importance of ancestral ties to be acknowledged by all the parties.

67 In its Investigation Report on the DRC forests operations, the Panel wrote:

> if access to these non-timber resources were considerably restricted by the timber operations, there would be no way of compensating for the loss. The Panel's expert notes that for the forest-living people who find difficulties in satisfying their subsistence needs, the promotion of logging industry, or commercialization for export products, is by no means the only way, nor the best way, to solve the problem of poverty.

68 Sarfaty (2009), 647–83.

69 The cross-fertilization of international and Bank standards highlights the prominent role that the Bank's operational policies may play in the development of customary rules of international law, in the opinion of Boisson de Chazournes (2000), 300. Cross-fertilization also occurs in the opposite direction, whereby the WB revises its policies to keep up with developments in organizations such as the UN and ILO. See, e.g., Kingsbury (1999), 341.

70 Sarfaty (2005), 1792. The WB policy on environmental assessment inspired similar guidelines at the Asian Development Bank, the European Bank for Reconstruction and Development and the Inter-American Development Bank, in several bilateral agreements and with various private-sector firms.

in project finance. Moreover, the WB often incorporates provisions from its policies into its loan and credit agreements.[71] By conditioning loans and thus promoting compliance with international standards and rules as part of its operational policies, the WB affects the domestic policy-making of borrower countries.[72] The Bank's mandatory policies call for application of the international standards when they are higher than domestic ones.[73]

WB and IFC are therefore crucial actors in developing international norms, and 'IFC can play an important role in helping its client companies implement [such] processes'.[74] With regard to direct investments, IFC's Performance Standards contain obligations imposed directly on clients by a lender. The need to comply with such Standards has led companies to improve their policies and practices. In order to be eligible for IFC funding, companies must prove that an 'integrated social environmental assessment'[75] is carried out in order to avoid adverse impact whenever feasible. In addition, IFC advocates that companies should provide an 'action plan' to communities affected by their operations.

Civil-society groups insist that the IFC be fully consistent with international human-rights standards, by making a definite commitment that it will not support activities likely to cause, or contribute to, human-rights abuses. The IFC could indeed have done much more to improve its monitoring and implementation procedures, had it made financial support to borrowing companies conditional on meeting the Performance Standards.

71 As part of its loan agreement, a borrower country may be required to adopt and implement a resettlement action plan designed in accordance with the WB operational policy on involuntary resettlement.

72 The 'policy conditionality' is 'a set of requirements and preconditions that the recipient country is expected to meet in order to receive financial assistance' (World Bank, 'Review of World Bank Conditionality', Issues Note 4, 2005). If the country fails to meet these conditions, the Bank has the right to stop disbursing funds.

73 The operational policies on environmental assessment and forests, for example, require that a 'project [be] consistent with domestic law and that it … not contravene any international [environmental] treaties to which the borrower country is a party', Operational Manual, OP 4.01 (Environmental Assessment); *ibid.* OP 4.36 (Forests). See Kingsbury (1999), 330–2.

74 See Office of the Compliance Advisor/Ombudsman, 'Advisory Note: Review of IFC's Policy and Performance Standards on Social and Environmental Sustainability and Policy on Disclosure of Information', 16 (2010), www.caoombudsman.org.

75 A two-year review of the IFC's Performance Standards on environmental and social sustainability – approved by the board in May 2011 and coming into force in January 2012 – adds new requirements relating to such social and environmental assessments.

CAO's inability to consider international rules unless explicitly directed to do so by IFC/MIGA policies and standards[76] prevents it from holding IFC/MIGA accountable in the light of widely accepted rules of international law, which may provide a larger human-rights protection than IFC/MIGA policies. IFC and CAO also fail to promote responsiveness by denying project-affected people or their representatives a share of the decision-making power. As CAO does not have the power to bind IFC, when IFC disagrees with CAO's findings or recommendations, it can simply decide to take whatever course of action it prefers.

With specific regard to indigenous peoples' concerns, while there is considerable overlap between IFC PS7 and Convention 169 in terms of issues covered and approaches required, there is also a fundamental difference between the two, as the latter is an agreement concluded among States. Client-compliance with PS7 is no substitute for a State's implementation of Convention 169.[77] If a State that is a party to Convention 169 has failed to implement it effectively, there may be risks for a client, irrespective of how well it complies with PS7.[78] Where States have not yet ratified Convention 169 and there is no obligation on them to implement its provisions, there may still be available relevant legislation and processes. In such cases, clients should undertake the same activities and behaviour set out above and comply with PS7 if seeking financing from IFC.

So, business and governments must recognize the social, economic and environmental impact of land-acquisition on people, especially the most vulnerable and marginalized. Businesses that do not engage with communities in land-related questions will find themselves exposed to the risk of greater liability. Guidelines such as the WB Policies and the IFC Performance Standards provide governments and investors with guidance on the responsible acquisition and use of land. Activities having

76 For example, if IFC policies call for an interpretation consistent with the UN Declaration on the Rights of Indigenous Peoples, the CAO might insist on having the free, prior and informed consent of indigenous communities facing displacement by an IFC project.

77 In the evolving debate, a consensus is emerging that private-sector companies should not act in a manner that would interfere with the State's discharge of its international treaty obligations.

78 If an IFC client is implementing a project where government actions mean that the project does not meet the requirements of the Convention, it can find itself accused of 'breaching' the principles of the Convention or of violating rights protected under the Convention. This has occurred in relation to several IFC-financed projects in Latin America, and such complaints have sometimes contributed to troubled community relations and project delays. For example, see the case of the Marlin Project in Guatemala.

potentially a significant and irreversible adverse impact on the environment and affected people are excluded from WB Program-for-Results financing.

Foreign direct investments[79] specifically might present both threats and opportunities to indigenous peoples. Unfortunately, the former all too often predominate over the latter because governments tend to prioritize economic development over indigenous rights, and existing domestic and international legal frameworks are incapable of appropriately balancing the two. Foreign investment increasingly presents a serious challenge to the implementation of internationally recognized rights of indigenous peoples.

According to the Inter-American Court of Human Rights case-law,[80] the duty to consult indigenous communities has become a general principle of international law by virtue of the broad and constant reference to it. The existence of such a principle might have implications for multinational corporations, as long as their transnational operations increasingly comply with standards that mirror the duties of States.[81] Undertaking meaningful consultation with potentially affected groups mitigates these risks and allows businesses the opportunity to respond before individuals and communities are affected. Recent findings from OECD National Contact

79 The term 'foreign direct investment' (FDI) refers to investments made by a person or company (the foreign investor) located in one country (the home state) in a company or productive assets located in another country (the host State), under circumstances in which the foreign investor has control over the local company or assets. Host States are often developing countries; even if authorities in such States are sensitive to human rights, either their protective efforts are ineffective or they are prone to giving priority to the economic benefits that corporate activities create and disregarding human-rights abuses.

80 Among other cases, see, first, *Mayagna (Sumo) Awas Tingni Community* v. *Nicaragua*, Inter-Am. Comm'n H.R., Report 27/98 (3 March 1998). Cf. Amiott (2002), 873; Appiagyei-Atua (2005), 303; Barume (2005), 365; Binder (2005), 249. Second, *Yakye Axa Indigenous Community* v. *Paraguay*, Inter-Am. Ct. H.R. (ser. C) No. 125 (17 June 2005), quoted by Willis and Seward (2006), and Pasqualucci (2006), 281–322. Third, *Saramaka People* v. *Suriname*, Inter-Am. Ct. H.R. (ser. C) No. 172 (28 November 2007). Recently, *Kichwa Indigenous Community of Sarayaku* v. *Ecuador*, Inter-Am. Ct. H.R. (ser. C) No. 245 (27 June 2012), and the comment by Brunner and Quintana (2012). See, in general, McHugh (2011) and Pentassuglia (2011).

81 See, in particular, Stavenhagen (2003), 70–2; World Bank Legal Department, Legal Note on Indigenous Peoples (April 2005); Inter-American Development Bank, Operational Policy on Indigenous Peoples and Strategy for Indigenous Development, OP-765 (July 2006); European Bank for Reconstruction and Development, Environmental and Social Policy (May 2008), Performance Requirement 7; Anaya (2011); Ruggie (2011). As regards, in general, breaches of human rights due to the activities of multinational corporations, see Acconci (2007b).

Points underline the increasing importance placed on businesses giving priority to local consultation in genuinely attempting to meet their human rights-responsibilities.[82] Effective consultations with indigenous peoples from an early stage may provide a pre-emptive remedy to ensure that rights are not undermined at any stage of the acquisition or use of land.[83]

Even if this chapter doesn't focus on the integration of indigenous peoples' concerns into international investment law,[84] it is worth underlining that on various occasions indigenous peoples' rights have been raised in opposition to foreign investors' claims in investment treaty arbitrations[85] or in opposition to States before human-rights courts. Despite their obligations to uphold the rights of citizens and indigenous groups to oppose investments on their lands, governments also try to ensure that protests do not derail foreign investments, as they have to honour the concession, or risk a large-scale lawsuit by the foreign investor.[86] States often justify their failure to act in favour of indigenous peoples by referring to bilat-

82 See final statement of Norwegian NCP Re Intex Resources (www.aippnet.org); revised final statement by the UK NCP on the complaint from *Corner House et al. against BTC Corporation* and final statement by the UK NCP, complaint from *Survival International against Vedanta Resources Plc* (both on www.oecd.org).

83 There are historic barriers (intentional or not) to effective community consultation and free, prior and informed consent of indigenous communities prior to undertaking operations, such as limits on community information and awareness, questions of trust or confidence, and a communication barrier because of language.

84 As to the matter of the integration of non-investment concerns into international investment law, see, the contribution by Acconci in this book.

85 First, human rights law have been considered in arbitration awards in relation to certain investor protections, such as those on property or due process. Second, notwithstanding this practice, there are emerging scenarios where the human rights of non-parties (someone other than the foreign investor) are implicated in investment treaty disputes. These scenarios include those where the rights of citizens to assemble, express themselves and protest government or investor decisions arise; where government policies have been designed to accord preferences to certain historically disadvantaged persons or groups; where indigenous rights or claims come into friction with the rights of foreign investors; and where government regulation of the water and sanitation industry are professed to be in furtherance of human rights obligations such as the right to health, right to food or right to water.

86 For example, the government of Guatemala has stated to being torn between its duties to provide security for a highly controversial foreign-owned gold and silver mine in the country's western region and the government's obligations to uphold the rights of citizens and indigenous groups to assemble and protest the mining operation. See Rights and Democracy, 'Mining a Sacred Mountain: Protecting the Human Rights of Indigenous Communities', 2006 case study in human rights impact assessment project (www.dd-rd.ca). For a notable example of an investment project where serious

eral investment treaties, which would not allow national authorities to expropriate the foreign investor's properties.[87]

The Inter-American Court rejected this line of argument, observing that BITs typically do not prohibit expropriation or nationalization of foreign-owned land when there is a 'public purpose'. While declining to articulate how the State should strike the balance between the indigenous peoples' property rights and the legal protection owed to foreign investors, the Inter-American Court observed that, if the State could not 'on objective and reasoned grounds' return the traditional lands to their previous owners, then it 'must surrender alternative lands of equal extension and quality, which will be chosen by agreement with the members of the indigenous peoples'.[88]

However, while allowing expropriation, the standards of compensation for the affected property-owner, such as provided under these BITs, may complicate the efforts of developing countries' governments that are contemplating land redistribution policies. In order to accommodate certain overriding social interests or purposes, BITs' compensation standards should be interpreted flexibly. The approach of the European Court of Human Rights[89] might lead to less than market-value compensation

breaches have occurred see: Amnesty International, 1997, 'India: The "Enron Project" in Maharashtra – Protests Suppressed in the Name of Development' (ASA 20/031/1997), web.amnesty.org.

87 A NAFTA arbitration, between the Canadian mining company Glamis Gold Ltd. and the United States government, involved a claim by the company that California state mining regulations violate the protection contained in the NAFTA. In particular, Glamis objected to requirements for back-filling and re-grading of open-pit mine sites which were in close proximity to Native American sacred sites. A US indigenous group (the Quechan), applying to intervene as *amicus curiae*, submitted that the tribunal should interpret Glamis's treaty-protection 'in a manner consistent with the (USA)'s conventional and customary international law obligations to preserve and protect indigenous peoples' rights to land and its resources' (Non-Party Submission, *Glamis Gold Ltd.* v. *United States of America*, Submission of the Quechan Indian Nation, 9–10).

88 Having done neither of these, the respondent State was held to have violated the indigenous peoples' property rights under the American Convention on Human Rights. Moreover, the Court noted that compliance with commercial treaties should always be compatible with the American Convention on Human Rights, 'which is a multilateral treaty on human rights that stands in a class of its own and that … does not depend entirely on reciprocity among States' (Inter-American Court of Human Rights, *Sawhoyamaxa Indigenous Community* v. *Paraguay*, Judgment, 29 March 2006, 135, 140).

89 The European Court has stated that the ECHR 'does not guarantee a right to full compensation in all circumstances, since legitimate objectives of "public interest" may call for less than reimbursement of the full market value'. (*Holy Monastaries* v. *Greece*, Judgment, 9 December 1994, echr.org).

being awarded in some investment treaty arbitrations, depending upon the circumstances motivating a given expropriation, for example where a government is pursuing *bona fide* land-reform measures in favour of indigenous people or local communities.[90]

National policy measures or preferences that are designed to enhance the position of certain marginalized or disadvantaged persons or groups – whether they be indigenous persons, ethnic minorities (or majorities) – could come into conflict with the investment-treaty protection accorded to foreign investors, particularly where certain duties or obligations are to be borne by foreign investors, or where certain benefits or preferences are denied to foreign investors. It may be necessary for investment treaties to offer much clearer guidance as to how investor protection is to be squared with indigenous rights, land-reform initiatives and the level of compensation to be paid to affected foreign landowners. At the present time, it is unusual for governments to insert a general exception into an investment agreement[91] that may be invoked with regard to special preferences or policies in favour of indigenous peoples.

References

Acconci, P. 2007a. 'Accountability for Multinational Enterprises for Human Rights: Is Anything Going Differently?'. Moreau, M.-A. and Francioni, F. (eds.), *The*

90 See the joint cases, submitted for arbitration before the ICSID on the basis of German and Swiss Bilateral Investment Protection Agreements with the Republic of Zimbabwe, concerning properties in Zimbabwe on which the claimants, European investors, operated timber plantations: *Border Timbers Limited and others* v. *Republic of Zimbabwe* (ICSID Case No. ARB/10/25) and *Bernhard von Pezold and others* v. *Republic of Zimbabwe* (ICSID Case No. ARB/10/15). These properties had been compulsorily acquired by the government of Zimbabwe as part of its land-reform programme. The chiefs of four indigenous communities inhabiting the affected area raised before the tribunal the fact that these properties were located on the ancestral territories of indigenous peoples with rights to their ancestral lands, and to consultation, under international law. Despite acknowledging that the proceedings might well impact upon the rights of the affected indigenous communities, in their Decision of 26 June 2012, the ICSID Tribunal rejected the claim affirming that international human-rights law had no relevance to the dispute.

91 Notably, the New Zealand government in an agreement with Thailand includes such a sweeping general exception, thus making clear that none of the investor-protection will override the government's capacity to accord special or more favourable treatment to the indigenous Maori people (see Art. 15.8 of the New Zealand–Thailand Closer Economic Partnership Agreement of 2005, on www.mfat.govt.nz/Trade-and-Economic-Relations).

Pluridisciplinary Dimension of Corporate Social Responsibility. Marseille: Presses Universitaires d'Aix, 117–54.

2007b. 'Le violazioni delle norme internazionali sui diritti dell'uomo derivanti da attività di imprese multinazionali. Possibili forme di prevenzione, repressione e riparazione'. *Itinerari giuridici. Per il quarantennale della Facoltà di Giurisprudenza dell'Abruzzo*. Milano: Giuffrè editore, 1–30.

Alfredsson, G. 2005. 'Minorities, Indigenous and Tribal Peoples, and Peoples: Definitions of Terms as a Matter of International Law'. Ghanea, N. and Xanthaki A. (eds.), *Minorities, Peoples and Self-Determination*, Leiden, Boston: Martinus Nijhoff Publishers: 163–72.

Amiott, J.A. 2002. 'Environment, Equality and Indigenous Peoples Land Rights in the Inter-American Human Rights System: Mayagna (Sumo) Indigenous Community of Awas Tingni v. Nicaragua'. *Environmental L* 32: 873–904.

Anaya, J. 2010. 'Report by the Special Rapporteur on the Situation of Human Rights and Fundamental Freedoms of Indigenous People', UN Doc. A/HRC/15/37. Available at www.un.org.

2011. 'Extractive Industries Operating Within or Near Indigenous Territories', UN Doc. A/HRC/18/35. Available at www.un.org.

Anaya, S.J. 2004. *Indigenous Peoples in International Law*. New York: Oxford University Press.

2009. *International Human Rights and Indigenous Peoples?* New York: Aspen Publishers.

Appiagyei-Atua, K. 2005. 'Self-Determination v. State Sovereignty: A Critique of the African Commission's Decision in the Ogoni Case'. Castellino and Walsh (eds.): 303–36.

Bankes, N. 2009–10. 'International Human Rights Law and Natural Resources Projects Within the Traditional Territories of Indigenous Peoples'. *Alberta L Review* 47: 457–80.

Barsh, R.L. 1994. 'Indigenous Peoples in the 1990s: From Object to Subject of International Law?'. *Harvard Human Rights J*, 7: 33–86.

Barume, A.K. 2005. 'Indigenous Battling for Land Rights: The Case of the Ogiek of Kenia'. Castellino and Walsh (eds.): 365–87.

Binder, C. 2005. 'The Case of the Atlantic Coast of Nicaragua: The Awas Tingni Case, or Realizing that a Good Legal System of Protection of Land Rights Is No Guarantee of Effective Implementation'. Castellino and Walsh (eds.): 249–68.

Bissell, R.E. and Nanwani, S. 2009. 'Multilateral Development Bank Accountability Mechanisms: Developments and Challenges'. *Manchester J International Economic L* 6: 2–55.

Boisson de Chazournes, L. 2000. 'Policy Guidance and Compliance: The World Bank Operational Standards'. Shelton, D. (ed.), *Commitment and Compliance: The Role of Non-Binding Norms in the International Legal System*. Oxford University Press: 281–302.

Bradlow, D.D. 1994. 'International Organizations and Private Complaints: The Case of the World Bank Inspection Panel'. *Virginia J International L* 34: 553–613.

1996. 'The World Bank, the IMF, and Human Rights'. *Transnational Law and Contemporary Problems* 6: 47–90.

Bradlow, D.D. and Hunter, D.B. (eds.). 2010. *The International Financial Institutions and International Law*. The Netherlands: Kluwer Law International.

Brunner, L. and Quintana, K. 2012. 'The Duty to Consult in the Inter-American System: Legal Standards after Sarayaku'. *ASIL Insights* 16: 35 (www.asil.org).

Castellino, J. 2005. 'The "Right" to Land, International Law and Indigenous Peoples'. Castellino and Walsh (eds.): 89–116.

Castellino, J. and Walsh, N. (eds.). 2005. *International Law and Indigenous Peoples*. Leiden; Boston: Martinus Nijhoff.

Charters, C. and Stavenhagen, R. (eds.). 2009. 'Making the Declaration Work: The United Nations Declaration on the Rights of Indigenous Peoples'. Document No. 127. Copenhagen: IWGIA. Available at www.iwgia.org/iwgia_files_publications_files/making_the_declaration_work.pdf.

Daes, E.-I.A. 2005. 'Indigenous Peoples' Rights to Land and Natural Resources'. Ghanea and Xanthaki (eds.): 75–92.

Dannenmaier, E. 2008. 'Beyond Indigenous Property Rights: Exploring the Emergence of a Distinctive Connection Doctrine'. *Washington University L Review* 86: 53–110.

Francioni, F. 2008. 'Riparazione per le violazioni dei diritti dei popoli indigeni: quale ruolo per il diritto internazionale?'. Palmisano, A.L. and Pustorino, P. (eds.), *Identità dei popoli indigeni: aspetti giuridici, antropologici e linguistici*. Roma: IILA, 33–52.

Gilbert, J. 2007. 'Historical Indigenous Peoples' Land Claims: A Comparative and International Approach to the Common Law Doctrine on Indigenous Title'. *ICLQ* 56: 583–611.

Ghanea, N. and Xanthaki, A. (eds.). 2005. *Minorities, Peoples and Self-Determination*. Leiden, Boston: Martinus Nijhoff Publishers.

Herz, S. and Perrault, A. 2009. 'Bringing Human Rights Claims to the World Bank Inspection Panel', October. Available at www.bicusa.org/en/Document.101841.pdf.

Kingsbury, B. 1999. 'Operational Policies of International Institutions as Part of the Law-Making Process: The World Bank and Indigenous Peoples'. Goodwin-Gill, G.S. and Talmon, S. (eds.), *The Reality of International Law: Essays in Honour of Ian Brownlie*. Clarendon Press: Oxford, 323–43.

2001. 'Reconciling Five Competing Conceptual Structures of Indigenous Peoples' Claims in International and Comparative Law'. *New York University J International L and Politics* 34: 189–250.

Lee, V. 2008. 'Enforcing the Equator Principles: An NGO's Principled Effort to Stop the Financing of a Paper Pulp Mill in Uruguay'. *Northwestern Journal of International Human Rights* 6: 354–73.

Lenzerini, F. (ed.). 2008. *Reparations for Indigenous Peoples: International and Comparative Perspectives*. Oxford University Press.

McBeth, A. 2009. 'A Right by Any Other Name: The Evasive Engagement of International Financial Institutions with Human Rights'. *George Washington International Law Review* 40: 1101–56.

MacKay, F. 2002. 'Universal Rights or a Universe unto Itself? Indigenous Peoples' Human Rights and the World Bank's Draft Operational Policy 4.10 on Indigenous Peoples'. *American University International L Review* 17: 527–624.

2005. 'The Draft World Bank Operational Policy 4.10 on Indigenous Peoples: Progress or More of the Same?'. *Arizona Journal of International and Comparative Law* 22: 65–98.

2010. 'Indigenous Peoples and International Financial Institutions'. Bradlow and Hunter (eds.): 287–320.

McHugh, P.G. 2011. *Aboriginal Title: The Modern Jurisprudence of Tribal Land Rights*. Oxford University Press.

McInerney-Lankford, S. 2010. 'International Financial Institutions and Human Rights: Select Perspectives on Legal Obligations'. Bradlow and Hunter (eds.): 239–86.

Neugebauer III, G.P. 2003. 'Indigenous Peoples as Stakeholders: Influencing Resource-Management Decisions Affecting Indigenous Community Interests in Latin America'. *New York University L Review* 78: 1227–61.

Pasqualucci, J.M. 2006. 'The Evolution of International Indigenous Rights in the Inter-American Human Rights System'. *Human Rights L Review* 6: 281–322.

Pentassuglia, G. 2011. 'Towards a Jurisprudential Articulation of Indigenous Land Rights'. *EJIL* 22: 165–202.

Rodríguez-Piñero, L. 2005. *Indigenous Peoples, Post-colonialism, and International Law*. Oxford University Press.

Ruggie, J. 2011. 'Report by the Special Representative of the Secretary-General on the Issue of Human Rights and Transnational Corporations and Other Business Enterprises. Guiding Principles on Business and Human Rights: Implementing the United Nations "Protect, Respect and Remedy" Framework', A/HRC/17/31.

Sanders, D. 1999. 'Indigenous Peoples: Issues of Definition'. *International J Cultural Property* 8: 4–13.

Saper, B.M. 2012. 'The International Finance Corporation's Compliance Advisor/Ombudsman (CAO): An Examination of Accountability and Effectiveness From A Global Administrative Law Perspective'. *New York University J International L and Politics* 44: 1279–329.

Sarfaty, G.A. 2005. 'The World Bank and the Internationalization of Indigenous Rights Norms'. *Yale LJ* 114: 1791–818.

2009. 'Why Culture Matters in International Institutions: The Marginality of Human Rights at the World Bank'. *AJIL* 103: 647–83.

Scheinin, M. 2005. 'What Are Indigenous Peoples?'. Ghanea, N. and Xanthaki, A. (eds.), *Minorities, Peoples and Self-Determination*, Leiden, Boston: Martinus Nijhoff Publishers: 3–14.

Shihata, I.F. 1988. 'The World Bank and Human Rights: An Analysis of the Legal Issues and the Record of Achievements'. *Denver J International Policy* 17: 39–66.

2000. *The World Bank Inspection Panel: In Practice*. Oxford University Press.

Spiliopoulou Akermark, S. 2005. 'The World Bank and Indigenous Peoples'. Ghanea, N. and Xanthaki, A. (eds.), *Minorities, Peoples and Self-Determination*, Leiden, Boston: Martinus Nijhoff Publishers: 93–112.

Stavenhagen, R. 2003. 'Report by the Special Rapporteur on the Situation of Human Rights and Fundamental Freedoms of Indigenous People', E/CN.4/2003/90.

Swepston, L. 2005. 'Indigenous Peoples in International Law and Organizations'. Castellino and Walsh (eds.): 53–66.

Thornberry, P. 2002. *Indigenous Peoples and Human Rights*. Manchester University Press.

Udall, L. 1995. 'Arun III Hydroelectric Project in Nepal: Another World Bank Debacle?' www.internationalrivers.org.

Ward, T. 2011. 'The Right to Free, Prior, and Informed Consent: Indigenous Peoples' Participation Rights within International Law'. *Northwestern J International Human Rights* 10: 54–84.

Willis, F.M. and Seward, T. 2006. 'Protecting and Preserving Indigenous Communities in the Americas'. *Human Rights* 33: 18–21.

Wolfrum, R. 1999. 'The Protection of Indigenous Peoples in International Law'. *Zeitschrift für ausländisches öffentliches Recht und Völkerrecht* 59: 369–82.

Xanthaki, A. 2007. *Indigenous Rights and United Nations Standards: Self-Determination, Culture and Land*. Cambridge University Press.

PART III

The protection of general interests of host States and the EU as a new player in the investment arena

11

The future of BITs between EU Member States: are intra-EU BITs compatible with the internal market?

PAOLA MARIANI

1. Introduction

According to the figures provided by the Commission[1] there are nearly 170 Bilateral Investment Treaties between EU Member States (intra-EU BITs). These bilateral treaties had been concluded at a time when one or both contracting parties were not yet members of the European Union. The parties bilaterally involved are 'old members' of the Union at fifteen together with 'new members' (the twelve additional States as a result of the last enlargement process), as well as two latest members. It has never occurred instead that two Member States of the EC/EU have entered into negotiations to conclude a Bilateral Investment Treaty on foreign investment.

After the fall of the Berlin Wall and in the course of the transition to a market economy, several of the Central and Eastern Europe countries concluded BITs with many countries throughout the world, including the old members of the EC. During the accession negotiations of these countries the issue of the destiny of the international agreements in force between Member States on a matter so sensitive for the economic integration of the Union was apparently not dealt with. The consequence of this omission is now a complex legal issue involving the allocation of powers and competence between the EU and its Member States and the approach of the EU legal order towards international law.

The legal issues arising from the intra-EU BITs are completely different from those arising from the BITs between a Member State and third countries (extra-EU BITs). In fact, when two Member States are involved, the legitimacy of the BIT's operation has to be evaluated mainly as a question

1 Commission Staff Working Document on Capital Movements and Investments in the EU: Commission Services' paper on Market Monitoring, SWD(2012) 6 final, 13.

of compatibility with the sound operation of the internal market. On the other hand, BITs concluded with third countries should be considered from the different perspective of the external action of the Union and under the new scope of the common commercial policy after the inclusion of foreign direct investment in the subject matters governed by Art. 207 TFEU.[2] Considering the uniformity of BITs' structure and contents,[3] some questions relating to the conflict between substantive EU law and BIT provisions can be the same for both kind of treaties, however, the status of the parties involved makes the difference. Methodologically, the analysis will be conducted exclusively on the intra-EU BITs while the legal examination of the extra-EU BITs concluded by Member States will be limited to the issues of relevance in assessing compatibility with regulation under international law of investment within the European Union.

2. Intra-EU BITs: how to assess the allocation of powers between Member States and the EU inside the Union in investment treaties

Since 1957 the core of the European integration has been the creation of the internal market. In the words of the Treaty 'the internal market shall comprise an area without internal frontiers in which the free movement of goods, persons, services and capital is ensured in accordance with the provisions of the Treaties' (Art. 26 TFEU). The internal market requires also a common commercial policy, a regulation ensuring that competition is not distorted and the approximation of the Member States' laws to the extent necessary for the functioning of the internal market (Arts. 3 and 6 TFEU).

The first aim of the European integration has been to merge the markets of the Member States into one market.[4] In 1985 the White Paper 'Completing the Internal Market' had clearly indicated that 'the objective of completing the internal market has three aspects: … the welding together of the … markets of the Member States into one single market;

2 See Anderer (2010), 851; Bischoff (2011), 1527; De Luca (2012), 165; Dimopoulos (2011); Eilmansberger (2009), 383; Lavranos (2012), 281; Shan and Zhang (2010), 1049.

3 See Lowenfeld (2008), 555. On the standardisation of the BIT's clauses see Sacerdoti (1997), 290. A very critical approach to the uniformity of the text of the treaties is in Torrent (2010–11), 1397.

4 In the early decisions of the ECJ the creation of a European market 'involves the elimination of all obstacles to intra-community trade in order to merge the national markets into a single market bringing about conditions as close as possible to those of a genuine internal market'. See, e.g., Judgment in Case 15/81, *Gaston Schul I* [1982] ECR 1409, 33.

... ensuring that this single market is also an expanding market; ... ensuring that the market is flexible'.[5]

The elimination of the internal frontiers means that the nationality of natural and legal persons[6] should no longer be significant because in the single market 'any discrimination on grounds of nationality shall be prohibited' (Art. 18 TFEU). Every Member State has to make sure that every EU national, whether natural person, corporation or firm, may carry on business 'under the conditions laid down for its own nationals by the law of the country where such establishment is effected' (Art. 49 TFEU). Finally, according to Art. 63 TFEU 'all restrictions on the movement of capital between Member States and between Member States and third countries shall be prohibited'.

For a Member State to be part of the European Union involves the acceptance of the sovereignty of the EU law over the policy-fields conferred to the Union by the Treaties. According to the primacy principle, EU law takes precedence over national law; in its jurisdictional dimension national courts have the duty to apply EU law and to set aside any provisions of national law that may conflict with it, whether enacted before or after the EU provision.[7] According to Art. 4 TFEU, the internal market is the first of the shared competence of the Union within the meaning of Art. 2.2 TFEU:

> When the Treaties confer on the Union a competence shared with the Member States in a specific area, the Union and the Member States may legislate and adopt legally binding acts in that area. The Member States shall exercise their competence to the extent that the Union has not exercised its competence. The Member States shall again exercise their competence to the extent that the Union has decided to cease exercising its competence.

5 EC Commission, *Completing the Internal Market: White Paper from the Commission to the European Council* (Milan, 28–9 June 1985), COM(85) 310, 14 June 1985. For a recent analysis of the single market see Monti (2010).

6 According to Art. 54 TFEU, companies or firms formed in accordance with the law of a Member State and having their registered office, central administration or principal place of business within the Union shall be treated in the same way as natural persons who are nationals of Member States. The corporate seat performs a function similar to that of the nationality of natural persons in that it serves as the connecting factor with the legal system of a particular State. Judgments in Case 270/83, *Commission* v. *France* [1986] ECR 273, 18; Case C-330/91, *Commerzbank* [1993] ECR I-4017, 13; Case C-264/96, *ICI* [1998] ECR I-4695, 20 and Case C-141/99, *AMID* [2000] ECR I-11619, 20.

7 Judgment in Case 106/77, *Amministrazione delle Finanze dello Stato* v. *Simmenthal SpA*. [1978] ECR 629, 21.

Thus, in the shared fields of competence Member States are allowed to legislate only to the extent that the Union has not legislated.

Finally, according to Art. 26.1 TFEU, it is for the Union to adopt 'measures with the aim of establishing or ensuring the functioning of the market'. This provision allows a wide power of intervention by the Union because the internal market is not only a subject matter of the Union's competence but also a goal to be pursued by EU legislation. Since 1985,[8] the freedom left to Member States to act autonomously in this sensitive area is so restricted that one can legitimately say that the Member States have surrendered jurisdiction to the Union even if we are not in the field of exclusive competence.

The combination of the European rules affecting the market, competition and monetary issues makes it impossible for a Member State to take economic decisions, even in local context, in autonomy without at least taking into consideration the consequences in the EU framework. Let us make the example of taxation. Direct taxation is under the jurisdiction of Member States; nevertheless national tax systems have to comply with European law.[9] While Member States are formally free to design their direct tax systems according to their domestic policy-goals, this freedom is limited by the superior duty to avoid the application of national tax treatment applied in a cross-border context giving rise to discrimination or additional costs for non-nationals, corporations and natural persons. Thus, as regards the taxation of undertakings, the Member States retain the freedom to determine the basis of assessment and rate of tax applied to company profits. However, the Member States must exercise their powers in the field of direct taxation in accordance with European law.[10] In particular, the freedom of establishment guaranteed by the Treaty has been interpreted so widely by the Court of Justice that every measure in

8 In 1985 the Single European Act introduced the majority rule for the adoption of European measures for the approximation of the provisions of Member States which have as their object the establishment and functioning of the internal market. See Ehlermann (1987), 361.

9 The field of direct taxation falls within the competence of the Member States. The TFEU does not confer any power on the EU in matters of direct taxation, with the exception of Art. 114 which permits the Council, acting unanimously in accordance with a special legislative procedure, to adopt directives which seek to approximate national laws in the fields which directly affect the establishment or functioning of the internal market.

10 Judgments in Case C-279/93, *Schumacker* [1995] ECR I-225, 21, 26; Case C-80/94, *Wielockx* [1995] ECR I-2493, 16; Case C-107/94, *Asscher* [1996] ECR I-3089, 36; Case C-250/95, *Futura Participations and Singer* [1997] ECR I-2471, 19; Case C-311/97, *Royal Bank of Scotland* [1999] ECR I-2651, 19 and Case C-319/02, *Manninen* [2004] ECR I-7477, 19.

force in the host State which, although applicable without distinction to all national and foreign undertakings, renders less attractive the establishment of a foreign undertaking falling within the scope of application of the Treaty.[11]

It follows that if a Member State decides to provide one or more undertakings with a more favourable tax treatment than that which is generally available in the Member State concerned in order to boost an industry sector, this conduct could involve the responsibility of the State for the infringement of the European rules relating to State aids or freedom of establishment. Not to mention that according to the Stability and Growth Pact the general national government deficit must not exceed 3 per cent of GDP and public debt must not exceed 60 per cent of GDP; Member States that have breached either the deficit or the debt criteria make them subject to the excessive deficit procedure (EDP). According to the new rules introduced at the end of 2011,[12] Member States must ensure that their fiscal rules are in line with the Treaty's reference values of debt and deficit. Considering that twenty-three out of the twenty-seven EU Member States are in the so-called 'excessive deficit procedure' (EDP), the freedom of the Member States to design their direct tax systems according to their domestic policy goal is thereby greatly reduced.[13]

The discussion on the continued existence of intra-EU BITs should take full account of the above described legal framework. When the intra-EU BITs had been concluded, all the States involved in the bilateral relationship were sovereign subjects free to determine their policies concerning

11 Case C-442/02, *CaixaBank France* [2004] ECR I-8961, 11.

12 These new measures, the so-called 'six-pack', are made up of five regulations and one directive proposed by the European Commission and approved in October 2011: Regulation (EU) No. 1173/2011 of the European Parliament and of the Council of 16 November 2011 on the effective enforcement of budgetary surveillance in the euro area, OJ L306, 23.11.2011; Regulation (EU) No. 1174/2011 of the European Parliament and of the Council of 16 November 2011 on enforcement measures to correct excessive macroeconomic imbalances in the euro area, OJ L306, 23.11.2011; Regulation (EU) No. 1175/2011 of the European Parliament and of the Council of 16 November 2011 amending Council Regulation (EC) No. 1466/97 on the strengthening of the surveillance of budgetary positions and the surveillance and coordination of economic policies, OJ L306, 23.11.2011; Regulation (EU) No. 1176/2011 of the European Parliament and of the Council of 16 November 2011 on the prevention and correction of macroeconomic imbalances, OJ L306, 23.11.2011; Council Regulation (EU) No. 1177/2011 of 8 November 2011 amending Regulation (EC) No. 1467/97 on speeding up and clarifying the implementation of the excessive deficit procedure, OJ L306, 23.11.2011; and Council Directive 2011/85/EU of 8 November 2011 on requirements for budgetary frameworks of the Member States, OJ L306, 23.11.2011. See Van de Gronden (2012), 4.

13 Ruffert (2011), 1777.

the treatment of foreign investments and free to grant different treatment on the basis of the national origin of the investment. In fact, on one hand the European States already members of the EC were free to decide the foreign investment policy with third States, since the Community lacked competence.[14] On the other hand the other European States were not involved in schemes of multilateral economic cooperation conditioning their foreign investment policy. Non-EC European States that entered into the bilateral agreements had at that time their own national market which they could legally regulate at will.

When all those States became members of the European Union in 2004 something changed radically: the internal market replaced their national markets and those States lost their regulatory power over the treatment of investments coming from other members. The investments within the same internal market ceased to be foreign and became internal. As recognised also by observers from outside the EU legal system, the

> European integration has profoundly transformed the nature of the legal relations between EU members. As the European Court of Justice famously pointed out, the founding treaties are more than international agreements – they are a kind of 'constitutional charter' of the EU. They have set up a special kind of legal order between the Member States and thus they are interpreted and applied in a manner that does not necessarily correspond to the way 'ordinary' agreements are interpreted and applied.[15]

3. The legal consequences of the accession of new members for bilateral treaties from an international law perspective

According to the Commission,

> BITs between Member States concern fields also covered by EU law and they contain serious incompatibilities with EU law. In particular, they imply discrimination among EU investors and, furthermore, as they provide for investor-to-state arbitration of a binding character which is not subject to review by the CJEU on issues of the interpretation of EU law. Based on these and other legal arguments, Member States have been requested to terminate Intra-EU BITs.[16]

14 See *supra* fn 2.

15 International Law Commission, 'Fragmentation of International Law: Difficulties Arising from the Diversification and Expansion of International Law', Report of the Study Group of the International Law Commission, finalised by Manti Koskenniemi, AlCN.4/L.682, 13 April 2006, 113.

16 Commission Document on Capital Movements and Investments in the EU, 13 see *supra* fn 1.

The position of the Commission seems to be that the BITs are contrary to EU law, so that Member States involved are requested to terminate those that are still in force.

The question of the compatibility of the BITs' provisions with EU law has already been ruled on by the ECJ. The Court in three judgments of 2009[17] against Sweden, Austria and Finland, held that provisions on free transfers with such third countries (commonly referred to as a 'transfer clause') contained in BITs with third countries are incompatible with EU law if they do not allow the application of potential EU measures restricting capital movements. The three cases concerned extra-EU BITs, but the same finding could apply as well to an intra-EU BIT.

The issue of the compatibility of the BITs with EU law is also fundamental in order to address the question of the implied termination of the BITs after the accession of the Central and Eastern Europe countries to the EU. The question has been raised in the arbitration procedure *Eureko NV* v. *Slovak Republic*,[18] where the Slovak Republic claimed termination of the Treaty under Art. 59 of the Vienna Convention on the Law of the Treaties (VLCT). The argument made was that subsequent accession to the EC Treaty had implicitly abrogated the previous BIT as being incompatible with the Community regime.

The arbitral tribunal hearing the dispute rejected the submission that the BIT had been terminated in accordance with the rules set out in VCLT, Art. 59 for three reasons: the first one is a procedural argument because the Slovak Republic did not comply with the procedure to be followed with respect to termination of a treaty (VLCT, Art. 65); the second argument relates to the scope of the two treaties involved because, according to the arbitrators, the two regimes can coexist; the last one concerns the 'investor's (absolute) right to initiate Uncitral arbitration proceedings' against a State party under the BIT.

Leaving aside the question of the procedure to be followed according to the Vienna Convention in order to claim termination of a treaty, and the investor's right to arbitrate disputes with the State in question, to be dealt with at the end of the chapter, it is worth considering the reasoning of the Tribunal on the more general subject of the relationship between BITs and EU law within the framework of the international law of the treaties.

17 See Judgments in Case C-205/06, *Commission* v. *Austria* [2009] ECR I-01301; Case C-249/06, *Commission* v. *Sweden* [2009] ECR I-01335 and Case C-118/07, *Commission* v. *Finland* [2009] ECR I-10889.

18 *Eureko NV* v. *Slovak Republic*, UNCITRAL PCA Case No. 2008–13, Award on Jurisdiction, Arbitrability and Suspension, 26 October 2010.

According to the Tribunal's view the two conditions alternately requested by Art. 59, i.e. the intention of the parties that the later treaty governs the same subject-matter and an incompatibility between the provisions of the treaties such as to preclude their concurrent application, are not met. These conclusions are not convincing.

On the common intention that the later treaty should 'govern the matter', the Tribunal assumes a formalist approach claiming that

> there is, however, no evidence of any intention that the provisions of EU law should result in the termination of the entire BIT. Nothing in the text of the EU treaties produces that result; and the necessary intention is not established by extraneous evidence. Indeed, such evidence as there is indicates that there was no or, at least, no clear intention that the BIT should be terminated by any one of the CSFR Association Agreement, the Association Agreement, the Accession Treaty or the Lisbon Treaty.[19]

This approach is not correct because according to the wording of VCLT, Art. 59 what has to be found is the intention of the parties to have the subject matter covered by the earlier treaty governed by the later treaty, and not the intention to terminate the earlier. 'When a later treaty regulates an identical object to that regulated by an earlier treaty, it may be presumed that the parties intended to replace the regime fixed in the earlier treaty, in the absence of any expressed intention to the contrary on the part of those State.'[20] Considering the chronological sequence of the treaties, the presumption is that the later treaty prevails over the earlier one; this presumption may be rebutted if the parties express the intention to maintain the earlier regime. Thus the investigation should be aimed at ascertaining that the parties intended to maintain the earlier treaty, derogating from the full application of the new regime. The Tribunal contradicts itself when it recognises instead that 'it is plainly established that the Parties to the BIT – Respondent and the Netherlands – subsequently intended that EU law should apply in full between them'.[21] On the contrary, evidence of the intention of the parties to maintain the regime of the BIT, in order to rebut the presumption, is not given.

Moreover, in the present case a previous bilateral regime was opposed to a later multilateral one, involving other States as well as the parties to the bilateral relation. The evaluation of the intention of the parties cannot avoid taking also into account the participation of the other States to the later multilateral system. The Tribunal should have looked for: 1) evidence

19 *Ibid.*, 244. 20 Corten and Klein (2011), 1339.
21 *Eureko* (fn 18), 244.

of the intention of the Slovak Republic and the Netherlands to derogate to EU law in case of investments falling within the scope of the BIT in order to ensure to their investors the broader protection of the BIT,[22] and 2) evidence of the consensus of all the other members of the European Union to possible modifications of the scope of certain provisions of the EU treaties for the EU Member States and their investors as parties of an earlier BIT. The absence of those two pieces of evidence should have been read as the implying abrogation of the previous treaty. Contrary to the conclusion of the Tribunal – even not considering for the time being the inadmissibility of such a derogation under the EU law in the absence of an *ad hoc* Protocol or a declaration upon accession – it is more reasonable to consider that at the time of accession in respect of all the members of the European Union, the old ones and the new ones, all investors, irrespective of their State of origin, were to operate in the internal market under the same regulatory conditions.

In the view of the Tribunal also the second alternative required by VCLT, Art. 59 to implicitly abrogate an earlier treaty, i.e. an 'incompatibility between the provisions of the treaties such as to preclude their concurrent application', is not met. The arguments of the Tribunal in favour of the concurrent application of the BIT and EU law do not seem convincing. In fact, the Tribunal recognises that the subject matter is the same but concludes that the BIT provides a broader protection of the investor's rights and this broader protection is not in conflict with EU law. This last conclusion cannot be shared for the many reasons we shall see in the next section, and moreover because one of the fundamental principles of the Union is the general prohibition of discrimination on the ground of nationality. According to Art. 18 TFEU, 'Within the scope of application of the Treaties, and without prejudice to any special provisions contained therein, any discrimination on grounds of nationality shall be prohibited'. Also the multilateral regime of circulation of investments inside the EU is governed by this fundamental principle and, again, there is no special Treaty provision exempting members of previous BITs. If a Member State allowed a 'broader protection of the investor's rights' only in favour of the investors of one Member State this conduct would be an infringement of EU law because of the evident discrimination against other EU investors.[23]

22 *Ibid.*, 245.

23 According to the case law of the ECJ, the balance and reciprocity of a bilateral international convention concluded between a Member State and a non-member country may constitute an objective justification for the refusal by a Member State to extend to

4. The legal consequences of the accession of new members for bilateral treaties from an EU law perspective

Looking at the problem from an EU perspective, compatibility between the BIT regime of protection of investment and the EU legal order is difficult to maintain, even if the few arbitral decisions reported[24] have concluded for the continuity of the special BIT regime inside the EU. The specificity of the EU legal order precludes a coexistence of a general EU framework governing foreign direct investment inside the Union with a relatively small number of old Bilateral Investing Treaties concluded prior to the existing composition of the European Union and involving a minority of the Union's Member States.

Before addressing the issue of the areas of potential conflict, the question whether an external source such as an international treaty may now regulate the relations between Member States in an area of Union competence should first be examined. Of course, since the beginning of the integration process in the areas of EC competence regulations, directives and decisions have been the only sources of law; however, in very few specific areas of the EC competence closely connected to the single market (personal protection, abolition of double taxation within the Community, mutual recognition of companies or firms and recognition and enforcement of judgments of courts or tribunals and arbitration awards), Member States were required by the EC Treaty itself to enter into negotiations for adopting international conventions.[25] Usually the agreements concluded

nationals of other Member States the advantages which its own nationals derive from the international convention (see Judgment in Case C-55/00, *Gottardo* [2002] ECR I-413, 36). Such a justification can concern only international agreements concluded with one or more non-member countries in order to prevent, according to the exception laid down in Art. 351 TFEU, the rights of a non-member country arising under such an agreement being affected (see Judgment in Case C-124/95, *Centro-Com* [1997] ECR I-81, 55, 56). In case of international agreements between only two Member States, the justification cannot be invoked because Member States are under the primary duty to take all appropriate measures to ensure fulfilment of the obligations arising out of the Treaties and to assist each other to that end (Art. 4 TEU).

24 *Eureko* (fn 18); *Eastern Sugar B.V.* v. *The Czech Republic*, UNCITRAL SCC No. 008/2004, Partial Award, 27 March 2007, *Loan Micula, Viorel Micula, S. C. European Food S. A., S. C. Stramill s.r.l. and S. C. Multipck* s.r.l., v. *Romania*, ICSID Case No. ARB/05/20, 11 December 2013.

25 The original Art. 293 EC Treaty reads as follow:

> Member States shall, so far as is necessary, enter into negotiations with each other with a view to securing for the benefit of their nationals:
>
> - the protection of persons and the enjoyment and protection of rights under the same conditions as those accorded by each State to its own nationals,

under the umbrella of old Art. 293 EC Treaty have been multilateral treaties between all the Member States, for example the Brussels Convention on Jurisdiction and the Enforcement of Judgments in Civil and Commercial Matters 1968. Only in the case of double taxation did the old Art. 293 EC Treaty become the legal basis for a high number of bilateral conventions.[26] Until the entry into force of the Lisbon Treaty, in the EC framework an international treaty was admitted as a source of law in the internal relations between Member States. It is worth pointing out that the treaties adopted in the context of Art. 293 EC Treaty have to comply with EU law and the Court of Justice was and is entitled to ensure that compliance by means of preliminary ruling judgments.[27]

Art. 293 EC Treaty has not been reproduced in the Lisbon Treaty. The abrogation of Art. 293 seems to put an end to the possibility to use an international treaty as an internal source of law within the EU legal system. After the Lisbon Treaty in the categories and areas of Union competence there are only two kinds of law sources in the relationship between Member States: national law and EU law. International law is suitable only

- the abolition of double taxation within the Community,
- the mutual recognition of companies or firms within the meaning of the second paragraph of Article 48, the retention of legal personality in the event of transfer of their seat from one country to another, and the possibility of mergers between companies or firms governed by the laws of different countries,
- the simplification of formalities governing the reciprocal recognition and enforcement of judgments of courts or tribunals and of arbitration awards.

26 There is a network of over 300 bilateral treaties governing cross-border tax relations in the EU of twenty-seven members. On 1 January 2011, only ten bilateral relations between EU Member States were not covered by double tax conventions, Communication from the Commission to the European Parliament, the Council and the European Economic and Social Committee, *Double Taxation in the Single Market*, Nov. 2011, COM(2011) 712 final, 9. See also Kemmeren (2012), 157.

27 In the case of double taxation conventions the Court of Justice has said repeatedly, despite the absence of harmonising measures and although 'direct taxation does not as such fall within the purview of the Community, the powers retained by the Member States must nevertheless be exercised consistently with Community law' (Judgment in Case C-279/93, *Schumacker* [1995] ECR I-225, 21; see also, *inter alia*, Judgments in Case C-80/94, *Wielockx* [1995] ECR I-2493 16; Case C-107/94 *Asscher* [1996] ECR I-3089). The Court has also detected cases of discrimination in the treatment of Community citizens and businesses, arising because treaties are formulated or applied in a way that is contrary to the principles of the Treaty. The Court has therefore required that certain provisions of the double taxation treaties and the national implementing provisions be adjusted to those principles. See, for example, the Court's Judgments in Case C-58/01, *Océ Van der Grinten* [2003] ECR I-9809, 54; Case C-385/00, *F.W.L. de Groot* v. *Staatssecretaris van Financiën* [2002] ECR I-11852, 84, 94, 99 et. seq; Case C-397/98, *Metallgesellschaft* [2001] ECR I-1727, 71 et seq; Case C-200/98, *(X AB et Y AB)* [1999] ECR I-8261, 10, 31.

to regulate the external relations with third States or international organisations.[28] Accepting this opinion, one may well argue that the regional network of BIT is no longer admissible as a way of regulating relations between EU members within the European Union.

Moving to the issue of the areas of potential conflict between the BIT regime of protection of investments and the EU regime of treatment of cross-border investment within the Union, it is necessary to point out the rights provided to investors according to the BIT regime in order to ascertain whether and to what extent they might be in conflict with the EU regime. BITs provide investors with rights to fair and equitable treatment, to full protection and security and to protection against expropriation. These rights are not *per se* in contrast with rights protected by EU law, but the problem of incompatibility may arise when a special treatment has been accorded by the host State to an investor by means of a BIT concluded before that State joined the EU. What if this treatment is in contrast with fundamental rules of the EU? What if this treatment infringes the EU law on State aids, competition rules, freedom of establishment, free circulation of capital or the Stability Pact? How is it possible to justify the unequal treatment accorded only to nationals of one Member State vis-à-vis nationals of other Member States? And finally, which forum has the power to provide a final answer to all these questions?

Let's take the case of Eureko against the Slovak Republic. Eureko, a Dutch financial services group operating in the Slovak Republic through Union Healthcare, a wholly owned subsidiary incorporated in 2006 and funded by Eureko, complained that various legislative reforms introduced by the respondent after a change in government in July 2006 constituted a systematic reversal of the 2004 liberalisation of the Slovak health insurance market that had prompted Eureko to invest in the Slovak Republic's health insurance sector. According to Eureko, these actions had destroyed

28 On the other hand, in the case of relations with third States, Member States may still conclude BITs although following the entry into force of the Treaty of Lisbon, foreign direct investment is one of the matters falling under the common commercial policy, an exclusive competence of the Union. Within the fields of exclusive competence only the Union may legislate and adopt legally binding acts. The Member States are able to do so themselves only if so empowered by the Union, in accordance with Art. 2 TFEU. Regulation (EU) No. 1219/2012 of the European Parliament and of the Council of 12 December 2012, establishing transitional arrangements for bilateral investment agreements between Member States and third countries, OJ L351, 20.12.2012 lays down the conditions under which Member States are empowered to conclude and/or maintain in force bilateral investment agreements and introduces an authorisation procedure under the control of the Commission.

the value of its investment, having constituted an unlawful indirect expropriation of its investment in Union Healthcare. 'Claimant further alleges that Respondent's conduct amounts to a violation of the BIT's standards of protection contained in its provisions on (i) fair and equitable treatment including as to non-discrimination (Art. 3(1) of the BIT), (ii) full protection and security (Art. 3(2) of the BIT), and (iii) free transfer of profits and dividends (Art. 4 of the BIT).'[29]

In 2004 the Slovak Republic introduced a series of reforms to liberalise the legal framework of the health insurance market, aimed at achieving a mix of public and private investment. In 2006, after the parliamentary elections, a new and different Slovak government amended the 2004 reforms.

> Claimant bases its claim on nine of these measures: (i) the cap on operating expenses, (ii) the ban on brokers, (iii) the repositioning of the Healthcare Regulator and the entire management board, (iv) the amended network requirements obliging health insurance companies to contract with specific state hospitals, (v) the ban on the distribution of profits to shareholders, (vi) the changes to the redistribution system, (vii) the scrutiny of the budgets of health insurance companies, (viii) the newly-introduced solvency requirements, and (ix) the ban on the transfer of insurance portfolios.

Even without entering into the details of the specific questions it is obvious that all the measures contested by the investor in this case fall within the scope of application of the EU Treaties and EU law in general. This was so evident that Eureko itself, before commencing the arbitration, filed a complaint with the European Commission claiming that the new Slovak government policies were not in line with basic EU law principles and the complaint led to the opening of an infringement procedure by the European Commission against the Slovak Republic under old Art. 226 of the EC Treaty in connection with the Slovak health care legislation. Currently the procedure would appear still to be pending.

EU Treaties are neutral as to company ownership. According to Art. 345 TFEU 'The Treaty shall in no way prejudice Member States' rules governing the system of property ownership'. No preference is expressed for either private or public ownership of companies. It is therefore for each Member State to decide to what extent it remains the owner of the traditionally state-owned industries (e.g. post, transport, energy, health). Neutrality on company ownership also implies that the same Treaty

29 *Eureko* (fn 18), 2.

obligations apply to public and private companies: no discrimination is allowed, in order to ensure private and public companies compete on an equal footing. If a Member State liberalises a particular sector, such as the case of the health insurance market of the Slovak Republic, the EU must ensure that the rules on competition in the internal market, both antitrust and state aids, apply without discrimination (Art. 106). The only possible exception could be found in the second paragraph of Art. 106 EU Treaty which provides for a narrow exception allowing only undertakings responsible for the operation of services of general economic interest to be exempted from compliance with the provisions of the Treaty insofar as their application would obstruct such operation.

In the Union, the health-care systems differ significantly between Member States. The degree to which different health-care providers compete with each other in a market environment largely depends on these specific differences. In some Member States, public hospitals are an integral part of a national health service and are almost entirely based on the principle of social solidarity. Such hospitals are directly funded from social security contributions and other State resources and provide their services free of charge to those entitled on the basis of universal coverage. In many other Member States, hospitals and other health-care providers offer their services for remuneration, be it directly from patients or from their insurers.[30] In such systems, there is a certain degree of competition and the only admissible exceptions to the regular interplay of the competition rules and market rules may be those that allow the State to ensure that health-care services, as services of general economic interest, 'operate on the basis of principles and conditions, particularly economic and financial conditions, which enable them to fulfil their missions' (Art. 14 TFEU). This means that exceptions to the sound operation of the internal market can be admitted in order to allow Member States to respect the responsibilities to define 'their health policy and for the organisation and delivery of health services and medical care' (Art. 168 TFEU).

The European Union law does not prevent a Member State from reforming its health-care system in order to attain health policy-goals of a higher level of protection of human health, under the condition that 'the development of trade must not be affected to such an extent as would be contrary to the interests of the Union' (Art. 106 TFEU).

30 Communication from the Commission on the application of the European Union State aid rules to compensation granted for the provision of services of general economic interest, Notice No. 2012/C 8/02, OJ C8/12, 11.01.12.

In some cases a legislative reform of the health insurance market could be imposed on a Member State by the European Union itself, or rather the Member State might not have any alternative to reforming its health-care system to comply with EU obligations and in order to avoid excessive government deficit.[31] If a Member State exceeds the deficit ceiling it becomes subject to an excessive deficit procedure (EDP). This procedure entails several steps under constant monitoring control by the Commission which must assess the action taken by the State in order to allow the Council to take a decision on the matter.[32] Not to mention that with the entry into force of the 'six pack'[33] Member States are expected to ensure public-finance sustainability and the new rules define the 'expenditure benchmark' to help assess progress towards sustainability. This expenditure benchmark places a cap on the annual growth of public expenditure by means of reference to a medium-term rate of growth. It means that the sovereignty of the Member States in freely deciding on the budgetary resources is effectively conditioned by the EU economic goals.

Coming back to the case concerning the reform of the Slovak health insurance market, it is interesting to observe that the Slovak Republic has been subject to EDP since 2004. There have been two procedures: one over the period 2004–8 and the second, still pending, started in 2009. In the first procedure, between the various steps taken by the State were

31 According to Art. 126 TFEU

1. Member States shall avoid excessive government deficits. 2. The Commission shall monitor the development of the budgetary situation and of the stock of government debt in the Member States with a view to identifying gross errors. In particular it shall examine compliance with budgetary discipline on the basis of the following two criteria:
   (a) whether the ratio of the planned or actual government deficit to gross domestic product exceeds a reference value, unless:
      - either the ratio has declined substantially and continuously and reached a level that comes close to the reference value,
      - or, alternatively, the excess over the reference value is only exceptional and temporary and the ratio remains close to the reference value;
   (b) whether the ratio of government debt to gross domestic product exceeds a reference value, unless the ratio is sufficiently diminishing and approaching the reference value at a satisfactory pace.

The reference values are specified in the Protocol on the excessive deficit procedure annexed to the Treaties. Article 1 of the Protocol 12 reads as follow: 'The reference values referred to in Article 126(2) of the Treaty on the Functioning of the European Union are: 3% for the ratio of the planned or actual government deficit to gross domestic product at market prices; –60% for the ratio of government debt to gross domestic product at market prices.'

32 Adamski (2012), 1319. 33 See *supra* fn 12.

a further intervention on health-care reform and the Commission in its assessment recognised that the 'Slovak authorities have implemented the measures envisaged in the May 2004 convergence program, in particular those related to further health care reforms'.[34] In the second EDP the Commission, with reference to the Slovak government budget, complained of the lack of figures relating to 'spending of social security funds, public health care insurances and local governments'.[35]

The legislative reform of the health insurance sector in the Slovak Republic which, in the words of the Dutch investor, would have constituted an unlawful indirect expropriation of foreign investment in this area, has to be measured not only against the EU rules concerning internal market and competition, but also with the commitments made by Member States to avoid excessive government deficit. It is clear that a judgment on a Member State's conduct such as a legislative reform of the health-care system, involves the evaluation and assessment of many different principles and values equally protected by EU law and the achievement of a none-too-easy balance between them. The question that now arises is: what is the appropriate forum competent to provide such a decision?

5. The compatibility of investment arbitration involving EU Member States and European investors

The question of the compatibility between the BITs and the EU legal system in the terms described, probably would have never been posed if the same issue had been decided by a national court or by the ECJ. In fact, a national court would probably decide by applying the general principles of EU law on conflicts between sources of law in the EU legal system. The ECJ is not new to these issues and has consistently held that, in matters governed by the EU Treaties, those Treaties take precedence over international agreements concluded between Member States before the Treaties entered into force.[36]

An essential characteristic of an investor's rights under almost all BITs is the right to initiate UNCITRAL and ICSID arbitration proceedings

34 Council Recommendation with a view to bringing an end to the situation of an excessive government deficit in Slovakia, 5569/05, Annex, at 11.

35 Communication from the Commission to the Council, Assessment of the Action taken by Belgium, the Czech Republic, Germany, Ireland, Spain, France, Italy, the Netherlands, Austria, Portugal, Slovenia and Slovakia in response to the Council Recommendations of 2 December 2009 with a view to bringing an end to the situation of excessive government deficit, COM (2010) 329 final, 43.

36 Judgment in Case 235/87, *Matteucci* [1988] ECR 5589:

against the State concerned. As stated by the Arbitral Tribunal in the *Eureko* case 'a consensual arbitration under well-established arbitration rules adopted by the United Nations, in a neutral place and with a neutral appointing authority, cannot be equated simply with the legal right to bring legal proceedings before the national courts of the host State'.[37] This can be true in a traditional international context, where every State exercises its sovereign jurisdictional power in order to ensure respect of its own national legal system, but in an integrated area such as the European Union, where its judicial authority (the Court of Justice) in cooperation with the courts and tribunals of the Member States must ensure individuals the uniform application and interpretation of EU law, this assumption seems inappropriate. Every Member State is at all times responsible towards all persons belonging to the EU, whether individuals or corporate bodies, for a breach of EU law, even if committed by a final judgment of a domestic court. Discrimination against investors from other EU States on the part of a Member State, not sanctioned by a domestic court, is a case of failure to comply with EU law allowing the Commission to start an infringement procedure against the Member State. The two grounds of

> Article [10] of the Treaty provides that Member States must take all appropriate measures, whether general or particular, to ensure fulfilment of the obligations arising out of the Treaty. If, therefore, the application of a provision of Community law is liable to be impeded by a measure adopted pursuant to the implementation of a bilateral agreement, even where that agreement falls outside the field of application of the Treaty, every Member State is under a duty to facilitate the application of that provision and, to that end, to assist every other Member State which is under an obligation under Community law."

See again, Judgment in Case C-546/07, *European Commission* v. *Federal Republic of Germany* [2010] ECR I-439:

> The Court has, admittedly, held that disturbing the balance and reciprocity of a bilateral international agreement concluded between a Member State and a non-member country may constitute an objective justification for the refusal by a Member State party to that agreement to extend to nationals of other Member States the advantages which its own nationals derive from that agreement (see, *inter alia*, Case C-307/97 *Saint-Gobain ZN* ECR I-6161, 60, Case C-55/00, *Gottardo* [2002] ECR I-413, 36). Nevertheless, contrary to the situations at issue in those cases and that which gave rise to the judgment in D., on which the Federal Republic of Germany relies, application of the German-Polish Agreement concerns, since the accession of the Republic of Poland to the Union, two Member States, with the result that the provisions of that agreement can apply to relations between those Member States only in compliance with Community law, in particular with the Treaty rules on the free provision of services (see, by analogy, *inter alia*, Case 235/87 *Matteucci* [1988] ECR 5589, 16, 19– 21; Case C-478/07 *Budějovický Budvar* [2009] ECR I-07721, 97, 98).

37 *Eureko* (fn 18), 264.

judicial review, national and supranational, dramatically reduce the risk of discrimination for foreign EU investors.

The same question should be considered also from the different perspective of the Member State party to a BIT. Is the investment arbitration an appropriate dispute-resolution procedure to assess the investor rights to fair and equitable treatment, to full protection and security, given the primary obligation of every EU Member State to take any appropriate measure, whether general or particular, to ensure fulfilment of the obligations arising out of the Treaties (Art. 5 TEU)? According to the principle of sincere cooperation, 'the Union and the Member States shall, in full mutual respect, assist each other in carrying out tasks which flow from the Treaties' and 'the Member States shall facilitate the achievement of the Union's tasks and refrain from any measure which could jeopardise the attainment of the Union's objectives'. Since the two Member States of an intra-EU BIT share the same obligation to remove every possible obstacle to the attainment of the Union's objectives, an arbitral decision that requires the host State to infringe EU law would also entail an infringement of EU law on the part of the investor's home State in not having assisted another Member State in carrying out obligations which stem from the Treaties. In an international perspective, in contrast to the EU perspective, a Member State of a BIT has an obligation towards the other Member State of the bilateral treaty to make possible a State–investor arbitration; this is not the same as saying there is an individual international investor's right towards the host State.

The privilege for some EU investors to enter into State–investor arbitration to seek protection of their rights is *per se* an infringement of EU law on the part of the EU Member State. The Arbitral Tribunal in the *Eureko* case recognised that 'Affording such wider protection to those investors while not affording it to investors of other EU States may violate EU law prohibitions on discrimination'.[38] According to the case law of the ECJ, a Member State could avoid the violation of the principle of equal treatment by extending to all EU nationals the advantages granted to nationals of the two States under the bilateral treaty.[39] But in this case this was not possible, because even considering that the object of a BIT may not fully coincide with the internal market's area of competence, the Treaty recognises the competence of the Union to adopt measures ensuring the functioning of the internal market (Art. 26 of the TFEU). The abrogation

38 *Eureko* (fn 18), 267.

39 Judgments in Case 235/87, *Matteucci*, at 16 and Case C-55/00, *Gottardo*, at 34.

of Art. 293 EC Treaty, which allowed Member States to enter into negotiations to conclude international agreements to regulate areas confining with the internal market, has eliminated the power of Member States to regulate issues affecting the market.

In the *Mox Plant* case the ECJ affirmed the exclusive nature of its jurisdiction to resolve disputes concerning the interpretation and application of provisions of European Union law. The Court considered that the institution and pursuit of proceedings before an arbitral tribunal involved a 'manifest risk that the jurisdictional order laid down in the Treaties and, consequently, the autonomy of the Community legal system may be adversely affected'.[40] It is true that the decision was given in relation to an arbitration between two States, but the same risk is involved in an investor–State arbitration. In fact, arbitrators in an intra-EU investment issue, when judging the State' conduct, cannot avoid facing the application and interpretation of EU law, doing so without any preliminary ruling, unlike the situation applying with a national court.[41]

Let us take once again the case of *Eureko* where the Tribunal had been requested to judge an EU Member State in respect of a reform of its healthcare insurance system, while the Commission brought infringement proceedings against the same EU Member State for the same reform. The lack of any mechanism of coordination between the two proceedings in order to avoid conflicting decisions is a real danger for the State involved. In fact, in case the Commission considered the conduct of the Member State to be in compliance with the EU legal order, the Arbitral Tribunal, on the other hand, in relation to the same conduct held the same State bound to pay compensation to the investors. However, the EU Member State could be forced to infringe EU law in order to comply with the award. Indeed, a high award, not legally justified in terms of EU law, could be considered as a State aid distorting competition and thus forbidden under Art. 107 TFEU.

40 Judgment (Grand Chamber) in Case C-459/03, *Commission* v. *Ireland* [2006] ECR I-4635, at 151, 152, 154.

41 The argument that the uniform application of EU law is safeguarded by national courts in exercise of their competence to set aside or refuse to enforce arbitral awards or in their capacity to submit preliminary questions to the ECJ, cannot be accepted because

> the control of the awards at the time of enforcement/setting aside proceedings depends on the behaviour of the parties to the dispute, is limited to specific grounds (which often do not include the error in applying the law), and is exceptional in its scope, since normally judges are bound not to re-examine the merits of the case and react only to grave and violations of interest of the forum.

See Benedettelli (2011), 597.

Finally, there are two further reasons for considering investor–State arbitration inadequate in the specific context of intra-EU investments: the conflict of interest and the potential confidentiality of the arbitral proceedings.

First, with respect to conflict of interest, the special mechanism of State–investor arbitration implies that only the investor has the right to initiate UNCITRAL or ICSID arbitration proceedings against a State that is a party to a BIT. The main argument in defence of the host State is the lack of jurisdiction of the Tribunal because of the implied termination of the same BIT and, because of the primacy of EU law, it is very unlikely that this argument will be upheld. Arbitrators who reject the claim of an investor on the basis of these general arguments would have an adverse influence on all the future investor–State disputes in intra-EU investments: what investor would have an interest in initiating an expensive arbitration if there were such a precedent? Which Arbitral Tribunal would reasonably assume the responsibility of giving a decision that would risk making investor–State arbitrations a useless instrument in a field, that of intra-EU investments, where 170 BITs are still in force?

The second reason is the usually confidential nature of arbitration. Lacking the consent of both parties to the proceedings, the award may legitimately remain secret. It means that there can be an area of EU law where an infringement of a Member State can legally be kept secret allowing a form of discrimination for the sole benefit of EU investors protected by a BIT.[42] This would impact negatively on competition and the integrity of the EU legal order.

6. Conclusions

The BITs' regime of foreign investments protection applied in an intra-EU context risks creating a privileged protection for the investors based in the richer 'old member States' and, what is worse, a detrimental position for the new Member States; they can be required to pay an unexpected *extra* cost of being a member of the EU and complying with the EU legal order as a result of high awards by an arbitral tribunal. If formally the BITs are a based on reciprocity, it has never occurred that an investor from a Central and Eastern Europe country has claimed a violation of the BITs' standard protection by a host State of the 'old Europe'. The reasons

42 In general on confidentiality in investment arbitrations see Knahr and Reinish (2007), 97.

for such imbalances should not be sought only in the State's policies, but also in FDI flows usually much more intense inwardly than outwardly for the new EU countries.[43] An imbalance that, in any case, conflicts with the principle of solidarity within the European Union.

In the absence of a solution built upon consensus among all Member States to terminate the intra-EU BITs, as suggested by the Commission,[44] a possible solution could be unilateral termination by the Central and Eastern Europe countries in accordance with VCLT provisions. In such a way the host State could avoid entering into State–investor arbitrations without incurring liability at the international level. EU investors, for their part, are protected by the judicial review of the national courts. Indirectly, they enjoy the protection of the European Court of Justice through the mechanism of infringement proceedings, which may be activated not only by the Commission, but also by the investor's home State.

References

Adamski, D. 2012. 'National Power Games and Structural Failures in the European Macroeconomic Governance'. *Common Market Law Review* 49: 1319–64.

Anderer, C.E. 2010. 'Bilateral Investment Treaties and the EU Legal Order: Implications of the Lisbon Treaty'. *Brooklyn Journal of International Law* 35: 851–82.

Benedettelli, M.V. 2011. 'Communitarization of International Arbitration: A New Spectre Haunting Europe?' *Arbitration International* 27: 583–622.

Bischoff, J.A. 2011. 'Just a Little Bit of Mixity? The EU's Role in the Field of International Investment Protection Law'. *Common Market Law Review* 48: 1527–69.

Corten, O. and Klein, P. 2011. *The Vienna Conventions on the Law of Treaties: A Commentary*. Oxford University Press.

De Luca, A. 2012. 'New Developments on the Scope of the EU Common Commercial Policy under the Lisbon Treaty, Investment Liberalization vs. Investment Protection?' Sauvant, K.P. *Yearbook on International Investment Law & Policy 2010–2011*. Oxford University Press.

Dimopoulos, A. 2011. *EU Foreign Investment Law*. Oxford University Press.

Eilmansberger, T. 2009. 'Bilateral Investment Treaties and EU Law'. *Common Market Law Review* 46: 383–429.

43 Eurostat, Statistics in Focus, 3/2012, available at eds-destatis.de/de/downloads/sif/KS-SF-12-003-EN-N.pdf.

44 Commission Document on Capital Movements and Investments in the EU, 13 see *supra* fn 1.

Ehlermann, C.D. 1987. 'The Internal Market Following the Single European Act'. *Common Market Law Review* 24: 361–409.

Kemmeren, C.C.M. 2012. 'Double Tax Conventions on Income and Capital and the EU: Past, Present and Future'. *EC Tax Review* 21: 157–77.

Knahr, C. and Reinish, A. 2007. 'Transparency versus Confidentiality in International Investment Arbitration – The Biwater Gauff Compromise'. *The Law and Practice of International Courts and Tribunals* 6: 97–118.

Lavranos, N. 2012. 'Member States' Bilateral Investment Treaties (BITs): Lost in Transition?'. *Hague Yearbook of International Law* 25: 281–311.

Lowenfeld, A.F. 2008. *International Economic Law*. Oxford University Press.

Monti, M. 2010. 'A New Strategy for the Single Market', Report to the President of the European Commission. Available at ec.europa.eu/bepa/pdf/monti_report_final_10_05_2010_en.

Ruffert, M. 2011. 'The European Debt Crisis and European Union Law'. *Common Market Law Review* 48: 1777–806.

Sacerdoti, G. 1997. 'Bilateral Treaties and Multilateral Instruments on Investment Protection'. *RCADI* 269: 255–463.

Shan, W. and Zhang, S. 2010. 'The Treaty of Lisbon Half Way Toward a Common Investment Policy'. *EJIL* 21: 1049–73.

Torrent, R. 2010–11. 'The Contradictory Overlapping of National, EU, Bilateral, and Multilateral Rules on Foreign Direct Investment: Who Is Guilty of Such a Mess?'. *Fordham International Law Journal* 34: 1397.

Van de Gronden, J. 2012. 'The Transformation of EU Competition and Internal Market Law by the Stability and Growth Pact: Competence Creep into the National Welfare States?' available at: ssrn.com/abstract=2190122 or http://dx.doi.org/10.2139/ssrn.2190122.

12

European Union restrictions to the free movement of capital v. BITs guarantees: learning from the European Court of Justice case law

ELSA MILANESI

1. Introduction

The Treaty of Lisbon, which came into effect on 1 December 2009, includes important news about foreign direct investment. The sector is indeed included in the Common Commercial Policy (Arts. 206–7 TFEU), therefore falling within the exclusive competence of the European Union pursuant to Art. 3 TFEU. In this field of competence only the EU is entitled to legislate and adopt acts with legally binding effect.[1]

The Member States, instead, are entitled to adopt acts authorised by the EU or acts enforcing the EU provisions. Such a modification is undoubtedly bound to have an impact both on bilateral investment treaties (BITs) that are currently in force between the Member States and on treaties undersigned between the Member States and the third countries as well as on the negotiation and achievement of future treaties related to this matter.[2]

1 For the negotiation and the conclusion of the international agreements Art. 207.4 TFEU sets forth the qualified majority. Some treaties about direct foreign investment contain provisions for which unanimity is required to adopt internal rules (Art. 207.4.2.c TFEU). The active role of the European Parliament in this matter can be assumed through an interpretation of the combined provisions of Art. 207.2 TFEU, which provides for compliance with the ordinary legislative procedure for the adoption of the regulations through which the framework for the implementation of the common commercial policy is defined, with Art. 218.6.*v* TFEU, which requires the approval of the EP for the agreements relating to the sectors in which the ordinary legislative procedure is applied in particular. With regards to this matter see Richardson (2012), 9 ff; Statella (2010), 135.

2 For an analysis of the changes introduced by the Treaty of Lisbon into the field of commercial policy see De Luca (2012), 165 ff; Shan and Zhang (2010), 1049 ff; Štěrbová (2010), 4 ff.

The real extent of such an impact, however, still cannot be properly evaluated since it mostly depends on the interpretation given to the provisions of the TFEU relating to the Commercial Policy. These provisions are not fully clear and their scope cannot be easily identified, with the result that the extent of the exclusive competence of the EU over investment matters is still disputed among the EU institutions.[3] This topic will not be investigated here. This chapter will focus on a more specific issue, namely the compatibility between BIT clauses on money transfer and the EU provisions on free circulation of capital and payments, in particular Arts. 64.2 and 3; 66 and 75 TFEU (ex Arts. 57. 2 and 3 EC, 59 and 60 EC, respectively). This is a very delicate and controversial issue about which the Court of Justice of the European Union has already given its opinion, though drawing conclusions that are not fully convincing. These conclusions shall have to be carefully evaluated since the issue could be re-proposed in similar terms with respect to the numerous other BITs.[4]

2. Provisions on capital transfers: scope and objectives

BITs generally contain a whole set of provisions aimed at guaranteeing the safety of foreign investments, by providing for standards of treatment and protection to the benefit of foreign investors. The BIT standards of treatment and protection generally assist the right of foreign investors to initiate an arbitral proceeding against the host State.[5]

3 Art. 207 TFEU gives no indication about 'foreign direct investment', a notion which can hardly be defined in international law as well as in the national legislations of single EU Member States. Properly defining this notion is important, since it would enable the identification of different categories of properties and rights which are the object of the future treaties on investments of the EU. In particular, from the meaning attached to such a notion it could be determined whether some forms of investment, such as for instance portfolio investments, still fall in the specific field of competence of EU Member States. See Denza (2010), 273; Dimopoulos (2010), 153 ff; Mauro (2003), 31 ff; Mauro (2010), 424 ff; Sacerdoti (1997), 251 ff.

4 See Case C-205/06, *Commission* v. *Austria* [2009] ECR, I-1301; Case C-249/06, *Commission* v. *Sweden* [2009] ECR, I-1135; Case C-118/07, *Commission* v. *Finland* [2009] ECR, I-1889.

5 The clauses concerning the settlement of disputes usually allow the foreign investor – the rights of whom have been violated against the provisions of the BIT – to initiate an arbitral proceedings, usually in the form of ICSID or *ad hoc* arbitration, as an alternative to internal jurisdiction. Such a tool, which has been long hindered by the States, indeed enables foreign investors to obtain more quickly and with no biases a protection for their interests; Shany (2007), 63 ff; Valenti (2009), 27 ff. When the BIT provides for an *ad hoc* arbitration or for the referral to a single arbitrator, the clauses in this matter also indicate the rules on arbitration. Such rules usually refer to UNCITRAL rules.

Among the various standards, the BIT provisions regulating money transfers undoubtedly have a prominent relevance for the safety and stability of foreign investments.[6] The opportunity to either repatriate or transfer to a third country the investment capital or the returns on a foreign investment, then, satisfies a precise need of the foreign investors and hence represents a condition which can remarkably affect the choice of the country where to make the investment. As a matter of fact, provisions concerning this matter are included in nearly all the legislations of the Member States.[7] This notwithstanding, they do not always represent a real guarantee for the safeguard and the protection of foreign investors' interests and, notably, the capital connected to the investment. In particular, investors still fear the introduction of changes which might worsen the conditions currently guaranteed by the host countries, should their need of attracting new capital or increasing the capital flows to their territories come to an end or decrease.[8] This explains the trend to include in BITs a more and more accurate and detailed formulation of the clauses on money transfers.[9] Such clauses establish the obligation for each contracting party to guarantee to the investors of the other contracting party the free transfer of payments in connection with an investment. Moreover, they refer to a wide list of transferable funds, such as the transfer 'of the capital and additional amounts to maintain or increase the investment; the returns; the repayment of loans; the proceeds from the sale of the whole or any part of the investment or from its liquidation'. This is the case for some clauses inserted in the BITs signed by some EU Member States.[10] In particular, clauses on the matter, included in the extra-EU BITs signed by Italy, are formulated as follows:

6 The clauses concerning money transfers had already been introduced in the Treaties of friendship, commerce and navigation that had been concluded at the end of the nineteenth century. For an analysis of such clauses, see Shuster (1973), 311–12; Sacerdoti (1997), 255 ff.

7 National legislation quite seldom allows for unconditional money transfers. Mauro (2003), 22.

8 Salacuse (2010), 191 ff.

9 Sometimes, on the contrary, the clauses concerning money transfers are formulated in completely generic terms. See, for instance Art. VI of the agreement between the United States and Panama of 1882 which provides as follows: 'Each Party agrees, with respect to investments made within its territory by nationals or companies of the other Party, that current and capital transactions shall remain unrestricted and that payments and other transfers with respect to such transactions shall continue to be free.'

10 See, e.g., Art. 5 of the Treaty concluded between the Federal Republic of Germany and Poland in 1989. See also Art. 4 of the agreement concluded between France and Hong Kong in 1995; Art. 5 of the agreement concluded between Poland and Jordan in 1997.

> Each of the Contracting Parties shall guarantee that after investors have complied with all their fiscal obligations, they may transfer the following abroad, without undue delay, in any convertible currency: (a) capital and additional capital amounts used to maintain and increase investments; (b) net income, dividends, royalties, payments for assistance and technical services, interest and any other profit; (c) the proceeds of the total or partial sale or liquidation of an investment; d) funds to repay loans relating to an investment and interest due thereon; (e) remuneration and allowances paid to nationals of the other Contracting Party in respect of subordinate work and services performed in relation to an investment effected in its territory, in the amount and manner prescribed by current national legislation and regulations.[11]

The terms of money transfer (currencies, exchange rates and deadlines) can be disciplined in one single clause[12] or in multiple and different articles, such as in the case of the BITs concluded by Germany.[13] Some BIT clauses specify the currency in which the transfers are to be carried out[14] as well as the exchange rates that are applicable to the transfer operations.[15]

As far as the transfer time schedule is concerned, detailed provisions exist in parallel with other regulations which merely establish that the transfer shall be carried out 'without delay', as it is the case of the agreements concluded by Sweden.[16] The clauses of this type guarantee anyway

11 Art. 6 of Treaty between Italy and Mongolia of 1993.

12 Art. X of the agreement concluded between Austria and China in 1988; Art. 6 of the agreement concluded between Italy and Bangladesh in 1990; Art. 7 of the agreement concluded between Italy and the Czech Republic in 1996 providing as follows.

> 1. Each of Contracting Parties shall guarantee that after inventors have complied with all their fiscal obligations, as well as all relevant administrative procedures, they may transfer the following abroad, without undue delay, in any convertible currency: (a) capital and additional capital amounts used to maintain and increase investments; (b) net income, dividends, royalties, payments for assistance and technical services, interest and any other profit; (c) the proceeds of the total or partial sale liquidation of an investment; (d) funds to repay loans relating to an investment and interest due thereon; (e) remuneration and allowances paid to nationals of the other Contracting Party in respect of subordinate work and services performed in relation to an investment effected in its territory, in the amount and manner prescribed by current national legislation and regulations.

13 Arts. 5 and 7 of the agreement concluded between Germany and Swaziland in 1990.

14 See Art. 6.1 of the agreement between Austria and Bulgaria of 1981.

15 Art. V.2.*a* of the agreement between United States of America and Cameroon concluded in 1986; Art. 7 of the agreement between Germany and Antigua and Barbuda of 1998 stating that the 'transfers shall be made without delay at the market rate of exchange applicable on the day of transfer'.

16 See the BITs concluded by Sweden with Vietnam in 1994, with Argentina in 1992, with Bolivia in 1992, with the Ivory Coast in 1966, with Egypt in 1979, with Hong Kong

the freedom to move not only the investment-related capital, but also the capital that is needed for the management and increase of the investment itself and for loan repayment, as well as the capital coming from the liquidation or the transfer of the investment.

Other clauses set out time limits for transfer performance, such as the money transfer clause of the agreement between Italy and Paraguay of 1999, which provides for a period of six months after fulfilling any fiscal requirement.[17]

Sometimes, however, the clauses concerning money transfers are formulated in completely generic terms, just providing for transfers 'in respect of investments'[18] or the right to transfer profits[19] or merely 'the free transfer of payments'.[20]

Finally, the same clauses often provide for the possible restrictions of the granted facilitations. To such an end, BIT clauses, in some cases, merely refer to the national regulations relevant to this matter or to an annexed list of measures;[21] in other cases, they provide for given safeguard measures for the host country that are to be enacted in the case of 'exceptional circumstances', that is in the case of particular problems in the balance of payments[22] or for the fulfilling of international obligations.[23] These restrictions have a limited duration and they are imposed in good faith and without discriminations.[24]

in 1994, with Indonesia in 1993, with China in 1982, with Madagascar in 1967, with Malaysia in 1979, with Pakistan in 1981, with Peru in 1994, with Senegal in 1968, with Sri Lanka in 1982, with Tunisia in 1985, with Yemen in 1983, and with Yugoslavia in 1979, and those renewed with Serbia and Montenegro.

17 Art. 7.3 of the treaty concluded between Italy and Paraguay.

18 Art. 6 of the treaty concluded between the United Kingdom and Nigeria in 1990. With regards to such agreements, see Mauro (2003), 238 ff.

19 Art. 6 of the treaty concluded between the Federal Republic of Germany and Poland in 1986.

20 Art. 5 of the agreement concluded between Switzerland and Uganda in 1971. For more on this issue see Mauro (2003), 236.

21 The restrictions to the transfer of capital adopted by the State can be, for instance, the prohibition to transfer the capital gain if lower than a given amount being proportional to the performed investment or the transfer by instalments. See Art. 6 of the treaty concluded between France and Nepal in 1983, which prohibits the transfer of gains if lower than a given amount being proportional to the performed investment.

22 See Art. VI of the treaty concluded between United Kingdom and Costa Rica in 1982.

23 See the treaty concluded between Japan and Egypt in 1977.

24 See the agreement concluded between Germany and Swaziland in 1990. After listing in Art. 5 the funds covered by the right of transfer, the contracting parties point out that the transfer 'shall be made without delay at the applicable rate of exchange'.

3. Compatibility of international rules on money transfers with the European rules on restrictions to movements of capital and payments: extra-EU BITs

The above-mentioned clauses, which tend to ensure an effective protection to the foreign investors, represent a suitable regulatory framework for the free movement of direct investment flows between the contracting parties to a BIT. Hence, these provisions, which fit very well into the frame of the European regulations as per the above-mentioned Arts. 63–6 TFEU. These EU provisions regulate the free movement of capital and payments between the Member States and between the latter and third countries. Despite this, in the past the Commission has stated that such clauses are incompatible with the European law. Such a rigid approach of the Commission to the above-mentioned issue reflected the difficulties and uncertainties met by the European Union in asserting and exercising its external competence in the sector of investments.[25]

It was in the context of the pre-Lisbon uncertainty about the scope of competence over investments that the Commission in 2002 invited some accession countries and some candidate countries for adhesion to the EU to renegotiate their BITs with the United States, since they contained provisions clashing with the European precepts.[26] In particular, according to the Commission, the provisions concerning the monetary transfers could interfere with the powers of the Council to restrict the free movement of capital under given circumstances.[27]

The European Treaties, besides guaranteeing the free movement of capital with the third countries, allowed – and still allow – the Union

25 Dimopoulos (2009), 101; Mauro (2010), 406 ff; Van Aaken (2008), 29.

26 The concerned countries were the following: the Czech Republic, Estonia, Latvia, Lithuania, the Slovak Republic (accession States); Bulgaria and Romania (candidates for accession). Such States, after the collapse of the socialist regimes and of the state-run economies, had concluded both among them and with the States that were already members of the EU numerous BITs in the aim of facilitating investments on their territories. Such treaties added to the two BITs already in force in the period before 2002, are the agreements concluded by Germany on 27 March 1961 and on 16 April 1980 with Greece and Portugal respectively, before their accession to the European Union. Following EU enlargements in 2004 and in 2007 approximately 190 BITs could be retrieved in the European Union. With regard to this matter, see Neumayer and Spess (2005), 1567 ff.

27 On such an occasion the non-discrimination clauses (in the form of most-favoured-nation treatment and national treatment) and the clauses relating to the prohibition of performance requirements had been deemed to be incompatible with the European law, too. On this matter, see Mauro (2003), 5–52.

to impose given restrictions.[28] More specifically, the Council can adopt 'measures which constitute a step backwards in Union law as regards the liberalization of the movement of capital to or from third countries' (Art. 64.3 TFEU, ex Art. 57.2 EC)[29] or safeguard measures in case of difficulties relating to the economic and monetary union (Art. 66 TFEU, ex

28 Art. 63 TFEU (ex Art. 56 EC) prohibits any kind of restriction on the movement of capital and payments between the Member States as well as between the Member States and the third countries. As a consequence – pursuant to a constant jurisprudential orientation – both discriminatory and indistinctly applicable measures are prohibited. These clauses have indeed been modified several times over the years due to the evolution in the matter. The Treaty of Rome, which founded the European Economic Community, distinctly regulated the movements of capital and payments. Art. 67 EEC ruled that current payments relating to the movements of capital between Member States were freed from any kind of restrictions by the first stage. Art. 106 EEC in this respect then set forth a more detailed discipline requiring the commitment of Member States to authorise, in the currency of the Member State where either the creditor or the beneficiary were residing, the payments relating to the trade of goods, services and capitals as well as the transfers of capital and wages as long as the free movement of goods, services, capital and people was set forth pursuant to the same Treaty. The discipline relating to the movements of capital was instead constructed more cautiously. The same Art. 67 EEC as a matter of fact provided that the Member States, among them, during the transitional period, shall gradually eliminate the restrictions on movements of capital belonging to persons residing in their territories and laid down that there shall be no discrimination based on the nationality or on the place of residence of the parties or on the place where such capital was invested, only to the extent necessary for the proper functioning of the common market. This principle affected the liberalisation of capital for a long time. As a matter of fact it was only enforced in the mid 1980s with the adoption of the Directive No. 88/361/EEC of 24 June 1988. See [1988] OJ L 178, 5 18. After this the Treaty of Maastricht reformulated the discipline in this matter by acknowledging the principle of free circulation of capital between the Member States themselves as well as between Member States and third countries. Yet this principle is subject to specific derogations. Among these are the exceptions provided for by Art. 65 TFEU (ex Art. 58 EC). Par. 4 of this article introduced by the Treaty of Lisbon lays down that the Commission or, failing a decision by the Commission within three months after the Member State has filed the request, the Council is entitled to adopt, by unanimous resolution by its Members, a decision to confirm the compatibility with the European law of the restrictive fiscal measures taken by one of the Member States with respect to one or more third countries.

29 The free movement of capital enacted by Art. 63 TFEU is not an absolute value. Art. 64.1 TFEU includes a grandfather clause covering

> any restrictions which exist on 31 December 1993 under national or Union law adopted in respect of the movement of capital to or from third countries involving direct investment – including in real estate – establishment, the provision of financial services or the admission of securities to capital markets. In respect of restrictions existing under national law in Bulgaria, Estonia and Hungary, the relevant date shall be 31 December 1999.

Art. 59 EC)[30] or again, measures which limit the economic relationships with the third countries, including the free movement of capital, in the aim of preventing and struggling against terrorism and related activities in the area of freedom, security and justice (Art. 75.1 TFEU, ex Art. 60.1 EC).[31]

Finally, further restrictive measures limiting the free movement of capital between the Member States and third countries may be adopted by the Council, on the basis of a previous resolution adopted in the frame of the CFSP (Art. 215.1 TFEU, ex Art. 301 EC).

Despite the Union not introducing any restriction that would affect free movement of capital to and from the United States, the former-socialist countries readily started to renegotiate their BITs with the US in order to remove any incompatibility between the provisions therein and EU law. However, in the additional protocols signed in 2003, amending the concerned bilateral investment treaties, changes have been introduced only relating to the enforcement of national treatment and most-favoured-nation treatment.[32]

With regard to the incompatibility with EU law of the clauses concerning money transfers, the negotiations started with the United States did not bring the desired outcome. The only solution envisaged was that of confirming the presence of a clause which had already been included in the BITs, and which enables the contracting parties to the agreement to take all the necessary measures for the protection of their own essential safety interests.[33]

Furthermore, Art. 64.2 TFEU states that whilst endeavouring to achieve the objective of free movement of capital between Member States and third countries, the European Parliament and the Council, acting in accordance with the ordinary legislative procedure, shall adopt the measures on the movement of capital to or from third countries involving direct investment – including investment in real estate – establishment, the provision of financial services or the admission of securities to capital markets. When such measures constitute 'a step backwards in Union law as regards the liberalization of the movement of capital to or from third countries', 'only the Council, acting in accordance with a special legislative procedure, may unanimously, and after consulting the European Parliament' adopt them (Art. 64.3 TFEU).

30 The Council, on a proposal from the Commission and after consulting the European Central Bank, may take safeguard measures with regard to third countries only for a period not exceeding six months if such measures are strictly necessary.

31 Art. 75 TFEU, differing from Art. 66 TFEU, the purpose of which relates to exceptional circumstances of an economic nature, has a more strongly political value by supplementing Art. 215 (ex Art. 301 EC).

32 See www.stategov./s/l2003/44366. See also the European Commission press release of 3 September 2003 (IP/03/1284) available at europa.eu/rapid/press-release_IP-03-1284_en.htm.

33 Potestà (2008), 1068 ff.

Some years later the issue of the incompatibility with the EU law of the clauses concerning money transfers was raised once again by the Commission itself with respect to Austria, Sweden and Finland. These countries, before accession to the European Union, had entered into some BITs with different third countries. These included clauses engaging each contracting party to ensure to the other contracting Party's investors, without undue delay, the transfer, in freely convertible currency, of investment-related payments. The Commission, deeming those clauses likely to prevent the enforcement of any possible restriction to the free movement of capital and payments, invited the concerned States to revise the terms of their extra-EU BITs.[34]

The Member States concerned, however, contested the request of the Commission, refusing to reduce the rights guaranteed by the BITs in the name of a mere assumption. As a matter of fact, the Community/Union, until then, had taken none of the above-mentioned restriction or safeguard measures in order to regulate the movement of capital and payments.[35] And the Council itself, which already in the past made use of the Art. 75 TFEU (ex Art. 60.1 EC), did not adopt any measure against any one of the countries which were parties to the BITs in question.[36]

Following the refusal to comply with its request by the three Member States, the Commission referred the case to the Court of Justice, which, in the relevant judgments of 2009, accepted the arguments of the Commission. On this occasion the European judges, with sometimes unclear argumentation and without deepening the issue of the relationship between international law and EU law, stated that Austria, Sweden and Finland failed to fulfil the obligations stemming from their EU membership.[37] Despite enabling the Member States to keep the international

34 In May 2004, the Commission sent two letters requiring the concerned Member States to remove the incompatibility pursuant to Art. 307 EC, Doc. IP/04/618 of 10 May 2004.

35 See the BITs concluded by Austria with China in 1986, Malaysia in 1987, the Russian Federation in 1991, Korea in 1991, Turkey in 1991 and Cape Verde in 1993.

36 Sanctions have already been introduced under Art. 60.1 EC against the Ivory Coast and Serbia and Montenegro, with which Sweden had concluded or continued agreements. However, the Commission has not alleged any conflict between those sanctions and Sweden's agreements.

37 Case C-205/06, *Commission* v. *Austria*, 33–4; Case C-249/06, *Commission* v. *Sweden*, 34–5; C-118/07, *Commission* v. *Finland*, 27–8. In the latter judgment, the Court separately examines the BITs concluded by Finland with Belarus, China, Malaysia, Sri Lanka and Uzbekistan – which contain the clause qualifying the obligation to permit free transfer of capital and payments with the words 'within the limits authorised under its own laws and decrees and in accordance with international law' – from the Treaty concluded with Russia, which instead did not include such a clause. As regards this Treaty,

commitments they undertook before their accession to the EU, the last provision of Art. 307 EC (now Art. 351 TFEU) compels them to act in order to eliminate incompatibilities between the same international commitments and the obligations deriving from the EU law.[38]

In the case in question, the incompatibility between the provisions regulating the transfers of capital included in the extra-EU BITs and the European measures imposing restrictions on the movement of capital – according to the Court – finds its *rationale* in the need to secure the effectiveness of these measures. Such regulations, indeed, to achieve the set-forth objective need an *immediate* implementation with respect to the States they are aimed at, which, *inter alia*, could also be the same contracting parties to the BITs.[39]

The international rules on the transfer of capital at stake – which did not contain any prescriptive reference aimed at allowing the Council enforcing measures under Arts. 64, 66 and 75 TFEU – could have prevented these Member States from implementing obligations deriving from their membership to the Union.

It is quite interesting to underline that the Court seems to exclude that the resort by Member States to international mechanisms such as the renegotiation and/or the termination or suspension of treaties could ensure the effectiveness of European legislation. In this respect, the Court outlines that any European restriction on capital movements – in case of adoption by the Council – require to be immediately applied and enforced by the Member States. This appears incompatible by its very nature with the time required for a *renegotiation* of the BITs concerned or with the uncertain outcomes of a *suspension/denunciation* of the international agreements, even if only relating to some of their clauses.

the Court retraces the judgments against Austria and Sweden (at 26–35). As far as the other agreements, the Court deems that the clause 'within the limits authorised under its own laws and decrees' that they include indeed was not able to ensure compliance by Finland with 'Community obligations which may arise from the adoption by the Council of measures restricting the free movement of capital' (at 42). The Court bases its statements on Art. 31 of the Vienna Convention on the Law of Treaties under which a Treaty is to be interpreted 'in accordance with the ordinary meaning to be given to its terms in their context and in the light of its object and purpose' (at 39). See Denza (2010), 269.

38 Case C-205/06, *Commission* v. *Austria*, 34; Case C-249/06, *Commission* v. *Sweden*, 35; Case C-118/07, *Commission* v. *Finland*, 28.

39 With regard to this matter, see Denza (2010), 263 ff; Galgano and Marrella (2011), 551; Koutrakos (2009), 2059 ff; Lavranos (2009), 716 ff; Moschetta (2009), 16 ff.

In particular, Advocate General Poiares Maduro, in his Conclusions of 10 July 2008 on the above-mentioned cases C-205/06 and C-249/06, also excluded the application to extra-EU BITs subscribed by Austria and Sweden of the *rebus sic stantibus* principle set forth by Art. 62 of the Vienna Convention of 1969 on the Law of Treaties.[40] According to this principle, any international treaty can be terminated, even partially, in case of a fundamental change of circumstances existing at the time of the conclusion of the treaty and constituting an essential basis of the consent of the parties.[41]

The EU judges would have decided otherwise if they had taken into consideration the customary nature of the *de quo* principle, highlighted several times by the International Court of Justice. The Court

> has several times had occasion to hold that some of the rules laid down in that Convention might be considered as a codification of existing customary law. The Court takes the view that in many respects this applies to the provisions of the Vienna Convention concerning the

40 Art. 62 of Vienna Convention states:

> 1. A fundamental change of circumstances which has occurred with regard to those existing at the time of conclusion of a treaty and which was not foreseen by the parties, may not be invoked as a ground for terminating or withdrawing from the treaty unless: (a) the existence of these circumstances constituted an essential basis of the consent of parties to be bound the treaty; and (b) the effect of the change is radically to transform the extent of obligations still to be performed under the treaty. 2. A fundamental change of circumstances may not be invoked as a ground for termination or withdrawing from a treaty: (a) if the treaty established a boundary; or if the fundamental change is the result of breach by the party invoked it either of an obligation under the treaty or any other international obligation owed to any other party to the treaty. 3. If, under the foregoing paragraphs, as a party may invoke a fundamental change of circumstances as a ground for terminating or withdrawing from treaty it may also invoke the change as a ground for suspending the operation of treaty.

41 AG Poiares Maduro Opinion (10 July 2008), Case C-205/06 and 249/06, [2009] ECR I-1301, 62. See also AG Sharpston, Opinion (10 September 2009), Case C-118/07, ECR [2009] I-889, 41–4 who restates that the

> mechanisms offered by international law, such as suspension of the agreement, or even denunciation of the agreements at issue or of some of their provisions, is too uncertain in its effects to guarantee that the measures adopted by the Council could be applied effectively … there is no international law mechanism which guarantees that Finland will be able to exercise its rights and to fulfil its obligations as a member of the Community.

As to the resort to the *rebus sic stantibus* principle by Sweden, see Case C-249/06, *Commission* v. *Sweden*, 23. As to the resort to the *rebus sic stantibus* principle by Finland, see Case C-118/07, *Commission* v. *Finland*, 17. In its judgment, the Court did not examine the effects of such a principle on the extra-EU BITs concluded by Finland.

> termination and the suspension of the operation treaties, set forth in Arts. 60 to 62.[42]

The European Court of Justice itself has assigned a significant role to general international law (and, more specifically to the *rebus sic stantibus* principle as codified by the Vienna Convention on the Law of Treaties) within the Community system.[43] The Racke judgment of 1997 is illustrative of the matter. The Court of Justice – on the request of the German *Bundesfinanzhof* – gave its judgment on the validity of a regulation of the Council, which suspended a cooperation agreement with Yugoslavia.[44] Racke, a company which imported wine from Serbia thus benefiting from tariff preferences on imports of wine from Yugoslavia until their suspension by a regulation adopted by the Council in 1961, claimed that such decision was not in conformity with general international law rules; in particular with procedural (Arts. 65 and 67) and substantive requirements (Art. 62) codified by the Vienna Convention on the Law of Treaties.[45] The Council claimed that the seriousness of the Yugoslavian situation,

42 *Legal Consequences for States of the Continued Presence of South Africa in Namibia (South-West Africa) notwithstanding Security Council Resolution 276 (1970)*, Advisory Opinion [1970] ICJ Reports, 47; *Fisheries Jurisdiction (United Kingdom* v. *Iceland), Jurisdiction of the Court*, Judgment [1973] ICJ Reports, 36 according to which 'Art. 62 of the Vienna Convention on the Law of Treaties, may in many respects be considered as a codification of existing customary law on the subject of the termination of a treaty relationship on account of change of circumstances'. See also *Interpretation of Agreement of 25 March 1951 between the WHO and Egypt*, Advisory Opinion [1980] ICJ Reports, 49–50; *Case concerning the Gabčíkovo-Nagymaros project (Hungary* v. *Slovakia)*, Judgment of 25 September 1997 [1997] ICJ Reports, 95–104.

43 The ECJ stated that 'the Community must respect International law in the exercise of its power'; see Case C-286/90, *Poulsen and Diva Navigation* [1992] ECR I-6019, 9. A similar approach has been taken by the Court of First Instance when it gave its judgment on the legitimacy of a Council regulation which cancelled tariff preferences assigned to Austria before its adhesion; see Case T-115/94, *Opel Austria GmbH* v. *Council* [1997] ECR II-39, 90–3. On such occasion, the European judge based his decision on the binding character of the customary international law by stating that the Community/Union was 'required to comply with the rules of customary International law when adopting a regulation suspending the trade concessions granted by, or by virtue of, an agreement'.

44 See Case C-162/96, *A. Racke GmbH & Co.* v. *Hauptzollamt Mainz* [1998] ECR I-3655. The agreement referenced here was a so-called mixed agreement to which Member States are also party. This agreement was signed by the Community and Yugoslavia on 2 April 1980 and concluded by the Council with Regulation (EEC) No. 314 of 24 January 1983.

45 Adhesion to the Vienna Convention is reserved exclusively to States (Art. 1 of the Convention). There exists a second Vienna Convention relating to the right of treaties concluded between States and international organisations, which however is not effective and was not signed by the European Union; see UN General Assembly, A/Conf. 129/15, 20 March 1986.

defined by the UN Security Council as a threat to international peace and security, represented a change in the circumstances affecting the cooperation with the Community and its Member States which therefore justified the adoption of the regulation for the suspension of the cooperation agreement. Consequently, on such occasion the Court claimed that the Community, although not being a party to the 1969 Vienna Convention, was in any case bound to it since a series of its provisions reflected the general international law.[46]

Following such statements (and contrary to the rulings of the Court on the BIT clauses on money transfer), a Member State hosting foreign investments could resort to the *rebus sic stantibus* principle in order to justify the temporary suspension of the provisions on money transfers set forth in a BIT in the presence of a change in the economic and financial or even political circumstances.[47] This would allow the Member State to fulfil obligations relating to its membership to the European Union without violating international obligations set forth by the BIT. This is even more true since the measures, to which Arts. 64.2 and 64.3 TFEU, 66 TFEU and 75 TFEU refer, represent by their very nature situations which are completely exceptional, urgent and unforeseeable in respect of the conclusion of BITs by the contracting parties. Furthermore, the immediate application of adopted measures pursuant to such articles is covered by Art. 65.2 of the Vienna Convention, which provides, in case of urgent circumstance, for an exception to the three-month delay required to the Party claiming termination, withdrawal or suspension of the treaty to apply the proposed measure.[48]

46 In this regard, it is worth mentioning the statement of Advocate General Jacobs in his Conclusions of 4 December 1997 in the Case C-162/96, *A. Racke GmbH*. According to him the Vienna Convention on the Law of Treaties of 1969, although not counting among the contracting parties of the Community/Union, 'is nonetheless relevant as it expresses of customary international law binding on the Community' since its aim is 'to code rules of customary international law'; such approach has been also applied by the Court in the judgment of 16 June 1998 which stated that 'even though the Vienna Convention does not bind either the Community or its Member States a series of its provisions, including Art. 62, reflect the rules of international law which lay down, subject to certain condition, the principle that change of circumstances may entail the lapse or suspension of treaty'.

47 Mauro (2010), 420.

48 Art. 65.2 of the Vienna Convention sets forth: 'If, after the expiry of a period which, except in cases of special urgency, shall not be less than three months after the receipt of the notification, no party has raised any objection, the party making the notification may carry out in the manner provided in Art. 67 the measure which it has proposed.'

4. Regulation (EU) No. 1219/2012

The three above-mentioned sentences of 2009 on the contents and scope of the principle of faithful cooperation between Member States pursuant to Art. 4.3 TFEU do not consider the effects of the *rebus sic stantibus*[49] principle on extra-EU BITs. The three rulings may be encompassed in the jurisprudential approach focusing on the reaffirmation of the special characters of EU law and its integrity.[50]

The above-summarized debate continued even after the Treaty of Lisbon and became high-pitched regarding the *status* attributed to currently in force extra-EU BITs. Facing the increasingly rigorous orientation of the Commission toward renegotiating/rescinding such Treaties if

49 In order to prove that the clauses on money transfer contained in some extra-EU BITs subscribed to by Austria and Sweden are incompatible with European rules on limitations on capital movements, the Court simply underlines that:

> Contrary to what is contended by the Republic of Austria, the measures put forward by it, in its view, are such as to enable it to fulfil its Community obligations do not appear to guarantee that this will be the case. In the first place, the periods of time necessarily involved in any international negotiation which would be required in order to reopen discussion of the agreements at issue are inherently incompatible with the practical effectiveness of those measures. In the second place, the possibility of relying on other mechanisms offered by international law, such as suspension of the agreement, or even denunciation of the agreements at issue or of some of their provisions, is too uncertain in its effects to guarantee that the measures adopted by the Council could be applied effectively.
>
> (Case C-205/06, *Commission* v. *Austria*, 38–40)

In this respect, see also Case C-249/06, *Commission* v. *Kingdom of Sweden*, 39–41.

50 In particular, after the well-known MOX Plant judgment, a rigorous interpretation of Art. 344 TFEU (ex Art. 292 EC) has gained ground, according to which Member States undertake not to submit a dispute concerning the interpretation or application of the Treaties to any settlement procedure other than those provided for therein. See Case C-459/03, *Commission* v. *Ireland* [2006] ECR, I-4635. In this regard, it is worth mentioning that a dispute between an investor and a host country concerns issues that are more delicate and complex than those relating to conflicts between Member countries. Art. 344 TFEU caters exclusively to the latter and, consequently, the statements included in the above-mentioned MOX Plant judgment – which finally prevent Member countries from applying settlement procedures set forth by BITs insofar the dispute falls under the competence of the Union – cannot engage any third party, such as the private investor protected by the BIT, to submit any possible dispute to the Court of Justice. As a consequence, a mechanism for the settlement of disputes provided for by the BITs in order to protect private investors does not interfere in any way with the European law, which, in the current historical phase, does not provide any tool equivalent to arbitration. Any investor willing to file a dispute against the host country of his investment, indeed, has no other possibility but to resort to the law of such country or to invite his own home country to take charge of the violated interests by applying to the Court of Justice.

incompatible with the European Treaties, one doctrinal contingent spoke up for their compatibility with the European provisions and hence stated support for their 'survival'.[51]

On 12 December 2012, the Union adopted Regulation (EU) No. 1219, entered into force on 9 January 2013, which establishes a transitional discipline – modelled on Art. 351 TFEU, as interpreted by the CJEU in its case law on BIT clauses on transfer of funds[52] – for extra-EU BITs of Member States, both existing and new.[53]

The text of the EU Regulation also establishes a transitional regime for BITs signed by Member States between 1 December 2009 (the entry into force of the Treaty of Lisbon) and 9 January 2013 (the entry into force of the Regulation).[54] Finally, the EU Regulation also specifies rules of conduct for the Member States with regard to their BITs.

Member States' BITs, signed before 1 December 2009 and notified by Member States to the Commission by 8 February 2013 (Art. 2),[55] remain effective until when they will be replaced by new BITs concluded by the Union and the same third country (Art. 3).[56]

The Regulation enables the Commission to assess the BITs notified pursuant to Art. 2, with a view toward their progressive replacement with EU agreements (Art. 5). In this respect, the Commission has to evaluate 'whether one or more of their provisions constitute a serious obstacle to the negotiation or conclusion by the Union of bilateral investment agreements with third countries'.

51 Mauro (2010), 418 ff.

52 Case C-205/06, *Commission* v. *Austria*; Case C-249/06, *Commission* v. *Sweden*; Case C-118/07, *Commission* v. *Finland*.

53 Regulation of the European Parliament and of the Council No. 2019/2012/UE of 12 December 2012 establishing transitional arrangements for bilateral investment agreements between Member States and third countries, [2012] OJ L 351, 40–6. De Luca (2013), 150–5.

54 The Regulation also regulates the conduct of Member States with regard to their BITs (Art. 13).

55 Art. 2 provides that:

> By 8 February 2013 or within 30 days of the date of their accession to the Union, the Member States shall notify the Commission of all bilateral investment agreements with third countries signed before 1 December 2009 or before the date of their accession, whichever is later, that they either wish to maintain in force or permit to enter into force under this Chapter. The notification shall include a copy of those bilateral investment agreements. Member States shall also notify the Commission of any subsequent changes to the status of those agreements.

56 Every twelve months the Commission shall publish in the OJ a list of the bilateral investment agreements notified pursuant to Art. 2, Art. 11.6 or Art. 1.6 (Art. 4.1).

To favour the negotiation or the conclusion of substitutive BITs by the Union, the Regulation provides for a cooperation mechanism (Art. 6), as well as the grandfather clause of Art. 3. Under such a mechanism, the Member States shall take any appropriate measure to ensure that their BITs do not constitute a serious obstacle to the negotiation or conclusion of bilateral investment agreements between the EU and any third country, in view of their gradual replacement (Art. 6.1).[57] As a consequence, such Member States will be able to avail themselves of measures such as renegotiation, suspension and denunciation of the BIT to fulfil the Commission requests in line with the case law of the CJEU on Art. 351 TFEU.[58]

However, the procedure for the maintenance or entering into force of extra-EU BITs signed between 1 December 2009 and 9 January 2013 is more complex. The Member States shall comply with a two-step procedure consisting first of notifying the Commission of the extra-EU BITs and then obtaining the Commission's authorisation (Art. 12).

In particular, such agreements should have been notified by Member States by 8 February (Art. 12.1) with the aim either of obtaining the authorisation of the Commission to keep them in force or of permitting them to enter into force (Art. 12.2). In accordance with Art. 12.2, the Commission's authorisation is then conditioned on a preventive evaluation of the compatibility of the agreement with the requirements of Art.

57 Art. 6.2 provides that:

> [I]f the Commission establishes that one or more of the provisions of a bilateral investment agreement notified pursuant to Art. 2 constitute a serious obstacle to the negotiation or conclusion by the Union of bilateral investment agreements with third countries, with a view to the progressive replacement of the bilateral investment agreements notified pursuant to Art. 2, the Commission and the Member State concerned shall enter into consultations expeditiously and cooperate with a view to identifying the appropriate actions to resolve the matter. Those consultations shall take no longer than 90 days.

Art. 6.3 goes on to state that: 'Without prejudice to paragraph 1, the Commission may, within 60 days of the end of consultations, indicate the appropriate measures to be taken by the Member State concerned in order to remove the obstacles referred to in paragraph 2.'

58 See in particular Case C-62/98, *Commission* v. *Portugal* [2000] ECR I-5171, 49. In its judgment the Court stated that, although, in the context of Art. 307 EC, the Member States have a choice as to the appropriate steps taken to eliminate any incompatibility between a pre-Community convention and the EC Treaty, if a Member State encounters difficulties which make adjustment of an agreement impossible, an obligation to denounce that agreement cannot be excluded.

9.1 and 2.[59] According to Art. 12.6, when the Commission grants the authorisation, the Member State concerned notifies the Commission of the entry into force of the authorised BIT and of any subsequent changes to its status. Once authorised, these BITs are subject to the same regime provided for BITs signed before the entry into force of the Lisbon Treaty laid down in Arts. 3, 5 and 6.[60]

Such an evaluation is also necessary for Member States to obtain authorisation to amend existing BITs or conclude new extra-EU BITs (Arts. 7–11). Notification and an authorisation shall be required at any step of their stipulation. In particular, Member States shall have to notify their intention to open negotiations with any third country to either amend or conclude a BIT (Art. 8.1).[61] During the examination of the provisions to be negotiated, the Commission is entitled to require additional information (Art. 8.4) and may request to participate in the negotiations of BITs between Member States and third countries (Art. 10). In order to grant the authorisation to open formal negotiations (Art. 9), the Commission may require the Member State to include and/or eliminate given provisions so

59 Authorisation to open negotiations, to amend or to conclude an extra-EU BIT can be denied in four different cases: in case of incompatibility with Union law other than the incompatibilities arising from the allocation of competences between the Union and its Member States (Art. 9.1.*a*); in case it is superfluous, because the Commission has submitted or has decided to submit a recommendation to open negotiations with the third country concerned pursuant to Art. 218.3 TFEU (Art. 9.1.*b*); in case it is inconsistent with the Union's principles and objectives for external action as elaborated in accordance with the general provisions laid down in Chapter 1 of Title V of the Treaty on European Union (Art. 9.1.*c*); or in case it constitutes a serious obstacle to the negotiation or conclusion of bilateral investment agreements with third countries by the Union (Art. 9.1.*d*). According to Art. 9.2, 'As part of the authorization referred to in paragraph 1, the Commission may require the Member State to include or remove from such negotiations and prospective bilateral investment agreement any clauses where necessary to ensure consistency with the Union's investment policy or compatibility with Union law'. When an authorisation is denied because the BIT conflicts with the above requirements, a Member State is not allowed to take any further measure in order to conclude the agreement, but it is only entitled to either repeal or nullify the measures taken until then (Art. 12.5).

60 The Commission shall take the decision within 180 days of receipt of the notification. Where additional information is needed, the 180-day period shall run from the date of receipt of this information. Decisions shall be taken in accordance with the advisory procedure referred to in Art. 16.2.

61 The notification – which must include relevant documentation and an indication of the provisions to be addressed in the negotiations or to be renegotiated, the objectives of the negotiations and any other relevant information – shall have to be transmitted at least five months before formal negotiations are to commence (Art. 8.2–3). In the event that the Commission does not grant an authorisation pursuant to paragraph 1, it shall inform the Member State concerned thereof and state the reasons therefore (Art. 8.5).

as to guarantee consistency with the investment policy or compatibility with EU law (Art. 9.2).

Once it has obtained the relevant authorisation to open formal negotiations with the third country, the Member State has to communicate to the Commission the results of the negotiations and the agreed-upon text (Art. 11.1). In case a Member State has been granted the authorisation to undersign and hence to conclude a BIT, such State has to notify the Commission of the conclusion and entrance into force of the bilateral agreement as well as of every subsequent amendment (Art. 11.6).[62]

5. Conclusions

It is still too early to express an opinion about the effects of the notification/cooperation and notification/authorisation mechanism provided for by Regulation (EU) No. 1219/2012.

This notwithstanding, the notification/cooperation mechanism ensures stability for European investments abroad, as well as foreign investments in Europe, by enabling Member States to maintain in force their BITs signed with third countries before 1 December 2009 (or before the date of their accession) without any authorisation by the Commission. This is because such BITs will certainly not shortly be replaced by agreements entered into between the Union and the same third countries.

The notification/authorisation mechanism, allowing Member States to amend the existing BITs, to conclude new ones and to maintain in force a bilateral investment agreement signed between 1 December 2009 and 9 January 2013, implements a rigorous procedure under which the Commission eliminates any hindrance to the conclusion to future extra-EU BITs by the Union. In its decisions, the institution has a great discretionary power, the exercise of which will imply evaluations of a political, economic and social nature; such evaluations shall then be done by considering all the relevant circumstances on a case-by-case basis.

In this context the Member States are likely to be required to amend the clauses concerning money transfers in their existing BITs so as to permit the immediate application of any restrictions which may be imposed by the Council under Arts. 64 TFEU, 66 TFEU and 75 TFEU. But the

62 The authorisation to open formal negotiations, granted in accordance with the advisory procedure referred to in Art. 16.2, shall have to be obtained within ninety days of receipt of the notification of the opening of the negotiations. Where additional information is needed to take a decision, the ninety-day period shall run from the date of receipt of the additional information.

consequences of such a request might be too uncertain. Suffice it to say that a third country party to a BIT seldom accepts, without imposing compensation, any amendment which gives the other contracting party a new right to freeze movements of capital and payments even if it is requested by EU obligations. On the contrary, such States are very likely to insist on a corresponding provision or exactly the same privilege from the other contracting party.[63]

In case of failure in the renegotiation process, it will be interesting to see whether the Commission will nevertheless require Member States to denunciate existing extra-EU BITs. In fact, such a request may not always be practicable.

Despite some consequences even potentially damaging the interests of the Union, the EU Regulation No. 1219/2012, providing for a control mechanism on both the existing and the new BITs, can contribute to make the international investment framework more consistent, homogeneous and reliable.

When Member States' BITs are replaced with European agreements foreign investors will no longer have to deal with a whole set of differing provisions depending on the Member country in which they decide to invest.

References

Carbone, S.M. and Verrucoli, P. 1978. 'La disciplina italiana relativa alla protezione degli investimenti'. *Rivista di diritto internazionale privato e processuale*: 681–700.

Cremona, M. 2010. 'Balancing Union and Member State Interests: Opinion 1/2008, Choice of Legal Base and the Common Commercial Policy under the Treaty of Lisbon'. *European Law Review* 35: 678–94.

De Luca, A. 2012. 'New Developments on the Scope of the EU Common Commercial Policy under the Lisbon Treaty: Investment Liberalization vs. Investment Protection?', Sauvant, K.P. (ed.) *Yearbook on International Investment: Law & Policy 2010/2011*. Oxford Universtiy Press: 165–215.

2013. 'The Legal Framework for Foreign Investments in the EU: The EU Internal Market Freedoms and the Destiny of Member States' BITs, and Future European Agreements on Protection of Foreign Investments', Trakman, L.

63 Denza (2010), 270–1. According to the author, following the renegotiation desired by the Commission the provisions 'guaranteeing free transfer and return of capital would lose their practical effectiveness as a bulwark for the Union's foreign investors simply in order to safeguard Council powers whose value is entirely theoretical'.

and Ranieri, N. (eds.), *Regionalism in International Investment Law*. Oxford University Press: 121–62.

Denza, E. 2010. 'Bilateral Investment Treaties and EU Rules on Free Transfer: Comment on *Commission* v. *Austria*, *Commission* v. *Sweden* and *Commission* v. *Finland*'. *European Law Review*: 263–74.

Dimopoulos, A. 2009. 'The Common Commercial Policy after Lisbon: Establishing Parallelism between Internal and External Economic Relations?'. *Croatian Yearbook of European Law and Policy* 4: 102–31.

2010. 'The Effects of the Lisbon Treaty on the Principles and Objectives of the Common Commercial Policy'. *European Foreign Affairs Review* 15: 153–70.

Galgano, F. and Marrella, F. 2011. *Diritto del commercio internazionale*. Milano: Cedam.

Juillard, P. 2000. 'Freedom of Establishment, Freedom of Capital Movements and of Investment'. *ICSID Review* 15: 322–39.

Koutrakos, P. 2009. 'Case C-205/06 *Commission* v. *Austria*; Case C-249/06, *Commission* v. *Sweden*'. *Common Market Law Review* 46: 2059–76.

Lavranos, N. 2009. 'World Trade Organization Panel Report on Intellectual Property Rights *Commission* v. *Austria*; *Commission* v. *Sweden*'. *AJIL* 103: 716–22.

Mauro, M. R. 2003. *Gli accordi bilaterali sulla promozione e la protezione degli investimenti*. Torino: Giappichelli Editore.

2010. 'Accordi internazionali sugli investimenti e Unione europea'. *Studi sull'integrazione europea*: 403–30.

Moschetta, M. 2009. 'L'effetto utile in materia di investimenti'. *Sud in Europa* X: 16–17.

Neumayer, E. and Spess, L. 2005. 'Do Bilateral Investment Treaties Increase Foreign Direct Investment to Developing Countries?'. *World Development* 33: 1567–85.

Pescatore, P. 1999. 'Opinion 1/94 on "Conclusion" of the WTO Agreement: Is There an Escape from a Programmed Disaster?'. *Common Market Law Review* 36: 387–405.

Potestà, M. 2008. 'Il caso Eastern Sugar: accordi bilaterali sugli investimenti, Unione europea e diritto comunitario'. *Rivista di diritto internazionale privato e processuale:* 1056–70.

Poulain, B. 2007. 'Quelques interrogations sur le statut des traités bilatéraux de promotion et de protection des investissements au sein de l'Union européenne'. *Revue Générale de Droit International Public* 111: 803–28.

Richardson, L. 2012. 'The Post-Lisbon Role of European Parliament in EU's Common Commercial Policy: Implication for Bilateral Negotiations'. Available at www.coleurope.eu/sites/default/files/research-paper/edp_5_2012_richardson.pdf.

Sacerdoti, G. 1982. 'Stati e imprese multinazionali', Picone, P. and Sacerdoti, G. (eds.) *Diritto internazionale dell'economia*. Milano: Franco Angeli.

1997. 'Bilateral Treaties and Multilateral Instruments on Investment Protection'. *RCADI* 269: 255–460.

Salacuse, J. W. 2010. *The Law of Investment Treaties*. Oxford University Press.

Shan, W and Zhang, S. 2010. 'The Treaty of Lisbon: Half Way Toward a Common Investment Policy'. *EJIL* 21: 1049–65.

Shany, Y. 2007. *Regulating Jurisdictional Relations between National and International Courts*. Oxford University Press.

Shuster, M. R. 1973. *The Public International Law of Money*. Oxford: Clarendon Press.

Statella, M. C. 2010. 'Il mercato interno e la politica commerciale comune', Draetta, U. and Parisi, N. (eds.) *Elementi di Diritto dell'Unione Europea. Parte speciale il diritto sostanziale*, Milano: Giuffrè editore: 99–191.

Štěrbová, L. 2010. 'Impacts of the Lisbon Treaty on the EU Trade Policy. Identification of Possible New Problems Related to the EU Competences, to the EU Membership in International Organizations and to the Role of the European Parliament'. Available at www.g-casa.com/conferences/budapest/papers/Sterbova.pdf.

Valenti, M. 2009. *Gli standard di trattamento nell'interpretazione dei trattati in materia di investimenti stranieri*. Torino: Giappichelli Editore.

Van Aaken, A. 2008. 'Fragmentation of International Law: The Case of International Investment Protection'. *Finnish Yearbook of International Law* 17: 91–130.

13

Ensuring the consistency of the EU investment policy within the EU external action: the relevance of non-trade values

ALESSANDRO PERFETTI

1. Introductory remarks

The attention paid to the protection of non-trade values – including, among others, environment, health and workers' rights – in the policy of the European Union in the field of foreign direct investment has become a significant aspect of the consistency of this policy with its external action following the entry into force of the Treaty of Lisbon.

The Treaty on the Functioning of the European Union (TFEU), indeed, vests the European Union with an explicit competence in the field of foreign direct investment, treating it as a single form of external action based on non-trade principles and values.[1] Recently, the EU institutions have

1 Before the entry into force of the Treaty of Lisbon, the regulation of foreign direct investment within the framework of the European Union would not appear to have been homogeneous, primarily because of a complex – and not always clear – division of powers between the Union and its Member States. The first only dealt with the liberalisation of foreign direct investment, through measures aimed at promoting it; States, on their part, regulated the treatment and protection of foreign direct investment on a bilateral basis with third countries. For this reason, in fact, it was not a matter of indifference for an investor (either European or non-European) to choose to operate in a certain State rather than in another, given the substantial differences of regime caused by the absence of exclusive competence on the part of the Union. From the point of view of the pre-existing provisions, the Treaty establishing the European Community indirectly governed foreign direct investment in the provisions on the right of establishment and capital movements, in particular the Arts. 43–8 and 56–60. Nevertheless, the Community was able to secure a limited number of agreements containing rules on foreign direct investment, but the Court of Justice tended to limit this practice, stating that competence to conclude international agreements on the protection of foreign direct investment was mainly a matter for Member States. The Community could only confirm the principles and standards bilaterally negotiated by the Member States and, at least, to improve market access,

shown that certain non-trade values should permeate the Union's action in the field of foreign direct investment.[2]

After an overview of the relevant provisions of the Treaties and of certain aspects of the European competence and legal framework in foreign direct investment, this chapter will offer some comments on these initiatives on the part of the institutions, in order to show how they aim to protect non-trade values.

In the light of Art. 206 TFEU, 'the progressive abolition of restrictions ... on foreign direct investment' is now part of the common commercial policy.[3] By virtue of Art. 207 TFEU, this latter is 'based on uniform principles, particularly with regard to ... foreign direct investment'.[4]

to promote capital flows related to foreign direct investment and to facilitate the movement of persons necessary for the effective implementation of investment measures. Such a legal orientation emerges from some judgments, including the Opinion of the Court 2/92, 'Competence of the Community or one of Its Institutions to Participate in the Third Revised Decision of the OECD on National Treatment', [1995] ECR I-558, where the Court found Art. 113 of the Treaty relating to the common commercial policy not to be a suitable and sufficient legal basis for this purpose. The literature focusing on the *status quo* of the European policy on foreign direct investment is vast. Among others, see Karl (2006), 414; Dimopoulos (2008), 101; Maydell (2008), 73; Shan (2011), 603. For a more recent analysis of the issues thus far examined, see Mauro (2010a), 403.

2 See section 2.

3 More specifically, Art. 206 TFEU provides that 'the Union shall contribute, in the common interest, to the harmonious development of world trade, the progressive abolition of restrictions on international trade and on foreign direct investment, and the lowering of customs and other barriers'. This provision, while replacing the previous Art. 131 of the Treaty establishing the European Community, inserts foreign direct investment in the provisions on the EU action aimed at liberalisation of international trade relations and removes any reference to the action of the Member States realised in the same field. Before the inclusion in the TFEU of a special provision concerning foreign direct investment, the EU (and the Community first) had sought to extend its powers through an extensive interpretation of the concept of common commercial policy or by introducing provisions on capital movements and the promotion of investment in agreements concluded in other fields, in particular development cooperation. On the first method, see Mauro (2010b), 55; on the second, Babarinde and Faber (2004), 33.

4 According to Art. 207(1) TFEU,

> the common commercial policy shall be based on uniform principles, particularly with regard to changes in tariff rates, the conclusion of tariff and trade agreements relating to trade in goods and services, and the commercial aspects of intellectual property, foreign direct investment, the achievement of uniformity in measures of liberalization, export policy and measures to protect trade such as those to be taken in the event of dumping or subsidies. The common commercial policy shall be conducted in the context of the principles and objectives of the Union's external action.

Although the TFEU expressly transfers the competence in the field of foreign direct investment to the Union, the extension and the effective sphere of application of such competence are problematic issues, still debated among legal writers[5] also because of the absence, within the Treaties, of any definition of 'foreign direct investment'.[6]

Certainly, at present it does not seem that Member States intend entirely to give up their power of intervention in the field of foreign direct investment.[7] Indeed, the large number of international treaties concluded for the promotion and protection of foreign investment still testifies to a pervasive presence on the part of Member States as privileged negotiators in this sector, at least from a quantitative point of view.[8]

On the basis of the provisions analysed, however, the competence of the Union would appear to be exclusive, since its competence in the field of the common commercial policy is of the same nature.[9]

With regard, more specifically, to the notion of 'foreign direct investment' in European law, the EU institutions – the Commission, mainly[10] – lean

5 For some examples of the literature on the topic, see Krajewski (2005), 112; Dutheil de la Rochère (2009), 27.

6 In international law the definition of foreign investment is still in part problematic, primarily because of the different and often opposite interests at stake – of the investor and of the host State – being at the basis of investment operations. The issue also reflects the high degree of fragmentation in the regulation of foreign direct investment at the international level, whose elements are, as is well known, the extreme difficulty of finding a system of generally accepted rules of general international law on the subject, the almost total failure of multilateral regulatory efforts and the present number of redundant bilateral agreements for the promotion and protection of investment. The literature focusing on the different forms of the international investment law is vast. See, among others, Schwarzenberger (1969); Laviec (1985); Migliorino (1989); Picone and Sacerdoti (1991); Marchisio (1993), 567; Shihata (1993); Juillard (1994), 9; Dolzer and Stevens (1995); Giardina (1996), 459; Sacerdoti (1997), 251; Mauro (2003); Carreau and Juillard (2007); Sornarajah (2010). For a more focused analysis of the issues related to the definition of foreign investment see, among others, Carducci (2011), 649.

7 In order to outline this approach, the current international practice of Member States with regard to the promotion and protection of their investment abroad is relevant. In this regard, De Luca (2011), 203, argues that it is a '"minimalist" interpretation of the Lisbon Treaty rules on Common Commercial Policy as focused on liberalization of restrictions on foreign direct investment'.

8 For a critical analysis of this international practice, see De Luca (2011), 204 and the literature at fn 161.

9 The common commercial policy is an exclusive competence of the Union, in accordance with Art. 3(1)(e) TFEU.

10 See the Communication from the Commission to the Council, the European Parliament, the European Economic and Social Committee and the Committee of the Regions 'Towards a Comprehensive European International Investment Policy', COM(2010)343 final, 2.

towards a fairly wide definition that covers any foreign investment aimed at establishing direct and durable links with the enterprise in whose favour the capital necessary to carry out an economic activity is made available.[11] If the investment consists of a corporate participation, such a link presupposes that the shares held allow shareholders to participate effectively in the management of the company and/or its control.[12]

Some doubts remain, however, regarding the 'portfolio investment', which certain Member States would claim not to be included in the concept of foreign direct investment as propounded by the European Union.[13]

Finally, it is by no means uncontested that the European Union's competence comprises both the promotion and the protection of foreign direct investment.[14]

Indeed, pursuant to Art. 206 TFEU, only the abolition of restrictions to foreign direct investment would fall within the common commercial policy.[15] In this regard, the Member States' provisions in matters of property

11 In the framework of the European Union Law, a definition of 'foreign direct investment' – although now outdated – can be drawn from the Council Directive 88/361/EEC of 24 June 1988 for the implementation of Art. 67 of the Treaty, under which,

> for the purposes of this Nomenclature and the Directive only, the following expressions have the meanings assigned to them respectively: direct investment, investment of all kinds by natural persons or commercial, industrial or financial undertakings, and which serve to establish or to maintain lasting and direct links between the person providing the capital and the entrepreneur to whom or the undertaking to which the capital is made available in order to carry on an economic activity. This concept must therefore be understood in its widest sense.
>
> (OJ L178/5, 8 July 1988)

By definition of the directive, the upheld notion is based upon the definitions commonly accepted by the IMF and the OECD. The Directive at issue has been also invoked and updated in part by the Court of Justice in: Case C-463/00, *Commission of the European Communities* v. *Kingdom of Spain* [2003] ECR I-4629; Case C-446/04, *Test Claimants in the FII Group Litigation* [2006] ECR I-11753, 181; Case C-157/05, *Holböck* [2007] ECR I-4051, 34; Case C-112/05, *Commission* v. *Germany* [2007] ECR I-8995, 18.

12 On the control criterion as applied to the definition of foreign direct investment, see, in addition to the case-law at fn 7, Case C-194/06, *Orange European Smallcap Fund* [2008] ECR I-3747, 101.

13 The Court of Justice upheld the notion of 'portfolio investment' as being referred to 'the acquisition of shares on the capital market solely with the intention of making a financial investment without any intention to influence the management and control of the undertaking' (Cases C-282/4 and C-283/0, *Commission* v. *Netherlands* [2008] ECR I-9141, 19).

14 On the lively debate see Bungenberg (2008), 3; De Mestral (2010), 390.

15 Nor does Art. 207 TFEU help to clarify the issue. However, it is interesting to note that, during the preparatory work of the TFEU, an explanatory note intended to exclude from

protection – left unaffected, on the other hand, by Art. 345 TFEU – could be also relevant.[16] In the light of this circumstance, a certain number of Member States have inclined towards a definition that does not include aspects of protection, which they argue should remain in effect a prerogative of the States themselves, that these already exercise to a wide extent in bilateral agreements for the promotion and protection of investment, when they regulate issues relating to property.[17]

The Commission has expressed an opposite view, according to which the competence of the Union extends to both spheres: promotion and protection.[18]

In any case, the effective implementation of EU competence in foreign direct investment will be largely conditioned by the different solutions adopted for the issues just described. At the moment, however, the practice in this regard is still too limited to allow a definitive opinion on the matter.

the scope of the common commercial policy the issue of protection of foreign direct investment was deleted. Ultimately, this circumstance might militate in favour of a notion of foreign direct investment that includes aspects related to the protection, as underlined by Balan (2008), 5.

16 Art. 345 TFEU provides that 'the Treaties shall in no way prejudice the rules in Member States governing the system of property ownership', making explicit the well-known principle of the 'neutrality' of EU law with respect to ownership of assets, both public and private, existing within national systems. Nevertheless, in order to narrow the scope of the principle of the 'neutrality', including with regard to foreign direct investment, the Court of Justice took the view that the provision at issue does not permit expropriation measures that are not consistent with the basic rules of the Treaties, such as those relating to freedom of establishment and free movement of services (see, in particular, Case C-452/01, *Ospelt* [2003] ECR I-9743, 24).

17 See Dimopoulos (2011), 408; Shan and Zang (2011), 1063.

18 The Commission has affirmed that the Union, in concluding agreements in the field of common commercial policy containing rules on foreign direct investment, should be guided by agreements such as that establishing the North American Free Trade Area (NAFTA) and those establishing the various Free Trade Areas (FTAs) created by the United States where, in addition to provisions for the promotion of foreign direct investment, there are others aimed at protection (in this regard, see Commission Staff Working Document 'External Sources of Growth. Progress Report on EU Trade and Investment Relationship with Key Economic Partners', at 3 (trade.ec.europa.eu); Bungenberg (2010), 142). Finally, it is worth noting that, from a practical perspective, the separation of the two issues is not always easy and/or possible. On this issue, see Mauro (2010a), 425. For a recent analysis on the complex binomial, promotion/protection, see De Luca (2011), 171.

2. The 'horizontal' consistency of the EU policy on foreign direct investment pursued by means of the protection of non-trade values

The inclusion of foreign direct investment in the European Union's external action raises various issues on the consistency of this new policy with other EU policies.[19]

With the entry into force of the Treaty of Lisbon, the European Union's external action has, at least formally, fallen within a unified legal framework. Art. 205 TFEU provides that 'the Union's action on the international scene ... shall be guided by the principles, pursue the objectives and be conducted in accordance with the general provisions laid down in Chapter 1 of Title V of the Treaty on European Union' (TEU).

Art. 21 states that the Union's external action is based on a set of principles and values, including democracy, the rule of law, the universality and indivisibility of human rights and fundamental freedoms, respect for human dignity, the principles of equality and solidarity, sustainable development, poverty eradication, environmental protection and the rational exploitation of natural resources.

The pursuit of the objective of consistency, on the other hand, is made explicit by providing that 'the Union shall ensure consistency between the different areas of its external action and between these and other policies'.[20]

It follows that the (external) EU action on foreign direct investment must necessarily be guided by and comply with the principles mentioned and non-trade values.

The Commission has shown itself to be aware of that connection, when, on 7 July 2010, it adopted a Communication entitled 'Towards a Comprehensive European International Investment Policy'.[21]

19 Consistency between different EU policies is here defined as 'horizontal' and is distinguished from 'vertical' consistency that should be pursued between the Union's action in a certain sector and the action of Member States in the same field. For a thorough analysis of the different implications of the principle of coherence in the European Union law, see Mignolli (2009), 223. For a general overview on the issues relating to the coherence of EU external action, see Cremona (2009), 251.

20 Art. 21(2)(3) TEU.

21 Communication COM(2010)343 final.

The Communication intended first to clarify the references to the promotion of foreign direct investment within the framework of the European Union, pointing out some essential aspects of the issue of 'horizontal' consistency between the policy conducted in this latter field and other policies of the Union itself.

In this regard, the assertion that the Union's policy on foreign direct investment 'has to fit with the way the EU and its Member States regulate economic activity within the Union and across our borders' is particularly relevant.[22] In the Commission's view, in fact, the policy on foreign direct investment 'should be consistent with the other policies of the Union and its Member States, including policies on the protection of the environment, decent work, health and safety at work, consumer protection, cultural diversity, development policy and competition policy'.[23]

The Commission's intention is clearly that of ensuring that the Union's action in the field of foreign direct investment should be permeated with certain of the well-known and commonly accepted non-trade values such as environmental protection, health and respect of certain labour standards.

The Council has dealt with the same matter in a similar manner, in its Conclusions 'On a Comprehensive European International Investment Policy', which were adopted at the end of the Meeting in Luxembourg on 25 October 2010.[24]

The Council recognised 'the importance of the social and environmental dimension of foreign direct investment'[25] and stressed 'the valuable contribution of organizations like the OECD, UNCTAD, the ILO and their international instruments to the EU investment policy, especially in the field of corporate social responsibility'.[26] At the same time, referring to practices carried out by the Member States and to provisions laid down in Articles 205 TFEU and 21 TEU, the Council stated that 'the new European international investment policy should be guided by the

22 *Ibid.* 3(c). 23 *Ibid.*

24 Conclusions of the Council of the European Union 'On a Comprehensive European International Investment Policy', 3041st foreign affairs Council meeting, Luxembourg, 15350/10.

25 *Ibid.* 16.

26 *Ibid.* The Council was also aware of the fact that 'the main focus of international investment agreements should continue to be effective and ambitious investment protection and market access'.

principles and objectives of the Union's external action, including the rule of law, human rights and sustainable development'.[27]

It is worth pointing out that the Council aims to consider non-trade values as (further) paradigms of Union's policy on foreign direct investment since the inclusion of the latter into the new 'Europe 2020: A Strategy for Smart, Sustainable and Inclusive Growth'.[28] In particular, the revitalisation of foreign direct investment is conceived as a success factor for the realisation of a European economic growth aiming to achieve higher levels of prosperity and competitiveness, at the same time avoiding environmental degradation, loss of biodiversity and the sustainable use of resources and strengthening economic and social cohesion.[29]

Also the European Parliament – in the work of the Committee for International Trade – addressed the issue of the relationship between foreign direct investment and the protection of non-trade values within the framework of the European Union, on the occasion of the debate on the results of a study on 'The EU Approach to International Investment Policy after the Lisbon Treaty'.[30]

The parliamentary debate underlined the important efforts made by the Commission in defining the face and nature of the new EU policy on foreign direct investment, focusing on the importance of the 'OECD Guidelines for Multinational Enterprises' as an irreplaceable tool for a correct balance of rights and responsibilities of investors.

The Committee has also expressed the commitment of the European Parliament to adopt rules that help to ensure the 'horizontal' consistency between foreign investment policy and other policies of the Union. Particular reference is made to values such as, among others, sustainable

27 The goal of coherence is even more enhanced when the Council reaffirmed that 'the European investment policy must continue to allow EU and Member States to adopt and enforce measures necessary to pursue public policy objectives' (at 17).

28 Communication from the Commission 'Europe 2020: A Strategy for Smart, Sustainable and Inclusive Growth', COM(2010)2020.

29 In the Communication, the Commission stressed that the European Union is 'the world's biggest trading bloc and leading destination for foreign direct investment' and can also rely 'on our strong values, democratic institutions, our consideration for economic, social and territorial cohesion and solidarity, our respect for the environment, our cultural diversity, respect for gender equality' (at 9).

30 The report 'The EU Approach to International Investment Policy after the Lisbon Treaty' (www.europarl.europa.eu) was elaborated by the Directorate-General for External Policies of the Union of the European Parliament and was completed on 21 October 2010.

development,[31] environmental protection,[32] decent work[33] and safety and health in the workplace.[34]

The European Parliament Resolution 'on the future European international investment policy' is the latest initiative adopted, in chronological

31 The study highlights that in some regions there is a growing consensus in considering sustainable development as a value that 'multilateral and bilateral investment agreements should promote ... in the host and investing countries' (at 49). The most sensitive issue in this regard seems to be a suitable notion of sustainable development. The study points out, in fact, that 'there is no single definition of "sustainable development" and there is no consensus on how that might be achieved'. As a solution to this problem, it suggests that the EU institutions clarify the meaning and scope of the concept of sustainable development to which the policy on foreign direct investment should refer. More specifically, the Union 'could adopt a "narrow" definition focusing on specific priority areas, such as labour standards and environmental protection that have already been included in some EU preferential trade agreements' (at 50).

32 The report analyses the issue of environmental protection in its various aspects: climate change, environmental degradation and loss of biodiversity. According to Art. 11 TFEU, 'environmental protection requirements must be integrated into the definition and implementation of the Union policies and activities, in particular with a view to promoting sustainable development'. In order to achieve this purpose, 'EU investment policy should therefore consider how it might promote the transfer of green technologies, infrastructure improvements and capacity building in the field of environment and consider ways of reducing the adverse impact of inward and outward flows, such as resource degradation, deforestation, water, air and land pollution' (*ibid.*).

33 From the final report 'Impacts of EU Outward FDI', published on 20 May 2010 by Copenhagen Economics (trade.ec.europa.eu), it emerges that 'low-skilled labour in the EU could lose jobs even if the aggregated impact of outward investment on EU employment is a neutral'. Starting from this finding, the Parliamentary Committee has outlined two possible alternatives in order to promote and ensure respect for 'labour standards' within the framework of the European foreign direct investment policy. A first option 'would be to follow the US model and adopt the "no lowering measures" principle that prohibits parties to encourage inward investment flows by weakening or reducing the existing levels of labour protection provided by domestic laws'. The other option would be to insert – in future EU agreements relating to foreign direct investment – references to specific standards such as 'the 1998 International Labour Organization's (ILO) Declaration on Fundamental Principles and Rights at Work or other core ILO labour standards as included in the US BITs and some but very few EU member state BITs' (at 51).

34 The Parliamentary Committee for International Trade has recently reaffirmed the need to combine the social and environmental issues in the EU action in the field of foreign direct investment. In its Working Document 'On the European Union's Future Investment Policy', of 18 November 2010 (www.europarl.europoa.eu), it stressed, in fact, that 'in addition to the necessary investor protection, the EU's future policy must promote investment which is sustainable, respects the environment (a particularly important area for extractive industries) and encourages good-quality working conditions in the enterprises targeted by the investment'.

order, in the field covered by this survey.[35] In line with what we have just described, it stresses that 'the EU's future policy must also promote investment which is sustainable, respects the environment (particularly in the area of extractive industries) and encourages good quality working conditions in the enterprises targeted by the investment'.[36]

To this end, the Resolution reiterates the opportunity of including clauses relating to corporate social responsibility as well as social and environmental clauses, in the investment sections of free-trade agreements.[37]

An important step towards the achievement of such an objective is the 'Statement of the European Union and the United States on Shared Principles for International Investment', signed on 10 April 2012. The parties, having recognised 'the critical importance of creating and maintaining an open and stable investment climate and policies, which contribute to sustainable economic development and growth, job creation, increased productivity, technological innovation and competitiveness',[38] agreed on the need 'to promote responsible business conduct, in general, and adherence by third countries to the OECD Guidelines for Multinational Enterprises, in particular'.[39]

This commitment was reaffirmed at the end of a recent meeting between the United States and the European Union held on 24 October 2012 within the Working Group on Investment. The two parties agreed on the desirability of maintaining and promoting investment policies that are open, transparent and non-discriminatory.

In a similar perspective, the European Commission decided on 23 May 2013 to ask the Member States for their agreement on a mandate to open negotiations on an investment agreement with China, in the belief that such an agreement will contribute 'to secure existing openness and deliver new liberalisation of the conditions for accessing each other's

35 European Parliament resolution 'On the Future European International Investment Policy', 2010/2203(INI), 6 April 2011.

36 At 27. In the same point of the resolution, the European Parliament asks the Commission 'to include, in all future agreements, a reference to the updated OECD Guidelines for Multinational Enterprises'.

37 The European Parliament requests that the 'Commission assess how such clauses have been included in Member State BITs and how they could be included in future standalone investment agreements as well' (at 29).

38 For the text of the 'Statement' see trade.ec.europa.eu.

39 At 6.

investment market [and to] improve the treatment of investors and their assets – including key technologies and intellectual property rights'.[40]

In conclusion, from the documents just examined it clearly emerges that 'respect non-trade values' in the policy on foreign direct investment is an expression of the consistency of the (external) action of the European Union that the Treaties seek to ensure.

3. The 'vertical' consistency of the EU policy on foreign direct investment pursued by means of the protection of non-trade values

As is well known, prior to the entry into force of the Lisbon Treaty, Member States have concluded a large number of bilateral agreements with third countries in the domain of investment (Bilateral Investment Treaties or BITs). According to the rules of international law, those agreements are binding on Member States although, since 1 December 2009, a problem arises in relation to the EU's (literally) exclusive competence in foreign direct investment, since only the latter may adopt valid and binding legal acts in the field concerned.

Because of this and in terms of such competence, many of the above-mentioned BITs could be found to contain matters of non-compliance with European Union law.

Due to the nearly total absence of EU agreements concluded in conformity with the competence at issue,[41] inconsistency may occur only with respect to the BITs actually in force.

In order to avoid such a circumstance, on 12 December 2012, the European Parliament and the Council adopted a Regulation 'establishing transitional arrangements for bilateral investment agreements between Member States and third countries'.[42]

The solutions adopted by this latter meet a clear need to promote the gradual implementation of the provisions introduced by the TFEU concerning foreign direct investment,[43] through the formulation and pro-

40 Speech of the EU Trade Commissioner Karel De Gucht (trade.ec.europa.eu).

41 On the first attempts of this practice, see section 4.

42 OJ L351/40, 20 December 2012.

43 The gradual implementation of EU policy on foreign direct investment retraces the mechanism created for a definitive introduction of the common commercial policy in the late 1960s. A similar aim is in fact to be found in the Council decision of 9 October 1961 'Concerning the Standardization of the Duration of Trade Agreements with Third Countries' (OJ L71/1274, 11 April 1961) and the Council decision 69/494/EEC 'On the

gressive development of a Union policy on investment, 'which is to serve all investors and investment equally'.

The purpose of the Regulation is to establish a system of authorisations for keeping in force the BITs under consideration and to lay down the conditions and procedures for the modification and conclusion of new BITs. The first aim of this Regulation is to preserve their guarantees as to investment conditions for the contracting parties ('grand-fathering').[44] The second aspect is ensuring compliance of the existing BITs with the rules of EU law.[45]

The process of authorising Member States to negotiate new agreements or to renegotiate existing ones has just started.[46] The Commission is about to grant its first authorisations, primarily with the view of ensuring that EU investment agreements negotiated at EU level are fully in line with EU law.[47]

By virtue of the fact that the EU competence in foreign direct investment is exclusive, the procedures provided in the Regulation should be considered as strictly transitional measures.[48]

For the purposes of this survey, the Regulation is relevant insofar as it would provide Member States with specific procedural instruments to ensure 'vertical' consistency in the field of foreign direct investment, in terms also of non-trade values. In the light of the Regulation, Member States might influence both the existing BITs and those yet to be concluded,

Progressive Standardisation of Agreements concerning Commercial Relations between Member States with Non-member Countries and the Negotiation between Community Agreements' (OJ L326/39, 12 September 1969).

44 According to Art. 3 of the Regulation, 'without prejudice to other obligations of the Member States under Union law, bilateral investment agreements notified pursuant to Art. 2 of this Regulation may be maintained in force, or enter into force, in accordance with the TFEU and this Regulation, until a bilateral investment agreement between the Union and the same third country enters into force'.

45 For the purposes of ensuring compliance of the BITs currently in force with EU law, it is relevant Art. 351 (2) TFEU which states that 'to the extent that such agreements are not compatible with the Treaties, the Member State or States concerned shall take all appropriate steps to eliminate the incompatibilities established. Member States shall, where necessary, assist each other to this end and shall, where appropriate, adopt a common attitude'. On the basis of that provision, Member States could be required to amend or terminate the BITs incompatible with EU law, until such time as they are replaced by new agreements concluded in the light of Arts. 206 and 207 TFEU.

46 So far, the Commission has received twenty-nine requests for authorisation to negotiate new agreements and thirty-six requests to open negotiations to amend existing BITs.

47 The Commission has included a specific reference to this objective in the recommendations for negotiating directives addressed to the Council and which have been shared with the European Parliament.

48 On the issue, see the contribution by Mariani in this book.

in order to make them compliant not only with the rules of European law relating to the aspects of the traditional ruling of foreign direct investment.[49] Compliance should be guaranteed, in fact, also with non-trade values promoted and protected by European Union law, including during its ongoing development in international investment law.[50]

The most relevant values taken as a limit to protection within European law, also in terms of the Commission's Communication, are the environment, health, the 'social' rights of workers, cultural diversity and sustainable development. By virtue of the adoption of the Regulation, these values should benefit from an additional safeguard, primarily at procedural level.

4. Final remarks: towards a global European international investment policy

The EU policy on foreign direct investment represents a new frontier of the common commercial policy, which has been extended and strengthened by the provisions introduced by the Treaty of Lisbon. In addition to being an essential tool for increasing productivity and competitiveness of the European market, foreign direct investment has a significant impact on the growth, development and employment, both within and outside the borders of the Union.

The numerical data speak for themselves: the globalisation of economic and trade relations has resulted in an exponential increase in investment flows. The European Union is playing a very crucial role in this context,

49 The principles or standards that characterise the practice of BITs are: the 'most-favoured-nation treatment', the 'national treatment', the 'fair and equitable treatment' and 'full protection and security'. Some BITs provide for a 'security clause', which is intended to protect the contractual rights that a host State has accorded an investor. Almost all the BITs also provide clauses which identify specific forms of arbitration for dispute resolution.

50 In a number of recent BITs the promotion and protection of foreign direct investment are pursued by taking other values, such as health, safety, environment and workers' rights, into account. A method aimed at achieving this result is to reaffirm – almost always in the preamble to the agreement concerned – that there should be no conflict between the obligations arising from the latter and the sovereign rights of the parties to protect one or more of the values just mentioned. As an alternative method, the parties undertake not to lower the level of protection of certain values as a tool to attract more foreign direct investment. While in the first case, non-trade values receive some kind of protection only from the point of view of interpretation, in the second case their protection – at least as 'minimum standards' – becomes the object of specific provisions of the Agreement. On the topic, see Kahn (2006), 95; Dupuy, Francioni and Petersmann (2009), 45; and the contribution by Acconci in this book.

placing itself as one of the key players in the field of foreign direct investment. The UNCTAD report on world investment of 2009 shows that over 2.4 trillion euros of the total amount of the world foreign direct investment relate to investment from and into the European Union, regulated by about 1200 BITs.[51]

The figures are moreover growing, as noted and highlighted by the Commission in its last Staff Working Document.[52]

Referring to this scenario, the same European Commissioner, Karel De Gucht, recently said that

> European investors need open, sound and predictable business environments to thrive and these proposals aim to strengthen the EU ability to ensure level playing fields for them. In the long run, a comprehensive investment policy will keep Europe as the world's number one player in the field of foreign direct investment, ensure the best deal for all European businesses, invigorate growth and create jobs at this crucial time.[53]

In conclusion, the actions and initiatives examined clearly show the efforts made by the Union's institutions in order to create a global European policy of foreign direct investment that provides for a common and reliable frame of reference for all EU investors in third countries and vice versa. In the current and future global scenario, a really effective European policy on foreign direct investment must retain the role of the Union as leader on a worldwide scale, but must also strive to combine two seemingly divergent purposes into one coherent goal: making the European market even more competitive but also increasingly permeated by social and environmental values.[54]

At this stage, the evaluation of the functioning of the 'new' European Union policy on foreign direct investment and on its degree of protection of non-trade values is necessarily entrusted to the first agreements

51 UNCTAD, 'World Investment Report 2009 – Transnational Corporations, Agricultural Production and Development' (www.unctad.org). See also the 2010 report on 'Investing in a Low-Carbon Economy' and the last one of 2011, on the topic 'Non-Equity Modes of International Production and Development'.

52 Commission Staff Working Document 'External Sources of Growth', which emphasises the effort of 'developing a comprehensive investment framework, including provisions for investment protection following the new competence granted to the EU by the Lisbon Treaty in this area' (at 15).

53 The speech is reported in a Commission press release, issued on the occasion of the adoption of the Communication 'Towards a Comprehensive European International Investment Policy' (europa.eu/rapid).

54 This change of approach has been recently argued by Titi (2013), 2.

with major investment partners such as Canada[55], as well as to the current negotiations with the United States on the Transatlantic Trade and Investment Partnership (TTIP).[56] The EU is increasingly concerned to ensure a balance between protecting foreign investors and "the right to regulate and to pursue legitimate public policy objectives such as social, environmental, security, public health and safety, and the promotion and protection of cultural diversity".[57]

References

Babarinde, O. and Faber, G. 2004. 'From Lomé to Cotonou: Business as Usual?'. *EFA Review* 9: 27–47.

Balan, G. 2008. 'The Common Commercial Policy under the Lisbon Treaty'. *Jean Monnet Seminar on Advanced Issues of European Law, 6th session, 20–27 April 2008, Dubrovnik, Re-thinking the European Constitution in an Enlarged European Union* (www.pravo.hr).

Bungenberg, M. 2008. 'Centralizing European BIT Making under the Lisbon Treaty' (www.asil.org).

2010. 'Going Global? The EU Common Commercial Policy after Lisbon'. *European Yearbook of International Economic Law*: 123–51.

Carducci, G. 2011. 'Defining "Investment" in Public and Private International Law and the Scope of ICSID, NAFTA and Energy Charter Treaty Investment Arbitration', Ligustro, A. and Sacerdoti, G. (eds.), *Problemi e tendenze nel diritto internazionale dell'economia.* Liber Amicorum *in onore di Paolo Picone*. Napoli: Editoriale Scientifica: 649–73.

Carreau, D. and Juillard, P. 2007. *Droit international économique*. Paris: Dalloz-Sirey.

Cremona, M. 2009. 'Economic and Social Rights in EU External Policy', Bestagno, F. (ed.), *I diritti economici, sociali e culturali. Promozione e tutela nella comunità internazionale*. Milano: Vita e Pensiero: 251–85.

De Luca, A. 2011. 'New Developments on the Scope of the EU Common Commercial Policy under the Lisbon Treaty: Investment Liberalization vs. Investment

55 See the last Draft of the 'Canada-European Union Comprehensive Economic and Trade Agreement' (13 October 2013) (available at www.bilaterals.org).

56 On 21 January 2014, the EU Trade Commissioner Karel De Gucht announced public consultations on the investment provisions of the TTIP, emphasizing that "Governments must always be free to regulate so they can protect people and the environment. But they must also find the right balance and treat investors fairly, so they can attract investment. International investment agreements like TTIP should ensure they do both" (the speech is available at europa.eu/rapid).

57 See the recent 'Fact Sheet' of the EU Commission on 'Investment Protection and Investor-to-State Dispute Settlement in EU agreements' (26 November 2013, available at trade.ec.europa.eu).

Protection?'. *Yearbook on International Investment Law and Policy 2010–2011*: 165–215.

De Mestral, A. 2010. 'The Lisbon Treaty and the Expansion of EU Competence over Foreign Direct Investment and the Implications for Investor-State Arbitration'. *Yearbook on International Investment Law and Policy 2009–2010*: 390–413.

Dimopoulos, A. 2008. 'The Common Commercial Policy after Lisbon: Establishing Parallelism between Internal and External Economic Policy?'. *Croatian Yearbook of European Law and Policy* 4: 101–29.

2011. 'Creating an EU Foreign Investment Policy: Challenges for the Future', Cardwell, P.J. (ed.). *EU External Relations Law and Policy in the Post-Lisbon Era*. The Hague: Springer: 401–22.

Dolzer, R. and Stevens, M. 1995. *Bilateral Investment Treaties*. The Hague: Kluwer Law International.

Dupuy, P.-M., Francioni, F. and Petersmann, E.-U. (eds.). 2009. *Human Rights in International Investment Law and Arbitration*. Oxford University Press.

Dutheil de la Rochère, J. 2009. 'Le pouvoir des États membres de l'Union européenne de conclure des traités bilatéraux d'investissement'. Kassedjian, C. and Leben, C. (eds.), *Le droit européen et l'investissement*. Paris: Pantheon-Assas Paris II: 27–39.

Giardina, A. 1996. 'Le *Guidelines* della Banca Mondiale sugli investimenti stranieri'. Giardina, A. and Tosato, G.L. (eds.). *Diritto del commercio internazionale*. Milano: Giuffrè editore: 459–70.

Juillard, P. 1994. 'L'évolution des sources du droit des investissements'. *RCADI* 250: 9–20.

Kahn, P. 2006. 'Investissement internationaux et droits de l'homme'. Horchani, F. (ed.), *Où va le droit de l'investissement?*. Paris: Pedone: 95–109.

Karl, J. 2006. 'The Competence for Foreign Direct Investment – New Powers for the European Union?'. *The Journal of World Investment & Trade* 3: 413–44.

Krajewski, M. 2005. 'External Trade Law and the Constitution Treaty: Towards a Federal and More Democratic Common Commercial Policy?'. *Common Market Law Review* 42: 91–127.

Laviec, J.-P. 1985. *Protection et promotion des investissements. Etude de droit international économique*. Paris: Presses universitaires de France.

Marchisio, S. 1993. 'Investimenti esteri nel diritto internazionale'. *Digesto discipline pubblicistiche* 7: 567–88.

Mauro, M.R. 2003. *Gli accordi bilaterali sulla promozione e la protezione degli investimenti*. Torino: Giappichelli editore.

2010a. 'Accordi internazionali sugli investimenti e Unione europea'. *Studi sull'integrazione europea* 2: 403–30.

2010b. 'La politica commerciale comune nel Trattato di Lisbona, con particolare riferimento agli investimenti stranieri', Traisci, F.P. (ed.). *Il 'Diritto privato europeo': dal mercato interno alla cittadinanza europea*. Napoli: Edizioni Scientifiche Italiane: 55–101.

Maydell, N. 2008. 'The European Community's Minimum Platform on Investment or the Trojan Horse of Investment Competence'. Reinisch, A. and Knahr, C. (eds.). *International Investment Law in Context*. Utrecht: Eleven International Publishing: 73–92.

Migliorino, L. 1989. *Gli accordi internazionali sugli investimenti*. Milano: Giuffrè editore.

Mignolli, A. 2009. *L'azione esterna dell'Unione europea e il principio della coerenza*. Napoli: Jovene editore.

Picone, P. and Sacerdoti, G. 1991. *Diritto internazionale dell'economia*. Milano: Franco Angeli.

Sacerdoti, G. 1997. 'Bilateral Treaties and Multilateral Instruments on Investment Protection'. *RCADI* 269: 255–460.

Schwarzenberger, G. 1969. *Foreign Investment and International Law*. London: Stevens & Sons.

Shan, W. 2011. 'Towards a Common European Community Policy on Investment Issues'. *The Journal of World Investment & Trade* 3: 603–25.

Shan, W. and Zang, S. 2011. 'The Treaty of Lisbon: Half Way Toward a Common Investment Policy'. *The European Journal of International Law* 21: 1049–73.

Shihata, I. 1993. *Legal Treatment of Foreign Investment: 'The World Bank Guidelines'*. Dordrecht: Martinus Nijhoff Publishers.

Sornarajah, M. 2010. *The International Law on Foreign Investment*. Cambridge University Press.

Titi, C. 2013. 'EU Investment Agreements and the Search for a New Balance'. *Columbia FDI Perspectives* 86: 1–3.

14

Non-financial concerns in the lending policy of the European Investment Bank in context

EMANUELA PISTOIA

1. Introduction

A common concern is currently shared among multilateral lending institutions (MLIs): their accountability vis-à-vis stakeholders for the impact of their statutory activities on the environment and/or on social communities of host/recipient countries. All MLIs adopted policy frameworks on environmental and/or social issues that they are committed to abide by. All of them have equipped themselves with compliant procedures whereby the adherence of their lending activities to those policy frameworks can be reviewed and possibly ensured.

A trend-setter in this field has been the World Bank Group, particularly the International Bank for Reconstruction and Development (IBRD), the International Finance Corporation (IFC) and the International Development Association (IDA). In the past decades those institutions, hereinafter comprehensively referred to as World Bank (WB), were confronted by civil society with sharp criticisms for supporting projects detrimental to local communities for their alleged adverse effects over the environment and/or individual rights. In response, the Bank developed safeguard policies requiring the prior assessment of a project's potential impact on local environment and communities.[1] However, the Bank long resisted acknowledging a responsibility in actively protecting the environment and promoting human rights. The Bank also resisted accepting that dealing with political and civil human rights was compatible with the prohibition to interfere in the political affairs of any member laid down in Art. IV(10) of the Articles of Agreement, read in combination

1 Despite the adoption of safeguard policies in both fields, the WB's approach to human rights has long been more cautious than that to environmental protection. Such sharp difference can easily be identified in the chapters respectively devoted to the two topics in Shihata (1991), 97–134 and 135–80.

with Art. III(5)(*b*).[2] A major response of the WB to the above-mentioned criticisms has been the establishment of the Inspection Panel in 1993, which raised a huge interest among scholars and stakeholders.[3] As an accountability mechanism aimed at the adherence to the Bank's policy documents, in terms of protection of human rights and the environment its advantage is to bypass the obligations of the Bank in these fields and its international responsibility for their breach, as well as the responsibility of its Member States.[4] In the wake of that, all regional banks adopted safeguard policies and set up their own accountability mechanisms largely mirroring the WB Inspection Panel as to their function and purpose.[5] In 1994, the Inter-American Development Bank (IDB) equipped itself with the Independent Investigation Mechanism, which was recently replaced by the Independent Consultation and Investigation Mechanism (ICIM) in an enhancement and lessons learnt perspective.[6] The Asian Development Bank's Accountability Mechanism (AM) was introduced in 2003, building on the Inspection Function established as early as 1995, and in the past months it was subject to a review which resulted in the proposal of a few important changes.[7] The African Development Bank, created in 1964, and the African Development Fund set up their Independent Review Mechanism (IRM) in 2006 and implemented some amendments thereto in 2010. The European Bank for Reconstruction and

2 The view that, based on Art. IV(10), the Bank could only consider social and economic rights was first and long upheld by the Legal Counsel of the IBRD, I.F.I. Shihata. See extensively Shihata (1991), 98–9 and 107–26. This view has been criticised on several grounds. Against the idea that human rights are politics see especially Ghazi (2005), 92–3 and 97. The path followed by the Bank towards overtaking such position is carefully traced in Sarfaty (2009), 659–82 and Maldonado (2010). For the sake of brevity, I should limit myself to recall the Bank's General Counsel Dañino's note entitled 'Legal Opinion on Human Rights and the Work of the World Bank', released in January 2006, for being a milestone in this field.

3 A major criticism to the widespread approach according to which, before the establishment of the Inspection Panel, the WB lacked accountability is in Shihata (1994), 115–16. This author also comments on the 'mounting demands' as a reason for the establishing an inspection function within the World Bank: *ibid.*, 8–13. The above widespread approach was taken, *inter alia*, by Rodgers (1990), 457 ff., and Cahn (1993), 159 ff.

4 A critical analysis of the problems unsolved in the recent legal literature in those fields is in De Sena (2011), 832–43.

5 A recent overview of regional banks and their accountability mechanisms is in Cafaro (2011).

6 'Policy Establishing the Independent Consultation and Investigation Mechanism of the Inter-American Development Bank', www.iadb.org.

7 Asian Development Bank, 'Review of the Inspection Function: Establishment of a New ADB Accountability Mechanism', May 2003, and ADB, 'Accountability Mechanism Policy 2012' (both on compliance.adb.org).

Development (EBRD)'s Project Complaint Mechanism (PCM) has also been operational since late 2000.

As the world's absolute major lender and as the largest lender in developing countries,[8] the European Investment Bank (hereinafter EIB or Bank) is naturally in the spotlight as far its accountability is concerned. However, as compared to the other MLIs it has a unique status because, unlike them, the EIB is not a self-standing international organisation. Established in the Treaty of Rome on the European Economic Community (EEC), its Statute currently being a protocol to the Treaty on the European Union (TEU) and the Treaty on the Functioning of the European Union (TFEU), the EIB is part of Europe's integration process and of the 'European Union family'. However, even within the EU its position is quite peculiar. While having its own legal personality and enjoying financial autonomy within the EU (Art. 308 TFEU), it is bound by the objectives set out in the EU treaties. This is clearly established in the TFEU as well as in the EIB Statute and acknowledged by the Court of Justice of the EU (CJEU)[9] and the EIB itself. To give an idea of how decisive that feature proves to be, suffice it to recall that the fact that the Bank carries out projects 'furthering EU policy objectives' is quoted as a background to the Memorandum of Understanding with the European Ombudsman on complaints against the Bank itself (hereinafter MoU EIB/EO). Quite similarly, the decision granting an EU guarantee to the Bank against losses under loans and loan guarantees for projects outside the Union ('the decision on the EU guarantee')[10] is based on the fact that the EIB 'contributes to the general guiding principles and policy objectives of the Union'.[11]

In line with the other MLIs, in the last two decades the EIB put a considerable effort in increasing its accountability vis-à-vis its stakeholders.

8 Data of the main MLIs are reported in CEE Bankwatch Network, 'European Investment Bank. Promoting Sustainable Development, "Where Appropriate". A Survey of the EIB's Social Guidelines for Project Financing Outside the European Union', 2007, 55. According to official EIB sources (www.eib.org/about/key_figures/index.htm), the Bank still directs the largest part of its lending effort to EU Member countries, while non-EU States currently receive nearly 15 per cent of its funding. A clear picture of the actual role of the EIB in the EU policy-making on grounds of its lending effort within the Union is carried out in Robinson (2009).

9 The duty of the EIB to contribute to the objectives of the EU is acknowledged in the case-law of the CJEU: Case 85/86, *Commission* v. *EIB* [1986] ECR 1281, 29–30; Case C-15/00, *Commission* v. *EIB* [2003] ECR I-7342, 102.

10 Decision of the European Parliament and of the Council 1080/2011/EU, 25 October 2011, repealing decision 633/2009/EC, OJ L280/1, 27 October 2011.

11 Recital 1.

Against the above background, the present chapter is primarily aimed at highlighting to what extent, based on the above-mentioned constraints deriving from the EU treaties, the EIB should take into account non-financial concerns while carrying out its mission and the tools by which it indeed does so. With a view to put the Bank in context, I intend to point out to what extent the EIB's link to the EU makes a difference for its environmental and social accountability as compared to that of the other MLIs. Accordingly, I will first go through the treaty provisions concerning the mission of the Bank and the latter's policy documents on social and environmental concerns. It is worth mentioning that those provisions and documents should be at the basis of a future reflection on whether a parallelism between the EIB practice on non-financial concerns and the role of the latter in the newly established EU investment policy might be identified. Turning to the toolbox available for their protection, I will first take an *ex ante facto* perspective and address the procedures applicable to the approval of loans and guarantees, to check whether they favour the implementation of the above concerns. I will then move into *ex post facto* control, i.e. review and enforcement mechanisms. Those certainly include the EIB Complaints Mechanism (CM) mentioned before, but the role of the CJEU will also be considered. Beyond the lights and the shadows of those procedures to the purposes of safeguarding social and environmental concerns, the inquiry into *ex post facto* control is to show what actors bear responsibilities or retain potentialities in this connection. Also in comparison with the experience of the other MLIs, the aim is to understand the positions respectively held, in this regard, by host/recipient States, individuals or groups of individuals and non-State actors such as non-governmental organisations or local organisations supporting civil or social rights and/or environmental sustainability.

2. Non-financial concerns in the statutory mission of the EIB: purposes of the Bank's lending policy…

The inquiry as to whether the EIB's ties with the EU are such that the Bank should take into account non-financial concerns while carrying out its mission, requires drawing a distinction between the internal and the external mandate of the EIB, i.e. between the financial support to investments to be carried out in the territories of Member States and, in whole or in part, outside the territories of Member States (Art. 16(1) EIB Statute).[12]

12 Both the internal and the external mandate are set out in Art. 16 EIB Statute. In Art. 309 TFEU, that is recalled in the Statute itself (Art. 2) as the basis of the Bank's mandate,

While the general objective of the EIB as laid down in Art. 309 TFEU is 'to contribute ... to the balanced and steady development of the internal market in the interest of the Union', the two above mandates rely on two different legal bases in the TFEU and therefore aim at different specific purposes.

The internal mandate is placed in the section on the economic, social and territorial cohesion of the EU, the Bank being included among the financial instruments that should support the promotion of the overall harmonious development of the latter, particularly the reduction of 'disparities between the levels of development of the various regions and the backwardness of the least favoured regions' (Art. 175 TFEU, read in combination with Art. 174).[13] Despite neither social concerns within these regions, nor sustainable development, nor economic, social, cultural or minority rights being part of these objectives, the EIB's internal mandate can be enlarged in such a way as to encompass such non-financial concerns because the overall task of the Bank is the contribution to the development of the internal market (Art. 309 TFEU). On these grounds, the Bank is naturally bound to implement all the non-financial values that are inherent in the concept of the internal market as laid down in Art. 3(3) TEU. They include the sustainable development of Europe, full employment and social progress, a high level of protection and improvement of the quality of the environment, scientific and technological advance, the fight against social exclusion and discrimination, social justice and protection, equality between women and men, solidarity between generations, protection of the rights of the child, the safeguard and enhancement of Europe's cultural heritage.

The pursuance of the above non-economic values by means of the internal mandate of the Bank is also required by the extension to the activity of this institution of the 'horizontal' provisions laid down in Part I, Title II, TFEU, including the promotion of a high level of employment, the guarantee of adequate social protection, a high level of education, protection of human health and the environment. Those provisions should apply

there is no mention to the external mandate. To the opposite, there the goal of the EIB is established with exclusive reference to the internal market properly so called, i.e. regardless to its external projection. Accordingly, as opposed to measures to be approved in pursuance with the internal mandate, those pertaining to the external one are to be approved by the Board of Governors (Art. 7(2)(*d*) at a qualified majority (Art. 16(1)).

13 However, as to the mission actually carried out by the Bank, it is worth recalling that, almost twenty years ago, an analysis of its lending activity within the EU found it 'hard to identify a public policy and a cohesion-promoting role' for it: Honohan (1995), 324.

to all categories and areas of Union competence with the sole limit of the principle of conferral of powers. Against that extension it might be argued that the general application affects *the Union*, whereas the Bank, thanks to its own legal personality, is distinct from the Union itself. On the other hand, the argument in favour of the extension to the Bank of the principles laid down for general application in the Union is the fact that, despite its autonomy, the former is fully 'part of the framework of the Union'.[14] From the CJEU's case-law it clearly emerges that the autonomous status of the Bank, including its distinct legal personality, is instrumental to its lending activities and to the related financial support, i.e. to its recourse to the capital market.[15] Consequently, such status in no way implies that the Bank is unrelated to the EU legal system. Instead, as an EU body its link to the purposes of the EU is tight. In practice, the EIB is ready to apply the horizontal principles listed in the TFEU with the result of expanding its internal mandate. This is best attested by the 2009 Statement of Environmental and Social Principles and Standards (hereinafter ESPS Statement),[16] which lays down the environmental policy of the EIB by referring *inter alia* to the principle of integration of environmental protection requirements laid down in Art. 11 TFEU.[17]

The external lending of the EIB is to contribute to the development cooperation policy of the EU (Art. 209(3) TFEU).[18] The role of the Bank in such policy is highlighted in the 'European Consensus on Development', where the strengthening of the synergies between the programmes supported by it and those financed by the EU is encouraged '[i]n order to guarantee a maximum impact for the beneficiary countries'.[19] Moreover, it is required that the development cooperation policy of the EU be conducted within the framework of the principles and objectives of the

14 Case 85/86, *Commission* v. *EIB*, 29; C-15/00, *Commission* v. *EIB*, 102. See extensively Hachez and Wouters (2012), 49–50.

15 Case 85/86 *Commission* v. *EIB*, 28; C-15/00, *Commission* v. *EIB*, 104.

16 Adopted in 2009, the ESPS Statement is an evolution of the Bank's Environmental Statement first issued in 1996 and then successively revised in 2002 and 2004. Intermediate between the two is a previous version of the ESPS Statement, which replaced the Bank's Environmental Statement and in 2008 underwent a thorough review guided by an *ad hoc* panel and based on a public consultation process. This review is described in the 'Consultation Report' (www.eib.eu).

17 'ESPS Statement', 23.

18 This is reiterated in decision 1080/2011/EU, recital 2.

19 Joint statement by the Council and the representatives of the governments of the Member States meeting within the Council, the European Parliament and the Commission on European Union Development Policy: 'The European Consensus', 2006/C 46/01, 119.

external action of the EU (Art. 208(1)). That is the reason why the above-mentioned MoU between the European Ombudsman and the Bank says that '[o]utside the EU, EIB lending ... is based on EU external cooperation and development policies'.[20]

The Bank is so closely associated with the Union external policies that, since 2007, the majority of its operations outside the Union have benefited from a budgetary guarantee of the latter, which is designed to cover risks of a political or sovereign nature. In turn, the granting of such guarantee led to the enhancement of the link between Union policy objectives and the Bank's external lending. This has been achieved through the establishment of high-level objectives for the related financing activity,[21] the development of regional technical operational guidelines for the same financing, which was entrusted to the Commission in cooperation with the Bank and in consultation with the European External Action Service (EEAS),[22] and through 'regular and systematic dialogue and early exchange of information' of the Bank with the Commission and the EEAS, which should be carried out on a region-by-region basis.[23]

The specific purpose of the development cooperation policy of the EU is the reduction and, in the long term, the eradication of poverty (Art. 208 TFEU(1)). Also in the wake of the Statement on Poverty adopted in 2001 by the Committee on economic, social and cultural rights,[24] both should be regarded as of a non-economic nature.

In turn, the principles and objectives of the external action of the EU include 'democracy, the rule of law, the universality and indivisibility of human rights and fundamental freedoms, respect for human dignity, the

20 See Case C-155/07, *European Parliament* v. *Council of the European Union* [2008] ECR I-08103, 59–61 and 66–7, where the CJEU acknowledged that the EIB financing operations covered by the EU guarantee provided for in decision 2006/1016/EC, currently replaced by decision 1080/2011, support both the development policy of the Union and its external action. This led the Court to annul the contested decision, that had been adopted on the sole legal basis of the development cooperation, in particular of *ex* Art. 181a EC.

21 See Arts. 2–3 of decision 1080/2011, and the related recital 18, establishing the 'General Mandate and the Climate Change Mandate', which will be dealt with below.

22 Arts. 6 and 8(1) of decision 1080/2011.

23 Art. 8 of decision 1080/2011.

24 'Substantive issues arising in the implementation of the International Covenant on economic, social and cultural rights: poverty and the International covenant on economic, social and cultural rights. Statement adopted by the Committee on economic, social and cultural rights on 4 May 2001', E/C.12/2001/10, 10 May 2001. The close links between development and human rights are thoroughly explored in legal literature and are showcased in a number of UN official documents that have gradually led many agencies of the UN system to adopt a 'human rights approach'.

principles of equality and solidarity, and respect for the principles of the United Nations Charter and international law' (Art. 21(1) TEU).

In light of the above, the Union elaborated a vision of development, which it and its Member States are committed to pursue, where non-economic concerns are of utmost importance. It is worth devoting attention to such vision because, as mentioned above, the related document fully associates the EIB to the implementation of the Union aid to developing countries. The major role acknowledged to non-economic values in the vision at issue primarily derives from the adoption of the Millennium Development Goals (MDGs) as objectives of the development cooperation pursued by the Union.[25] Beyond the eradication of extreme poverty and hunger that would be the purpose of the EU development policy in its own right, the MDGs include achieving universal primary education, promoting gender equality, reducing the mortality rate of children, improving maternal health, combating HIV/AIDS, malaria and other diseases and environmental sustainability. Second, the European consensus identifies a number of 'common values' that the EU and its Member States should pursue in partnership and dialogue with third countries. They are as follows: respect for human rights, fundamental freedoms, peace, democracy, good governance, gender equality, the rule of law, solidarity, justice and respect for international law.[26] The commitment to sustainable development is also remarkable. The Union is to carry out initiatives aiming at the preservation of natural resources, particularly at halting biodiversity loss and promoting bio-safety and sustainable management of biodiversity. The Union cooperation policy also includes efforts to keep climate change under control: the EU Action Plan on Climate Change should be implemented in this context, too.[27] Moreover, the development cooperation pursued by the EU is keen on the proper supply of water and energy to the population of the beneficiary countries.[28] In the framework of rural development and support to agriculture as tools for poverty reduction and growth, other specific non-economic concerns are identified. They are food security, the quality of nutrition and the sustainable intensification of production.[29]

25 The 'European Consensus', 42 and, as to the coordinated action between the Union and the Member States, especially 5–6.

26 The 'European Consensus', 13, 53 and 86.

27 The 'European Consensus', 75–6.

28 The 'European Consensus', 80–2.

29 The 'European Consensus', 83–5.

3. ...and limits thereto

There are also non-financial concerns that operate as limits to the activity of the EIB, i.e. that should not be adversely affected by projects supported with its loans or guarantees. They are surely the human rights enshrined in the Charter of Fundamental Rights of the European Union (hereinafter the Charter), but they include also the values upon which the EU and its policies are founded.[30]

Starting with the restrictions that the EIB derives from the Charter, the fact that the Bank is bound to the latter clearly emerges from Art. 51 on its scope. According to this provision, the Charter is addressed not only to the 'institutions of the Union', that do not include the EIB (Art. 13(1) TEU), but also to its bodies. The EIB surely qualifies as such because, as clarified in the 'Explanations', this expression covers all entities established in the treaties as well as in the EU secondary legislation. A 'body' of the EU is the way the CJEU usually refers to the EIB.[31]

The fact that Bank should abide by the Charter is also indirectly laid down in Art. 1 of its Statute, according to which the Bank should act 'in accordance with the provisions of the Treaties': it is well known that the Charter has the same legal value as the Treaties (Art. 6(1) TEU).

Especially insofar as the internal mandate is concerned, it should be pointed out that it is not being argued here that the Charter designates objectives for the Bank. In other words, being bound to the Charter does not entail that the Bank is required to actively promote the rights enshrined therein through its loans and guarantees. This would be clearly in contrast with Art. 51(2) of the Charter. Rather, the latter should not support projects that have a negative impact on those rights.

A clear acknowledgement by the Bank of the role that the Charter plays in its activity is contained in the ESPS Statement. There, the principles of the Charter of fundamental rights of the European Union, along with the UN Universal Declaration of Human Rights, are referred to as the source of the Bank's 'rights based approach when considering the social aspects of a project'.[32]

More generally, none of the principles and values upon which the Union is founded should be endangered by the activity of the EIB, be it

30 See Hachez and Wouters (2012), 59–62, who also argue that, beyond being bound to the EU Treaties and the Charter, the EIB should carry out its activities '*with due regard for* EU legislation' (61). On this point see below, in this section.

31 Case 15/00, *Commission* v. *IEB*, 75 and 98.

32 'ESPS Statement', 30.

addressed within or outside the territory of the Union. This can be argued because, as acknowledged by the CJEU and already recalled in the previous section, despite its functional and institutional autonomy the Bank 'forms part of the framework of the Union'.[33] Provided that this status in principle allows the adoption of EU secondary legislation directed to the Bank,[34] *a fortiori* it is compatible with the assumption that the latter should not run counter to the EU fundamental principles and values. As pointed out above, these include, beyond the human rights enshrined in the Charter, peace, security, democracy, sustainable development, solidarity and mutual respect among peoples, free and fair trade, eradication of poverty.[35]

Ultimately, concerning the external mandate, all of the non-economic concerns that the EIB should pursue also operate as limits to its activity. This is made clear in decision 1080/2011 on the EU guarantee to the EIB against losses under loans and loan guarantees for projects outside the Union, whose preambular paragraph 21 recalls the principles of the European Consensus on Development in this connection.

4. Non-financial concerns in the actual lending policy of the EIB

An overview of the implementation of the EIB's non-economic mandate should rely primarily on some policy documents dealing with the matter. As to the activity addressed to non-EU countries, the decision on the EU guarantee should also be considered.

The most comprehensive, ambitious and clear-cut policy document with a focus on non-financial concerns is the above-mentioned ESPS Statement. According to the definitions adopted there, environmental standards are those that 'aim to protect and improve the natural and built environment', whereas social standards 'aim to protect the rights and enhance the livelihoods of people … and are intended to promote outcomes to the benefit of individual well-being, social inclusion and sustainable communities'.[36] The Statement includes them among the purposes of the Bank's lending and also regards them as values that the latter

33 Case 15/00, *Commission* v. *IEB*, 102.

34 In Case 15/00 (fn 33) the CJEU denied that being addressed by some EU secondary legislation was incompatible with the EIB autonomous status after engaging in a thorough analysis as to whether such legislation practically hindered the Bank's financial and operational autonomy.

35 See Art. 3 TEU.

36 'ESPS Statement', 45.

should not jeopardise. These two different roles are first outlined in the preamble, where it is stated:

> The EIB requires that all the projects it is financing are acceptable in environmental and social terms by applying appropriate safeguards to all its operations. The Bank also finances projects that contribute directly to environmental sustainability and social well-being in support of sustainable development, by virtue of their positive contribution either to the protection and enhancement of the natural or built environment and/or to the promotion of sustainable communities.[37]

Another policy document worth mentioning in the present analysis is the Statement on Corporate Social Responsibility (CSR),[38] which indeed applies also to the European Investment Fund (EIF) because the EIB is its majority shareholder.[39] The EIB definition of CSR as 'sound business practice' is multi-faceted as it covers both the content of the Bank's activity, including the goals that its lending policy pursues, and the way the former is carried out in terms of governance (including anti-fraud and anti-corruption measures). Accordingly, the Bank's CSR affects the direct pursuance or at least the safeguard of non-financial concerns under its first facet. Indeed, the Statement on CSR emphasises that 'social cohesion' and 'a better environment', i.e. precisely the two issues that are the focus of the ESPS Statement, are main concerns in the Bank's lending activity.[40]

Concerning the direct commitment to the promotion of environmentally and socially sustainable projects, in the ESPS Statement social and environmental matters are not subject to separate assessments, but they are integrated in a single sustainability concept. However, the Bank itself points out that they are treated 'differently in manner, scope and intensity'.[41]

As to the support for environmental sustainability, projects that are designed to meet this target should pursue one of the following four objectives: to tackle the threat of climate change, to support sustainable natural resource management, to improve the quality of urban life or to safeguard

37 'ESPS Statement', 1. The two different roles played by environmental and social matters are stated again at 10.

38 'EIB Group Statement on Corporate Social Responsibility', May 2005, www.eib.eu.

39 The EIF is a public-private partnership with legal personality and financial autonomy, whose other shareholders are the European Union and several financial institutions from EU Member States.

40 As the first point of the description of the Bank's commitment to CSR, it is stated: 'The EIB Group aims to integrate environmental and social concerns into its business activities.' See 'EIB Group Statement on Corporate Social Responsibility', 2, and also 4, 3–5.

41 'ESPS Statement', 6.

human health.[42] Environment-oriented projects include those aimed at fostering markets in environmental goods and services 'that serve to correct for under-investment (e.g. the carbon market in the case of low carbon technologies, and the emerging market in ecosystem services)'.[43] Conversely, no specific objectives pertaining to the support of social well-being can be identified in the Statement. It follows that the EIB's concept of integration of social and environmental matters amounts to a functional relation between improvement of social well-being and environmental protection: in other words, the latter is a factor of the former. As pointed out in the Statement: 'The environmental standards of the EIB are intended to protect and enhance the natural environment, not only for its own sake but also to improve the quality of life, economic development and social well-being *that result from environmental sustainability.*'[44]

In the Statement on CSR, too, environmental and social matters apparently hold a different role, the former undoubtedly attracting most of the Bank's effort. Suffice it to recall that, the first pillar of the Bank's strategy reportedly being 'value added', the Statement explains that '[t]he EIB adds value in particular through its appraisal and follow-up of investment projects and programmes – which must be viable not only economically, technically and financially but *also as regards the environment.*'[45] However, despite the document's brevity on this point, it seems to refer to the need for the Bank's lending to have no negative impact on the environment, more than to environmental sustainability as a direct purpose of such lending.

Particularly keen on environmental protection is also the European Parliament and Council decision on the EU guarantee. This decision breaks down the maximum ceiling of the EIB financing operations in third countries under EU guarantee into two parts corresponding to two different mandates: the General Mandate and the Climate Change Mandate.[46] The latter is designed to support projects contributing to the objective of the United Nations Framework Convention on Climate Change, i.e. by 'avoiding or reducing greenhouse gas emissions in the areas of renewable energy, energy efficiency and sustainable transport, or by increasing resilience to the adverse impacts of climate change on vulnerable countries, sectors and communities'.[47] Not only does the goal of

42 'ESPS Statement', 10. 43 'ESPS Statement', 14.

44 'ESPS Statement', 31 (emphasis added).

45 See 'EIB Group Statement', 3 (emphasis added).

46 Art. 2. 47 Art. 2(4).

protecting the environment take advantage of one specific line of action, but it is also pursued through the other. Two out of the three specific objectives of the General Mandate pertains to environmental protection, one being entirely devoted to it – climate change mitigation and adaptation, as referred to in the related *ad hoc* mandate – and one partially – the development of social and economic infrastructure, including environmental infrastructure.[48] On the other hand, the objective consisting in the local private sector development, in particular support to small and medium enterprises (SMEs),[49] stimulates economic growth with an eye on social well-being. As pointed out in the preamble of decision 1080/2011, the support to SMEs is a tool for combating unemployment.[50]

In line with the policies outlined above, environmental protection and, to a slightly minor extent, social well-being are priorities in the Bank strategy in the EU and Pre-Accession (Candidate and Potential Candidate) Countries. Among the six objectives set out for the Bank's lending activities one is protecting and improving the environment and promoting sustainable communities. Environmental protection is also a component of the objective of supporting the establishment of a sustainable, competitive and secure energy supply. Related to the improvement of social well-being in the manner described above is the objective of providing support to SMEs. The other three strategic objectives are connected with social well-being as understood in a broad sense. They are as follows: economic and social cohesion and convergence, implementation of the knowledge economy and development of Trans-European Networks (TENs).

Turning now to the standards and principles that all the projects financed by the Bank – not just those of an environmental and/or social nature – should meet, the approach taken in the ESPS Statement is inspired to flexibility and pragmatism more than to the highest possible level of protection. It will be shown below that this is true particularly for social well-being.

On the environment side, projects should show no negative impact on the environment either as regards their own technical characteristics, e.g. emissions, or as to characteristics of the host environment and its immediate neighbourhood, or in connection with project development, implementation and operation.[51] In general terms, the applicable principles are as follows: the principle of aiming at a high level of environmental protection, the precautionary and the prevention principles, the principle

48 Art. 3(1)(c) and (b) respectively. 49 Art. 3(1)(a).
50 Recital 18. 51 'ESPS Statement', 31.

that environmental damage should be rectified at source.[52] More specifically, projects within the EU and candidate or potential candidate countries can be financed only insofar as they comply with applicable national environmental law, with applicable EU environmental law, particularly some specified directives among which is the EU EIA Directive, and the principles and standards of relevant international environmental conventions incorporated into EU law.[53] Projects in the rest of the world can be financed only if compliant with national legislation, including international conventions ratified by the host country, and EU standards, especially if more restrictive than those established in national legislation.[54] In case this is not practical or even desirable, a phased approach to higher standards should be conceived.[55]

On the social well-being side, the adverse effects that projects financed by the Bank should not produce are violation of human rights[56] and giving rise to conflicts or intensifying them.[57] As to involuntary resettlements and the rights of indigenous people and other vulnerable groups, to gaps in the implementation of the ILO core labour standards, to risks to worker and/or community health and threats to the integrity of sites that have a high level of protection for reasons of cultural heritage, including UNESCO World Heritage Sites, projects with a negative impact upon them are not totally excluded. Rather, in order for such negative impact to be minimised, project promoters are required to plan their activities in those regards and to submit the related documents to the Bank: respectively, the Resettlement Action Plan, the Indigenous Peoples Development Plan, programmes and procedures to ensure that project implementation is compliant with the core labour principles and standards and, ultimately, programmes and procedures to ensure that good international practices in matters of community and occupational health and safety standards are adhered to.[58] As to projects involving threats to cultural heritage sites, they can be financed only if the promoter can demonstrate that certain conditions are met, e.g. that there is no feasible alternative, that the overall socio-economic benefits from the project substantially outweigh the costs, that adequate restoration measures are adopted and are adequately

52 'ESPS Statement', 23–9. 53 'ESPS Statement', 36.

54 'ESPS Statement', 36. 55 'ESPS Statement', 40.

56 'The Bank will not finance projects which result in a violation of human rights': 'ESPS Statement', 6.

57 'The EIB does not finance projects that give rise to conflicts or intensify existing conflicts': 'ESPS Statement', 47.

58 'ESPS Statement', 51–5.

funded and maintained, and that stakeholders have been consulted and the relevant authorities have granted approval.[59]

5. Implementing the non-financial mandate of the EIB: its impact on the Bank's decision-making

The decision-making of the EIB inspires a few comments on its potentialities for the implementation of the 'non-financial mandate' of the Bank, i.e. the active promotion of environmental sustainability, individual well-being and social inclusion as well as protection of these values in projects aimed at different purposes.

Such decision-making is partially different with respect to the internal or the external mandate. According to Art. 19 of the EIB Statute applicable to the former, it includes the compulsory opinion of both the Commission and the Member State in whose territory the investment will be carried out.[60] In more detail, applications made through the Commission shall be submitted for an opinion to the said Member State, while applications submitted through the Member State shall be submitted for an opinion to the Commission. Last, as undertakings and public or private entities may apply for a loan directly to the Bank, in those cases the opinion of both the Member State concerned and the Commission should be needed. Given the Commission's role in the EU system and the natural interest of the State in whose territory the investment will be carried out to protect *its own* environment and *its own* residents and local communities, the procedure set up in Art. 19 provides a tool for the implementation of the Bank's environmental and social policy. This tool is particularly effective as far as the host Member State is concerned by reason of the EIB's inability to finance, in whole or in part, any investment opposed by this State.[61] Instead, the Commission's unfavourable opinion may be ignored by the Board of Directors provided that it reaches unanimity, the director nominated by the Commission abstaining.[62]

59 'ESPS Statement', 58.

60 Those opinions are to be compulsorily sought but they are not binding insomuch as either they are released within two months or the Bank may proceed without after the above time-period has elapsed (Art. 19(2)).

61 EIB Statute, Art. 18(6).

62 EIB Statute, Art. 19(6). According to Art. 19(7), the Commission's negative opinion prevents the Bank from financing a project in absolute terms just if coupled with the negative opinion of the Bank's Management Committee. As this provision does not prescribe that the two oppositions to the project be backed by converging reasons, it may

On the basis of the various successive acts granting an EU guarantee to the EIB against losses under loans and loan guarantees for projects outside the Union, the consultation laid down in Art. 19 also applies to decisions pertaining to the external mandate, at least as far as the Commission is concerned.[63] Indeed, those acts provide that the Union guarantee shall not cover an EIB financing operation about which the Commission delivered an unfavourable opinion, so that the role of this institution under the external mandate proves to be more effective than in the framework of the internal mandate. Instead, no role is left to the non-Member State in whose territory the investment will be carried out. This confirms that the rationale behind the Art. 19 consultative contribution of the host State is merely financial, although the latter could well avail itself of this chance for the safeguard of general interests as pointed out above. Indeed, according to Art. 16(3), for loans to be granted to an undertaking or to a body other than a Member State, the guarantee of the host Member State is required. Conversely, in the framework of the external mandate, no guarantee of the host (non-member) State is required, such guarantee being ensured by the Union itself: accordingly, no opinion of such State should be delivered.

Also in the light of the above observations, one may wonder whether the enhanced role of the Commission in the decision-making applicable to external mandate financing operations should serve purely financial reasons or whether it may work as a tool to check the adherence of those financing operations to the EU external policy objectives, too. An argument in favour of the first option might be that, based on Art. 6(3) of decision 1080/2011, the consistency of the Bank's financing operations with the EU external policy objectives is to be monitored in accordance with Art. 11 of the same decision. However, this is apparently not a sound basis for excluding that further tools may be used in this connection. The rationale behind the extension of the consultative role of the Commission

well happen that the Commission's negative attitude based on environmental and/or social concerns halts the decision-making process of the Bank.

63 Decision 1080/2011/EU, Art. 6(3). An identical provision was also in decision 633/2009/EC of the European Parliament and of the Council of 13 July 2009, repealed by the former (there it was Art. 3(3)), and in Council decision 2006/1016/EC of 19 December 2006, annulled by the ECJ by its judgment of 6 November 2008 in Case C-155/07, *Parliament* v. *Council*, and later replaced by decision 1080/2011 (here it was Art. 3(3)). The Memorandum of Understanding between the EIB and the Commission of 26 May 2008, in respect of cooperation and coordination in the regions covered by Council decision 2006/1016/EC, reiterated Art. 3(3) of the latter (section 4.2.4). The MoU is published at www.eib.org.

in the Bank's decision-making to the latter's external mandate operations can be inferred from recital 4 of decision 1080/2011, which points out that the EU budgetary guarantee supporting this mandate is 'administered by the Commission'. Such administration may be deemed to cover both the financial side of the guarantee and the characteristics of the EIB operations selected for the support through it. According to Art. 1(2) of decision 1080/2011, the related eligibility includes three requirements: the EIB loans or loan guarantees should be granted for projects carried out in the countries listed in Annex III of the decision, in accordance with the EIB's own rules and procedures 'including the EIB's statement on social and environmental standards' and in support of the EU external policy objectives. Should one of those requirements prove unsatisfactory, a negative opinion from the Commission, in the framework of the EIB's decision-making, would well be feasible. All the more so because the 'European consensus on development' calls upon the Commission to ensure that all its services and delegations managing programming and implementation of Community development assistance use its own provisions 'as the key reference' for their action.

The Commission plays a prominent role also in the procedure specifically set up in the above-mentioned Art. 11 of decision 1080/2011 for monitoring the contribution of the EIB financing operations covered by the EU guarantee to the fulfilment of the latter's external policy objectives. It should produce an annual report to the European Parliament and to the Council on those operations which is to include an assessment of the above contribution, particularly 'the extent to which the EIB has taken into account environmental and social sustainability in the design and monitoring of the projects financed'.[64] Art. 11 is complemented by Art. 7(3), which obliges the EIB to submit to the Commission annual reports on the estimated development impact of the operations financed during the year.

The Commission may also take active steps to ensure the contribution of the EIB to the implementation of the Union external policy objectives. First, as it is empowered to adopt delegated acts amending Annex III on regions and countries eligible for EIB financing under EU guarantee, it may exclude those where democracy, human rights and fundamental freedoms are endangered. According to Art. 4(2) of decision 1080/2011, the Commission's decisions on the matter shall be based *inter alia* on this sort of assessment. A further tool entrusted to the Commission to the same

64 Art. 11(1).

aim is the development of regional technical operational guidelines in pursuance of Art. 6 of decision 1080/2011. Those guidelines aim precisely at that consistency purpose.[65] They should be developed by the Commission itself, together with the EIB, and should be transmitted to the European Parliament and to the Council. They set out the framework for the EIB to define its financing strategies and ensure their implementation.

The final remark is about the possibility for other stakeholders to influence the EIB's decision-making in such a way as to enhance or to safeguard the protection of local environment and communities. This possibility is provided for by the Social and Environmental Statement, which requires that Environmental Impact assessment (EIA) procedures be carried out for all projects potentially affecting the environment as a condition for the EIB's support. Moreover, decision 1080/2011 obliges the EIB, 'where appropriate and in line with Union social and environmental principles' to 'require the presence of appropriate local public consultation, on development-related aspects of projects covered by the EU guarantee'.[66]

6. Enforcing the non-financial mandate of the EIB: the role of the complaint mechanism and the Ombudsman...

Once loans or loan guarantees are granted, the actual adherence of supported projects to those non-financial values that they purportedly pursue and/or their adverse effects upon those values can be reviewed through a half internal/half external procedure known as the EIB CM. The half internal section of the CM is operated by the competent office of the Bank, the EIB Complaints Mechanism Division (the CM Division). The half external section, which can be activated only if the former proves unsatisfactory, is entrusted to the European Ombudsman (EO). The abovementioned MoU EIB/EO deals with the topic, which is also regulated by Principles, Terms of Reference and Rules of Procedure unilaterally adopted by the Bank.[67] Complaints can be lodged with the EO provided that they have exhausted the internal procedure.[68] The EO is not to make an entirely new assessment of the substantive questions that may have

65 Art. 6(1). 66 Art. 7(1).

67 See the document titled 'EIB Complaints Mechanism. Principles, Terms of Reference and Rules of Procedure', approved by the EIB Board of Directors in 2010 and revised in 2012. Published at www.eib.eu, this document is said to formalise the practice of the EIB Complaints Office with a view to strengthen the latter and to raise public awareness of the CM.

68 See 'EIB Complaints Mechanism', Part III – 6.1, and MoU EO/EIB, 2.IV.

been tackled by the CM Division on environmental, social and developmental matters, its role being to review 'whether the EIB has provided a consistent and reasonable explanation of its position in relation to such matters'.[69]

Such a two-tier procedure featuring an external component is unique among the accountability mechanisms active within MLIs since the last two decades, starting with the well-known World Bank Inspection Panel. Those mechanisms are entirely internal to the development bank they pertain to, because they are led or operated by individuals appointed by the banks' bodies, often beyond encompassing a role for staff members.[70] Nevertheless, their respective establishing instruments ensure that they act independently. Suffice it to say that the sole or the main body of all mechanisms always consists of individuals who should not be part of the related bank's governing bodies and should be selected among non-staff members. The role of the WB's officers within the accountability mechanisms at issue, if any, is limited to minor tasks and sometimes merely to administrative support. In any event, members of accountability mechanisms are usually required to act independently of the related bank's management.

The difference with the EIB CM in this connection is striking and it is completely dependent on the Bank's link with the EU. The CM Division, responsible for the internal section of the mechanism, entirely consists of Bank employees. As pointed out in the terms of reference, its independence relies on the fact that it is not responsible for operational activities of any kind and that it holds the status of an *ad hoc* department, being a part of the Inspectorate General of the Bank and under a functional responsibility of a Vice President. Therefore, despite this care in the designation of appropriate institutional features for the CM, it is thanks to the EO that the EIB's accountability mechanism aligns itself with the corresponding MLI's mechanisms. As compared to the latter, indeed the role of the EO is an added value for the EIB CM in terms of transparency, expertise and democratic control of the Bank's adherence to its mission. This is due to its link with the European Parliament.[71]

A major parallelism among all existing accountability mechanisms relates to the subject of the complaints which they are entrusted to deal with: whether MLIs have acted in accordance with their respective policies

69 MoU EO/EIB, 2, EO Declaration, 2.
70 For the sake of brevity examples are omitted.
71 See extensively Adam (1992), 928 ff. and more recently Romito (2011), 62.

and procedures 'with respect to the design, appraisal and/or implementation of a project'[72] financed by themselves, i.e. whether they accomplished their mission as established and regulated in their own internal policy documents. As all MLIs have introduced safeguards against abuses in the field of environmental sustainability and human rights of local communities, their accountability mechanisms end up contributing to the protection of those concerns. This is true also for the EIB CM, although its mission is indeed broader inasmuch as, mirroring the mandate of the EO in accordance with the EU Treaties, it is entrusted to detect maladministration of the EIB.[73] According to the definition reproduced in the EIB CM Principles, maladministration 'occurs when the EIB Group fails to act in accordance with the applicable legislation and/or established policies, standards and procedures', plus when it 'fails to respect the principles of good administration or violates human rights'.[74]

On the first set of standards, one main difference with other accountability mechanisms is that they should include legal rules.[75] Moreover, in several decisions on complaints against the EIB concerning the environmental impact of projects financed by the Bank, the EO pointed out that such projects should comply with both national and EU environmental law because this is required in the EIB's relevant policy documents. Accordingly, although it is not the task of the EO to check whether national authorities correctly applied national or European law, the latter ended up closely examining actions and omissions of those authorities particularly in the light of the 'EIA Directive'.[76] This practice shows that, based on clear references made in the EIB policy documents, the Bank's accountability mechanism is capable of reviewing also the latter's adherence to legal instruments otherwise not applicable to its activity. Furthermore, the concept of good administration – i.e. the second standard relevant under 'maladministration' – proved sometimes to lower, sometimes to raise the threshold potentially provided for by the requirements recalled

72 Quoted from resolution 'The World Bank Inspection Panel', section 12.

73 The EO's ownership of the mission to fight maladministration is due to the origin of this institution, which is inspired by a Scandinavian model subsequently spread all around the world: Condinanzi (2001), 701 ff.; Casolari (2006), 3607. The concept of maladministration within the EO cannot be fully investigated here. It has been outlined by the EO itself in its annual reports.

74 'EIB Complaints Mechanism', section 1.2.

75 See Pliakos (1994), 563; Casolari (2006), 3610; Romito (2011), 70.

76 Council Directive of 27 June 1985 on the assessment of the effects of certain public and private projects on the environment, 85/337/EEC, OJ L 175, 5 July 1985, 40, as amended.

before, thereby at the same time narrowing or broadening the scope of the protection ensured by the EIB policy documents. Examples are shown in the Polish 'Transport projects' case[77] and in the Polish 'Flood Damage Reconstruction II project' case,[78] on the one hand, and in the Spanish 'High-speed railway project' case,[79] on the other hand. In the Polish cases, the EO's concern was not to understand whether the Polish authorities had wrongfully implemented the EIA Directive but to ascertain whether 'the EIB could reasonably expect that the Polish authorities would act according to the spirit of the Europe Agreement and would not apply the national EIA procedure in a manner not consistent with EU law'[80] and whether the EIB could safely rely on some explanations given by those authorities. Consequently, in the 'Transport projects' case no instance of maladministration was found because, on the basis of the explanations received by the Polish authorities it was reasonable for the EIB to conclude that compliance of the Project with the national law was ensured.[81] Conversely, but based on an equivalent line of reasoning, in the 'Flood Damage Reconstruction II project' case the EIB was found to have committed an instance of maladministration because it failed to react to two reports of the Polish authorities where they appeared to have disregarded the EIA Directive procedure.[82] Instead, the Spanish 'High-speed railway project' case shows the opposite trend. There, regardless of the fact that the Spanish authorities carried out the EIA procedure properly, according to the EO good administrative practice required the EIB to document its review of that procedure appropriately.[83]

The accountability mechanisms of all MLIs mirror one another also with regards to their main purpose, which is to review the compliance of assisted projects with their policy documents. All of them may also engage in problem solving or mediation, with relevant differences concerning the flexibility between those two activities and the subjects – the complainant or the mechanism itself – enabled to select which should be preferred.[84]

77 Decision of the EO on complaint 1779/2006/MHZ against the EIB, 17 December 2007, www.ombudsman.europa.eu.

78 Decision of the EO on complaint 1807/2006/MHZ against the EIB, 17 December 2007, www.ombudsman.europa.eu.

79 Decision of the EO closing his inquiry into complaint 244/2006/(BM)JMA against the EIB, 4 May 2009, www.ombudsman.europa.eu.

80 Decision 1807/2006/MHZ, 1.3.

81 Decision 1779/2006/MHZ, 2.15–17.

82 Decision 1807/2006/MHZ, 1.16.

83 Decision 244/2006/(BM)JMA, 29–31 and 51–3.

84 The EIB CM is 'compliance focussed', but for each admissible complaint it shall determine if, beyond the compliance, there is room for problem solving and/or mediation: 'EIB Complaints Mechanism', chapter III, section 1.2.

Another close similarity of the mechanisms under discussion is the outcome of their compliance review, which is typically a report in which they describe the results and often make recommendations with no binding effects upon the banks' management. The existing differences raise no particular interest here because they are not apparently due to structural/institutional reasons. Above all, they are not such as to oppose the EIB to the other MLIs.

A further major similarity among the accountability mechanisms is that they are available to private parties only. Therefore, States hosting projects supported by MLIs are unable to take advantage of the institutional procedures designed to provide protection in case those projects adversely affect local environment and communities.

Focusing on the private parties eligible to trigger the above mechanisms, the latter differ either as to whether they allow some sort of *actio popularis* or not, or as to whether they are open to individual complainants beyond groups or not.

The EIB's CM is surely at the forefront in all respects. First and foremost, it allows a sort of *actio popularis*: 'Any person or group, including civil society organisations, who allege there may be a case of maladministration within the EIB Group, can lodge a complaint.'[85] The same applies to complaints lodged with the EO in connection with those previously dealt with the CM Division, which have not allegedly been dealt with 'in a timely and/or in correct manner':[86] as recalled in the Rules of Procedures, complainants can take action 'in accordance with Article 228 of the Treaty on the Functioning of the European Union *and regardless of a direct concern in the alleged maladministration*'.[87] That paves the way to requests from non-governmental organisations, as shown in practice.[88] Moreover, individuals – not just groups or legal persons – are eligible to take action: they will typically (but not necessarily) take advantage of this possibility in case projects supported by the EIB have directly and materially damaged them.[89] It is noteworthy that the MoU between the EO and

85 'EIB Complaints Mechanism', chapter IV, section 2.1. See Casolari (2006), 3607.

86 'EIB Complaints Mechanism', chapter V, section 1.1.

87 *Ibid.* (emphasis added).

88 In the two Polish cases referred to before, the complainant was a Polish NGO dealing with environmental issues named *Polska Zielona Siec*.

89 This happened in the Spanish case referred to above, where the individual complainant – while arguing that the segment of the high-speed railway project going through Barcelona, 'by means of several tunnels between the stations of *Sants* and *Sagrera*, could cause serious social and environmental damage, including noise and vibrations, which

the Bank provides a remedy to the problem that, in accordance with Art. 228 TFEU, just EU citizens or natural or legal persons residing or having their registered office in an EU Member State can complain to the EO. This rule would have prevented the availability of the CM's highest tier in connection with projects carried out in the framework of the EIB's external mandate. Therefore, with the objective to 'raise the bar' in relation to stakeholders' engagement and protection as regards the EIB's activities and, in particular, to extend such protection to physical and legal persons who are not citizens or residents of one of the Member States of the EU, or who do not have a registered office in one of the EU Member States,[90] the EO is committed to use its own power of initiative to open an inquiry 'whenever the only reason not to inquire into a complaint alleging maladministration by the EIB is that the complainant is not a citizen or a resident of the EU'.[91]

A look at the accountability mechanisms of the other MLIs shows that, as to the admissibility of *actio popularis*, the EIB's CM is indebted to the EO. Indeed, no other MLI allows it, so that the related rule within the EIB can be deemed to have been inspired by Art. 228 TFEU, which required coordination. The other accountability mechanisms are open to applicants whose rights or interests have been or are likely to be directly affected by an act or omission of the relevant bank in connection with the assisted project[92] or, in the cases of the EBRD's PCM and the Asian DB's Office of the Special Project Facilitator (OSPF), to applicants to whom such project caused, or is likely to cause, a harm.[93] However,

might endanger the nearby buildings and be a nuisance for their inhabitants' – noted that 'he would be one of the citizens whose home would be affected by the project' (decision 244/2006/(BM)JMA, 10). It is worth observing that, even when a complainant would have *locus standi* to lodge his/her complaint anyway, the advantage of *actio popularis* is that he/she need not provide evidence of his/her situation.

90 MoU EO/EIB, section 1.

91 MoU EO/EIB, section 2. See also 'EIB Complaints Mechanism', chapter III, section 6.3.

92 Resolution 'The World Bank Inspection Panel', section 12; IDB, 'Policy Establishing the ICIM', section 38 (concerning the Consultation Phase) and section 53 (concerning the Compliance Review Phase); 'African DB-African DF', 'Resolution Instituting the IRM', section 11. Within the African DB's IRM, the determination of a 'prima facie evidence that the affected parties have been harmed or threatened with harm by a Bank Group-financed project' is part of the eligibility assessment (*ibid.*, section 22). As to the WB Inspection Panel, on the restrictions originating from the concept of 'affected party' see Shihata (1994), 54–7.

93 Concerning the EBRD's PCM, this requirement applies to complaints pertaining to both the 'Problem-solving Initiative' (PCM: Rules of Procedure, section 18 c)) and the 'Compliance Review' (*ibid.*, section 19 b)). As to the Asian DB's OSPF, the relevant information is published on adb.org.

the fact that those mechanisms extend their scope to potential adverse effects or harm, 'raises the bar' of the protection that they provide to private stakeholders.[94]

Last, the EIB's CM is available also to individuals. The same rule is laid down within the IDB's ICIM and within the EBRD's PCM,[95] while all other mechanisms are open to collective complaints only.

7. ... and the role of the CJEU

The CJEU has jurisdiction on claims against the EIB in accordance with Art. 271 TFEU. In this section the possibility that this may help safeguard environmental and social concerns adversely affected or not duly protected by the Bank's action will be explored. Attention will also be devoted to the possibility that other provisions of the TFEU on the CJEU may serve the same purpose.

Starting with Art. 271, both decisions implementing the external and the internal mandate are eligible for review by the Court: Art. 271(*b*) and (*c*) respectively allows actions against decisions of the Board of Governors and the Board of Directors under the conditions laid down in Art. 263 TFEU on legality review. A main difference can be detected though. While no restrictions concerning the grounds of illegality are laid down for actions against decisions of the Board of Governors (Art. 271(*b*)), the decisions of the Board of Directors can be questioned solely for non-compliance with the procedure established in Art. 19(2), (5), (6) and (7) of the EIB Statute. These include the provisions on the consultative role of the Commission and the host State, with the exception of the prohibition on the Bank to finance investments opposed by the latter, which is laid down in Art. 18(6). As a result, the judicial review of EIB's financing operations on substantial grounds is admissible just in the framework of the external mandate, being the decisions of the Board of Governors on financing limited to investments to be carried out, in whole or in part, outside the territories of Member States.[96]

Claims against the decisions of the Board of Governors can be brought by Member States, the Commission and the Board of Directors, while the

94 See Seatzu (2008), 209, who underlines the parallelism between the requirement of actual harm and that of potential harm.

95 IDB, 'Policy Establishing the ICIM', section 30; EBRD, 'PCM: Rules of Procedure', sections 1–2.

96 Art. 7(2)(*d*) and Art. 16(1), which establishes that the Board of Governors should act 'at a qualified majority on a proposal from the Board of Directors'.

annulment of the latter's decisions can be sought by a Member State and the Commission only.

The question arises as to whether Art. 271 is to be regarded as an exception to Art. 263, which lays down broader rules on the matter. Indeed, Art. 263 potentially covers claims against the EIB's decisions on loans and loan guarantees because among the reviewable acts it includes 'acts of bodies, offices or agencies of the Union intended to produce legal effects vis-à-vis third parties' (par. 1). Art. 271(*b*) and (*c*) would establish an exception to Art. 263 inasmuch as they do not grant the capacity to bring proceedings to institutional actors such as the Parliament and the Council, they leave aside natural and legal persons and they narrow down the grounds of review as reported above.

Since the provisions in Art. 271(*b*) and (*c*) are contained in the more general Art. 263(2) and (3), the former cannot but be regarded as *lex specialis* to the latter, laid down with the purpose of limiting the institutional actors capable of bringing actions against decisions of the EIB and the related grounds of review by reason of the special status of the Bank. Conversely, Art. 271 does not apparently affect non-institutional actors.[97] The first argument in support of such conclusion is that it does not even mention natural and legal persons, while following the amendments to Art. 263 introduced by the Treaty of Lisbon,[98] the action for annulment against acts of 'bodies, offices and agencies of the Union' is in principle open to the above subjects. Consequently, the total preclusion of the latter from taking advantage of the annulment action would require an explicit provision. Second, Art. 263(5) leaves room to special rules on actions for legality review taken by such actors against bodies, offices and agencies of the Union, but indeed not to their exclusion. Last, such exclusion would be patently in contrast with Art. 47 of the Charter of Fundamental rights of the European Union, on the right of everyone 'whose rights and freedoms guaranteed by the law of the Union are violated' to an effective remedy before a tribunal.

97 Likewise, in Marchegiani (2012), 76, it is stated as follows: 'it seems by now undisputable that judicial actions under Arts. 263 and 265 TFEU can also be lodged by natural and legal persons against any measure adopted by any decision-making body of the Bank which is intended to produce legal effects vis-à-vis those persons'.

98 The Treaty of Lisbon introduced in Art. 263 the last sentence at 1 ('[The CJEU] shall also review the legality of acts of bodies, offices or agencies of the Union intended to produce legal effects vis-à-vis third parties') and at 5 ('Acts setting up bodies, offices and agencies of the Union may lay down specific conditions and arrangements concerning actions brought by natural or legal persons against acts of these bodies, offices or agencies intended to produce legal effects in relation to them').

However, the further question arises as to the actual feasibility of the action for annulment as a remedy against adverse effects on local environment and/or local communities and/or individual rights for natural and legal persons different from the recipients of EIB financial support. Indeed, the CJEU pointed out that '[t]he EIB … does not adopt decisions having legal effects vis-à-vis third parties who are not in receipt of EIB loans or guarantees'.[99] In other words, those subjects would never be in the position described in Art. 263(1) TFEU. In addition, they would never be in the position described in Art. 263(4) either: since projects producing adverse effects are usually implemented following the decision of a local authority, they could never be of direct concern to 'third parties who are not in receipt of EIB loans or guarantees'.[100] The two above observations would lead to the conclusion that the subjects under consideration would never be able to institute proceedings against the EIB before the CJEU. Along with the impossibility for non-governmental organisations to lodge claims, which emerges from the well-established Court's case-law, such conclusion would seriously compromise the effectiveness of the judicial remedy as a tool to enforce the protection of human rights and the environment.

On the first obstacle identified by the Tribunal it could be observed that decisions of the EIB which infringe natural and legal persons' rights established in the Charter of fundamental rights and/or in the TFEU do have legal effects vis-à-vis those parties. Differently, it is true that third parties are not directly affected by the EIB's decisions, their alleged harm stemming from decisions approving the project and not from those providing support to it. Those allegedly harmed by a project financed by the EIB should consequently lodge their claims before a national court. However, it is also true that, should the EIB's financial support prove essential to the implementation of the project, the CJEU could positively assess the requirement of being 'directly concerned' with a decision of the EIB. The Court should elaborate criteria in this connection.

The fact that the EIB's decisions are not usually of direct concern to third parties is also an obstacle to actions for damages.

As to the further requirement that third parties should be 'individually concerned' with a decision of the EIB, it obviously prevents *actio popularis*,

99 Case T-460/93, *Étienne Tête* v. *EIB* [1993] ECR II-1258, 18.

100 In *Étienne Tête*, the Court noted that '[o]nly the decisions taken by the various French authorities with a view to the construction of the ring road in question, for example compulsory-purchase decisions, are liable to affect the applicants' legal situation' (fn 99) 22.

including the lodging of claims by non-governmental organisations,[101] and leaves room just to claimants whose position vis-à-vis projects is different to that of anyone else. To draw a parallel with the practice of the EIB's CM, in principle, a resident of the area where a motorway financed by the EIB is under construction, particularly if his/her health is adversely affected by the project, might be in such a position.

8. Conclusions

The above analysis shows that the EIB's link to the EU does make a difference for its environmental and social accountability in comparison with that of the other MLIs.[102]

First, the Bank's mandate includes the protection of the environment and human rights and, at the same time, the Bank is subject to clear obligations in both fields, which projects financed by it should not infringe, whatever purpose they serve. To stress this point, the Bank's obligation of due diligence established in Art. 7 of the decision on the EU guarantee applicable to external mandate operations should be recalled. According to due diligence, '[t]he Bank as a whole is called on to devote attention to its environmental and social mandate'.

Not only do the close links to the EU result in obligations and constraints for the EIB in the fields of environmental and human rights protection. Thanks to such obligations and constraints laid down in the EU treaties and in EU secondary legislation, the Bank's conduct in disregard of its non financial mandate or resulting in adverse effects on the local communities and environment may be subject to judicial review. That would not be possible on the basis of the sole policy documents which, as also the EO noted, are not a source of legal obligations.[103] In more detail, should a Bank's decision prove to be in contrast with the above obligations, it may be annulled by the CJEU on grounds of 'infringement of the Treaties or of any rule of law relating to their application'.[104]

101 Case C-321/95 P, *Stichting Greenpeace Council (Greenpeace International) and Others v. Commission of the European Communities* [1998] ECR I-1702.

102 In my view, this remains true despite 'more advantage should be taken of the EIB's being part of the EU legal order to guarantee effective accountability to external stakeholders': Hachez and Wouters (2012), 95. The fact that this conclusion is well-founded clearly emerges from a number of points made in the present chapter.

103 Decision of the EO on complaint 1807/2006/MHZ, 1.5.

104 Art. 263(2) TFEU.

While third parties adversely affected by the Bank's action have limited access to the Court, if any, the Commission is in the position to trigger judicial control. Given that the role of this institution within the EU is focused on ensuring 'the application of the Treaties' and 'of Union law', the protection of human rights and the environment in connection with possible infringements of the related provisions of EU law originated from the EIB's financing operations is firmly in the Commission's hands. Consequently, thanks to the strong links between the Bank and the Union, the accountability of the former in terms of judicial control is mostly, if not only, internal to the Union. In other words, it is an accountability vis-à-vis its shareholders more than vis-à-vis its stakeholders. Moreover, the Commission is in the position to carry out an *ex ante facto* control over the implementation of the non-financial interests included in the Bank's mandate which is surely unparalleled in any other MLI. This is undoubtedly an added value of the EIB being part of the 'EU family' and, again, it is a feature of the internal accountability of the Bank.

States in whose territory the projects supported by the EIB are carried out are also involved both in the *ex ante facto control* and in the triggering of judicial protection.

However, remarkable differences are to be noticed among member and non-Member States. The latter are excluded from the decision-making process and they can lodge complaints with the CJEU as 'legal persons' within the meaning of Art. 263 TFEU, whereas Member States fall within the scope of Art. 271.

The protection of human rights and the environment in connection with the EIB's financial operations benefits from the Bank's close links to the EU also as far as its non-judiciary accountability mechanism is concerned. The role of the EO therein is surely an added value both for its overall role within the Union and for including *actio popularis*. Since the CM is the sole real tool for the Bank's external accountability, this is of utmost importance.

As a last point, despite its status as a self-standing MLI with its own legal personality, the fact that the EIB is bound to the Union's objectives brings about a further feature with no correspondence in similar financial Institutions. The latter are usually keen on maintaining their neutrality vis-à-vis host States on policy grounds. Conversely, the EIB is bound to political considerations before granting a loan or a loan guarantee. In the framework of the external mandate, '[t]he Bank does not finance projects located in countries declared "off-limits" by the European Council for EU financing, particularly due to violations of human rights'.[105] Nor does it finance projects 'that give rise to conflicts or intensify existing conflicts'.[106] Moreover, the EU guarantee covering projects outside the Union relies on a dual list of countries, one containing those potentially eligible for EIB financing under EU guarantee (Annex II) and one including countries actually eligible for such financing (Annex III), which is based of the former. The Commission is empowered to amend the Annex III list, based on an economic *and political* assessment, 'including aspects related to the democracy, human rights and fundamental freedoms as well as the relevant European Parliament resolutions and Council decisions and conclusions' (Art. 4(1) and (2)).

References

Adam, R. 1992. 'Il Mediatore europeo: organo di tutela del singolo o strumento di controllo parlamentare?'. *Rivista internazionale dei diritti dell'uomo* 5: 928–35.

Cafaro, S. 2011. 'Le banche internazionali'. *Enciclopedia del diritto, Annali*. Milano: Giuffré editore: 171–91.

Cahn, J. 1993. 'Challenging the New Imperial Authority: The World Bank and the Democratization of Development'. *Harvard Human Rights Journal* 6: 159–94.

Casolari, F. 2006. 'Mediatore europeo', Cassese, S. (ed.), *Dizionario di Diritto pubblico*. Milano: Giuffré editore, IV: 3607–12.

Condinanzi, M. 2001. 'Art. 195 TCE', Pocar, F. (ed.), *Commentario breve ai Trattati dell'Unione e della Comunità europea*. Padova: Cedam: 701–4.

De Sena, P. 2011. 'Fondo monetario internazionale, Banca mondiale e rispetto dei diritti dell'uomo'. Ligustro, A. and Sacerdoti, G. (eds.), *Problemi e tendenze del diritto internazionale dell'economia*. Liber amicorum *in onore di Paolo Picone*. Napoli: Editoriale Scientifica: 829–58.

Ghazi, B. 2005. *The IMF, the World Bank Group and the Question of Human Rights*. New York: Transnational Publishers.

Hachez, N. and Wouters, J. 2012. 'A Responsible Lender? The European Investment Bank's Environmental, Social and Human Rights Accountability'. *Common Market Law Review* 49: 47–96.

Honohan, P. 1995. 'The Public Policy Role of the European Investment Bank within the EU'. *Journal of Common Market Studies* 33: 315–30.

Maldonado, N. 2010. 'The World Bank's Evolving Concept of Good Governance and Its Impact on Human Rights'. Unpublished paper presented at the

105 'ESPS Statement', 46. 106 *Ibid.*, 47.

doctoral workshop on development and international organizations, www2.warwick.ac.uk.

Marchegiani, G. 2012. 'The European Investment Bank after the Treaty of Lisbon'. *European Law Review* 37: 70–8.

Pliakos, A. 1994. 'Le Médiateur de l'Union européenne'. *Cahiers de droit européen* 30: 563–606.

Robinson, N. 2009. 'The European Investment Bank: The EU's Neglected Institution'. *Journal of Common Market Studies* 47: 651–73.

Rodgers, P.A. 1990. 'Looking a Gift Horse in the Mouth: The World Bank and Environmental Accountability'. *Georgetown Environmental Law Review* 3: 437–56.

Romito, A.M. 2011. 'Il Mediatore europeo nel Trattato di Lisbona', Triggiani, E. (ed.), *Le nuove frontiere della cittadinanza europea*. Bari: Cacucci: 61–84.

Sarfaty, G.A. 2009. 'Why Culture Matters in International Institutions: The Marginality of Human Rights at the World Bank'. *American Journal of International Law* 103: 647–83.

Seatzu, F. 2008. *Il Panel di ispezione della Banca mondiale. Contributo allo studio della funzione di controllo nelle banche internazionali di sviluppo*. Torino: Giappichelli.

Shihata, I.F.I. 1991. *The World Bank in a Changing World. Selected Essays*. Dordrecht: Martinus Nijhoff Publishers.

1994. *The World Bank Inspection Panel*. Oxford University Press.

PART IV

The protection of general interests of host States in the trade and investment context: other regional perspectives

15

The protection of general interests of host States in regional agreements in the Asia-Pacific Area*

CLAUDIO DORDI AND HAI YEN TRINH

1. Introduction

This chapter analyzes the provisions to improve regulatory discretion of member States included in regional investment agreements of the Asia-Pacific region. The analysis will be limited to the regional agreements only, excluding the Bilateral Investment Treaties which, in general, do not contain relevant derogatory provisions.[1] In this context, a central role is played by the Association of South East Asian Nations (ASEAN) that, since 1987, promoted the conclusion of an Investment Guarantee Agreement among the six States that were at the time members of ASEAN.[2] However, only after the conclusion of the ASEAN Charter in 2008, which provided a more solid institutional profile to ASEAN as well as the international legal personality,[3] ASEAN concluded a number of investment agreements: the ASEAN Comprehensive Investment Agreement (among ASEAN members), and a number of agreements with third countries (China, Korea, Australia and New Zealand). All the agreements are focused exclusively on investment, with the exception of the agreement with Australia and New Zealand, which is part of a more comprehensive free trade agreement.

2. Heterogeneity of states and fragmented trade and investment agreements in the region

The main features of regional investment agreements in the Asia-Pacific region (as defined in the introduction above) reflect the heterogeneity and the dynamism of the countries involved as well as the huge differences among their legal systems.[4] Indeed, in the region there are well-established

* Select material for this chapter is based on Trinh Hai Yen, 'The Interpretation of Investment Treaties: Problems and Solutions' (Brill/Nijhoff, forthcoming 2014).

1 Ranjan (2009), 217–219. 2 Desierto (2012), 1–3.

3 Chesterman (2008), 1–5. 4 Malanczuk (2008), 1.

developed countries (Japan, Australia, New Zealand and, of course, the US), relatively new developed States (Singapore, South Korea), developing countries at a quite advanced stage of economic development (China, Thailand, Malaysia, Indonesia), countries which are stuck in the so-called middle-income development trap (Philippines and, likely, Vietnam) and, finally, countries still struggling to escape from the bottom line of economic development (Cambodia, Laos and Myanmar). The ASEAN countries feature also different political, legal and economic systems. All the spectrum of economic organizations is covered: from advanced market economies (US and Singapore) to socialist-(market) oriented economies (China and Vietnam). Last, it should be considered that some countries of the region, traditionally seen as capital-importing, showed a progressive increase in investment outflows (e.g., China, Malaysia and Indonesia).[5]

The main consequence of the above-mentioned situation is the legal fragmentation of most of the regional Asia-Pacific treaties dealing with economic issues (trade and investment); indeed, these treaties are characterized by a list of sectors excluded from the scope of the agreements, provisions to ensure the special and differential treatment for less developed countries, special derogations for least developed members and systems of "modular" commitments for States depending on their economic development. For example, all the ASEAN Free Trade Agreements (the ASEAN FTA and the five other FTAs concluded by ASEAN with, respectively, China, South Korea, Japan, India, Australia and New Zealand) provide different obligations and deadlines for trade liberalization of the most advanced countries (Singapore, Brunei, Thailand, Indonesia, Malaysia and Philippines and the non-ASEAN counterparts) and the four less advanced (the so-called CMLV countries, i.e., Cambodia, Myanmar, Laos and Vietnam). The number of exemptions and exceptions specifically tailor-made to the exigencies of the members as well as the extensive use of reservations produced a sort of bi-lateralization of the obligations of the regional agreements:[6] in the ASEAN–China FTA, for example, the level of liberalizations provided in China's schedule of commitments is applicable to individual ASEAN members only on a reciprocity basis.

While States of the Asia-Pacific concluded a high number of BITs, with the exceptions of the Trans Pacific Partnership Agreement, ASEAN is the only entity in the region having promoted the conclusion of regional investment agreements, i.e., the ASEAN Comprehensive Investment Agreement (ACIA), the two external investment agreements with Korea

5 UNCTAD (2012), 5. 6 Yen (2011), 183–185.

and China and Chapter 11, focused on investment, of the ASEAN–Australia and New Zealand Free Trade Agreement.

3. The long tradition of ASEAN regional investment agreements

The Association of South East Asian Nations (ASEAN) is a dynamic international organization, created in 1967 and presently participated by ten countries. Known for its loose approach to integration, the so-called "ASEAN way," is based on: "a strict interpretation of the principle of non-interference in the domestic affairs of the other ASEAN members," emphasizing the "informal efforts looking for consensus and relying on confidence-building, instead of moving forward through legally binding and enforceable commitments or agreements."[7] ASEAN members have been quite active in negotiating and concluding a number of trade and investment agreements. The ASEAN agreements have some peculiar features: first, only ASEAN member States are part of the agreement and not the organization. Indeed, as thoroughly discussed in the doctrine, at least before the conclusion of the ASEAN Charter in 2008 (but even afterwards), the legal international personality of ASEAN was highly questioned.[8] Second, the trade agreements concluded by ASEAN members do not contain provisions focused on investment, with the exception of the mentioned Chapter 11 of the ASEAN–Australia and New Zeland FTA. Third, ASEAN members were among the first countries to experience a regional investment agreement (i.e., a non-bilateral investment treaty).

Indeed, the first investment agreement in the region was concluded in 1987 (the ASEAN Investment Guarantee Agreement – IGA) and it was participated by six States which at that time were members of ASEAN. IGA was an agreement with a wide scope of application, with standard clauses on fair and equitable treatment and Most Favored Nation and National Treatment. The agreement was particularly generous in terms of repatriation of capital and earnings of FDIs and it provided standard procedures for settling disputes, both for State disputes (the party could submit the dispute to the ASEAN Economic Ministers, where decisions were taken with consensus, after the amicable solution did not succeed) and State–investors disputes (where amicable solution and conciliation were not practicable, the ICSID or UNCITRAL arbitration was made

7 Malanczuk (2008), fn. 3. 8 Chesterman (2008), 199–201.

available). After a Protocol concluded in 1996 which modified the original text of the IGA (among others, the Protocol added the newly created ASEAN Dispute Settlement Procedure to the other dispute settlement systems already provided), ASEAN members, deeply affected by the financial crisis, concluded in 1998 a new Framework ASEAN Investment Agreement (AIA) introducing a number of restrictions on the protection of other investment from ASEAN members. In particular, the new agreement reduced the scope of application of IGA, limiting the extension of the investment and ASEAN investors covered by the agreement. Moreover, the AIA introduced flexibility for the application of the National Treatment provision for the new ASEAN members (which are also the less developed – i.e., Cambodia, Laos, Myanmar and Vietnam) and further restrictions to the application of National Treatment provision through a list of temporary excluded sectors and a list of sensitive sectors. Furthermore, the AIA introduced a number of exceptions to the protection granted by the agreement, i.e., general exceptions modeled on Art. XX of GATT, emergency safeguard measures as well as balance of payment restrictions.

After the entry into force of the ASEAN Charter, on December 15, 2008, a number of new international investment agreements were concluded in 2009 by ASEAN members: the ACIA (ASEAN Comprehensive Investment Agreement), the ASEAN–China, the ASEAN–Korea and the Chapter 11 of the mentioned ASEAN–Australia and New Zealand Free Trade Agreement. As mentioned above, ASEAN is not part of these agreements, as only ASEAN individual member States (and third countries) are contracting parties.[9] Another investment agreement with India was concluded in December 2012 but is not yet in force. Moreover, a number of ASEAN members (Brunei, Singapore, Vietnam and Malaysia) are part of the Trans Pacific Partnership (TPP) ongoing negotiations. TPP will include a chapter dedicated to investment.

4. Background of ASEAN investment agreements

Only in 2008 the members decided to provide ASEAN with international legal personality through the conclusion of the ASEAN Charter (Art. 3). ASEAN members committed, according to Art. 5.2 of the ASEAN Charter, to take all necessary measures, including the enactment of appropriate domestic legislation, to effectively implement the provisions of the

9 Cfr. Art. 41.4 of the ASEAN Charter.

Charter and to comply with all obligations of membership. Although some ASEAN members still have not completed the transition to a full-fledged market-economy, the provisions in Art. 2 (n) of the Charter obliges the members to adhere "to multilateral trade rules and ASEAN's rules-based regimes for effective implementation of economic commitments and progressive reduction towards elimination of all barriers to regional economic integration, in a market-driven economy." The ASEAN Charter set up a number of organs (the ASEAN Summit, the ASEAN Coordinating Council and the ASEAN Community Councils) and formalized the existence of the ASEAN Secretariat.

Limiting the analysis to the economic-related topics, the main objective of the ASEAN Charter (Art. 1.5) is that to "create a single market and production base which is stable, prosperous, highly competitive and economically integrated with effective facilitation for trade and investment in which there is free flow of goods, services and investment; facilitated movement of business persons, professionals, talents and labour; and freer flow of capital." These objectives shall be achieved within the framework of another ASEAN agreement, the ASEAN Economic Community Blueprint, setting the agenda and the deadlines of the measures to be implemented.

All the investment agreements concluded after the entry into force of the ASEAN Charter reflect the general principles enshrined in the Blueprint, which are, in general, in line with the recognized principles of international investment law. It is not within the scope of this chapter to analyze all the provisions of the Blueprint related to investment; the Blueprint is particularly focused on Investment protection to all investors, facilitation, cooperation among members and liberalization.

5. ACIA and other ASEAN agreements: the result of a longstanding experience in including exceptions in regional investment agreements

All the ASEAN investment agreements include provisions leaving member States discretion to apply domestic regulatory measures. Indeed the Framework ASEAN Investment Agreement (AIA) concluded in 1998 already included a number of exceptions which have been lately reproduced in the investment agreements concluded after the ASEAN Charter. As pointed out above, the local doctrine clarified that the precocity of ASEAN members in limiting the protection afforded to foreign investors to increase the reserved domain of States was the direct effect of the financial crisis,[10] which forced ASEAN members to include a number of restrictive provisions in the AIA. Indeed, the comparison between the IGA (1988) and the AIA (1998) is paradigmatic as it shows how a group of States reacted, in an investment agreement, after a severe financial crisis. Indeed, in the AIA there can be found a list of measures which have the consequence of restricting the openness towards foreign investors. Most of the restrictive provisions applied in the AIA have been lately reproduced in the ACIA and in all the other regional agreements participated in by ASEAN members. The following subsections will analyze the provisions of ASEAN investment agreements which carve out space for regulatory discretion of member States, therefore extending their ability to achieve legitimate policy objectives.[11]

5.1 Elements to increase the regulatory discretion in the preamble of the agreements

The preamble of most of the ASEAN investment agreements, which is a well-known support to interpret treaty provisions, includes reference showing the intention of members to widen their regulatory discretion; first, all the agreements (i.e., ACIA, ASEAN–China and ASEAN–Korea and the preamble of the ASEAN–Australia and New Zealand FTA) recognize in the preamble the "different stages and pace of development among the parties and the need for special and differential treatment and flexibility for the newer ASEAN Member States."[12] A more clear reference to the regulatory discretion of members can be found in the preamble of the

10 Besides the legal instruments aimed at regulating investment, right after the financial crisis ASEAN implemented a number of measures to control the movement of capital. Indeed, three main measures have been implemented: the "ASEAN Surveillance Process," i.e., "a framework for closer consultations on economic policies," the ASEAN+3 Financial Cooperation, consisting of regular consultations between ASEAN countries and China, Japan and Korea, and The Chiang Mai Initiative, set up by the ASEAN+3 finance ministers consisting of "an expanded ASEAN Swap Arrangement and a network of bilateral swap arrangements among ASEAN countries, China, Japan and the Republic of Korea." Quotation from the document "ASEAN Response to the Financial Crisis," www.aseansec.org/7660.htm.

11 Mann (2007), 1–17, introduced an interesting system of classification of restricting provisions usually included in international investment treaties. This chapter partially adopts that system of classification.

12 Preamble of the Agreement on Investment of the Framework Agreement on Comprehensive Economic Cooperation between the Association of Southeast Asian Nations and the People's Republic of China, www.asean.org/22974.pdf. The other agreements mentioned in the text show similar provisions.

ASEAN–China investment agreement, where the parties reaffirmed the commitment to establish the ASEAN–China FTA, "while allowing flexibility … to address their sensitive areas as provided in the Framework Agreement, in the realization of the sustainable economic growth and development goals on the basis of the equality and mutual benefits so as to achieve a win-win outcome." It should be noted that the definition of "sustainable development" included in the ASEAN–China Investment Agreement diverges from the commonly shared interpretation of "sustainable development" terms developed since the well-known Declaration of Rio of 1992 and mainly referring to sustainable environmental development or, as in the last generation of FTA concluded by the EU, extended also to some social-related topics.

5.2 *Regulatory measure provisions included in the text*

The ASEAN investment agreements do not contain regulatory measure provisions. This definition identifies a statement similar to the following provided in Art. 43 of the ESFTA (EFTA–Singapore Free Trade Agreement) signed in 2002:[13] "nothing in this Chapter shall be construed to prevent a Party from adopting, maintaining or enforcing any measure consistent with this Chapter that is in the public interest, such as measures to meet health, safety or environmental concerns." This provision mirrors the well-known NAFTA Art. 1114 and similar provisions of a number of FTAs participated in by the US and Canada. However, differently from Art. 1114 of NAFTA, the scope of Art. 43 goes beyond the environmental concerns, covering also the health and safety-related measures.[14]

5.3 *Limitations on the scope of expropriation*

ACIA includes special provisions interpreting the commitments on expropriation and compensation modeled on the interpretation of expropriation provisions provided in Annex B of the US Model BIT[15] with two substantial differences: first, the ACIA does not refer (as in the US Model

13 The ESFTA entered into force January 1, 2003. See www.fta.gov.sg/fta_esfta.asp?hl=11.

14 Article 1114 of NAFTA states that "nothing in this Chapter shall be construed to prevent a Party from adopting, maintaining or enforcing any measure otherwise consistent with this chapter that it considers appropriate to ensure that investment activity in its territory is undertaken in a manner sensitive to environmental concerns."

15 See US Model Bilateral Investment Treaty, Annex B, Expropriation www.ustr.gov/sites/default/files/BIT%20text%20for%20ACIEP%20Meeting.pdf. Here following the text:

BIT) to the fact that the article on expropriation and compensation "is intended to reflect customary international law concerning the obligation of States with respect to expropriation." Second, the application of non-discriminatory measures by an ACIA member aimed "to protect legitimate public welfare objectives, such as public health, safety and the environment" do not constitute an indirect expropriation; in the US Model BIT this provision is more flexible as it recognizes the existence of "rare circumstances" where the cases described above might be considered an indirect expropriation.

It is interesting to note that the ASEAN–China (Art. 8.4) and the ASEAN–Korea (Art. 12.4) investment agreements foresee the application of the domestic laws of the expropriating party to the measures regarding the expropriation of lands, which is an exception to the normal regime usually adopted for expropriation in the IIA. Chapter 11 of the ASEAN–Australia and New Zealand agreement includes a similar provision in Art. 9.6.[16]

The Parties confirm their shared understanding that:

1. Article 6 [Expropriation and Compensation] (1) is intended to reflect customary International law concerning the obligation of States with respect to expropriation.
2. An action or a series of actions by a Party cannot constitute an expropriation unless it interferes with a tangible or intangible property right or property interest in an investment.
3. Article 6 [Expropriation and Compensation] (1) addresses two situations. The first is direct expropriation, where an investment is nationalized or otherwise directly expropriated through formal transfer of title or outright seizure.
4. The second situation addressed by Article 6 [Expropriation and Compensation] (1) is indirect expropriation, where an action or series of actions by a Party has an effect equivalent to direct expropriation without formal transfer of title or outright seizure.

(a) The determination of whether an action or series of actions by a Party, in a specific fact situation, constitutes an indirect expropriation, requires a case-by-case, fact-based inquiry that considers, among other factors:
   (i) the economic impact of the government action, although the fact that an action or series of actions by a Party has an adverse effect on the economic value of an investment, standing alone, does not establish that an indirect expropriation has occurred;
   (ii) the extent to which the government action interferes with distinct, reasonable investment-backed expectations; and
   (iii) the character of the government action.

(b) Except in rare circumstances, non-discriminatory regulatory actions by a Party that are designed and applied to protect legitimate public welfare objectives, such as public health, safety, and the environment, do not constitute indirect expropriations.

16 This particular exception has been included to acknowledge the specific regime of real estate rights in the two countries. It enlightens the situation of real estate rights

5.4 *Exclusions through annexes*

The effective scope of application of the investment agreements and, therefore, the extent of the regulatory discretion of the hosting State in the region largely depends on the presence of annexes listing sectors which are completely or partially excluded from the application of part or the entire agreement. The ACIA, the ASEAN–Korea agreement and Chapter 11 of the ASEAN–Australia and New Zealand FTA include an article on "reservations" leaving the members the possibility to exclude the application of the National Treatment and the nondiscriminatory provisions on the senior management and board of directors for specific sectors listed in each member's reservation schedule.[17] In the ACIA, for example, members made an extensive utilization of the reservations list; a look at the schedules shows that the number of notifications listed in the schedules limiting the application of the agreement varies from the 7 of Cambodia to the 26 of Vietnam. The schedule of Vietnam is illustrative of the significant restrictions of the scope of ACIA. In practice, Vietnam excludes the application of National Treatment and of the Senior Management and Board of Directors in the following cases:

- Any measure in relation to the employment of expatriates, with the indication that restrictions may be imposed on the ratio of Vietnamese employed in a foreign invested company, on minimum wages and on the duration and type of expatriates employed.
- Portfolio investment.
- Investment licenses issued before the entry into force of ACIA.
- Specific measures related to the establishment, acquisition, organization and operation of foreign invested enterprises or foreign invested

in Vietnam, described by the US Department of State report on investment climate in 2013:

> real estate rights in Vietnam are divided into land ownership, which is collective, and land-use and building rights, which can be held privately. All land in Vietnam is owned collectively and managed by the State and, as such, neither foreigners nor Vietnamese nationals can own it. In addition to land, collective property includes forests, rivers and lakes, water supplies, wealth lying underground or coming from the sea, the continental shelf and the air, the funds and property invested by the State in enterprises and works in all branches and fields – the economy, culture, society, science, technology, external relations, national defense, security – and all other property determined by law as belonging to the State.
>
> (www.state.gov/e/eb/rls/othr/ics/2013/204760.htm)

17 The text of the ASEAN investment agreements regarding reservations is modeled on Art. 14 of US Model BIT.

projects (e.g., foreign investors investing in Vietnam must have an investment project and perform the procedures for investment registration or evaluation of investment at the State administrative body for investment in order to be issued with an investment certificate).

- Measures related to State-owned enterprises and small and medium enterprises.
- Land, property and natural resources associated with land.
- "Conditional investment" (i.e., Vietnam established a list of sectors where investment is conditional, i.e., to be carried out at the specific conditions provided by the national legislation).
- A number of manufacturing, agriculture and forestry services, fishery sectors and specific sensitive sectors (i.e., manufacturing of explosives, automobile and motorcycles assembly and manufacture).
- Food security.

ACIA and the ASEAN–Korea investment agreement members have committed to progressively reduce the exemptions listed in the reservation schedule;[18] while in the ASEAN–Korea investment agreement the progressive elimination of the restrictions shall be carried out in accordance to a work program to be discussed by the parties within five years from the date into force of the agreement, in the ACIA the procedure for the "reduction or elimination" of the reservations shall be in conformity with the "Strategic Schedule of the ASEAN Economic Community Blueprint," one of the most important documents aimed at providing the steps for the creation of the ASEAN Economic Community by 2015, "a region with free movement of goods, services, investment, skilled labor and freer flow of capital."[19]

It should be pointed out that the wide scope of the reservation list of a member State does not necessarily imply a restriction to foreign investment but only a larger regulatory discretion of local government: if a government is particularly liberal in a certain period, the perceived level of restrictions will be quite low. However, this situation might be particularly worrying for foreign investors, as they invested in a country favoring the inflow of investment without a concrete legal protection. Therefore, the FDI restrictive index, often utilized to assess the level of openness to foreign investment of a specific country, cannot be utilized to

18 Cf. ACIA, Art. 9.4 and ASEAN–Korea, Art. 27.
19 ASEAN (2012), 4; ERIA (2012), 6.

measure the effective level of implementation of international investment agreements.[20]

5.5 *Other relevant provisions carving out discretionary space to the host State*

In some of the investment agreements participated by ASEAN members (ACIA and ASEAN–Australia and New Zealand Chapter 11) specific provisions limit the applicability of the agreements to investment "specifically approved in writing by the competent authority of a member State"[21] when the legislation of a member requires so. This obviously allows the host State a huge discretion in rejecting foreign investment, even if the mentioned agreements set out specific procedures to ensure transparency (e.g., inform all the members about the reasons for rejecting an investment; "notify the applicant in writing within one month … of all the additional information required" and, in case the application is denied, "inform the applicant in writing of the reasons of such denial"[22]).

All the agreements analyzed, moreover, exclude taxation measures, government procurement, supply to service to government, subsidies and trade in services from their scope of application.[23]

5.6 *Special and differential treatment for less developed members*

The different level of development of ASEAN members and the necessary flexibility to be granted to the new ASEAN member States (i.e., Cambodia, Myanmar, Laos and Vietnam: CMLV) are already addressed in the preamble of the ACIA and ASEAN–Korea Investment Agreement. The two mentioned agreements and the ASEAN–Australia and New Zealand Chapter 11 contain a specific provision on special and differential treatment for the above-mentioned four new ASEAN members:[24] besides the

20 ERIA (2012) assessed the level of implementation of the AEC Blueprint for the liberalization of investment through the investment restrictive index. According to this index, for example, Vietnam, which is the country with the wider level of restrictions provided in the reservation schedule, results in being one of the most liberal countries in terms of investment inflows.

21 See ACIA Art. 3 and ASEAN–Australia and New Zealand Art. 2.

22 See ACIA, Annex 1, Approval in Writing.

23 See ACIA, Art. 3.4; ASEAN–Korea, Art. 2.2; ASEAN–China, Art. 3.4; ASEAN–Australia and New Zealand, Chapter 11, Art. 1.2.

24 ACIA, Art. 23; ASEAN–Korea, Art. 16; ASEAN–Australia and New Zealand, Art. 15.

commitment of members to provide technical assistance to strengthen the capacity of CMLV in relation to investment policies and promotion, ACIA members engaged to liberalize to investment areas which are of interest of ASEAN member States; moreover, commitments by each newer ASEAN member "may be made in accordance with its individual stage of development." It is not clear how the special and differential treatment provisions have been concretely applied: for example, taking into consideration the reservations schedules mentioned above, it seems that only Vietnam decided to take full benefit from the special and differential treatment provisions, presenting reservations in 26 different fields, while Myanmar, Laos and Cambodia included only 11, 8 and 7 reservations.

5.7 Measures to safeguard the balance-of-payments

All the ASEAN investment agreements, with the exception of ASEAN–Australia and New Zealand include an exception for measures to safeguard the balance-of-payments of members, modeled on Art. XVIII, section B of GATT 1994 (Governmental Assistance to Economic Development). Indeed, the ASEAN investment agreements balance-of-payment provisions, while recognizing the right of all the members to "adopt or maintain restrictions on payments or transfers related to investments" in the "event of serious balance-of-payments and external financial difficulties or threat thereof," is particularly focused to member states "in the process of development," which "may necessitate the use of restrictions to ensure … the maintenance of a level of financial reserves adequate" for the implementation of their programs of economic development.[25] The language adopted by the ASEAN investment agreements balance-of-payment provisions remind one of GATT 1994 language: indeed, measures shall "be consistent with the Articles of Agreement of the IMF … avoid unnecessary damage to the commercial, economic and financial interests of another Member State … be temporary and be phased out progressively" and "be applied such that any one of the other member States is treated no less favorably than any other Member State or non-Member State."

5.8 General exceptions

The ACIA reformulates the provision on general exceptions of the ASEAN earlier agreement, the AIA,[26] which adopts with modification

25 See ACIA, Art. 16. 26 See ACIA, Art. 17 and AIA, Art. 13.

Art. XIV of the WTO General Agreement on Trade in Services (GATS) and Art. XX of the WTO General Agreement on Trade and Tariffs (GATT).[27] It borrows the wording of the GATS Art. XIV and combines it with two additional exceptions from the GATT Art. XX with respect to the protection of national treasures of artistic, historic or archaeological value and the conservation of exhaustible natural resources.[28] ASEAN Agreements on Investment with China and South Korea contain the same formulation. Instead of restating the WTO formulas, the ASEAN–Australia and New Zealand Free Trade Agreement (AANZFTA) refers to the same rules of the GATS and GATT as part of its Chapter 11 on Investment.[29] The state parties to these agreements would likely advocate for the inclusion of a similar rule. However, TPP members, who have opted to omit general exceptions in their model investment treaties, would possibly disapprove of the incorporation of such provisions in the TPP.[30] Future negotiations on the TPP investment issues would unavoidably have to deal with these competing policies.

There has been no arbitral jurisprudence on provisions on general exceptions in investment treaties. Relevant WTO jurisprudence would shed some light on future application of these provisions. However, interpreting the provisions under investment treaties could lead to conclusions different from those within the WTO realm because they have distinct interpretive guidance including the treaty preamble, context, object and purpose, and supplementary means of interpretation.[31]

27 Yen (2012), 3–50. See ACIA, Art. 17(1); see also GATT, Art. XX.

28 Yen (2012), 3–60. See also ASEAN–Korea Agreement on Investment, Art. 20(1); ASEAN–China Agreement on Investment, Art. 16(1).

29 AANZFTA, Chapter 15, Art. 1(2) provides that: "[f]or the purposes of Chapter 8 (Trade in Services), Chapter 9 (Movement of Natural Persons) and Chapter 11 (Investment), Article XIV of GATS including its footnotes shall be incorporated into and shall form part of this Agreement, *mutatis mutandis*." Paragraph 4 of the same article states that

> [f]or the purposes of Chapter 8 (Trade in Services) and Chapter 11 (Investment), subject to the requirement that such measures are not applied in a manner which would constitute a means of arbitrary or unjustifiable discrimination between Parties where like conditions prevail, or a disguised restriction on trade in services or investment, nothing in these Chapters shall be construed to prevent the adoption or enforcement by a Party of measures necessary to protect national treasures or specific sites of historical or archaeological value, or measures necessary to support creative arts of national value [footnote omitted].

30 See, e.g., the 2012 US Model Treaty.

31 VCLT, Arts. 31 and 32.

Under the Asia-Pacific investment treaties, a measure that falls under one of the enumerated clauses of the provision on general exceptions must be:[32]

(a) necessary to protect public morals or to maintain public order;
(b) necessary to protect human, animal or plant life or health;
(c) necessary to secure compliance with laws or regulations which are not inconsistent with the provisions of this Agreement including those relating to:
   (i) the prevention of deceptive and fraudulent practices to deal with the effects of a default on a contract;
   (ii) the protection of the privacy of individuals in relation to the processing and dissemination of personal data and the protection of confidentiality of individual records and accounts; and
   (iii) safety;
(d) aimed at ensuring the equitable or effective imposition or collection of direct taxes in respect of investments or investors of any other Party;
(e) imposed for the protection of national treasures of artistic, historic or archaeological value; or
(f) relating to the conservation of exhaustible natural resources if such measures are made effective in conjunction with restrictions on domestic production or consumption.

Two clarifications from Art. XIV of the GATS are incorporated in this provision. The public order exception may be invoked by a member State only where a genuine and sufficiently serious threat is posed to one of the fundamental interests of society.[33] A nonexhaustive list of measures aimed at ensuring the equitable or effective imposition or collection of direct taxes is also provided.[34]

The WTO Appellate Body noted the use of different terms in respect of various categories of policy objectives such as "necessary," "for the protection of," and "relating to." It concluded that "[i]t does not seem reasonable to suppose that the WTO Members intended to require, in respect of each and every category, the same kind or degree of connection or relationship between the measure under appraisal and the state interest or

32 ACIA, Art. 17; AANZFTA, Chapter 15, Arts. 1(1) and (2); ASEAN–China Agreement on Investment, Art. 16; ASEAN–Korea Agreement on Investment, Art. 20.
33 ACIA, fn. 12. See also fn. 5 of the GATS.
34 See ACIA, fn. 13.

policy sought to be promoted or realized."[35] The WTO Appellate Body (AB) and panels interpreted in detail such qualifications in the relationship between a measure and a policy in some cases.[36] For example, the Appellate Body stated:[37]

> The word "necessary" normally denotes something "that cannot be dispensed with or done without, requisite, essential, needful" … We believe that, as used in the context of Article XX(d), the reach of the word "necessary" is not limited to that which is "indispensable" or "of absolute necessity" or "inevitable." Measures which are indispensable or of absolute necessity or inevitable to secure compliance certainly fulfil the requirements of Article XX(d). But other measures, too, may fall within the ambit of this exception. As used in Article XX(d), the term "necessary" refers, in our view, to a range of degrees of necessity. At one end of this continuum lies "necessary" understood as "indispensable"; at the other end, is "necessary" taken to mean as "making a contribution to." We consider that a "necessary" is, in this continuum, located significantly closer to the pole of "indispensable" than to the opposite pole of simply "making contribution to."

In the WTO jurisprudence, its Members have the right to determine the level of protection of the interests falling within the scope of the GATT provision on general exceptions.[38] Considering the context of this provision, the AB emphasized that it "may not be read so expansively as seriously to subvert the purpose and object" of the general rule of the GATT; nor may other provisions be given "so broad a reach as effectively to emasculate" the general exceptions and the policies and interests it embodies.[39] The specific meanings of undefined terms such as public order, public morals[40] and exhaustible natural resources have been discussed in several WTO rulings.[41]

Under the investment treaties, which do not have a clear provision exempting states from liability under other substantive standards, some

35 WTO, Appellate Body Report, *US – Gasoline*, WT/DS2/AB/R, May 20, 1996.

36 WTO, Appellate Body Report, *US – Gasoline*; Appellate Body Report, *Korea – Various Measures on Beef*, WT/DS161/AB/R and WT/DS169/AB/R, January 10, 2001; Appellate Body Report, *EC – Asbestos*, WT/DS135/AB/R, April 5, 2001.

37 WTO, Appellate Body Report, *Korea – Various Measures on Beef*, 160–161.

38 WTO, Appellate Body Report, *EC – Asbestos*, 168.

39 WTO, Appellate Body Report, *US – Gasoline*, 18.

40 WTO, Appellate Body Report, *US – Gambling*, WT/DS285/AB/R, April 7, 2005, 291 and 296; Panel Report, *US – Gambling*, WT/DS285/ARB, December 21, 2007, 6.465. See also Choudhury (2011), 689.

41 WTO, Appellate Body Report, *US – Shrimp*, WT/DS58/AB/R, November 6, 1998. See also Jackson, Davey and Sykes (2002), 550–552.

state parties faced difficulties in defending their public welfare measure that did not violate the rules on expropriation or fair and equitable treatment.[42] By adopting the WTO expansive exhaustive list of exceptions for noneconomic regulatory objectives, the recent Asia-Pacific regional investment treaties show a new trend of making detailed and balanced international commitments to protect foreign investment. It opens the gate for the host State's new defenses in taking action to protect general interests.

5.9 *Requirements to balance with the objectives of Asia-Pacific investment treaties*

To prevent the abuse or misuse of these exceptions, which might erode or render naught the substantive treaty rights,[43] the introductory clause to the provision on general exceptions lays down some conditions. They ensure that the measures, which are invoked as a general exception, are "applied reasonably, with due regard both to the legal duties of the party claiming the exception and the legal rights of the other parties concerned."[44]

The introductory clause requires that the application of such measure does not constitute either a means of arbitrary or unjustifiable discrimination between the parties or their investors where like conditions prevail or a disguised restriction on investors or investments made by investors of any other party.[45] The language prescribing these conditions is the same as the chapeaux of the provisions on general exceptions of the GATS and GATT except that the former address foreign investment and the latter deal with international trade. The Appellate Body noted the clause prohibits *arbitrary* and *unjustifiable* discrimination, rather than discrimination *per se*.[46] Therefore, this requirement is interpreted differently from other substantive standards in the Most Favored Nation and National Treatment clauses. The protective application of a measure will also constitute an abuse if its design, architecture and structure demonstrate a disguise to conceal the pursuit of trade-restrictive objectives.[47] Each of

42 Moloo and Jacinto (2011), 1–65.
43 WTO, Appellate Body Report, *US – Shrimp*, 156.
44 WTO, Appellate Body Report, *US – Gasoline*, 22.
45 ACIA, Art. 17(1); AANZFTA, Chapter 15, Arts. 1(1) and (2); ASEAN–China Agreement on Investment, Art. 16(1); ASEAN–Korea Agreement on Investment, Art. 20(1).
46 WTO, Appellate Body Report, *US – Gasoline*, 23.
47 See WTO Panel Report, *EC – Asbestos*, 8.236.

the listed exceptions is, therefore, "a *limited* and *conditional* exception from the substantive obligations" contained in the same treaty.[48]

The structure of the provision on general exceptions of the Asia-Pacific regional investment treaties, like their model formulations in the GATS and GATT as interpreted in the WTO jurisprudence, sets out a two-tier test for any invocation of a general exception: (i) specific qualifications of each enumerated exception and (ii) requirements to balance with the substantive protection of foreign investment in the introductory clause.[49] With the incorporation of these exceptions in the treaty text, new defenses are now available for the host State in taking measures to protect general interests.

5.10 *Protecting security interests with security exceptions*

Security interests are of paramount significance to the survival of all countries and take priority over economic objectives, including attracting investment.[50] Therefore, many investment treaties have introduced exceptions to protect the host State's security interests.[51] For example, Art. XI of the US–Argentina BIT provides:[52] "This Treaty shall not preclude the application by either Party of measures necessary for the maintenance of public order, the fulfillment of its obligations with respect to the maintenance or restoration of international peace or security, or the Protection of its own essential security interests."

This formulation exempts state liability from measures taken for both international and national security objectives. State defense regarding national security in international investment arbitrations has led to arbitral quests for two issues: the meaning of "essential security interests" and the authority determining the necessity of the measures at issue.[53] The new design of the provisions on security exceptions in the Asia-Pacific

48 *Ibid.*, 157 (original emphasis).

49 WTO, Appellate Body Report, *US – Gasoline*, 23.

50 Yen (2012), 65.

51 Burke-White and Von Staden (2008), 319–320. See also Sornarajah (2010), 457.

52 Treaty Concerning the Reciprocal Encouragement and Protection of Investment between the US and Argentina, Art. XI, November 14, 1991.

53 *CMS Gas Transmission Company* v. *Argentine Republic*, ICSID Case No. ARB/01/18, Award, May 12, 2005, 373; *LG&E Energy Corp. and others* v. *Argentine Republic*, ICSID Case No. ARB/02/1, Decision on Liability, October 3, 2006, 212–214; *Enron Corporation and Ponderosa Assets, L.P.* v. *Argentine Republic*, ICSID Case No. ARB/01/3, Award, May 22, 2007, 339–342; *Sempra Energy International* v. *Republic of Argentina*, ICSID Case No. ARB/02/16, Award, September 28, 2007, 388–389; *Continental Casualty Company* v. *Argentina*, ICSID Case No. ARB/03/9, Award, September 5, 2008, 187–188.

regional investment agreements provides guidance to reduce such uncertainties in interpretation. By specifying that nothing in the relevant investment treaty "prevent[s] any Member State from taking any action *which it considers necessary* for the protection of its essential security interests,"[54] these provisions expressly provide that the state is the judge of the necessity of its measures. They reject the tribunal's conclusion of the non-self-judging nature in arbitrations interpreting the above-mentioned US-Argentina BIT.[55]

Although the provisions do not define essential security interests to preserve flexibility in determining diverse factual situations, they contain a nonexhaustive list of actions relating to such interests. Four types of measures listed are: (i) action relating to fissionable and fusionable materials or the materials from which they derived; (ii) action relating to the traffic in arms, ammunition and implements of war and to such traffic in other goods and materials as is carried on directly or indirectly for the purpose of supplying a military establishment; (iii) action taken in time of war or other emergency in domestic or international relations; (iv) action taken so as to protect critical public infrastructure, including communication, power and water infrastructures, from deliberate attempts intended to disable or degrade such infrastructure.[56] The national security exceptions under these investment treaties are broader than those of the GATT 1994 and the GATS because the latter exhaustively list the first three types of actions in the former's illustrative list.[57]

Notwithstanding the self-judging characteristics of the necessity test, the provision on the national security exception provides for a judicial determination on which situations fall within their scope. Some tribunals have concluded that a severe economic crisis could constitute an essential security interest.[58] Therefore, they both preserve regulatory space for

54 ASEAN–China Agreement on Investment with China, Art. 17(b); ASEAN–South Korea Agreement on Investment, Art. 21(b); AANZFTA, Chapter 15, Art. 2(1)(b); ACIA, Art. 18(b) (emphasis added). Other treaties also explicitly indicate the self-judging nature of the security exception by using the same phrase as in the Asia-Pacific regional investment treaties, "it considers necessary." See Arts. 18 of the US Model Treaties of 2004 and 2012 and Art. 14(1) of the US–Bahrain BIT of 1999.

55 See arbitral decisions in *supra* note 53; see also Gazzini (2010), 242.

56 See *supra* note 54.

57 See Art. XXI of the GATT 1994 and Art. XIV *bis* of the GATS.

58 See *CMS* v. *Argentina* (fn 55) 359; *LG&E* v. *Argentina* (fn 55) 238; *Enron* v. *Argentina* (fn 55) 332; *Sempra* v. *Argentina* (fn. 55) 374; *Continental* v. *Argentina* (fn 55) 174.

states to protect their national security and allow an objective assessment of states' invocation of the exception.

The ASEAN–Australia and New Zealand Free Trade Agreement, unlike other Asia-Pacific regional investment treaties, designs an institutional mechanism to observe the security measures of state signatories. It provides that "[t]he FTA Joint Committee shall be informed to the fullest extent possible of measures taken under Paragraph 1(b) and (c) [identical to Article 18(b) and (c) of the ACIA] and of their termination."[59] In addition to the exception for the protection of national security, these provisions have the exception relieving a state party from any requirement to disclose information, which "it considers contrary to its essential security interests."[60] The international security exception under the Asia-Pacific investment treaties is clarified to be based on obligations of the State Parties under the United Nations Charter for the maintenance of international peace and security. The formulation on security exceptions of these treaties, therefore, provides clear guidance to ensure a balanced application of such exceptions.

6. Conclusions

The world trading and investment system has envisaged the necessity to provide detailed rules on the protection of some important noneconomic societal interests since its inception.[61] International investment law, however, emerged from the main concern of the rising nationalization trend of foreign investment. The vast majority of investment treaties do not incorporate general exceptions.[62] Capital-importing and exporting countries have reached a compromise with short and general formulations of substantive protection of investment and virtually left out a mention of exceptions to undertake measures for the sake of other interests for decades. Arbitral tribunals have found regulatory measures for non-investment objectives such as environment protection in breach of treaty provisions.[63] To secure regulatory space for different societal values and

59 AANZFTA, Chapter 15, Art. 2(2).

60 ASEAN–China Agreement on Investment with China, Art. 17(a); ASEAN–South Korea Agreement on Investment, Art. 21(a); AANZFTA, Chapter 15, Art. 2(1)(a); ACIA, Art. 18(a).

61 See GATT 1994, Art. XX.

62 The few exceptions include, e.g., the 1998 Framework Agreement on the ASEAN Investment Area (AIA). See AIA, Art. 13.

63 See, e.g., *Methanex* v. *United States of America*, Award, August 9, 2005, available at http://ita.law.uvic.ca.

interests, some recently concluded treaties, including the regional ones in the Asia-Pacific Area, have introduced provisions on general exceptions. The four investment agreements participated by ASEAN members all contain general and security exceptions modeled, respectively, on Arts. XX and XXI of GATT 1994. They also include balance-of-payment provisions modeled on the similar discipline of GATT 1994 (especially Art. XVIII, Section B). Moreover, ASEAN members adopted a number of other treaty provisions to extend their regulatory powers: indeed, many sectors have been excluded from the scope of application of ASEAN investment agreements through specific exclusion (or reservation) lists and the special and differential treatment allows a particular flexibility to less developed ASEAN members.

References

ASEAN, 2012. *ASEAN Economic Community Blueprint*, Jakarta: ASEAN. www.insaps.org/portaladmin/uploads/Download/1366608631.pdf.

Burke-White, W.W. and Von Staden, A. 2008. "Investment Protection in Extraordinary Times: The Interpretation and Application of Non-Precluded Measures Provisions in Bilateral Investment Treaties." *Virginia Journal of International Law* 48: 319–320.

Chesterman, S. 2008. "Does ASEAN Exist? The Association of Southeast Asian Nations as an International Legal Person." New York University School of Law: Public Law & Legal Theory Research Paper Series. Working Paper 8–26. ssrn.com/abstract=1113612.

Choudhury, B. 2011. "Exception Provisions as a Gateway to Incorporating Human Rights Issues into International Investment Agreements." *Columbia Journal of Transnational Law* 49: 689.

Desierto, D.A. 2012. "Investment Treaty Regulation Under the New ASEAN Charter Regime." Asian Development Bank. papers.ssrn.com/sol3/papers.cfm?abstract_id=1963563.

ERIA, 2012. "Mid-term Review of the Implementation of AEC Blueprint." Kyoto Eria Publications. www.eria.org/publications/key_reports/mid-term-review-of-the-implementation-of-aec-blueprint-executive-summary.html.

Gazzini, T. 2010. "Interpretation of (Allegedly) Self-judging Clauses in Bilateral Investment Treaties," Fitzmaurice, M., Elias, O. and Merkouris, P. (eds.), *Treaty Interpretation and the Vienna Convention on the Law of Treaties: 30 Years on*. Leiden and Boston: Martinus Nijhoff Publishers, 242.

Jackson, J.H., Davey, W.J. and Sykes, A.O. (eds.) 2002. *Legal Problems of International Economic Relations: Cases, Materials and Text on the National and International Regulation of Transnational Economic Relations*, St. Paul, MN: West Group, 550–552.

Malanczuk, P. 2008. "Association of South East Asian Nations (ASEAN)." Max Plank Encyclopedia of Public International Law.

Mann, H. 2007. "Investment Agreements and the Regulatory State: Can Exceptions Clauses Create a Safe Haven for Governments?" Issues In International Investment Law, Background Papers for the Developing Country Investment Negotiators' Forum, Singapore. iisd.org/pdf/2007/inv_agreements_reg_state.pdf.

Moloo, R. and Jacinto, J. (eds.) 2011. "Environmental and Health Regulation: Assessing Liability under Investment Treaties." *Berkeley Journal of International Law* 29: 1–65.

Ranjan, P. 2009. "Definition of Investment in Bilateral Investment Treaties of South Asian Countries and Regulatory Discretion." *Journal of World Trade* 26: 217–235.

Sornarajah, M. 2010. *The International Law on Foreign Investment*. New York: Cambridge University Press: 457.

UNCTAD, 2012. *World Investment Report*. Geneva: United Nations Publications.

Yen, T.H. 2011. "East Asian Investment Treaties in the Integration Process: Quo Vadis?" Buckley, R.P., Hu, W. and Arner, D.W. (eds.), *East Asian Economic Integration*. Cheltenham, UK: Edward Elgar Publishing, 183–199.

2012. "The ASEAN Comprehensive Investment Agreement." Davidson, P. (ed.), *Trading Arrangements in the Pacific Rim: ASEAN and APEC*. New York: Oceana Publishing, 3–59.

16

The regulation of foreign investments in Mercosur: failed attempts and challenges ahead

ARNO DAL RI JR AND PAULO POTIARA DE ALCÂNTARA VELOSO

1. Introduction

Created amidst a market liberalisation wave at the end of last century, Mercosur[1] tried in its first years of activity to launch the basis of a regional system of foreign direct investments (FDIs) regulation, regarding the flow of investments among member States, as well as the reception of investments from third countries. Such regulation was materialised in two protocols signed by the four member States, but, with the exception of Argentina, the National Parliaments refused to ratify them and the initiative did not succeed.

Only in 2010, after sixteen years of frustrated initiatives on this matter, was a new regulatory project launched, this time by national governments with foreign policies considerably different from the ones of the previous decade. In addition, the economic policy of Mercosur's member States had also suffered many changes, which had a direct impact on the initiatives concerning FDIs in the regional bloc, resulting in a document with more conservative and traditional characteristics than its predecessors.

2. Dilemmas faced by Mercosur

After almost two decades of unsuccessful attempts to put into force the Protocols of Colônia[2] and Buenos Aires,[3] finally in a meeting of Mercosur's Heads of State, which took place at Foz do Iguaçú on 16 December 2010, a

1 Mercosur was established in 1991 with the Treaty of Asuncion by Argentina, Brazil, Paraguay and Uruguay.

2 'Protocol for the Promotion and Reciprocal Protection of Investments in Mercosur', signed on 17 January 1994 in Colônia do Sacramento, Uruguay.

3 'Protocol about the Promotion and Protection of Investments from non State Parties of Mercosur', signed in Buenos Aires on 5 August 1994.

new action plan was launched, focusing on trade, investment and immigration issues, in order to take advantage of the growth phase in the region. Concerning specifically FDI matters, it was decided on the occasion that the regional bloc institutions should prepare a new draft of an agreement and this text should be negotiated by the parties in 2011.

The failure of the previous attempts to regulate investments in the region[4] has always been a source of embarrassment in the corridors of the bloc's institutions, especially due to the endless critics from the internal and external economic sectors of Mercosur that were interested in the regulation of the subject. As a result of a determination of the Common Market Council (CMC),[5] both documents have been reviewed, since 2004, by the relevant sub-workgroup.

With the exception of the issue concerning the dispute settlement between host States and foreign investors, the new text, still not presented, tends not to depart from the wording of the Colonia Protocol. Generally speaking, the political scenario and the position of the member States appear to point towards a more modest solution regarding the former failed experience.

2.1 *Reasons for a foretold failure*

The Colonia Protocol envisaged instituting a law statute of freedom of investment in each of the member States' territory. This is one of the biggest innovations of the instrument in study. Influenced by the United States' practice on the subject, the free movement of investments would prevail before the State sovereignty.

Once approved, the Protocol would allow foreign investors from a Mercosur member State to settle in the territory of another member State, under the same conditions of its nationals. Investments from third countries would be regulated by the Buenos Aires Protocol. As has been noticed in doctrine, '(t)he Colonia Protocol adopts thus the approach of the United States Bilateral Investment Treaties (BITs), while the Protocol of Buenos Aires, a peculiar example of multilateral (regional) treaty in favour of third States, follows the pattern of the other BITs mentioned

4 Such failure was due to the lack of deposit of ratification instruments by the member States of the 1994 Protocols. In fact, only Argentina, in 1997, incorporated in its laws the Colônia Protocol.

5 Mercosur body whose function is the political pursuit of the process of integration. It is formed by the Ministers of Foreign Affairs and Treasury of the member States, who communicate among themselves through decisions.

before, in referring the matter of the entry of FDI to the law of the host State'.[6]

The premises of the US model can be found in other provisions of the Colônia Protocol, e.g. in the clause that forbids controls by the host State when admitting investments in its territory, as well as the prohibition of performance requirements. The latter prohibition, in particular, would be equivalent 'to the freedom of access for foreign investors, excluding certain sectors from the national economy'.[7]

With regard to dispute resolution, the Colonia Protocol envisaged mechanisms of international arbitration, including the International Centre for Settlement of Investment Disputes (ICSID). However, the latter could be used only if the member States had ratified the Washington Convention or the Additional Facility.

The Protocol of Buenos Aires reveals an ambiguous content, presenting both conservative and liberal elements, depending on the subject matter. Among the conservative elements, one may highlight the granting of national treatment only for the post-establishment phase.[8] Among the liberal aspects of the Protocol one may find the availability for the investor by his own choice of an arbitral proceeding against the host State, without the prior exhaustion of domestic remedies.

The texts of both Protocols also contained mechanisms trying to avoid the emergence of 'tax wars' within the agreement.[9]

Among the reasons that hindered the adoption of the two Protocols by Mercosur member States, it has been argued that both would be 'hazardous to national sovereignty, also for the fact that, in some cases, they provide a more favourable treatment to foreign investors than the one given to local investors'.[10] Moreover, States were concerned about the availability for foreign investors of international arbitration without the need to exhaust domestic remedies.[11]

The impasse experienced in these years, as well as the differences between national policies on the subject seem to allow for the 'absence of a sub-regional harmonized strategy' focused in the use of the 'international

6 Sacerdoti (1997), 334. 7 Ramina (2009), 76–7.

8 Art. 2.B.1, of the Protocol. Thus, the right of the host State to regulate the entry of foreign investments in its territory according to its interests would be preserved. On this matter, see Schlee (2005), 82 ff.

9 Flôres (2005). 10 Pontes (2009), 128 ff.

11 As previously seen, this possibility was provided for by both the Colonia Protocol (Art. 9) and the Protocol of Buenos Aires (Art. 2.h).

judicialisation as an instrument of harmonising liberalisation, minimal standards and even, the international protection of foreign investment'.[12]

The worsening of the economic situation of some member States and some political problems in the region caused the abandonment of the initiatives after ten years of negotiations. The considerations developed in a 2005 essay by Renato Flôres, economist of the Fundação Getúlio Vargas, presented at the time of the official announcement of the abandonment of these initiatives, are interesting. The essay pointed out the need to restructure both protocols, merging them in a single document, contemplating the following points:

> a) the associated mechanism for resolving disputes, rather than resorting to ICSID ..., as earlier versions of both protocols proposed, it must refer to the system now in force in Mercosul, improved significantly after the creation of the court standing in Asuncion; b) with respect to fiscal wars, something similar and not much beyond the Code of Conduct for Multinational Enterprises of the OECD should be implemented, as it has been suggested by Brazil, with respect to Argentinean complaints regarding tax competition, c) particular attention and a modern approach should be devoted to the definition of investments and the true scope of the concepts of MFN and national treatment for foreign direct investment within the bloc. Attention should extend to the restrictions imposed by the WTO TRIMS Agreement, with due qualifications included in the protocol, if necessary.[13]

2.2 *Old risks in new robes*

Even after the initiative launched in Foz de Iguaçú in 2010, it remains difficult to foresee the approval in the short or medium term of an effective

12 Costa (2006), 76. Along the same lines, the author states that

> the Appri's cannot be considered as relevant instruments of international cooperation for the establishment of a good investment climate. First, although there are agreements involving many ALADI countries, as the analysis of the Argentinean network of agreements reveals, these do not exist between the Mercosur countries. Except for an agreement between Paraguay and Uruguay, the failure of the Protocols of Colonia and Buenos Aires, fueled by the Brazilian antipathy to these agreements, resulted in the Appri's international network and particularly TBIs, not being extended into the sub-region. Meanwhile, these instruments were not replaced by any joint strategy for the establishment of a sub-regional system of promotion, protection and regulation of investments. That, at least to some extent, can be attributed to the liberal perception of the Treaty of Asunción, which puts great emphasis on the commercial aspects, ignoring the needs of concerted policies and regulatory strategies.

13 Flôres (2005).

regulatory framework for FDIs within the bloc. Three strong reasons support this perspective.

The first reason is the negative impact of the various moments of stagnation experienced in intra-bloc trade negotiations during 2011 and 2012. This context is reflected in the negotiations aimed at liberalising investments, preventing them from prospering.

Secondly, the positioning of the current national governments and parliaments of Argentina, Brazil and Uruguay – and now also of Venezuela – which are marked by ideological discourses and in many ways have refractory responses to market liberalisation and tend to implement conservative or even restrictive policies on FDI matters.

Finally, the current apprehension relating to certain international arbitration mechanisms relating to investments contributes to the caution in the approval of the current framework. If by the end of the 1990s a positive attitude led to the conclusion of numerous BITs by most South American States and to the accession by some of them to the ICSID, the first decade of the twenty-first century was permeated with a feeling of perplexity that in many cases rapidly developed into suspicion. Such suspicion was caused, for instance, by controversial arbitral decisions, such as *Maffezini*[14] and *Vivendi*,[15] where ICSID arbitrations went far while interpreting the Washington Convention of 1965 concerning the State's consent, resulting in the return, in some aspects, of certain postulates of the Calvo doctrine.

Such concerns were increased before the Colonia Protocol, which presented a tendency favourable to investors when choosing the jurisdiction before which to present a possible dispute against the host State, pointing towards the ICSID arbitration as one of the possible mechanisms. Thus, if the new document has a provision similar to the one of the Colonia Protocol it could bind indirectly the Mercosur member States to ICSID jurisdiction. This would be valid for countries such as Brazil, which is not a party to the Washington Convention and has never ratified a single BIT. If this framework were adopted, disputes against investors

14 *Emilio Agustín Maffezini* v. *Kingdom of Spain* ICSID Case No. ARB/97/7, Award, 9 November 2000.

15 *Compañia de Aguas del Aconquija S.A. & Compagnie Générale des Eaux* v. *Argentine Republic* ICSID Case No. ARB/97/3, Award, 21 November 2000. See also *Southern Pacific Properties Ltd.* v. *The Arab Republic of Egypt* ICSID Case No. ARB/84/3, Award, 20 May 1992, and *Asian Agricultural Products Limited* v. *Democratic Socialist Republic of Sri Lanka* ICSID Case No. ARB/87/3, Award, 21 June 1990.

from Argentina, Uruguay or Paraguay could be submitted to the ICSID Additional Facility.[16]

A simple reading of Art. 9.4 of the Colonia Protocol and the results of the *Maffezini* and *Vivendi* cases is enough to notice that each member State would be consenting, by signing the Protocol, to submit itself to the ICSID arbitration in disputes with investors from other member States. This context is further aggravated with the draft of the Protocol of Buenos Aires that, as seen before, contained the advanced consent of member States to submit any dispute between the host State and investors of third countries directly to international arbitration, such as the ICSID, at the choice of the foreign investor (Art. 2.h).[17]

The insertion of the same provisions contained in the Protocols of Colonia and Buenos Aires into a new document, which is still being drafted, would collide with the current tendencies dominating the bloc internally. Therefore, the proposal for a new regulatory framework of investments will probably have a more conservative approach compared to the previous ones.

The absence of an FDI policy in Mercosur – the bloc is formed by countries of a presidential regime, where foreign policy bears the mark of each President's choices – could be better understood if studied as a result of the approaches of the two main member States, namely Brazil and Argentina, as well as the influence of the choices by Chile, the most important associated State of the bloc.

3. Brazilian controversies

Brazil, Mercosur's largest economy, has an ambivalent position when addressing the FDI regulation. As indicated previously, while the governmental and parliamentary approaches to this matter have been characterised by actions seen as conservative to a certain degree – influencing, clearly, the decisions taken also at a regional level – the case-law has presented the necessary elements to generate confidence among the foreign investors and has been consolidated by the Brazilian superior courts. The success of this unexpected formula can be demonstrated in numbers: Brazil has received an amount of US$66.7 billion[18] in FDIs in 2011, which reinforces its image as one of the world's largest FDI receptors.

16 Ramina (2009), 76–7.

17 About the drafting of the Protocol of Buenos Aires, see Sacerdoti (1997), 428.

18 Banco Central do Brasil (2012).

In the Brazilian legal system, FDIs are regulated by three internal sources. In the Constitution, relevant are Arts. 172[19] on the incentive for FDI; and 173[20] on the State intervention in the economy. Both aim at setting patterns for foreign investments in the country, which consequently set the fundamental principles of the national economy as well as regulate the access to justice. These, in turn, indirectly impact on the Brazilian policies of attraction and protection of FDIs.

At an infra-constitutional level, the legislation is very specific, being formed by Law 4,131 of 1962 on the investment of foreign capital and the remittance to foreign countries, as well as Law 11,371 of 2006 which deals with exchange operations and the registration of foreign capital. Law 4,131 of 1962 was amended in 1964 by Law 4,390, and finds itself overcome by the current praxis, establishing merely criteria for the record of FDIs in Brazil and the remittance of profits and dividends to foreign countries. In fact, there is no regulation stating the validity criteria to be used for the entrance of investments in the country or regulations limiting the remittance of profits to foreign countries. However, the Law in Art. 28 provides for the possibility of restrictions on the remittance of income from foreign capital in case of imbalance or disequilibrium eminence of the balance of payments.[21]

Considering the administrative sphere, the regulatory legislation is under the responsibility of the Central Bank, and, in a tenuous way, also under the responsibility of the Secretariat of Federal Revenue of Brazil. The subjects related to FDIs are regulated, almost entirely, by ordinances and regulations from these two governmental bodies. These administrative norms, however, sometimes are contrary to the aforementioned legislation, mainly when they refer to provisions of Law 4,131 of 1962.

As far as international law rules on the protection of foreign investments, Brazil is not bound by any treaty on the subject. In fact, the country seems not to be affected by the international pressure exerted on

19 Art. 172 of the Constitution provides as follows: 'The law shall regulate, based on national interest, capital investments abroad, encourage reinvestments and shall regulate the remittance of profits.'

20 Art. 173 of the Constitution provides as follows: 'Except for the cases provided in this Constitution, the direct exploitation of economic activity by the State shall be permitted only when necessary to the imperatives of national security or the relevant collective interest, as defined by law.'

21 In this case, Law 4,131 of 1962 leaves these restrictions to be applied by an administrative entity called, in 1965, the Financial Oversight Council (in Portuguese – Conselho da Superintendência da Moeda e do Crédito), which is now extinct. This competence has been now absorbed by the Central Bank.

developing countries to conclude International Investment Agreements (IIAs) with investment exporting countries. Brazil has not become part of a single BIT yet, and has not ratified the ICSID Convention. Therefore, in principle, it could be argued that it would not be possible to give international protection to foreign investors that may eventually be harmed by actions of the Brazilian government.

In addition, Brazilian regulatory restrictions are also rare in relation to the presence of FDIs. Indeed there are express constitutional provisions prohibiting such restrictions and aiming at attracting FDIs in a largely favourable regulatory framework.

Regarding demands involving FDIs and the Brazilian government, there is no way to analyse objectively the posture assumed by the country in the international sphere. This is due to the fact that Brazil has not yet become part of the safety measures for international investments concerning FDIs. This phenomenon might lead to the conclusion that the only legal remedy for the resolution of disputes between foreign investors and the Brazilian government is the Brazilian judiciary. However, the analysis of some case-law from the Brazilian superior courts seems to point to another direction.

In Brazil, Law 9,307 of 1996 (Arbitration Law) establishes the criteria for arbitral procedures in the Brazilian legal system. These rules limit the admissibility of international and national arbitral procedures to disposable property rights (Art. 1). They establish the full validity of arbitration clauses in contracts (Arts. 3 and 4) and stipulate that an arbitral decision, in Brazil, has the status of a court sentence enforceable as such (Art. 31). In addition, other provisions help to strengthen these rules of arbitration. One example is Art. 267(VII), of the Brazilian Civil Procedure Code, which establishes the extinction of proceedings, without a decision on the merit, when there is a dispute resolution clause opting for arbitration. Brazil has also adopted some of the international mechanisms that guarantee the recognition of foreign arbitral decisions in its internal sphere.[22]

Besides that, the Law 9,307 of 1996 seems to indicate that Brazil can be demanded on an arbitral case, given that the law does not appear to distinguish between private companies and State-owned enterprises. Moreover,

22 Inter-American Convention on International Commercial Arbitration, signed in 1975, promulgated in 1996; the Montevideo Convention on extraterritorial validity of foreign judgments and arbitral awards, signed in 1979, promulgated in 1997; and the Convention on the Recognition and Enforcement of Foreign Arbitral Awards, signed in New York in 1958, and promulgated in 2002.

as already mentioned, the Brazilian Constitution clearly states that semi-public enterprises must be submitted to the legal regime of private companies (Art. 173). Similar provisions can be found also in the ordinary legislation, such as Law 11,079 of 2004 on Public–Private Partnerships, and Law 6,404 of 1976 on Public Limited Companies.

Moreover, the possibility of Brazil participating in arbitral procedures is confirmed by the case-law of national superior courts as decided in the leading case *Electric Power State Company* v. *AES Southern Power Distribution Company of Rio Grande do Sul and others.*

This case refers to a damages action for breach of contract between a semi-public enterprise, the Electric Power State Company, and the subsidiary company controlled by the American company AES, the AES Uruguaiana Enterprises Ltd.[23] Appealing to the Brazilian national courts, the Electric Power State Company aimed at discussing the breaching of contract by AES. AES, however, requested the court the extinction of proceedings without deciding on the merits of the case, based on the contract of power supply agreed by both parties. This contract had an arbitration clause, indicating arbitration as the adequate way to solve omitted or doubtful issues about the execution of the contract. Although the first and second instance judges were against such understanding, the decision of the Brazilian Superior Court of Justice[24] validated the arbitration clause stated in the contract.

Thus, the Brazilian Superior Court has indicated clearly that public companies can, in fact, take part in international arbitral procedures that involve foreign investors. In this sense, according to the Presiding Judge: 'when the contracts celebrated by State-owned-enterprises address the economic activity in the strict sense – that is, public services from industrial nature or economic activity of production or trade of goods, likely to generate income and profit – rights and obligations derived from it will be transferable, disposable, and, therefore, liable to arbitration procedures.'

Hence, it may be argued that although there are no specific provisions about the regulation of FDIs, a high level of legal certainty for foreign

23 The company integrates the holding of the Electric Power Brasiliana Company (Companhia Brasiliana de Energia), composed by AES Corp, that holds 50.01 per cent from the voting capital, and by the National Bank of Economic and Social development (BNDES – Banco Nacional de Desenvolvimento Econômico e Social), with 49.99 per cent from the voting capital. See: www.aesbrasil.com.br/ogrupo/Paginas/aesnobrasil.aspx.

24 *Decision on Recurso Especial (REsp) 612.439*, Superior Tribunal de Justiça, 14 September 2006. See also *Decision on Recurso Especial (REsp) 606.345*, Superior Tribunal de Justiça, 8 June 2007.

investors exists. In other words, national laws, mainly after the constitutional reforms in the 1990s, establish an effective protection for foreign investors, foreseeing the possibility of different types of arbitration procedures for the resolution of litigations that might arise from the enforcement of a contract. In addition, the government cannot excuse itself for not meeting its obligations provided for in the arbitration clauses. In accordance to that, the case-law tends to follow the decision taken by the Brazilian Superior Court discussed previously.[25] These factors, together with the stability of the Brazilian macro economy, seem to be an excellent indicator for the attraction of FDIs, and they also constitute important elements for the comparison of the Brazilian policy in relation to other States that that are part of Mercosur.

4. Argentinean inconstancies

Argentina, Mercosur's second largest economy, has an important role in the attraction of FDIs to the region. However, after the country became a large receptor of FDIs in the 1990s as a result of the great number of privatisations implemented by the Carlos Menem government, it experienced an inconstant flux of investments at the beginning of this century.

The country is considered one of the most open economies in the world, a fact constantly mentioned in the last few months by the Argentinean government. In the OECD rank, the country is the eleventh most open economy on the planet[26] (and the second most open in Latin America[27]). Within Mercosur, Argentina is the country that has enacted the strongest measures for the protection of foreign investors. In line with the policy of trade liberalisation implemented in the 1990s, the country has signed many treaties aiming at protecting foreign investments, including fifty-eight BITs.[28] In 1994, the country also ratified the Washington Convention of 1965. In addition, as already mentioned, Argentina is the only country that has ratified the Colonia Protocol for the Promotion and Protection of Investments in Mercosur.

Despite this scenario, one may identify large uncertainties resulting from the constant crises that the country has experienced, particularly in recent decades. In this sense, the crisis of 1999 represents an important element for this study, since in this period (1999–2004) one could see a profound change in the macroeconomic data that directly impacted

25 *Decision on REsp 612.439* (fn 24). 26 Timerman (2012).
27 The first one being Colombia. 28 Data provided by the Argentinean government.

foreign investors. The debt crisis at the beginning of the twenty-first century caused deep financial and structural problems that led to the change of position of the government with regard to FDIs. The abandonment of the fixed exchange rate system that had been in place for ten years provoked a large depreciation of the peso's value that reached rates nearly four pesos per dollar. Having taken place in the context of an economic plan called *corralito*, the devaluation of the peso occurred with other economic measures, such as the *pesificación* (obligatory conversion of dollar to pesos at an official rate) and the nationalisation of industrial production. These policy changes occurred in 2002 – during Eduardo Alberto Duhalde's government – and directly affected the policy context for FDI inflows into Argentina and still have been reflected in recent years.

Nevertheless, the regulatory framework seems to ensure a favourable scenario for foreign investors. Although there is not a legal basis for the legal equality between national and foreign investors, the Argentinean Constitution provides, in Art. 20, for the extension of all national rights to foreigners. Moreover, the country counts with a specific legislation regulating FDIs: Law 21,382 of 1993 (*Inversiones Extranjeras*). This law establishes the conceptual basis for what is understood as productive FDI. In its first article, the statute stipulates the equality between national and foreign investors, and Art. 5 states the freedom of repatriation of investment or the remittance of profits abroad.

Since the beginning of this decade, however, a great inconsistency in the FDI inflow numbers in Argentina has been observed. In 1990, when the scenario was absolutely diverse to the current circumstances, the country received a total of US$75.5 million, with a peak of US$24 million in 1999.[29] However, in the period between 2001 and 2011, Argentina received around US$50 million in FDIs,[30] 50 per cent less than the previous period.

Although the governmental statements have indicated that lower values reflect more qualified FDIs invested in setting up new ventures rather than FDIs designated to mergers and acquisitions and privatisations as in the 1990s, this is not what is seen in practice. Although Argentina has been found as the destination of some high quality investments, such as the ones related to research, only Brazil has positioned itself as a relevant place for this matter.[31] Besides, in 2011 Argentina received US$7.2 billion in FDIs, in which only one acquisition operation corresponded to US$2.45

29 Vismara (2008). 30 CEPAL (2011), 34. 31 *Ibid.*, 18.

billion,[32] and another to US$480 million.[33] Together they added up to around 40 per cent of the total numbers of FDI received in that year.

The phenomenon that can be found, therefore, is the mismatch between the official speech, indicating a positive direction, and the State practices, which follow in a completely different direction. At the same time that agents of the Argentinean government indicate a significant increase of FDI inflows in 2011 compared to 2010, the government nationalises companies in order to fit within its ideological discourses. In this controversial scenario, actions like the nationalisation of the YPF (*Yacimientos Petrolíferos Fiscales*), like many others,[34] may influence, in a decisive way, the flux of investments to Argentina.

The great number of arbitral procedures in which Argentina was involved at the ICSID level reflects the inconsistency of the governmental policies at an international level. Since the entry into force of the ICSID Convention for Argentina (in 1994), the country has already played the defendant role in forty-nine cases, from a total of 395 cases held by ICSID in its whole history. Argentina, alone, therefore, accounts for more than 12 per cent of all cases in the Organization, which counts with 158 signatory States. Considering that this mechanism is triggered by State practices which apparently harm foreign investors' rights, this data is alarming.

5. Chile's stability

Invited to join Mercosur as a member State in 1991, and maintaining the status of regional associated member, Chile has always followed closely the development of policies on international trade and investment matters discussed above. Among the reasons for the country not to join the bloc is the concern that the policies resulting from the integration agreement and its protocols might restrict the freedom of action of the government in the investments field, in which Chile has obtained significant success since the early 1990s. Even today, as an associated member, Chile participates in the implementation of certain measures adopted within

32 Acquisition operation of the company Occidental Argentina by the Chinese company Sinopec. *Ibid.*, 39.

33 *Ibid.*, 61.

34 The government of Cristina Fernández de Kirchner has nationalised, apart from YPF, the airline company Aerolíneas Argentinas and the private pension and retirement funds. The previous government, of Néstor Kirchner (2003–2007), had also nationalised, e.g, the water and courier companies.

Mercosur, but maintains firmly its exclusion from topics considered sensitive, such as services, the automotive sector and FDIs.[35]

In 1996, the Economic Complementation Agreement number 35, signed between Mercosur and Chile, introduced into the Chilean legal framework Mercosur's Common External Tariff (TEC), and also tried to create the base for a policy of a reciprocal treatment of investments from investors of the parties.

The Chileans' liberal policy on investments matters – one of the reasons for its non-complete membership in Mercosur – has acquired over the years an important role in the international community. For two years, 2009 and 2010, in particular, its policy was used as an example by the United Nations Conference on Trade and Development (UNCTAD) in its 'Best Practices in Investment for Development' report regarding investments in the areas of infrastructure and mining.[36] The Economic Commission for Latin America and the Caribbean (CEPAL), in its document 'La Inversion Extranjera Directa en América Latina y el Caribe 2010', highlighted that Chile held the highest percentage of FDI in relation to national GDP in the region, approaching 8 per cent. The World Investment Report of 2010 showed that the stock of FDIs in Chile was US$121,640 million in 2009, the second highest in the region, figuring behind only Brazil. CEPAL's 2011 report on FDIs in Latin America and the Caribbean[37] also shows the amount of US$17,299 million as the inflow of FDI in Chile in the same year, representing a growth of 15 per cent over the previous year. With these numbers, Chile stands as the third country in South America in FDI growth, and the second largest receiver of FDI in the region.[38]

The Decree-Law No. 600 ('Estatuto de Inversión Extranjera') can be considered as one of the reasons for the current positive scenario of investments in Chile. The act creates a mechanism for the protection of investors, which is valid for those that signed an investment agreement with the Chilean government and establishes the guarantees, rights, duties and authorises the transfers of capital or other forms of investment in the country. Since 1974, when it came into force, most foreign investors have been using it.[39]

35 Stefoni and Fuentes (1996), 25. 36 UNCTAD (2009, 2011).

37 CEPAL (2010), 11. 38 CEPAL (2011), 14.

39 From US$15,095 million, the total FDI that came into Chile via DL 600 in 2010 was US$2,304 million according to the Central Bank of Chile. By 2010 this figure was US$77,261 million, representing 62.7 per cent of the total capital inflows in Chile. See Comitè de Inversiones Extranjeras (2012).

The statute clearly expresses the equal treatment between foreign and domestic investments. Therefore, it does not have clauses that exclude foreign investors from activities reserved to the Chilean State or to private entities. It also does not restrict the participation of FDI to specific activities or corporate types. Art. 9, in particular, provides that when a treatment is considered discriminatory:

> The laws or regulations relating to certain productive activities shall be considered discriminatory if they are to be applied to all or to the majority of the productive activities in the country, except for FDIs. Similarly, laws or regulations that establish exceptional arrangements for sectors or zones shall be considered discrimination if the foreign investments cannot reach them even though these follow the same conditions and requirements imposed on domestic investments for their use.

Art. 10, in turn, provides ways for foreign investors, or companies whose capital belongs to foreign investors, to request the elimination of discrimination stemming from existing laws and regulations.

Furthermore, Art. 3 sets out the deadlines that foreign investors shall follow for their investments, establishing a minimum period of one year to initiate the repatriation of profits derived from FDI. In addition, among other provisions, Art. 16 creates the '*Comite de Inversiones Extranjeras*' and defines the cases in which FDIs will require the approval from the committee.

In the country's national legislation there is also, as an alternative investment protection to the DL 600, Chapter XIV of the Compendium of International Trade Standards (CNCI) of Chile's Central Bank. It is entitled 'Normas Aplicables a los Creditos, Depositos, Inversiones y Aportes de Capital Provenientes del Exterior' and is a mechanism through which foreign investors can protect their investments.[40]

With the end of the dictatorship in Chile in the 1990s, in addition to the domestic legislation favourable towards the investment, the country began a process of intense negotiations and subscription of bilateral and multilateral agreements relating to trade and investment. The wide commercial and financial opening, allied to the new political landscape, facilitated Chile's international integration and made the country a highly attractive destination for investments.[41]

40 This chapter establishes the standards for international trade operations relating to loans, deposits, investments and capital contributions coming from abroad, as well as other foreign obligations.

41 Rodas (2003).

The number of BITs signed by Chile is significant: a total of thirty-nine at June 2013. In general, the treaties present certain common features among themselves. The investments covered by these agreements are those made in accordance with the national legislation of the contracting parties.[42] Once admitted, foreign investments have to be granted some advantages such as the fair and equitable treatment, the national treatment and the most-favoured-nation treatment.[43] Moreover, as is usual in BITs, some conditions are envisaged in order to consider legitimate measures of expropriation taken by the host contracting State.[44] Some BITs also regulate the issue of compensation in cases of losses resulting from war, revolution, a state of emergency.[45] The BITs signed by Chile establish the right of investors to make money transfers freely, and reserves to the country the right for the internalised capital to only be remitted abroad after a year of its entry, in line with Chilean domestic law.[46] Finally, BITs concluded by Chile usually provide for international arbitration or, alternatively, for

42 See e.g. Art. 1(2) of the Chile–UK BIT: 'This Agreement shall apply to investments in the territory of one Contracting Party made in accordance with its laws, prior to or after the entry into force of this Agreement, by investors of the other Contracting Party.'

43 See e.g. Art. 4 of the Chile–Greece BIT:

> 1. Each contracting party shall ensure fair and equitable treatment for the investments made by investors of the other contracting party in its territory, and will ensure that the exercise of the rights recognized in these terms is not hindered in practice. 2. Each contracting party shall ensure for investments made in its territory by investors of the other contracting party a treatment no less favourable than the one given to investments of investors of any third State or of any party, whichever is more favourable.

44 See e.g. Art. 4 of the Chile–Germany BIT:

> (2) Investments of nationals or companies of either contracting party shall not, in the territory of the other party, be expropriated, nationalised or subjected to other measures that would be the equivalent to expropriation or nationalisation, but for the common good, in which case compensation would be compulsory. These measures must be authorised by law. Compensation shall correspond to the value of the investment immediately before the date of the expropriations, nationalisation or comparable measure actual or imminent are made public.'

45 See e.g. Art. 5 of the Chile–UK BIT:

> Compensation for Losses (1) Investors of one Contracting Party whose investments in the territory of the other Contracting Party suffer losses owing to war or other armed conflict, revolution, state of national emergency, revolt, insurrection or riot in the territory of the latter Contracting Party shall be accorded by the latter Contracting Party treatment, as regards restitution, indemnification, compensation or other settlement, no less favorable than that which the latter Contracting Party accords to its own investors or to investors of any third State.

46 As an example, D.L. 600, Art. 4: 'Capital remittances may be made after one year from the date of the investment has entered the territory. The capital gains made with utilities,

domestic jurisdiction for the settlement of disputes between the host contracting State and an investor of the other contracting State.[47]

Over the last decades, Chile also became signatory to a large number of Free Trade Agreements (FTAs). Although they have wider objectives than those provided by the BITs, the FTAs also deal with FDIs. At a first glance, it can be argued that the main difference between BITs signed by Chile and the approach to investments by the FTAs is the fact that the latter not only aim at protecting the investments once they have entered the country, but also ensure the right of access of the investments into the other party of the treaty. Once again, the internalisation of investments occurs through the use of the international principles of national treatment[48] and most favoured nation.[49] Moreover, like the BITs, FTAs establish standards with

capable of being sent outside the territory may be remitted without being subject to any time limit upon fulfilment of tax obligations.'

47 See e.g. Art. 7 of the Chile–UK BIT:

> Settlement of Disputes between a Contracting Party and an investor of the other Contracting Party 1. With a view to an amicable solution of disputes, which arise within the terms of this Agreement, between a Contracting Party and an investor of the other Contracting Party consultations will take place between the parties concerned. 2. If these consultations do not result in a solution within three months from the date of request for settlement, the investor may submit the dispute to the International Centre for the Settlement of Investment Disputes (hereinafter referred to as "the Centre") for settlement by arbitration under the Convention for the Settlement of Disputes between States and Nationals of other States open for signature at Washington DC on 18 March 1965. 3. Notwithstanding the provision of paragraph (2) of this Article the Centre shall not have jurisdiction if the investor has already submitted the dispute to the courts of the Contracting Party which is a party to the dispute.

48 See e.g. Art. 3.3 of the Chile–Malaysia FTA:

> National Treatment 1. Each Party shall accord national treatment to the goods of the other Party in accordance with Art. III of GATT 1994, including its interpretative notes, and to this end, Art. III of GATT 1994 and its interpretative notes are incorporated into and made part of this Agreement, mutatis mutandis. 2. Paragraph 1 shall also apply to a regional level of government.

49 See e.g. Art. 10.3 of the Chile–USA FTA:

> Most Favoured Nation Treatment 1. Each party shall confer investors of another party a treatment no less favourable than the one given, under similar circumstances, to investors of any non-party with respect to the establishment, acquisition, expansion, management, conduct, operation and sale or other disposition of investments in its territory. 2. Each party shall confer covered investments a treatment no less favourable than the one given, under similar circumstances, to investments in its territory of investors of any non-party with respect to the establishment, acquisition, expansion, management, conduct, operation and sale or other disposal of investments inversions.

a view to compensation in cases of expropriation,[50] define international arbitration as a means of dispute resolution[51] and innovate by prohibiting requirements of performance and of nationality of top officials.

In this context, it is important to emphasise that the FTAs signed with Mercosur, and the one with the European Union, have maintained the validity of BITs of Chile with the member States of those economic blocs.[52]

For the government of Chile, the good performance of the country in attracting international investors is mainly due to four factors: political stability, efforts on social issues, serious and responsible macroeconomic policies and austerity in the management of the fiscal policies. For those reasons, and maybe others that might be elaborated, it is undeniable that Chile is currently the best evaluated emerging economy in Latin America and figures prominently among economies worldwide.

The good results obtained by Chile in the recent decades are, precisely, one of the factors that hinder the possibility of it sharing the regulations of Mercosur. Unlike Brazil, which became one of the top recipients of FDI only a few years ago and Argentina, which was a big investment receiver but is passing through a sharp drop in FDI, Chile remains stable and has had continuous positive entries since the early 1990s. Therefore, it becomes really questionable to what extent would the Chilean government agree to share with Mercosur any initiative in the field of investments.

50 See e.g. Art. G-10 of the Chile–Canada FTA:

> Expropriation and Compensation 1. Neither party may expropriate or nationalise directly or indirectly an investment of an investor of another party in its territory or take a measure tantamount to nationalisation or expropriation of such investment ('expropriation'), except: (a) for a public purpose, (b) on a non-discriminatory basis, (c) in accordance with the due process of law and Art. G-05 (1), and (d) conferring the payment of compensation in accordance with paragraphs 2–6. 2. Compensation shall be equivalent to the fair market value of the expropriated investment immediately before the expropriation has taken place (date of expropriation) and shall not reflect any change in value occurring because the intended expropriation had become known before the date of expropriation. Valuation criteria shall include the ongoing business value, asset value including declared tax value of tangible property, and other criteria, as appropriate, to determine a fair market value.

51 See e.g. Art. 13.3 of the Chile–Panama FTA: '1. Disputes arising under the provisions of this Treaty, the WTO Agreement, and any other trade agreement on which the parties are members, may be submitted to the dispute resolution mechanisms of either forum at the discretion of the complaining party.'

52 See e.g. Art. 41 of the Chile–Mercosur FTA: 'Bilateral agreements on the promotion and reciprocal protection of investments, signed between Chile and MERCOSUR member States shall remain in full force.'

6. Final considerations

Mercosur can be seen as a hostage of the foreign policies of its five member States, which are characterised by strong presidential regimes and largely have taken conservative positions regarding the regulation of FDIs. Due to these political issues one can allege that it seems remote that a liberal regulatory framework on investments will be soon put into force by the bloc. Even if currently there is a propitious atmosphere in the bloc's economy in general for the opening of the member States to FDIs and even though the judiciary of some of these countries seem to slowly demonstrate the sensitivity and maturity needed to deal with disputes of this nature, the path towards a regulation of the issue at the regional level still seems to be long and tortuous.

Such a regulation, however, could have some chances of success only if States will leave aside the most controversial issues that hindered the adoption of past proposals, such as the availability of international arbitration to settle disputes between investors and host States. This contribution has argued that Mercosur would continue to assume conservative positions and would not in the near future adopt a liberal framework following the example of the European Union or the NAFTA. Therefore, unless different positions are taken, the new proposal emerged in the 2010 Foz do Iguaçú summit is doomed to failure such as its antecedents.

References

Banco Central do Brasil. 2012. *Relatório de Inflação Junho de 2012*. BCB. Available at: www.bcb.gov.br/htms/relinf/port/2012/06/ri201206c5p.pdf.

CEPAL. 2010. *La Inversion Extranjera Directa en América Latina y el Caribe*. Naciones Unidas. Available at: www.eclac.cl/publicaciones/xml/9/43289/2011-322-LIE-2010-WEB_ULTIMO.pdf.

2011. *La Inversion Extranjera Directa en América Latina y el Caribe*. Naciones Unidas. Available at: www.eclac.cl/publicaciones/xml/0/46570/LIE2011esp.pdf.

Comité de Inversiones Extranjeras. 2012. *Origen de la IED*. CIE Chile. Available at: www.inversionextranjera.cl/index.php?option=com content&view=article&id=133&Itemid=102.

Costa, J. A. F. 2006. 'Proteção e Promoção do Investimento Estrangeiro no Mercosul: uma Ferramenta para a Implementação de um Bom Clima de Investimentos?'. *Revista Brasileira de Política Internacional* 49: 60–77.

Flôres, R. G. 2005. 'Investimento Direto Estrangeiro no Mercosul: Uma Visão Geral'. *Ensaios econômicos* 598. EPGE-FGV.

Pontes, K. D. S. 2009. *Mercosul: a Dimensão Econômico-Comercial.* Instituto Rio Branco. Available at: pt.scribd.com/doc/30827809/Mercosul-PDF.

Ramina, L. 2009. *Direito Internacional dos Investimentos: Solução de Controvérsias entre Estados e Empresas Transnacionais.* Curitiba: Juruá.

Rodas, M. 2003. *Cláusulas Ambietales y de Inversión Extranjera Directa em los Tratados de Libre Comercio Subscritos por México e Chile.* Santiago de Chile: CEPAL.

Sacerdoti, G. 1997. 'Bilateral Treaties and Multilateral Instruments on Investment Protection'. *RCADI* 269: 255–460.

Schlee, P. C. 2005. 'Padrões de Tratamento do Estrangeiro e Sua Propriedade em Matéria de Investimento: Análise da Jurisprudência do ICSID', *DeCita* 3: 82–105.

Stefoni, C. and Fuentes, C. 1996. 'Chile y Mercosur: ¿Hasta dónde queremos integrarnos?', *UNESCO Documentos de debate* 25: 1–43. Available at: www.iadb.org/intal/intalcdi/PE/2007/00139.pdf.

Timerman, H. 2012. *Inversión Extranjera Directa (IED) en Argentina.* Ministerio de Relaciones Exteriores y Culto. Available at: www.mrecic.gov.ar and www.slideshare.net/mrecicarg/indice-de-restricciones-a-la-ied-ocd-vc-miercoles-6.

UNCTAD. 2009. 'Best Practices in Investment for Development. Case Studies in FDI. How to Utilize FDI to Improve Infrastructure – Electricity: Lessons from Chile and New Zealand'. *Investments Advisory Series* 1. United Nations.

2011. 'Best Practices in Investment for Development. Case Studies in FDI. How to Attract and Benefit from FDI in Mining: Lessons from Canada and Chile'. *Investments Advisory Series* 7. United Nations.

Vismara, J. P. C. 2008. *Evolución de la Inverión Extranjera Directa en Argentina. Una Comparación entre la Década del'90 y el Periodo Post-Crisis.* Universidad Nacional de Mar del Plata. Available at: nulan.mdp.edu.ar/643/1/calvo_vismara_jp.pdf.

PART V

The protection of general interests of host States from the Italian perspective

17

Italy's treaty practice and case-law: what balance between investors' protection and general interests of host States?

FEDERICO ORTINO AND DOMENICO DI PIETRO

1. Introduction

Since the mid 1960s Italy has concluded bilateral investment treaties (BITs) with almost 100 countries. The first was the Italy–Guinea BIT signed on 20 February 1964 and the latest is the recent Italy–Iraq BIT signed on 8 June 2011 (an Additional Protocol was signed on 18 October 2012). The great majority (approximately 90 per cent) of Italian BITs were concluded between 1987 and 2004 and have actually entered into force.

In terms of content, BITs signed by Italy present the following key features. Firstly, practically all BITs signed by Italy include provisions on the promotion of foreign investment, expropriation, most-favoured-nation (MFN) treatment, transfer of funds and the settlement of disputes between the contracting parties (so called State–State dispute settlement). In other words, these provisions represent the core of Italian BITs. Secondly, most Italian BITs include provisions on fair and equitable treatment (FET), national treatment, prohibition of arbitrary (or unjustifiable) or discriminatory measures, and the settlement of disputes between a contracting party and an investor of the other contracting party (so called investor–State dispute settlement). Thirdly, a minority of Italian BITs include provisions on right of access (so-called liberalization commitments or pre-establishment rights), full protection and security (FPS), umbrella clauses, stabilization, performance requirements, transparency and general exceptions. Unsurprisingly, all of these provisions are reflected (in one form or another) in the 2003 Italian Model BIT, with the exception of provisions on full protection and security, transparency and general exceptions.

There have also been in excess of twenty (known) international arbitrations brought under Italian BITs in the last fifteen years (see appendix at the end of the chapter).

The underlying aim of the chapter is to assess the balance between investment protection and the sovereign right to regulate in the public interest that Italian BITs have struck. Such assessment will be carried out on the basis of an analysis of the content and evolution of Italy's investment treaty making over the last forty years as well as an examination of the way Italian treaties have been interpreted and applied by investment tribunals over the last two decades. The main findings of this chapter are as follows: while Italian BITs show some form of evolution in terms of scope of protection, the balance between investment protection and the sovereign right to regulate remains an open question as the interpretation of Italian BITs by arbitral tribunals settling disputes between Italian investors and a variety of host States has been influenced by the diverse and evolving arbitral case-law relating to the broader world of investment treaties.

2. Key substantive protection

2.1 *Promotion and admission*

As noted above, Italian BITs invariably include, often at the very beginning of the treaty itself, an obligation on each contracting party to promote the investments of the other party. In *Toto Costruzioni Generali S.p.A.* v. *Lebanon*,[1] the parties argued the issue whether such a provision in the Italy–Lebanon BIT imposes an obligation of due diligence. The tribunal briefly concluded that '[e]ven if "due diligence" were to be required, Toto has not submitted evidence that Lebanon had not behaved in a diligent way'.[2]

Additionally, most Italian BITs require each contracting party to admit the investments of the other party 'in accordance with its laws and regulations'[3] or 'in the exercise of powers conferred by its laws'. This is the traditional approach taken in BITs concluded by (in particular) European countries leaving to each host State the discretion to admit a foreign investment in accordance with its own legislation and focusing instead on

1 *Toto Costruzioni Generali S.p.A.* v. *The Republic of Lebanon*, ICSID Case No. ARB/07/12, Award, 7 June 2012.

2 *Toto Costruzioni Generali S.p.A.* (fn 1) 187.

3 2003 Italian Model BIT, Art. II.6.

providing protections to foreign investors once they have been admitted to the host State (so called post-entry or post-establishment rights).

However, from the mid 1990s, some Italian BITs have granted to investors of one of the contracting parties the right of access to the investment activities in the territory of the other contracting party pursuant to conditions that are not less favourable than those enjoyed by investors of the other contracting party and/or of third states. Those treaties thus grant pre-entry or pre-establishment rights.

Some Italian BITs (often those that contain the above-mentioned qualified right to access) also include a prohibition of certain so-called 'performance requirements'. For example, Art. 2(b) of the protocol to the 1997 Italy–Georgia BIT provides that 'Neither of the Contracting Parties will set any condition for the creation, the expansion or the continuation of investments, which may imply the taking over or the imposing of any limitation to the sale of the production on domestic and international markets, or which specifies that goods must be procured locally, or similar conditions.'

2.2 *Expropriation*

As noted above, practically all Italian BITs prohibit each contracting party from nationalizing, expropriating or subjecting investments of investors of the other contracting party to any measure having equivalent effect, except in the public interest and upon payment of compensation. Art. IV of the 1964 Italy–Guinea BIT, for example, provides that investments of the other contracting party 'ne pourront être expropriés ni soumis à d'autres restrictions, que dans le cas d'un intérêt public évident et démontré et contre versement d'une indemnité égale à la valeur des biens expropriés [...] Le terme "expropriation" comprend également tout acte ou toute mesure ayant un effet analogue à celui de l'expropriation et de la nationalisation.' Later treaties have also required that the expropriation be carried out 'on a non-discriminatory basis and in conformity with legal procedures'.

Italian BITs have normally adopted a fairly broad notion of what constitutes expropriation. In addition to a reference to 'measures having an equivalent effect'[4] to expropriation or nationalization, many Italian

4 2003 Italian Model BIT, Art. V.2.

BITs expressly include 'de jure or de facto'[5] and/or 'direct or indirect'[6] measures.

Investment tribunals have in general struggled to distinguish between an indirect or de facto expropriation and a legitimate regulatory measure. Two recent tribunals constituted on the basis of two Italian BITs seem to have adopted the view that, in order to demonstrate the existence of an expropriation, the investor needs to establish that the adverse effect of the host State measures has rendered the investment useless for all practical purposes. In *Consortium RFCC* v. *Morocco*,[7] for example, the tribunal stated that an indirect expropriation exists in case the measures have 'substantial effects of an intensity that reduces and/or removes the legitimate benefits related with the use of the rights targeted by the measure to an extent that they render their further possession useless'.[8]

The tribunal in *Impregilo* v. *Argentina*,[9] having noted the absence of a definition of expropriation in Art. 5 of the 1990 Italy–Argentina BIT, put forward the following general statements. First, it emphasized that expropriation involves the deprivation of the investor's property and that in this context property should be given a broad meaning covering any material and immaterial assets having an economic value, including concessions and contractual rights belonging to the investor. The tribunal further noted that, while less far-reaching measures which regulate or restrict the right to use property may also have serious economic effects for the investor, they do not constitute expropriation. However, in the view of the tribunal, there are borderline cases where restrictions on the use of property go so far as to leave the investor with only a nominal prop-

5 For example, Italy–Lithuania BIT 1994, Italy–Croatia BIT 1996, Italy–Uganda BIT 1997, Italy–Armenia BIT 1998, Italy–Zimbabwe BIT 1999, Italy–Slovenia BIT 2000, Italy–Ecuador BIT 2001, Italy–Syrian Arab Republic BIT 2002, Italy–Guatemala BIT 2003 and Italy–Yemen BIT 2004.

6 For example, Italy–Egypt BIT 1989, Italy–Jamaica BIT 1993, Italy–Lithuania BIT 1994, Italy–Hong Kong BIT 1995, Italy–Kenya BIT 1996, Italy–Latvia BIT 1997, Italy–Mozambique BIT 1998, Italy–Zimbabwe BIT 1999, Italy–Qatar BIT 2000, Italy–Ecuador BIT 2001, Italy–Syrian Arab Republic BIT 2002, Italy–Guatemala BIT 2003, Italy–Nicaragua BIT 2004 and Italy–Bahrain BIT 2006.

7 *Consortium RFCC* v. *Kingdom of Morocco*, ICSID Case No. ARB/00/6, Award, 22 December 2003.

8 *Consortium RFCC* (fn 7) at 69 (English translation). French original reads as follows: 'avoir des effets substantiels d'une intensité certaine qui réduisent et/ou font disparaître les bénéfices légitimement attendus de l'exploitation des droits objets de ladite mesure à un point tel qu'ils rendent la détention de ces droits inutile'.

9 *Impregilo S.p.A.* v. *Argentine Republic*, ICSID Case No. ARB/07/17, Award, 21 June 2011.

erty right that this, in appropriate cases, could be regarded as indirect expropriation.[10]

Interestingly, a few Italian treaties have attempted to provide further details on the kind of measures that fall under the provision on expropriation, for the most focusing on the host State measure's adverse effect. Clause 4 of the Protocol to the 1994 Italy–Peru BIT, for example, provides that 'any measure that causes substantial prejudice to the value of [the enterprise controlled by the investor]' shall be considered as a nationalization or expropriation.[11]

With regard to the amount of compensation, and independently of the language used in the treaty (very often either 'full' or 'adequate' compensation), Italian BITs further specify that compensation shall be equivalent to the real (or fair) market value of the investment.

It should also be noted that many Italian BITs include, as the first paragraph of the article on expropriation, a prohibition on subjecting investments to any measure, which might limit the right of ownership, possession, control or enjoyment, whether permanently or temporarily. While this prohibition is in principle quite broad, it is invariably limited by the following provision: 'unless specifically provided for by applicable laws and by orders issued by tribunals having jurisdiction'.

2.3 *Standards of protection*

With only minor textual variations, most Italian BITs contain a broad fair and equitable treatment (FET) provision. The first such provision was adopted in the 1975 Italy–Egypt BIT, where Art. I stipulated that each contracting party shall in any case accord investments of the other contracting party 'fair and equitable treatment'. By the 1989 Italy–Egypt BIT the clause read as one would find it in most Italian BITs: 'Each Contracting State shall at all times ensure fair and equitable treatment to the investments of investors of the other Contracting State.'

The FET clause in the 1989 Italy–Egypt BIT was at issue in *Siag and Vecchi* v. *Egypt*.[12] The tribunal there noted the breadth of the FET standard and the importance of the particular facts of each case. However, in line with past arbitral tribunals, the tribunal noted that the principle of good

10 *Impregilo S.p.A.* (fn 9) 270.

11 See Italy–Kazakhstan BIT 1994, Clause 4 of the Protocol; Italy–Saudi Arabia BIT 1996, Clause 4 of the Protocol; Italy–Georgia BIT 1997, Clause 4 of the Protocol.

12 *Waguih Elie George Siag and Clorinda Vecchi* v. *The Arab Republic of Egypt*, ICSID No. ARB/05/15, Award, 1 June 2009.

faith underlies FET and that 'the host State's duty to respect the investor's legitimate expectations arises from its more general duty to act in good faith towards foreigners'.[13] In the tribunal's view, while its precise ambit is not easily articulated, the following notions have been linked with the FET in past cases: transparency, protection of legitimate expectations, due process, freedom from discrimination and freedom from coercion and harassment.[14]

The tribunal in *Impregilo* v. *Argentina* adopted a similarly broad reading of the FET provision in the 1990 Italy–Argentina BIT. While it noted that the term cannot be easily defined, and that it requires at least respect for the customary international minimum standard of protection, the tribunal stated that FET 'is intended to give adequate protection to the investor's legitimate expectations'.[15] The tribunal, however, clarified that the investor's legitimate expectations need to be evaluated considering all circumstances and that FET 'cannot be designed to ensure the immutability of the legal order, the economic world and the social universe and play the role assumed by stabilization clauses specifically granted to foreign investors with whom the State has signed investment agreements'.[16] In the view of the tribunal, while the legitimate expectations of foreign investors cannot be that the State will never modify the legal framework, especially in times of crisis, investors must be protected from unreasonable modifications of that legal framework.

A similar approach was also followed by the tribunal in *Toto Costruzioni* v. *Lebanon*. The tribunal there noted that, in the absence of a stabilization clause or similar commitment, changes in the regulatory framework would be considered breaches of the duty to grant FET only in case of a drastic or discriminatory change in the essential features of the transaction.[17]

Often within the same sentence or paragraph providing for FET, many Italian BITs contain the prohibition of arbitrary or discriminatory measures with regard to the management, maintenance, use, enjoyment or disposal of investments. The tribunal in *Siag and Vecchi* v. *Egypt* found a similarly worded provision in the 1989 Italy–Egypt BIT disjunctive in the sense that measures that are either unreasonable or discriminatory will found a claim, and thus contravene, this provision. Having also noted that a direct expropriation clearly affected the 'management, maintenance, use, enjoyment or disposal' of claimants' investment, the *Siag* tribunal

13 *Waguih Elie George Siag* (fn 12) 450. 14 *Waguih Elie George Siag* (fn 12) 450.

15 *Impregilo S.p.A.* (fn 9) 285. 16 *Impregilo S.p.A.* (fn 9) 290.

17 *Toto Costruzioni Generali S.p.A.* (fn 1) 244.

concluded that many of the measures taken by Egypt in the course of this dispute were 'unreasonable in the ordinary meaning of that term'.[18] The tribunal simply limited itself to list a few examples of such unreasonable measures noting that any one of them would constitute unreasonable behaviour:

> Egypt expropriated Claimants' investment in May 1996 on the purported grounds that Siag Touristic had not met its construction deadlines when those deadlines had in fact not arrived; in June 1996 Egypt seized control of Claimants' investment on the back of Resolution No. 83 at a time when Claimants' application to enjoin Resolution No. 83 was pending; it re-took Claimants' investment in August 1996 despite the fact that Resolution No. 83 had been enjoined by the Cairo Administrative Court; and it failed to comply with the several judicial rulings invalidating Resolution No. 83 and its successor.[19]

As noted above, when it comes to most-favoured-nation (MFN) treatment and national treatment, while practically all Italian BITs include the former, a small number of Italian BITs do not contain the latter. The two provisions may be contained in the same sentence or in two successive paragraphs. Most Italian BITs include two versions of the MFN and/or national treatment provision: in addition to requiring that MFN treatment and/or national treatment be accorded to 'investments effected by investors of the other Contracting Party', Italian BITs expressly extend the two standards either to 'the activities connected with an investment of the other Contracting Party' or to 'the investors of the other Contracting Party'.

Exceptionally, a few Italian BITs have attempted to further define the meaning of 'less favourable treatment'. For example, clause 2 of the protocol to the 1975 Italy–Egypt BIT provided a list of measures that would be deemed treatment less favourable if directed in a discriminatory way against nationals or companies of the other contracting party. Clause 3 of the protocol to the 1996 Italy–Saudi Arabia BIT provides that 'measures that have to be taken for reasons of public order, public health or morals shall not be deemed "treatment less favourable"' within the meaning of the MFN and national treatment provision.

Invariably, all Italian BITs include the usual exceptions to the MFN clause with regard to the advantages and privileges granted to investors of third States by virtue of customs or economic unions, free trade areas, regional or sub-regional agreements, double taxation treaties and

18 *Waguih Elie George Siag* (fn 12) 459.

19 *Waguih Elie George Siag* (fn 12) 459.

agreements to facilitate cross-border trade.[20] The reference to 'regional or sub-regional agreements' is curious, as it apparently does not specify the subject matter nature of such agreements creating some interpretative difficulties. A few Italian BITs contain further limitations (particularly with regard to the national treatment obligation): for example, the 1990 Italy–Morocco BIT includes an exemption for national development policies.[21]

As noted above, a provision on the transfer of funds is also one of the hallmarks of Italian BITs. For example, Art. IV of the 1975 Italy–Egypt BIT provided that each contracting party grant in respect of investments by nationals or companies of the other contracting party the free transfer of returns, royalties, instalments in repayment of loans, amounts spent for the management of the investment, additional funds necessary for the maintenance of the investment, or the value of partial or total liquidation of the investment. Like the 1975 Italy–Egypt BIT, the majority of Italian treaties appear to include a closed-list of funds (including for example, capital, dividends and proceeds of total or partial sale or liquidation of the investment). While earlier treaties often subject the free transfer guarantee to applicable domestic laws and procedures, several later treaties only condition the guarantee to compliance with the host State's fiscal legislation.[22] Exceptionally, some Italian BITs include a broader exception clause to address balance of payments problems.[23]

As noted above, umbrella and stabilization clauses may be found only in a minority of Italian BITs, particularly in those concluded from the mid 1990s. With regard to the former, it should be emphasized that only a few Italian treaties contain the typical formulation according to which each contracting party shall observe any obligation it has assumed with

20 2003 Italian Model BIT, Art. III.3.

21 Italy–Morocco BIT 1990, Art. 3(3) [original French version]: 'Les investisseurs des deux Parties Contractantes ne peuvent se prévaloir du traitement national pour bénéficier des aides, dons, prêts, assurances et garanties accordés par le Gouvernement de l'une des Parties Contractantes exclusivement à ses propres ressortissants ou sociétés dans le cadre des activités des programmes de développement national.'

22 See, for example, Art. 5 of the Italy–Lebanon BIT 1997.

23 See, for example, Art. 6.3 of Italy–Argentina BIT 1990, Art. 6.4 of the Italy–Mexico BIT 1999 ('In case of serious balance of payments difficulties or the threat thereof, each Contracting Party may temporarily restrict transfers, provided that such a Contracting Party implements measures or a programme in accordance with the International Monetary Fund standards. These restrictions would be imposed on an equitable, non- discriminatory and in good faith basis'), and Art. VI.4 of the Italy–Nicaragua BIT 2004.

regard to investments in its territory by investors of the other contracting party. A few other treaties include a rather different version according to which each contracting party 'shall create and maintain in its territory a legal framework apt to guarantee to investors the continuity of legal treatment, including the compliance, in good faith, of all undertakings assumed with regard to each specific investor'. In *Salini* v. *Jordan*,[24] the tribunal found that such treaty provision in the 1996 Italy–Jordan BIT was 'appreciably different' from the language of umbrella clauses discussed in other cases and accordingly held that it did not have any effect similar to an umbrella clause.[25] Accordingly, the tribunal excluded the possibility that the clause could transform contractual obligations into treaty obligations, and thus confer jurisdiction over a mere contractual dispute to the investment treaty tribunal.

Stabilization clauses found in Italian BITs invariably tend to protect the investor against regulatory changes that may intervene after the start of the investment. The variations in the formulation of these clauses appear to focus on the kinds of regulatory changes for which protection is granted through the stabilization clause. For example, the 1994 Italy–Peru BIT adopts a broad definition of regulatory changes as it provides that 'Whenever, after the investment has been made, regulatory change takes place in the country where the investment has been made, the investor's rights acquired on the basis of the previous regulation will not be modified.'[26] The 1996 Italy–Jordan BIT provides a narrower set of regulatory changes as it provides that 'Whenever, after the date when the investment has been made, a modification should take place in laws, regulations, acts or measures of economic policies governing directly or indirectly the investment, the same treatment will apply upon request of the investor that was applicable to it at the moment when the investment had been carried out.' More recently, the 2004 Italy–Nicaragua BIT provides that 'After the date when the investment has been made, any substantial modification in the legislation of the Contracting Party regulating directly or indirectly the investment shall not be applied retroactively and the investments made under this Agreement shall therefore be protected.'[27]

24 *Salini Costruttori S.p.A. and Italstrade S.p.A.* v. *The Hashemite Kingdom of Jordan*, ICSID Case No. ARB/02/13, Award, 31 January 2006.

25 *Salini Costruttori S.p.A.* (fn 25) 126.

26 Italy–Peru BIT 1994, Art. 12(3).

27 Italy–Nicaragua BIT 2004, Art. 12(3).

3. General dispute resolution features of Italian BITs

One of the main features of BITs is the dispute resolution system for the settlement of disputes between foreign investors and Contracting States. Most BITs allow private foreign investors to engage in some means of dispute resolution directly against the State where the investment was made. If not an entirely new feature, this is a ground-breaking development in international law in terms of scope and magnitude.

The type of protection available under BITs has developed over the years both in terms of scope and choice. Most of the BITs entered into in the 1960s and the 1970s provided for direct claims and arbitration only in the event of claims dealing with quantification of compensation for expropriation. Modern BITs, especially those entered into from the beginning of the 1990s, have extended such 'procedural' protection to any breach of the relevant BIT and do tend to provide ample choice as to the means of dispute resolution. Most BITs nowadays do indeed provide foreign investors, as far as arbitration is concerned, with a choice between arbitration under the 1965 Washington Convention (so-called ICSID Convention), arbitration administered by a reputable arbitral institution or *ad hoc* arbitration, mostly under the rules of UNCITRAL.

Generally, the dispute resolution provisions contained in the BITs entered into by Italy reflect the above-mentioned trend. As a result, it is not uncommon for BITs entered into by Italy in the 1960s and early 1970s not to have any dispute settlement provisions between foreign investors and the relevant host State.

The BIT between Italy and Gabon of 1968 as well as the BIT between Italy and Egypt of 1975, for example, provided no investor–State dispute resolution mechanism. Only State to State means of dispute resolution were contemplated. Similarly, the BIT between Italy and the Republic of Guinea of 1964 as well as the BIT between Italy and Malta of 1967, contained no dispute resolution mechanism between the investor and the host State. They only provided for State to State *ad hoc* arbitration with the International Court of Justice acting as appointing authority for the Chairperson of the tribunal. There were of course already some exceptions at that time. Indeed, the BIT between Italy and Chad of 1969 allowed for recourse to International Centre for Settlement of Investment Disputes (ICSID) arbitration while any disputes between the Contracting States should be settled through diplomatic channels.

Similarly to other States, and as we have seen above, Italy has produced a Model BIT that is used in negotiations with potential contracting partners. As far as the investor–State arbitration options are concerned, Art. X of the Italian Model BIT provides, amongst other things, that the investor may submit the dispute to either 'an *ad hoc* Arbitration Tribunal, in compliance with the arbitration regulations of the UN Commission on International Trade Law (UNCITRAL)'; or 'the International Centre for Settlement of Investment Disputes, for the implementation of the arbitration procedure under the Washington Convention of 18 March, 1965, on the Settlement of Investment Dispute between State and Nationals of other States (ICSID arbitration), if or as soon as both Contracting Parties have acceded to it'.

4. Investment protection: the requirements

Most BITs, including those entered into by Italy, make their protection available to foreign investors on condition that certain requirements are fulfilled. Such requirements are normally sorted into four conditions: (i) requirements *ratione materiae* (relating to the nature and characteristics of protected investments); (ii) requirements *ratione personae* (pertaining to the characteristics of protected investor); (iii) requirements *ratione temporis* (relating to the temporal application of the BIT); and (iv) requirements *ratione voluntatis* (jurisdiction over issues encompassed in the consent of the parties). The first two requirements are by far the two most important and, in any event, those that are more frequently the object of debate in investment arbitrations. Our analysis, therefore, will focus on those two requirements.

4.1 The rationae materiae *requirement*

The current Italian Model BIT reflects the international practice aimed at providing a rather broad definition of what is a protected investment. Art. I of the Italian Model BIT is no exception.

The interpretation of such broad provisions would normally generate few problems. A degree of uncertainty, however, might arise where such provisions are to be applied within the legislative and procedural framework of ICSID arbitration. It is indeed generally accepted that for ICSID arbitration to be validly accessed, the investment should not only fall within the scope of application under the relevant BIT or investment contract but, in case protection is sought under the aegis of the ICSID Convention, it should also comply with the scope of application of the latter. This second layer of analysis – which is sometimes also referred to as the 'double keyhole approach' or 'double-barrelled test' – has been the object of heated debate in the last few years.[28] Indeed, such an additional layer has materialized in the jurisprudence of ICSID tribunals since neither the Convention (apart from some limited statements in its preamble) nor the Convention's *travaux préparatoires* deal with this issue at length.

Pursuant to the 'double-barrelled test', in analysing their jurisdiction under the ICSID Convention, ICSID arbitral tribunals should not limit themselves to the notion of investment stipulated in a BIT by the two contracting States or in the investment contract entered into by the host State and the foreign investor. ICSID tribunals are expected to undertake further analysis aimed at establishing the compatibility of the investment with the 'spirit' of the ICSID Convention.

As is well known, however, while the concept of investment is central for the jurisdiction of ICSID arbitral tribunals to be established, the ICSID Convention does not contain any definition or even description of what amounts to an investment for the purpose of the Convention being applied.

In *Salini* v. *Kingdom of Morocco*[29] the two Italian companies Salini S.p.A and Italstrade S.p.A. had successfully submitted a joint tender for the construction of one section of a highway in Morocco. When a dispute about the performance of the contract arose, the Italian companies commenced ICSID arbitration proceedings pursuant to Art. 8 of the Italy–Morocco BIT.

One of the issues to be ascertained by the tribunal was its jurisdiction *rationae materiae* over the dispute. The tribunal was faced with the task of assessing the existence of an investment, both within the meaning of the BIT and the ICSID Convention. According to Art. l(c) and (e) of the Italy–Morocco BIT, the definition of investment entailed 'rights to any contractual benefit having an economic value' and 'any right of an economic nature conferred by law or by contract'.

As the relevant contract gave the claimants a right of an economic nature, the issue of fulfilling the *rationae materiae* requirement under the BIT could be positively resolved with comparative ease. However, the tribunal also noted that, insofar as the option of jurisdiction had been exercised in favour of ICSID, the rights in dispute must also constitute an investment pursuant to Art. 25 of the Washington Convention.

28 See UNCTAD (2003); Gaillard (2009).

29 *Salini Costruttori S.p.A. and Italstrade S.p.A.* v. *Kingdom of Morocco*, ICSID Case No. ARB/00/4, Decision on Jurisdiction, 23 July 2001, 42 ILM 609 (2003).

The tribunal noted that the existence of an investment under the ICSID Convention necessitated: (i) contributions by the investor; (ii) a certain duration of performance of the contract; (iii) a participation in the risks of the transaction; and, as an additional requirement which could be inferred by analysing the Convention's preamble, (iv) the need for the contribution to the economic development of the host State of the investment.

It was not disputed that the claimants: (i) used their know-how, provided the necessary equipment and qualified personnel for the accomplishment of the works; (ii) set up the production tool on the building site; (iii) obtained loans enabling them to finance the purchases necessary to carry out the works and to pay the salaries of the workforce; and (iv) finally agreed to the issuing of bank guarantees. The Italian companies, therefore, made contributions in money, in kind and in industry.

As far as the duration was concerned, the performance of the contract was finally fixed, after a four-month extension, at thirty-six months, which, in the opinion of the tribunal, constituted a long enough period of time.

Finally, the tribunal noted that the contribution of the contract to the economic development of the Moroccan State could not be seriously questioned as the highway in question served an obvious public interest. As a result, the tribunal deliberated that the contract entered into between ADM and the Italian companies amounted to an investment both under the Bilateral Treaty between Italy and Morocco and Art. 25 of the ICSID Convention.

In *Saipem* v. *Bangladesh*,[30] Saipem entered into a contract with Petrobangla for the construction of a natural gas and condensate pipeline. Following disputes over performance under the contract, Saipem initiated arbitration proceedings under the rules of the International Chamber of Commerce (ICC). The relevant tribunal found in Saipem's favour.

In April of 2004, the Bangladeshi courts, upon Petrobangla's application for the setting aside of the award, held that there was no award capable of being annulled, as the ICC proceedings had proceeded illegally. Having taken into account such a ruling and Petrobangla's persistent unwillingness to meet its obligations under the arbitral award, Saipem resorted to ICSID, arguing that it had suffered expropriation by Bangladesh in breach of the Italy–Bangladesh BIT of 1990.

30 *Saipem S.p.A.* v. *The People's Republic of Bangladesh*, ICSID Case No. ARB/05/07, Decision on Jurisdiction, 21 March 2007.

To determine whether Saipem had made an investment within the meaning of Art. 25 of the ICSID Convention, the arbitral tribunal applied the well-known criterion developed in the case of *Salini* v. *Jordan*,[31] according to which the notion of investment implies the presence of the following elements:

a) a contribution of money or other assets of economic value;
b) a certain duration;
c) an element of risk; and
d) a contribution to the host State's development.[32]

The tribunal approached the analysis as to whether there was an investment under Art. 25 of the ICSID Convention by considering the entire operation. Interestingly, with regard to the ICC arbitral award, the tribunal observed that the rights embodied therein had not been created by the award itself but were rather the effect of the rights and obligations created by the parties through the contract. The ICC award, therefore, crystallized the existing rights and obligations of the parties. As a result, the tribunal held that the entire operation qualified as an investment for the purpose of Art. 25 of the ICSID Convention.

4.2 *The* rationae personae *requirement*

Under most BITs, each Contracting Party undertakes to provide certain protection to natural and legal persons who are nationals of the other Contracting Party. The issue of nationality of investors is also addressed under the ICSID Convention. The Convention follows the traditional definitions of nationality adopted under international law as well as under most domestic laws.[33]

31 *Salini Costruttori S.p.A. and Italstrade S.p.A.* v. *The Hashemite Kingdom of Jordan*, ICSID No. ARB/02/13, Decision on Jurisdiction, 9 November 2004.

32 Even though the need for such last element is sometimes put in doubt – see *ASTALDI S.p.A.* v. *People's Democratic Republic of Algeria*, ICSID Case No. ARB/05/3, Decision [on Jurisdiction], 12 July 2006, 72.

33 According to Art. 25(2) 'National of another Contracting State' means:

> a) any natural person who had the nationality of a Contracting State other than the State party to the dispute on the date on which the parties consented to submit such dispute to conciliation or arbitration as well as on the date on which the request was registered … but does not include any person who on either date also had the nationality of the Contracting State party to the dispute; and
> b) any juridical person which had the nationality of a Contracting State other than the State party to the dispute on the date on which the parties consented to

The issue of nationality was addressed in the well-known case of *Soufraki* v. *the United Arab Emirates*.[34] The dispute concerned a concession between the Dubai Department of Ports and Customs and the claimant, who described himself in the contract as a Canadian national. A dispute arose as a result of the cancellation of the concession. Hussein Nuaman Soufraki submitted the dispute to ICSID claiming to be an Italian national for the purposes of the Italy–UAE BIT.

Because of the incongruent nationality asserted by Mr Soufraki in the concession and in the arbitration, the UAE raised a number of jurisdictional objections.[35] The respondent's challenge was supported by Professor Giorgio Sacerdoti's expert witness statement on, *inter alia*, the two 1912 and 1992 Italian laws on nationality.

The core issue was whether the tribunal could make an independent determination of the nationality of the claimant or whether it was bound by the determination made by the Italian municipal and consular authorities through the different documents, such as passports and certificates of nationality, issued to the claimant. The answer of the tribunal to this central question is contained in paragraph 55 of the Award where it is stated that:

> It is accepted in international law that nationality is within the domestic jurisdiction of the State, which settles, by its own legislation, the rules relating to the acquisition (and loss) of its nationality. Article 1(3) of the BIT reflects this rule. But it is no less accepted that when, in international arbitral or judicial proceedings, the nationality of a person is challenged, the international tribunal is competent to pass upon that challenge. It will accord great weight to the nationality law of the State in question and to the interpretation and application of that law by its authorities. But it will in the end decide for itself whether, on the facts and law before it, the person whose nationality is at issue was or was not a national of the State in question and when, and what follows from that finding. Where, as in the instant case, the jurisdiction of an international tribunal turns on an issue of nationality, the international tribunal is empowered, indeed bound, to decide that issue.

submit such dispute to conciliation or arbitration and any juridical person which had the nationality of the Contracting State party to the dispute on that date and which, because of foreign control, the parties have agreed should be treated as a national of another Contracting State for the purposes of this Convention.

34 *Hussein Nuaman Soufraki* v. *The United Arab Emirates*, ICSID Case No. ARB/02/7, Award, 7 July 2004.

35 Mr Soufraki was indeed born in Ethiopia during the Italian occupation. He had never spent time in Italy nor had he exercised any rights as an Italian citizen.

A similar issue was addressed in the already mentioned *Siag and Vecchi* v. *Egypt*,[36] a case brought under the Italy–Egypt BIT. In that case the Egyptian Ministry of Tourism had sold a parcel of property to the company Siag Touristic. The purpose of the sale was to permit Siag Touristic to develop a tourist resort. However, in 1996 the property was confiscated by the Egyptian government.

Siag Touristic was controlled by Mr Siag and Mrs Vecchi. Mr Siag was born an Egyptian national but claimed Lebanese and Italian nationality at the time of the arbitration. He claimed to have lost Egyptian nationality in 1990 when his formal request for permission to obtain Lebanese nationality was granted. Under Egyptian law, once permission to obtain another nationality was granted, the grantee could retain Egyptian nationality by making a declaration of such retention within one year. Mr Siag claimed that he did not make a formal declaration, and therefore he lost his Egyptian nationality.

Mrs Vecchi, originally an Italian national, had gained her Egyptian nationality in 1957, after marrying Mr Siag's father. Mrs Vecchi acquired her Italian nationality once again in 1993, which she claimed terminated her Egyptian nationality at that time pursuant to Egyptian law.

Egypt argued that Mr Siag's and Ms Vecchi's continued use of their Egyptian nationality, as evidenced by several official documents, was decisive in determining their nationality for purposes of the arbitration. The claimants' position in this regard was that such documents were no more than '*prima facie* evidence of nationality', and the final determination of nationality could only be made by the tribunal.

The tribunal ruled in favour of the claimants noting that it was uncontested that they had Italian nationality. The tribunal found that Egypt had not demonstrated that the claimants acquired Italian nationality as a mere expedient in order to bring ICSID proceedings pursuant to the BIT. Both claimants acquired Italian nationality in 1993, a long time before they commenced their claims against Egypt. Furthermore Italian nationality had also been acquired for recognized reasons, i.e. marriage to an Italian in the case of Mr Siag and reacquisition following the death of a husband in the case of Mrs Vecchi.

36 *Waguih Elie George Siag and Clorinda Vecchi* v. *The Arab Republic of Egypt*, ICSID No. ARB/05/15, Decision on Jurisdiction, 11 April 2007.

4.3 *Extension of protection to joint venture partners*

In *Impregilo* v. *Pakistan*[37] the tribunal rejected the argument according to which the fulfilment of the *rationae personae* requirements cannot be automatically extended to or benefited from other members of a joint venture through which an investment has been carried out.

The tribunal explained that it had no jurisdiction in respect of claims on behalf of, or losses incurred by, any of Impregilo's joint venture partners. It clarified that it had jurisdiction *ratione personae* over Impregilo's claims, only insofar as such claims concerned Impregilo's own alleged loss, being (at most) proportionate to its pro-rata participation in the joint venture.

5. The problem of mass claims

The problem of mass claims in investment arbitration has arisen in connection with the alleged breach of Argentina's obligations in relation to bonds ultimately held by Italian nationals.

As is well known, Argentina defaulted in 2001 on over US$100 billion of external bond debt owed to both non-Argentine and Argentine creditors. Argentina proceeded with a restructuring of its debt culminating in the launching, in January 2005, of an exchange offer, pursuant to which bondholders could exchange existing series of bonds, on which Argentina had suspended payment, for new debt that Argentina would issue.

In 2006, some of the bondholders who had not participated in the restructuring filed a request for arbitration with ICSID pursuant to the Argentina–Italy BIT of 1990. The case is now known as *Abaclat* v. *Argentina*.[38]

Argentina objected to ICSID's jurisdiction, *inter alia*, on the argument that the conditions for ICSID jurisdiction were not fulfilled as the claims were an unprecedented abuse of the investment treaty regime. According to Argentina such claims were being brought without legal basis and for a fundamentally illegitimate motive.

Amongst other things, Argentina observed that the claim – originally brought by about 180,000 (eventually 'only' about 60,000) unrelated

37 *Impregilo S.p.A.* v. *Islamic Republic of Pakistan*, ICSID Case No. ARB/03/3, Decision on Jurisdiction, 22 April 2005, 223.

38 *Abaclat and Others* v. *The Argentine Republic*, ICSID Case No. ARB/07/5, pending case, registered 7 February 2007.

claimants – had arisen out of different purported investments that had been brought individually by each claimant at different times and under different circumstances. According to Argentina it should not be possible to turn a sovereign's non-payment of external debt, that is governed by other States' laws providing for remedies in the courts of those other States, into a violation of an investment treaty.

The tribunal noted that, while commencement of ICSID arbitration proceedings by multiple claimants has occurred in the past, this appeared to be the first case in the ICSID's history that mass claims were brought before it. The tribunal recognized that the large number of claimants raised a series of questions and challenges. In particular, the large number of claimants made it impossible to treat and examine each of the thousands of claims as if it were a single claim. As a result, a degree of generalization and/or group examination would be unavoidable.

Having said that, the task to be tackled by the tribunal was whether the characteristics of such mass claims might constitute a hurdle to the ICSID's jurisdiction and/or to the admissibility of the claims. The tribunal noted in that regard that neither the ICSID framework nor the BIT address the issue of such mass proceedings and therefore fail to provide a clear answer to this question. The parties unsurprisingly disagreed on how that silence should be interpreted.

The tribunal observed in that respect that the mass aspect of the case related to the modalities and implementation of the ICSID proceedings and not to the question of consent to ICSID arbitration. According to the tribunal, in light of the absence of a definition of investment in the ICSID Convention, it would be contrary to the purpose of the BIT, and to the spirit of the ICSID, to require in addition to the consent to ICSID arbitration in general, a supplementary express consent to the form of such arbitration.[39]

Similarly, in *Ambiente Ufficio S.p.A.* v. *Argentina*,[40] ninety Italian claimants brought a claim against Argentina for harm arising from Argentina's default and subsequent restructuring of its sovereign debt in 2001. As in the *Abaclat* decision, the claimants alleged that Argentina had breached its international obligations under the Argentina–Italy BIT. Also as in *Abaclat*, Argentina objected to the tribunal's jurisdiction on the basis that it had never consented to multi-party claims under the ICSID.

39 *Abaclat and Others*, Decision on Jurisdiction and Admissibility, 4 August 2011, 518.

40 *Ambiente Ufficio S.p.A. and Others* v. *The Argentine Republic*, ICSID No. ARB/08/9, Decision on Jurisdiction and Admissibility, 8 February 2013.

Also the *Ambiente Ufficio* tribunal faced the issue of whether it had jurisdiction to hear a claim with multiple claimants. Although the tribunal dismissed Argentina's jurisdictional objections, the tribunal distinguished between the 'mass claim-type collective proceedings' in *Abaclat*, and the 'multi-party' character of the proceedings in *Ambiente Ufficio*, suggesting that a distinction may lie between the two decisions. The tribunal subsequently decided, after consideration of a series of factors, that multi-party proceedings were 'perfectly compatible' with ICSID arbitration and that no consent beyond that given by Argentina under the BIT was necessary to trigger ICSID's jurisdiction.[41]

6. Most-favoured-nation treatment: procedural issue

As is well known, most BITs include a most-favoured-nation (MFN) clause. Pursuant to that clause, foreign investors are to accord the highest standard of treatment that is available or might be made available in the future by the Contracting States to investors from any other third State.

Such clauses have for some time been the object of heated debate as to their scope of application. In other words, it is debated whether they should only apply to the substantive protections contained in BITs or they should extend to any provisions contained in such instruments including protections of a procedural nature such as the dispute resolution provisions.[42]

The issue arose following the arbitration in *Maffezini* v. *Spain*,[43] where an Argentine national, who had brought a claim under the Argentina–Spain BIT, was allowed to rely on a more favourable time requirement in the arbitration process found in the Chile–Spain BIT. The tribunal accepted this as an application of the MFN principle. Other cases since then have tackled the same issue. As far as Italian BITs are concerned, in *Salini* v. *Jordan*,[44] it was stated that the extension of protection depends on the actual wording of the relevant clause. In that specific case the tribunal found that, on the basis of the specific language employed in the clause, the extension of protection could not be granted.[45]

41 A thorough analysis of the problematic issues connected to mass claims in investment arbitration have been tackled by De Luca (2011). See also Levesque (2012), 1–8.

42 Amongst the most recent contributions on the issue see Acconci (2008), 363–406; Schill (2009), 193; Santiago Tawil (2009); Douglas (2011), 97–113; Parker (2012), 30–63.

43 *Emilio Agustín Maffezini* v. *The Kingdom of Spain*, ICSID No. ARB/97/7, Award, 13 November 2000.

44 *Salini Costruttori S.p.A.* (fn 32) 115–18.

45 It was observed in that regard that:

In *Impregilo* v. *Argentina*,[46] Argentina challenged the tribunal's jurisdiction on the basis that the investor had failed to observe a requirement in the BIT (Italy–Argentina and Germany–Argentina, respectively) according to which any disputes should be litigated before the domestic courts for eighteen months prior to instituting international arbitration proceedings. The investor countered that it could avoid the pre-arbitration requirement by virtue of the MFN clause in the respective basic treaty, through which it could import a more favourable dispute resolution clause from a third-party treaty.

The majority held that the tribunal had jurisdiction over the claim through the operation of the MFN clause. The majority of the tribunal attached 'special weight' to the wording of the MFN clause, which provided in Art. 3 that the MFN treatment was to be accorded to 'investments [...] to the income and activities related to such investments and to all other matters regulated by this Agreement'.

The majority thus endorsed the decision in *Maffezini*[47] where the relevant tribunals had adopted a different stance on the scope of application of MFN clauses.

7. Closing remarks

The Italian investment treaty practice has experienced marked evolution. The 2003 Italian Model BIT represents the apex of this evolution. The 2003 Model includes pre-establishment rights on a national treatment and MFN basis, all of the traditional investment protection guarantees

> The current Tribunal shares the concerns that have been expressed in numerous quarters with regard to the solution adopted in the Maffezini case. Its fear is that the precautions taken by authors of the award may in practice prove difficult to apply, thereby adding more uncertainties to the risk of 'treaty shopping'. The Tribunal also observes that bilateral investment treaties carry varying provisions that address this issue. Some of those treaties provide expressly that the most-favored-nation treatment extends to the provisions relating to settlement of disputes [...] In other treaties, the MFN clause does not contain such a provision, but refers to 'all rights' contained in the agreement, or to 'all matters' subject to the agreement [...] The Tribunal observes that the circumstances of this case are different. Indeed, Art. 3 of the BIT between Italy and Jordan does not include any provision extending its scope of application to dispute settlement. It does not envisage 'all rights or all matters covered by the agreement'. Furthermore, the Claimants have submitted nothing from which it might be established that the common intention of the Parties was to have the most-favored-nation clause apply to dispute settlement [...] From this, the Tribunal concludes that Art. 3 of the BIT does not apply insofar as dispute settlement clauses are concerned.

46 *Impregilo S.p.A.* (fn 9). 47 *Emilio Agustín Maffezini* (fn 44).

(with the curious exception of the full protection and security clause but the inclusion of a stabilization clause), and both State–State and investor–State arbitration.[48] The Italian Model BIT is in line with that of other States even though some States have more recently undertaken some form of review of their investment policies. For example, in the last ten years, Canada and most notably the United States have put forward new Model BITs clarifying scope and extent of the protection actually afforded to foreign investors in significant part to achieve a better balance between the protection afforded to investors and the ability of host States to regulate in the public interest. Notable examples are the linking of the FET and FPS clauses to customary law, the omission of the umbrella clause and the inclusion of a self-judging security exception. The fact that Italy has not yet been on the receiving end of a BIT claim may explain why Italy has not yet recalibrated the content of its BITs.

Following the recent grant of exclusive competence to the EU with regard to FDI, Italy's foreign investment policy is now inevitably linked with the formulation of an investment policy at the EU. The core challenge remains undisputed: to afford the maximum protection to investors while at the same time guaranteeing host States' ability to regulate in the public interest.[49] That process is complex and still ongoing and one cannot but wait and see what will be the role that Italy will play therein.

Appendix

Italy–Albania BIT

Burimi S.r.l. and Eagle Games SH.A. v. *Republic of Albania*, ICSID Case No. ARB/11/18

Italy–Algeria BIT

L.E.S.I. S.p.A. and ASTALDI S.p.A. v. *République Algérienne Démocratique et Populaire*, ICSID Case No. ARB/05/3

Consortium Groupement L.E.S.I.-DIPENTA v. *République Algérienne Démocratique et Populaire*, ICSID Case No. ARB/03/08

Italy–Argentina BIT

Abaclat and Others v. *Argentine Republic*, ICSID Case No. ARB/07/5

Impregilo S.p.A. v. *Argentine Republic*, ICSID Case No. ARB/07/17

48 See Ortino (2013), 321–46.

49 See EU–US Statement on Shared Principles for International Investment of 10 April 2012.

Ambiente Ufficio S.p.A. and Others v. *Argentine Republic*, ICSID Case No. ARB/08/9
Alemanni and Others v. *Argentine Republic*, ICSID Case No. ARB/07/8
Italy–Bangladesh BIT
Saipem S.p.A. v. *The People's Republic of Bangladesh*, ICSID Case No. ARB/05/07
Italy–Cuba BIT
Italian Republic v. *Republic of Cuba*, *ad hoc* State–State arbitration
Italy–Egypt BIT
Siag and Vecchi v. *Egypt*, ICSID Case No. ARB/05/15
Italy–Honduras BIT
Astaldi S.p.A. v. *Honduras*, Award, ICSID Case No. ARB/07/32
Italy–Jordan BIT
Salini Costruttori S.p.A. and Italstrade S.p.A. v. *The Hashemite Kingdom of Jordan*, ICSID Case No. ARB/02/13
Italy–Ivory Coast BIT
Adriano Gardella S.p.A. v. *Côte d'Ivoire*, ICSID Case No. ARB/74/1
Italy–Lebanon BIT
Toto Costruzioni Generali S.p.A. v. *The Republic of Lebanon*, ICSID Case No. ARB/07/12
Italy–Morocco BIT
Consortium RFCC v. *Royaume du Maroc*, ICSID Case No. ARB/00/6
Salini Costruttori S.p.A. and Italstrade S.p.A. v. *Kingdom of Morocco*, ICSID Case No. ARB/00/4
Italy–Pakistan BIT
Impregilo S.p.A. v. *Islamic Republic of Pakistan*, ICSID Case No. ARB/03/3
Italy–Russian Federation BIT
Cesare Galdabini S.p.A. v. *Russian Federation*, UNCITRAL proceedings
Italy–South Africa BIT
Piero Foresti, Laura de Carli & Others v. *The Republic of South Africa*, ICSID Case No. ARB(AF)/07/01
Italy–United Arab Emirates BIT
Hussein Nuaman Soufraki v. *The United Arab Emirates*, ICSID Case No. ARB/02/7

References

Acconci, P. 2008. 'Most-Favoured-Nation Treatment', Muchlinski, P., Ortino F. and Schreuer C. (eds.), *The Oxford Handbook of International Investment Law*. Oxford University Press: 363–406.

Binder, C., Kriebaum, U., Reinisch, A. and Wittich, S. (eds.), 2009. International Investment Law for the 21st Century: Essays in Honour of Christoph Schreuer. Oxford University Press.

De Luca, A. 2011. 'Collective Actions in ICSID Arbitration: The Argentine Bonds Case'. *Italian Yearbook of International Law* XXI: 211–39.

Douglas, Z. 2011. 'The MFN Clause in Investment Arbitration: Treaty Interpretation Off the Rails'. *Journal of International Dispute Settlement* 2: 97–113.

Gaillard, E. 2009. 'Identify or Define? Reflections on the Evolution of the Concept of Investment in ICSID Practice', Binder, Kriebaum, Reinisch and Wittich (eds.): 403–16.

Levesque, C. 2012. '*Abaclat and Others* v. *Argentine Republic*: The Definition of Investment'. *ICSID Review* 27: 1–8.

Ortino, F. 2013. 'Italy', Brown, C. (ed.), *Commentaries on Selected Model Investment Treaties*. Oxford University Press: 321–46.

Parker, S.L. 2012. 'A BIT at a Time: The Proper Extension of the MFN Clause to Dispute Settlement Provisions in Bilateral Investment Treaties'. *The Arbitration Brief* 2.1: 30–63.

Santiago Tawil, G. 2009. 'Most Favoured Nation Clauses and Jurisdictional Clauses in Investment Treaty Arbitration', Binder, Kriebaum, Reinisch and Wittich (eds.): 9–41.

Schill, S.W. 2009. *The Multilateralization of International Investment Law*. Cambridge University Press.

UNCTAD. 2003. *Dispute Settlement: ICSID Requirement Ratione Materiae*. New York and Geneva: United Nations (UNCTAD/EDM/Misc.232/Add.4).

18

Diplomatic intervention and State-to-State arbitration as alternative means for the protection of foreign investments and host States' general interests: the Italian experience

MATILDE RECANATI

1. Introduction

The International Centre for Settlement of Investment Disputes (ICSID) investor–State arbitration system has been recently criticized as a system favouring investors' interests at the prejudice of States' interests. The current 'backlash' against investor–State arbitration is perceived to have begun with a number of ICSID awards[1] against measures that host States have defended as designed to achieved legitimate domestic policy objectives.[2] This has appeared especially in relation to cases involving Argentina.

There are several State 'general interests', the protection of which may limit the rights of foreign investors. They may consist of needs of the population and of economic policy measures as it was in the ICSID Arbitral cases involving Argentina's financial crisis;[3] host State general

1 See, e.g., *Piero Foresti et al.* v. *South Africa* ICSID Case No. ARB(AF)/07/1, Award and Concurring Statement of Arbitrator Matthews, 4 August 2010; *Desert Line Projects LLC* v. *Yemen* ICSID Case No. ARB/05/17, Award, 6 February 2008; *Victor Pey Casado* v. *Chile*, ICSID Case No. ARB/98/2 Award, 8 May 2008; *ADC Affiliate Ltd* v. *Hungary* ICSID Case No. ARB/03/16, Award, 2 October 2006; *Aguas del Tunari SA* v. *Bolivia* ICSID Case No. ARB/02/3, Decision on Jurisdiction, 21 October 2005; *Biwater Gauff* v. *Tanzania* ICSID Case No. ARB/05/22, Award, 26 July 2008; *Vattenfall et al.* v. *Germany* ICSID Case No. ARB/09/6, Award, 11 March 2011.

2 Nelson (2010), 555.

3 See *Compañia de Aguas del Aconquija SA and Vivendi Universal* v. *Argentina* ICSID Case No. ARB/97/3, Award, 20 August 2007; *Enron Corporation and Ponderosa Assets, LP* v. *Argentina* ICSID Case No. ARB/01/3, Award, 22 May 2007; *Sempra Energy International* v. *Argentina* ICSID Case No. ARB/02/16, Award, 28 September 2007; *Azurix Corp.* v. *Argentina* ICSID Case No. ARB/01/12, Award, 14 July 2006; *CMS Gas Transmission Co* v. *Argentina* ICSID Case No. ARB/01/8, Award, 12 May 2005; *LG&E* v. *Argentina* ICSID

regulatory action; the protection of the host State national security; the protection of non-economic concerns like sustainable and human development, the protection of human rights and environment, as well as the control of the production and sale of harmful substances. Also in the field of intellectual property rights, the standard of IPRs' protection (TRIPs-plus regime) may result in limiting the rights of host States to rely on the exceptions and flexibilities under the TRIPs (Trade-Related Intellectual Property Rights) in order to address public interests concerns.[4]

The reasons of the so called 'legitimacy crisis'[5] have been identified by a group of academics in the 'Public Statement on the International Investment Regime, 31 August 2010' as coming from the pro-investor interpretation of investment treaties and from the legal framework and dispute resolution of investment treaties.[6]

As for the 'pro investor interpretation of investment treaties', it is argued in the document that 'Awards issues by international arbitrators against States have in numerous cases incorporated overly expansive interpretations of language in investment treaties' which 'have prioritized the protection of the property and economic interests of transnational corporations over the right to regulate of States and the right to self-determination of people'.[7] Moreover, according to the document 'the award of damages as a remedy of first resort in investment arbitration poses a serious threat to democratic choice and the capacity of government to act in the public interest by way of … policy making in response to changing social, economic and environment conditions'.[8]

As for the legal framework and dispute resolution, it is argued that 'investment treaty arbitration as currently constituted is not a fair, independent and balanced method for the resolution of investment disputes'.[9]

States' reactions to concerns about the potential for investment law to favour the protection of the investors' interests against the ones of the host State have been different. Some countries especially in Latin America, have responded by denouncing or insisting on the renegotiation of some of their International Investment Agreements (IIAs) and by

Case No. ARB/02/1, Decision on Liability, 3 October 2006. See for comments: Alvarez and Khamsi (2008–9), 379; Kurtz (2010), 325; Sacerdoti (2013) 351.

4 Di Blase, in this volume.

5 Schill (2012).

6 Public Statement on the International Investment Regime, 31 August 2010, available at www.osgoode.yorku.ca/publicstatement/documents/Public%20Statement%20%28June%202011%29.pdf

7 *Ibid.*, 5. 8 *Ibid.*, 6. 9 *Ibid.*, 8.

withdrawing from the ICSID Convention or seeking to limit the jurisdiction of the Centre established by the Convention.[10] Countries in Southern and Eastern Africa have adopted a comprehensive investment promotion treaty among themselves, with different provisions from traditional IIAs.[11] Other States through joint interpretations have clarified the substantive provisions of their existing IIAs or adopted new IIAs with provisions that seek to reconcile the tension between the principles of investment protection and host States' general interests.[12] Over the last two years, the United States[13] and Norway[14] have undertaken official reviews of their IIAs to determine whether they now strike an appropriate balance between these competing interests.[15]

This alleged legitimacy crisis bring us to wonder whether, on the one hand, treaties predating BITs and, on the other hand, the resort to diplomatic protection of aggrieved investors by their home State against the host State, either through diplomatic means or by interstate adjudication, might protect States' general interests better than the current investment regime does.

10 In May 2007, Bolivia gave notice under Art. 71 of the ICSID Convention that it was withdrawing from the Convention ('Bolivia Submits a Notice under Art. 71 of the ICSID Convention' (16 May 2007), icsid.worldbank.org); see also *Investment Treaty News*, 'Bolivia Notifies World Bank of Withdrawal from ICSID, Pursues BIT Revisions' (9 March 2007). In December 2007, Ecuador unilaterally modified its submission to ICSID jurisdiction by excluding any disputes involving Ecuadorian natural resources ('Ecuador's Notification under Art. 25.4 of the ICSID Convention' (5 December 2007) icsid.worldbank.org). In April 2008, Nicaragua also threatened to withdraw from ICSID and in July 2009 Ecuador to do so; see also F. Cabrera-Diaz, 'Ecuador Continues Exit from ICSID', *Investment Treaty News* (8 June 2009) available at: www.iisd.org/itn/2009/06/05/ecuador-continues-exit-from-icsid. Meanwhile Venezuela and Bolivia have manifested hostility to the current system of BITs to which they are party, and Venezuela has withdrawn from the 'Group of Three' free trade agreement with Colombia and Mexico. See Gaillard (2008).

11 See Agreement Establishing the Common Market from Eastern and Southern Africa Common Investment Area (22–3 May 2007) COMESA CIAA; Muchlinski (2008–9), 37.

12 See Vandevelde (2008–9), 283; Schwebel (2009), 519; Spears (2011), 271.

13 See US Department of State, Office of the United States Trade Representative, Public Notice 6693, 74 Fed. Reg., 14 July 2009; D. Vis-Dunbar, 'United States Reviews its Model Bilateral Investment Treaty', *Investment Treaty News* (5 June 2009).

14 See L. E. Peterson, 'Norway Proposes Significant Reforms to its Investment Treaty Practice', *Investment Treaty News* (27 March 2008); D. Vis-Dunbar, 'Norway Shelves its Draft Model Bilateral Investment Treaty', *Investment Treaty News* (8 June 2009); Draft Agreement between the Kingdom of Norway and [Country] for the Promotion and Protection of Investment (Draft Norway Model BIT), ita.law.uvic.ca/investment-treaties.htm.

15 Spears (2011), 271.

Reference is made to treaties of Friendship, Commerce and Navigation (FCNs) typically entered into by the USA, or Consular and Establishment treaties, some of them going back to the nineteenth century. Their relevance appears to be residual in comparison with the elaborate substantive and procedural provisions of BITs, on the other hand since many of these treaties are still in force, often between countries which are not bound by reciprocal BITs, they may still be of value, as confirmed by recent cases in which they were resorted to through diplomatic protection by the home countries of aggrieved investors as the sole available international means of redress.

This was the case of the well known *ELSI* dispute,[16] in which the United States invoked against Italy certain provisions of the bilateral FCN treaty of 1948 before the ICJ in 1986–9. In another case Italy successfully exercised diplomatic protection towards Switzerland in 1991–2 in favour of Italian citizens faced with confiscation of immovable property, because of alleged violations of Swiss legislation restricting acquisition of land by foreigners. In this case Italy relied on the bilateral treaty of establishment of 1868,[17] which guarantees to the nationals of either country an unlimited right to acquire real estate.

Another avenue is the invocation of the BIT by the home country in diplomatic protection of aggrieved national investors against the host country in a State-to-State arbitration. As known, in addition to investor–State arbitration, bilateral investment treaties generally provide for arbitration between two contracting States, by which disputes concerning the interpretation and application of the treaty can be brought before arbitral tribunals established under the BIT.[18] This is provided in BITs but rarely resorted to. One such case is the recent dispute between Italy and Cuba, where Italy espoused the claims of several Italian investors against Cuba in a direct State-to-State arbitration pursuant to Art. 10 of the BIT of 1993 between the two countries.[19]

16 *Elettronica Sicula S.p.A. (ELSI)* (*United States of America* v. *Italy*), ICJ Judgment, 20 July 1989, ICJ Reports 1989, 15.

17 Establishment and Consular Convention between Italy and Switzerland, signed on 22 July 1868 and entered into effect on 1 May 1869, available at: itra.esteri.it/itrapgm/Visualizza.asp?ID=45862. For a more detailed exam of this dispute see Sacerdoti (2014): 403.

18 See US–Ecuador investment treaty, according to which: 'Any dispute between the Parties concerning the interpretation or application of the Treaty, which is not resolved through consultation or diplomatic channels, shall be submitted, upon the request of either parties, to an arbitral tribunal for binding decision in accordance with the applicable rules of international law.' See Roberts (2010), 179.

19 Preliminary Award of 15 March 2005; Final Award of 15 January 2008, available at www.italaw.com/documents/Italy_v_Cuba_FinalAward2008.pdf made in the French

There is finally a further alternative to the agreements mentioned above, namely reliance by the host State on customary international law. This was the case in the *Barcelona Traction* case[20] and in the more recent *Diallo* case.[21] Since the analysis of this point is beyond the scope of the present contribution, references to those cases will be made only where appropriate. A common feature to all these different avenues is the resort to diplomatic protection of aggrieved investors by their home State against the host State, whether a claim is pursued by diplomatic means as was the case of the Italian-Swiss dispute of 1991–2, or by adjudication, such as in the *ELSI* case and in the Cuba–Italy case.

The aim of this contribution is trying to analyse whether treaties different from BITs and recourse to diplomatic protection can be a real alternative to investor–State arbitration under the ICSID, which better serves the protection of States' interests in respect of the investors' ones.

2. The dispute between Italy and Switzerland (1990–2) on the right to acquire property under the 1868 bilateral establishment and consular treaty

'Establishment Conventions' or 'Establishment and Consular Conventions' were frequently entered into by European countries in the second part of the nineteenth century and the first part of the twentieth century, some of which are still in force. The 1868 Convention between Italy and Switzerland conforms to a common pattern of such treaties entered by the newly formed Kingdom of Italy (1861) but also by the Italian Republic recently with friendly countries of Europe and Latin America.[22]

language. The dissenting opinion of Professor Tanzi to the Final Award is available at www.italaw.com/documents/Italy_v_Cuba_FinalAward2008_Dissent.pdf.

20 *Barcelona Traction, Light and Power Company Limited* (*Belgium* v. *Spain*), ICJ Judgment, 5 February 1970, ICJ Reports 1970, 3.

21 *Ahmadou Sadio Diallo* (*Republic of Guinea* v. *Democratic Republic of Congo*), ICJ Judgment, Preliminary Objections, 24 May 2007, ICJ Reports 2007, 1; *Ahmadou Sadio Diallo* (*Republic of Guinea* v. *Democratic Republic of Congo*), ICJ Judgment, Merits, 30 November 2010, ICJ Reports 2010, 1.

22 From the database of the Italian Ministry of Foreign Affairs it appears that similar treaties, currently still in force, had been entered by Italy with France, 23 August 1951; Belgium, 22 July 1878; Bulgaria, 21 February 1968; Czech Republic, 10 October 1975; Costa Rica, 12 December 1933; El Salvador, 25 January 1876; France, 12 January 1955; United Kingdom, 1 June 1954; Libya, 4 July 1998; Netherlands, 3 August 1865; Poland, 9 November 1973; Romania, 8 August 1967; Slovakia, 10 October 1975; Greece, 27 November 1880; Portugal, 30 September 1868; Spain, 21 July 1867; United States, 8 May 1878; Ukraine, 23 December 2003; Hungary, 16 October 1969; Turkey, 9 September 1929.

Inspired by liberal economic and trading policies, typical of that period, the provisions of this treaty go beyond the protection usually offered by BITs since it does not only protect property once acquired, but includes a right to market access and the making of investment, specifically in real estate. Art. 1 grants reciprocally, in great detail, to Italians in Switzerland and to Swiss nationals in Italy full freedom of travelling, establishment, trade and commerce, access to professions and equality of treatment with nationals as to persons and property. More specifically, Art. 3 grants them 'full and entire right to acquire and own by sale, inheritance, donation or in any other manner, all kinds of movable or immovable property, ownership of which is open to nationals and to dispose thereof'. Art. 6 ensures, moreover, to the beneficiaries 'the most constant and complete protection of their persons and property', including 'easy and free access to justice'.

2.1 The object of the dispute: restrictions to acquisition of immovable property in Switzerland and confiscation of property not duly authorized

The dispute at issue concerned the right of Italian nationals to own 'secondary residences', that is holiday apartments and houses, in Switzerland following a stream of Swiss statutes that had progressively restricted from 1961 the access of non-resident foreigners to immovable property in Switzerland. Restrictive regulation of acquisition by non-resident foreigners of real estate in coveted touristic areas has been adopted in other European countries, such as Greece, Austria, Denmark: in some instances derogations from national treatment and freedom of capital movement have led to disputes as to their legality before the European Court of Justice.[23]

The last such Swiss law at the time of the dispute was that 'on the acquisition of real estate by persons from abroad' of 16 December 1983 explicitly aimed at 'preventing excessive foreign domination of national soil'.[24]

23 Protocol 32 to the European Union (Maastricht) Treaty of 1992 allows Denmark to maintain existing restrictive legislation on the acquisition of real estate by non-resident citizens of other EU countries. Austrian restrictions applicable to ownership in Tirol has come before the Court of Justice, see Case C-302/97, *Klaus Konle* v. *Republik Österreich*, [1999] I-ECR 3099.

24 The Statute (so-called 'Authorization Law'), SR 211.412.41, published in the Swiss Official Journal 1984, 1148, is commonly known as *Lex Friedrich* after its proponent and currently Lex Koller, following subsequent modifications that have lifted some of the restrictions of the previous text. On March 2012 the Swiss Parliament rejected a proposal by the government to abrogate Lex Koller (www.swissinfo.ch of 12.03.2012) while the Swiss electorate in a referendum has approved a proposal to limit secondary housing to 20 per cent of the total in each municipality.

The statute provided for a limited number of authorizations to be distributed each year by individual Swiss cantons as a requirement to acquire secondary residences by non-resident foreigners. After a lax application of this legislation for many years, the turning point occurred in the first case brought by the canton Grisons against a bearer's share corporation in which the ownership of shares corresponded to an exclusive right to an apartment in a multi-storey building built and owned by the corporation. The Swiss Federal Tribunal declared the corporation illegal and ordered its dissolution under Art. 57.3 of the civil code, confiscating its assets in favour of the canton.[25] Following such favourable decision, the canton started to press all other foreign owners of apartments (not just Italians) in the same situation, offering them a 'settlement' which would have entailed them to relinquish their property without compensation against just a long-term lease of same.

The claimants had not invoked the treaty[26] but the invocation of the accepted doctrine that a treaty prevails on domestic law under the Swiss constitution had been rejected by the Swiss Federal Tribunal in a previous case concerning a German investor which had invoked the corresponding provision of the German-Swiss treaty. The Tribunal had relied on the jurisprudential exception that in Switzerland treaties do not prevail against contrary legislative provisions where the legislator had clearly stated that it intended a provision to be enacted irrespective of treaty obligations to the contrary.

2.2 *Italy's intervention in diplomatic protection and the settlement of the dispute*

The Italian Ministry of Foreign Affairs accepted to extend diplomatic protection to the group of Italian owners and complained with the Swiss Ministry of Foreign Affairs in June 1991 of the breach of the 1868 treaty provision granting full right of property to Italian nationals. Italy hinted that in absence of a friendly solution, Italy would have resorted to the

25 Decision of the II Chamber of 13 October 1989 (5C.4/1989/cb) *Sud Provizel SA* v. *Kanton Graubünden*, holding that Art. 57.3 was applicable by implication under the previous legislation on foreign owned real estate in place when the acquisition had been made.

26 BGE 112, II, 13. The Italian-Swiss treaty was invoked in a later case by another Italian-owned corporation also threatened with dissolution (BGE, 5C.137/1991/tb of 29 November 1991, *Gordona SA* v. *Kanton Graubünden*), but the Federal Tribunal, while recognizing that the treaty was applicable, evaded the issue, finding that the treaty should have been invoked at an earlier stage of the proceedings.

bilateral treaty of conciliation and judicial settlement of 1924, which ultimately provided for recourse to the International Court of Justice.

While central Swiss authorities expressed the wish to settle the matter in a satisfactory way for both parties, the canton proceeded further with its confiscatory actions after the Swiss Federal Tribunal had issued further decisions upholding the application of Art. 57.3 of the civil code. Finally, the Swiss government obtained the agreement of the canton on a settlement proposal acceptable to the Italian owners. The Swiss government was to allocate to the Grisons an extra number of authorizations to be distributed with retroactive effect to the individual owners affected so that they would be able to retain their property in conformity with Swiss law. The latter would have pay to the canton a 'compensation for administrative costs' of about 12 per cent of the official value of each property and would transform their bearer shares into nominative.[27]

A key factor in reaching the settlement was, however, the fact that Italian civil code at Art. 16 of its preliminary provisions grants full civil rights to foreigners 'under condition of reciprocity': Swiss nationals became unable to acquire holiday houses in Italy once the Italian Ministry made known to notaries that reciprocity was lacking as to Switzerland in respect of real estate acquisitions by non-residents. This proved a powerful incentive to Swiss authorities to resolve the matter notwithstanding opposition from various domestic circles against 'bowing to foreign pressure', including complaints that the executive branch was showing disrespect for a final decision of the highest court of the country.[28]

At the end the settlement of the dispute was in favour of the foreign investors but the general interests of the host State were also protected. On the one hand, bilateral treaties of the type dealt with here do afford protection to foreign investors of one party threatened with confiscation, expropriation or discriminatory treatment by authorities of the other party. On the other hand, diplomatic negotiations between the home and

27 Press Notice of the Swiss Ministry of Foreign Affairs of 1 April 1992 and Decision n. 1224 of the Canton Grisons of 14 April 1992.

28 See the official statement of the Swiss Foreign Ministry by its Director for Legal Affairs, Mathias Krafft, Neue Zuercher Zeitung n. 96, 25–6 April 1992, at 24, upholding the application of the 1868 Treaty. The 1983 legislation has since been made more flexible and permits made more readily available. Moreover under the later bilateral agreements between Switzerland and the European Union citizens of the EU may obtain residence in Switzerland more easily than was the case in 1990 and as such may acquire dwellings as a matter of right, and vice versa. This right does not accrue however to Swiss corporations in the EU, Case C-541/08, *Fokus Invest AG* v. *Finanzierungsberatung-Immobilientreuhand und Anlageberatung GmbH (FIAG)*, [2010] ECR I-1025.

the host country may turn to the advantage also of the last one through a practical solution. In the case at issue the general requirement of Swiss law that an authorization is required remained in place, safeguarding Swiss policy choices restricting the unfettered right of property granted by the 1868 treaty. Moreover, the canton obtained that until then anonymous owners would declare themselves, besides cashing from them an 'indemnity' of a considerable global amount.

3. Protection of investments under FCN treaties: the *ELSI* case

Also bilateral Friendship Commerce and Navigation Treaties (FCN Treaties) such as the one between United States and Italy of 2 February 1948,[29] which was unsuccessfully invoked by the United States before the ICJ in the *ELSI* case,[30] afford protection to foreign investors through their broad terms and coverage as to the rights that each signatory State's nationals and legal entities may acquire and enjoy in the other State's territory.[31] FCN Treaties ensure rights as to the acquisition, establishment and operations of business enterprises (but also of non-profit organizations), as well as guarantees against interferences and takings carried out in the absence of due process of law and compensation.

The *ELSI* dispute is too well-known as an example of 'investment dispute' to require extensive description of the facts and of the decision. We will, therefore, summarize the main aspects of this case hereunder for the purpose of our comparative analysis.

The USA filed a claim following the requisition by Italian local authorities of the plant and related assets of Raytheon-ELSI S.p.A. (previously Elettronica Sicula S.p.a. or 'ELSI'), an Italian corporation wholly owned by the United States corporations Raytheon Company ('Raytheon') and its subsidiary the Machlett Laboratories ('Machlett') established in Palermo where it produced electronic components. The requisition had been ordered by the Mayor of Palermo on 1 April 1968 for six months, in response to Raytheon's decision to close the ailing plant. The plant was

29 Treaty of Friendship, Commerce and Navigation, Protocol, Additional Protocol and Exchange of Notes, 2 February 1948, Italy–United States, 79 UNTS 171; Agreement Supplementing the Treaty of Friendship, Commerce and Navigation of 2 February 1948, 26 September 1951, United States–Italy, 404 UNTS 326.

30 For comments on this case see: Spota (1989), 320; Seidl-Hohenveldner (1990), 261; Stern (1990), 897; Kubiatowski (1991), 215; Mann (1992), 92.

31 The first Friendship commerce and navigation Treaty was signed between the United States and France on 6 February 1978. See on this Treaty: Preiswerk (1979), 7; Wilson (1949), 262; Wilson (1951), 83; Walker (1956), 229; Wilson (1956), 927; Schill (2009), 29.

occupied by workers and soon thereafter ELSI filed petition in bankruptcy. The order of requisition was justified among other reasons by the fact that in the particular instance there was a grave public necessity and urgency to protect the general economic public interest and public order.[32]

Before the ICJ the USA claimed that Italy had breached Art. III(2) of the Treaty, which grants to companies the rights to organize, control and manage corporations; Art. V(1) and (3) of the Treaty, providing for the protection and security of nationals of the other contracting party and their properties; Art. V(2) of the Treaty prohibiting the taking of properties of nationals, without due process of law and without the prompt payment of just and effective compensation; and Art. VII of the Treaty, providing for the right of corporations of either contracting parties to acquire, own and dispose of immovable property or interests. Finally, the USA claimed the violation by Italy of Art. I of the Supplementary Agreement of 1951, which prohibits arbitrary or discriminatory measures.

The position of the United States was that the requisition order issued by the Mayor of Palermo caused an economic situation of such gravity that it immediately and directly triggered the bankruptcy of the company.

On the merits, the majority of the Chamber found that Italy had not violated the FCN Treaty and therefore rejected the US claim for reparation,[33] based on the facts of the case: since the feasibility of an orderly liquidation had not been sufficiently established, the requisition order could not interfere with control and management in any real sense. Therefore, the requisition while ultimately found to be unlawful and annulled under Italian law was not the cause of ELSI's bankruptcy and did not entail a breach of Art. III(2) of the 1948 Treaty[34] nor of the other Treaty provisions invoked by the USA.[35]

3.1 Issues raised in the ELSI *case under FCN treaty: exhaustion of local remedies*

As a defence against US claims Italy raised the objection that the two corporations for which the USA was acting had not exhausted the local remedies available to them in Italy,[36] while the United States disputed that the

32 *ELSI* (fn 16) 30.

33 For a critical viewpoint on the Court's findings see Mann (1973), 259.

34 *ELSI* (fn 16) 92.

35 *Ibid.*, 108. The Court concluded further dismissing on factual grounds the US claim that the national treatment obligation of Art. V(1) and (3) had been breached by Italy in the handling of the occupation, the requisition and related proceedings.

36 *Ibid.*, 49.

requirement applied at all. The USA argued first that the relevant article of the FCN Treaty did not make any reference to the local remedies rule, second that it was acting for a declaratory judgment of a direct injury to the United States by infringement of its rights under the FCN Treaty.

As to the first US argument the Chamber ruled that, although the parties to a treaty can agree that the local remedies rule shall not apply to claims based on alleged breaches of the treaty, such a rule cannot be tacitly disposed of.[37] Nevertheless, the Chamber rejected Italy's objection, considering that Italian municipal courts had been fully seized of the matter which was the substance of the Applicant's claim before the Chamber.[38] The Chamber rejected also the second US argument since it was clear in its views that the United States was espousing the claims of Raytheon and Machlett.[39]

As the case shows, under FCN treaties the requirement of prior exhaustion of local remedies is not waived if this is not explicitly provided therein, nor can it be circumvented by claiming that the claimant State acts in its own interest. By contrast, BITs are more favourable to aggrieved foreign investors in admitting direct arbitration of disputes, independently from recourse to domestic courts and exhaustion of local remedies. On the other hand BITs often contain a 'fork in the road provision' making recourse to domestic court alternative to such arbitration. The exclusion of the local remedy requirement in BITs as a condition precedent to international direct arbitration is reinforced by the provision of Art. 26 of the ICSID convention to the same effect.[40]

37 It has been submitted that the approach taken by the Chamber of the ICJ in the *ELSI* case is inconsistent with the canons of treaty interpretation under the Vienna Convention on the Law of Treaties in that the latter does not support the incorporation of unexpressed rules of customary international law where these might not represent the plain meaning of the text of the treaty; see Murphy (1991), 409–11; McLachlan (2008), 361. The strict approach adopted by the Chamber should be therefore considered with some caution by future international tribunals which must look at the precise wording of any treaty before them; Muchlinski (2009), 341.

38 *ELSI* (fn 16) 58–9. In its Draft Articles on Diplomatic Protection, the International Law Commission has followed the view adopted by the Chamber of the International Court of Justice in the *ELSI* case. While some room for implied waivers to the exhaustion of local remedies rule can be found in an arbitration agreement entered into after the dispute in question has arisen, a strong presumption exists against implied waivers when the parties have agreed to submit disputes to arbitration that may arise in the future (see International Law Commission, Draft Articles on Diplomatic protection with Commentaries, UN Doc. A/61/10 (2006), Art. 15, at 16, available at untreaty.un.org/ilc/texts/instruments/english/commentaries/9_8_2006.pdf).

39 *Ibid.*, 50–2.

40 See to this effect Art. VII.2 and 3 of the US–Argentina BIT of 1991.

3.2 Issues raised in the ELSI case under FCN treaty: the admissibility of claims on behalf of shareholders for damages suffered by a local subsidiary

As general rule, a corporation is to be protected by the State of nationality of the corporation and not by the State of nationality of the shareholders in a corporation. This basic principle of diplomatic protection of corporations was confirmed by the ICJ in the *Barcelona Traction* case, where the Court concluded that in the event of an injury to a foreign company endowed with independent legal personality,[41] its shareholders of another nationality have no right under customary international law to claim damages on their own behalf,[42] other than when the act complained of is aimed at the direct rights of the shareholder as such.[43] The State(s) of nationality of the shareholders may exercise diplomatic protection on their behalf only where the company had ceased to exist or this right has been established by treaty.[44]

Although Italy objected that the company, whose rights were alleged to have been violated, was incorporated in Italy, in the *ELSI* case the Chamber accepted that the United States was entitled to bring the claim against Italy. The *ELSI* decision has, thus, recognized the right of the national State of the shareholders of a company incorporated under the laws of another State to espouse their claims for damages inflicted by the host State to their locally incorporated subsidiary, which represents the most common way to carry out direct investment abroad.

It has been questioned whether the *ELSI* case represented a departure from the principles of diplomatic protection of corporations set forth in the *Barcelona Traction* judgment or rather an application of one of the exceptions to the general rule established by the Court in that case.[45] The

41 *Barcelona Traction* (fn 20) 40. Abi-Saab (1971), 121; Briggs (1971), 327; Caflisch (1971), 162; De Visscher (1971), 1; Higgins (1971), 327; Mann (1973), 259; De Velasco (1974), 87.

42 *Barcelona Traction* (fn 20) 44. See also at 46, where the Court has stated: 'Not a mere interest affected, but solely a right infringed involves responsibility, so that an act directed against and infringing only the company's rights does not involve responsibility towards the shareholders, even if their interest are affected.'

43 *Ibid*., 47.

44 *Ibid*., 64–8. In the *Barcelona Traction* case the Court rejected the less stringent test which allowed intervention on behalf of shareholders when the company was 'practically defunct' as inadequate and ruled. See also Separate Opinion of Judges Nervo, *ibid*., 256–7 and Ammoun, *ibid*., 319–20, 25–6.

45 The relevant exception would be that which allows the State of shareholders in a corporation to intervene when the State whose responsibility is invoked is the national State

most common view seems to be that the *ELSI* judgment did not rely on customary international law but that it was based on the interpretation of the bilateral treaty, which provides explicitly for the protection of the shareholders.[46] This view has been confirmed by the International Court of Justice in the recent *Diallo* case.[47] It cannot thus be concluded that the *ELSI* case has represented a departure from the basic principles on diplomatic protection of corporations expressed in the *Barcelona Traction* judgment.[48]

In the *Diallo* case Guinea claimed the right to exercise diplomatic protection of Mr Diallo both in respect of the violation of his direct rights as shareholder of companies established in Zaire and in respect of the injuries suffered by them (so-called protection by substitution). The Court has reaffirmed the right of the national State of the shareholders to diplomatic protection for injuries to the direct rights of the shareholders.[49] It has categorically denied, instead, the right of Guinea to protect the company as a matter of customary international law, which according to the Court has not changed in this matter.[50]

In this respect the FCN model represents a clear advantage for investors in respect of customary rules. BITs have further expanded the coverage of treaty-based protection by clarifying in the definitions that investments covered include companies established by investors of one State (home State) in the other (host) State and shareholding therein. Art. 25(2)(b) of the ICSID Convention has expanded this concept to open direct arbitration to

> any juridical person which had the nationality of a Contracting State other than the State party to the dispute on the date on which the parties consented to submit such dispute to conciliation or arbitration and any juridical person which had the nationality of the Contracting State party to the dispute on that date and which, because of foreign control, the parties have agreed should be treated as a national of another Contracting State for the purposes of this Convention.[51]

of the company and the foreign shareholders do not have other means of protection on the international level but through their State of nationality (Dinstein 1998, 512). Alternatively it has been held that the claim of the United States on behalf of shareholders could rely on the fact that the company, once gone into liquidation, had ceased to exist (Stern 1990, 897).

46 Draft Articles on Diplomatic Protection (fn 38) Art. 11, at 11; Lowe (2002), 269.

47 *Diallo*, Preliminary Objections (fn 21) 87. Okowa (2008), 219.

48 Stern (1990), 897; Amerasinghe (2008), 129; *contra* Murphy (1991), 391.

49 *Diallo*, Preliminary Objections (fn 21) 64–7. 50 *Ibid.*, 90.

51 Sacerdoti (1987), 289.

In this respect, therefore, in absence of specific treaty provisions, an ICSID investor–State arbitration would seem more favourable to the protection of investor interests than an interstate dispute in front of the ICJ.

4. State-to-State arbitration under BITs as a means of redressing individual investors' losses in breach of BITs: the arbitration between Italy and Cuba (2003–8) under the BIT of 1993

Apart from providing for direct arbitration by foreign investors against the host State in case of alleged breaches of the protection standards to the detriment of their investments, bilateral investment treaties provide also for State-to-State arbitration to settle disputes concerning the interpretation or application of the BIT itself between the Contracting Parties. Although rarely resorted to, as far as it is known, in a recent dispute between Italy and Cuba this procedure has been used also for the purpose of protecting investors of the contracting State initiating the proceedings.[52]

Other cases of interstate arbitration are *Peru* v. *Chile* and the *Ecuador* v. *United States* disputes.

In the first case the arbitral proceeding was initiated by the Republic of Peru against the Republic of Chile in 2003 as an attempt by Peru to block or hinder an earlier-initiated investor–State arbitration brought by the Chilean investor, Lucchetti, against Peru. The State to State arbitration was *inter alia* designed to resolve a disagreement between Peru and Chile as to the proper interpretation of the Peru–Chile BIT. However, this State-to State arbitration was discontinued after the arbitrators in the separate *Lucchetti* v. *Peru*[53] investor–State case declined to suspend their own proceedings so that the State-to-State proceeding could be pursued.[54]

The second case arises out of Ecuador's dissatisfaction with the interpretation given by an earlier investor–State arbitral tribunal in *Chevron*

52 Dolzer and Stevens (1995), 120; Vandevelde (2010), 499.

53 *Empresa Lucchetti S.A. and Lucchetti Perù S.A.* v. *Perù* ICSID Case No. ARB/03/4, Award 7 February 2005, 9.

54 See UNCTAD, Latest Developments in Investor–State Dispute Settlement, IIA MONITOR No 4, 2005, 2, n. 3, available at bit.escwa.org.ib/CMSPages/GetFile.aspx?nodeguid=a7831054-0ed6-4040-8480-4b2c7a16116e.

and Texaco Petroleum Company v. *Republic of Ecuador*[55] to Art. II(7) of the US–Ecuador BIT.[56] Such a clause is unusual in BITs, requiring signatories to provide foreign investors with 'effective means' for asserting claims and enforcing rights.[57] The investor–State tribunal found that Ecuador's courts' failure to adjudicate the claims brought by the claimant constituted a violation of Art. II(7) of the BIT. The Tribunal held that Art. II(7) protected foreign investors against 'undue' delay in local court systems, and this obligation might be more easily breached than a standard claim for denial of justice under international law. Following this award, Ecuador informed the USA that it disagreed with the interpretation given by the Tribunal in that case and asked the USA to state whether it agreed with Ecuador's interpretation according to which Art. II(7) of the Treaty was an expression of the international customary rule on denial of justice. Since the USA had refused to respond to Ecuador's request, the Republic of Ecuador instituted arbitral proceedings via the UNCITRAL Procedural rules concerning the interpretation and application of Art. II(7) of the BIT pursuant to Art. VII. The arbitral tribunal resolved the dispute on 29 September 2012 rejecting Ecuador's claim as far as is known.[58]

In the three cases at issue was the interpretation of the standard compromissory clause in these treaties according to which jurisdiction is granted to an international tribunal over disputes between the parties concerning 'the interpretation or application of the treaty'. While in *Peru* v. *Chile* at issue was an attempt to block an ongoing investor–State arbitration and in *Ecuador* v. *US*, Ecuador sought to obtain an abstract interpretation

55 *Chevron and Texaco Petroleum Company* v. *Republic of Ecuador*, Partial Award, 30 March 2010, available at italaw.com/sites/default/files/case-documents/ita0151.pdf. In the *Chevron* case, because of a breach of contract, TexPet filed seven cases in Ecuadorian courts against Ecuador in the 1990s. However, the Ecuador courts did not adjudicate the cases. In 2006 Chevron and TexPet started arbitral proceedings under the US–Ecuador BIT claiming the Ecuador's courts' failure to adjudicate the cases equated to a violation of Art. 2.7 of the BIT. According to the claimants' view, Art. II.7 does not reflect customary international law. According to the respondent, instead, there was 'no indication whatsoever that the parties to the Treaty contemplated lowering the standard for establishing a denial of justice through the Treaty provisions' (at 219). The Tribunal found that Art. II.7 of the BIT is 'an independent, specific treaty obligation and does not make any explicit reference to denial of justice or customary international law' (at 242–4).

56 Treaty between United States of America and the Republic of Ecuador Concerning the Encouragement and Reciprocal Protection of Investment, 27 August 1993.

57 Art. II(7): Each party shall provide effective means of asserting claims and enforcing rights with respect to investment, investment agreements, and investment authorizations.

58 See at www.italaw.com/cases/1494.

of the BIT, in the *Italy* v. *Cuba* case the recourse to interstate arbitration under the BIT had the purpose to protect investors as an alternative to the investor–State arbitration provided under the BIT.[59]

4.1 *The arbitration between Italy and Cuba (2003–8) under the BIT of 1993*

Italy initiated in 2003 arbitration against Cuba under Art. 10 of the BIT between the two countries,[60] both on behalf of 16 Italian investors and in Italy's own name for breaches of the BIT by Cuba.[61]

The dispute was heard by an *ad hoc* arbitral tribunal, constituted in accordance with Art. 10, which first issued a preliminary award on several issues among which whether Italian nationals and companies, whose claims Italy was espousing, had made an investment as defined by Art. 1 of the BIT.[62]

Through a textual and teleological approach to the interpretation of the Treaty provisions, the Tribunal excluded that the notion of investment in the Treaty could be established by reference to Cuban domestic law.[63] Relying on ICSID case-law (the so-called *Maffezini* doctrine), the Tribunal defined the investment as: 'toute operation économique réunissant un apport, une certaine durée et une participation aux risques de l'operation', thus excluding sales agreements.[64] It invited the claimant to file only those cases which could be regarded as investment according to the criteria set forth in the preliminary award.[65] Italy, therefore, submitted on the merits only six cases involving small Italian companies operating in the health, beauty, pasta sauce manufacturing, tourism and glass production industries.

59 Orecki (2013).

60 Italy–Cuba Bilateral Treaty on the Protection and Promotion of Investments, 7 May 1993, entered into effect on 23 August 1995, available at itra.esteri.it/itrapgm/Visualizza.asp?ID=43878. See on this case Potestà (2012), 341.

61 Italy claimed the breach by Cuba of several obligations of the Treaty, including the obligation of encouraging foreign investments (Art. 2(1)); of fair and equitable treatment of foreign investments (Art. 2(2)); of the most favoured nation treatment and national treatment (Art. 3); and of no-direct or indirect expropriation (Art. 5).

62 The Tribunal was constituted by Prof. Attila Tanzi and Dr Olga Miranda Bravo, respectively appointed by Italy and Cuba, and Mr Yves Derains appointed jointly by the parties. The Tribunals seat was in Paris and the awards were made in the French language.

63 *Italy–Cuba*, Preliminary Award (fn19), 82–3.

64 *Ibid.*, 81. 65 *Ibid.*, 85.

The Tribunal found that it had jurisdiction only in respect of two cases out of the six. It considered that two instances did not involve an investment but were commercial operations,[66] while two other corporate investors were found not protected by the treaty since Art. 1 of the BIT was found to exclude from its coverage investments made through third countries, as was the case here.[67]

Italy's action failed however altogether also in respect of the only two investors, whose position was examined in the merits (Finmed S.r.l. and Caribe and Figurella) since the Tribunal concluded that no internationally wrongful act had been shown to exist in respect of them.

Both claims involved the issue of whether the action of the local partners of the two Italian investors, which were State-owned companies in the tourism sector, were attributable to Cuba governmental authorities. In the first case the Tribunal found that the alleged injury suffered by Finmed and its shareholders was due to the inability of the representatives of Finmed to show their powers of representation, and not to acts committed either by the State-owned company Cubacan or by Cuba. As to the claim relating to Caribe and Figurella, the Tribunal concluded that the action of the State-owned company, which had brought to the discontinuance of the operations, causing the loss of the investment, did not imply Cuba's responsibility in the light of a 'functional criterion', since the hotel's operations involved were essentially of a commercial non-governmental nature.[68] In so deciding, the Tribunal held that in order to determine whether the acts or omissions committed by a company entirely owned by the State could be a cause of State responsibility it was not sufficient to look at domestic law but reference needed to be made to the principles developed by the international case-law.[69]

4.2 *Relevant legal issues in the Italy–Cuba arbitration*

The arbitral Tribunal had to resolve a number of legal issues of general interest.

First of all whether a clause, which permits State-to-State arbitration of disputes on the interpretation and application of the Treaty, implies a State's consent to arbitrate investors' claims filed by a home State;[70]

66 See *Italy–Cuba*, Merits Award (fn 19), 195–9 and 212–21, respectively in relation to *Icemm S.r.l.* and *Menarini Società Farmaceutica*.

67 *Ibid.*, 200–11. 68 *Ibid.*, 161–3. 69 *Ibid.*, 160.

70 Due to the number of bilateral investment treaties in effect between States and the means of investors' protection provided therein part of the scholarship has underlined

secondly, the possibility of tacitly disposing of the rule of prior exhaustion of internal remedies. Finally, the Tribunal had to decide on whether investments of a contracting party's nationals through juridical persons of a third country fell into the scope *rationae personae* of the treaty.

The Tribunal resolved the first issue in favour of the admissibility of Italy's action under Art. 10, referring by analogy to Art. 27 of the ICSID Convention. It took the view that Italy would have been precluded from exercising diplomatic protection only if the investors themselves had consented to resort to or had already resorted to the investor–State arbitration under Art. 9(2) of the BIT. Since this was not the case, the majority of the Tribunal held that Italy could exercise diplomatic protection of the Italian investors under Art. 10.[71]

As to Cuba's objection that the investors concerned had not previously exhausted the local remedies, the Tribunal made reference to the *Interhandel* case[72] to assert the relevance of the rule of exhaustion of internal remedies in the case.[73] It rejected Italy's argument that 'silent waiver' to the rule could be inferred from Art. 9(2) of the Treaty, which allows investors to choose between internal courts or the *ad hoc* arbitral tribunal. The Tribunal ruled that the issue was rather to be examined in relation to each claim together with the merits of the case.[74]

Finally, in relation to the claims of two companies owned by Italian citizens but incorporated respectively in Panama and Costa Rica, the final award stated that the BIT was only applicable to investments made in Cuba by natural or legal Italian persons directly; so that the Italian nationality of the shareholders of these corporations could not be taken into account. The Tribunal reached this conclusion through a textual interpretation of Art. 1 of the Treaty and considered its interpretation consistent with the concept prevailing in 1993 when the principles set

the residual character of diplomatic protection: Kokott (2002), 21; The Final Report of the International Law Association, Toronto Conference 2006, Diplomatic Protection of Person and Properties, available at: www.ila-hq.org/pdf/Human%20Rights%Law/Report%202006.pdf. *Contra*, Condorelli (2003), 5. See also Pustorino (2006), 68.

71 *Italy–Cuba*, Preliminary Award (fn19), 65.

72 *Interhandel* (*Switzerland* v. *United States of America*), ICJ Judgments, 21 March 1959, ICJ Reports 1959, 6, 27.

73 *Italy–Cuba* Preliminary Award (fn19), 90. On the condition of the exhaustion of local remedies rule in State-to State arbitration see Tejera-Pérez (2012), 445.

74 On the issue of the nature of the local remedies rule as a substantive or procedural requirement see Kriebaum (2009), 818.

forth in *Barcelona Traction* were not seriously disputed, as well as with the object and purpose of the Treaty.[75]

The case between Italy and Cuba shows that resort to inter-State dispute settlement mechanisms under a BIT may be used to exercise diplomatic protection of an investor, but it entails, however, the pitfalls of the nationality link and of the previous exhaustion of local remedies. These requirements may well defeat, as in that case, the action by the State of the investors.

5. Conclusions

The examination of instances in which treaties other than BITs have been invoked through diplomatic protection by the home States of the investors, whether the action resulted in judicial action (as in *ELSI*) or was resolved diplomatically (Italy–Switzerland dispute) indicates that bilateral treaties other than BITs afford valuable protection to investors in various instances.

The Swiss dispute shows that invocation by the home State of a treaty protecting investors may lead to a settlement by diplomatic means which protects the latter while, at the same time, safeguards the general interests of the home State.

At the same time, the features and outcomes we have set forth above show that in State-to-State disputes under these treaties the claims of the investors are subject to pitfalls and hurdles from which resort to direct investor–State arbitration are exempted, especially the requirement of prior exhaustion of local remedies.

In fact in the Italy–Cuba case, while the Tribunal has made extensive reference to the ICSID case-law on investor–State disputes to solve some of the legal issues that have arisen,[76] it has looked at the more restrictive ICJ

75 In his dissenting opinion Arbitrator Tanzi has criticized the restrictive view of nationality adopted by the majority of the Tribunal. In his view the BIT's provision permitting claims by legal persons of a contracting State did not strictly mention nationality and expressed protection of investments regardless of the legal form chosen or of the legal system in question. Arbitrator Tanzi also disputed the majority's interpretation of Art. 9 of the ILC Draft Articles as reconfirming the rule of Barcelona Traction. According to Tanzi's view, Art. 9 provided an exception to the rule and was directly applicable in the two cases. Prof. Tanzi Dissenting Opinion, 33–4.

76 The reference to ICSID case law is open to criticism insofar as arbitration between Italy and Cuba was of course not subject to the ICSID. Moreover Cuba is not even part of the ICSID Convention.

jurisprudence on State-to-State disputes to apply the requirements of the previous exhaustion of internal remedies and nationality of companies.[77]

It can thus be concluded that procedural requirements of a State-to-State dispute, whether in front of the ICJ or in front of an arbitral tribunal, together with the tendency to a restrictive interpretation of these requirements and of the text of treaties seem to favour an outcome of the dispute more favourable to the protection of the host State regulatory powers rather than the investors' interests. This would seem to come from the interstate nature of these proceedings irrespective of the nature of the body settling the dispute.

References

Abi-Saab, G. 1971. 'The International Law of Multinational Corporations: A Critique of American Legal Doctrines'. *Annals of International Studies* 2: 121.

Alvarez, J.E. and Khamsi, K. 2008–9. 'The Argentine Crisis and Foreign Investors: A Glimpse into the Heart of the Investment Regime'. *Yearbook on International Investment Law and Policy*: 379–478.

Amerasinghe, C.F. 2008. *Diplomatic Protection*. Oxford University Press.

Binder, C., Kriebaum, U., Reinisch, A. and Wittich, S. (eds.) 2009. *International Investment Law for the 21st Century: Essays In Honour of Christoph Schreuer*. Oxford University Press.

Briggs, H.W. 1971. 'Barcelona Traction: The *Jus standi* of Belgium'. *American Journal of International Law* 65: 327–45.

Caflisch, L. 1971. 'The Protection of Corporate Investment Abroad in the Light of the Barcelona Traction Case'. *ZAöRV* 31: 162–96.

Cohen, S. 2009. 'Claims of Shareholders in International Investment Law', Binder, Kriebaum, Reinisch and Wittich (eds.): 363–76.

Condorelli, L. 2003. 'La protection diplomatique et l'évolution de son domaine d'application', *Rivista di Diritto Internazionale*: 5–26.

De Velasco, D. 1974. 'La protection diplomatique des sociétés et des actionnaires'. *RCADI* 141: 87–185.

De Visscher, C. 1971. 'La notion de référence (renvoi) au droit international dans la protection diplomatique des actionnaires'. *Revue Belge de Droit International*: 1–6.

77 For a view according to which indirect ownership is permitted so long as it is not excluded see *Siemens AG* v. *Argentina* ICSID Case No. ARB/02/8, Decision on Jurisdiction, 3 August 2004; *Kardassopoulo* v. *Georgia*, ICSID Case No. ARB/05/18, Decision on Jurisdiction, 6 July 2007 commented by Cohen (2009), 363.

Dinstein, Y. 1998. 'Diplomatic Protection of Companies under International Law', Wellens, K. (ed.), *International Law: Theory and Practice, Essay in Honor of Eric Suy*. The Hague: Martinus Nijhoff Publishers: 505–18.

Dolzer, R. and Stevens, M. 1995. *Bilateral Investment Treaties*. The Hague: Martinus Nijhoff Publishers.

Gaillard, E. 2008. 'Anti Arbitration Trends in Latin America', *New York Law Journal* 239 – No. 108, available at: www.shearman.com/files/Publication/33b80659-ac58-4ffd-8217-2af9205ff1c2/Presentation/PublicationAttachment/db188d5f-038b-4950-a9cf-2b7a752cd94b/IA_070208_03.pdf.

Higgins, R. 1971. 'Aspect of the Case Concerning the Barcelona Traction Company'. *Virginia Journal of International Law* 11: 327–43.

Kokott, J. 2002. 'The Role of Diplomatic Protection in the Field of the Protection of Foreign Investment', *International Law Association, Report on the Seventieth Conference* (New Delhi), London: 21–31.

Kriebaum, U. 2009. 'Local Remedies and the Standards for the Protection of Foreign Investment', Binder, Kriebaum, Reinisch and Wittich (eds.): 818–29.

Kubiatowski, S.A. 1991. 'The Case of Elettronica Sicula S.p.A. toward Greater Protection of Shareholders' Rights in Foreign Investments'. *Colum. J. Transnat'l. L.* 29: 215–44.

Kurtz, J. 2010. 'Adjudging the Exceptional at International Investment Law: Security, Public Order and Financial Crisis'. *ICLQ* 59: 325–71.

Lowe, V. 2002. '"Shareholders" Rights to Control and Manage: From Barcelona Traction to ELSI', Ando, N., McWhinney, E. and Wolfrum, R. (eds.), *Liber Amicorum Judge Shigeru Oda*. The Hague: Kluwer Law International: 269–84.

Mann, F.A. 1973. 'Protection of Shareholders' Interests in the Light of the Barcelona Traction Case'. *American Journal of International Law* 67: 259–74.

1992. 'Foreign Investment in the International Court of Justice: The *ELSI* Case'. *American Journal of International Law* 86: 92–102.

McLachlan, C. 2008. 'Investment Treaties and General International Law'. *ICLQ* 57: 361–401.

Muchlinski, P. 2008–9. 'Trends in International Investment Agreements: Balancing Investor Rights and the Right to Regulate: The Issue of National Security'. *Yearbook on International Investment Law and Policy*: 37–45.

2009. 'Diplomatic Protection of Foreign Investors: A Tale of Judicial Caution', Binder, Kriebaum, Reinisch and Wittich (eds.): 341–62.

Murphy, S.D. 1991. 'The *ELSI* Case: An Investment Dispute at the International Court of Justice'. *Yale Journal of International Law* 16: 391–452.

Nelson, T.G. 2010. '"History Ain't Changed": Why Investor–State Arbitration will Survive the "New Revolution"', Waibel, M., Kaushal, A., Chung, K. and Balchain, C. (eds.), *The Backlash against Investment Arbitration: Perceptions and Reality*. The Netherlands: Kluwer Law International BV: 555–75.

Okowa, P.N. 2008. 'Case Concerning Ahmadou Sadio Diallo (*Republic of Guinea* v. *Democratic Republic of the Congo*) Preliminary Objections'. *ICLQ* 57: 219–24.

Orecki, M. 2013. 'State-to State Arbitration Pursuant to Bilateral Investment Treaties: The Ecuador-US Dispute', available at: www.youngicca-blog.com/state-to-state-arbitration-pursuant-to-bilateral-investment-treaties-the-ecuador-us-dispute.

Potestà, M. 2012. 'Italy-Cuba, *Ad Hoc* Arbitration'. *American Journal of International Law* 106: 341–7.

Preiswerk, R. 1979. *La Protection des Investissements Privés dans les Traités Bilatéraux' Nendeln/Leichtestein*. Zurich: Éditions polygraphic.

Pustorino, P. 2006. 'Recenti Sviluppi in tema di Protezione Diplomatica'. *Rivista di Diritto internazionale*: 68–104.

Roberts, A. 2010. 'Power and Persuasion in Investment Treaty Interpretation: The Dual Role of States'. *American Journal of International Law*, 104: 179–225.

Sacerdoti, G. 1987. 'Foreign and Foreign-Owned Corporations in International Economic Law', Dicke, D.C. (ed.), *Foreign Investment in the Present and a New International Economic Order*. Switzerland: University Press Fribourg: 289–309.

2013. 'BIT Protections and Economic Crises. Limits to their Coverage, the Impact of Multilateral Financial Regulation and the Defence of Necessity'. *ICSID Review* 28: 351–383.

2014. 'Diplomatic Conciliation of Investment Disputes: the Italian-Swiss Controversy on Secondary Residences in Engadine (1990–1992) and its Lessons, N. Lavranos and P. Mavroidis (eds.) Fetschrift H.-U. Petersmann. Brill: 403–418.

Schill, S.W. 2009. *The Multilateralization of International Investment Law*. Cambridge University Press.

2012. 'The Public Law Challenge: Killing or Rethinking International Investment Law?' *Columbia FDI Perspective*, 58, available at www.vcc.columbia.edu/content/public-law-challenge-killing-or-rethinking-international-investment-law.

Schwebel, S.M. 2009. 'The United States 2004 Model Bilateral Investment Treaty and Denial of Justice', Binder, Kriebaum, Reinisch and Wittich (eds.): 519–24.

Seidl-Hohenveldner, I. 1990. 'ELSI and Badger, the Two Rayetheon Cases', *RDIPP*: 261–76.

Spears, S.A. 2011. 'Making Way for the Public Interest in International Investment Agreements', Brown, C. and Miles, K. (eds.), *Evolution in Investment Treaty Law and Arbitration*. Cambridge University Press: 271–97.

Spota, G.D. 1989. 'Note'. *ICSID Review*: 320–9.

Stern, B. 1990. 'La Protection Diplomatique des Investissements Internationaux. de Barcelona Traction à Elettronica Sicula ou les Glissements Progressifs de l'Analyse'. *Journal du droit international*: 897–945.

Tejera-Pérez, V.J. 2012. 'Diplomatic Protection Revival for Failure to Comply with Investment Arbitration Awards'. *Journal of International Dispute Settlement*: 445–75.

Vandevelde, K.L. 2008–9. 'A Comparison of 2004 and 1994 US Model BITs: Rebalancing Investor and Host Country Interests'. *Yearbook on International Investment Law and Policy*: 283–316.

2010. *Bilateral Investment Treaties*. Oxford University Press.

Walker, H. 1956. 'Treaties for the Encouragement and Protection of Foreign Investment: Present United States Practice'. *American Journal of Comparative Law*: 229–47.

Wilson, R.R. 1949. 'Postwar Commercial Treaties of the United States'. *American Journal of International Law* 43: 262–87.

1951. 'Property Protection Provisions in the United States Commercial Treaties'. *American Journal of International Law* 45: 83–107.

1956. 'A Decade of Commercial Treaties'. *American Journal of International Law* 50: 927–33.

INDEX

CPSIA information can be obtained at www.ICGtesting.com
Printed in the USA
BVOW11*2235180514

353786BV00006B/92/P

9 781107 050235